World Politics
in a
New Era

World Politics in a New Era

Second Edition

Steven L. Spiegel
University of California at Los Angeles

Fred L. Wehling
Monterey Institute of International Studies

Harcourt Brace College Publishers

Fort Worth   Philadelphia   San Diego   New York   Orlando   Austin   San Antonio
Toronto   Montreal   London   Sydney   Tokyo

Publisher	Earl McPeek
Acquisitions Editor	David C. Tatom
Product Manager	Steve Drummond
Developmental Editor	Stacey Sims
Project Editor	Charles J. Dierker
Art Director	Don Fujimoto
Production Manager	Serena Barnett
Art & Design Coordinator	Florence Fujimoto

ISBN: 0-15-505625-5

Library of Congress Catalog Card Number: 98-84609

Address for Editorial Correspondence:
Harcourt Brace College Publishers, 301 Commerce Street, Suite 3700, Fort Worth, TX 76102

Address for Orders:
Harcourt Brace & Company, 6277 Sea Harbor Drive, Orlando, FL 32887-6777. 1-800-782-4479

Web site address: http://www.hbcollege.com

Harcourt Brace College Publishers may provide complimentary instructional aids and supplements or supplement packages to those adopters qualified under our adoption policy. Please contact your sales representative for more information. If as an adopter or potential user you receive supplements you do not need, please return them to your sales representative or send them to:

Attention: Returns Department, Troy Warehouse, 465 South Lincoln Drive, Troy, MO 63379

Printed in the United States of America

8 9 0 1 2 3 4 5 6 7   039   10 9 8 7 6 5 4 3 2 1

About the Authors

STEVEN SPIEGEL

Steven L. Spiegel, professor of political science at UCLA and associate director of the Center for International Relations there, specializes in the analysis of world politics, American foreign policy, and American foreign policy in the Middle East. In addition to *World Politics in a New Era*, he is now working on a volume about the Middle East in the post–Cold War era. Dr. Spiegel is the director of the Middle East peace pulse project, co-sponsored by the Israel Policy Forum and the UCLA Center for International Relations. He also serves as the international chair of the Middle East Cooperative Security Program for the statewide Institute on Global Conflict and Cooperation of the University of California. His other books include *The Other Arab-Israeli Conflict: Making America's Middle East Policy, from Truman to Reagan* and *The International Politics of Regions* with Louis Cantori.

FRED WEHLING

Fred Wehling is Senior Research Associate with the Center for Nonproliferation Studies (CNS) at the Monterey Institute of International Studies, Monterey, California. His current fields of research include implementation of international nonproliferation agreements, nuclear issues in the former Soviet states, and transfers of weapons and related technology to the Middle East and South Asia. Before coming to CNS in 1998, Wehling was a consultant at RAND, Coordinator of Policy Research for the University of California's Institute on Global Conflict and Cooperation (IGCC), and a researcher at the Cooperative Monitoring Center (CMC) at Sandia National Laboratories. After receiving his Ph.D. in political science from UCLA in 1992, Wehling taught courses on international security and Russian foreign policy at UC San Diego. His recent writings include *Irresolute Princes: Kremlin Decision Making in Middle East Crises* (1997).

Preface

Conceived, organized, and written after the end of the Cold War, this book addresses a critical question: "What is the nature of world politics in a New Era?" We embarked on this project because we could not find a book that satisfactorily serves the introductory course on world politics at the University of California, Los Angeles. We searched in vain for a volume that deals comprehensively with all major aspects of contemporary international politics: history, economics, military strategy, theory, major global issues, and fundamental ideas about the patterns of international relations.

ORGANIZATION

In writing this book, we have tried to make sense of these issues through two unifying themes: the contrasting dynamics between globalization and fragmentation, and between cooperation and conflict. Although interdependence and increased communications are yielding new areas of unimagined contact and collaboration between peoples, there are also continuing trends in world politics that yield fragmentation, conflict, violence, and chaos. Why is current international politics distinguished by these countervailing pressures? This book seeks to provide students with the basic knowledge and skills needed to address this question.

Aside from its themes, another distinguishing feature of this book is its "building block" organization. In teaching the introductory course, we have found that students often do not have the background necessary to integrate the variety of theories, facts, and issues that are covered in this course. Thus, this book is organized to first provide concrete basics (history, global and regional politics, trade and economics), then acquaint the student with the issues and institutions that shape global politics (environment, security, international law and organizations) and finally move toward more abstract and theoretical topics (policy and levels of analysis). This is a reversal of the organization presented in many other textbooks. Here, the later theoretical chapters use the earlier descriptive chapters ("building blocks") as a base to illustrate the application of the abstract and theoretical topics, thus enabling the student to better comprehend the usefulness of theory at a more advanced level.

However, this book has been written so that instructors can use its contents in an order different from that in the table of contents. A course could be designed so that the theoretical material at the end of the book could be used initially. Alternatively, a course could be organized around an early analysis of history, followed by the theoretical material, and then the chapters on global issues. Because the materials in this book are integrated and cross-referenced, an instructor need not pursue the precise order of presentation used here.

In approaching the subject matter, we strove to provide comprehensiveness. Although many instructors may wish to use ancillary volumes, our aim was to provide an entire course in a single book. Thus, after the introductory chapter outlines the book's goals and organization, Part I reviews the history of international politics from 1648 to 1998. In this process, we discuss the origins of the modern international system (Chapter Two), the two World Wars (Chapter Three), the Cold War (Chapter Four) and the post–Cold War New Era (Chapter Five).

Part II deals with the other set of "building blocks"—economics, trade and development. The basic concepts of global economics are set forth in Chapter Six, which includes a very elementary overview of theories of international trade. Chapter Seven then traces the evolution of the modern international economic system. Chapter Eight concludes the unit with an examination of North-South economic relations.

Moving to a higher level of abstraction, Part III surveys the issues and institutions that comprise the structure and content of global politics. Chapter Nine covers international law and organizations, particularly the United Nations system. Next, Chapter Ten offers capsule descriptions of global issues critical to comprehending world politics in the New Era, including population, migration, food and hunger, the environment, drugs, terrorism, energy, and natural resources. Chapter Eleven then covers fundamental concepts of national and international security, including conventional and nuclear weapons, deterrence, proliferation of mass destruction weaponry, and emerging security challenges such as environmental and information security.

Finally, Part IV introduces students to international relations theory and levels of analysis. Chapter Twelve provides a concise survey of the major systemic, domestic, and individual level theories applied to world politics, highlighting both established lines of inquiry such as structural realism and game theory and newer approaches such as critical theory. Chapter Thirteen suggests how students can use both factual building blocks and theoretical approaches to think analytically and critically about the future of world politics, comparing several scenarios and outlining how students can develop their own evaluations of trends in the global political and economic system.

Throughout this book, a variety of paradigms are covered, including idealism and realism, modernization and dependency theories, feminist theory, the impact of interdependence, and neoliberal explanations for why cooperation is possible even within an anarchic world. Numerous non-European events and perspectives are stressed, including Third World complaints about Western dominance of the international economic system. There is also a strong emphasis on the continuing impact of environmental change and ethnic conflict on world politics.

FEATURES

Such a comprehensive tableau could not be presented without features in addition to the printed text. "At A Glance" boxes summarize complex phenomena and issues and provide a hook for major points in different sections of the chapters. "What Would You Do?" boxes provide a critical-thinking component that asks the student to assume the role of a decision maker and to resolve a dilemma after analyzing countervailing arguments and options. "Spotlight" boxes examine important international events and colorful personalities in greater depth or focus on precise points of complex conflicts and theories. Historical maps help students grasp the ebb and flow of geopolitics over the centuries, while thematic maps reinforce key points visually, and graphs, charts, and tables summarize statistical information. Bold-faced key terms appear in text where initially mentioned, and definitions are collected in a glossary at the end of the book. Each chapter ends with a list of key terms and a numbered "Principal Points" summary that highlights the major concepts and ideas of the text. The book also includes a chronology of selected pivotal events in international politics from 1453 to 1998. We hope these features will help students comprehend the many themes and topics that form the foundations of an introductory exploration of world politics.

CHANGES TO THE SECOND EDITION

In addition to updated material on recent international events and issues present throughout the book, this second edition of *World Politics in a New Era* includes a number of major changes designed to enhance the value of the text for both teachers and students:

- A new chapter on the contemporary international system, including sections on regional relations, ethnic conflict, collective security, and the evolving roles of the nation-state and international organizations (Chapter Five)
- Expanded presentation of economic issues at an introductory level, including chapters on trade and finance, economic history, and development, focusing on economic globalization and regional integration (Part III)
- A new concluding chapter emphasizing the application of theory to both history and current trends (Chapter Thirteen)
- Concise surveys of theoretical perspectives on international relations, including features on critical and feminist theory (Chapter Twelve)
- Integration of imperialism and colonialism into global political and economic trends in the historical chapters (Part II)
- New and updated maps, tables, diagrams, "At a Glance" and "Spotlight" boxes, and profiles of leaders, with special attention to environmental and humanitarian issues and women in world affairs

ANCILLARIES

Harcourt Brace College Publishers offers a variety of ancillaries for instructors who use this book and provides copies of them free of charge to those instructors qualified under its adoption policy. Please contact your sales representative to learn how you may qualify.

- **Instructor's Manual with Test Bank**   For each chapter of the textbook, the Instructor's Manual with Test Bank includes a description of the scope, objectives, and approach presented; what students should learn at the foundation, enrichment, and mastery levels; an outline of the core material presented; a brief description of how the material relates to the central themes of the text; suggested lecture topics; study and exam questions; and recommended enrichment readings. A separate test bank at the end of the volume provides on average a hundred additional multiple choice, essay, and true/false questions per chapter.

- **Computerized Test Bank**   The last section of test materials in the Instructor's Manual is available in computerized form for IBM and Macintosh users. This software has many features that facilitate test preparation, scoring, and grade recording. It also offers great flexibility. The order of text questions can be altered to create different versions of any given test, and it is easy to modify questions.

ACKNOWLEDGMENTS

We have been assisted by a unique team of individuals who made this book possible by serving as research and writing assistants, editors, feature analysts, and as a focus group for testing chapters and concepts.

UCLA has a marvelous undergraduate student research program. Elizabeth Matthews supervised the students' efforts with good cheer, and despite enormous pressures. We deeply appreciate her wisdom, vision, patience, and perspicacity.

David Tatom, senior acquisitions editor for political science at Harcourt Brace, convinced us to undertake this task. He was a stern taskmaster—always reminding us about deadlines and difficulties, but always holding out the light at the end of the tunnel as well. We are also indebted to Fritz Schanz, developmental editor for the first edition, and Chris Nelson and Stacey Sims on the second edition, for their guidance and contribution to the content, visual material, and features. Charles Dierker served as project editor for both editions, and we are grateful for his perseverance and patience.

We hope readers find this book useful in creating new perspectives on the evolution of world politics in a truly New Era, and that these perspectives influence students, scholars, and policy makers as we all attempt to deal with challenges and opportunities no one thought possible even a decade ago. We fully realized how complex this New Era has become only after we began preparing the manuscript for this text. We found that many old methods, approaches, and concepts used for the analysis of international politics are clearly outdated or inadequate. A new, comprehensive conception is necessary, and in writing this book we have worked to provide students with a foundation for that conception. While we strongly affirm the value of studying history, our real aim in writing this book is to help students equip themselves to make history in a complex and interdependent world.

Table of Contents

List of Maps

World Politics
in a
New Era

WORLD POLITICAL SYSTEMS

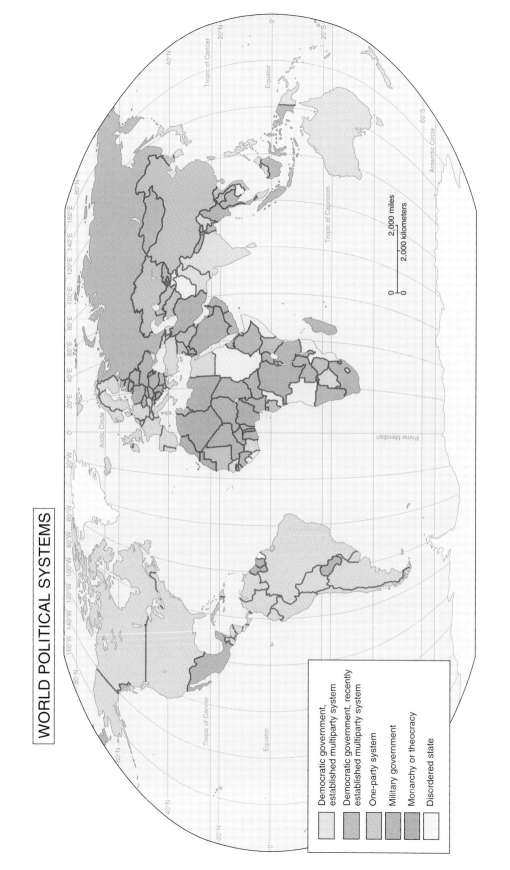

Democratic government,
established multiparty system

Democratic government, recently
established multiparty system

One-party system

Military government

Monarchy or theocracy

Disordered state

2,000 miles

2,000 kilometers

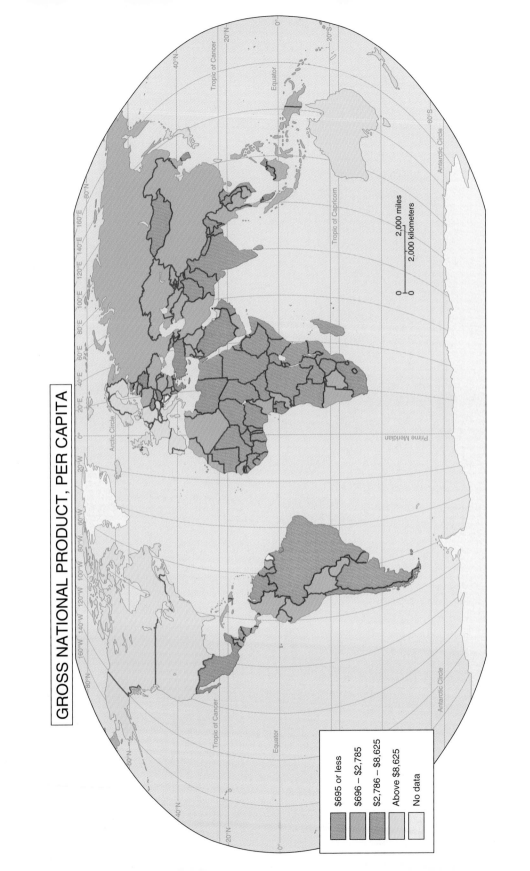

GROSS NATIONAL PRODUCT, PER CAPITA

$695 or less
$696 – $2,785
$2,786 – $8,625
Above $8,625
No data

NORTH AND SOUTH AMERICA

EAST ASIA
AND OCEANIA

WORLD DEFORESTATION AND DESERTIFICATION

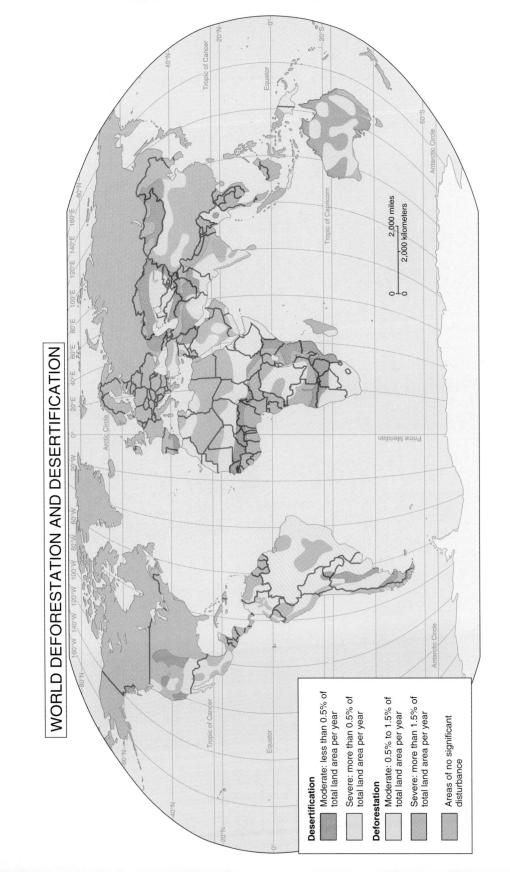

Desertification

Moderate: less than 0.5% of total land area per year

Severe: more than 0.5% of total land area per year

Deforestation

Moderate: 0.5% to 1.5% of total land area per year

Severe: more than 1.5% of total land area per year

Areas of no significant disturbance

0   2,000 miles

0   2,000 kilometers

□ □ □ □

PART

I

Introduction

CHAPTER 1
World Affairs in Our Lives

World Affairs in Our Lives

In more ways than we realize, our lives have become international-ized. The news media have played a significant role in narrowing the information gap between nations. Simply by turning on a television, we can witness a war, a riot, an earthquake, a military coup, a rebellion, a sports event, a protest, or an election thousands of miles away in a distant part of the world, live via satellite. In the next few days, you may eat pizza, egg rolls, tacos, crepes, falafel, and hamburgers, each reflecting the food and culture of very different people. We may purchase a car thinking we are buying an American or Japanese product, but it may be composed of parts produced in several countries. In the market for a new car? General Motors automobiles are manufactured or assembled in one of thirty-four countries, including Brazil, Finland, Kenya, Tunisia, South Korea, and Poland. Your local music store probably stocks CDs featuring musicians from South Africa, released by Sony, a Japanese company, manufactured in Singapore using technology originally developed in the

Netherlands. Very soon, Britain, France, Germany and the other countries of the **European Union** may all adopt a common currency, regulated by a European central bank. Consumers in Australia, Canada, Malaysia, the Philippines, or Taiwan can buy Wrigley's chewing gum or Johnson & Johnson medical and surgical products. In Beijing you can eat at the largest McDonald's in the world, or you can sample the food at Taco Bell in London, or eat pizza at Pizza Hut in Osaka. Then you can share your culinary experiences with fellow gourmands in Argentina and India on an Internet chat room, where other users may complain about American cultural imperialism. Elsewhere on the World Wide Web, environmental activists in Estonia can exchange data on deforestation and discuss possible solutions with their counterparts in South Korea and Tanzania. Ask your parents how many of these activities, which we take for granted today, would have been impossible or inconceivable a generation ago and you will begin to appreciate the increasing impact of world events and global trends on our daily lives. Map 1.1, a political map of the world, shows the borders between the world's nations as if they were solid lines on the globe, but these boundaries seem to mean less with each passing day.

POPULAR IMAGES OF WORLD POLITICS

It's a Small World, after All

From the obvious impact of news agencies and trade to the more subtle influence of cultural exchange, internationalism is as much a factor today as nationalism was in the past. Many readers may have visited either Disney World in Florida or Disneyland in California, or perhaps Tokyo Disneyland or even Eurodisney near Paris. One of the attractions, "It's a Small World," involves a boat trip through a variety of cultures. Along the riverbank, singing and dancing dolls dressed in myriad traditional costumes represent the earth's cultural diversity. As the music plays, the rider visits far-off lands and is told, "It's a world of laughter, a world of tears / It's a world of hopes and a world of fears / There's so much that we share / That it's time we're aware / It's a small world after all." [1] The rider departs amid fond farewells in several languages—*adios, ciao, auf Wiedersehen, sayonara*. Upon disembarking from this ten-minute journey, he or she may feel uplifted and reassured that the world is a happy place where people are sympathetic with one another and united despite their differences. This message encapsulates one particular understanding of the world in which the normal condition is one of harmony and accord, where people are naturally good and kind. From this perspective on international politics, cooperation is normal, understanding between people is easy once we get to know one another, and disputes are superficial anomalies that can be resolved amicably.

Lest the reader believe that this understanding of the world is reserved for the fantasies of Disney, we can also cite other examples in popular culture. For example, during the Ethiopian famine of 1985—which was caused not only by large-scale drought, but also by political factors, including civil war and authoritarian rule—a song was written as a rallying cry for popular worldwide assistance. "We

Map 1.1 Political Map of the World, 1998

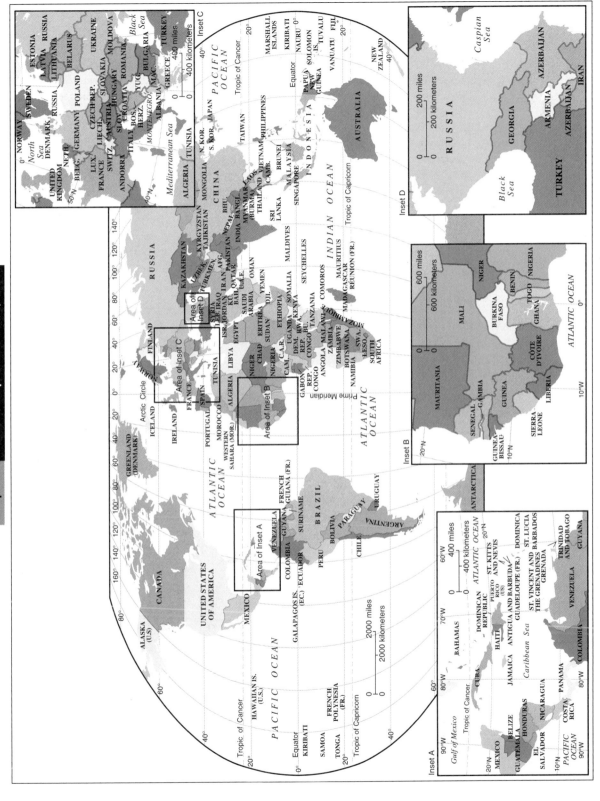

Are the World" expresses a sense of humanitarian universalism with verses that remind people of a shared sense of responsibility and an obligation to render assistance when others face the life or death agonies of famine. Inherent in its message is the notion that people can and ultimately must understand and accommodate each other.

The British singer Sting expressed similar notions when he wrote his song "Russians" in the 1980s, at the height of a particularly cold phase of the Cold War between the United States and the former Soviet Union. The words express the notion that we are essentially the same, that "we share the same biology / Regardless of ideology."[2] This song calls on us to empathize with the problems faced by individuals in both societies rather than concentrating on the preoccupations of the leaders of states with their political "hang-ups" and controversies. This idealistic view of the world is taken to its ultimate conclusion in the famous song "Imagine," by John Lennon, in which he expresses a view that is wistfully anti-state, anti-church, anti-political, anti-international structure: "Imagine there's no countries / It isn't hard to do / Nothing to kill or die for / And no religion too."[3] Lennon's lyrics evoke the image of a unified world of blissful anarchy in which all are one, living in harmony.

Pop stars record the song "We Are the World" in 1985. The group USA for Africa used proceeds from the recording to aid victims of African famine.   SOURCE: © JetSet / Sygma

Star Wars

A very different view of the world is also present in popular culture. Movies such as *Star Wars* and *Rambo* depict an inherent conflict between good and evil. This perspective is the exact opposite of the idealistic view in which conflicts are resolvable by peaceful means and all people are naturally sympathetic with one another. In this *Star Wars* view of the world, evil persons create conflicts and seek to defeat the forces of truth, justice, and (in the American imagination) the American Way. (The Soviet film *Solo Voyage*, produced in response to *Rambo*, features the heroic acts of a Russian commando fighting evil American agents in Afghanistan.) The *Star Wars* approach holds that **world politics** is fundamentally a struggle between evil states and good states. Tension in the world is created by evil states that seek to gain at the expense of weaker nations. When a conflict arises, one **nation** (or a group of nations) must be at fault. Wars do not start because of the situation in which states find themselves, but rather because of the aggressive intentions of evil states or leaders.

Former President Ronald Reagan's view of the world seemed to follow this line of thinking. During Reagan's presidency he labeled the Soviet Union the "Evil Empire." From his perspective, the USSR sought to destroy democracy in Europe and America. The "good guys" had to defend against this threat by standing firm politically and increasing their military power. Sizable U.S. military budgets were justified using this type of rationale throughout the Cold War. When Soviet President Mikhail Gorbachev adopted less confrontational policies in the late 1980s, Reagan claimed that America's vigilance and military strength had caused the USSR to give up and reform its evil ways. From this perspective, when the USSR collapsed at the end of 1991, the "good guys" finally won, but the possibility of new threats to world peace arising from other "bad guys" remained.

These two views represented in popular culture suggest either that the natural order of humanity is harmonious, or that history is a conflict between the forces of light and those of darkness. We will see these views recurring in the sources of conflict and cooperation in international relations, the causes of war and peace, and the functioning of world politics. These contrasting interpretations are necessitated by the fact that there is no automatic order in the **international system**. In domestic politics, there are legal **norms** that are enforceable on individuals. In world politics, however, no one rules over states.

ANARCHY VERSUS AUTHORITY

Consider the differences between behavior in the jungle and on the soccer field. Both are arenas of intense competition and often violent conflict. On the field, players are supervised by referees, and the athletes abide by specific rules of the game. If they break a rule, a penalty will be assessed. They can attempt to score at will, but only within the confines of accepted patterns of behavior. In the jungle,

Terminology

We should take an opportunity to define some important terms used throughout this book. All the states of the world, including the international organizations to which they belong, compose the **international system**. World politics refers to the competition for and exercise of power and authority in the international system, while the broader term *international relations* refers to the totality of interactions among states and nonstate actors. Ob-

viously, world politics and international relations are closely related, but they are not entirely synonymous; a performance by a Nigerian dance troupe in Toronto and the opening of a McDonald's in Jakarta are part of international relations, but not of world politics. *Foreign policy* refers to the actions and positions on issues taken by an individual state regarding other states or groups outside its boundaries.

by contrast, there are no referees and no rules. The survival of the fittest is the law of nature, and there is no higher authority than instinct and the struggle between predator and prey.

Similarly, the unique characteristic that makes international politics so complex is that it takes place in an environment of **anarchy.** There is no world government or higher authority policing nation-states. This is the fundamental difference between international and domestic politics. In domestic politics, there is a system that establishes law and order of some kind. Although this system may be different for each state, each government in its own way provides enforcement of laws to maintain a more or less orderly society.

When we think of domestic politics we might think of a centralized government with a large bureaucracy. This bureaucracy is the machine that runs the everyday business of government. A leader such as a prime minister or a president is to ensure that the government functions properly. A country also usually has a set of laws, as well as a constitution. These laws guide and constrain the behavior of its citizens. Even in a totalitarian regime, where individuals do not have rights, a system of authority prevails. In a democracy, authority to govern is granted through the means of popular elections and political campaigns. In the United States, for example, a presidential election occurs every four years. Billboards dot the landscape, and interviews, endorsements, and commercials are transmitted incessantly from television and radio. In any national political system, order arises because of laws and authorities that enforce those laws, namely the courts and the police. If you disobey laws, there is always a possibility that you will be caught and punished.

In the international system, however, states worry less about "being caught," as there are no "police" to enforce the laws of international politics. Saddam Hussein, in deciding to invade and annex Kuwait, mistakenly calculated that his actions would not result in any significant response from the rest of the world, or at least he thought he could handle whatever protests emerged. Sometimes other nations, or groups of nations, such as the **United Nations** (UN), choose to act as police, as happened in the case of the Iraqi invasion of Kuwait, yet there is no certainty that this will occur. Examples of successful aggression include China's forcible absorption of Tibet in 1950, the Soviets' assumption of control of the Baltic states in 1940, the Indian takeover of the tiny Portuguese enclave of Goa in 1961, and the Vietnamese capture of Cambodia in 1978. As is so often the case in international politics, aggression is in the eye of the beholder. In each of these examples, some believed that the military action was justified. Thus international action against aggression often resembles vigilante justice, where innocents are harmed in clumsy attempts to find and punish the guilty. Additionally, the posse may not arrive in time to save the day; by the time an international response could be coordinated to deal with the self-destruction of Yugoslavia in 1991–95 or the genocide in Rwanda in 1994, hundreds of thousands had lost their lives to aggression and hatred.

The Security Dilemma

This anarchic nature of world politics leads to a situation known as the **security dilemma.** The security dilemma arises when a state feels insecure and decides that its best policy is to increase its military strength. Its objective in so doing is not to enhance its aggressive power, but only to increase its ability to defend against attack. Unfortunately, a neighboring country may then feel threatened by this increase of armaments near its border. The second state, fearing that it has been made more vulnerable by the increase in the first state's military power, initiates a military buildup of its own. As more and more states witness this increase in military potential, they consider themselves threatened by the possibility of aggressive action. An unintended spiral thus occurs, where every nation grows more and more insecure and seeks to stay equal to its neighbors in military strength.

This unfortunate situation arises despite the fact that none of the states involved intends to threaten the security of its neighbors. Each state, acting in its own self-interest, helps to create a potentially dangerous buildup of weapons. We recently witnessed this effect of the anarchic world system during the Cold War between the United States and the former Soviet Union from 1945 to 1991 (described in Chapter Four) and in the Arab-Israeli disputes of the post–World War II period (outlined in Chapter Five). The security dilemma explains how conflicts can arise even when states do not harbor aggressive intentions toward one another.

Of course, some people with a *Star Wars* view believe that the Americans or the Soviets, the Arabs or the Israelis, did or do indeed have aggressive intentions toward their adversaries. But, to those who believe in the security dilemma, conflict occurs not because states are fundamentally antagonistic, but because of the conditions in which they find themselves. That is, conflict stems from an anarchic world where the possibility of aggression is ever present. States hope for the best, but expect the worst, and thus arm themselves as a precautionary measure.

Nations all seek **power** over one another, and must either conquer or die. The popular film series about the British spy-hero James Bond similarly suggests a world where nations that are basically good must sometimes resort to intrigue, subterfuge, and controlled force in order to survive and prevail against evil. In the same vein, many Cold War–era movies such as *The Spy Who Came in from the Cold,* in which innocent people are used as pawns and sacrificed in order to save a reprehensible but indispensable British spy behind the Iron Curtain, present an image of world politics in which the ends sometimes justify the means—that is, it is necessary to commit sins in order to overcome evil. (The security dilemma and its effects are discussed further in Chapter Eleven.)

Common Interests and Cooperation under Anarchy

Even in an anarchic world dominated by the security dilemma, however, there is far more cooperation than conflict between nations. Because wars and crises make the headlines and catch our attention, it is easy to overlook the fact that relations between states are usually positive and friendly, and rarely lead to violence. The national interests that all states pursue will frequently conflict with the goals and interests of other states, but the leaders know that they are more likely to attain their goals through cooperation and reciprocal behavior. As a result, states, in interacting with one another, establish rules and norms that reinforce cooperation.

One such time-honored norm is that of **diplomatic immunity.** One of the reasons the seizure of the American Embassy in Teheran in 1979 by the Iranian revolutionary guards caused outrage in the United States and elsewhere is that it violated this time-honored principle. According to international convention, diplomatic personnel enjoy freedom from arrest and prosecution, and are allowed to conduct their business unmolested even in times of crisis. Iran decided against voluntarily complying with international norms of conduct and took over the embassy. If all states took the representatives of nations with whom they had relations hostage, normal diplomatic interchange could not exist. Chapter Nine describes how states develop the practice of diplomatic immunity and other norms of cooperative behavior.

Similarly, no country has all the resources or products that it requires. As Chapter Seven shows, many states specialize or have particular products they can produce more efficiently than other countries. If states could not trade products or resources they have in surplus for those they do not produce or possess, all would be poorer. Thus, states find that they have complementary economic interests and realize that cooperation can provide mutual benefits. In international politics, it often pays to cooperate in such areas as diplomatic and economic relations. Trade provides gains for all sides. Diplomatic relations are useful to all states. Most states realize that they would have difficulty pursuing their own interests without economic relations and diplomatic exchanges.

States also share common problems. Pollution in the air or water affects many countries. The accident at the nuclear reactor in Chernobyl in 1986 in the former Soviet Union increased the radiation over many nearby countries. Pollution of a river like the Rhine or the Danube that runs through several countries affects many neighbors downstream. Use of **fossil fuels** produces hydrocarbons, which alter the earth's atmosphere and may cause temperatures around the globe to rise. Many industrial chemicals adversely affect the ozone layer, which protects the earth from harmful radiation. Because many nations derive short-term economic benefits from ignoring pollution regulations or chopping down forests for wood products, environmental degradation is a global problem about which nations must cooperate in order to solve. (Chapter Ten surveys environmental concerns, drug trafficking, terrorism, and other global issues.)

Therefore, although the nature of international politics is anarchic and encourages conflict, the nature of some of the problems that governments face encourages cooperation. The security dilemma does not prevent nations from working together to address concerns that affect them all. Simply put, nations need each other. Benjamin Franklin's remark about the leaders of the American Revolution is even more applicable to the states in the contemporary international system: "We must indeed all hang together, or, most assuredly, we shall all hang separately." Order in the international arena is thus established not through enforcement, as is the case in the domestic arena, but rather through reciprocal compliance by nations explicitly or tacitly adhering to agreements, norms, and **regimes** of cooperation. (Chapters Six, Nine, and Twelve discuss how these cooperative arrangements can work.)

COOPERATION VERSUS CONFLICT

Given the anarchy of international politics, cooperation and conflict are frequently intertwined. In theory, since World War II there has been a concerted effort in economic matters to promote and establish an international trading order to the benefit of all involved. As noted in Chapter Five, however, many countries in the **Third World** have resented the economic success of the West and have argued that it has been achieved in large measure by exploitation of their resources without adequate or fair remuneration. For example, a South American country may feel that U.S. firms exercise excessive control over its natural resources, such as copper in Chile or oil in Peru. Countries of the former communist bloc, after decades of imposed isolation from this trading order, are attempting to integrate themselves into the global economy. Many of these states have begun to model themselves after the capitalist democracies, but these moves are bringing domestic political and ethnic conflicts to the forefront. The effects of cooperation are thus not invariably positive; cooperation itself may cause tensions in other sectors of international affairs.

As nations modernize and society becomes more complex, states begin to interact more frequently with other states for a variety of reasons and in a variety of ways, such as trade, diplomacy, and environmental protection. Economies become linked to those of other states. This pattern of linkage is called **interdependence.** For most industrial countries, foreign trade has become increasingly more important to their economies as their exports have grown faster than their **GNP** (gross national product, the total sum of all goods and services produced by a nation) for at least the last two decades. Perhaps more significant is the dependence of many countries on foreign sources of raw materials. Japan's reliance on imports for practically all of its energy needs, especially petroleum, has influenced its foreign policy towards oil-producing states. Manufacturers in the United States, Japan, and the European Union are also dependent on foreign supplies of minerals like bauxite, manganese, and chromium.[4]

Economies are further connected by foreign investment. Multinational corporations such as Ford, Sony, Philips, and BASF have vested interests in the stability of the world economy; their investments in factories, offices, and other business expenses in countries ranging from Australia and Japan to Pakistan and Venezuela depend on friendly and stable diplomatic and economic relations being maintained. The sums of money involved in international trade and finance are truly staggering. In all, the U.S. government and private American investors owned more than $4 trillion in foreign assets at the end of 1996, while the total of foreign assets in the United States exceeded $5 trillion.[5] As states become more intertwined in their relations with other states, they develop greater stakes in international cooperation even though their specific economic interests may conflict.

Cooperation and conflict also coexist when nations are confronted by an event of paramount proportions, namely war. In these instances, cooperation between states emerges. In World War II, the United States, Great Britain, and the Soviet Union worked together to prevent the Nazis from conquering all of Europe. The formation of **NATO** (North Atlantic Treaty Organization) by the United States, Canada, and Western European nations in 1949 arose from post–World War II apprehensions concerning possible Soviet aggression. This perceived threat prompted former World War II allies and enemies alike to cooperate against a new common adversary.

Therefore, although world politics is anarchic, it is not disorderly. Order exists in the international system and constrains the behavior of states. Although there is no world government to enforce laws, if states violate international rules, this can lead to negative outcomes that far outweigh any potential gains from such behavior. Thus many states that could easily conquer their weaker neighbors do not do so because they fear retaliation or political or moral isolation from the international community.

DOMESTIC FACTORS IN INTERNATIONAL RELATIONS

Other constraints on the actions of states and leaders are rooted in domestic politics. The U.S. antiwar movement impeded the ability of both the Johnson and Nixon administrations to conduct military operations in Vietnam as they pleased. Even the former Soviet Union's military actions in Afghanistan were restricted by domestic popular discontent with the uncertainty of prolonged combat in that forlorn country. Indeed, the Afghan War was a factor in the collapse of Soviet **communism.** Another famous example of domestic politics limiting the ability to act in the international arena was the widespread pacifism in Britain and France prior to World War II. This pacifism interfered with the British and French governments' abilities to counter the rise of Hitler. The popularity of isolationism in the United States during this period played a similar role (see Chapter Three).

Additionally, modern communications make it easier for citizens to obtain the information necessary to question their leaders' policies. In the highly complex environment in which we live today, we can fly to another country in a few hours, call overseas and transmit documents in an instant. Communication is cheaper and easier than before. Satellite coverage allows us to watch events around the world as they are happening. The Vietnam War was the first conflict seen on television, with full reports of the gore and uncertainty of combat. The result was a devastating decline in support for the war in the United States and in support of American policy generally. More recently, the Tiananmen Square Massacre in China, when students who were demonstrating in favor of democracy were gunned down (while other protesters faxed reports of repression to the outside world), had a temporarily devastating impact on China's ability to pursue its diplomatic and economic goals, because widespread revulsion against the bloodshed led nations like the United States to modify their relations with the Chinese government. The Persian Gulf War in the Middle East affected hundreds of millions of people around the world because they could see and experience it. When a CNN (Cable News Network) journalist wearing a gas mask reported impending Scud missile attacks on Saudi Arabia and Israel during the Gulf War, viewers felt as if they were the victims. (Some Americans even bought gas masks out of fear that the United States would suffer terrorist attacks.)

Thus we see that international relations are a confusing blend of both the domestic and the international, and of cooperation and conflict. On the one hand, the nature of world politics is an anarchic system in which no higher authority can enforce laws upon the individual states. On the other hand, cooperation and order emerge from mutual interests, international institutions, and constraints on action.

WHO PARTICIPATES IN INTERNATIONAL POLITICS?

The primary type of actor in international relations today is the **nation-state,** around which the world is organized. The nation-state is a relatively new idea whose origins are rooted in the American and French revolutions at the end of the eighteenth century. A state is an independent political entity with institutions and an authority in a specific territory. A nation is a group of people who view themselves as having a common heritage, a common destiny, and a sense of mutual identification based on language, history, and culture. The nation-state fuses these two concepts; it is a state structure in which a nation resides and that exists (ideally) to protect and promote the interests of that nation. Modern examples of nation-states include France, Turkey, Japan, and Brazil. The concept of the nation-state is directly related to much of the conflict in international politics for the last two hundred years and still accounts for much of the continuing conflict today.

A man stands passively before a convoy of Chinese army tanks on the Avenue of Eternal Peace in Beijing on June 2, 1989. The next day government troops attacked pro-democracy demonstrators in Tiananmen Square.　　　　SOURCE: © Reuters / Bettman

Throughout history, many bitter conflicts have arisen when nations (such as Greece, Poland, and Croatia) attempted to create their own states, and when states (such as Germany, North Korea, and Serbia) sought to unify all members of a nation. For these reasons, more will be said about the definition and origin of the nation-state in Chapter Two.

While the nation-state is the basic organizing principle of world politics, **nationalism** (the belief that a nation should have its own state) is one of the main motivating factors. National groups such as the French-speaking Quebecois in Canada, the Kurds, the Tibetans, and the Muslim Slavs in Bosnia all claim the right to "self-determination," or to have their own independent states. The situation is reversed in numerous African countries. When European states controlled much of Africa, they divided territories according to their convenience without reference to the interests or history of indigenous peoples. We therefore see conflicts in many African states due to the colonial powers' arbitrarily cutting borders across ethnic boundaries, such as the Yoruba in Benin and Nigeria, the Somali in Somalia and Ethiopia, the Hutu and Tutsi in Rwanda, Burundi, and Zaire, and the Swazi in Swaziland and South Africa (see Chapters Two and Five).

Although the nation-state is the primary actor in the international arena, other entities can influence world politics. These may be grouped into the two broad categories of **intergovernmental organizations** (IGOs) and **nongovernmental organi-**

zations (NGOs). IGOs, as the name implies, are groups of states or governments organized for a common purpose, while NGOs are groups not directly related to governments but organized to take an active part in international affairs. (IGOs, NGOs, and a whole alphabet soup of other nonstate actors on the world stage are discussed further in Chapter Nine.)

IGOs can provide a diplomatic and legal framework for political interaction among nations (in which case they are usually termed international organizations) or they may be designed to foster cooperation in specific fields such as trade, security, health, transportation, arms control, and human rights. Some examples are the United Nations, the best-known and most important international organization; the Organization of Petroleum Exporting Countries (**OPEC**) and the Organization for Economic Cooperation and Development (**OECD**), which are primarily economic organizations but which frequently have political goals as well; the North Atlantic Treaty Organization (NATO), which is a defense alliance; and the International Atomic Energy Agency (**IAEA**), which monitors nuclear weapons proliferation and the safety of nuclear power plants.

The impact that IGOs have in the international arena ranges from minimal to quite substantial, depending on their cohesion and resources. For example, the regulation of oil prices by the OPEC nations in 1973 raised oil prices, created economic hardship in both the Third World and industrialized countries, and had a considerable political impact on world affairs due to Western demands for and dependence on oil. By contrast, the United Nations offers a forum for dialogue on controversial issues that in some circumstances leads to conflict resolution, and the UN Security Council can dispatch peacekeeping forces to areas of conflict— if UN member states agree to supply the troops and finance their operations. However, many UN resolutions are often ignored by states that do not agree with them. Institutions affiliated with the UN, such as the **World Health Organization** (WHO), the **Food and Agriculture Organization** (FAO), and the United Nations Relief and Works Agency (UNRWA) also provide services in specific areas such as health care, famine relief, and protection for refugees.

NGOs come in a wide variety of types. **Multinational corporations** (MNCs) are one type. With the increasing world interdependence and a liberal international economic order that supports **free trade** (trade without **tariffs** or similar barriers), the twentieth century has seen the rise of multinational corporations as international participants. Although they may be based in one particular nation, referred to as the MNC's home country, they have operations and production plants in many other nations, or host countries. Famous examples include IBM, the Mitsubishi group, Shell Oil, Volkswagen, Coca-Cola, ICI, and General Motors. Their influence over governments and in the international arena is generated by their financial resources and economic power, which are often quite extensive.

Terrorist groups are extremist political factions that use violence to achieve political gains. This category encompasses the underground terror wings of political organizations, such as Hezbollah and the Irish Republican Army (IRA), as well as groups operating only as violent militarists, such as the Red Brigades in Italy and Peru's Tupac Amaru. Often, these groups exert influence by frightening civilians with the threat and practice of violence in order to persuade others to support their political aims. Terrorists are often supported by states, or governments, many times serving the goals of those states. For example, competing factions of the Palestine Liberation Organization (PLO) who oppose the peace process are actively sponsored and housed by Syria and other Arab regimes. Iran's active participation throughout the Middle East has included its sponsorship of hostage-taking in the 1980s, and its support of various radical Islamic terrorist groups. North Korea is another state accused of supporting acts of terrorism like the bombing of a Korean Air Lines jet in 1987. When these groups engage in terrorist activity, they further the goals of individual states and their quest for power in the region. The difference between terrorism and resistance to conquest is often a matter of perspective; one side's "terrorists" may be another's "freedom fighters."

Various other types of organizations also play a role in world politics. These include the news media, the Catholic church, Greenpeace, **Amnesty International,** the International Olympic Organizing Committee, and the International Committee of the **Red Cross.** From time to time, these organizations can influence international relations that deal with their specific interests. For example, Greenpeace's active pursuit of laws against whaling has contributed to negotiations between Japan, the former USSR, and the United States over whaling practices in the Pacific Ocean. The Vatican seeks to improve the human condition through religious teaching and moral persuasion, but it engages in some political activity as well. For example, it placed its own kind of sanctions against the white-dominated South African regime, denouncing apartheid as a moral evil and refusing to include the country on the pope's itinerary. Amnesty International lobbies for an end to capital punishment and focuses publicity on individuals who are victimized by their governments, sometimes resulting in their release from prison. Amnesty International campaigned for the release of Vaclav Havel of the Czech Republic and Nelson Mandela of South Africa while they were incarcerated as political prisoners; soon after they were released, they were elected to the presidency of their countries.

The news media draw attention to particular states, personalities, and problems. By raising global awareness of specific concerns, the media can bring issues to the forefront of national and international political debate and can affect the perceptions of millions toward specific events. When Mikhail Gorbachev resigned the presidency of the now defunct USSR in December 1991, the event was covered by teams of journalists, relayed instantly around the world, followed by hours of commentary, background reports, and speculation on the impact the event would have on world politics. (One news service executive even provided a pen when Gorbachev's failed.) The Internet now offers even more immediacy and intimacy of international communication, and anyone who can create a home page on the World Wide Web can present his or her case to the world. This reminds us that in a very real sense, we all participate in international politics in one way or another.

LEVELS OF ANALYSIS IN INTERNATIONAL RELATIONS

These global connections enable states that are small in terms of area, population, or GNP, as well as NGOs, which have none of the above, to exert a major impact on world politics. This leads us to ponder a question: exactly what does determine how a state will act in the international system? As the chapters in this book will show, there is little that is either exact or predictable about world politics. Although analysts of international affairs can rarely find definitive explanations for historical events or current policies, they can at least tell us where to look. The plethora of factors influencing world politics may be grouped into **levels of analysis,** which may be thought of as categories of variables that can help us decide where to search for explanations of world affairs. Chapter Twelve will discuss levels of analysis in more detail, but it will be useful to briefly introduce them here before the book embarks on a survey of events and issues in international politics.

Experts in the field of international relations disagree on the number of levels of analysis. (This should begin to give you an idea of how little they agree on anything else.) It is most convenient for the purposes of this book to assign the various influences on state behavior to one of three levels: the international systemic (systemic, for short), the domestic, or the individual.[6] The international **systemic level of analysis** claims that states are essentially similar. They are moved by the situation in which they find themselves and react to similar situations in the same way as others. Thus how the state is organized or who is in charge doesn't matter very much. Present any state with an external challenge, systemic theorists argue, and it will react in a particular manner determined largely by its role and influence in the global political or economic system.

The systemic level covers factors which come into play in the interactions between states. These include the number of major political actors in the system and their strengths and weaknesses relative to one another (often referred to as the **balance of power**), the rules and norms that govern the relations between states, as well as international organizations, and similar influences operating "above" or "outside" specific nation-states. In general, these factors affect all states in the system; the impact on each state may vary, but the nature of the influence is the same for the entire system. For example, the United Nations influences all countries, although it may have a different impact on stronger states than on weaker states. Moreover, a system cannot have more than one structure at the same time. For example, it cannot simultaneously be **bipolar** (dominated by two actors of relatively equal power that overshadow all the rest) and **multipolar** (containing several more or less equal actors). (These concepts will be discussed further in Chapter Twelve.)

In many ways, the systemic level considers the ways in which factors common to all states prompt them to behave similarly toward one another. By contrast, the **domestic level of analysis** deals with influences that operate within nation-states and thus examines how different attributes of states lead them to act differently. The domestic level looks at individual nations' political and economic systems, government structure, bureaucracy, history, and culture. Analysis from the domestic level considers how each state's unique characteristics give it a particular orientation toward or outlook on world politics and how these traits define a state's specific interests, goals, and concerns. Chapter Twelve will also examine how the features of a state that distinguish it from other actors in the international system can cause it to relate to other states in a manner different from what an analysis at the systemic level might lead us to expect.

Just as states share universal characteristics while possessing unique features, people are alike in many important ways and very different in others. Recognizing this, Chapter Twelve will consider how individual leaders' backgrounds, experiences, gender, styles of leadership, and personal goals and beliefs can affect the decisions they make regarding their countries' foreign policies. All too often, these decisions must be made under extremely stressful conditions, and the **individual level of analysis** explores how situations of confrontation and crisis can affect the decision-making process. The final sections of Chapter Twelve will therefore attempt to put a human face on world politics by looking at how leaders and the citizens they lead can shape international relations.

After Chapter Twelve's brief introduction to theories of international relations, Chapter Thirteen will discuss how levels of analysis can help us think about the future of world politics. For now, it is most important to remember that levels of analysis are basically categories of explanations for the actions of states in the international system. Taken together, they provide an organizational scheme for theories of international relations. As such, they help analysts to formulate and test explanations for the behavior of states and nonstate actors in the international system. The levels do this by indicating what sort of data is most relevant to a particular theory and identifying the competing explanations an analyst must contend with in order to prove his or her case. They can also help us to understand events by classifying the plethora of factors that may have prompted a state to take an action or a leader to make a decision. The At a Glance box "Levels of Analysis" summarizes the main features of the three levels of analysis.

THEMES AND CONTROVERSIES

Regardless of whether one concludes that the most important influences on world politics are found at the systemic, domestic, or individual level of analysis, the history of international relations has a puzzling and often depressing regularity to it. Periods of peace alternate with destructive wars; conflicts of economic interest wax and wane; political issues that were believed put to rest in one era resurface again in another. Part of the reason why we can sometimes observe cycles or patterns in international affairs is that many of the same problems crop up in the relations between different states, and many of the disputes that are central to the making of all nations' foreign policies have never been satisfactorily resolved. Opposition between contending perspectives on international politics and economics is a recurring theme in both the history of interactions between states and in contemporary debates over **foreign policy.** Before embarking on an examination of

At a Glance

Levels of Analysis

Systemic	Domestic	Individual
Basic Explanation for State Actions		
All states are essentially similar. State behavior results from the operation of the international system.	All states are unique. State behavior is an outgrowth of a state's characteristic features.	State behavior is determined by decisions made by individual leaders.
Examples of Theories		
Balance of power	Peace among democracies	Cognitive theories
Long cycle	Military-industrial complex	Attribution theory
Hegemonic stability	Bureaucratic politics	Crisis decision making
Security dilemma		Operational code
Types of Data Considered		
Military strength	Form of government	Leadership style
Nuclear deterrence	Political institutions	Leaders' beliefs, goals, and
Gross national product (GNP)	Economic structure	values
Number of major powers	Ideology	Generational experience
	History	Personal relationships
	Culture	
	Public opinion	

world politics past and present, it may be helpful to outline a few of the major controversies that, in different forms and with reference to various specific issues, have animated the theory and practice of international relations for many years.

Perhaps the most fundamental controversy in world affairs is the clash between **realism** and **idealism.** In general terms, realists believe that the security dilemma cannot be completely overcome. From this perspective any increase in one state's power, no matter how well-intentioned, threatens the interests of other states to some degree. Therefore, states have no choice but to "look out for number one" by seeking power and independence in order to protect their vital interests. This viewpoint promotes policies that seek to maximize a nation's security and power in a cold, cruel world in which all other states have no choice but to do the same; such a policy course is commonly termed **realpolitik,** literally the "policy of realism." Idealists, on the other hand, refuse to believe that the security dilemma is inescapable. The fact that states do cooperate shows that cooperation is possible, and suggests that the right conditions can foster greater cooperation. The game of international relations may not always be zero-sum; interdependence may make it necessary and possible for countries to collaborate in order to solve common problems. If the structure of the international system, or human nature, leads to recurrent conflict, perhaps either or both can be improved in order to create an environment more favorable to cooperation.

A related dispute exists between **internationalism** and **isolationism.** Internationalists conclude that states have no choice but to participate actively in world politics in order to pursue their basic interests. Regardless of whether the world is fundamentally conflictual or harmonious, problems in one part of the globe, if left unchecked, can eventually spread to every corner, so states ignore the outside world at their peril. Essentially, therefore, internationalists believe that regardless of geography, no state is an island. Nations must open their doors and minds to the world for security, economic, political, or moral reasons, whether they like it or not. Isolationists, on the other hand, regard engagement with other nations as an inherently risky enterprise that affords more dangers than opportunities. Because the world is such a complex and unpredictable place, and each state's resources are limited, it is better to concentrate on solving problems at home and improving the welfare of one's fellow citizens. Isolationists, therefore, generally counsel "live and let live" in foreign policy. They argue that the best course is to keep the national nose out of another nations' business and thank other countries to do the same.

Two other fundamental controversies center around economic issues. The most common difference of opinion on a state's external economic affairs is the opposition between free trade and **protectionism.** Advocates of free trade argue that removal of all trade barriers will allow each state to produce goods and services most efficiently, according to its **comparative advantage.** If trade is unhindered by tariffs, **import quotas,** and other restrictions, products will flow freely between nations, world prices will be lower, resources will be allocated more efficiently by the free market, and everyone will be better off. Supporters of protectionism, or managed trade, counter that this would allow other states to drive key industries out of business by undercutting the prices of domestically produced goods. After disposing of the competition, and in the process eliminating good jobs in the targeted industry, foreign companies could then raise prices at will and squeeze excess profits out of domestic consumers. To avoid this, protectionists argue, trade barriers should be erected to protect important industries and high-paying jobs, even if this means that consumers will have to pay higher prices or pay for subsidies with increased taxes. (For more on these issues, see Chapters Six and Seven.) Conflicts between advocates of free trade and supporters of protected or managed trade have been waged for centuries. A more modern economic controversy that arose in the wake of the Industrial Revolution (see Chapter Two) stems from the antagonism between **capitalism** and **socialism.** To oversimplify (as has been done for all of the viewpoints considered in this section), capitalists believe that the means of production of goods and services should be owned privately, so that the desire for profit will lead to greater efficiency and thus benefit consumer and producer alike. The free market, according to this viewpoint, will reward productivity, and the world economic system will become more productive as a result. Socialists, in contrast, contend that productive assets should be owned collectively (which in practice means by the state) in order to maximize the benefits to society. Economic rewards should be allocated according to human need rather than corporate greed, so that wealth may be distributed more equally. In terms of international trade, free-market capitalism would tend to benefit industrialized nations (which use capital and labor most efficiently), while socialism would tend to benefit states that export natural resources and labor (which, on average, have more uneven economic development and suffer more from poverty).

These disputes have taken many forms over the centuries. Idealists argued after World War I that creating a strong League of Nations would prevent another catastrophic world war, while realists argued that the League could not stop nations from seeking to maximize their power in pursuit of their own security and prosperity (see Chapters Three and Nine). In the 1990s, internationalists shared the conviction that the United States and other countries had both a strong interest and a moral duty to intervene military to stop civil wars in Bosnia, Haiti, Somalia, and elsewhere, while isolationists were equally convinced that both interest and morality argued against intervention. Britain sought to open world markets to free trade in the nineteenth century, while many continental powers erected tariff barriers (Chapters Two and Seven). Proponents of a New International Economic Order in the 1960s argued that Northern capitalism was destroying the economies and societies of Southern developing countries and demanded a global redistribution of wealth (see Chapter Eight).

One of the reasons why these controversies have not been resolved is that they are in large measure irresolvable. Arguments and analyses used in support of all of them ultimately depend on perceptions and assumptions, and reasonable people continue to disagree about them. The reader cannot expect that this book (or any other) will present a resolution of these disputes, but should expect to encounter them repeatedly as recurring themes in the making of foreign policy and the conduct of world politics. The At a Glance box "Opposing Themes" summarizes these themes and controversies.

THE CONTEMPORARY INTERNATIONAL ARENA— GLOBALIZATION AND FRAGMENTATION

The global trends toward cultural, economic, and environmental interdependence, balanced by the natural desire of nations and individuals to maintain their autonomy and identity, create a contemporary international system dominated by opposing trends toward **globalization** and **fragmentation.** On the one hand, the world seems to be shrinking with every year. You can turn on your television and watch an American football team playing a game in Tokyo. During commercial breaks, multinational corporations will tell you how you can fly almost anywhere in the world quickly and comfortably, call or fax someone on the other side of the globe instantly, or send a package to practically any city on the planet in a few days. You can use VCRs or computers manufactured in distant lands, eat fruit or vegetables grown thousands of miles away, take brief vacations in faraway exotic resorts, and your financial future can be determined in part by decisions of governments in Paris or Singapore. Regions that were isolated just a few years ago, such as the Amazon River in South America, the remote forests of Siberia, and

At a Glance

Opposing Views of World Politics

Realism

States have no choice but to pursue self-interest and power without regard to moral considerations. The security dilemma cannot be completely overcome. International security is a zero-sum game. This viewpoint is also known as realpolitik.

Idealism

States have the ability to pursue moral values as well as material goals. The security dilemma is not inescapable, and cooperation is possible. The right conditions can foster greater cooperation.

Internationalism

States have no choice but to participate actively in world politics. Problems in one part of the globe, if left unchecked, can eventually spread to every corner. Regardless of its geographic situation, no state is an island.

Isolationism

Engagement with other nations is inherently risky. The world is a complex and unpredictable place. It is better to concentrate on one's own problems and not those of others.

Free Trade

The removal of all trade barriers will allow each state to produce goods and services most profitably. Products will flow freely between nations, prices will be lower, resources will be allocated more efficiently, and everyone will be better off.

Protectionism

Trade barriers should be erected to protect important industries and high-paying jobs. Consumers will have to pay higher prices or pay for subsidies with increased taxes.

Capitalism

In society, the means of production of goods and services should be privately owned. The desire for profit will lead to greater efficiency and thus benefit consumer and producer alike. The free market will reward productivity. As a result, the world economic system will become more productive. Industrialized nations will benefit from this system.

Socialism

Productive assets should be owned collectively (which in practice means by the state) in order to maximize the benefits to society. Economic rewards should be allocated according to human need rather than corporate greed, so that wealth may be distributed more equally. States that export natural resources and labor will benefit from this system.

parts of the Indonesian archipelago, are now readily accessible—and of great concern to environmentalists.

The media can report on events in other nations that in the past would either have gone unnoticed or would have been reviewed days afterward. In particular, international services like CNN and the Sky Channel provide information instantaneously around the world to a growing global elite that watches the same news programs, wears the same clothes, and eats the same food. Recall CNN's reporting of the U.S. bombing of Baghdad in January 1991. Recall, too, reports about the aborted coup in the former USSR that August. We experienced these events as if they were happening in our back yard. Compare this immediacy to Hawaiian television broadcasts when, as late as the early 1970s, Hawaiians received only day-old images of world events, because the film had to be flown in from the mainland. By contrast, in the 1990s anyone with a home computer could join in a live chat session over the Internet with participants in Vancouver, New York, Hong Kong, and Amsterdam.

Travel, communications, and high technology have therefore reduced the size of the world map both practically and psychologically. As the USSR collapsed, people in the West could see the gripping events unfolding on their television screens, accompanied by constant reminders of the effects on their own lives. The old superpower threat might have collapsed, we were told by Russian and American analysts, but the control of nuclear weapons was now more uncertain and diffused. But other signs of globalization are not so easily dramatized. Rising unity in Western Europe means a more powerful political partner and economic competitor on the world stage, in part through the ever increasing maze of economic entanglements among the advanced industrial nations. And globalization means an easier time for criminals, as the large volume of travel and trade among countries makes trafficking in drugs and arms, as well as movement of terrorists, more difficult to monitor.

Those who believed that progress toward "one world" would cure the world's conflicts and tensions have been proven wrong. Instead, the constant homogenization process of globalization, creating one culture and shared experiences for hundreds of millions of people, creates a backlash in the form of a fragmentation process. Ironically, it seems that many people around the world have been frightened by increased communication and consolidation of world affairs. They seek to retain their own identities in order to resist the possibility of everyone becoming alike. Thus we have a fragmentation process in which states are breaking up, as in multinational states such as Ethiopia and the former component republics of the Soviet Union and Yugoslavia. In other cases, such as India, divisions seem

In world politics, stronger states often use local conflicts as an arena in which to fight their own battles by proxy.
Source: © Jerry Robinson, © Cartoonists & Writers Syndicate

under control, but the potential for ethnic strife and violence remains high. Europe is filled with groups that seek autonomy, including Basques in Spain, Hungarians in Romania, and Bretons and Corsicans in France. Even proverbially calm and stable Canada has a long-standing separatist movement in French-speaking Quebec.

Thus, current world politics is dominated by two countervailing processes. Even as globalization continues, divisive tendencies may be omnipresent. Interdependence coexists with constant conflict. The advanced technology that makes globalization possible also aggravates tensions. International politics is ripe with contradictions that deepen the complexity of, and the fascination with, the processes that we address in this volume.

To understand these dynamic complexities, we will embark on an exploration of world politics that is based on a building-block approach. First, we will present the historical background essential for understanding international relations. Part II of the text (Chapters Two through Five) outlines the history of world politics from the rise of the nation-state in the seventeenth century, to the decline of the nation-state and the rise of the global information society on the eve of the twenty-first century. Once we have examined the historical record, we will step back and consider the operation of the international system. Accordingly, Part III (Chapters Six, Seven, and Eight) gives a basic introduction to international economics, including the special problems and challenges faced by the developing world.

Moving on to a higher level of abstraction, Part IV (Chapters Nine, Ten, and Eleven) presents key concerns that supersede problems specific to nation-states. Chapter Nine discusses international law and organizations, setting out the "rules of the game" of international politics, and Chapter Ten surveys contemporary global issues on which states frequently disagree but cannot resolve without cooperation. Chapter Eleven proceeds to explore the dynamics of security and power, which, for better or worse, remains an overriding concern of all participants in world politics.

After considering these issues and concepts, we will be ready to introduce the theoretical analysis international relations in Part V. Chapter Twelve shows how theories derived from the three levels of analysis can offer explanations for the patterns of cooperation and conflict observed in earlier chapters. Finally, in Chapter Thirteen, we use all of the tools and information provided in earlier material to speculate on the future of world politics in a new and uncertain era.

Essentially, this book's approach to international relations may be likened to a newspaper article. Part II gives the basic historical information necessary for understanding the "story" of world politics—answering the initial journalistic questions of who, what, and where. Parts III and IV then examine how things happen in the international system—how states determine their goals and priorities, how they attempt to achieve their aims, and how they resolve, through fair means or foul, the conflicts that inevitably occur. Following this, Part V tackles the complex and controversial question of why things happen the way they do in world politics, presenting theories from the systemic, domestic, and individual levels of analysis. Our story's last chapter, which looks at the future of international politics, attempts to take on the most difficult question of all, the one that is both most mysterious and most urgent: what next?

International politics is changing rapidly in our day, and technological and political developments are accelerating the rate of change. The world is coming together, and flying apart, faster than ever before. These changes create dangers and opportunities for all of us, but it isn't always easy to tell the two apart. Many readers of this book may be wondering how developments on the international scene will affect their lives: Should I be worried that a Japanese automaker is planning to open a plant in my home town, or should I apply for a job there? Will Chile's entry into the **North American Free Trade Agreement** (NAFTA) create or destroy American jobs? Can an international convention to reduce carbon emissions stop global warming, or is climate change really not a problem? Will my company be able to sell its products in the European Union, or will it face insurmountable non-tariff barriers? Will terrorists strike my hometown if the United States bombs a suspected North Korean nuclear weapons laboratory?

The answers to such questions are not in this book—but the historical background, theoretical concepts, and analytical tools that one must have in order to attempt to answer them are here. The purpose of this text is to help readers develop the skills necessary to make sense of a complex and constantly changing world. It is hoped that readers will use the information and ideas presented here to make their own analyses of the ongoing events that shape world politics and increasingly affect our lives.

KEY TERMS

Amnesty
  International
anarchy
balance of
  power
bipolar
capitalism
comparative
  advantage
communism
diplomatic
  immunity
domestic level of
  analysis
European Union
Food and
  Agriculture
  Organization

foreign policy
fossil fuels
fragmentation
free trade
globalization
GNP
IAEA
idealism
import quotas
individual level
  of analysis
interdependence
intergovern-
  mental
  organizations
internationalism
international
  system

isolationism
levels of analysis
multinational
  corporations
multipolar
nation
nationalism
nation-state
NATO
nongovern-
  mental
  organizations
norms
North American
  Free Trade
  Agreement
OECD
OPEC

power
protectionism
Red Cross
realism
realpolitik
regimes
security
  dilemma
socialism
systemic level of
  analysis
tariffs
Third World
World Health
  Organization
world politics
United Nations
zero-sum game

□ □ □ □

PART

II

The History of World Politics

Origins of the Modern International System

The central term in the expression "**international relations**" is "nation," but the **nation-state** has not always been the central focus of **world politics**. In fact, before the seventeenth century, the nation-state as we know it did not exist. The change in the nature of world politics from relations between rulers to relations between nations was a historical development of tremendous importance. It had a powerful impact not only on politics, security, and commerce, but on every field of human endeavor. As the system of nation-states is now the primary organizational structure of the world, the time and place where it originated is the logical point from which to begin our study of world politics. This chapter will outline the development of the nation-state from its beginnings in seventeenth-century Europe, through its expansion throughout the world in the eighteenth and nineteenth centuries, and to the point which many regard as its ze-nith, the eve of the twentieth century.

The sovereign nation-state originated in Europe and subsequently spread to other parts of the globe, making the European nation-state system the blueprint for the rest of the world. This fact requires the historical chapters of this book to concentrate heavily on Europe. The European focus of the history of seventeenth-through nineteenth-century international relations presented in this book should not be construed to mean that nothing important was happening outside Europe during this period—far from it. Chapter Four will show how Europe was eclipsed after 1945 as the center of world politics, and Chapter Five will discuss how de-velopments outside of Europe created the economically globalized but politically fragmented world of the late twentieth century. For better or worse, however, Eu-rope set the pattern for the organization of and interaction among nation-states that persists to the present day. Any examination of how world politics came to attain its present form must therefore begin in Europe.

POLITICS BEFORE NATIONS

Politics has existed as long as human beings have, but the nation as we know it has not. From earliest times until the seventeenth century, political entities were basically defined by the **power** of ruling elites and/or by religion. Territory was not divided into independent countries with precisely demarcated, recognized bound-aries, but into a variety of constantly shifting and often ambiguous units, includ-ing city-states, duchies, principalities, kingdoms, or **empires.** In this complex and confusing situation, the area over which a ruler could exercise authority was usu-ally determined in practice by the ability of his or her soldiers to keep the forces of other rulers out. Rulers of smaller political units, such as city-states, counties, or duchies, often owed allegiance to the rulers of larger principalities or kingdoms and were granted title over their lands in return for promises of money or military service. This arrangement was known as the feudal system. Local authorities of-ten owed varying degrees of allegiance or types of service to more than one ruler, and these multiple divided loyalties led to bitter struggles over territory.

Leaders could sometimes point to laws or treaties to legitimize their con-trol over a territory, but these were rarely universally recognized and were often imprecise. With no central authority to adjudicate legal disputes and enforce judg-ments, such international laws as existed were usually worth less than the parch-ment they were written on. (Shakespeare's play *Henry V* and the modern drama *The Lion in Winter* brilliantly depict how the complexities of inheritance and pas-sionate disputes over land often led to intrigue, violence, and war in the Middle Ages.) As a result, there was hardly any globalization and a great deal of **frag-mentation** while the feudal order prevailed in Europe and similar arrangements governed the rest of the world.

Of course, a leader's territorial claims could be greatly strengthened if he could plausibly claim that God was on his side. This was relatively easier to do before the seventeenth century than it is now, because religious authorities played a much more active role in politics. The Roman Catholic Church controlled a substantial amount of territory directly, recognized one European monarch as head of the Holy Roman Empire (which was intended to unite all Christian lands but usually was confined to what is now Austria and Germany), and could legitimize or terminate claims to land by papal writ. Empires throughout history have frequently claimed religious backing for their right to rule. The Roman emperors and Muslim caliphs were religious officers as well as secular leaders, and the emperors of China based their authority on the "Mandate of Heaven." Spiritual and temporal leaders alike could claim the right to intervene in or conquer neighboring lands for religious reasons, which offered a convenient pretext for expanding territorial holdings. Sacred authority often meant little without profane power, however, and Niccolò Machiavelli's notorious "how to" guide to power politics, *The Prince*, was aimed at "Princes of the Church" as well as budding secular tyrants. (It was also designed to show that although kings and princes had no choice but to act ruthlessly, democratic leaders were capable of acting in the interests of the people.)

With leaders of church and state acting as Machiavelli described, it was not surprising that the inhabitants of the crazy quilt of territories usually did not feel any special loyalty to their rulers, even when they could be sure who their leaders were. There was little sense of connection between rulers and ruled, and no concept of national identity, save perhaps in those few areas (usually city-states) that were organized as republics, such as pre-imperial Rome or medieval Venice. Individuals felt and swore loyalty to individual kings or princes or to God rather than to nations, the very idea of which (other than as the place of one's birth) was meaningless. It was much easier to think of one's self as a citizen of a city with precisely delineated boundaries, common interests, and walls for mutual protection, than to feel loyalty toward an ill-defined and frequently invaded country with rulers who could change with marriages and murders. There were no constitutions, and rulers rarely felt bound by laws. Most could demand taxes at will, without reference to any law (which was how the legend of Robin Hood got started). In the absence of enforceable laws and treaties, foreign rulers could demand taxes or tribute as well—there was no concept of national sovereignty defined as the inviolable authority of a legitimate government within the territory of a state.

With no rules or conventions to regulate commerce, trade was a very risky business, and ruinous taxation was often a greater danger than piracy or shipwreck. The fact that each of the many picturesque castles overlooking the Rhine River imposed tolls on boat traffic in the Middle Ages illustrates the political and economic fragmentation of the period. Nevertheless, the potential rewards of trade were great, particularly after explorers such as Dias, Columbus, and Magellan discovered sea routes to East Asia and the "New World" of North and South America. The expansion of seagoing trade in the fifteenth and sixteenth centuries began to convince many Europeans that the confusing and fragmented feudal order was stifling commerce and economic development.[1] A major political and social upheaval would be required, however, before a more stable system could be established.

Spotlight

A Very Great Princess

When Elizabeth, daughter of Henry VIII and Anne Boleyn, was crowned Queen of England in 1558, few predicted that she would survive, let alone succeed, as the monarch of a nation in crisis. Religious divisions between Catholics and adherents of the official Church of England established by her father racked the country, aggravated by persecutions on both sides carried out by her predecessors. The treasury was almost bankrupt and foreign policy was a shambles, with the country threatened from invasion by France or by Spain, the dominant powers in Europe, and by intrigues to replace the young queen with a Catholic sovereign. But through her shrewd political skills and unsurpassed charisma, Elizabeth led England to new levels of prosperity, political influence, and cultural achievement.

PHOTO SOURCE: By kind permission of the Marquess of Tavistock, of the Trustees of the Bedford Estates.

Elizabeth was a superb judge of character, courageous, highly educated (speaking six languages) and a political virtuoso, qualities which served her well throughout her reign. She chose excellent advisors, tamed rival factions of nobles and magnates, and worked constructively with Parliament to enact economic and fiscal policies that put the country on a sound financial footing. Her religious policies were remarkably tolerant in an era when brutal persecution was the norm; consequently, England did not experience the savage wars of religion that raged throughout much of continental Europe. Though her aides and courtiers were often targets of her violent temper, she took care to cultivate a benevolent public image, requiring all the artists who painted portraits of her to work from a template that depicted her in the youthful flower of her regal beauty.

Elizabeth adroitly played the established great powers against each other. She supported the Protestant revolt against Spanish rule in the Netherlands and promoted the development of English trade and sea power, which culminated in the near-miraculous defeat of the formidable Spanish Armada launched against England in 1588. As the invasion force approached, she gave an inspired address to

THIRTY YEARS' WAR AND PEACE OF WESTPHALIA

That upheaval was the Reformation, the Protestant revolt against the religious authority of the Roman Catholic Church, which began in the early sixteenth century. Through the writings of Luther, Calvin, Zwingli, and other Protestant theologians, the Reformation created a spiritual challenge to the Catholic church's religious domination of Western Europe. A popular backlash against widespread corruption in the Church added fuel to the doctrinal fire, and political leaders exploited this religious schism to further their own ambitions. One example was Henry VIII of England, who in 1534 created the Church of England and declared himself its head. The claims of authority over most of Europe asserted by the popes and the Holy Roman emperors became more burdensome to European kings as these monarchs expanded their realms of authority. Worried that

her troops, speaking directly to the era's prejudices against women in authority and dispelling any doubts as to her ability to lead her country in war in well as in peace:

> I have but the body of a week and feeble woman, but I have the heart and stomach of a king, and a king of England, too, and think foul scorn that any prince in Europe should dare to invade the borders of my realm.

Elizabeth defied convention on the role of a female ruler in another way: She never married. She earned her sobriquet, "the Virgin Queen," through a series of strategic decisions. Her perpetual marriageability was an asset in both domestic and foreign politics, and she entertained many suitors and their offers of political and dynastic alliance during her reign. She also dallied with a number of favorites, including Sir Walter Raleigh; Robert Dudley, Earl of Leicester; and Robert Devereaux, Earl of Essex. However, her experience as a young princess in turbulent Tudor politics probably had a strong impact as well because both her mother and stepmother had literally lost their heads to royal marriages.

Her refusal to choose a husband illustrates that decisiveness was conspicuously absent from her many qualities of leadership. She typically waited until the last minute to make up her mind. Her indecision hampered her ability to control the threat to her reign represented by her cousin Mary, Queen of Scots, who (because the Virgin Queen had no children) was the heir presumptive to her throne and the focus of conspiracies to overthrow her. In 1587, after Mary was convicted in a plot to depose and murder her, Elizabeth signed her death sentence but never ordered it carried out. She subsequently became hysterical when her advisors executed Mary in her name. Later, she vacillated until the very moment of her death on whether to acknowledge Mary's son, James, as heir to the English throne, and even then her final decision was ambiguous.

The final verdict on Elizabeth I, returned by the people of England, was one of overwhelming love and admiration. Elizabethan England enjoyed a period of relative civil peace, unprecedented prosperity, and a cultural awakening marked by the literary works of Christopher Marlowe, Edmund Spenser, Francis Bacon, and William Shakespeare. Adored at home, where she was called "Good Queen Bess" and "Gloriana," and respected throughout Europe (a French ambassador esteemed her "a very great princess, who knows everything") she also became a legend in the New World with the founding of the English colony of Virginia. When her long and successful reign ended in 1603, she was revered as the sovereign who led the transformation of England from a strife-torn insular kingdom into a world power.

religious fragmentation and growing autonomy of secular European leaders were undermining their spiritual and political authority, popes and emperors sought to crush these challenges, and the challenges and repressions culminated in the Thirty Years' War (1618–1648).

This war was a catastrophic conflict that wiped out more than a third of Europe's population; nearly 8 million people died from the devastation it caused. Originally sparked off by the religious conflict between Catholics and Protestants within the German lands of the Holy Roman Empire and the revolt of the Protestant estates of Bohemia against Prussia's Ferdinand II (then Catholic king of Bohemia), the war came to involve the military forces of Austria, England, France, the Netherlands, Spain, and Sweden. Religion did not provide the major motivation for most of these combatants, who were far more interested in preserving their own political power.

After many bloody battles, horrendous massacres, and sudden shifts in alliances, the Thirty Years' War finally ended with the signing of the **Peace of Westphalia** in 1648. This treaty established two important principles regarding the relations between states, **sovereignty** and **collective security,** both of which remain the foundations of contemporary international politics. First, the treaty acknowledged that states are to be sovereign in their internal affairs. In an obvious blow to the church, this meant that kings could decide domestic policy, such as the official religion within their domains, free from outside interference. Second, in attempting to establish a system of collective security, the treaty provided that whenever a state displayed blatant aggression toward another, all states were to unite in opposition to the offender in order to restore the status quo. The events in the Persian Gulf in 1990–1991 show how these principles are still important to contemporary international relations. In reaction to Iraq's invasion of Kuwait, global condemnation focused on Iraq's destruction of Kuwait's independence. However, although the United Nations sanctioned the use of military force in order to restore Kuwait's sovereignty, it refused to intervene in Iraq's domestic affairs.

The principle of sovereignty recognized in the Peace of Westphalia represents an essential element in the creation of the modern nation-state. The idea that political legitimacy could derive from secular legal authority rather than from divine sanction paved the way for the development of constitutional government. The high cost of waging the Thirty Years' War also aided in the creation of the modern nation-state because it forced monarchs to consolidate control over their territories in order to extract greater resources from their respective populations. This need required levying higher taxes, for example, and enforcing their collection. Tasks such as these usually mandated the creation of a more efficient and stable state organization—that is, a centralized bureaucracy. Increasingly, with the rise in importance of trade and manufacture (most of which would today be called "cottage industry"), the cooperation of a variety of institutions outside the church and state (especially banks and trade guilds) became more important for the functioning of a country's military and economy. In order to rule effectively, monarchs could no longer keep their entire ruling apparatus inside their castles and occasionally send out soldiers to knock the peasants' heads together, but had to either respond to or suppress the demands of the citizens. In other words, the focus of state activity shifted from kingship to government. The agony of the Thirty Years' War and its conclusion with the Peace of Westphalia thus inaugurated the modern nation-state.

The imperfections of the peace soon became apparent, however. Although the Peace of Westphalia established sovereignty and collective security as key principles of international law, these principles contradict each other. In an anarchic world (that is, one in which there is no world government), sovereignty dictates that actors must look out for their own interests first and foremost, as no power can compel others to come to their aid. If self-interest motivates nation-states, then achieving a consensus among states with conflicting interests becomes increasingly difficult, as the interests of one state often fail to mesh well with those of others. For example, rather than trying to judge "objectively" which state is the

Map 2.1	Europe in 1648

aggressor after the onset of war, states frequently side with those belligerents who best serve their interests. Shifting alliances and ongoing conflict often result, making international politics inherently complicated. These complex and contradictory forces governed relations between European states and their interactions with the wider world.

ORIGINS OF EUROPEAN IMPERIALISM

Imperialism is a process of extending a nation's authority by territorial acquisition or by the establishment of political and economic hegemony over other nations. Throughout history, empires have risen and fallen. The Egyptians, Persians, Romans, Chinese, Mongols, Aztecs, and Incas all established extensive empires dominating their local regions of the world. However, these empires were isolated from one another by what probably seemed to be insurmountable geographical barriers—vast mountain ranges, oceans, and deserts. By "discovering" the Americas in 1492, Christopher Columbus proved that these barriers were not so insurmountable after all. Yet Columbus' voyage was only one dramatic result of decades of European efforts to expand and control trade with Africa and Asia. These efforts were the first major steps toward the political and economic globalization of the modern world.

Europeans had traded with Asia for thousands of years before Columbus. For centuries, the European demand for spices and other valuable commodities from the Orient was supplied via a land route across Asia and the Middle East, and then transported through the Mediterranean by Italian, primarily Venetian, merchants. Prompted by the expansion of the Empire of the Ottoman Turks, which gained control of the traditional trade routes to Asia and posed a serious strategic threat to Europe, Prince Henry the Navigator of Portugal formed a special center for navigation designed to expand Portuguese trade and dominion overseas. One advance in navigation—the sextant—enabled sailors to plot direction by use of the stars. This invention allowed explorers to travel farther, to heretofore unknown waters, while still being able to return home with some degree of certainty. Once the Europeans got where they wanted to go, the emerging military technologies of cannons and firearms provided superior means of defense or conquest.[2]

In an effort to break into the oriental spice trade, both Spain and Portugal commissioned sailors to use the new technology in order to find alternative routes to the Orient. The Portuguese explorers Bartholomeu Dias and Vasco da Gama revolutionized world trade when, from 1487 to 1498, they led the first European expeditions to round the Cape of Good Hope at the southern tip of Africa, thereby opening up a new route to India and China through the Indian Ocean. The need for fresh water and food led the Portuguese to establish supply stations along the western and eastern coasts of Africa, as well as on the Indian subcontinent and in Southeast Asia.

Although the Portuguese developed trade routes to the east and south, Christopher Columbus, a navigator and trader from Genoa, had a crazy idea: reach the east by sailing west, directly from Europe to Japan or China. Critics who argued that such a voyage was impossible were correct, as the ships of the time could not carry enough supplies to sail as far as Columbus hoped to go. But although Columbus did not find an alternative route to the Orient, he stumbled onto the Americas, two continents rich in natural resources and fertile land, if not in silks and spices. Subsequent explorers found that although the New World did not

This sixteenth-century sketch depicts the lucrative silver mines of the Cerro Rico, the fabulous mountain of silver at Potosi in the Andes Mountains (now Bolivia). Conscripted Indian slaves worked the mines under extremely harsh conditions.

SOURCE: © Hulton Deutsch Collection Limited London

produce the luxury goods that Europeans coveted, it did offer many opportunities for trade and conquest, which Spain and Portugal were quick to exploit.

In order to avoid conflict over their competing expansion, in 1494 Spain and Portugal signed the Treaty of Tordesillas, which purported to divide up the world along an imaginary north-south line approximately 300 miles west of the Azores Islands (a Portuguese possession in the Atlantic Ocean). Spain was granted possession of all lands to the west of this line, Portugal the lands to the east. The treaty thus established the authority of Spain in the New World except for what is now Brazil, which Portuguese sailors discovered on their side of the line in 1500. The Portuguese, in turn, gained supremacy over Africa and the Indian Ocean, indeed a lucrative trade route. At first, it seemed that Spain was left with a less appealing territory, but the vast wealth of what Europeans came to call the New World soon became apparent. Spanish conquest of the Aztec and Inca Empires in the early sixteenth century meant fabulous riches for the Spanish crown, though for many indigenous peoples it also meant subjugation and, for some, near extinction.[3] Many

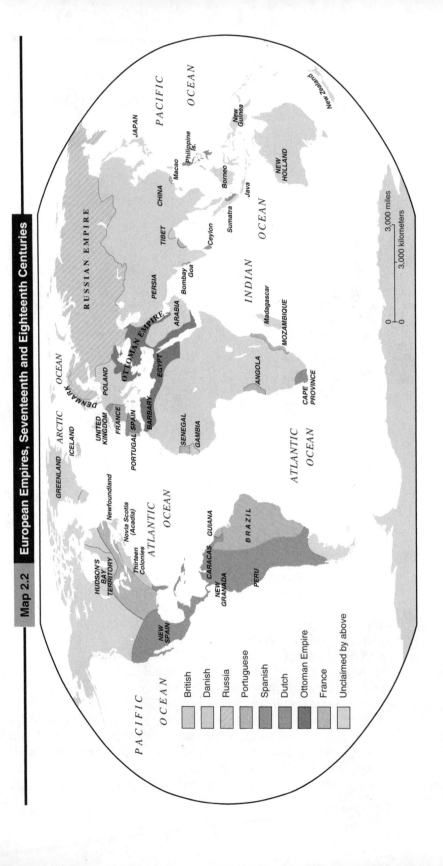

Map 2.2   European Empires, Seventeenth and Eighteenth Centuries

Spanish conquistadors went about their empire-building with religious zeal, and saw no conflict between their sacred and profane motives: as one put it, "We came here to serve God and his majesty [the king of Spain], to give light to those who were in the darkness, and to get rich, as all men desire to do." Faced with shortages of labor for their mines and plantations in the New World, the Spanish and Portuguese began buying millions of African slaves from African and Arab agents and transported them to the Americas, a practice that British, French, Dutch, and later American traders would continue until the mid-nineteenth century.

Gained by fair means and foul, wealth from the New World would finance Spain's many military endeavors and make Spain the most powerful state in sixteenth-century Europe. Spain's vast empire soon became overextended, however, and after an attempt to conquer England failed in 1588 (with the famous defeat of the Spanish Armada), Spanish power rapidly declined. A new rising power, Holland, attempted to build a trading empire in the seventeenth century and succeeded in establishing control over most of the spice-rich East Indies (known now as Indonesia). As trade and technology developed, however, Portugal and Holland did not have the population or resources to defend and extend their colonial outposts. By 1700, therefore, Britain and France emerged as the leading colonial competitors.

Britain and France brought different strengths and weaknesses to their struggle. As an island nation, Britain could focus its energies on the Royal Navy and neglect creating a large standing army. Moreover, Britain had to trade for many raw materials and a significant portion of its food, increasing its motivations to expand and protect trade. By contrast, France was a continental power with vulnerable borders and designs on expanding its territory in Europe, and therefore had to devote large amounts of its resources to a standing army. As a result, the French navy was never able to overcome British seapower. In addition, French self-sufficiency in food meant that France was consistently more inward-looking in economic matters, while British population pressure encouraged emigration to overseas colonies. The combination of these factors gave Britain consistent advantages over France in their colonial competition, which became a driving force in world politics in the eighteenth century.[4]

EIGHTEENTH-CENTURY EUROPE

Much as they do today, the opposing forces of globalization and fragmentation contributed to conflict in the eighteenth century. While trade and **colonialism** were strong forces for globalization in Asia, Africa, and the Americas, fragmentation was occurring in the political center of the newly emerging European system. In central and eastern Europe, the disintegration of the Holy Roman Empire (known as the Hapsburg Empire, after its ruling dynasty of the era) and the weakening of the Ottoman Empire after 1700 meant that new actors, mainly Prussia and Russia, emerged to challenge Austria, which had been the dominant power in the region. (See Map 2.1.) European states became less isolated from one another and from the rest of the world, and more and more, European politics became an integrated system in which developments in one area affected events in other nations.

International and Domestic Politics in the Eighteenth Century

A few characteristics of eighteenth-century Europe had profound effects on international relations. The first of these was social stratification. Autocratic monarchs ruled most of the European states, with the exception of the Netherlands and Britain, and despite all their rivalries, these monarchs had more in common with one another than with their own subjects. All of the rulers spoke French, practiced Christianity (save for the Ottomans), and were often related by blood or marriage. As a consequence, virtually every aspect of their lives was subject to an elaborate set of rules and mores. They enjoyed a luxurious life with sumptuous balls and feasts, complete with strict codes of conduct concerning who sat where at the table and who danced with whom. The aristocracy proudly patronized music and the arts although many of their subjects worked hard and lived miserably.[5] The films *Dangerous Liaisons* and *The Madness of King George* depict the life-styles, mores, and mind-set of many eighteenth-century aristocrats, all of which were quite different from those of ordinary Europeans.

The common culture of the European rulers did not keep their states from fighting one another, but it did contribute to keeping wars more circumscribed than later conflicts among modern nation-states. In general, eighteenth-century war was limited, fought by limited means for limited objectives. The expense of maintaining standing armies and the difficulty of supplying troops over long distances meant that armies could not engage in sustained combat for long periods, so most campaigns were short and sharp. States rarely fought to annihilate one another, and were usually willing to sue for and negotiate peace when their immediate territorial objectives were achieved. Another factor restrained the scope and destructiveness of eighteenth-century warfare: Sometimes monarchs, such as Britain's William III (who was Dutch by birth) and George I (who was German-born and never bothered to learn English) and Russia's Catherine the Great (born a German princess), ascended to the thrones of foreign countries. Because most rulers were related to one another and could marry only within their class, monarchs had an overriding interest in maintaining the legitimacy of the institution of monarchy by not completely destroying any ruling family or toppling crowned heads from their thrones.

Domestic conditions also often restricted the foreign policy-making latitude of a monarch. The inability to extract sufficient resources (namely taxes) from the populace limited a monarch's capability to wage war. The general populace consisted of peasants engaged in subsistence agriculture, which made tax collection inherently difficult and inefficient. (As in medieval times, taxes were often collected in kind—that is, in heads of livestock or bushels of grain rather than in money.) Because life was centered on the village, peasants often did not identify with the monarch's personal objectives and therefore had little incentive to sacrifice for the state. War drained the royal treasuries. To fight their wars, rulers generally relied on mercenaries, hired soldiers who often came from foreign states (like the Hessians hired by the British crown to fight rebellious American colonists). It was common for officers to serve wherever they could find opportunities for profit or adventure, regardless of the nationality of the troops they commanded or the monarch they served; late in his career, American naval hero John Paul Jones sailed for the tsar of Russia. Mercenary armies required great expenditures to hire and supply, and entire units would desert if not paid on time or if the enemy offered a better deal. Monarchs therefore had to husband their resources carefully, and wars often resembled chess games, decided by maneuver or positioning rather than intense combat.

Because of the keen competition for power and influence among states, and the fact that monarchs could not always extract enough resources out of the domestic population to match or prevail over their rivals, these rulers often resorted to obtaining resources through expansion, either in Europe itself or overseas through colonization. States gained or lost extensive territories through war or diplomacy, but rarely were completely conquered or ceased to exist. The principal exception to this rule was Poland. Prussia, Russia, and Austria divided Poland among themselves three times, in 1772, 1793, and 1795; in the last partition Poland disappeared entirely. Given the close relationship between territory and power, any gain by one state would lead its competitors to seek compensation, frequently at the expense of weaker states. However, the lack of sophistication of available weaponry and battlefield techniques usually prevented conflicts from being particularly decisive or destructive.[6]

Despite these political, economic, and technological limitations, most eighteenth-century rulers could conduct foreign policy unhindered by democratic controls or the interests of the general population. As a result, the personalities and ambitions of the autocrats and their top advisers figured prominently in the policies pursued by individual states. A change of rulers could lead a country to reverse alliances, go to war, or sue for peace. Not surprisingly, kings and queens, especially Louis XIV of France (the "Sun King"), Prussia's Frederick II ("the Great"), and Russia's Catherine II (also called "the Great"), are famous for how they conducted their countries' policies in this period. All monarchs sought to increase their power through territorial expansion, increased repression at home, or alliances with other monarchs, which marriage or installing a relative on the throne of another state helped to accomplish. The fear that another ruler would gain enough power and territory to dominate all of Europe dwarfed the other worries of a monarch, except perhaps the fear of widespread popular revolt. Throughout much of the century, the state that seemed most capable of dominating Europe was France.

Great Powers

Although the status of individual states fluctuated constantly during the eighteenth century, at no point did fewer than four **great powers** compete against one another. The **international system** during this period was therefore **multipolar** (containing more than two major actors). Not dependent on other states for security and militarily and economically stronger than other countries, the great powers played a major role in the security calculations of other countries. Only other great powers could threaten a great power militarily or challenge it politically, and most great powers could exert considerable influence beyond their own borders. In modern parlance, they possessed capabilities for **power projection** that less powerful countries could not match.

The exact qualifications for great-power status have always been imprecisely defined, but it is generally agreed that to be a great power, a state needs a relatively large territory and population, a well-organized military, and a strong economy. To have only one of these attributes without the others means that the state cannot sustain its influence in the international system for very long. For example, seventeenth-century Holland, in spite of its prosperous economy, had the misfortune of being located next to much larger France and having to compete with England for overseas trade. Similarly, despite Sweden's wealth and capable army and navy at the end of the Thirty Years' War, its small population prevented it from maintaining great-power status after the early eighteenth century.

States possessing all of the necessary factors of power, on the other hand, could exercise political influence for long periods. Russia, though isolated and undeveloped at the start of the eighteenth century, became a great power as the century progressed, largely because of its huge population and vast natural resources. Austria controlled extensive territories with a large population, particularly after the Hapsburg armies recaptured Hungary from the Ottomans in 1699. Beginning in the mid-seventeenth century, England became a major player in world politics because of its strong economy, powerful navy, and extensive empire. (England's status as an island nation also aided it in its quest for power and security, because it could depend on the "wooden walls" of the Royal Navy for defense without having to maintain a large and expensive standing army.) Spain also had an extensive overseas empire that reached its zenith in the 1500s and 1600s, and France had a large population and abundant wealth beginning in the seventeenth century.[7]

The influence of each great power upon the others linked their fates together. The elimination of any one power by another could threaten the interests, and possibly even the survival, of others. Therefore, most major powers sought to prevent the domination of the continent by any single state. In other words, the great powers tried to preserve a **balance of power** by allying with weaker powers against stronger states in order to protect themselves from present and future threats. Furthermore, alliances fluctuated constantly and unpredictably. They proved to be fragile and of short duration, and usually did not form until after a war had already been initiated. For instance, the common interests of England and Austria led to those countries repeatedly allying in the first half of the century. This coalition broke down in the 1750s as Austria and France grew increasingly concerned about the rise of Prussia, and in 1756 an Austro-French alliance faced England and Prussia. The multipolar nature of the eighteenth century meant, as we shall see, that alliances shifted often and wars were frequent, although limited in scope.

As was touched on earlier, the intensity of conflict was restricted by the "common culture" among monarchs, the limited capabilities of the available technology, and the use of a large number of mercenaries to fill out standing armies. Despite these hindrances, the great powers managed to involve themselves in three major wars during the course of the eighteenth century. As one might expect from monarchs, two of these were provoked by dynastic struggles.

"World Wars" of the Eighteenth Century

The eighteenth century saw three major wars resulting from the way the great powers responded to one another's attempts to dominate Europe.[8] Although these wars resulted primarily from European conflicts, a small portion of the fighting took place outside of Europe as well. These struggles thus may be considered the first global wars, though unlike their twentieth-century counterparts, they were limited in their scope and objectives.

The century began with the War of the Spanish Succession (1701–1714), the bloodiest conflict since the Thirty Years' War. As the name implies, the War of the Spanish Succession developed out of a controversy over who would inherit the Spanish throne when King Charles II of Spain died without an heir. King Louis XIV of France, with Spanish support, attempted to crown his grandson Philip king of Spain, but he was opposed by the "Grand Alliance" of Austria, Britain, and the Netherlands, which was later joined by Portugal and other states. (In most eighteenth-century wars, you can't tell the players without a scorecard.) Although neither side could decisively defeat the other, the terms of the treaties that concluded the fighting favored the Grand Alliance, and thus both France and Spain made territorial and trade concessions to Britain and Austria.

Another major conflict erupted in 1740, when the death of the Austrian King Charles VI, who was also the Holy Roman emperor, severely weakened Vienna's power. The ensuing confusion provided the opportunity for King Frederick II of Prussia, better known as Frederick the Great, to seize the prosperous territory of Silesia from Austria. The other great powers were alarmed at this action, not because Prussia had only a vague historical claim to Silesia (rulers had started wars on flimsier pretenses before), but because Frederick had violated a treaty that pledged to uphold the integrity of Austrian possessions.[9]

Frederick dismissed the indignation of the other European monarchs as so much hypocrisy. He saw himself as a master of realpolitik, which we saw in Chapter One is a view of world politics that holds that in the anarchic international system, states have no choice but to preserve their vital interests through whatever means are available. Like many leaders before and since, Frederick the Great used diplomacy when possible and war when necessary to achieve his goals and protect his state's interests. He summarized his policies succinctly and frankly: "If we can gain something by being honest, we will be it, and if we have to deceive, we will be cheats."[10]

When the time came for the Great Powers to put up or shut up on the issue, the Prussian takeover of Silesia was supported by France and Spain, but opposed by England and Austria. The result was the War of the Austrian Succession (1740–1748), which was fought in the Americas and Asia as well as in Europe. Yet another stalemate resulted from the fighting. The Treaty of Aix-la-Chapelle in 1748 called for a general return to the *status quo ante bellum* (literally "the situation before the war"), but Prussia retained control of Silesia. The fact that "upstart" Prussia had successfully challenged Austria's dominant position in Germany, however, put the stability of central Europe under a cloud.

Eight years later, in a move that demonstrated how rapidly alliances could shift during the eighteenth century, Austria realigned itself with France and Russia, leaving Britain (whose naval power could do Prussia little good in continental Europe) as Prussia's only major-power ally. Prussia was thus surrounded by enemies, who took advantage of the situation to launch the Seven Years' War (1756–1763), the war known in North America as the French and Indian War. Combined attacks by Austria, France, and Russia put Prussian forces on the defensive, but superior organization and the military genius of Frederick the Great won Prussia some spectacular victories. While Prussia fought its adversaries to a standstill in Europe, England concentrated on attacking French possessions in the West Indies, Canada, and India. In the peace settlements that followed, France regained some of the overseas possessions it had lost during the war, but England was established as the dominant power in India and North America, where it was awarded all of Canada.

At the end of the Seven Years' War, England, France, and Russia had important interests both within and outside Europe, but Prussia and Austria were solely European powers. During the war, Britain had severely weakened France's position on the continent and eclipsed France in the competition for empire. The reduction in the threat posed by France led Britain to devote less energy to European affairs in order to tend to domestic concerns. In addition, although it had won vast territories in North America and Asia, Britain's colonial affairs would soon become increasingly troublesome.

Aftermath of War and Prelude to Revolution

At first, Paris had no realistic means of directly challenging England's gains in North America because of British control of the seas. Meanwhile, the American colonists grew resentful of Britain's efforts to retire its war debt by increasing tax levies on its colonies. Much of the "taxation without representation" decried by Americans in the 1760s and 1770s was levied to pay for the Seven Years' War, and so helped to make the resulting British supremacy in North America short-lived. With the start of the American War of Independence in 1776, France saw a golden opportunity to weaken England. By assisting the rebels, France sought to shift the balance of power in its favor. Paris assisted the colonists by providing them money and arms and by engaging in active military support. This forced

What Would You Do ?

You are the king of France in the late 1770s. During the last decade, Britain's King George III imposed highly unpopular taxes on the American colonists in order to pay for the expenses Britain incurred fighting your forces during the Seven Years' War, which ended in 1763. You have gradually received word from overseas that these taxes have stirred unrest among the colonists and that the British crown's use of troops to quell this incipient rebellion has succeeded in transforming it into a full-blown war of independence. You are trying to decide whether to assist the colonists by declaring war on Britain.

By declaring war, you can aid the colonists by forcing the British government to move its redcoats to other military fronts. Winning such a war would also force the British crown to concede important overseas territories to you. Territorial concessions could yield valuable riches to fill your greatly depleted royal treasury (this is important because it is getting more difficult to increase your resources by taxing the peasantry), brighten your waning glory abroad, and quell growing unrest at home.

However, even if victory is achieved against the British, you may drain your already depleted treasury to the point of bankruptcy. Thus, even victory abroad may not increase your people's love for you and your royal house. If you lose this war, you probably will ensure bankruptcy of the royal treasury and darken the glory of your reign. You face a tough decision. You need a victory over Britain to fill your coffers and increase domestic popularity without risking greater losses to both.

What would you do ?

England to divert resources to other fronts and made the resupply of its forces in North America more difficult.

The Treaty in Paris in 1783, which recognized an independent United States of America, also forced Britain to concede several other overseas possessions to France. These losses weakened Britain's position in North America, which was even more precarious because the new United States now represented a threat to Britain's remaining colony, Canada. This Peace of Versailles might thus have represented a major victory for Paris, but France's triumph would prove pyrrhic. The war with Britain had postponed important domestic reforms and dramatically escalated government debt. (The king's grandfather, Louis XIV, had severe debt problems as well; huge budget deficits were a problem for European monarchs long before they became a headache for American presidents.) When King Louis XVI sought to impose new taxes to bring down the debt, a political and financial crisis broke out in France. Within a few years, this crisis erupted into a revolution that would transform not only French politics and society, but also the concept of the nation-state and the relations between them as well.

FRENCH REVOLUTION AND NAPOLEONIC WARS

Throughout the eighteenth century, France was the most powerful state in Europe. More populous than any nation except Russia, France was often led by ambitious and highly capable kings and its government was usually well organized for administration at home and the exercise of its influence abroad. As a result, French domination over the European continent remained a worrisome possibility for the other great powers during the 1700s. At various times, England, Austria, Prussia, and Spain tried to prevent a decisive French victory in Europe. Although the supremacy of the British navy weakened France in Asia and the Americas, its European position remained strong. France's global influence did not come without a price, however, and by the end of the century the tremendous costs of maintaining France's military and international political power caused a severe social and economic crisis that culminated in the French Revolution of 1789. One of the most momentous events in world history, the Revolution and the conflicts that followed represented a radical departure from the rule of autocratic monarchy (the *ancien régime*) and from the balance of power that defined eighteenth-century European politics.

French Revolution

The immediate cause of the French Revolution was the debilitating debt accumulated by France during the American War of Independence. In May 1789, in order to gain support for increased taxation, King Louis XVI called a meeting of the Estates-General (the Parliament), which represented the nobility, clergy, and townspeople but which had not met since 1614. The nobility and clergy, who controlled the meeting, sought not just to prevent a deterioration of their own status in French society, but also to enhance those positions at the expense of royal power. They were willing to relinquish their privileged immunity from taxation only if they could enlarge their say in governing.

By challenging the king's authority, however, the upper classes set in motion forces beyond their control, as the politically and economically disenfranchised middle and lower classes seized the opportunity to assert their own demands. Riots and protests swept through Paris, and on July 14, 1789, a mob stormed the Bastille, a prison where many political prisoners were held. Rioting spread throughout the country, and an attempt to set up a constitutional monarchy failed to quiet protests and restore order. France was proclaimed a republic in 1792, and the king and his queen, Marie Antoinette, were guillotined in 1793.

The revolution was inspired by two political ideologies. One of them, liberalism, held that the power of government should reside in the people and that government should, to the greatest extent possible, allow individuals responsibility for controlling their own actions. (Eighteenth- and nineteenth-century liberals, such as the writers of America's Declaration of Independence and constitution, would probably be called "conservatives" today. They did not advocate redistribution of wealth or "big government," as do many modern liberals. The political "conservatives" in the 1700s and 1800s would today be called "monarchists" or "authoritarians.") The second ideology, **nationalism,** called for popular loyalty to focus on the nation rather than on the monarch. This was a radical departure from previous ideas of the state and government. It was a concept of political order that, for the first time, defined a country in terms of its people rather than in terms of its rulers.[11] Ideology aside, several political factions struggled for control of the new Republic. Radicals, such as Robespierre, demanded the sovereignty of the people, which presented a fundamental challenge to the established order in Europe. Less extreme factions called for an aristocratic republican form of government.

The very existence of the French Republic challenged monarchical legitimacy and caused Europe's kings and emperors to fear for their thrones. France was also considered, with good reason, to be a destabilizing influence, particularly after Robespierre's Reign of Terror resulted in thousands of deaths after 1793. Even earlier, Leopold II, the Holy Roman emperor and monarch of Austria, and Prussia's King Frederick William II declared, in August 1791, that the "restoration of the monarchy in France was in the common interest of all of the European powers."[12] Although debate still surrounds the question of whether Austria and Prussia intended to act on their statements, it seemed clear to the French that these other states were hostile to the revolution and would attempt to support counterrevolutionaries in France or even invade France to save the king and restore the monarchy.

To respond to these foreign threats, the republic needed an army, and fast. It raised one by ordering the *levée en masse* in August 1793. This decree called for universal conscription (what would later be called simply "the draft") and the consolidation of all of France's resources under the authority of the government. Levies of troops and taxes had been commonplace since ancient times, but attempting to create an army of citizen-soldiers loyal to the nation, rather than a king, was a profound change from the use of mercenary armies by European monarchs. The truly radical development, however, was the mobilization of the entire nation's resources in defense of the vital interests of the nation, rather than paying for war out of the king's treasury to serve the king's objectives. In this sense, France's attempt to create a "nation in arms" was indeed an innovation.

Although weak and inexperienced at first, by 1794 France's conscript army had more than half a million soldiers, far outmanning its opponents. Now feeling that it had a stake in its country through the achievements of the Revolution, the French populace rallied to arms under the slogan *liberté, égalité, fraternité* ("liberty, equality, brotherhood"). In addition, the radicals in the French government declared that they would assist revolutionaries everywhere, thus making the threat to the monarchical order especially urgent. The other European powers feared the "export of revolution" throughout Europe, just as American administrations feared the export of Soviet- and Cuban-style Communist ideology to Latin America during the Cold War (see Chapter Four).

Warfare convulsed Europe for more than two decades after the French Revolution. The radical regime believed that it could compensate for its weakness at home by waging war, or that foreign expansion would enhance its domestic legitimacy. It also feared that bringing the troops back home would inevitably destabilize French politics. The conquered territories increasingly bore the costs of the war and also provided spoils to the French government. Continued French aggression led the other European powers to contain it. Yet each coalition opposing the revolution suffered from a fundamental weakness: the interests of each member state were quite different and frequently at odds. Britain, in particular, had little sympathy for the absolute monarchs whom authoritarian Austria, Prussia, and Russia were trying to restore, and the fear of republicanism did not eliminate the continental empires' old rivalries over territory. If one source of France's strength stemmed from its revolutionary form of mobilization, the other originated in the divisions among its opponents.

Napoleonic Era

The turmoil of revolution and war brought many opportunities to the daring and ambitious, and at the end of the eighteenth century no one in Europe was bolder or more ambitious than Napoléon Bonaparte. Though he began his military career as a corporal in Louis XVI's army, Napoléon became a member of the radical Jacobins and rose rapidly in rank and fame because of the ingenuity he had displayed in battle during the French Revolution. (He particularly impressed the Jacobins with his pragmatism and resolve when he stopped a riot in Paris by firing cannons into the mob.) In the wake of France's military setbacks and increased domestic disorder, Napoléon led a successful coup in 1799 and quickly seized dictatorial power.

The Revolution had laid strong military foundations for France, and now the nation would be led by a brilliant strategist and capable administrator with a vision of a Europe united under French domination. Once Napoléon completely consolidated his control of France in 1802, he then began to wage the Napoleonic Wars (1803–1815), campaigns that abandoned the eighteenth-century norms of limited war. In a deliberate return to the practices of the Roman Empire, Napoléon accepted only the complete submission and occupation of a defeated country. He made countries that remained formally independent either into satellites or allies of France. He often installed members of his own family as nominal rulers of conquered territories—one of his brothers ruled Spain, and his brother-in-law became king of Naples. Formally ratifying a status Napoléon had achieved in fact, in May 1804, the French Senate proclaimed him Emperor Napoléon I.

His control of Europe almost complete, Napoléon banned the importation of British goods to the continent in 1806, creating the Continental System, a means of expanding French economic control of Europe and weakening the British. By 1810, at the height of his power, Napoléon's empire controlled Spain, western and southern Germany, most of Italy, the Netherlands, Switzerland, and the Grand Duchy of Warsaw (the Polish state that he reestablished) and maintained alliances with Austria, Denmark, Norway, and Prussia. (See Map 2.3.) Although Britain retained its naval supremacy after decisively defeating the combined French and Spanish fleets at the Battle of Trafalgar in 1805, France dominated continental

Napoléon Bonaparte looks benign in this period painting. At the height of his power, however, Napoléon turned the idealistic principles of the French Revolution (*Liberté, Egalité, Fraternité*) into a battle cry threatening all of Europe.

SOURCE: © Culver Pictures, Inc.

Europe. Three factors, however, undermined Napoléon's power. First, while the Continental System posed a threat to Britain, it also created considerable resentment in French-controlled territories, which had profited from trade with Britain and its colonies. Second, France was unable to defeat Spain and Portugal in the long and bloody Peninsular War. Napoléon invaded Spain late in 1808 to quell a popular revolt against his brother, whom he had installed as king, and at the same time attempted to force Portugal out of its alliance with Britain and bring it into line with the anti-British Continental System. Spanish forces were weak and incompetently officered, but Britain intervened on Spain's behalf, and irregular fighters known as guerrillas (the origin of the modern term) opposed French forces at every step. By 1812 Napoléon had committed more than 300,000 troops to the conflict. During the bitter fighting, both sides committed atrocities, which the Spanish artist Goya depicted in his series of drawings, *The Disasters of War*. The endeavor drained Napoléon's resources substantially. The conflict was referred to at the time as "the Spanish ulcer," but in modern parlance it might well be called "Napoléon's Vietnam."

Third, Napoléon's boundless ambition led him to make a disastrous strategic blunder. In June 1812 Napoléon invaded Russia with an army of more than 500,000 troops. At first, his forces drove the Russians farther and farther east, and by September the French occupied Moscow. In retreat, however, Russian troops destroyed and burned anything that might have been useful to the conquerors in the policy of "scorched earth," and even the fall of Moscow did not cause them to submit. Overextended, far from its bases of supply, and unable to decisively defeat the Russians, Napoléon's army was forced to withdraw. As they stumbled back toward Poland, the emperor's forces were decimated by Cossack cavalry and the severe Russian winter. By the end of 1812, only 40,000 men, less than one out of ten of those who had originally invaded, crossed back into Poland. (Leo Tolstoy depicts Napoléon's attempt to capture Russia in his epic novel *War and Peace*.)

Exhausted by the fighting on two fronts (Russia and the Iberian peninsula), the French forces began to collapse. Then, France's allies and satellites turned against Napoléon. Although exhausted and reluctant to pursue Napoléon through Central Europe, Russian, Austrian, Prussian, and Swedish forces, with financial and material assistance from Britain, continued the fight. By 1814 Napoléon's armies in both the east and south retreated. In March the anti-French allies occupied Paris, and on April 6 Napoléon abdicated. The First Peace of Paris, signed on May 30, forced France to give up most of the territory it had taken since 1792 and restored Louis XVIII to the French throne.

But the Napoleonic era was not quite over. With divisions among the victorious allies and domestic instability in France, Napoléon escaped from exile on the island of Elba and returned to power in March 1815. Quickly rallying the tattered remnants of the French army, he again threatened the peace of Europe. This time, however, the allies quickly sent their armies against him. On June 18 Napoléon's final Hundred Days of glory came to an end when British, Prussian, and Dutch forces led by Generals Wellington and Blücher defeated him at Waterloo. The victorious allies then exiled him to the South Atlantic island of St. Helena, where he died in 1821.

Napoléon's Legacy

Napoléon was as ruthless as any European monarch of his day, but he had tremendous energy, drive, and charisma. He literally became a legend in his own time, and he inspired works (not all of which were flattering) by generations of Europe's creative geniuses, including Goethe, Beethoven, Hugo, and Tolstoy.[13] (Inspired by

Map 2.3 Napoleonic Europe

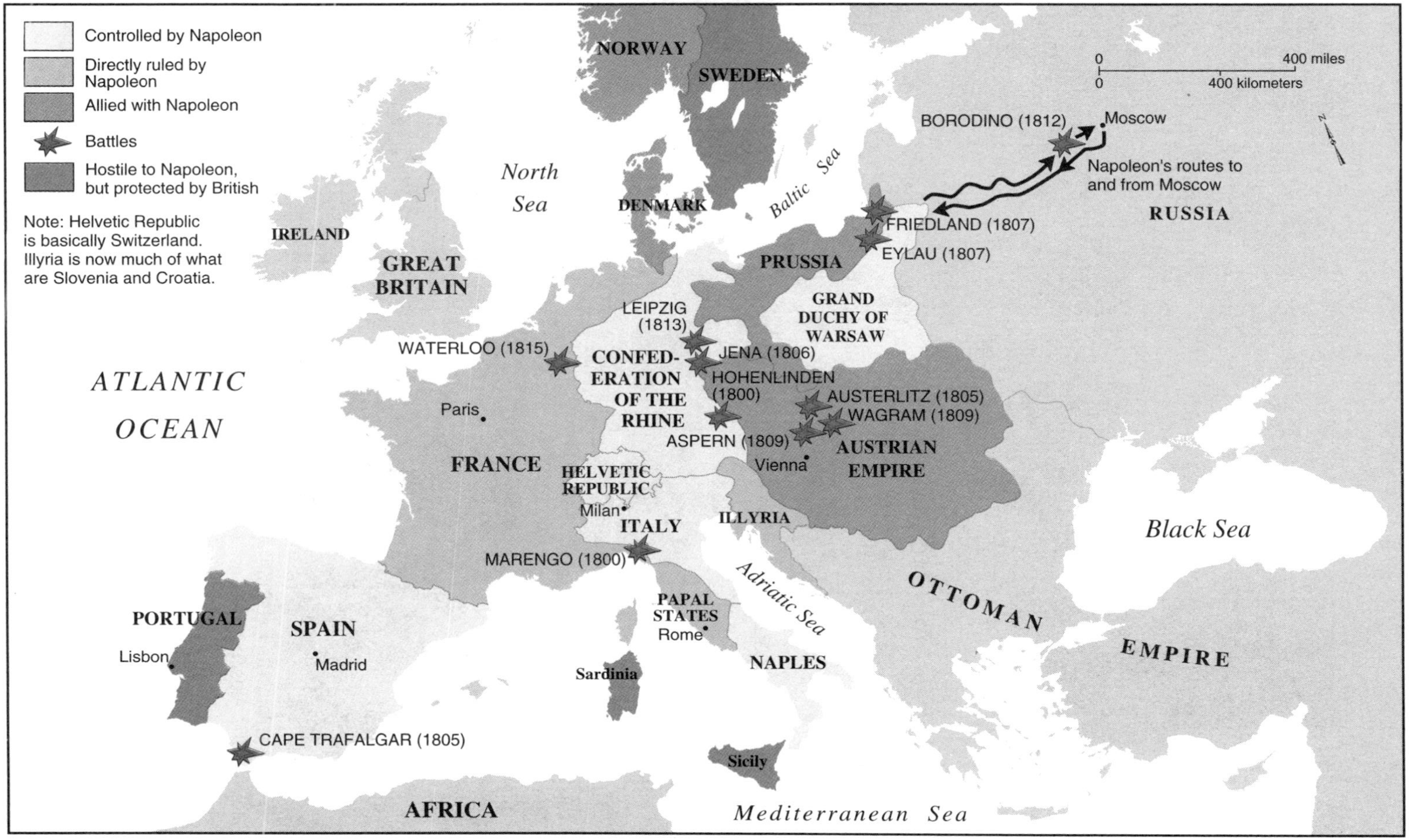

Controlled by Napoleon

Directly ruled by Napoleon

Allied with Napoleon

Battles

Hostile to Napoleon, but protected by British

Note: Helvetic Republic is basically Switzerland. Illyria is now much of what are Slovenia and Croatia.

400 miles

400 kilometers

Napoleon's routes to and from Moscow

RUSSIA

Moscow

BORODINO (1812)

FRIEDLAND (1807)

EYLAU (1807)

Baltic Sea

PRUSSIA

GRAND DUCHY OF WARSAW

AUSTERLITZ (1805)

WAGRAM (1809)

AUSTRIAN EMPIRE

JENA (1806)

HOHENLINDEN (1800)

Vienna

ASPERN (1809)

ILLYRIA

OTTOMAN EMPIRE

Black Sea

Adriatic Sea

NAPLES

Sicily

Mediterranean Sea

LEIPZIG (1813)

CONFEDERATION OF THE RHINE

HELVETIC REPUBLIC

Milan

ITALY

MARENGO (1800)

PAPAL STATES

Rome

Sardinia

SWEDEN

NORWAY

DENMARK

North Sea

WATERLOO (1815)

FRANCE

Paris

GREAT BRITAIN

IRELAND

ATLANTIC OCEAN

SPAIN

Madrid

PORTUGAL

Lisbon

CAPE TRAFALGAR (1805)

AFRICA

This portrait of Simón Bolívar, styled after a famous painting of Napoléon crossing the Alps, emphasizes his admiration for, and emulation of, the Emperor of the French.

SOURCE: Culver Pictures

Napoléon's success as a revolutionary leader, Beethoven composed his "Eroica" ["heroic"] symphony in the French emperor's honor; later, when he became disillusioned with Napoléon the dictatorial ruler, Beethoven entitled one composition "Wellington's Victory" and wrote "The Glorious Moment" to celebrate the capture of Paris by the armies of the anti-French coalition.)

Spotlight

The Liberator

The ideas that Napoléon promulgated and the example of leadership he set continued to have great influence long after his defeat and the collapse of his empire. Many leaders who were exposed to the nationalist fervor of Napoleonic Europe attempted to supplant the old order in their countries with nationalist institutions. The unsuccessful Decembrist Revolt of 1825 was an attempt to create a constitutional monarchy in Russia, and Muhammad Ali, seeking to imitate Napoléon's example, carried out many reforms in Egypt and helped that nation win autonomy from the Ottoman Empire.

The leader who brought the fire of nationalism to Latin America was Simón Bolívar. Born in Venezuela in 1783, Bolívar was a student in Paris when Napoléon was crowned emperor of the French in 1804. He was an eager convert to the philosophy of the Enlightenment that energized the French Revolution, and he admired Napoléon's boldness and drive, but was disappointed by the emperor's dictatorial rule. Nevertheless, he committed himself to the cause of nationalism and vowed that he would liberate his homeland from the Spanish colonial empire.

From 1810 to 1814, Bolívar fought tirelessly for Venezuela's independence, helping to form two republican regimes (one of which gave him the title of Liberator) only to see both of them crushed by Spanish troops. Bolívar was undismayed, however, and he set forth a vision of a free community of independent states from Mexico to Argentina. "A people that love freedom will in the end be free," he wrote of Latin America in 1814. "We are a microcosm of the human race. We are a world apart, confined within two oceans, young in arts and sciences, but old as a human society. We are neither Indians nor Europeans, yet we are a part of each." In a series of daring campaigns, his forces freed New Granada (now known as Colombia), Venezuela, Ecuador, and Peru from Spanish control. (Upper Peru was named Bolivia in his honor.) By 1824, Bolívar was president of Colombia and Peru, northern South America was brought together in the Union of Grand Colombia, and he proposed a cooperative alliance among all the nations of North and South America (similar to the modern Organization of American States) at the Congress of Panama in 1826.

The Liberator soon came to emulate Napoléon more closely than he intended, however. Bolívar established an authoritarian dictatorship over the countries he led and quarreled with other revolutionary leaders, and internal dissension soon split Grand Colombia. Beset by revolts, assassination attempts, and tuberculosis, the gallant adventurer resigned his leadership post in 1830 and died a broken man later that same year. Although Bolívar the president was a failure, Bolívar the Liberator is revered throughout the Western Hemisphere as a hero of Latin American independence.

The order Napoléon imposed changed Europe dramatically and had a profound impact on the rest of the world. The governing institutions he set up in French satellites greatly increased the efficiency of government and were much more responsive to the needs of broader segments of society than the old feudal order had been. Even his enemies copied Napoleonic innovations; Prussia's *landwehr* militia system (similar to the modern U.S. National Guard) was inspired by the *levée en masse,* and many nations to this day have legal systems based on the Napoleonic Code.

The Napoleonic Era also saw independence for Latin America. Brazil, Portugal's huge South American colony, achieved independence peacefully. When French forces invaded Portugal, the Portuguese monarchy was whisked away by British ships to Brazil. Throughout the French occupation, the center of the Portuguese empire resided in its colony, and the Portuguese king, João IV, allowed Brazilians to trade freely with other countries, particularly England. When Dom João returned to Portugal, he left his son Dom Pedro in charge, but the Brazilians chafed at the new trade restrictions the Portuguese wished to impose. In 1822 Dom Pedro bowed to domestic social pressure and peacefully announced the formation of the independent Brazilian Empire.

The story in the former Spanish colonies was different. For three centuries, the Spanish monarchy attempted to keep close tabs on its far-flung possessions, prohibiting trade with countries other than Spain and reserving for itself control of the lucrative mines. The proscription on **free trade,** especially with other colonies and with England, irritated many of the elites in the colonies. Despite festering discontent within the colonies, rebellion did not break out until events in Europe created an opening. Napoleon's attempt to place his brother on the Spanish throne made refusal to obey Napoleonic rule a patriotic endeavor in the colonies, and elites in the colonies took advantage of the situation to press for independence. The struggle for independence was encouraged by Britain, which welcomed the opportunity to harm Spain, now a French ally, by removing a critical source of its wealth. In addition, England was eager to trade freely with the colonies, and thus preferred to have them be independent countries.

The Monroe Doctrine, proclaimed by the young United States in 1823, attempted to prohibit efforts by European powers to recapture their former colonies in the Western Hemisphere, and British backing gave the prohibition considerable weight. Nevertheless, Spain was not willing to blithely relinquish its possessions, and the fight for independence lasted roughly from 1810 to 1825. Most of Spain's South American colonies (excluding the islands of Puerto Rico and Cuba) achieved political independence under the leadership of the legendary Símon Bolívar, the "Great Liberator" of South America. Bolívar hoped to unify the continent in a United States of South America, but the divisions among Latin Americans proved too great to overcome (see box).

CONCERT OF EUROPE

After Napoléon's defeat in 1814, the great powers of Europe (Austria, Prussia, Russia, England, and France) gathered in a critical meeting in Vienna to chart the future of the continent. The conference sought first and foremost to restore Europe to what it considered to be "normalcy," meaning a return to the old monarchical system. Ideological consensus, revulsion at the horrors of war, and economic exhaustion after the upheaval of the past two decades fostered cooperation among the states on forming a new international system. Prince Klemens von Metternich, chief minister of the emperor of Austria, played host at the Congress of Vienna and worked to promote his own view of a new European order. Supported solidly by British Foreign Minister Castlereagh, Prussian King Frederick William III, and Russian Czar Alexander I, Metternich firmly believed that the immediate peace and security of the other states demanded the restoration of Europe to the monarchical status quo that had preceded the French Revolution.

Largely because of Metternich's unflagging efforts and uncommon political instincts, the Grand Alliance had been able to survive the infighting that had threatened to tear it apart even before it had defeated Napoléon.[14] Czar Alexander I desired a "Holy Alliance" of all Christian powers, but the other rulers humored him while not taking his romantic ideas seriously. Defeated France was represented by the unctuous diplomat Talleyrand, who had survived both the revolution and Napoleon's downfall by knowing when it was time to switch allegiances. At the Congress, he put his political instinct to work safeguarding France's survival as a major force in Europe, and he cajoled the allies into granting Louis XVIII the succession to the French throne.[15] Talleyrand's negotiating skill helped to ensure that even in defeat, France would not lose its great-power status.

The Treaty of Vienna of 1815 was an attempt to incorporate the lessons of twenty-two years of nearly constant warfare against France by Britain, Russia, Prussia, and Austria, and it reflected the leading role of Russia and Britain in the alliance that defeated Napoléon. The great powers were to contain France by establishing and guaranteeing the neutrality of buffer states, such as Switzerland, between France and the other great powers. (See Map 2.4.) Britain's demands for restoring the independence of the Netherlands and Belgium (which France had absorbed) as a unified state reinforced France's confinement. The victors also forced France to pay an indemnity, further eroding its gains from the war.

These realpolitik steps did not fully satisfy the various states that had attempted to defeat France over the years, however. Many leaders believed there would have to be cooperation among the great powers to prevent another recurrence of any such threat. They agreed to meet periodically to review developments in Europe in order to pursue their common interests and the peace of the continent. Thus the Vienna settlement established the **Concert of Europe,** in which the great powers sought to cooperate in maintaining peace and order on the continent. Comprising the Quadruple Alliance, the four other major states, Britain, Russia, Prussia, and Austria, agreed that an attack on one—by France—constituted an attack on all.

They had also learned a valuable lesson from years of war: that because domestic developments had international repercussions, they had to be contained. Therefore, they agreed that the great powers could regulate domestic disturbances. In other words, they reserved the right to intervene in countries where liberalism appeared to be emerging as a threat. With the peace of Europe restored at such considerable expense, the powers sought to ensure that its repose was not again threatened. They sought to maintain the status quo against any possible challenge. The Concert of Europe thus became the world's first international security organization. As such, it was a major step toward the globalization of world politics.

From the start, however, the Concert contained more discord than harmony. Despite the apparent unity among the great powers, dissension roiled just beneath the surface. Specifically, it was Russia and Austria that had demanded that the

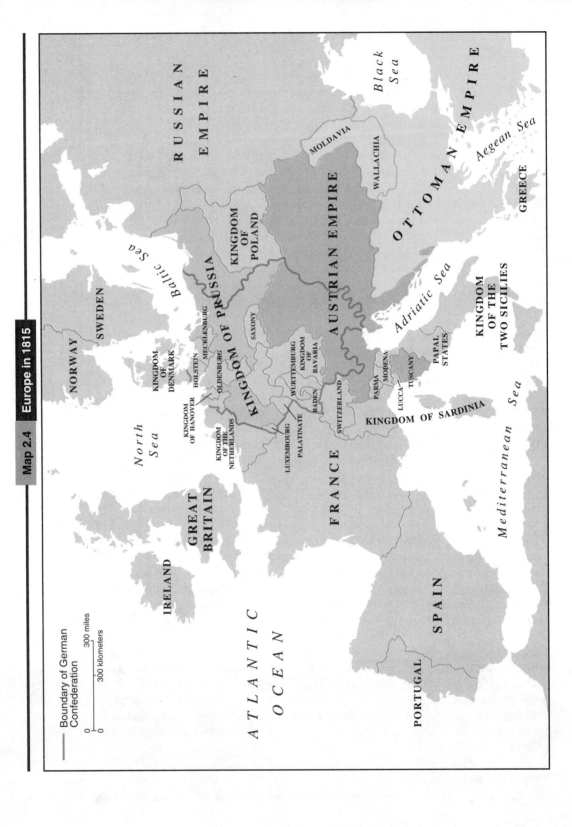

Map 2.4 Europe in 1815

Boundary of German Confederation

300 miles

300 kilometers

ATLANTIC OCEAN

IRELAND

GREAT BRITAIN

North Sea

NORWAY

SWEDEN

Baltic Sea

RUSSIAN EMPIRE

KINGDOM OF PRUSSIA

KINGDOM OF POLAND

KINGDOM OF DENMARK

HOLSTEIN

MECKLENBURG

OLDENBURG

KINGDOM OF HANOVER

KINGDOM OF THE NETHERLANDS

LUXEMBOURG

PALATINATE

SAXONY

WURTTEMBURG

KINGDOM OF BAVARIA

BADEN

SWITZERLAND

AUSTRIAN EMPIRE

MOLDAVIA

WALLACHIA

OTTOMAN EMPIRE

Black Sea

Aegean Sea

GREECE

Adriatic Sea

FRANCE

PARMA

MODENA

LUCCA

TUSCANY

PAPAL STATES

KINGDOM OF SARDINIA

KINGDOM OF THE TWO SICILIES

Mediterranean Sea

SPAIN

PORTUGAL

great powers agree to intervene in the domestic affairs of others should revolution threaten; Britain disagreed. In spite of Britain's opposition, the states reached a settlement. Ideologically, the British differed from the three conservative powers of the East (Austria, Prussia, and Russia). Britain was a country that had strong democratic traditions and it was gradually developing liberal ideas on trade and human rights. Although Britain sought to ensure the continued weakness of France for geopolitical reasons, British political ideas were basically compatible with the French Revolution's notions of liberty, equality, and fraternity and sprang from many of the same sources in the philosophy of the Enlightenment (especially the works of Locke and Montesquieu). Britain's implacable enmity with revolutionary and Napoleonic France was one of history's greatest ironies, and, along with the settlement of the Congress of Vienna, an example of the triumph of realpolitik over idealism.

STABILITY AND CHANGE IN THE NINETEENTH CENTURY

The Vienna settlement marked a restoration of the old order on two levels. First, many dethroned monarchies came back into power (most importantly, in France). Second, the dispensation of territory was again used to reward victors and punish losers. The settlement also changed past practice in that it explicitly sought to institutionalize the supremacy of particular great powers through the Concert of Europe. Despite the new accord on the future of Europe, the terms of the settlement represented a patchwork of compromises among the great powers, which were still looking out for their own interests. The restoration of the old order was more apparent than real, however, for the French Revolution had unleashed new forces of nationalism and liberalism that could not be ignored.

Nationalism in the New Europe

Nationalism, which held the self-determination of nations as its highest ideal, would increasingly threaten the established order in Europe throughout the nineteenth century. Advocates of national independence frequently supported the classical liberal ideas of the free market and individual liberty as well, which posed an additional challenge to monarchical authority. Nationalism most acutely threatened empires, states that encompass many ethnic and linguistic groups, or in other words, many nations. Many of these groups increasingly demanded independence from imperial rule. As a result, it became more and more difficult for the Concert of Europe to contain the political struggle between nationalism and monarchical imperialism and to prevent the gradual dissolution of Europe's great empires. Some nationalist issues were resolved peacefully: Belgium's achievement of independence from Holland in 1830 did not provoke a war, and Norway split from Sweden in 1905 without resorting to violent conflict. On the other hand, the prolonged disintegration of the Ottoman Empire bedeviled European politics for much of the century, and the Austrian Empire's nationality problems increasingly weakened it and seriously threatened its survival.

Nationalism also served as a unifying force, especially in Italy and Germany, which did not exist as unified political entities at the start of the nineteenth century. After the Congress of Vienna, Italy consisted of a number of independent city-states, although Austria controlled many territories, such as Trieste, where Italians constituted the majority of the population. Germany after 1815 was a patchwork of thirty-nine states (down from approximately 300 in 1648) ranging in size from city-states and principalities to Austria and Prussia, which were recognized as great powers. Many German and Italian nationalists called for the unification of their respective nations into independent nation-states, greatly worrying neighboring states and empires (especially Austria and France). At the start of the nineteenth century, therefore, nationalism had the potential to be a force for both unification and fragmentation, and this potential would frequently be realized as the century progressed.

Disharmony in the Concert

The years 1815–1914 were in an important sense the most peaceful in the period between 1600 and 1945. Although wars continued to be fought, they were limited both in duration and geographic area. During the ninety-nine-year period after 1815, no large-scale European wars occurred. During at least the first half of the nineteenth century, the relative absence of conflict may be attributed to the exhaustion of the great powers after the French Revolution and the Napoleonic Wars. The dynasties that ruled Europe's monarchies also needed to reestablish their domestic authority and fend off the challenges of nationalism and liberalism. Their preoccupation with domestic situations left little time or resources for engaging in foreign conflicts. The system of conflict management through the Concert of Europe and the decline of Anglo-French colonial rivalry also contributed to the relative peace and stability of the first half of the nineteenth century.

Tensions arose, however, between the principle of collective security (which was one of the founding principles of the Concert of Europe) and the self-interests of the great powers. In the fifteen years following the Congress of Vienna, differing ideological and geopolitical perspectives caused independent action by the major states to replace concerted endeavors. These divisions helped France to resume a role co-equal with that of the other great powers. The conservative states of Austria, Prussia, and Russia almost always firmly opposed any challenge to the status quo. They wished to intervene in the domestic affairs of other states if liberals or nationalist movements threatened to overthrow the entrenched monarchies. Conversely, France almost always sided with the liberals. Britain shifted its allegiance, at times aligned with France and at others with the conservative states, in order to preserve the balance of power on the continent that Britain felt was vital to its security.

At the same time, political ambitions motivated each of the five great powers at the expense of ideological consistency. For example, the Concert did not function as planned during conflicts in the southern Italian state of Naples and in Spain. In the latter case, France intervened in support of the monarch, contradicting its own policies of nonintervention and liberalism in pursuit of its security and economic interests.

Perhaps the most poignant demonstration of state interest taking precedence over ideology came in the great powers' reaction to the Greek effort to secede from the Ottoman Empire, which began in earnest in 1821. Austria, too weak to take advantage of the Ottoman Empire's internal problems and fearful that its own multinational empire might erupt in revolt, worried that Russia would use the opportunity to improve its position in the Balkans. Austria thus opposed Greek independence on the principle that existing regimes and the territorial status quo should not be threatened. Although a conservative power, Russia supported Greek independence, both out of self-interest and in Orthodox Christian solidarity against the Muslim Ottomans. Britain, fearing Russian ambitions, opposed a war that would weaken the Ottoman Empire as a counterweight to Russia. (Not all Britons shared this realpolitik outlook on the conflict; the romantic poet Lord Byron died in Greece in 1824 fighting for the Greek cause.) In 1826, after Canning replaced Castlereagh as foreign minister, Britain modified its policy and sided with Russia in supporting Greece's autonomy while allowing the country to remain technically under Turkish suzerainty (a type of feudal overlordship). The following year, France joined them, and all three destroyed the Ottoman fleet at Navarino, preventing a joint Turkish-Egyptian force from subduing Greece. Thus a strange alliance between liberal Britain and France and conservative Russia resulted in Greece gaining its independence in 1830. (Curiously, though nationalism fueled the struggle for Greek independence, the great powers installed a German prince as the first king of Greece.)

The twin fears of French power and of domestic revolution that underlay the establishment of the Concert of Europe reasserted themselves with the July 1830 "revolution" in France when Louis XVIII was overthrown and replaced by a new king, Louis Philippe, who was more liberal than his predecessor. In August that same year, Belgium, which had been part of a united Netherlands under Dutch rule after 1815, rose up against the forced union with Holland, and the fear that France would take advantage of the situation heightened tensions throughout Europe. The eastern monarchs opposed Belgian efforts at independence on the principle that the Concert should preserve the territorial status quo. Yet their distance from Belgium, as well as nationalist problems in their own backyards (namely Italy and Germany), meant they had little influence over events. In January 1831 Britain and France gained the other great powers' acquiescence to Belgium's independence and recognition of its neutrality.

The year of 1830 also saw conservative Russia and Austria facing the first serious challenges from the incipient nationalism of some of their subject peoples. The liberal regime in France provided some support to these nationalist movements. While the French government made statements in support of nationalist objectives and protested Russia's harsh treatment of Polish rebels trying to regain their independence, the tsar's forces crushed the Poles in September 1831, after ten months of fighting. Thus began a series of smaller-scale rebellions and their repression,

At a Glance

Political Entities Over Time

Pre-Seventeenth Century

Territory is not divided into independent countries. Divisions are defined by the power of ruling elites and/or by religion. Feudal system is in use. Leaders are stronger if they can claim that God is on their side. Loyalty is to individual kings rather than to nations. Leaders can demand taxes at will. There are no rules to regulate commerce. Great political and economic fragmentation exists.

Late Seventeenth Century

The Peace of Westphalia in 1648 establishes ideas of sovereignty and collective security. Problems result from the fact that sovereignty and collective security are contradictory principles. Yet sovereignty is important for the creation of the nation-state because leaders are forced to consolidate control over their territories. Kings can determine domestic policy, which is a blow to the Church. State activity has shifted from kingship to government. All states are encouraged to unite against any aggressor state.

Eighteenth Century

Advances in transportation and finance accelerate the spread of European influence and facilitate colonial-

ism. Social stratification prevails. Wars are fought by limited means for limited objectives. Most nations cannot extract sufficient resources to wage major wars. Rulers rely on mercenaries. The international system is multipolar. Alliances are short-lived. A severe social and economic crisis culminates in the French Revolution of 1789. This results in ideologies of liberalism and nationalism.

Nineteenth Century

Many nations base their political systems on the Napoleonic system. The Concert of Europe is designed by the great powers to cooperate in the control of Europe. It becomes the world's first international mechanism designed to guarantee collective security. Nationalism becomes stronger. The Industrial Revolution begins. Manufacturing moves out of the home and into factories. Cities grow rapidly. War becomes deadlier because of more lethal weapons. Uneven population growth leads to domestic instability. The Bismarckian system leads Germany to a powerful position internationally.

which, while frequently bloody, did not generate any serious threat to the general peace.

Industrial Revolution

In addition to ideological and political change, the nineteenth century also witnessed rapid economic change. The French Revolution was paralleled by the Industrial Revolution, which began in Britain in the late eighteenth century. The Industrial Revolution moved manufacturing out of the home and into factories, where it became more efficient through the use of mass production and interchangeable parts. As well as radically changing the organization of industrial production, the Industrial Revolution harnessed new sources of energy, especially steam power, which enabled manufacturing to be increasingly mechanized. Beginning with textiles and food processing and expanding into the iron and steel, machine building, transportation, and communication industries, the Industrial Revolution made it possible for more people to make more things faster and better than ever before.

The Industrial Revolution changed everything. Populations exploded as new farming techniques grew more food, railroads reliably transported it to where it was needed, and sanitation and medicine lowered infant mortality and raised life expectancy. Cities grew rapidly as workers flooded in from the countryside in search of better-paying jobs. Successful investors in industry made huge sums of money, amassing fortunes that rivaled and ultimately dwarfed those of the traditional aristocracy, whose wealth was usually obtained from farming on large estates. Technology improved at a pace unsettling to many, as railroads and the telegraph allowed goods and information to move faster than had ever been dreamed possible. Families were transformed from the extended family group suited to a sedentary, agricultural way of life into what was later called the "nuclear family" of one couple and its children, which moved frequently as one or both parents sought jobs. Growing shortages of skilled workers encouraged women to enter the labor force for the first time in substantial numbers (though the radical idea of women being able to earn their own money was often slow to catch on in traditional societies). The rich enjoyed the opportunity to make unprecedented profits, though often at considerable risk; a new urban middle class of small investors, technicians, and managers flourished. Workers earned higher wages and could buy more consumer goods, but faced the possibility of unemployment if businesses lost money or failed.

The benefits of the increase in material wealth during the Industrial Revolution were numerous and widespread, but unevenly distributed, as factory owners became wealthy while many of the jobless and the working poor continued to eke out a bare existence. The rich got richer faster than ever before, and the middle classes prospered, but the living conditions of the poor were slower to improve. One British government official, Charles Dickens, was inspired by the plight of London's urban underclass to write novels, such as *Nicholas Nickleby, Little Dorrit,* and *Oliver Twist,* depicting the social and economic conditions of nineteenth-century England, and Victor Hugo did the same with his classic *Les Miserables* in France. In time, rich and poor alike would suffer from another legacy of the Industrial Revolution—deforestation and pollution.[16]

The development of industry changed war and politics as well as economics. With the increased lethality and range of weapons made possible by new technology, wars became deadlier. New types of weapons, which by the end of the nineteenth century included machine guns and long-range artillery, enabled and later required states to raise mass armies much larger than had been fielded before the industrial era. Armored steam-powered warships gave navies greater range and striking power, and naval powers raced with one another to match their adversaries' most advanced ship designs. Armies increasingly directed violence not only at military targets, but at economic and civilian ones as well, as a state's industrial capacity became a vital part of its military strength. With the growing reliance on large conscripted armies, the support of the general public became more important for the success of military campaigns, thus accelerating the entrance of a greater proportion of the population into the political arena.[17] Rulers progressively required the economic and political support of the captains of industry, labor unions, and the newly emerging mass media (newspapers) for foreign escapades as governments needed to raise more funds—and thus needed the support of financiers and the population as a whole for more expensive conflicts. Politics as well as production began to take on many modern characteristics.

Yet this increased involvement of civil society in politics did not immediately bring about greater democratization, as many liberals had hoped. The rapid pace of industrialization often led to social dislocation and turmoil. In a precursor of modern conflicts over workplace automation, "Luddites" (followers of a mythical leader named "Ned Ludd" or "King Ludd") smashed textile machinery that they feared would make their jobs obsolete. The landed aristocracy was usually less than comfortable with the rising political importance of industrial capitalists and often resented the nouveaux riches who made their money in trade and industry. The threat posed by industrialization to the established order was occasionally ameliorated by attempts to focus popular attention on foreign enemies and the glory of the nation—some rulers resorted to foreign wars and colonial expansion to distract the populace from the growing trouble at home. At the same time, industrialization increased competition for markets and sources of raw materials, which provided a powerful impetus for European colonization in Asia and Africa (see below).

The spread of the Industrial Revolution slowly but inexorably changed the European system. With its origins in Britain, the Industrial Revolution was a major source of that country's strength. Industrialization spread very unevenly, depending on social and political conditions within particular countries. France industrialized slowly, Austria even more so, and Russia had barely begun the process of industrial development by the end of the nineteenth century. Prussia, on the other hand, industrialized rapidly. With increased production came increased opportunities for trade, and the Industrial Revolution increased British support for a liberal trade regime under which goods could be freely bought and sold between countries (see Chapter Six). Seagoing commerce expanded rapidly, and trade forged economic and political links among nations all over the globe. Britain sought to maintain the system of free trade with its financial, industrial, and naval strength, and innovations in manufacturing, communications and finance promoted international borrowing and investment throughout nineteenth-century Europe. The Industrial Revolution was thus a major impetus for the globalization of the world economy.

The uneven spread of industrialization also contributed to increased domestic instability, especially in the German states. More and more, peasants moved to the cities, where they became better organized to present their demands and to protest when their demands were ignored. This posed a threat to many ruling authoritarian regimes, which tried to preempt the challenge by focusing attention on often exaggerated foreign threats. In addition, the changing domestic balance of power between rival economic interests led to increased demands for government interference in the economy—in particular, protection from imports. Although these factors existed in all of the European states, they were most influential in Germany, which by mid-century would become a center of violent unrest.

Revolutions of 1848

The next major turning point in nineteenth-century European politics came when a wave of popular discontent crested in 1848. Protests, motivated by nationalist demands and the social and economic upheaval caused by the Industrial Revolution, erupted across the continent from France to Austria and Hungary. These uprisings threatened to shake the crowns off many European monarchs. Although King Frederick William IV of Prussia initially promised reforms, he postponed his plans after confrontations between troops and demonstrators led to pitched battles in the streets of Berlin. Widespread revolts in the Austrian Empire led Emperor Ferdinand to issue a manifesto in April promising to free the Austrian peasants from all services and duties incumbent upon them. This edict helped turn the peasants to the emperor's side, but his forces proved incapable of controlling the uprisings, and the rebellion continued until it was crushed with the aid of Russian intervention in 1849.

Only in France did the revolution meet with success, in that Louis Philippe abdicated the throne and fled to England, and a provisional government proclaimed a republic. This event raised the concerns of the other monarchs, who recalled the events following 1789 all too well. The new French government did not, however, seek confrontation with the other powers. It feared that conflict would lead to conditions similar to those that had led to the radical takeover of 1793.[18] Throughout Europe, the excesses of industrial capitalism inspired an upwelling of **socialism** and led to the origin of **communism,** expressed in the writings of the German political economist Karl Marx (see Chapter Six).

The violent events of 1848 showed that the Concert of Europe was incapable of controlling the internal threats faced by the conservative monarchies. In state after state, the urban working class rose up to demand increased political rights, which could come only at the expense of the monarchs' power. The social divisions generated by the Industrial Revolution created tensions between the rising bourgeoisie (the middle class of industrialists and small business owners), the landed aristocracy, and the working classes. These divisions and the spread of liberal ideas were growing in impact.[19] The revolutions of 1848 represented not only demands for greater democracy, but increasingly politically active publics demanded the revision of the 1815 settlements in order to unify nations in some cases (such as Italy and Germany) or gain their independence in others (such as Hungary and Poland).

The monarchists and the landed gentry won out for the time being, largely because the liberals were not able to maintain their initial gains and were crushed with the aid of external conservative powers—especially Russia, the "Gendarme of Europe." The potential for domestic unrest to spill over into international conflicts remained, however. In the mid-nineteenth century, the Concert of Europe deliberated on the possibility and desirability of international intervention to prevent nationalist conflicts in Poland, Austria, Hungary, and elsewhere from escalating into international war. (More than a century later, another collective security institution, the United Nations, would debate the same problem with regard to conflicts in Bosnia and Croatia.)

A PERSPECTIVE AT MID-CENTURY

By 1850 the revolutions of 1848 had failed. The monarchist regimes in central and eastern Europe regained control of events and either destroyed or delegitimized the liberals. Because the demands of many liberal ideologues led to increased radicalism on the part of the working class, this same radicalism scared the middle classes. Willing to sacrifice political freedoms for the sake of stability, they accepted monarchical reaction and repression in many countries. Yet the stability that had been reestablished was palpably fragile, and many recognized it as only the calm before the storm. The forces of liberalism and nationalism had been released, and proved to be impossible to contain in the long run.

In the first half of the century, rulers feared nationalism because it threatened a revision of the territorial status quo and it was tied to liberalism. Notwithstanding the early association between liberalism and nationalism, the relative degree of fear of nationalism greatly depended on the previous history of the various parts of Europe. In western Europe, the state and the nation were essentially contiguous by the mid-nineteenth century, so ruling elites had little reason to fear that the extension of political rights to the working class would lead to the dissolution of the state. Germany and Italy profited from the growing force of nationalism, using it to unify their nations into single states.

In central, eastern, and southern Europe, the situation was quite different. The growing strength of nationalism threatened the future of the Austrian Empire, which included Hungarians, Poles, Czechs, and others. In the Russian empire, the increased nationalist activity of the Poles, Balts, Finns, Armenians, and others subject to Russian control constituted a drain on the energies of the monarchy. It effectively suppressed any attempt at rebellion as it had the Decembrist Revolt of 1825, when liberal army officers attempted to force the tsar to accept a constitutional monarchy. However, with the defeat of the liberals in 1848, imaginative conservatives came to the realization that they could use nationalism for their own purposes.

Crimean War

If the strength of Russia and Britain had been a stabilizing force in the first half of the century, the increased tensions between them boded ill for continued European security, as those two great powers disagreed over the future of the territories controlled by the decrepit Ottoman Empire. Meanwhile, after almost forty years of relative quiet from France, fear of the former revolutionary state had subsided.

Yet the France of President Louis Napoléon Bonaparte (Napoléon Bonaparte's nephew), who took office in December of 1848, was a dissatisfied power. By restoring France to what he considered to be its proper status as a leading power in Europe, Louis Napoléon (who was crowned Emperor Napoléon III in 1852) hoped to improve his domestic legitimacy as well as gain more respect from other European nations.[20]

Seeking to demonstrate France's renewed strength, Napoléon III adroitly took advantage of the infirm Ottoman Empire. In 1852 he demanded that guardianship of the Christian holy places in Jerusalem be given to Roman Catholic rather than Orthodox clerics. This seemingly innocuous incident eventually precipitated the Crimean War (1853–1856), the first between the great powers since 1815. In 1853 Russia sent troops to occupy Moldavia and Walachia, two Ottoman provinces in the Balkans. (Both areas were later incorporated into Romania when that state gained independence from Ottoman rule.) Britain and France intervened in order to bail out the Ottomans, attacking Russia in the Crimean Peninsula on the northern shore of the Black Sea. The protracted siege warfare that ensued (the futility of which is captured in Tennyson's poem "The Charge of the Light Brigade") bore little resemblance to the swift, dramatic campaigns of the Napoleonic Wars. The fighting dragged until 1856, when Russia agreed to withdraw its troops from Moldavia and Walachia, which were granted autonomy under Ottoman suzerainty. Although Russia's defeat spurred on some liberalizing reforms in that country, the Crimean War had little lasting impact on European politics. It did, however, demonstrate that the Concert of Europe was no longer able to maintain collective security when the interests of the great powers conflicted. Ultimately, it proved to be little more than a costly sideshow, while the main event was about to begin in central Europe.

UNIFICATION OF ITALY AND GERMANY

From 1815 to about mid-century, Britain and Russia had effectively stabilized Europe. Both counterbalanced France, while Russia shared Austria's conservative revulsion to challenges to the territorial and political status quo. Their resources depleted by their exertions in the Crimean War, both Russia and Britain reduced their involvement in continental affairs. As a result, Paris obtained greater freedom of action and Vienna could no longer rely on Russia for support against nationalist demands inside Austria and in neighboring Italy and Germany.

Italian Unification

France did not delay in taking advantage of Austria's vulnerability. Napoleon III moved quickly to assist the movement for unity among the Italian city-states, or Risorgimento, as the Count di Cavour of Piedmont-Sardinia assumed leadership of the Italian unification movement. In July 1858 Cavour and Napoleon agreed that France would support Piedmont's cause in return for French acquisition of

Nice and Savoy. In 1859 French forces intervened to push Austrian troops out of northern Italy. Nationalist troops led by Giuseppe Garibaldi won control of Sicily and Naples in 1860, paving the way for their union with Piedmont, which dominated northern Italy, and an Italian parliament proclaimed a unified kingdom of Italy in 1861.

The unification of Italy produced a profound revision of the territorial settlement of 1815. It also removed a significant source of friction between Paris and Vienna, which had previously competed for influence among the republics, principalities, and city-states of the peninsula. The new state at first was too weak to pose a major threat to either France or Austria, and it provided a useful buffer between these two powers. Italy had achieved territorial unity but remained politically divided and economically underdeveloped, and so it never attained the great-power status to which its leaders aspired.

German Unification

Italy's unification left one major European nation, the Germans, still divided. In 1862 King William I of Prussia appointed Otto von Bismarck as his chancellor. The dominant personality of Europe during the second half of the nineteenth century, Bismarck was a conservative *junker* (aristocratic landlord) who sought to protect and improve the position of the monarchy, mainly in order to raise funds for a reformed army, at the expense of a liberal parliament that had limited powers. Because they had associated nationalism with liberalism since the French Revolution, many conservatives feared that unification would threaten the status quo and their entrenched positions. Bismarck had no particular interest in German unity initially, but he gradually realized that nationalism could become the means of assuaging the masses while preserving most of the aristocracy's prerogatives and expanding Prussia's international power and prestige.

Bismarck was committed to realpolitik in foreign policy. He was concerned only with advancing the state interest by whatever means: diplomacy if possible, war if necessary. Bismarck had no qualms about resorting to military means if that would provide an opportunity to strengthen the domestic position of conservatives, the monarchy, and the army. He agreed with the German military theorist Clausewitz that "war is nothing but the continuation of politics by other means."[21] Thus, Bismarck was known as the "Iron Chancellor" for his determination to unite Germany under Prussian domination and for his statement that "it is not by speeches and resolutions that the great crises of the times are decided, but by iron and blood."[22]

While serving as chancellor, Bismarck came to believe that the most practical way to unify Germany would be to exclude Austria, which was only partially German. Austria was an empire consisting of many ethnic groups, including Czechs, Slovaks, Poles, Croats, Hungarians, and diverse others. A unified Germany could never incorporate the myriad ethnic groups in the Austrian Empire. Additionally, the prospect of a unified "greater Germany" including both Prussia and Austria

Otto von Bismarck created a unified Germany through three quick, carefully calculated wars in the 1860s. The "Iron Chancellor" dominated European politics for the next twenty years.　　　　SOURCE: © Culver Pictures, Inc.

would alarm the other European powers, which would probably go to war to prevent the union of the two major German states.

In 1864 the king of Denmark handed Bismarck a golden opportunity to further his goal of German unification. The Danish king, under the mistaken impression that Britain supported him, attempted to fully incorporate the autonomous duchies of Schleswig and Holstein into his kingdom. Bismarck quickly signed an alliance with Austria for the purpose of gaining control over these largely German-speaking areas, and in 1864 Austrian and Prussian forces marched in and won a quick victory. Berlin and Vienna soon fell out, however, over the agreement on joint control of the territories won from the Danes, and in June 1866 Austria broke off diplomatic relations and began to mobilize its army. Bismarck used the Austrian mobilization as a pretext for war. With superior organization, and by clever use of the emerging technologies of the railroad and telegraph, Prussia could mobilize and concentrate its forces more rapidly. This advantage proved decisive, and Prussia soundly defeated Austria within two months. In the peace settlement, Austria gave up its authority in German and Italian affairs (the Italian city of Venice, at various times part of the Austrian empire, was finally transferred to the kingdom of Italy), and the northern German states were incorporated into the Prussian-dominated North German Confederation.

Prussia's victory fundamentally challenged the previous order in central Europe. Austria's weakness forced it to accept the demands for political equality from its Hungarian provinces, and in 1867 the Austrian Empire became the "dual monarchy" of Austria-Hungary. The rapid growth in Prussia's power caused great consternation among the other great powers, but Bismarck was able to isolate France and neutralize Britain and Russia through diplomatic maneuvering. On June 14, 1870, after tensions had been exacerbated by a dispute over the succession to the Spanish throne, Bismarck leaked a telegram from Kaiser Wilhelm that the Iron Chancellor edited to make it look as if the kaiser and the French ambassador had insulted each other. Pressure for war mounted in both Vienna and Berlin, and five days later Napoléon III played right into Bismarck's hands by declaring war on Prussia.

Again making good use of new technology and its army's superior organization, Prussia rapidly defeated the French forces within a matter of weeks. Neither Britain nor any of the other great powers could come to France's aid in time. The Prussians captured Napoléon III, and after a four-month siege, took Paris as well.[23] France was forced to pay a huge indemnity and cede to Prussia the provinces of Alsace and Lorraine, which had long been part of France. Although the German annexation of Alsace could be justified on nationalist grounds, as the majority of the population was German, the population of Lorraine was largely French. The loss of both troubled the French for decades thereafter.

The harsh terms and humiliation imposed on France signaled a departure from Bismarck's previous habit of tolerance toward defeated opponents, whom he well knew might be potential allies in the next conflict. By declaring the formation of the new German Empire on January 18, 1871, from the Palace of Versailles, a symbol of French power built by Louis XIV just outside Paris, Bismarck added insult to the injury of losing Alsace and Lorraine. He acted in deference to pressure from the kaiser and a public enraptured with victory and impatient with the subtle workings of his diplomacy. This uncharacteristic triumph of nationalism and chauvinism over realpolitik in Bismarck's policy would later cost Germany and the rest of Europe dearly. Nevertheless, in 1871 the aspirations of generations of Germans for a unified German nation-state had been realized.

The unification of Germany under the Prussian crown profoundly affected European politics and radically shifted the balance of power. Through these short wars based on rapid mobilization and decisive battles, the process of German unification influenced strategy and military organization in virtually all of the European states. It also sped the innovation of new weapons technology, including

Map 2.5   Europe after German and Italian Unification, 1872

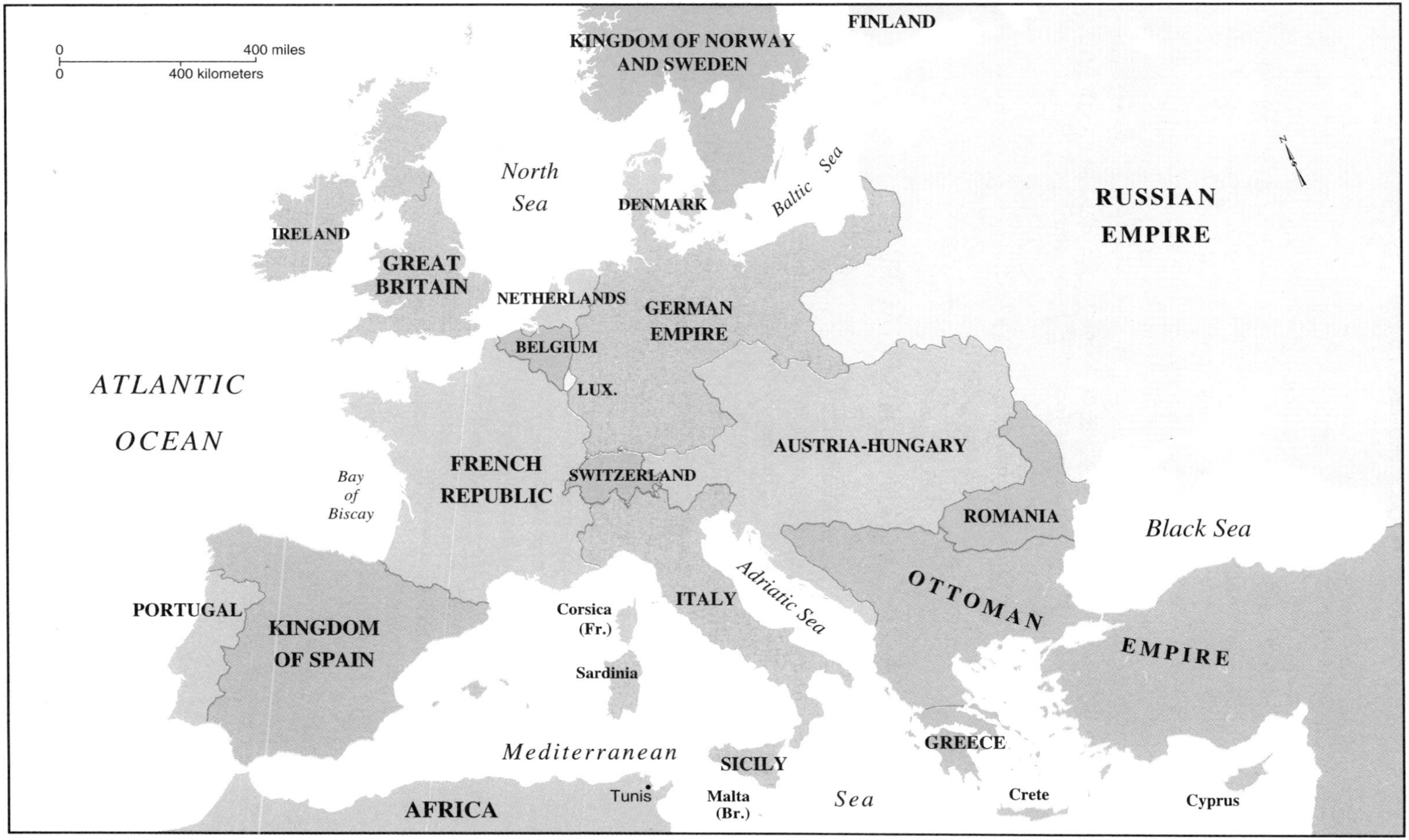

both the breech-loading rifle and machine gun, and spurred the development of railroads. (For the changes German and Italian unification brought to European political geography, see Map 2.5.) The new German Empire was now the strongest country in continental Europe. Resentment smoldered in France, but that nation was too weak to act alone and could find no allies. Austria accepted its irreversible loss of influence in Germany and turned its focus to the Balkans, a step encouraged by the demands of Hungary. Because the Crimean War blocked Russian expansion to its south, Russia increasingly focused on expanding into Asia and trying to improve its domestic economy. Finally, Britain saw little reason to involve itself on the continent as long as Belgium and the Netherlands were not threatened. Instead, it focused on strengthening its colonial and commercial empire. Thus, the achievement under Bismarck's leadership of a unified German nation was secure for the time being.

IMPERIALISM IN THE INDUSTRIAL ERA

As nation-states were being built in Europe, empires were built in the wider world. The industrial revolution greatly expanded the industrializing states' demand for raw materials, labor, and markets. In the minds of many European leaders, the only way to secure access to materials and markets was to establish political control of the territories in which they were located. Far-flung colonies and imperial territories therefore became vital strategic and economic interests that had to be secured, protected, and denied to potential rivals or enemies. Control of resources and markets was seen as a method of expanding political power as well as economic strength. Industrialists sought to make huge profits from exploiting natural resources and exporting manufactured goods and to keep their competitors away from the most lucrative opportunities, and they often found that the best way to do both was to influence governments to grant preferences, concessions, or monopolies. For these reasons, industrialization could make imperialism an almost irresistible temptation.[24]

At the same time, new technologies and mass production greatly increased industrializing states' abilities to build and project military power. Repeating rifles, machine guns, improved artillery, railroads, the telegraph, and armored steamships gave the European powers decisive strategic advantages over traditional African and Asian states. The superiority of industrial-era military technology was demonstrated in battles like that at Omdurman in the Sudan, where in 1898 British, Egyptian, and Sudanese forces, outnumbered by 2 to 1 by Sudanese rebels, killed 11,000 enemy soldiers while losing only 48 of their own. Although resistance to colonial conquest was frequent and sporadically successful, many indigenous cultures were simply overwhelmed by the expanding European powers, and some were forced to choose between acceptance of foreign rule and virtual annihilation. However, an industrialized military required bases, secure lines of communication, and strategic resources. For example, unlike the sailing ships of previous eras, steamships required coaling stations at fairly frequent intervals, and both armies and navies needed iron for guns, copper and nitrates for ammunition,

This painting of a Belgian officer settling a tribal dispute in the Congo in 1885 illustrates the attitude of superiority many Europeans felt towards the colonial world during the era of imperialism.   SOURCE: © Hulton Deutsch Collection Ltd. London

and coal for fuel. Maintenance of military power thus created its own incentives for imperial expansion.

Pax Britannica

During the nineteenth century, with Latin America independent and open to British trade and India under British rule, Britain generally refrained from adding new territories to its empire, concentrating instead on consolidating its overseas possessions. However, the rise of Germany, continental expansion of Russia, and the renewed push by France for colonies in the early 1880s posed a difficult problem for Britain, as these states usually closed their imperial territories to British trade and threatened to challenge British influence over areas London considered vital. Therefore, when renewed exploration and the discovery of mineral resources resulted in the "scramble for Africa" in the 1880s, Britain again adopted a policy of imperial expansion. Though British industrial production would be surpassed by Germany and then the United States as the nineteenth century drew to a close, Britain's naval power and its position as the world's center of trade and finance enabled it to impose the *Pax Britannica* ("British peace"), discouraging major war by threatening aggressors with embargoes on trade and other economic sanctions.

Britain used its superior naval and industrial power to secure the proverbial "lion's share," especially in eastern and southern Africa.[25] The most ambitious "man on the spot" in Africa was Cecil Rhodes, an English chauvinist and white supremacist who began his colonial career as an impoverished diamond prospector in South Africa. Rhodes founded the DeBeers company (which still controls most of the world's supply of diamonds), became prime minister of Cape Colony, and dreamed of "painting the map red" (establishing British dominion) from the mouth of the Nile River to the Cape of Good Hope. Rhodes gained most of central Africa for British influence by establishing Northern and Southern Rhodesia, which today are Zambia and Zimbabwe, respectively. Though his career ended in scandal and disgrace, many of his dreams for British control of Africa were fulfilled, as Britain dominated the whole of the Nile Valley, including Egypt, the Sudan, Uganda, and Kenya. (In his will, Rhodes established the Rhodes Scholarships for students from America, Germany, and the British colonies to study at Oxford University, in the hope of strengthening political and cultural ties within the Anglo-Saxon world.)

Britain's most important and costly colonial war, the Boer War, took place in South Africa. Disputes between the Dutch Afrikaners and British in South Africa increased after huge deposits of gold were found in the nominally independent Dutch Boer republic of the Transvaal. Rhodes tried to engineer British control over the Transvaal with a raid in 1895; his attempt to foster a coup failed disastrously and increased antagonism between Britain and Germany, Britain's main rival for influence in the region. Anglo-Boer tensions finally broke into warfare in 1899. When the war with Boer guerrillas became increasingly unpopular and expensive, Britain agreed to a compromise peace in 1902, and years later the Boer republics were absorbed into the newly created Union of South Africa, which was granted self-governing dominion status (though only whites enjoyed full civil and political rights).

Britain also secured some of the most fertile areas of the West African coast in the colonies of Nigeria, the Gold Coast (modern Ghana), and Sierra Leone. In Asia, British rule was extended to Aden and Burma, and Britain established exclusive "spheres of influence" over parts of Persia (modern Iran) and China. By the time of Queen Victoria's Diamond Jubilee in 1897, the "sun never set" on a British Empire of 500 million inhabitants, extending from the South Pacific islands to Singapore, India, and the hinterlands of Africa, through the British Isles, and on to Canada. The ethos and spirit of the empire were reflected in the popular adventure writings of Rudyard Kipling (born in British India) and H. Rider Haggard, and were later captured in films such as *The Four Feathers, The Man Who Would Be King, Zulu, The Far Pavilions,* and *The Ghost and the Darkness.* Britain's primacy in the colonial world was indisputable, though its ability to keep this vast empire together was open to question.

Imperial Rivals

Other imperial endeavors were not as successful as Britain's, but nonetheless had a significant impact on the international system.[26] After the Napoleonic Wars, France again began to build an overseas empire, this time in Africa, Southeast

Asia, and the Pacific. In 1830, motivated in part by the need to stop raids by the Barbary pirates, France conquered Algeria in North Africa. Elsewhere, in West Africa, the French extended their influence inland, coming to dominate a vast region of little economic value due to the arid climate and sparse population. In Asia they were able to colonize Indochina and a number of Pacific islands such as Tahiti. French colonialism of this era has often been characterized as "direct rule," driven by the ideological rationale of a *mission civilatrice*. The French saw their role as bringing culture and civilization to backward peoples and thus attempted to assimilate and colonize them to the French way of life. This French Empire was extensive in its territory, covering large areas of Africa. Moreover, in light of France's protectionism, virtually all trade involving French colonies was conducted with France.[27]

Germany and Italy also sought colonial empires in Africa, though Italy's imperial adventures were generally thwarted until the twentieth century. Germany sought a "place in the sun" alongside other European powers in Africa, and came out of the "Scramble for Africa" with Cameroon, Tanganyika (modern Tanzania) and South-West Africa (modern Namibia), though it could not hope to hold its possessions for long against British naval supremacy. Meanwhile, Russia secured dominion over the Caucasus and Central Asia and sought to extend its influence farther south, though Russian ambitions in South Asia were consistently thwarted by the British, who viewed Russian expansion as a threat to British India.[28]

While the British, French, German, and Russian empires expanded, one great empire steadily declined. In the mid- to late nineteenth century, the weakened Ottoman Empire increasingly came under attack from Russia and Austria, both of which vied for control over the former Ottoman territories. As the century proceeded, the Ottoman decline accelerated despite internal attempts at reform and the efforts of different European countries—especially Britain—to prevent a total collapse. The British saw the Ottoman Empire as a critical counterweight to Russian expansion. The increasingly obvious weakness of the empire only encouraged external intervention on the part of European powers eager for some of the spoils left by the crumbling Ottoman authority. Yet, because each of the European great powers had interests to protect in Ottoman-controlled areas, all sought to ensure that none would gain the upper hand. They thus tended to counterbalance one another, and all the while the "sick man of Europe" gradually continued to deteriorate.

Though the Ottoman Empire progressively sought to adopt Western military technologies, its fate was no longer in its own hands. It had fallen too far behind, and the social, educational, and technical obstructions to modernization were too difficult to overcome. As we noted earlier, intensification of nationalism in Greece and the Balkans led to a series rebellions, which the Ottomans attempted to violently repress. Russia, which claimed to be the protector of fellow Slavs, responded with force in 1877, only to be restrained by other great powers. The power vacuum left by the continuing Ottoman decline in the Balkans exacerbated rivalries between the other imperial powers, and the combination of revolutionary nationalism and imperial maneuverings began to pile up the tinder for a conflagration on an unprecedented scale.

Spotlight

The Balkans

Be prepared to hear a lot about the Balkans in this book. This geographic expression refers to the area of southeastern Europe now consisting of Albania, Romania, Bulgaria, Greece, Yugoslavia, and the former Yugoslav states of Slovenia, Croatia, Bosnia, and Macedonia. The sheer number of nations located in this relatively small area indicates the intense political fragmentation that has plagued the region.

The Balkans are a melange of intermingled ethnic and religious groups, many of whom harbor old hatreds and quarrels with one another. Complicating the situation even further, the area has been conquered and reconquered over the centuries by many outside powers (including Austria, Russia, Turkey, and Hungary). The result has been the reinforcement of deep divisions among the many nationalities that inhabit the region. By the nineteenth

century, competition among the declining Ottoman Empire and the Austro-Hungarian and Russian empires frequently combined with indigenous nationalism and ethnic strife to turn the Balkans into the "tinderbox" of Europe. (See Map 2.5.)

This chapter and the next will show that throughout the nineteenth and early twentieth centuries, the Balkans repeatedly exploded into violent conflict and crisis. As Chapter Four will relate, conflict in the Balkans was more or less frozen by the Cold War. With the end of that global political struggle, however, the forces of fragmentation have once again seized the Balkans with paroxysms of violence, particularly in Croatia and Bosnia. At times, it almost seems as if the flames of nationalism and ethnic hatred burn so brightly in the Balkans that those who remember the fragmentation of the past condemn the region to repeat it.

BISMARCKIAN SYSTEM

The last decades of the nineteenth century saw a succession of alliances known collectively as the **Bismarckian system.** Germany used these defensive alliances to moderate the demands of its allies, prevent the formation of coalitions of opponents that could seriously threaten its vital interests, and forestall the escalation of local conflicts into general war. A delicate balancing act performed by a master political acrobat, Bismarck's system worked splendidly for a time, but it could not resolve the domestic and international conflicts that ultimately led to his downfall and his system's collapse.

The strategic objective of Bismarck's alliance system was to keep Germany, Austria-Hungary, and Russia together and France isolated. This was no easy task, because the goals of Bismarck's two major allies, Austria-Hungary and Russia, were opposed. Bismarck had been able to ally with both of these adversaries—first with Austria-Hungary in the Dual Alliance in 1879, then with both in the Three Emperors' Alliance in 1881—but this balancing act was threatened by political developments, particularly in the Balkans. Independence movements challenged Turkish control of the Balkans, and the weakening Ottoman Empire could neither suppress nor satisfy nationalist demands. As a result, Austria-Hungary and

Russia increasingly supported various Balkan nationalist movements in a competition for territory and influence in the region. Agreements brokered by Bismarck at the Congress of Berlin in 1878 temporarily stabilized the Balkans, but issues of Austro-Hungarian and Russian competition had still failed to resolve themselves and overlapped with the tensions among the states emerging after the Ottoman Empire's disintegration. Seeking to reduce the tensions caused by territorial disputes between Rome and Vienna, Bismarck brought Italy into his alliance system in 1882 with the Triple Alliance between Germany, Austria-Hungary, and Italy.

Bismarck's position was strengthened by disagreements between France and Britain over another part of the declining Ottoman Empire, Egypt, which Britain regarded as an area of vital interest (particularly after the opening of the Suez Canal in 1869). When France did not join with Britain in putting down an Egyptian rebellion in 1882, British troops occupied Egypt, and Britain established a de facto protectorate over the country. (It remained a nominal part of the Ottoman Empire until 1914.) This action severely alienated France and consequently removed another possible ally for Paris in its attempts to pursue its revanchist hopes against Germany. (**Revanchism** is the desire for revenge, particularly for a defeat in war.)

By 1888, however, Bismarck's system was struggling to hold itself together. Russia became increasingly distrustful of German diplomacy, which effectively prevented St. Petersburg from actively pursuing its goals in the Balkans. In its competition with Russia, Austria-Hungary grew increasingly dependent on Germany as a protector. Bismarck tried to juggle Russian and Austrian interests, but none of the great powers could control events in the Balkans, which were largely driven by the ambitions and antagonisms of the local peoples fighting for greater autonomy from Ottoman suzerainty. This mixture of independent action on the part of the Balkan states and the irreconcilable interests of Austria-Hungary and Russia in this region played a major role in the decline of Bismarck's system.[29]

With formidable skill, Bismarck was able to temporarily manage the many conflicts between the interests of the great powers. Yet, by the late 1880s domestic pressures for a more assertive German policy multiplied and became more difficult to contain. The flexibility of Bismarck's policies meant that other powers were neither overly disgruntled nor particularly pleased with Germany. Once alternative sources of support became available to the dissatisfied powers, alliance with Germany looked less attractive. Meanwhile, within Germany, groups seeking protective tariffs and favoring aggressive colonialism increased their political clout. (Bismarck himself was not enthusiastic about German colonialism outside Europe, but his successors espoused the view that Germany needed colonies to maintain its "place in the sun" alongside the most active colonizers, France and Britain.) These internal developments affected Germany's external position, as its expanding role in world politics increasingly infringed on the established interests of the other European powers. German domestic politics eventually undermined Bismarck's position, and he was removed from office in 1890. By the time of his dismissal, most of Europe had enjoyed almost two decades of peace, but the seeds of a great-power war had been sown.

Spotlight

Does the Balance of Power Promote Peace?

Both theorists and practitioners of international politics frequently use the expression *balance of power*. This term has a number of meanings, which are discussed in more detail in Chapters Eleven, Twelve, and Thirteen, but in eighteenth- and nineteenth-century Europe it usually referred to an equilibrium, or at least a rough equivalence, in the relative economic and military strengths of the great powers.

Politicians justified many actions and much expenditure by claiming that alliances, arms buildups, and almost anything else they could think of were necessary to "preserve the balance of power." In particular, when one leading great power (such as France under Louis XIV or Napoléon or the newly united Germany after 1871) threatened to outstrip the capabilities of the others to the extent that it could impose its will throughout Europe, the other major states would ally against it to prevent it from achieving domination over the continent.

As mentioned earlier, throughout the nineteenth century Britain pursued a policy designed to ensure that no single power could dominate Europe, and all the major powers acted to counterbalance one anothers' strengths so that (it was hoped) none

would feel strong enough to launch a major war.

Should they have bothered? Some international relations theorists, such as Hans Morgenthau and Morton Kaplan, argue that an equivalence of power among major states is the most effective way of preventing major war in the anarchic international system. From this viewpoint, war is caused by an *imbalance of power*—if one state or alliance feels that it can defeat its opponents, it will attempt to force them to do as it wishes and will attack if they resist.

Other analysts, however, contend that peace is maintained most effectively when a single power becomes dominant. A. F. K. Organski, George Modelski, and others (see Chapter Twelve) argue that war becomes less frequent if the strongest power achieves **hegemony**, or recognized leadership, making the international system somewhat less anarchic. The hegemon can then impose peace on other states through economic sanctions (such as an embargo, or forcible cutoff of trade) or the threat of military force. In their view, major wars break out when the dominant power becomes too weak to fend off challengers, and its rivals launch wars with it and among themselves to see who will be the next

CONCLUSION

The International System on the Eve of the Twentieth Century

Toward the end of the nineteenth century, the stability that the Concert of Europe had imposed on Europe was rapidly disappearing. Shared interests among the great powers disintegrated into local conflicts that proliferated, especially in the Balkans, serving as a constant reminder of conflicting objectives. The community of fundamental interests envisioned in the Concert of Europe, a precursor of modern political and economic globalization, was being rapidly overcome by the fragmentation caused by the conflicting interests of Europe's many nationalities. In the final analysis, Bismarck's system served only to prolong the calm before the storm.

"king of the hill." Thus, a balance of power would actually encourage war as many states would feel they had a fighting chance of coming out on top.

Unfortunately, the historical evidence on whether a balance of power promotes or prevents war is supremely equivocal. When Napoleonic France dominated continental Europe militarily and imposed the Continental System to prevent trade with its rival Britain, Europe enjoyed a brief lull in the Napoleonic Wars. French hegemony soon broke down, however, as French power became overextended, and the continent plunged back into war.

During the mid- to late nineteenth century, when British naval power was able to threaten any state with an embargo on trade, no major wars occurred, and as a result the period was referred to as the *Pax Britannica* (the "British Peace"). However, although the great powers looked to Britain for leadership, they recognized one another as ostensible equals in the Concert of Europe, and no power (including Britain) achieved military domination on the continent. Later, Bismarck's system of alliances designed to maintain a balance of power avoided large-scale war for almost twenty years, but minor conflicts were frequent and the system eventually broke down. War and peace have thus occurred under both a balance and an imbalance of power.

Given that the evidence is so inconclusive, what good, if any, does the balance of power do? While theorists will probably continue to debate this point as long as there is an international system upon which to disagree, the one behavior that appears constant among all major powers is that none will willingly allow any of the others to achieve domination. States will thus try to balance one another regardless of whether theorists recommend it. In an anarchic international system where all states face the security dilemma (see Chapter One) and each state must look out for its own interests first, they have little choice.

This situation may not last forever; strong international institutions that can guarantee collective security may help states escape the security dilemma, and there is significant evidence that democratic states do not fight with one another, regardless of their **relative power** (see Chapter Twelve). Until the world becomes less anarchic, or more democratic, however, leaders seem likely to continue to pursue a balance of power much as they did throughout the eighteenth and nineteenth centuries, whether international relations specialists approve or not.

Perhaps, however, this was all that it could have been expected to do. Institutions such as the Concert of Europe and Bismarck's alliances had proven capable of resolving conflicts between nations that arose from the security dilemma or from calculations of strategic interest. But they had repeatedly shown themselves to be incapable of resolving conflicts, which frequently have deep historical and cultural roots and all too often resist solution through rational compromise. These nationalist conflicts were destined to worsen as the twentieth century approached, because although some European nations, such as France, Italy, and Germany, had achieved independent statehood, many subject nations of the Austro-Hungarian, Ottoman, and Russian empires had not. Additionally, many nations in Asia and Africa were denied independence by European colonialism.

The conflicts inherent in the international system in the late nineteenth century were thus covered by a veneer of stability which was wearing precariously thin. Europe was gradually moving toward an increasingly dangerous situation, and the spread of European power and influence throughout the globe ensured that any major conflict in Europe would threaten the peace of the entire world.

PRINCIPAL POINTS OF CHAPTER TWO

1. Generally speaking, in the period 1648–1890, great leaders such as Louis XIV, Frederick the Great, Napoléon, and Bismarck had a major impact on international politics, and the balance of power operated among the great powers to prevent a single empire from dominating Europe.

2. Spain and Portugal, seeking new routes to the Orient for the lucrative spice trade, began the race for colonies in the late fifteenth century.

3. The concept of the sovereign nation-state was codified by the Peace of Westphalia, which ended the Thirty Years' War in 1648.

4. The period 1648–1789 was one of competition among the primary monarchies of Europe. Wars among the great powers were frequent but limited. France made major efforts to become paramount, but the balance of power operated to block French expansion.

5. After the decline of the Spanish and Portuguese empires, the principal colonial competition through most of the eighteenth and nineteenth centuries was between Britain and France. Britain won decisive victories in India and North America, but lost its American colonies in the American Revolution.

6. In 1789 the French Revolution challenged the European monarchies with a new wave of political ideas, including liberalism and nationalism. Nationalism holds that each nation deserves an independent state of its own.

7. After years of turmoil, Napoléon took charge of France, declared himself emperor, and embarked on a series of wars to dominate Europe and spread the ideas of the revolution.

8. With Napoléon's defeat in 1815, the major powers formed the Concert of Europe, designed to prevent the resurgence of French power and the spread of liberalism and nationalism. Ousted monarchies were returned to power.

9. The Concert of Europe established the principle of collective security and demonstrated that cooperation was possible among the great powers, but it was only partially successful. The great powers often disagreed among themselves, and the ideas of liberalism and nationalism spread.

10. Yet, major war between the great powers did not occur in the remainder of the century. Instead, violence within states over nationalism and liberalism contributed to the fragmentation of empires. France quickly returned to great-power status, and the European powers frequently disagreed over whether to intervene to prevent rebellions.

11. Globalization of European politics was accelerated by the Industrial Revolution, which led to mass production in manufacturing, new forms of transportation, growth of cities, social dislocations, domestic instability,

and new and more lethal weaponry. Major political and social upheavals occurred within states, particularly the revolutions of 1848. New technology and economic imperatives pressed forward the process of globalization, and the search for colonies and additional markets began anew.

12. Bismarck, chancellor of Prussia, harnessed the conservative agenda of keeping the aristocracy in power while promoting the liberal nationalist aim of German unification. He also proved adept at diplomacy with the other great powers. Through three quick and successful wars against Denmark, Austria, and France, he united Germany in 1871 under Prussian leadership.

13. Driven by the perceived strategic and economic imperatives of industrialization, the competition between the European powers for colonial empires continued in the late nineteenth century. France and Germany won colonies in Africa and the Pacific, and Russia gained territory in Asia, but Britain's economic and naval power ensured its predominance outside Europe.

14. Bismarck maneuvered to maintain the stability of the European system from 1870 to 1890, but he could not contain growing opposition at home and increasing competition among the European powers.

15. The net result of the spread of nationalism in the nineteenth century was that Italy and Germany were unified, but the multinational Austrian and Ottoman (Turkish) Empires began to come apart.

16. As the twentieth century approached, industrialization, the competition between monarchy and liberalism, and nationalism combined to create a new, turbulent, and potentially explosive international system.

KEY TERMS

balance of
  power
Bismarckian
  system
collective
  security
colonialism
communism

Concert of
  Europe
empires
fragmentation
free trade
great powers
hegemony
imperialism

international
  relations
international
  system
junker
multipolar
nationalism
nation-state
Peace of
  Westphalia

power
power
  projection
relative power
revanchism
socialism
sovereignty
world politics

SOURCE: Imperial War Museum/Archive

The World Wars

At the start of the twentieth century, world leadership was vested in Europe. Through military power, economic strength, and colonial empires, the European great powers dominated the world's political and economic system. By the middle of the century, however, Europe was struggling to recover from catastrophic devastation, and political and economic leadership had passed from London, Paris, and Berlin to capitals thousands of miles away from Europe's center of gravity. This radical change in the structure of world politics was brought about by two horrific wars, unequaled before or since in scope or destructiveness. World War I (1914–1918) and World War II (1939–1945) were the means by which the Eurocentric world order self-destructed and was replaced by a globalized economic and political system. The exact number of people killed in these two wars will never be known, but it certainly exceeds 55 million. This chapter will examine the causes and consequences of the world wars and their impact on world politics. Our discussion of these complex conflicts will not go into great detail on how they were fought, but will instead concentrate on why they occurred and what the fighting and the peace settlements that followed did to change the nature and structure of world politics.

Wars have always been the cause and effect of political changes, as Chapter Two has outlined. The world wars, however, were unprecedented not only in their carnage and scale, but in the degree to which they brought about political, economic, technological, and social change. They were fought not just in Europe, but also in Africa, Asia, the Pacific Islands, and the Americas, and no corner of the world was sufficiently remote to remain unaffected by the conflicts and their resolution. Men were mobilized in record numbers, which meant that equally large numbers of women entered the industrial workforce; this development in turn strengthened the case for women's political and social equality. Similarly, the wars' insatiable demands for workers and soldiers brought ethnic and racial minorities into the military and the industrial economy, bringing to the forefront social tensions that could be resolved only by the extension of political and civil rights.

The ramifications of the technological advances spurred on by the world wars were at first not fully comprehended either by soldiers or by military strategists. Barbed wire, invented on the American plains to fence in cattle, would be employed in Europe to confine entire armies to their trenches. The machine gun, perfected in the late nineteenth century, would become the weapon of choice in the twentieth, and dramatic developments greatly increased the ranges and firepower of artillery. World War I introduced the tank and changed the airplane from a curiosity to a tactical and strategic weapon, though the impact of both was marginal at first. These war machines would become decisive during World War II, an all-encompassing struggle that engendered a plethora of devices that now shape modern life, from the jet engine to the computer to the atomic bomb.

The two world wars thus had a deep and profound impact on almost every aspect of global civilization. An appreciation of the conditions that led to them and the legacy of their outcome is therefore necessary for an understanding of contemporary world politics. Although the effects of World War I and World War II are well known, many questions remain about their causes. This chapter cannot and should not attempt to answer these questions; instead, it will outline the salient facts and contending theories about the origins, conduct, and aftermath of these catastrophic conflicts. The choice of which facts and which theories are most relevant, and the determination of whether or not these long and bloody wars could have been avoided, will be left as an exercise for the reader.

CAUSES OF WORLD WAR I

The devastation wrought by the four years of World War I has led to a continuing and at times bitter debate as to its causes. Debate also focuses on the question of responsibility for the war. In the 1919 **Treaty of Versailles,** which officially ended the war, Germany and its kaiser, Wilhelm II, were held responsible for deliberately starting it. Yet, some scholars feel that none of the states, including Germany, had intended to go to war, but were instead caught up in events beyond their control. As the diplomatic historian René Albrecht-Carrié wrote, "If the outbreak of war in [1914] may be explained as but the logical outcome of long-maturing trends and forces, it may be said with equal truth that Europe in 1914 accidentally stumbled into a catastrophe from which all her members recoiled."[1] Although opinions thus differ about the causes of the Great War, it is clear in hindsight that the complex relations among the European states prior to 1914 created the context for the crisis that arose in July 1914. The decisions made by European leaders during that crisis led to a war that none of them wanted and that would destroy the world as they knew it.

Amidst all the controversy over the origins of World War I, six factors are recognized as playing an important role in European politics and diplomacy in the years leading up to the outbreak of war in 1914:

1. The growing power of Germany.
2. The system of alliances designed to protect the security and interests of the great powers.
3. The changing balance of economic power.
4. Ascendant nationalism.
5. Heightened competition for empire within and outside of Europe.
6. The **cult of the offensive**—the belief that the next European war would be short and that rapid mobilization and attack would be decisive.

As this section will illustrate, all of these contending explanations for the Great War follow the same basic pattern: the potentially far-ranging impact of a political, social, or technological development was not recognized until it was too late. The significance of these developments is obvious in hindsight, but in the early years of the twentieth century, diplomatic and strategic thinking in European capitals failed to keep pace with political and economic changes. It is difficult to determine which factor contributed most to the outbreak of war in 1914, as any one of them alone would have increased tensions among the European states. Together, they overwhelmed the relative peace Europe had enjoyed in the decades after 1815.

Rise of Germany

With the stunning defeat of France in 1871 and Germany's subsequent unification (see Chapter Two), Germany took center stage in European international relations. Being at the center of Europe had both advantages and disadvantages for German diplomacy. The advantages were that Germany was well situated to expand trade, investment, and political contacts with the whole of Europe and could concentrate its military forces rapidly to meet a threat from any direction. The disadvantage was that Germany's central location meant that it had more points of potential conflict with other states than any other great power, and thus it feared encirclement by hostile neighbors. At the same time, Germany's neighbors became alarmed by Germany's growing economic and military strength—particularly France, which sought the return of Alsace and Lorraine, annexed by Germany as a result of the Franco-Prussian War.

From 1870 until 1890, when he was dismissed from office, Chancellor Otto von Bismarck was able to use Germany's central position to its advantage. After 1890, however, the foundations of Bismarck's success were gradually undermined. Kaiser Wilhelm II, who came to the throne in 1888, disagreed with Bismarck's methods and felt that the chancellor had too much influence on German foreign policy, so he dismissed him at the first opportunity. As the new kaiser felt that Germany's natural affinity was with other Germans, Germany began to tie itself closer to Austria-Hungary, and Russo-German relations consequently deteriorated. The kaiser also believed, contrary to Bismarck, that Germany required a powerful navy in order to maintain its status as a great power, and Admiral Tirpitz and many other officials in Berlin concurred. Thus, after Bismarck was sacked, the way was cleared for a buildup of naval power, and in 1898 Germany initiated a rapid expansion of its fleet.

News of the ambitious German naval construction program was received with great apprehension in London. From the British perspective, there was no logical reason for Germany to construct a large fleet unless it planned to challenge the dominant position of the Royal Navy. Britain regarded its naval supremacy as absolutely necessary in order to protect the island nation from invasion and to guard its extensive overseas empire. The kaiser's policies thus heightened the security dilemma in Europe on both land and sea. By 1914 Germany was engaged in a naval arms race with Britain and, together with its ally Austria-Hungary, in a ground-forces arms race with Russia and France.[2]

Alliance System

France, tired of diplomatic isolation and intent on replacing Bismarck's system of alliances with one that better protected its interests, seized the opportunity to court Russia when antagonism between Berlin and St. Petersburg began to increase. Although reluctant at first to make an alliance, Russia agreed in 1894 to a defensive treaty with France that explicitly sought to counter the increased power of Germany.[3] This treaty put an end to Bismarck's Triple Alliance and marked the beginning of an alliance system locking the great powers into commitments to intervene if their alliance partners were threatened. The agreement was designed to make Russia and France feel more secure, but to the Germans it represented the first step in a hostile encirclement.

Germany hoped to counter the Franco-Russian alliance with closer ties to Britain, but played its diplomatic hand poorly. Ill-conceived attempts to convince Britain that it needed German support to protect its colonial empire backfired (see the following section on imperialism). Germany's heavy-handed policy worsened relations by arousing public opinion in both countries against an Anglo-German alliance.

One up-and-coming nation with which Britain did share strategic interests, however, was Japan. Both Britain and Japan were concerned about Russian expansion in Asia, and in 1902, the two nations signed a treaty in which they agreed to remain neutral if either country fought one other major power and to support each other should either be at war with two other powers. This Anglo-Japanese alliance presented France with a dilemma. If Japan and Russia went to war, French failure to support Russia would antagonize an ally crucial for the balance of power in Europe. If France actively assisted Russia, it would, at minimum, alienate Britain and, at most, lose a naval war to it. As France had plans for colonial expansion in North Africa (discussed in Chapter Two), it could ill afford to antagonize Britain, and so it had to take steps to improve Anglo-French relations.

Therefore, in April 1904 the two countries signed an entente (diplomatic French for an agreement or understanding) in which France recognized British supremacy in Egypt and Britain recognized France's predominant role in Morocco. The entente bound England into an alliance with the nation that had been its perennial enemy, France, and drew London closer to another ancient British foe, Russia. England had several conflicts with Russia, especially over the Turkish Straits and Persia, but events in Europe would continue to bring the two together.

The Bismarckian system of flexible alliances that was set up to prevent a major war in Europe was thus followed by a rigid system ensuring that if two of the great powers went to war, the rest would quickly follow. None of the countries wanted a general European war, but each had its own designs and fears. Some, such as Germany, wanted to increase their influence, while others, like Austria-Hungary and Russia, sought to recapture their failing great power status. Russia, Austria-Hungary, and the Ottoman Empire were the last of the antiquated autocratic monarchies of Europe and were rapidly being eclipsed by the other great powers in terms of economic development, military strength, and political and social organization.[4] This trend became even more apparent with Russia's humiliating defeat in the Russo-Japanese War of 1904–1905, the first loss in modern times by a European power to a non-European state, which sparked off an unsuccessful but debilitating revolution in 1905. As the Russian, Ottoman, and Austrian situations became increasingly desperate, their leaders became prepared to risk anything, up to and including war, to hold on to their internal cohesion and international stature. The rigid alliance system that existed in Europe after about 1909 virtually ensured that if one of the decaying empires fell into war, the other great powers would be dragged down with it.

Economic Change and Competition

The foreign and domestic political problems confronting the European powers in the late nineteenth and early twentieth centuries were compounded by the wrenching changes brought about by industrialization. Among its many other effects (see Chapter Two), the Industrial Revolution led to massive growth in Europe's population. In the first years of the new century the population of Europe was 50 million; in 1870 it was roughly 200 million, and by the eve of war in 1914 the population had soared to 300 million.[5] This population explosion generated great pressures on the economic systems of states, which had to reconcile competing demands for civilian consumption, capital investment, and military spending. Particularly in the economically and politically backward Austro-Hungarian, Russian, and Ottoman empires, it became increasingly difficult to simultaneously satisfy the resource requirements for foreign, domestic, and security policy.

The only thing that outstripped the population growth was the growth in industrial production. This growth was not evenly spread either among countries or within them. Italy, Russia, and Austria-Hungary lagged behind Britain, France, and Germany in industrial development. As the twentieth century opened, Britain, as the first state to industrialize, was declining relative to late-developing states such as Germany and the United States. In 1850 Britain was the undisputed world industrial leader and France the continental powerhouse. In that year, Britain alone accounted for over one-third of the combined manufacturing output of the great powers. During the Bismarckian period, however, Germany emerged as the most powerful continental state, and by the end of the century Germany was encroaching on Britain's lead as well, surpassing the United Kingdom in steel production and overall manufacturing.[6] During the same period, another up-and-coming power, the United States, was beginning its takeoff, and by 1914 would evolve into an industrial giant. Table 3.1, which traces the major powers' share of world manufacturing output from 1880 to 1913, gives a rough indication of how the European powers and the United States stacked up against one another in terms of economic power as European conflicts intensified.

As the industrial capacity of states grew, their ability to challenge the other great powers for political leadership grew correspondingly. As Germany's economic strength approached and then surpassed Britain's, the main objective of European alliances changed from containment of France and Russia (as had been the case in the eighteenth and early nineteenth centuries) to containment of Germany. Meanwhile, increased industrial output was intensifying competition for resources and markets. Industrialization thus heightened the potential for conflict among the great powers at the same time that it enhanced their capacity to make war.[7]

Perceptions of political power often lagged behind changes in relative economic strength, however. Prior to the outbreak of World War I, few European leaders looked to the United States as a potential counterweight to Germany or other expansionist states. Public and congressional opinion in the United States at that time ran toward **isolationism,** and most Americans thought it best to stay well clear of the rivalries, conflicts, and "entangling alliances" of the European powers. On both sides of the Atlantic, leaders were slow to recognize how changes in the global economic system created new dangers and opportunities and made the collective security system originally envisioned in the Concert of Europe increasingly difficult to manage.

Table 3.1	Relative Shares of World Manufacturing Output, 1880–1913		
Country	1880	1900	1913
Britain	22.9%	18.5%	13.6%
United States	14.7	23.6	32.0
Germany	8.5	13.2	14.8
France	7.8	6.8	6.1
Russia	7.6	8.8	8.2
Austria-Hungary	4.4	4.4	4.4
Italy	2.5	2.4	2.4

SOURCE: P. Barioch, "International Industrialization Levels from 1750 to 1980," *Journal of European Economic History* 11 (1982), pp. 292, 299.

Nationalism

The most powerful political doctrine of the nineteenth and early twentieth centuries was nationalism. The French Revolution largely put an end to the idea of class, religion, or locality as the primary focus of loyalty for most people. The nation-state was now the supreme focus of allegiance. Those who clung the tightest to the ideas of nationalism in the early twentieth century, however, were people whose nations did not have independent states, namely those in Eastern Europe and the Balkans. These regions were dominated by competing powers, the Russian, Austro-Hungarian, and Ottoman empires, which were convinced that suppressing nationalism within their borders was necessary for their survival as political entities. As a result, campaigns of persecution were launched against minorities who did not seem to belong to the national image. Moscow forced the Poles in its empire to conform, the Jews in eastern and central Europe were persecuted, and all over Europe attempts were made to crush nationalist forces.

One of the greatest victories for nationalism was the unification of Germany, but its effect was not limited to the creation of the German Empire. The nationalism of the various ethnic groups within the many empires of Europe became a pressing issue in the twentieth century. The empires of eastern Europe were threatened by groups demanding separation and independence. These included Poles in Prussia and the French in Alsace and Lorraine who desired freedom from the German Empire; Serbs, Czechs, Romanians, and many others from the Austro-Hungarian Empire; Finns, Poles, and Balts from the Russian Empire; and Bulgarians, Greeks, Serbs, and Arabs from the Ottoman Empire.

The empire that felt most threatened by nationalist movements was Austria-Hungary. Here was the only country in Europe that was held together not by national identity, but by the principle of personal dynastic rule. Emperor Franz Josef I had ruled over the numerous nationalities within the empire since 1848. The Hungarians and the Austrians were actually minorities in a patchwork of Slavic groups, including Poles, Czechs, Slovaks, Slovenes, Croats, and Serbs. Austria was opposed to Russian encroachment in the area and was even more concerned about further independence in the Balkans. Vienna was afraid that the independent Balkan states, especially Serbia, would stir up trouble within the empire. The various nationalities under Austrian rule longed for independence and needed little encouragement from their brethren, but many independent Balkan states supported nationalist agitation in hopes of unifying all people of their respective nationalities. In particular, the domestic problem presented by Slavic nationalism was exacerbated by the desire of Serbia, aided and abetted by Russia, to expand at Austria-Hungary's expense.

In general, empires tended to suppress nationalists within their own borders while encouraging those in neighboring empires, hoping to make political gains at the expense of their imperial rivals. This created an explosive situation in the ethnically diverse and politically fragmented Balkans, where, as will be shown later, a dispute over nationalism provided the spark that ignited the First World War.

Imperialism

Empires were not confined to Europe. By 1900 most of the world outside Europe (except the Americas) was under the domination of some European power. Nearly all of Africa had been partitioned without regard to national or ethnic boundaries, and most of Asia as well was under de facto if not de jure control by European colonial regimes.[8] Because power and security depended on having control of resources, acquisition of colonies for their resources and markets was considered essential by many European leaders. But with most of the world already divided between the colonial empires, there was nowhere left to colonize. The states that felt left out of the colonial race, especially Germany, thought they deserved more and worried that without colonies they would not be able to obtain enough raw materials or have sufficient trading partners to remain competitive with the other great powers. The breakup of the "sick man of Europe," the faltering Ottoman Empire, presented an opportunity to acquire more territory (especially in the Middle East) that some states found irresistible.[9]

Many conflicts over colonial interests in Africa and Asia heightened tensions among the great powers in Europe. Britain and France frequently clashed over colonies and **spheres of influence,** as did Britain and Russia, but these great powers avoided war with each other over colonial disputes in the nineteenth century. As the twentieth century approached, however, colonial problems intensified the mutual antagonism between Britain and Germany. In particular, German support for the Boer republics increased efforts to resist British control of South Africa (see Chapter Two) and aroused public opinion in Britain against German meddling in a region that Britain saw as its rightful sphere of influence. The incident added to growing Anglo-German tensions.

Cult of the Offensive

Meanwhile, back in Europe, the improved relations between Russia and France generated great concern in Germany, especially among its top military leaders.

The worst nightmare of every German leader, as of Prussian leaders before them, was the possibility of a two-front war with both Russia and France simultaneously, which would divide and thus weaken Germany's army. With the advent of new technology, it appeared that the side that could swiftly mount an effective offensive would win, offering a tempting solution to this strategic problem. In the late nineteenth and early twentieth centuries, most European strategists ascribed to this belief in what modern strategic analysts refer to as the cult of the offensive.[10] There were two main reasons why this became the primary strategic doctrine for European military planners. The first, as mentioned, had to do with technology. The expansion of railroads, among other technological improvements, enabled states to rapidly deploy troops to the front, and the telegraph allowed generals to receive reports and transmit orders faster, enabling them to control larger armies more effectively. Also, the breech-loading rifle and the machine gun were widely thought to increase the ability of attacking troops to concentrate their firepower at the point of assault. (For some reason, the ability of defending troops to do this as well was downplayed.)

Second, recent experience with wars in Europe seemed to indicate that the side that "landed the first blow" would win. Prussia defeated its adversaries in 1866 and 1870–1871 quickly and with relatively few **casualties** (see Chapter Two). Most European generals expected the next great power war to resemble the last, and accordingly based their strategies on rapid mobilization and offensives. The economic pressures inherent in maintaining a large conscript and reserve army mobilized for long periods also made striking first more attractive, as leaders could promise that the boys would be home by Christmas. The same leaders chose to ignore the experience of the American Civil War (1861–1865) and the Boer War (1899–1902), both of which were protracted struggles and, especially in the American Civil War, produced a frightening number of casualties.

The inherent dangers of the cult of the offensive were not fully realized at the time. When political and military leaders believe that war will bring great gains at little cost, war becomes more likely. States act more aggressively by increasingly challenging their neighbors through military buildups and coercive threats of war. As these neighbors grow more fearful, they, too, build up their forces and seek stronger alliances in order to better secure themselves in the event of war. Even if none of the states actually seek war, this spiral of tension makes conflicts of interest more severe and likely to lead to violence. The cult of the offensive thus enhances the security dilemma (see Chapter Eleven) and encourages preemptive attacks, because when crises threaten to escalate into war, states have great incentives to strike first and defeat their enemies before their enemies can defeat them.

The cult of the offensive influenced the military plans of most of the European great powers. Beginning in 1892, German Chief of Staff Alfred von Schlieffen changed Germany's strategy. Previously, in the event of a two-front war with Russia and France, Germany planned to attack Russia first while German forces stood on the defensive against France. The new **Schlieffen Plan** called for Germany to knock out France with a fast-moving offensive, just as Prussia had done in the Franco-Prussian War, and then shift its troops by rail to the eastern front to fight the slower-moving Russian forces.

The Schlieffen Plan thus intended to use Germany's ability to mobilize troops and equipment faster than its adversaries to defeat first France and then Russia. To be successful, Germany had to mobilize at the first sign of Russian preparations for war, as any delay would shorten the window of opportunity for a quick victory and increase the chances of a two-front war, which would put Germany at a disadvantage. Russia and France, however, had similar plans for rapid mobilization and offensive in the event of a war with Germany. The cult of the offensive thus put the massive military machines of the great powers on a hair trigger.

PATH TO WAR

As the preceding section has outlined, there are plenty of possible explanations for *why* World War I occurred. Taken together, German expansion, the alliance system, economic competition, imperialism, nationalism, and the cult of the offensive offer more than enough reasons why Europe was pushed over the brink of war in 1914. In order to explain *how and when* World War I broke out, it is necessary to look at the string of crises that arose from the conflicting interests and aspirations of the great powers in the early twentieth century. There had been several regions of conflict throughout the century before 1914, but in the decade before the war, international attention was particularly focused on two areas, North Africa and the Balkans.

Moroccan Crises

At the start of the twentieth century, France was trying to draw the kingdom of Morocco under its wing in the hopes of adding it to France's African empire. In March 1905 Kaiser Wilhelm, looking for a way to break up the friendship between Britain and France and ensure German economic access to Morocco, visited Tangier in support of Moroccan independence. This catalyzed the First Moroccan Crisis, which the great powers decided to resolve at a diplomatic conference at Algeciras, Spain, in 1906. Germany's allies failed to support it at this conference, which recognized French dominance in Morocco. (In keeping with how the great powers viewed the world outside Europe, the interests of the Moroccans were given little attention.)

When French troops occupied the Moroccan capital of Fez in May 1911 to quell a revolt, Germany perceived the move (correctly) as an attempt to establish a protectorate over Morocco. To emphasize that its interests had to be taken into consideration, Germany sent a gunboat to the Moroccan port of Agadir, thereby beginning the Second Moroccan Crisis. The crisis was resolved by November with a compromise in which the Germans agreed to drop their objection to a French protectorate in Morocco in exchange for the acquisition of a slice of French colonial territory in the Congo. Nonetheless, the agreement satisfied neither France nor Germany and angered public opinion in both nations. Many people in France resented what they regarded as another humiliation of their country, while Germans regarded the incident as another denial of Germany's rightful "place in the sun." Meanwhile, taking advantage of the distraction provided by the crisis, Italy declared war on the Ottoman Empire in September 1911 and seized Tripoli (then an Ottoman domain, now the capital of Libya). In the short run, this was a sideshow for the great powers, but Italy's victory displayed the inherent weakness of the Ottoman Empire, which further encouraged nationalist demands in the Balkans.

Balkan Powder Keg

While imperialism was heightening conflicts between the great powers in Asia and Africa, nationalism was gaining momentum in Europe. In 1908, 1912, and 1913, several crises and two wars in the Balkans created a situation of rising tensions (see Map 3.1). The heart of the problem was the conflict between German-backed Austria-Hungary and Russian-backed Serbia, which were competing for the spoils of Ottoman decline. By 1914 the stage had been set for a showdown between Austria-Hungary and Serbia.

The sequence of events that finally put out the lights of Europe is convoluted, but it is worth recounting in detail, as it is one of history's greatest tragedies. On June 28, 1914, Archduke Franz Ferdinand, heir to Austria-Hungary's crown, was assassinated while on a visit to Sarajevo (then as now the capital of Bosnia) on a Serbian national holiday. Austria-Hungary had annexed Bosnia in 1908, but it was an area claimed by Serbia. Vienna held Serbia responsible for the assassination, and Austria's foreign minister, Count Berchtold, decided to use the incident as an opportunity to "settle accounts" with Serbia. Austria did not dare act without German support, however, so on July 5 the Austrian ambassador to Berlin met with Kaiser Wilhelm II to discuss the matter. Without consulting his military advisors, the kaiser not only promised Germany's support, but also pressed Austria-Hungary to take quick action and capitalize on the public outcry generated by the assassination. Thus Germany, one of the strongest countries in Europe, essentially gave a blank check to the weak and unstable Austro-Hungarian Empire to deal with Serbia as it saw fit.

On July 23, Austria-Hungary issued an ultimatum to Serbia and gave Belgrade forty-eight hours to reply. The terms of the ultimatum were extremely harsh, and most of Europe expected that Serbia would have no choice but to reject it—as did Austria, which was simply looking for an excuse to invade Serbia. The Russian government, believing that it needed to stand firm in support of Serbia in order to preserve Russia's great-power status, resolved that Russia would not be humiliated as it had been in the Balkan crisis of 1908, when it accepted Vienna's annexation of Bosnia. When he saw the Austrian ultimatum, Russian Foreign Minister Sazanov exclaimed, "This means a European war."[11]

On July 25, Russia issued orders to prepare for the mobilization of its army. That same day, Serbia responded to the ultimatum, surprisingly accepting most of

| Map 3.1 | The Balkans Before World War I |

Croatia-Slavonia

AUSTRO-HUNGARIAN EMPIRE

Dalmatia

Bosnia and
Herzegovina
administered by Austro-
Hungarian Empire since 1878;
annexed 1908

SERBIA
autonomous within Ottoman
Empire since 1830;
independent since 1878

ROMANIA

San Stefano Bulgaria
(March-July 1878)

Adriatic
Sea

MONTENEGRO
independent
since 1878

acquired by Mont. 1913

OTTOMAN EMPIRE

BULGARIA
autonomous within Ottoman
Empire 1878-1908;
gained independence 1908

Treaty of Bucharest, 1913
(disposition of Macedonia
and neighboring territory)

Ceded to Serbia

Ceded to Greece

Ceded to Bulgaria

International boundary
1908–1913

ALBANIA
declared
independence
1912

MACEDONIA

Aegean
Sea

0   100 miles
0   100 kilometers

GREECE   GR

Austria-Hungary's demands. Austria-Hungary, however, preferred to resolve the crisis by force. It rejected Serbia's response, broke off diplomatic relations, and, despite the fact that its army was not prepared to take action, declared war on Serbia on July 28. The following day, Tsar Nicholas ordered a partial mobilization of the Russian army directed against Austria-Hungary in an attempt to deter an attack against Serbia, but he still hoped to avoid war with Germany.

In Berlin, the chief of the German General Staff, Helmuth von Moltke, wanted to mobilize the army immediately. The kaiser and chancellor, Bethmann-Hollweg, however, tried furiously to gain time for more negotiations. The kaiser wrote a note to the tsar pleading for restraint, but Tsar Nicholas was under great pressure from his own military leaders, who did not have any plans for a partial mobilization and also thought Germany was likely to intervene in any war between Russia and Austria-Hungary.[12] On July 30, after much vacillation, the tsar agreed to full mobilization. The next day, July 31, Germany sent Russia an ultimatum stating that Germany would be forced to mobilize against Russia if Russia moved against Austria and warned that if this occurred, "European war could scarcely be prevented." [13]

Germany also requested French assurances of neutrality in the event of a Russo-German war, but the expectation of a major war was rapidly becoming a self-fulfilling prophecy. At 3:55 A.M. on August 1, France responded to the German request by ordering a general mobilization. Five minutes later, Germany also issued orders for a general mobilization, and at 7:00 A.M. declared war on Russia. [14] The initial conflict between Austria-Hungary and Serbia had escalated into a confrontation between the continental great powers.

For each nation, mobilization was an expensive move that could not be sustained for long without causing significant economic damage. But the great powers all subscribed to the cult of the offensive described earlier—they believed that whoever attacked first would gain a decisive advantage. Belief in the power of the offensive was particularly strong in Germany, which was now faced with a two-front war. The Schlieffen Plan, which anticipated this contingency, dictated that the main French forces be circumvented, so on August 2 Germany demanded free passage for its troops through Belgium. Consistent with its neutral status, Belgium refused, but on August 3 Germany declared war on France and sent troops through Belgium anyway. Britain, which regarded Belgian neutrality as a vital interest, declared war on Germany on August 4. World War I had begun. [15]

THE GREAT WAR

All of the great powers had expected a short and relatively bloodless war. Germany hoped to defeat France as rapidly as it had in 1871. Had the war been between only these two countries, Germany's hopes might have been realized, for the initial German attack threatened to take Paris. (During the First Battle of the Marne in 1914, German troops were able to see the Eiffel Tower before they were forced to retreat.) However, the assumptions of the cult of the offensive did not prove correct. The technology that seemed to favor the offense could be used even more effectively by the defense. European armies had learned to employ the machine gun, which was devastating against massive infantry offensives.

After the initial German attack failed, the armies on the western front dug in to hold their positions, and there the fighting stayed until the closing months of the war. The trench lines eventually reached more than 300 miles from the coast of Belgium to the Swiss Alps, and through most of the four years of fighting the front lines never shifted more than ten miles. On the eastern front, the initial Russian attack on Germany was halted by a spectacular German victory near Tannenberg, in eastern Prussia, and trench warfare soon set in there as well.

Instead of the quick war of maneuver that European strategists had counted on, the conflict became a **war of attrition** in which thousands of men would die fighting for advances measured in yards rather than miles. [16] During the war's major battles, the numbers of men killed for minuscule gains defy comprehension. At the five-month Battle of the Somme in 1916, British forces gained 120 square miles at the cost of 420,000 casualties, or roughly 3500 casualties per square mile, while

What Would You Do ?

You are the tsar of Russia in early August 1914. You are backing the Serbians, your Orthodox Christian brethren, whom Austria, and by extension, Germany, have threatened over the assassination of the heir to the Austrian throne on his visit to Bosnia, an Austrian province that Serbia covets. You are trying to decide whether to order full mobilization of your forces against Austria.

You are aware that mobilization may precipitate the next war. You have suggested to your military commanders that the country partially mobilize, thereby keeping its options open. If the crisis abates, you can easily de-mobilize; if the crisis leads to war, you will at least be partially ready. But your generals tell you that this is not possible: No one ever devised a scheme for partial mobilization; it is either all or nothing. Mobilization will threaten Germany and will likely lead to war. If you wait a few years until you are stronger industrially, you may be in a better position to fight and win.

Although you have made great strides in bringing your country into the industrial age in the last twenty years (such as building more munitions factories, steel mills, and kilometers of railroads), you have also heightened expectations on the part of the working classes for greater economic and political reform. The Japanese defeat of your armies in 1905 revealed your country's lack of military and economic preparation, and it incited a domestic revolt. You do not want to risk a repeat of this event.

On the other hand, you want to maintain your alliance with France, which opposes Germany. Your military experts tell you that if you do not mobilize your forces to thwart a possible Austrian attack against Serbia, the Austrians and their patrons, the Germans, could easily win a war. Your military officers keep saying that the first country to mobilize will win the next war. Six years ago during a similar crisis in the Balkans, you caved in and your position, and that of your clients, the Serbs, only deteriorated. If you wait too long to decide, you may appear weak and indecisive to both client and foes.

You face a dilemma. The war could be lost if you decide not to mobilize, but mobilization could lead to war. If it leads to a war that you lose, it could mean your downfall.

What would you do ?

the Germans suffered 445,000 casualties (casualties refers to the total number of wounded or killed). On July 1, the first day of the British offensive, 60,000 British soldiers died (more than the number of Americans killed during the entire Vietnam conflict); 21,000 were killed in the first hour of the attack, possibly within the first few minutes.[17] Attempting to break through defensive lines, both sides used poison gas, a new weapon that caused agonizing deaths and crippling injuries but did not alter the stalemate. Tanks and aircraft were introduced in further attempts to generate offensive momentum, but these military machines were still in early stages of development and had only a marginal effect on the fighting. At sea, the fleets of British and German dreadnoughts fought only one major battle (the Battle of Jutland, in 1916), which proved indecisive. Most of the naval war was fought between German U-boats (submarines, another new tool of warfare) and British convoy escorts.

Italy joined the Entente Powers—France, Russia, Britain, and Serbia (collectively referred to as the Allies)—in 1915, and by 1917 Montenegro, Romania, Greece, Portugal, and Japan had joined the Allies. Germany and Austria-Hungary (the Central Powers) were joined by the Ottoman Empire in October 1914 and by Bulgaria in 1915. These new entrants to the war had little effect on the fighting on the main eastern and western fronts, however. Fighting spread throughout the Balkans, the Middle East, and even to German colonies in Africa and the Pacific, but the deadlock on the primary fronts continued. The prolonged stalemate prompted peace efforts, including those initiated by U.S. President Woodrow Wilson, who argued for ending the war with "no victor and no vanquished." None of the peace proposals, however, could resolve the basic problem: "Germany would not surrender territorial gains while there was a hope of victory, while the Entente could not contemplate peace without the restoration of French territory and Belgian independence at a minimum." [18]

Although neither side was willing to make peace, the human, material, economic, and social costs of the war were increasing for both. The fruitless slaughter and deprivation reduced the morale of both front-line troops and the civilians at home. In the spring of 1917 many units of the French army mutinied, and the German army also faced disciplinary problems, including mutinies and desertions. The great powers were all nearing their breaking points when, in 1917, two dramatic developments changed the course of the war.

Russian Revolution

The war with Germany and Austria created additional pressures on the decrepit tsarist regime in Russia. By the end of 1916, the Russian army had suffered many defeats and more than 3.6 million casualties, with another 2.1 million Russian soldiers taken prisoner. These losses prompted St. Petersburg to drastically increase draft calls, which in turn increased unrest among the peasants and urban workers. Additionally, food supplies were not getting to the cities due to an inadequate transportation system, and inflation had skyrocketed. Finally, insufficient supplies of weapons, ammunition, and food were reaching soldiers at the front. Strikes, mutinies, and rioting culminated in the overthrow of Nicholas II in March 1917. The new Provisional Government, a coalition of democratic, socialist, and communist parties headed by Alexander Kerensky, continued the war, a decision that increasingly incurred the wrath of soldiers and the civilian population. In November the Bolshevik (Communist) Party seized power, and the revolutionary leader Vladimir Lenin assumed leadership on a platform of "land, bread, and peace." The Bolsheviks delivered on one plank of their platform; they signed an armistice with Germany in December, and in the March 1918 Treaty of Brest-Litovsk, the Bolshevik government signed a separate peace with Germany, relinquishing Russian claims to the Baltic States of Latvia, Lithuania, and Estonia, as well as Finland, Poland, and other territories in eastern Europe. German forces remained in occupation of the western portions of Ukraine and Russia.

United States Enters the War

With Russia eliminated from the fighting, Germany now faced a one-front war, though ironically the result was opposite to that envisioned in the Schlieffen Plan (which called for France to be defeated first). Had Germany faced only France and Britain in the west, it might have forced the Allies to sue for peace. But while Russia was leaving the war, another major power was entering on the allied side.

Neutral since 1914, the United States grew increasingly annoyed with both Britain and Germany, as the two warring powers interfered with American trade and shipping. The United States at that time was still pursuing a policy of isolationism; Washington hoped to steer clear of the tangled political conflicts that had dragged the European powers into war in 1914. (This did not stop the United States from lending billions of dollars to Britain and France to finance their war efforts, however.) America was perfectly happy to trade with other countries, including the belligerents, but few Americans saw any reason why their country should get involved in a European war.

American attitudes changed markedly, however, after Germany's January 1917 decision to launch unrestricted submarine warfare, in which ships were attacked without warning regardless of nationality. This action greatly angered the U.S. government and inflamed public opinion against Germany. Berlin was taking a calculated risk: The German high command predicted that unrestricted submarine warfare would eventually bring the United States into the war. However, they believed that they would be able to prevail in the conflict by strangling Britain's supply lines before U.S. aid or intervention could make a substantial impact. The first prediction proved true: In April 1917 the United States declared war on Germany. The second German prediction, however, was not correct. The entry of the United States provided the impetus to break the long and bloody stalemate. By the autumn of 1917 some 300,000 American troops were arriving in Europe every month, and the United States was contributing its huge productive capacity to the Allied cause.[19]

Armistice

By August 1918 the Allies halted the last major German attack and went on the offensive. The number of troops America committed to the war was not large compared to the French and German armies, but U.S. entry gave the Allies a decisive advantage in industrial capability and boosted the morale of Allied soldiers and civilians. As Germany's armies were being pushed back, Berlin concluded that there was no hope of avoiding defeat, although as yet German territory had not been invaded. On October 3, Germany sought an armistice (agreement to stop fighting), which was signed on November 11, 1918.

Most wars in Europe since 1648 had been limited wars that did not cause widespread devastation or huge numbers of military and civilian casualties. World War I, however, was a total war, in which the whole of each involved nation's human and material resources were devoted to the conflict, and defeat threatened national survival. The destruction caused by the war was overwhelming. An estimated 8 million soldiers were killed during the war, with another 7 million permanently disabled. In addition, more than 5 million civilians were killed in Europe outside Russia, and the number of Russian civilian casualties is probably much higher.[20] An entire generation of young Europeans was all but destroyed. The agony of the war was later captured in literary works such as the poetry of Wilfred Owen, Erich Maria Remarque's novel *All Quiet on the Western Front*, and Ernest Hemingway's *A Farewell to Arms*. Stanley Kubrick's film *Paths of Glory*, Peter Weir's *Gallipoli* (named for the site of a bungled British attempt to capture the Turkish Straits), and the documentary series *The Great War and the Shaping of the Twentieth Century* offer powerful depictions of the physical and psychological horrors of trench warfare. The world sighed with relief when the Great War ended in 1918, but winning the peace would prove to be a struggle in itself.

VERSAILLES SETTLEMENT

With the destruction caused by the Great War fresh in their minds, the victorious Allies took upon themselves the responsibility for bringing order and stability to Europe and the rest of the world. In January 1919 the United States, Britain, France, and Italy convened the Paris Peace Conference at the palace of Versailles. The conference was attended by a number of smaller states, but neither Germany nor Austria-Hungary was invited. Because France had suffered the most during the war, it played a leading role at the conference, as did the United States, in recognition of its military and economic clout. French goals were relatively straightforward: punish Germany and take revenge not only for the losses incurred between 1914 and 1918, but also for the humiliation of 1871. Prime Minister David Lloyd George of Britain was also bent on exacting punishment to a lesser degree, but Britain and Italy, along with the smaller Balkan states, were mainly there to gain territory from the division of the fallen empires. The goals of the European conferees were thus in line with old-fashioned realpolitik as it had been practiced at the Congress of Vienna (see Chapter Two).

The goals of the United States were distinctly different. President Wilson argued that America had entered the war not out of a narrow self-interest, but in order to make the world "safe for democracy." In January 1918, before Germany's defeat, Wilson had enunciated fourteen points on which he believed the peace settlement

Map 3.2   Versailles Settlement after World War I

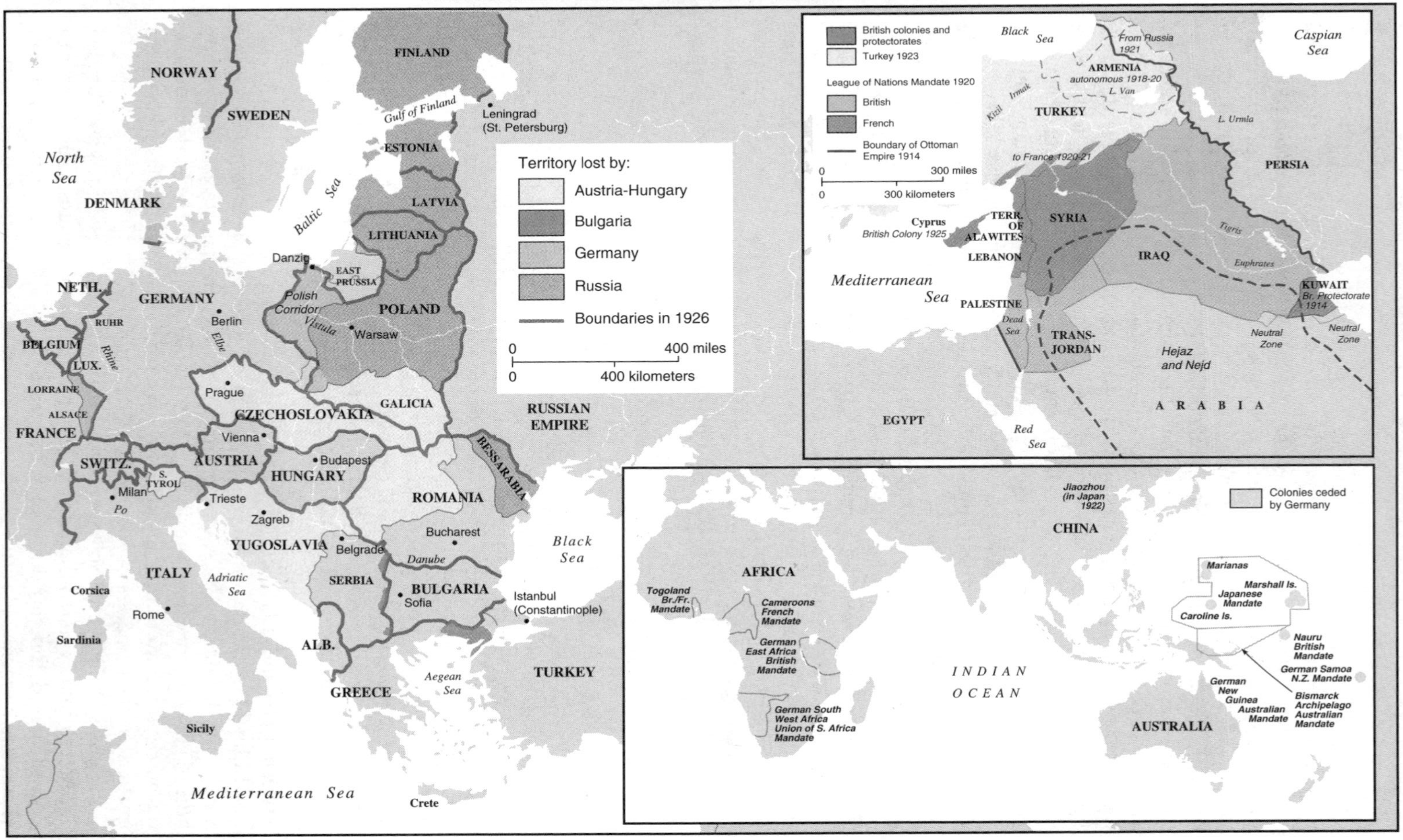

Caspian Sea

PERSIA

KUWAIT
Br. Protectorate 1914

Neutral Zone

Neutral Zone

From Russia 1921

ARMENIA
autonomous 1918-20

L. Urmia

L. Van

Tigris

Euphrates

TURKEY

to France 1920-21

Kizil Irmak

ARABIA

IRAQ

Hejaz and Nejd

Black Sea

SYRIA

TERR. OF ALAWITES

LEBANON

TRANS-JORDAN

PALESTINE

Dead Sea

Red Sea

EGYPT

Cyprus
British Colony 1925

Mediterranean Sea

British colonies and protectorates
Turkey 1923

League of Nations Mandate 1920
British
French

Boundary of Ottoman Empire 1914

0   300 miles
0   300 kilometers

Colonies ceded by Germany

Marianas

Marshall Is.
Nauru British Mandate
German Samoa N.Z. Mandate

Japanese Mandate

Caroline Is.

Bismarck Archipelago Australian Mandate

German New Guinea Australian Mandate

AUSTRALIA

Jiaozhou (in Japan 1922)

CHINA

INDIAN OCEAN

AFRICA

Cameroons French Mandate

German East Africa British Mandate

German South West Africa Union of S. Africa Mandate

Togoland Br. Fr. Mandate

Territory lost by:
Austria-Hungary
Bulgaria
Germany
Russia

Boundaries in 1926

0   400 miles
0   400 kilometers

RUSSIAN EMPIRE

NORWAY

SWEDEN

FINLAND

Leningrad (St. Petersburg)

Gulf of Finland

ESTONIA

LATVIA

LITHUANIA

Baltic Sea

EAST PRUSSIA

Danzig

Polish Corridor

Vistula

POLAND

Warsaw

DENMARK

North Sea

NETH.

BELGIUM

LUX.

GERMANY

Berlin

Elbe

RUHR

Rhine

LORRAINE

ALSACE

FRANCE

SWITZ.

Prague

CZECHOSLOVAKIA

Vienna

AUSTRIA

S. TYROL

Milan

Po

ITALY

Rome

Corsica

Sardinia

Sicily

GALICIA

HUNGARY

Budapest

Zagreb

Trieste

YUGOSLAVIA

Adriatic Sea

BESSARABIA

ROMANIA

Bucharest

Danube

Belgrade

SERBIA

BULGARIA

Sofia

Black Sea

ALB.

GREECE

Aegean Sea

Istanbul (Constantinople)

TURKEY

Crete

Mediterranean Sea

should be based. These "Fourteen Points" called for open diplomacy, free trade, arms reductions, the self-determination of nations, and, perhaps most importantly, a League of Nations designed to ensure collective security. Basically, Wilson hoped to use the conference to create a new world order based on mutual respect and cooperation between nations (see box). His position was thus an idealistic one, as it proposed a means for overcoming the security dilemma that had created so many dangerous conflicts in prewar Europe. Some of the younger delegates from Britain were also adherents to the Wilsonian crusade. But from the perspective of the European powers, particularly France and its leader Georges Clemenceau, the American proposals appeared naive and unrealistic, although they could not be ignored given the extent of American power.

The delegates to the conference spent months arguing amongst themselves.[21] Finally, after resolving their many differences, the Allies presented Germany with a treaty. This document took Wilson's idealistic proposals and Clemenceau's vengeful demands and combined them to form a compromise that satisfied no one.

■ Woodrow Wilson making a whistlestop speech. SOURCE: Culver Pictures

Spotlight

An Idealist at Versailles

President Woodrow Wilson's leadership style contained an intriguing mix of traits that paradoxically prevented him from achieving his major foreign-policy objectives. Idealistic, moralistic, and self-righteous, Wilson was also an activist, a genuine product of the Progressive Era in America. The influence infused him with a desire to take part energetically in various problem areas of policy in order to come up with the best possible remedy. Unfortunately, this essentially optimistic desire to "fix" problems was counterbalanced by a negative "inflexibility"—a lack of willingness to reach a bargain or compromise solution with one's political opponents. A political scientist by profession and former president of Princeton University, Woodrow Wilson was elected president of the United States in 1912 on a platform emphasizing the reform of American domestic politics. Shortly after his election, he remarked to a close friend, "It would be an irony of fate if my administration had to deal chiefly with foreign affairs." Fate wasted little time in handing him an irony. After campaigning for re-

election in 1916 with the slogan, "He kept us out of war," Wilson reluctantly decided to take the United States into World War I within a few months of the start of his second term.

After the war, President Wilson took a leading position at the Paris Peace Conference. "To make the world safe for democracy," he proposed a new world system in which states "all act in the common interest and are free to live their own lives under a common protection."* Wilson's vision of a collective-security community was the League of Nations, intended to maintain peace by ensuring justice and self-determination for all peoples and envisioned in his "Fourteen Points."

Many Americans criticized Wilson for his decision to personally go to Versailles to participate in the peace settlement (he was the first American president to cross the Atlantic while in office). He also had to reassure Congress that he was not trying to usurp its role in international politics, but was going to secure a just and lasting peace.

The peace conference became in effect a battle

The treaty called for Germany to return Alsace-Lorraine to France, cede some of its eastern territory to the recreated state of Poland, permit French and British occupation of the economically vital Saar region, and demilitarize the Rhineland (the portion of Germany bordering France). In addition, Germany was required to adhere to strict disarmament provisions that limited the size of its army; forbade it to possess submarines, tanks, or an air force; and outlawed conscription.

Consistent with the principle of national self-determination, the Austro-Hungarian Empire was divided into a number of successor states: Austria, Hungary, Czechoslovakia, and Yugoslavia (which united Serbs, Croats, Slovenes, Montenegrins, and Muslim Slavs among others in an artificial kingdom). Poland, which had been partitioned out of existence in 1795, was reunited and joined Italy and Romania in claiming other parts of the former Hapsburg Empire. Austria, most of whose population was Germanic, was forbidden from joining with Germany, and a large German population was incorporated into Czechoslovakia in an area known as the Sudetenland. (Map 3.2 shows how the Versailles Treaty redrew the map of Europe.)

between Wilson and representatives of the other Allied powers, led by French Premier Georges Clemenceau, who favored the maintenance of a balance-of-power system (see Chapter Twelve). Wilson, considered by his fellow peacemakers to be an upstart American with little practical experience in world affairs, was never able to convince his colleagues to agree to a system of collective security. When he returned to the United States in February 1919, he remained confident that he would be able to secure Senate support for the Versailles Treaty. Yet, Republicans in the Senate, led by Henry Cabot Lodge, argued that the League would lead the United States back into war, give Britain too much influence and, most importantly, threaten the nation's isolationist tradition. They would not accept the treaty without an overhaul of the League of Nations Covenant, which Wilson had just helped write.

In an effort to gain Republican support, Wilson returned to Paris in March 1919 and secured amendments to the League's Covenant. But Republican opposition remained steadfast and public sentiment grew increasingly negative. Failing to garner public support for the treaty upon his return to the United States, Wilson refused to compromise with the Republicans and asked Senate Democrats to vote against the Senate's proposed version of an amended League of Nations Covenant because it did not incorporate the strong provisions for **collective action** against aggression that he insisted upon. His lack of flexibility, no doubt tied to his strong sense of self-righteousness, prevented the United States from signing the treaty and joining the League, which became ineffective without U.S. involvement. As a result, the United States retreated into its prewar isolationist mode and played a relatively minor role in world politics during the tumultuous 1920s and 1930s. Wilson also refused to recognize the American public's weariness with its involvement in Europe's affairs and lack of enthusiasm for any role as global policeman.

* Quoted in Gordon A. Craig and Alexander L. George, *Force and Statecraft* (New York: Oxford University Press, 1983), p. 52.

Despite all the talk about self-determination of nations, the treaty granted self-determination to some nationalities but not to others; and, in particular, the doctrine was not applied to the Germans. Much to the dismay of the Arabs and the European colonies, the principle was not applied at all outside Europe. The British had promised the Arabs independence if they aided in the fight against the Ottoman Turks, but this turned out to be an empty promise, as Britain, France, and Russia had made plans to carve up the Ottoman Empire among themselves before the war had even finished.[22]

Finally, Germany was held responsible for the war and forced to pay extensive reparations to the Allies, particularly France. Germany objected to many parts of the treaty, but no clause did more to create a lasting sense of betrayal and resentment than Article 231. This article was the "war guilt" clause, which held Germany and its allies wholly responsible for the war and all the damage it caused. The clause would foster rage and resentment among the German people that nationalist extremists were quick to exploit. Germany had little choice but to accept the treaty, as the Allies continued to blockade German ports and maintained large forces in position to strike at German territory until the treaty was signed.

On June 28, 1919, the five-year anniversary of the assassination of Archduke Franz Ferdinand, Germany reluctantly signed the treaty of peace. The onus of accepting the punitive treaty fell to the new Weimar Republic, which had replaced the German monarchy after the kaiser's November 1918 abdication. The signing of the peace agreement discredited the infant democratic regime in the minds of many Germans. The treaty was signed in the Hall of Mirrors at the Palace of Versailles, where in 1871 Bismarck had proclaimed the German Empire that was now no more. The Great War was officially over, but the peace settlement was soon to create almost as many problems as it had solved. In the words of one British observer, "After the 'War to end War' they seem to have been pretty successful in Paris at making a 'Peace to end Peace.' "[23]

THE FALSE PEACE OF THE 1920s

Niccolò Machiavelli once noted that a victor should either conciliate his enemy or destroy him. The Treaty of Versailles accomplished neither. Germany was left scourged, humiliated, and resentful but not permanently weakened. The country lost territory, but it was not actually partitioned, and it retained most of its industrial potential and resource base. A great many Germans felt it was unjust for Germany to be held directly responsible for the war, because (as recounted earlier in this chapter) the actions of many countries contributed to the outbreak of fighting. The reparations payments were also seen as unfair and were greatly burdensome to the German economy, which was weak and in need of extensive rebuilding. Furthermore, German armies had not been driven from France, nor had German territory been invaded; this made both the defeat and the harsh peace terms especially difficult to accept. The denial of self-determination for many ethnic Germans added to the widespread resentment of the peace settlement.

In addition, the splitting of the former Austrian Empire into a number of small states actually left Germany as the strongest continental power, because France was virtually exhausted. These newly formed countries were weak and unable to protect themselves, and so had to rely upon the support of the great powers in order to survive as sovereign states. This left the new states vulnerable to renewed German expansion, which remained a possibility, because the Versailles Treaty did not greatly reduce Germany's economic and military potential. Disarmament and reparations, which were the harshest measures in the treaty, were left completely up to German cooperation. Allied commissions were set up to monitor German compliance, but there was nothing to back up these commissions.

A Weak League

One of the reasons why the details for enforcing the provisions of the Versailles Treaty were so feeble was the weakness of the League of Nations. The hope of establishing peace and stability through the League was thwarted by the decision of the United States not to join. The U.S. Senate refused to ratify the Treaty of Versailles. Aside from the Senate's fear of "entangling alliances," some senators demanded an amendment asserting the primacy of the U.S. Constitution, which would protect Congress' prerogative to declare war. (These arguments foreshadowed American resistance in the 1990s to placing U.S. troops under United Nations command; see Chapter Five.) Wilson refused to compromise, the Senate refused to ratify the treaty, and the United States remained outside the League. The absence of the United States, which had proposed and been a driving spirit of the League, left it a body without substance. Without the world's largest industrial power, the League of Nations was weakened to the point that many doubted its capability to satisfactorily resolve the many challenges to the new political order established at Versailles. The global security system Wilson envisioned thus never got off the ground.

In sum, the potential for an upsurge in German resentment, the American return to isolationism, the revolution and civil war in Russia (renamed the Union of Soviet Socialist Republics by the Bolshevik government in 1922), and the splintering of eastern Europe made the European balance of power inherently unstable. Europe became more fragmented in political, economic, and security terms than it had been before 1914.

In response to the uncertain situation, European diplomats scrambled to set up new security agreements. France established a network of defense pacts with Poland, Czechoslovakia, Romania, and Yugoslavia in an attempt to contain Germany should the need arise. (Because the reliability of these alliances was questionable, however, France began in 1930 to build an extensive system of defensive fortifications, called the **Maginot Line,** on its border with Germany.) Britain, Italy, France, Belgium, and Germany addressed security concerns in western Europe in the Locarno Treaties of 1925, and in 1926 Germany was allowed into the League of Nations.

These international security arrangements, however, would soon be undermined by domestic developments in the various European great powers. Hoping to avoid a recurrence of the devastation that the Great War had brought to all of Europe, postwar public opinion in Britain and France was strongly against spending money on defense. The desire to avoid war at any cost was fed by a growing belief that weapons and arms races lead to war, by disgust with "merchants of death" who reaped huge profits from manufacturing weapons and war material, and by reassessments of the war's origins that did not heap all of the blame on Germany. (As the earlier sections on the causes of World War I recount, there was plenty of blame to go around.) Antiwar sentiments would later guide the proponents of the policy of **appeasement,** a policy dissuading aggressors from attacking by conceding part of their demands in order to satisfy their appetite for expansion.

In contrast to the growth of pacifism in the West, many Italians and Germans, feeling cheated (for different reasons) by the outcome of World War I, increasingly turned to radical forms of nationalism as their social and economic situation led to disillusionment with democracy. In Italy, social upheaval nearly led to civil war. Fearing the possibility of a communist-inspired revolution, King Victor

Emmanuel III appointed Benito Mussolini, head of the ultraconservative and nationalist Fascist party, prime minister in 1922. Mussolini, called *Il Duce* (the leader), soon established a dictatorial regime promising to end the social and economic chaos and "make the trains run on time."[24]

Similarly, economic problems in Germany during the 1920s placed enormous strains on its fragile democratic institutions. Saddled by the Allies with crushing reparations, the German government recklessly printed money to make the payments required by the Versailles Settlement and cover its other debts. The immediate result was hyperinflation (an extreme, rapid, and uncontrolled rise in prices), which wiped out savings and drove millions of Germans into poverty. Housewives had to take wheelbarrows with them to do their shopping—not to carry their purchases home, but to carry enough money to buy groceries.[25] This financial disaster would soon lead many Germans to listen to extremist politicians who proposed radical solutions to the economic crisis.

The Great Depression

The already shaky global economy was dealt a crushing blow when the American stock market crashed in 1929. The crash hurled first the United States and then Europe into the Great Depression, the worst economic disaster in modern times. Banks failed, the supply of capital dried up, investments and savings vanished, and millions of workers lost their jobs. Almost overnight, international trade broke down as nations erected trade barriers to protect jobs and domestic markets. The 1930 Smoot-Hawley Tariff dramatically increased American import duties and aggravated the situation by closing off the U.S. market from industrial imports. The closing of world markets spread, further exacerbating Germany's inability to pay its war debts.[26] Unable to get new loans from America, Germany renounced payment of war reparations, which in turn led France and Britain to default on their debts. (For more on these issues, see Chapter Seven.)

The Great Depression exacerbated political and economic conflicts all over the world. The German economy, in particular, was devastated, and its political system was paralyzed. Many Germans looked for a strong hand to lead them out of the crisis, and the National Socialist (Nazi) Party, led by Adolf Hitler, offered one. In elections held from 1930 to 1933, the Nazis continuously gained seats in the Reichstag (parliament) until they controlled more seats than any other party, thus clearing the way for Hitler to become chancellor in January 1933. The man who would become the world's most infamous dictator thus came to power through the democratic process.

What Caused World War II?

The reasons for the outbreak of the Second World War have not been debated as extensively or enthusiastically as the causes of the First World War. In general, its origins are less complex and mysterious than those of World War I, and it is almost universally accepted that if Germany, Italy, and Japan had not pursued expansionist policies in the mid- to late 1930s, World War II might well have never occurred or at least would not have become such a massive conflict. Nevertheless, five factors may be identified as candidates for the prime cause of World War II. Some of these factors, particularly the aforementioned expansionism on the part of Germany, Italy, and Japan and the rise of **fascism** in Europe, may have had greater influence than others, and each factor when taken individually may not have been necessary or sufficient to cause a global war. All, however, are likely to have exerted some influence on the rapid collapse of the fragile peace of the 1920s and 1930s.

The first possible reason for the outbreak of another world war was that the terms of the Versailles Treaty were too harsh. As discussed earlier, the self-determination granted to many of Europe's nationalities was not extended to the German people; many of the treaty's provisions infringed on German sovereignty; and many Germans came to support a revision of the terms of the peace, by force if necessary. On the other hand, it has been argued that a second major war occurred because the terms of the Versailles Treaty were not enforced. As the following sections will show, the European powers were reluctant to use force to compel Germany to adhere to the treaty's provisions, which may have encouraged progressively greater violations of the peace treaty. Additionally, the League of Nations never functioned as it was designed to and was severely weakened by the nonparticipation of the United States, and thus it was unable to deter aggression or maintain collective security in Europe and elsewhere.

Third, the changing balance of power may have played an important role in the outbreak of a new world war. In particular, Japan, Germany, and the Soviet Union became markedly stronger during the 1930s, which may have made conflict with the other great powers inevitable as the rising stars on the world scene challenged Britain, France, and the United States for world leadership. However, as mentioned in Chapter Two, changes in the balance of power do not always lead to war; this has led some analysts to contend that German, Italian, and Japanese expansionism was the deciding factor in the eruption of a global conflict. These states, this argument runs, decided to expand their territory and global reach in order to resolve or avoid a variety of domestic and international political problems. If Berlin, Rome, and Tokyo had chosen different solutions for their internal difficulties, war might not have resulted.

Finally, many of the same pressures that prompted the Axis powers to expand before the war prompted the rise of fascism in a number of European states and in Japan. The authoritarian and militaristic ideology of fascism was anathema to the Western democracies (as was the totalitarian communism practiced in the Soviet Union under Stalin). Perhaps if Hitler and Mussolini had not come to power, or if the Nazi party had not stamped out democracy and human rights so brutally, the great powers would have been able to resolve their differences without resorting to war.

Considering how many possible reasons there were for their outbreaks in both 1914 and 1939, the world wars may have been overdetermined. Perhaps, in both cases, the preceding peace was only an illusion waiting to be shattered. For whatever reasons, by the end of 1939 it was obvious that the "war to end all wars" was nothing of the kind and that the collective security system envisioned by the victorious allies at Versailles was a grandiose failure.

RISE OF THE THIRD REICH

Essentially, Hitler's rule can be divided into two phases.[27] In the first, roughly from 1933 to 1935, the German dictator did not seem especially threatening. During this period, many viewed Hitler as a basically reasonable leader, in spite of his Nazi party's repression of opponents, discrimination against Jews, and other anti-democratic policies. After all, under his leadership Germany was clearly getting back to work, and the poverty and suffering of most of the population were greatly alleviated. He seemed to be resolving the chaotic social and economic crisis that Germany had endured. Many dismissed his objectives as set forth in his prison memoir, *Mein Kampf* ("My Struggle"), as empty rhetoric.[28]

Hitler's ultimate goals, however, were extremely ambitious at best and frightening at worst. Hitler sought to restore Germany to its original borders, which meant a rejection of the territorial settlement in the Versailles Treaty. After restoring its borders of 1914, Germany would then expand to include all Germans, which meant the annexation of Austria, the Sudetenland in Czechoslovakia, and the German parts of Poland before 1914. But this would still not be enough. To Hitler, the German people were the "master race," for whom the borders of even a greater Germany were insufficient. What was needed was *lebensraum* ("living space"), which necessitated expansion to the east at the expense of Poles, Russians, and other Slavs, who were considered *untermenschen* ("subhumans"). These "inferior races" would be reduced to slavery, while those considered "inhuman," including Jews, Gypsies, and homosexuals, would be eliminated from Hitler's Third Reich. (According to the Nazis, the "First Reich" was the medieval German empire founded by Kaiser Otto I; the "Second Reich" was the German Empire forged by Bismarck in the nineteenth century, as described in Chapter Two.) In the early years of Hitler's regime, it was never made clear how these goals were to be achieved, but the Nazis later decided on a "final solution" to the "Jewish problem" (see the section on the Holocaust).

When Hitler came to power, however, Germany was still too weak to pursue his expansionist agenda. It was necessary to appear moderate and play on Germany's grievances stemming from the Versailles Treaty and Germans' demands for self-determination, which many considered legitimate. In 1935 Hitler received a great boost to his power and popularity when the people of the Saar region voted overwhelmingly to rejoin Germany. The holding of the **plebiscite** had been mandated in the Versailles Treaty sixteen years before, but because it occurred during Hitler's tenure he was able to take credit for it. Meanwhile, Hitler began to take steps forbidden by the Versailles Settlement. In 1935 compulsory conscription in Germany was reinstated, and in March of that same year Hitler revealed the previously secret existence of the *Luftwaffe*, the German air force.

Adolf Hitler addresses a Munich Nazi party meeting in November 1934. Chancellor of the Third Reich from 1933 to 1945, Hitler was perhaps the most destructive political genius in history.   SOURCE: © Culver Pictures, Inc.

Hitler thus began to openly defy the Versailles Treaty and to enter the second, more menacing phase of his regime. Having encountered little international opposition thus far, he sent German troops back into the demilitarized Rhineland in 1936. Emboldened by the other European powers' failure to respond effectively, Hitler accelerated the buildup of the German military. France and Britain were well aware of this buildup, but their domestic political and economic situations constrained their ability to match Germany. In 1937 Germany spent 23.5 percent of its national income on the military, while France spent 9.1 percent and Britain only 5.7 percent.[29] In absolute terms, the gap becomes even clearer: In the same year that Germany was spending more than $3 billion on the military, France was spending $890 million and Britain $1.2 billion.[30] In short, Germany alone spent more than France and Britain combined. (Keep in mind, however, that Germany faced a potential threat from the Soviet Union, which was also spending more than $3 billion.)

The imbalance in military expenditures contributed significantly to the continuation of the British and French policy of appeasement. Both countries sought to avoid antagonizing Hitler by agreeing to his initial demands, hoping that this would encourage him to moderate his ultimate objectives. At the time, appeasement was a popular policy; it was consistent with the widespread desire to avoid war. Concern in Paris over developments in Germany, however, led France to seek protection through cooperation with the USSR, which also had good reason to fear Germany and was alienated by Hitler's rabid anticommunism.

Growing German strength and belligerence also led to improved relations between France and Italy, because Mussolini was concerned about Hitler's ambitions towards Austria. Since the 1860s there had been some desire for German-speaking Austria to unify with Germany, but Bismarck had rejected this notion and few Austrians supported the idea. In the 1930s, however, nationalist sympathies in both Germany and Austria led to demands that the two countries become unified in a single German-speaking nation. Hitler, an Austrian by birth, gave support to Austrian Nazis, who assassinated Austrian Chancellor Engelbert Dollfuss in July 1934 during an unsuccessful coup attempt.

China, Ethiopia, and Spain

While developments in Europe had whittled away at the new world order envisioned at Versailles, the first genuine challenge to the League of Nations' principle of collective security came not in Europe, but in Asia. By the early 1930s Japan was the only Asian country able to industrialize and avoid colonial domination by the European powers. Instead, it had embarked on an imperial course itself. Largely bereft of raw materials necessary for industrial production, Japan sought to expand its sphere of control in Asia in order to ensure their availability and guarantee markets for its goods. In addition to these economic goals, territorial expansion was advocated by the Japanese military establishment, which began to play an increasingly important role in Japan's authoritarian government.

In 1931 Japan seized Manchuria from China, and in 1932 it established the nominally independent state of Manchukuo, which was actually a Japanese protectorate. The League of Nations duly condemned Japan's actions, but it was unable to impose effective economic or military sanctions, as the Soviet Union and the United States, which were not members of the League, refused to accept its recommendations. The United States feared that military sanctions against Japan might precipitate a U.S.-Japanese war in Southeast Asia and that economic sanctions against Japan would hurt the U.S. economy at the depth of the Great Depression.

In 1937, Japanese forces invaded China from Manchuria. China's weak and poorly organized army was unable to stop the Japanese advance, but continuing the offensive and garrisoning the conquered territory became an expensive burden for Japan. Temporarily shocked out of its isolationism, the United States responded by demanding that Japan withdraw from China and imposing limited sanctions. The Japanese government, heavily influenced by its army, ignored the sanctions and the condemnation of the League of Nations, and went on with the war.

The League's weakness soon became apparent in other parts of the world. Germany's increased power posed a threat to Italy, but this ironically enhanced Italy's status in Europe because France and Britain saw Mussolini's government as an important counterweight to Hitler's expansionist designs. This gave Mussolini the opening to pursue his own imperial ambitions in Abyssinia (Ethiopia), the domination of which had long been an Italian goal. (Abyssinian troops had defeated an invading Italian force In 1896, one of only a few defeats suffered by a European power in Africa.) In October 1935 Italian troops invaded Abyssinia from their base in the neighboring Italian colony of Somaliland (now part of Somalia). When the initial attack was unsuccessful, Italian forces resorted to poison-gas attacks to bring the Abyssinians to submission. Western nations were appalled, but neither France nor Britain wanted to alienate Italy as long as Germany constituted a growing threat. Consequently, when Abyssinian Emperor Haile Selassie asked the League of Nations to halt the Italian aggression, the League imposed only limited economic sanctions. Selassie's efforts failed to stop Italy's annexation of Abyssinia. He made a final appeal to the League in 1936, but the assembled nations ignored his warning: "It was us today. It will be you tomorrow."

The League had again proven ineffective; in fact, its limited sanctions were worse than useless, as they were sufficient to alienate Italy from Britain and France. As a result, Mussolini improved relations with Germany. In 1936, Italy, Japan, and Germany signed the Anti-Comintern Pact, in which all agreed to fight communism and support one another in case of war with the Soviet Union. After discussions between Italian and German diplomats, both sides tacitly recognized Italy's sphere of influence in the Mediterranean and Germany's in central Europe.

The Spanish Civil War (1936–1939) provided another prelude to the wider conflict that was to come. Italy and Germany gave extensive assistance to the right-wing Nationalist forces, led by Francisco Franco, who were fighting against the Republican government. Hitler and Mussolini hoped that if the Nationalists won, Spain would ally with them against France. Spain also provided a proving ground for new German and Italian military hardware. The terrible destructive potential of aerial bombing was demonstrated in 1937 when German aircraft devastated the city of Guernica. (Picasso's renowned painting of the same name commemorates the atrocity.) As had been the case throughout the 1930s, the other European powers refused to take part in the conflict. The Soviet Union provided aid to the Republican forces (who counted socialists and Communists among their supporters), but all others remained steadfastly neutral. Franco's Nationalist forces won the Civil War, and though Spain remained neutral during World War II, the victory of fascism in Spain testified to the failure of isolationism and appeasement. But the worst was still yet to come.

Anschluss

German power was still growing in Europe. The next step in Hitler's plan was the fulfillment of his dream to unify all Germans. Hitler had consistently supported the Austrian Nazis and used nationalist appeals to press for unification, but the Versailles Treaty expressly forbade any such union. In 1936, Hitler had backed down on the issue of a German-Austrian union in the face of opposition from the other European powers. At that time, he even went so far as to explicitly recognize Austria's independence and provide assurances that Germany would not intervene in Austria's internal affairs. In March 1938, however, Hitler bullied the Austrian chancellor into resigning, then used his resignation as a pretext to order German troops into Austria. The *anschluss*, or annexation of Austria by Germany, was declared on March 13, and Austria ceased to exist as an independent state.

Yet again Hitler had violated the mandate of the Versailles Treaty, and once again the other great powers refused to take action. In spite of the widespread concern over Hitler's intentions, the *anschluss* was relatively easy to justify, as Austrians were arguably ethnic Germans. Besides, Hitler reassured other European leaders that his intentions were benign and professed that all he wanted to do was to right the wrongs committed against Germany at Versailles.

Czech Crisis and Munich Conference

With the union of Austria and Germany accomplished, Hitler turned his attention to the Sudetenland, a part of Czechoslovakia inhabited by large numbers of ethnic Germans. He had encouraged the Sudeten Germans to press demands for union with Germany, and the pressure on Czechoslovakia to cede the territory reached a fever pitch after the *anschluss*. In May 1938 Czechoslovakia mobilized its forces on the German border in response to reported German military troop movements. Both France and Britain cautioned Germany not to aggravate the situation, but simultaneously they pressured the Czech leaders to make concessions.

Hitler was determined to force a confrontation over the Sudetenland, but Britain and France earnestly hoped to avoid one. The British foreign office explicitly warned Paris that Britain would not support France in a war over Czechoslovakia. Public opinion in Britain was still strongly opposed to involvement in another continental conflict, especially because Hitler's demands did not seem unreasonable: He was attempting to achieve self-determination for all Germans. British Prime Minister Neville Chamberlain especially made it clear that he wanted to

British Prime Minister Neville Chamberlain holds a copy of the Munich Agreement, which he claimed would result in "peace for our time." Events were soon to prove him disastrously wrong.

SOURCE: © UPI/Corbis-Bettmann

avoid war at all costs, describing the crisis over Czechoslovakia as "a quarrel in a faraway country among people of whom we know nothing." For their part, the Soviets indicated that they would honor a treaty commitment to come to Czechoslovakia's aid, but because the treaty predicated Soviet action on French involvement, they waited for the French response. France, however, was unwilling to support Czechoslovakia without British help.

The crisis continued through the summer of 1938. Holding out one last hope to avoid war, Chamberlain proposed in September that Britain, France, Italy, and Germany meet to settle the Czech issue. Hitler, Mussolini, Chamberlain, and French Prime Minister Edouard Daladier subsequently met in Munich, Germany, where they agreed that the Sudetenland would be turned over to German control. (The Czech government was not asked for its opinion on the matter; in fact,

The Munich Analogy

Munich was an experience seared into the memory of all who witnessed the promises made and broken in 1938. The Munich Conference became synonymous with the discredited appeasement policy of British Prime Minister Neville Chamberlain. Adolf Hitler, Chamberlain, French Prime Minister Edouard Daladier, and Italian Prime Minister Benito Mussolini met in Munich on September 29, 1938, to resolve the crisis over the Sudetenland of Czechoslovakia. Hitler was threatening to go to war in order to annex the Czech territory, where 3 million ethnic Germans lived. Chamberlain and the others sought to appease Hitler by agreeing to cede the Sudetenland to Germany, on the basis of Hitler's guarantee not to attack the remaining portion of Czechoslovakia. Chamberlain was greeted as a hero when he returned to Britain, for it was believed that war had been averted.

At the time, appeasement was a popular policy, credited with keeping Europe out of another ruinous war. Within six months, however, Chamberlain and his appeasement policy were thoroughly discredited when Hitler invaded the rest of Czechoslovakia. "Appeasement" became a dirty word, and Munich became a metaphor for encouraging aggression by giving in to an aggressor.

In later years, leaders have referred to Munich in attempts to win support for standing firm against an opponent's challenges. During the Cold War, many policies designed to contain the Soviet Union were justified by citing the Munich analogy, most notably the decisions to send forces to counter Communist threats in Korea in 1950 and Vietnam in 1965. U.S. President George Bush invoked the Munich analogy to convince Congress to authorize the use of force against Iraq in 1991 and called Iraqi President Saddam Hussein a "new Hitler."

Ever since Munich, it appears, politicians have consistently painted their enemies as Hitlers while doing as much as they are able to avoid being remembered as Chamberlains.

Czechoslovakia was not even invited to participate in the conference that would decide its fate.) It appeared as if war had been averted. Upon his return to Britain, Chamberlain proclaimed that the Munich Agreement meant "peace for our time." Opposition Member of Parliament Winston Churchill, on the other hand, thought the agreement would only encourage Hitler's ambitions: "The German dictator, instead of snatching the victuals from the table, has been content to have them served to him course by course."[31]

The leaders of Britain and France hoped that Hitler would now be satisfied, having incorporated virtually all German-speaking areas into the Third Reich. However, rather than achieving peace, Britain and France had merely postponed war. Czechoslovakia and the USSR had been willing to take a stand against Germany, but instead, Czech territory had been handed over to Hitler without a fight. In March 1939 German troops invaded and took over what remained of Czechoslovakia.

THE APPROACH OF WAR

The invasion of Czechoslovakia proved to be a turning point in European acceptance of German aggression. First, Britain and France were outraged. Unlike Germany's annexation of Austria and the Sudetenland, the conquest of Czechoslovakia could not be justified by national self-determination. Second, London and Paris had lost a potentially helpful ally, and Czech military industries were now at Hitler's disposal. Third, neither France nor Britain had defended Czechoslovakia, even though that nation as well as the USSR had been prepared to fight. This signaled to Hitler that France and Britain were unlikely to go to war over small countries in eastern Europe. The situation was especially worrisome for Poland, which seemed the next likely target for German expansion because it included areas taken from Germany by the Treaty of Versailles. In an attempt to reassure Warsaw and deter Hitler from further aggression, in March 1939 British and French leaders pledged their assistance to Poland if Germany attacked.

Although the Warsaw government felt reassured by British and French pledges, the Soviet Union remained skeptical. What could Britain and France do for Poland? Both were separated from Poland by Germany, Britain was primarily a naval power with only a small army, and France cowered behind its defensive Maginot Line with no plans to attack Germany. Absent any credible French threat to Germany in the west, French assurances to Poland were meaningless. In April 1939 the Soviet Union nevertheless began discussions with Britain and France regarding a defensive alliance against Germany. Although the Western powers favored such an alliance, Poland and Romania's leaders remained opposed. Remembering all too well their former domination by Russia, they refused to accept Soviet assistance if it meant bringing Soviet troops into their countries. Meanwhile, in May, Hitler and Mussolini sealed their alliance in the Pact of Steel, later known as the Rome-Berlin Axis.

Because of Soviet premier Joseph Stalin's distrust of the French and British, Moscow also began to seek improved relations with Germany. (Stalin suspected and distrusted everyone; for more on this Soviet leader, see Chapter Four.) Although initially suspicious himself of Soviet intentions, Hitler found an agreement with the Soviet Union more attractive as his plans to invade Poland progressed. When France and Britain balked at signing an agreement with the Soviet Union in deference to the objections of their eastern European allies, Stalin accepted the idea of a nonaggression pact with Germany. The Nazi-Soviet pact, also known as the Molotov-Ribbentrop Pact after the two foreign ministers (Vyacheslav Molotov of the USSR and Germany's Joachim von Ribbentrop) who negotiated it, was signed on August 23, 1939.

The world was stunned. Two leaders who espoused implacably hostile ideologies, fascism and communism, had signed an important treaty with each other. The pact served the pragmatic self-interests of both sides, however, as it temporarily alleviated the threat of a two-front war for both countries. Hitler knew that without the USSR, France and Britain lacked the military strength to invade

Germany in order to protect Poland. In this regard, Hitler was following the same policy as Bismarck had before him. From Stalin's perspective, the pact gained the Soviet Union time to build up its military strength to prepare for the possibility of war with either Germany or Japan. In addition, the agreement included secret protocols that provided for the division of Poland between Germany and the USSR and secured German consent to Soviet control of the Baltic states (Latvia, Lithuania, and Estonia) and parts of Finland and Romania.

With the signing of the Nazi-Soviet pact, Hitler no longer needed to fear war with the Soviet Union over Poland. The failure of Britain and France to support Czechoslovakia suggested that they might not support Poland either, and in any case there was little they could do to stop an invasion of Poland without Soviet help. The groundwork for Hitler's next move was thus in place. Germany attacked Poland on September 1, 1939, and France and Britain declared war on Germany two days later. Twenty-one years after the first great European war of the twentieth century had ended, the second had begun.

WORLD WAR II

Though their combined armies and navies were larger than Germany's in September 1939, the Western Allies were unprepared for the outbreak of World War II. The Allies were slow to recognize the implications of advances in military tactics and technology, but they would soon learn all too well that the use of mechanized forces and aircraft allowed advancing armies to move much faster than had been possible in the Great War.[32] In September 1939 Poland was rapidly defeated, which was no real surprise given Germany's superiority in numbers and technology. The German **blitzkrieg** ("lightning war") strategy of armor and air attacks overwhelmed the obsolete Polish army; there wasn't much that horse cavalry could do against tanks. On September 17, the Soviet Union also overran eastern Poland and the Baltic States, as the Molotov-Ribbentrop Pact allowed. The USSR subsequently attacked Finland on November 30, but the Finns fought stalwartly against the Soviet attack.

As Hitler had anticipated, neither France nor Britain took immediate measures to aid Poland. What ensued has come to be known as the "phony war" in which both sides barely fought. France and Britain sought only to blockade Germany and prevent it from obtaining crucial raw materials, and France made sure its Maginot fortifications were at full strength. It was not even clear whether a major confrontation would occur. In October Hitler proposed that the Western powers accept the new situation in exchange for peace, but, with Hitler's actions after Munich still in mind, the offer was rejected.

The strategy of London and Paris focused on a war of attrition. The French and British leaders believed that a Germany denied of raw materials crucial to war fighting would accept a settlement returning territory to the status quo ante.[33] They therefore deemed it necessary to maintain control of the North Sea and the Mediterranean. Recognizing this strategy, Germany invaded Denmark and Norway in April 1940. Both were quickly defeated. In reality, there was little that Britain and France could do at this time to combat the Germans because of the lack of military preparation in the two countries.

This weakness became apparent when the war turned "real" for the British and French in May 1940. On May 10, Germany launched its blitzkrieg on France, sending its tanks through Belgium and thereby bypassing the Maginot Line. The original German battle plan was essentially similar to the Schlieffen Plan of 1914, but a copy of the plan fell into Allied hands. Germany was forced to come up with a new scheme that surprised the Allies by sending armored divisions through the Ardennes Forest, thought to be tank-proof. France managed to survive for five short weeks, only two weeks longer than Poland.[34]

Thus, the beginnings of both the world wars stunned strategic planners. In 1914 Germany hoped to achieve a quick victory over France as it had in 1871, but its forces soon bogged down into immobile trench warfare. In 1940 the Allies expected trench warfare and thought France would be safe behind the formidable Maginot Line, but German armies circumvented French defenses and smashed through to Paris much as they had in 1871. Confident that France was done for, Italy joined the war on Germany's side in June. (Germany and its allies were thereafter referred to as the Axis, after the Rome-Berlin Axis signed in May 1939.)

Hitler contemplated an invasion of Britain, but the English Channel remained a substantial obstacle and the British navy a formidable opponent. He decided to prepare for an invasion with demoralizing air attacks on British shipping, airfields, and cities, thus initiating the Battle of Britain between the Royal Air Force (RAF) and the German Luftwaffe. Although inflicting heavy casualties, the air raids only strengthened the resolve of the British people, led by Churchill, who replaced Chamberlain as prime minister. The German air force was unable to win the conflict, which took place from July to October 1940. In this case, Britain's delay in rearming after World War I was a benefit: The newer British airplanes were able to outmaneuver their German counterparts. Key to the British success, however, was the new top-secret radar that warned them of the impending German attacks.[35]

Britain remained stalwart against Germany, but by the end of 1940, Hitler dominated the Continent in a manner not seen since Napoleon. Churchill tried to enforce a blockade, again as in the Napoleonic Wars, but it posed no real threat to Germany's control of the Continent. Besides, there was little to no possibility of a British invasion of Europe. In fact, despite its tenacity, Britain was rapidly nearing the end of its endurance. Germany continued to try to force a British surrender through submarine warfare, as German U-boats and surface raiders fought British naval forces in the Battle of the Atlantic. The only hope for Britain at this dark hour was the isolationist great power across the Atlantic, the United States. The U.S. president, Franklin Delano Roosevelt, wanted to come to the aid of the British, but public and Congressional opinion prevented him from doing so.

Meanwhile, a bungled Italian invasion of Greece prompted Hitler to invade the Balkans in 1941. German forces quickly overwhelmed Yugoslavia and subdued Greece, but partisan fighting would continue in those countries throughout

The Last Lion

It would be difficult to invent a fictional character who embodied the ruling class and spirit of the British Empire as much as Sir Winston Leonard Spencer Churchill (1874–1965). The son of an American heiress and an English lord, direct descendant of the renowned eighteenth-century British general the Duke of Marlborough, Churchill nevertheless needed three attempts to pass the entrance exam to the Royal Military Academy at Sandhurst.

He craved action as a young officer, but saw less fighting as a soldier in India than he did as a war correspondent in Cuba and South Africa (after being captured by Boer commandos, he escaped from military prison within a month). He had an equally adventurous career in politics, changing parties several times and serving as First Lord of the Admiralty during World War I. (The disastrous Allied invasion at Gallipoli was his idea.) He lost elections almost as often as he won, and once remarked, "Politics are almost as exciting as war, and quite as dangerous. In war, you can only be killed once, but in politics many times."

Churchill had a boy's impetuousness, a teenager's smugness, and an old man's arrogance throughout most of his life. In his later years, however, he suffered from alcoholism and periodic bouts of severe depression. He preferred big ideas to small details, and he pursued both his causes and his avocations (painting and polo) passionately. The quality that served him best throughout his career, however, was his tenacity, which he lent to his country as prime minister in the darkest days of World War II.

When he succeeded Neville Chamberlain in that post after the debacle in France, many Britons were considering the possibility of asking Adolf Hitler for peace terms. But Churchill was convinced that accepting German domination of Europe would be tantamount to national suicide, and after the evacuation of British troops from Dunkirk his oratory rallied Britain to go on, or go down, fighting:

> *We shall not flag or fail. We shall go on to the end. We shall fight in France, we shall fight on the seas and oceans, we shall fight with growing confidence and growing strength in the air, we shall defend our island, whatever the cost may be, we shall fight on the beaches, we shall fight on the landing grounds, we shall fight in the fields and in the streets, we shall fight in the hills; we shall never surrender.* *

Later in 1940, during the Battle of Britain, Churchill again exhorted the nation to keep its fighting spirit:

> *Let us . . . brace ourselves to our duties, and so bear ourselves that if the British Empire and its Commonwealth last for a thousand years, men will still say: "This was their finest hour."* †

Churchill may have believed the Empire could last that long, but by the end of the war it was clear that British power had been eclipsed by that of the United States and the Soviet Union. Churchill argued that Britain should try to retain its empire, or at least divest itself of it slowly ("I have not become the King's First Minister in order to preside over the liquidation of the British Empire," he declared in 1942), but he was voted out of office before the war's end. (He would serve again as prime minister from 1951 to 1955.) He warned the West to beware of Soviet expansion after the war, but he believed the USSR could be contained through the same political, military, and economic means that Britain had used to contain continental threats for 150 years.

Although he is regarded as one of the greatest leaders of modern times, many of his beliefs were better suited to the period of Queen Victoria and the *Pax Britannica* than to the era of total war. In this respect, by the mid-twentieth century he was, like the British Empire, a glorious anachronism.

---

* Winston Churchill, Speech on Dunkirk, House of Commons, June 4, 1940.
† Churchill, Speech in the House of Commons, June 18, 1940.

■ Winston Churchill flashing V for Victory.

the war. (In Yugoslavia, Croatian units organized by the Nazi occupation regime aided German forces in persecuting Serbs who cooperated with the resistance, creating a bitter legacy of ethnic violence that would tear the benighted country apart fifty years later.) After the blitzkrieg in the Balkans, Britain again stood alone, besieged by U-boats and fighting desperately in North Africa to keep German and Italian forces from capturing the strategically vital Suez Canal.

Barbarossa

The pressure on Britain, however, was ultimately relieved by Hitler's own doing. Like Napoléon, Hitler felt that a war with Russia was inevitable, and so he decided to strike at the eastern colossus before it could build up its forces. On June 22, 1941, Germany launched Operation Barbarossa, the invasion of the Soviet Union. Germany's Axis partners Hungary, Romania, and Finland also joined in the attack. At first, the offensive was highly successful. In the first four months of the war, German troops killed or captured 3 million Soviet soldiers and rapidly forced the Soviet army into retreat.

But in spite of tremendous losses, the Soviet Union was not defeated. The Germans reached the outskirts of Moscow, but the Soviets' huge territorial expanse effectively neutralized the German blitzkrieg. The same difficulties that had plagued Napoléon revisited the Nazis, including troubles with supplying troops across the great expanse of Soviet territory and especially the rigors of the great Russian winter. By 1943 the war on the eastern front thus became one of attrition in which German forces were at a disadvantage.

Pacific War

In the fall of 1941, though the situation looked bleak in Europe, it still appeared unlikely that the United States would intervene. President Roosevelt had already proposed that some economic and military aid to be sent to Britain, but even these limited measures met with opposition in Congress. America had the potential to become a predominant military power, but it remained a basically isolationist "sleeping giant." It would not be long, however, before it received a rude awakening.

On December 7, 1941, the Japanese navy launched a surprise attack on Pearl Harbor, Hawaii, which was the principal American naval base in the Pacific. The attack was executed perfectly and sunk or put out of action most of the battleships of the U.S. Pacific Fleet.[36] The next day, the U.S. Congress declared war on Japan, but there was still some doubt as to whether America would go to war against the European Axis partners. On December 11, however, Germany and Italy, in accordance with their alliance with Japan, declared war on the United States, bringing the United States fully into the conflict.

The Japanese attack on Pearl Harbor seems inexplicable at first glance. Not only was America's gross domestic product seventeen times the size of Japan's, but

Map 3.3 Height of Axis Expansion in the European Theater

America had nearly twice the population of Japan and its overall military potential was greater by a factor of ten.[37] Why would Japan attack a nation more powerful than itself? Throughout the 1930s, Japanese expansion in Asia aggravated Tokyo's relations with the United States. The United States condemned Japan's 1931 invasion of Manchuria, but took no action; in 1937, however, when Japan invaded China, the United States imposed economic sanctions. When Japan occupied French Indochina (which included Vietnam, Laos, and Cambodia) in September 1940, the Japanese leadership hoped the raw materials and strategic bases afforded by this new conquest would help bring the war in China to a speedy end. But the United States slapped Japan with an embargo on scrap metal and steel, materials sorely needed for its war effort. The costs of the war and the effects of the sanctions mounted, but from Tokyo's standpoint, withdrawal from China under foreign pressure would have been unacceptably humiliating.

By the end of 1940, therefore, Japan's leaders found themselves on the horns of a dilemma. One horn was the fact that 80 percent of Japanese oil imports came from the United States, and they feared that the United States would embargo this vital resource in an attempt to compel Japan to withdraw from China. Japan could counter this threat by invading the oil-producing Dutch East Indies (now Indonesia). But this was the other horn: It was almost certain that the United States would intervene against Japan should it expand further in Asia, particularly the Dutch East Indies.

In July 1941 Tokyo's fears came true. In a further effort to pressure Japan to pull its forces out of China, the United States halted its oil exports to Japan and froze Japanese assets, thus restricting Japan's ability to pay for imports. Because the Japanese government still adamantly refused to end the intervention in China, war with the United States now appeared inevitable. Given this conclusion, Japan's leaders decided that their only chance to avoid total defeat was to launch a preemptive strike against U.S. naval forces, hoping that this initial blow would gain time for Japan to further build up its forces and convince the American government and people that a long, costly war would not be worth fighting.

Japan's subsequent surprise attack on Pearl Harbor was planned brilliantly and carried out masterfully. Nevertheless, it failed to achieve its primary strategic objective, as it galvanized the American public's determination to fight a war to the finish. As Japan's Admiral Isoroku Yamamoto remarked, the attack only awakened the sleeping giant.[38]

Arsenal of Democracy

The United States' entrance into the war dramatically changed its course, as had the introduction of American troops in 1917. But this change would be slow in coming, as it took time for the American economy to shift from peacetime to wartime production. The considerable unused production capacity that existed as a result of the Depression lessened the dislocation in the United States caused by this shift. In the meantime, Germany maintained its advances in the Soviet Union and also in North Africa, while Japan increasingly took control of the Pacific (see Map 3.4).

That the United States eventually fought a successful two-front war, alone in the Pacific and with Britain and the Soviet Union in Europe, indicated the extent to which it had become a world power. However, the alliance with which the United States joined was not always free of problems. Strains emerged that

Map 3.4   Height of Japanese Expansion in the Pacific Theater

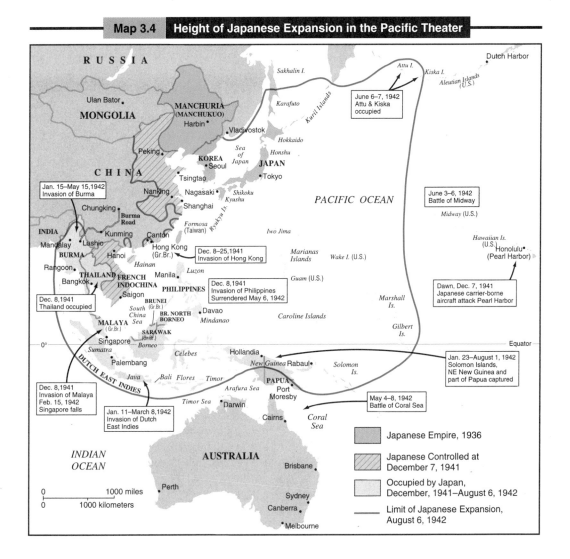

affected America's relations with its allies, particularly the Soviet Union. Moscow was fending off the Nazi onslaught alone and persistently called for the opening of a second front in western Europe to draw off some of the German forces. Stalin grew resentful and suspicious of American and British unwillingness to open a second front on the European continent. However, to the Americans, and especially to the British, it appeared essential that any attempt to invade Europe wait until Germany's strength was eroded. The Soviets' resentment was not soothed by the infusion of almost $11 billion of **lend-lease** aid.

The British and American leaders thought that in order to weaken Germany, its forces would first have to be driven from North Africa, and then its infrastructure and economy would have to be crushed by extensive bombing. Ostensibly, the latter would also destroy the German people's willingness to continue fighting. By 1943 German forces were driven from North Africa, but the bombing of Germany proved unsuccessful. Postwar analyses revealed that German production of military equipment was higher in 1944 than in 1941.[39] The bombing also failed to seriously affect civilian morale. So, in spite of the destruction of its cities, with 135,000 civilian casualties lost in the firebombing of Dresden alone, the German government continued the fight. The Western Allies became convinced that only an invasion of continental Europe could push Germany over the edge of defeat.

Second Front

Consequently, the United States and Britain invaded Italy in 1943. Few German troops were diverted to Italy, however, as the German High Command was still waiting for the main blow to fall in the west. Italy surrendered later that year. Mussolini tried to escape capture but was caught and killed by antifascist partisans, and Italy subsequently joined the Allies. Finally, on June 6, 1944 (D-Day), the United States and Britain began the liberation of France with the invasion of Normandy. Germany now fought a two-front war (actually a two and one-half–front war, counting the Mediterranean) against far superior enemies. The Allies had command of the air and were slowly progressing toward Berlin. The German defeat by now seemed a foregone conclusion, but Hitler was determined to fight to the bitter end. Indeed, the Allies wanted an unconditional surrender from their foes, believing that the Germans had not been sufficiently convinced of their defeat in World War I. Allied forces pushed on through Europe, heading for Berlin. On April 20, 1945, the Soviets reached the German capital, and the Allies met at the Elbe River on April 28. On May 8, eight days after Hitler committed suicide in his Berlin bunker, Germany unconditionally surrendered, and the Allies declared victory in Europe. Hitler's Thousand-Year Reich had collapsed within twelve years.

Uneasy Alliance

The end of the war in Europe created new political problems for the Allies. Not the least of these was resolving the question of what to do with the defeated Germany. Throughout the war the major Allied powers held a series of summit conferences to discuss strategy and other war concerns. Until the conflict's final stages, little thought was given to what Europe would look like after the defeat of the Axis Powers, as the immediate goal was to win the war. On this score the Allies were united. However, once the common enemy was eliminated, the wartime consensus began to break down. This became evident in the two main conferences held in 1945 at Yalta and Potsdam.[40]

Churchill, Roosevelt, and Stalin, the "Big Three" leaders, met for the final time at Yalta in the Soviet Crimea in February 1945 to address some important issues regarding postwar Europe. The most significant of these was the fate of the liberated nations of eastern Europe. It was important to the Allies, and especially to the Americans, that the countries liberated by the Soviets be granted self-determination and that they be able to choose their own (preferably democratic) governments. After all, the fate of Poland was the reason for the war in the first place.

Stalin agreed to elections in the eastern European countries, but he did not take the issue seriously. He was more concerned with Soviet security and German reparations. In both world wars Russia had been invaded through eastern Europe and hence he sought to maintain effective control over these countries so that they could never again support Germany against Russia. The Big Three also differed on the issue of war reparations, with sharp disagreement occurring between the Soviets, who demanded huge reparations, and the United States and Britain, who did not want to permanently cripple Germany. In the end, the decision was postponed until the next meeting. As will be seen in the next chapter, these hurried decisions had a fateful impact on post–World War II relations that the three leaders could not foresee.

In July 1945, shortly after the end of the war in Europe, the Allies met again to discuss the postwar settlement, this time in Potsdam, a Soviet-occupied German town near Berlin. Of the former Big Three, however, only Stalin remained. Roosevelt had suddenly died of a cerebral hemorrhage in April, leaving Vice President Harry Truman to be the new president. Churchill's Conservative party was voted out of office during the proceedings, so the new prime minister, Clement Atlee, replaced him in mid-conference. At this meeting it was confirmed that Germany was to be disarmed and that British, American, and Soviet troops would each occupy part of Germany. Berlin, located within the area to be occupied by the USSR, would also be divided among the three nations. Under pressure from Paris, Britain and the United States added France as a participant in the occupation, so Germany was divided into four zones of occupation, as was Berlin (see Map 3.5). Once again the issue of war reparations was discussed, and it was agreed that the Soviets would be able to take reparations and booty out of their own German zone of occupation and would receive a quarter of any reparations assessed in the American, British, and French zones.

The distrust brewing among the Allies was all the more apparent by the time of the Potsdam meeting. In particular, the Allies were concerned about the Soviet occupation of eastern Europe. Despite glossing over their animosity toward the Soviets during the war (to the extent that Stalin was portrayed as "Uncle Joe" to the Americans), the British, French, and Americans were wary of Moscow. Fresh on their minds were Stalin's brutal political purges and his forced collectivization of Soviet agriculture in the 1930s, which killed millions. The strains between the wartime allies were exacerbated, however, by the change in personnel at the top.

| | Map 3.5 | A Divided Germany, Post–World War II |

Truman, Atlee, and Stalin did not have the same history of communication and co-operation that Roosevelt, Churchill, and Stalin had enjoyed.

Atomic Bomb

At Potsdam, Truman was still eager to gain Soviet engagement in the fight against Japan. The United States had been fighting essentially alone against an implacable enemy in the Pacific throughout the war. Eventually, the United States gained the upper hand and secured bases from which bombing raids could be launched against the Japanese home islands. In an attempt to undermine the Japanese people's will to fight, most of Japan's major cities were extensively bombed; the firebombing of Tokyo alone killed about 200,000 people in only one week in

Spotlight

The Holocaust

The Holocaust was the genocide of 6 million European Jews committed by the Third Reich. It was the official policy of the Nazis, who made the Jewish people the scapegoat for most of Germany's post–World War I hardships. They considered Jews, Gypsies, and homosexuals "inhuman" and likened their murder to the extermination of pests. Millions of Jews and other victims were captured, transported, enslaved, and gassed to death in concentration camps such as Auschwitz, Buchenwald, Dachau, and Bergen-Belsen.

The concentration camps had one aim: the murder of those who entered. Either one faced outright gassing, was worked to death in slave labor, or died of starvation or disease. The killings occurred on a scale unseen before in human history, using the organized and methodical techniques of mass production for murder.

Accompanying the undeniable horror of the "Final Solution," Hannah Arendt has described the banality of the evil that took place.* The German railroads were paid full fare for transporting victims to the camps, and large corporations located factories near the camps to take advantage of the free forced labor. Gruesome as well were notorious medical experiments attempting to prove twisted genetic theories and the making of soap, candles, and even lampshades out of the remains of human beings. The gold retrieved from victim's teeth also was a ghastly booty. Bodies were either buried in mass graves or were cremated in huge ovens, spreading a pall of ash over the surrounding area.

The Holocaust ended with the end of the war. None of the Allied troops who liberated the camps were prepared for what greeted them: the sight of skeleton-like prisoners and their accounts of grisly horror. The Nazi leaders responsible for this crime against humanity (with the exception of those who escaped or committed suicide) were tried and convicted after the war at a special war-crimes tribunal at Nuremberg, and all the world's nations vowed that such horrors should never be allowed to happen again. Yet part of the tragedy of the Holocaust is that although it was unique in scope, method, and its attempt to exterminate an entire people, the Jews, other genocides have also occurred in the twentieth century. From the massacre of Armenians in the Ottoman Empire during World War I to the "killing fields" of Cambodia in the 1970s, to "ethnic cleansing" in the former Yugoslavia, twentieth-century humanity has repeatedly proven itself capable of terrible crimes of hatred when the civilized world is unable or unwilling to intervene.

*Hannah Arendt, *Eichman in Jerusalem: A Report on the Banality of Evil* (New York: Penguin Books, 1977 c. 1964).

1945. But, as in Germany and in England, the bombing of civilians did not break the will of the Japanese, and they continued to resist.

This left the United States with a fearsome prospect: the invasion of Japan itself. Truman recognized the political cost of transferring a large number of American troops to Asia for an invasion of Japan. With the war in Europe over, the American people were reluctant to continue fighting and were certainly hoping to bring home their soldiers unharmed from the Pacific. Furthermore, U.S. military leaders had calculated that such an invasion would result in more than 1 million American casualties, as the Japanese could be expected to defend their home islands with ferocious tenacity. Although the Soviets would be likely to exact concessions and try to establish lasting control over whatever territory they occupied,

At a Glance

The World Wars

WORLD WAR I, 1914–1918

Nations Involved
- *Central Powers:* Austria-Hungary, Germany, Bulgaria, Ottoman Empire, their allies
- *Allied Powers:* British Empire, France, Russia, Serbia, Italy, United States, their allies

National Goals
- Austro-Hungarian nationalism and territorial expansion. German colonial expansion for raw materials and markets. British concern for the rise of the German expansion. France sought revenge for defeat in 1870–1871. Russia wanted to protect Serbia in order to expand its line of defense against Austria and Germany.

Key Leaders
Austria-Hungary: Emperor Franz Josef
British Empire: David Lloyd George
France: Georges Clemenceau
Germany: Kaiser Wilhelm II
United States: Woodrow Wilson
Russia: Tsar Nicholas II

Causes of the War
1. The growing power of Germany
2. The system of alliances designed to protect the great powers
3. The social changes wrought by industrialization
4. Nationalist challenges to the Ottoman and Austro-Hungarian Empires
5. The impact of heightened competition for imperial gains outside of Europe on inter-European affairs
6. The belief that the next European war would be short and that rapid mobilization and attack would be decisive

Inventions
- Tank, machine gun, airplane for military use, poison gas and chemical weapons, large-scale assembly-line industry, shipping (tankers)

Ideas
- Cult of the offensive, nationalism, imperialism, communism in Russia

Civilian and Military Deaths
- 15 million

Political Results
- Germany, the Ottoman Empire and the Austro-Hungarian Empire are divided into smaller nations, Communists take over Russian monarchy. The United States remains isolationist. The League of Nations is created.

Major Conferences
- Versailles

Terms of Peace
- Germany must limit armaments, pay reparations, admit guilt in starting the war, and treat minorities fairly. Germany is demilitarized. Germany, Austria-Hungary and the Ottoman Empire lose territories and colonies. The latter two empires collapse.

Winners
- Britain, France, and the United States. Britain loses its hegemony. The United States returns to isolationism after the war.

Losers
- Germany, Austria-Hungary, and the Ottoman Empire

WORLD WAR II, 1939–1945

Nations Involved
- *Axis Powers:* Germany, Italy (changed sides in 1943), Japan, their allies
- *Allied Powers:* United States, France, Britain, USSR, their allies

National Goals
- Hitler wanted to restore Germany to its former glory, purify the "master race," unify all Germans, and expand the German empire. Japan wanted access to raw materials, markets, and colonies.

Key Leaders
- Germany: Adolf Hitler
- Great Britain: Winston Churchill
- Italy: Benito Mussolini
- Soviet Union: Joseph Stalin
- United States: Franklin Roosevelt
- Japan: Hideki Tojo

Causes of the War
1. German, Italian, and Japanese expansionism
2. The authoritarian and militaristic ideology of fascism in these countries, led by vicious and resolute leaders
3. Changes in the economic strength of the great powers as the growth of Japan, Germany, and the Soviet Union posed a challenge to Britain, France, and the United States
4. The harsh terms of the Versailles Treaty
5. The ineffective enforcement of the Versailles Treaty

Inventions
- Atomic bomb, radar, jet engine

Ideas
- The "master race," blitzkrieg ("lightning war"), carpet bombing

Civilian and Military Deaths
- 40–50 million

Political Results
- United States and the Soviet Union become superpowers. Two rival power blocs form, the Western (NATO) and the Eastern (Warsaw Pact). With the exception of East Germany, the German, Italian, and Japanese dictatorships are replaced with democracies. The League of Nations is replaced by the United Nations. The Cold War starts.

Major Conferences
- Casablanca, Yalta, Potsdam

Terms of Peace
- Guarantees are required against racial and religious discrimination, and fascist parties are banned. Each defeated nation has to pay reparations and limit the size of its military. Japan has the right to self-defense, to develop an economy, and to join in defense and trade agreements. Germany is divided after the war.

Winners
- The Soviet Union and the United States and their allies. The United States becomes the Western hegemon while the USSR emerges as the Communist hegemon.

Losers
- Germany and Japan are occupied by the Allies. Germany is divided after the war. West Germany and Japan are educated for democracy.

as they had done in Europe, Truman still considered their participation in the war essential if American casualties were to be contained.

At this point, however, another option became available. Fearing that Nazi scientists were working to develop a nuclear weapon, the United States started the top-secret Manhattan Project in 1942 to produce an atomic bomb before the Germans did. This project was so secret that not even the vice president knew about it—Truman learned of the work on the atomic bomb only when he assumed the office of president upon Roosevelt's death. (For more on the Manhattan Project, see Chapter Eleven.) The German atomic bomb project never got off the ground, but on July 16, 1945, while Truman was in Potsdam, Manhattan Project scientists detonated the first atomic bomb near Alamogordo, New Mexico.[41]

The development of the new weapon made Truman's dilemma much easier. If Japan were to surrender once it had seen the devastating potential of the atomic bomb, American lives would be spared. Other benefits included the saving of Japanese lives (compared with the staggering death toll that an invasion would have caused) and being relieved of the disadvantages of Soviet participation in the war. But for Truman, sparing American casualties was the essential point. He therefore decided to use the new weapon.[42] On August 6, 1945, an American B-29 bomber, the *Enola Gay,* dropped the "Little Boy" atomic bomb on the Japanese city of Hiroshima. In the blinding flash and subsequent firestorm, 80,000 to 100,000 Japanese were killed. The explosive force of the atomic bomb was equivalent to 14,000 tons of TNT, ten times more powerful than had been predicted. In the absence of an immediate Japanese surrender, the Soviets declared war on Japan on August 8, and a second atomic bomb (the "Fat Man") was dropped on the city of Nagasaki on August 9. The following day, the Japanese government decided to sue for peace, and Japan formally surrendered on September 2. Humankind's most terrible weapon had ended its most terrible war.

CONCLUSION: THE END OF TWO WARS— AND THE BEGINNING OF ANOTHER?

The Second World War was even more destructive than the first. It is estimated that the war killed at least 40 million to 50 million people. The USSR alone suffered 7.5 million to 11.5 million soldiers killed and 6 million to 8 million direct civilian deaths, although the total of all Soviet war-related deaths is probably between 20 million and 25 million.[43] Entire cities in Europe and Asia were destroyed by aerial bombing, ground combat, or by occupying forces as reprisals for resistance activity. Most of the combat and devastation occurred in central and eastern Europe, but the war was fought everywhere, from the frozen tundra of Lappland to the sweltering jungle of Burma, from the Aleutian Islands in the North Pacific to the estuary of the Río de la Plata in the South Atlantic. Only nine sovereign states remained neutral by the end of the war, though many nations that declared war on the Axis committed few troops to combat. World War II was truly a global war.

The experience of the war is captured in a large number of firsthand accounts by persons who participated in the war at every level, from supreme commander (Churchill's memoirs) to innocent victim (*The Diary of Anne Frank*). World War II fiction also abounds, among which James Jones' novel set on Guadalcanal, *The Thin Red Line,* stands out as a depiction of the war from a soldier's perspective. The war spawned a myriad of films as well, but most are propagandistic or tendentious in one way or another (Hollywood spent the war perfecting the art of the propaganda film). The German films *Stalingrad,* which depicts combat on the Russian Front, and *Das Boot,* which follows the crew of an ill-fated U-boat, and the Finnish *Talvisota,* which portrays combat between Finnish and Russian forces in 1939–1940, are notable exceptions that can make the war seem all too real to modern audiences. The British documentary series *The World at War* and *Battlefield* illustrate the strategies, tactics, and consequences of the war less graphically. Steven Spielberg's *Schindler's List* has provided millions with new understanding of the Holocaust. Perhaps more than any other conflict, World War II has made a lasting impression on world culture; more people know the name of Adolf Hitler than that of any other historical figure.

Together, World Wars I and II combined to fundamentally alter world politics. Except for the Soviet Union, the old empires were now gone, replaced by a growing number of states claiming to represent a particular nation. Moreover, the European powers no longer had the ability (whether they recognized it or not) to maintain their colonial holdings. The age of European political and economic domination was thus over, as the combat begun in 1914 had resulted in an astonishing process of self-destruction. One of the most important results of the Second World War was a much higher degree of globalization of world politics. The European powers and Japan had suffered staggering human and material losses from which they would need decades to recover.

At the end of the war, only the United States and the Soviet Union had the resources to contend for global leadership. It was not immediately clear, however, that the two massive powers would be adversaries. On the one hand, both nations (as well as Britain, France, and China) had seats on the newly formed Security Council of the United Nations, which was designed to facilitate cooperation among the great powers in resolving conflicts. Washington and Moscow thus recognized each other as partners in maintaining world peace just as they had been partners in victory during the world war. On the other hand, the United States and the USSR had very different political and economic systems, and their leaders espoused beliefs and values which were diametrically opposed. These political differences created a climate of mistrust that had already prompted the two countries to view each other's actions with suspicion. The world wars had decisively destroyed the old world order, but they built the foundations of a new system for resolving global issues. Whether the new order would be cooperative or conflictual, however, remained to be seen.

PRINCIPAL POINTS OF CHAPTER THREE

1. In two terrible wars in the first half of the twentieth century, Europe devastated itself and destroyed its dominant position in world politics.
2. Six main reasons are advanced for the outbreak of World War I:
   a. German expansionism.
   b. The rigid alliance system that developed in the early years of the twentieth century, with Britain, France, and Russia on one side and Germany and Austria-Hungary on the other.
   c. Changes in the relative economic strength of the great powers, as Britain's share of world industrial production declined and that of Germany, Russia, and the United States expanded.
   d. The challenge posed by nationalism to decrepit empires, especially in the Balkans.
   e. Colonial rivalries and the end of opportunities for colonial expansion.
   f. The cult of the offensive, a widespread belief that wars would be brief and the side that was first to mobilize and attack would win.
3. World War I ended with the victory of the Entente Powers (Britain, France, Italy, the United States, and their allies) over the Central Powers (Germany, Austria-Hungary, and the Ottoman Empire). The victorious allies imposed the terms of the Versailles Treaty on Germany.
4. The League of Nations was established to preserve peace through collective security, but consistently failed in this task throughout the 1930s.
5. Five factors are candidates for the primary cause of World War II:
   a. German, Italian, and Japanese expansionism.
   b. The authoritarian and militaristic ideology of fascism in these countries, led by vicious and resolute leaders.
   c. Changes in the economic strength of the great powers, as the growth of Japan, Germany, and the Soviet Union posed a challenge to Britain, France, and the United States.
   d. The terms of the Versailles Treaty being too harsh.
   e. The terms of the Versailles Treaty not being effectively enforced.
6. The Allies (Britain, France, the Soviet Union, the United States, and their allies) defeated the Axis (Germany, Italy, Japan, and their allies) in World War II.
7. At the end of World War II, the victorious United States and the Soviet Union emerged as superpowers, but conflicts between them arose immediately.

KEY TERMS

appeasement
blitzkrieg
casualties
collective action

cult of the
   offensive
fascism
isolationism
lend-lease

Maginot Line
plebiscite
Schlieffen Plan
spheres of
   influence

Treaty of
   Versailles
war of attrition

SOURCE: UPI/Corbis-Bettmann

The Cold War

International politics during the post–World War II period was dominated by the struggle for power between the United States and the Soviet Union: the Cold War. The term describes a situation in which the two superpowers were locked in an apparently intractable conflict, punctuated by crises and haunted by the danger of nuclear war, but nevertheless managed to avoid direct combat. Despite the intense and extensive competition between the two superpowers, the Cold War period, which extended roughly from 1945 to 1990, was relatively stable compared to the shifting alliances and frequent wars of earlier years.

For more than four decades, the Cold War endured periods of rising tension followed by waves of relaxation. The particular pattern was shaped by various factors, including the personalities and beliefs of Soviet and American leaders, domestic politics, economics, and unanticipated events on the world stage. Often these events prompted each of the superpowers to take actions benefiting its own interests at its adversary's expense. This chapter begins by advancing six explanations for why the

Cold War began, next traces the ebb and flow of the Cold War from its origins in the aftermath of the Second World War in 1945 to its end with the collapse of the Soviet Union in 1991, and finally concludes by discussing why the Cold War ended.

WHO OR WHAT CAUSED THE COLD WAR?

In the aftermath of World War II, the world became divided into two camps, the U.S.–led Western democracies and the Communist regimes, led by the Soviet Union. Rightly or wrongly, conflicts throughout the world came to be viewed in the context of the relations between the two superpowers. The bipolar structure of the international system (meaning the system was dominated by two major powers—see Chapter Twelve) seemed at the time to be the culmination of an ultimate logic to world politics: from the ashes of World Wars I and II, out of a world of "Lilliputians," two giant "Gullivers" were destined to emerge.

Was this bipolar logic inescapable? Were the superpowers predestined to be hostile to each other? This question is likely to occupy students of world politics long after the Cold War itself has faded from living memory. The various explanations that have been advanced for why the Cold War began may be summarized in six main lines of argument, each of which fits into one of the images of world politics discussed in Chapter One. For some, the Cold War was a struggle between the forces of truth and justice on one side and an "evil empire" on the other; while for others, it was the same dog-eat-dog world it had always been, but only the two biggest dogs were still standing. Each explanation also argues from a frame of reference provided by one of the levels of analysis of international relations presented in Chapter One. Accordingly, some contend that individual leaders were responsible (the individual level), others point to specific national characteristics of the United States or USSR (the domestic level), while still others look to the structure of the international system itself (the systemic level) for the reasons why the Cold War broke out. This section outlines the six basic explanations for the start of the Cold War.

It Was Moscow's Fault

First, the conventional American view is that the Soviet Union was primarily responsible for the Cold War. From this perspective, if the Soviets had not been bent on territorial acquisition, especially their subjugation of Eastern Europe, the United States would have retreated into its prewar position of isolationism. This explanation paints the USSR as an "evil empire" that may well have intended to conquer Western Europe as well. Without American efforts, the Soviets would have taken advantage of Western Europe's war-torn and desolate conditions to do just that. Note that this is a domestic-level argument, as it contends that the USSR was inherently aggressive and expansionist.

According to this interpretation of the Cold War's origins, the United States was correct to adopt the policy of containing Soviet attempts to expand. Without an activist American **containment** policy, the Soviets would have continued to expand in Europe, the Middle East, and Asia. Particular blame is placed in this view upon the dictator Joseph Stalin, whose brutal policies and paranoid personality contributed to a sense of "encirclement" and an interest in expanding wherever possible to prevent a weakening of power. Many contemporary Russian analysts agree that Stalin's expansionist policy provoked widespread hostility toward the USSR, which contributed to its ultimate collapse. According to this argument, without Stalin's aggressive policies in the years following World War II, exemplified by Soviet actions in Eastern Europe, the Cold War would not have evolved, or at least it would not have been as vehement.

No, It Was Washington's Fault

A second interpretation of the origins of the Cold War takes the opposite position. Here the United States is to blame for the outbreak of the Cold War because it insisted on trying to expand its overseas export markets in Eastern Europe after World War II, and because it failed to comprehend the severe security problems facing the Soviet Union at the end of the war. After all, this argument goes, because the USSR suffered about 20 million deaths in the war, amounting to almost 10 percent of its population, it was understandable that the Soviets would want to protect their territory by controlling countries such as Poland, which twice within half a century had been the invasion route for Germany against Russia. Stalin thus demanded that the USSR possessed the right to have "friendly" nations on its borders. Note that this explanation is also a domestic-level analysis.

This perspective therefore contends that the United States mistook legitimate security precautions as aggressive designs and thereby initiated the Cold War, to which the Soviets were forced to react. A variant position maintains that American use of the atomic bomb at the end of World War II caused the USSR to look to its own security. It has been argued that the United States used the atomic bomb on Japan not to quickly end the war, which was already nearing its conclusion, but as a warning to the USSR not to encroach further into Asia and as a demonstration of the destructive power of the new American weapon. Though he would never admit it publicly, Stalin was very concerned by the fact that the war ended with the United States in sole possession of **atomic weapons.** When President Harry Truman mentioned to him at the Potsdam summit that the United States had developed a powerful new weapon (of which he had already been informed by Soviet intelligence), Stalin replied only that he hoped the United States would make good use of it. Upon his return to Moscow, however, he told Soviet military industrial officials, "You know that Hiroshima has shaken the whole world. The balance has been destroyed. Provide the bomb—it will remove a great danger from us."[1] Until Soviet science was able to fulfill Stalin's order, the American nuclear monopoly could only have exacerbated Soviet security concerns.

Ideological Conflict

A third explanation for the origins of the Cold War claims that the difference in ideologies and ways of life that the Soviet and American political systems represented was the primary cause for the conflict between these nations. According to this explanation, it would have been impossible for two potential competitors to avoid conflict when one represented an open democracy and the other a closed totalitarian system. For each, the other presented a threat of immense proportions; each saw the other as expansionist and bent on ideologically converting the world. This is another domestic-level argument, portraying the Cold War as a clash of political ideas and forms of government.

This explanation views the conflict as driven by the vast differences between **capitalism** and **communism.** Capitalism is a system based on markets, competition, and individual choice. For it to function properly, it requires trading partners, open world markets, and international stability. Its essence is the private ownership of the means of production and the existence of a mobile labor force. Western democracy is anchored in the protection of individual rights and freedom. From the West, communism was perceived as monolithic, antidemocratic, and totalitarian. The Communist system rejected private property, required a centralized system of production and distribution of resources, and enforced narrow limits on individual rights such as freedom of religion, assembly, and speech. Soviet ideologues supported the explanation of ideological incompatibility, though they naturally portrayed capitalism as reprehensible.

Marxist-Leninist ideology shaped Soviet perceptions of world politics. According to socialist ideology, capitalism was the cause of war and conflict, and peace would come only with the worldwide overthrow of the capitalist system. Stalin expressed this viewpoint in a February 1946 speech declaring that "war was inevitable as long as capitalism existed."[2] Until it was eradicated, "capitalist encirclement" would threaten the gains of the 1917 revolution. Cooperation with the capitalist powers could therefore be only a temporary expedient, as a final violent struggle of socialism against capitalism would eventually come. Many Communists also sought to spread their ideology to other countries throughout the world, advocating a global Communist revolution, and viewed any Western resistance to this idea as evidence of the intent of Western governments to destroy Soviet communism.

Leadership or the Lack Thereof

A fourth explanation for the Cold War focuses on individual leaders in both the United States and the Soviet Union. In both states, according to this argument, foreign policy is ultimately the responsibility of one person, the leader. In the United States, for example, the president has considerably more leeway in foreign affairs than in domestic politics, where he competes with Congress, the Supreme Court, and special-interest groups. Consequently, his personality, beliefs, and image can

Winston Churchill, Franklin Roosevelt, and Joseph Stalin put on a show of accord and friendship at the Yalta Conference.   SOURCE: AP/Wide World

significantly affect foreign policy and the nature of interstate relations. According to this explanation, President Franklin Roosevelt knew (or at least thought he knew) how to handle Stalin and believed that "if he could just have an opportunity to exert his powers of personal charm and persuasion on the Russian dictator . . . Stalin would be disarmed and his lasting friendship secured."[3] Roosevelt's intention was to demonstrate that the United States could be trusted and its commitments would be fulfilled. (See the Spotlight box for more on FDR's ideas for collective security in the postwar world.)

However, Harry Truman, who had replaced Roosevelt upon his death in April 1945, had little experience in foreign affairs and was more suspicious of Soviet intentions. Truman, according to this line of reasoning, relied heavily on the many Roosevelt aides who were similarly suspicious of the Soviet leadership—more so than Roosevelt had been. This resulted in unnecessarily harsh policies that strained Soviet-American relations. Examples include Truman's tough conversation with Soviet Foreign Minister Molotov a few days after he had taken office, strict Marshall Plan regulations that made it impossible and even insulting for the USSR to accept American aid, and the withholding of economic assistance.

Stalin also plays a role in this explanation. This brutal, increasingly paranoid dictator had already been responsible for the death of millions of his own citizens even before World War II started. His totalitarian rule and brutal practices at

The Big Three and The Great Design

The leaders of the major Allied nations in World War II, Roosevelt, Churchill, and Stalin, the "Big Three," developed out of necessity a close working relationship, in spite of American and British distrust of the Soviet premier. The serious threat posed by the Axis Powers increased the importance of such a relationship, for if the Allies were significantly divided in terms of their objectives and strategies, they would be weakened severely. The Allied leaders' ability to work together on most issues of strategy and tactics was an invaluable factor contributing to their eventual victory.

The war resulted not only in an unprecedented level of death and destruction, but also in the creation of atomic weaponry that threatened incomprehensible devastation in the case of a future worldwide conflict. Allied leaders thus became convinced that another global war must not occur. In 1941, before the United States even entered the war, Roosevelt and Churchill agreed to the establishment of a "permanent international body" to provide "a wider and permanent system of general security" at the war's end. Inspired by Wilson's vision of international peace, and aware of the League of Nations' failure to guarantee it, President Roosevelt committed himself to a more realistic plan for collective security. In fact, Roosevelt devised his

"Great Design" for the postwar international system as an antidote for the ailing League of Nations, basing it on a continuation of the wartime alliance among the United States, Britain, and the Soviet Union, rather than on ideals (see Chapters Three and Nine). A necessary part of the plan, however, was a continuation of a working relationship, like that which Roosevelt, Churchill, and Stalin had developed, into the postwar period.

The key component of Roosevelt's global security plan was a basic agreement among the leaders of the great powers to oppose aggression. His concept of an Anglo-American international police force was expanded to include the Soviet Union and eventually China, a state he believed would become a major power and in any case would play a pivotal role in the future security of Asia. These "four policemen" would become permanent members of the Security Council of the United Nations, a forum that, not unlike the nineteenth-century Concert of Europe, would provide an institutional framework for those powers to cooperate in maintaining world peace. (France was added to the Security Council after the war.) The United States, Britain, France, and the Soviet Union would collectively decide territorial and political issues in postwar Europe, preventing further conflict in that region. All other

home and abroad were likely to raise fears among democracies that had just fought the most horrible war in history, which had been caused in part by their failure to respond in time to actions of a vicious autocrat. Though Stalin framed his actions in a Marxist-Leninist context, his primary concern may have been the maintenance of his own power and strength and the security of the Soviet state. But his suspicious nature, which undoubtedly magnified his perceptions of the threats to the USSR posed by Western actions immediately after World War II, led to responses by the Western powers that only reinforced his paranoia.

The argument that the Cold War was primarily the fault of individual leaders therefore does not necessarily portray United States or Soviet leaders as heroes or villains; rather, it emphasizes that they were fallible human beings. Of course,

states would be prohibited from establishing military forces large enough to threaten their neighbors. Though Roosevelt's plan may look antiquated and Eurocentric in the New Era, Churchill, Stalin, and China's President Chiang (who were, after all, leaders of states that had governed great empires in previous centuries) responded favorably to the plan in principle.

The devil, of course, was in the details. Stalin maintained that the USSR had special security requirements, which called for a zone of Soviet-controlled states on the Russian frontier as a buffer against future invasions. This requirement was the basis for an earlier informal agreement between Churchill and Stalin on the principle of "spheres of influence" for each of the major powers in an updated balance-of-power system. Although Roosevelt understood Stalin's concerns, he felt that the American public would not support U.S. participation in a system of European-style "entangling alliances," especially one premised on the blatant denial of national self-determination in Europe. Thus Stalin's insistence on pro-Soviet regimes in Eastern Europe was doubly problematic. By imposing a form of government dictated from Moscow, it ran counter both to the concept of an international body intended to preserve the sovereignty of independent states and to American ideals; thus, it jeopardized U.S. membership in the anticipated United Nations.

Finally persuaded by Roosevelt of the material and political value of cooperating with the United States in establishing the UN, Stalin pledged to hold "free" elections in Poland and other Eastern European states. The February 1945 Yalta Declaration on Liberated Europe was true in principle to the Atlantic Charter and the basic idea behind the United Nations, though it merely delayed Communist takeovers in Eastern Europe. The Soviets' violation of the Yalta agreements confirmed Western suspicions about Stalin's lack of commitment to Western political ideals. Yet, the Big Three leaders had overcome deep differences in order to cooperate against the Axis during the war, and these veterans of global politics might have been able to work out a compromise that would have allowed the UN to function as Roosevelt envisioned. But by the end of the war, Churchill had been voted out of office, Roosevelt was dead, and his successor Truman was inexperienced, unknown, and therefore not widely respected. The UN was eventually established in a much weaker form than had been originally conceived. Roosevelt's vision of collective security based on great-power agreement might have been difficult to implement, but the end of the working relationship between the Big Three wartime leaders ensured that it would never get the chance to prove itself.

consistent with this explanation, one could (and many did) blame either Truman or Stalin as responsible for starting the Cold War.

One World Divided by Two Superpowers Equals Conflict

A fifth explanation for the origins of the Cold War concentrates on the fact that the United States and the Soviet Union had emerged after World War II as the two dominant powers in the world. They were the only two capable of projecting influence and of challenging each other for global leadership; and ultimately, they were the only states that could threaten the other's survival. As such, they were destined to be natural adversaries. Note that this is a systemic-level argument, fitting into the **realpolitik**, or "everybody wants to rule the world," view of world politics, in which states by their very nature seek power in the international system. Accordingly, this argument holds that had Britain emerged more powerful than the USSR at the end of World War II, the Cold War would still have occurred, with London and not Moscow perceived as the main threat to American security, because only Britain would have had the capability to challenge American survival.

As Chapters Two and Three have shown, great powers have always rivaled one another throughout the history of world politics. At the end of World War II, only two superpowers remained, and it would have been unprecedented if their relations had been purely amicable. As Chapter Twelve will explain, **bipolarity** promotes a **zero-sum** view of world politics. Each superpower saw a gain for the other side, no matter how small, as a loss for itself, and vice versa. Some form of conflict between the United States and the USSR was therefore inevitable as neither side could afford to let the other attain a decisive advantage in the bipolar competition

The position that the Cold War started because of the great-power conflict based on the bipolar structure that emerged after World War II is also in keeping with the **security dilemma** discussed in Chapters One and Eleven. The action-reaction spiral of the bipolar security dilemma encouraged intensive competition between the two superpowers. For example, when the U.S. first tested and then used atomic weapons in 1945, the USSR stepped up its program to develop an atomic bomb, which culminated in a Soviet nuclear test in 1949; the Soviet test prompted U.S. efforts in the early 1950s to develop the even more powerful thermonuclear bomb. As we will see in this chapter, a similar action-reaction dynamic would often drive the superpowers to engage in a strategic arms race.

From this systemic perspective, there is no point in assigning blame, as the two powers became locked in conflict as a consequence of their circumstances and the structure of the postwar international system. Like two gunslingers in a Western film, the superpowers both knew that "this town ain't big enough fer the both of us," and it didn't matter who was wearing the black or the white hat.

It Was All a Misunderstanding

There is a sixth explanation for the origins of the Cold War, also fitting into the systemic-level framework, which suggests that each side misperceived the intentions of the other. On the one hand, the United States misunderstood that Soviet actions were designed to guarantee the USSR's security after the trauma inflicted by Hitler's surprise attack and the devastation the Soviet people suffered. On the other hand, according to this argument, the Soviets also misunderstood American interests and concerns, seeing U.S. efforts to aid its allies and trading partners as an attempt to encircle and challenge the USSR. Each superpower assumed the worst about its adversary and acted accordingly. This process led to a series of events that eventually solidified into a worldwide competition. Although theories

At a Glance

Alternative Causes of the Cold War

Soviet Actions

If the Soviets had not been bent on territorial acquisition, the United States would have retreated into its prewar position of isolation. The USSR was intent on conquering Western Europe.

American Actions

If the United States had not insisted on trying to expand its overseas export markets in Eastern Europe and had recognized the Soviet security dilemma, the Cold War would have been avoided. Instead, the Soviets felt that they needed Eastern Europe as a buffer. The Allies should have helped the USSR by opening a second front against Germany more quickly during World War II. According to this view, the United States used the atomic bomb on Japan to scare the Soviets out of Asia.

The Behavior and Interaction of Stalin and Truman

President Truman had little experience in foreign affairs and expected the worst from the Soviets. He followed a "get tough" strategy. Stalin was a brutal dictator who killed millions of his people before World War II in order to preserve his totalitarian rule at home. Western actions only increased his paranoia that his leadership was being undermined.

The Competing Ideologies of Communism and Capitalism

Capitalism is an international system that needs trading partners, open world markets, and international stability. It is based on a privatized economy, a mobile labor force, and individual rights and freedom. The Communist system rejects private property, requires a centralized economic system, and adheres to a narrow definition of individual rights. Communism is designed to be spread around the world. These two ideologies are polar opposites. Each side thought that it was right.

The United States and the USSR Were the Only Remaining Nations that Were Great Powers

The United States and the USSR could challenge each other for global leadership, project influence around the world, and threaten the other's survival. In a bipolar system, the two leading nations inevitably oppose each other in a total confrontation.

Each Side Misperceived the Other's Actions

The Americans interpreted Soviet actions that were designed for security as Communist expansion. The Soviets misunderstood American efforts to aid its allies and trading partners as an attempt to encircle and challenge the USSR. A process of action-reaction resulted in a worldwide competition.

of bipolarity conclude that superpower rivalry and conflict were inevitable, the misperception thesis argues that it could have been avoided through better communication and mutual understanding. The Cold War thus developed out of a vicious circle of mutually reinforcing misperceptions. If only both powers had comprehended the basic defensive nature of the policies of the other, the Cold War would never have occurred, or at least the competition between the superpowers would have been defused. Because the information upon which each group of leaders had to base its policies was often very limited, however, particularly with respect to its adversaries' intentions, it is not easy to see exactly how Soviet and American leaders could have broken the circle of misperception.

Who or What Was to Blame?

The reasons for the Cold War have been debated from the outset. In the late 1940s some Americans on the left of the political spectrum argued that the United States had overreacted to Soviet actions. This position was reinforced by revisionist historians after the Vietnam War who argued that the United States was guilty. By contrast, the end of the Cold War has bolstered the view of many that the Soviet Union was responsible for the conflict. With the end of Soviet aggression, these analysts argue, competition ended; the change in Soviet rather than American policy implies that the Soviet Union was at fault. These analysts are reinforced by Russian scholars in the era of *glasnost* (political openness) who criticize the Stalin era. Even with the new information available to historians with recent declassification of archives in Moscow and Washington, the question of the origins of the Cold War is likely to remain an open debate for many years.[4] The reader is invited to draw her or his own conclusion from the events and personalities involved in the conflict, to which this chapter now turns.

HEATING UP THE COLD WAR, 1945–1953

World War II ended with tensions increasing between the Soviet Union and the Western allies, especially over the future of Eastern Europe and Germany, but the wartime allies did not immediately become bitter enemies. The prospect of impending conflict between the United States and the USSR, let alone the shape that conflict would take, was not yet apparent. Postwar events, however, soon propelled the two emerging superpowers into confrontation.

Initial Confrontations: Iran, Greece, and Turkey

During World War II, both the USSR and Britain feared the expansion of Nazi influence in the Middle East. In 1941 the Soviets and British agreed to jointly occupy Iran—the Soviets in the north and the British in the south—with the intent of protecting Iran from Nazi influence and securing supply lines to Russia during the war. The agreement specified that both Soviet and British troops were to be removed after the war. When the war ended in May 1945, the British pulled out, but Stalin refused to withdraw the Soviet troops. President Truman resolved to confront Soviet obstinacy with a "get tough" stance: A warning was dispatched to Moscow, and an aircraft carrier was sent to the eastern Mediterranean to maintain an American presence. For a time, it looked as if the wartime allies might be drawn into serious conflict less than a year after the end of World War II, but the crisis was defused in April 1946, when the Soviets pledged to leave Iran after Teheran agreed to set up a joint Iranian-Soviet oil company.

Why did Moscow retreat? According to historian Adam B. Ulam, the involvement of the American government was the primary cause. The Soviets were not willing to risk even a minor confrontation with America for fear of threatening their interests in more crucial regions.[5] Whatever the real reasoning behind the Soviet withdrawal may have been, Truman and his advisors determined that the best way to check Soviet expansion and the possibility of Soviet control of Western Europe was to directly counter Stalin's actions and stand firm against Soviet demands.

The United States and Britain hoped that a similar "get tough" stance would convince the USSR to stop allowing the newly established Communist governments in Eastern Europe to supply Communist partisans in Greece. They also wanted the USSR to cease pressuring Turkey for territorial concessions and access to the Mediterranean through the Dardanelles, because London and Washington viewed these actions as attempts to expand Soviet control into new areas.

The Iron Curtain Descends

By the end of 1945 it was clear that the USSR had firmly established itself as the dominant power in Eastern Europe. Many Western leaders, alarmed by Soviet efforts to expand into the Middle East and Mediterranean, and by the presence of massive Soviet forces in Eastern and Central Europe, began to perceive a growing Soviet threat. In 1946, at a speech in Fulton, Missouri, Winston Churchill warned Americans that "from Stettin in the Baltic to Trieste in the Adriatic, an iron curtain has descended across the continent."[6] Using the example of Munich, he pleaded for an alliance of Western democracies to exert influence over Russia and thwart further Soviet expansion.

In early 1947 the British government informed Washington that it would no longer be able to maintain its presence in Greece and Turkey due to economic concerns and the unwillingness of the Labour government to risk British troops in foreign civil wars. The British concluded that they could not be responsible for countering Soviet advances in the region and feared that unless the United States stepped in, a power vacuum would develop and lead to dangerous consequences.

This was a dramatic change in the international system. At the end of World War II, it was widely believed that there would be three superpowers in the postwar world: the United States, the Soviet Union, and Great Britain.[7] Britain, however, had been devastated and exhausted by the effort needed to withstand the Nazi onslaught, and consequently began to relinquish political control and withdraw its forces from India, Palestine, Iraq, Jordan, and other former colonies. The British now concluded that it was necessary to reduce their role in areas such as Greece and Turkey that were independent, but in which Britain still had important interests.

To the Truman administration, the British decision came as a shock, especially because the president believed that Greece and Turkey were still threatened by the possibility of Soviet encroachment. American officials decided that the Soviet

Union had to be blocked and that the United States would have to replace the British power vacuum in the region. Many in Washington felt that Moscow was trying to pull an "end run" around Europe, and as Undersecretary of State Dean Acheson put it, "We and we alone are in a position to break up the play." [8] The Truman administration's willingness to assume greater responsibilities in world affairs marked a major turning point in the foreign policy of the traditionally isolationist United States.

Truman Doctrine

In essence, the Truman administration had decided it would have to deny the Soviets any possibility of expansion, especially in Europe. This aim would necessitate an unprecedented engagement of the United States abroad in peacetime, as it would require abandonment of its traditional isolationist stance. Yet, as Truman and his aides soon found when they began to brief Congress, to place this issue in purely realpolitik terms would not satisfy the American people. There was a strong movement in the United States to return to its prewar position of isolation. Republican Senator Arthur Vandenberg, chairman of the Senate Foreign Relations Committee, advised Truman that he would have to "scare the hell out of the American people" to make them receptive to his plans.[9] Therefore, the president rose before Congress on March 12, 1947, and introduced the **Truman Doctrine,** which some regard as an American "declaration of the Cold War." Truman's speech concentrated on the ideological conflict between freedom and totalitarianism:

> At the present moment in world history nearly every nation must choose between alternative ways of life. The choice is too often not a free one. One way of life is based upon the will of the majority, and is distinguished by free institutions, representative government, free elections, guarantees of individual liberty, freedom of speech and religion, and freedom from political oppression. The second way of life is based upon the will of a minority forcibly imposed upon the majority. It relies upon terror and oppression, a controlled press and radio, fixed elections, and the suppression of personal freedoms. I believe that it must be the policy of the United States to support free peoples who are resisting attempted subjugation by armed minorities or by outside pressures.[10]

To gain domestic support, the president thus couched his appeal for economic and financial aid to Greece and Turkey in terms of global and moral responsibility. The United States would now be called upon to help the nations of the free world gain and keep their freedom. Critics were concerned about the manner in which the Truman Doctrine was to be defined. Did this mean that the United States would intervene anywhere at any time? The president's aides had to admit that the United States would not be able to involve itself in every situation worldwide, but were unable to clarify the limits of commitment. Despite these uncertainties, Congress overwhelmingly approved the Truman Doctrine and authorized a $400 million program of assistance for Greece and Turkey.

Spotlight

Mr. X and Containment

The Truman Doctrine and the Marshall Plan were based on the philosophy of containment, which was developed by George Kennan, a Soviet specialist based in the American Embassy in Moscow. His "Long Telegram" of February 1946 alerted American officials to the threat they faced from Soviet insecurities and expansion and suggested possible solutions.

In July 1947 Kennan published an article in *Foreign Affairs* under the pseudonym "X," which delineated the policy of **containment,** the basis for future American actions in the Cold War.* He argued that the Soviets threatened free institutions throughout the Western world and were determined to fulfill the Marxist-Leninist desire for worldwide revolution. "X" claimed that Soviet actions could be contained by the "joint and vigilant application of counterforce at a constantly shifting series of geographical and political points around the world."

Kennan later regretted using the term "counterforce," because he advocated economic and political, rather than military, instruments for dealing with the Soviets. This distinction would become a major controversy in the conduct of American foreign policy.

In essence, Kennan argued that the Soviets would seek to expand until counteraction from the United States forced them to retreat. Ultimately, he believed that the containment approach would cause the Soviet Union to collapse internally and force it to negotiate, a prediction that would prove accurate forty years later. Kennan's containment theory provided American decision makers with a critical vision for organizing U.S. foreign policy and remained the centerpiece of American grand strategy for the next four decades.

* "X" [George F. Kennan], "The Sources of Soviet Conduct," *Foreign Affairs* 20, no. 4 (July 1947), pp. 556–582.

Marshall Plan

In 1947 the Truman administration was also confronting economic decline in Europe. Social and economic institutions had been demolished by the war; an unusually severe winter and meager harvest compounded the crisis. France and Italy were internally besieged by Communist parties, and economically exhausted Britain was retreating from its empire abroad. Winston Churchill described Europe as "a rubble heap, a charnel house, a breeding ground of pestilence and hate." [11] There was widespread fear in Washington that Communist agents would topple the governments of Western Europe in preparation for a Soviet invasion, and the war-ravaged countries would be unable to purchase American goods, which would threaten the American economy and perhaps would return the world to its prewar state of depression.

The response to this potential catastrophe was the Marshall Plan, named after Secretary of State George C. Marshall, who announced the plan in an address at Harvard University's commencement exercises as a way to "help start the European world on its way to recovery." [12] Because the United States had emerged from

World War II an economic superpower and had escaped the destruction of war at home, it was in a strong position to take this action.

The Marshall Plan, perhaps the most successful U.S. foreign policy program in history, offered American economic and military assistance to promote free-market economies within Europe. The plan was originally offered to the Soviet Union and its satellites, but in July 1948 Soviet Foreign Minister Molotov declared that the program would infringe on the sovereignty of the European states, and thus Moscow would not participate. Various reports and documents declassified years later reveal that Stalin's true concerns were that American revitalization of Great Britain, France, and Germany would restore their great-power status and return the world to the pre-1939 political system. Soviet leaders feared what they perceived as America's "intention to restore the economy of Germany and Japan on the old basis, provided it is subordinated to interests of American capital." [13] Stalin believed that this would be detrimental to Soviet vital interests, especially in Eastern Europe; it represented, he thought, a threat to the security of the USSR. As a result, Marshall Plan aid, which was administered through the Economic Co-operation Act of 1948 and comprised 2.75 percent of America's gross national product, was transferred only to the democracies of the West. [14]

The Marshall Plan had three main effects. First, it revitalized European economies and restored Britain, France, and eventually Germany to major-power status (although not to the level of the United States or USSR). Second, it thwarted Communist control within the Western European countries as it helped end the economic hardships that served as a breeding ground for discontent and increased the influence of communist parties, particularly in France and Italy. Finally, it helped to create the basis for a movement toward European economic integration we now know as the European Union, and it facilitated the eventual integration of West Germany into the European economy.

Stalin and Tito

In the early years of Soviet domination of Eastern Europe after World War II, Moscow allowed a considerable degree of latitude to the Communist regimes that it supported. Elections were held in several countries and noncommunist parties could compete in them, but their role was kept marginal. Communist parties that attained power largely through their own efforts rather than Soviet pressure, however, maintained a degree of independence from Moscow. As the tensions surrounding the Cold War increased, Stalin became obsessed with the possibility that these regimes could prove to be unreliable.

His fears were heightened by the growing friction between the Kremlin and the Communist government of Yugoslavia. Josip Broz Tito, the leader of Yugoslavia, had come to power with his own unique mix of communism and nationalism. The ethnic conflicts among the dominant Serbs and their neighbors, which had catalyzed World War I, were kept below the surface under Tito's leadership. (They would resurface in the years after Tito's death.) Stalin became ever more concerned about Tito's independent power and legitimacy in Yugoslavia and his challenges to Moscow's influence over the policies of East European Communist parties. As a result, Stalin began to crack down on other states in Eastern Europe in order to prevent any other independent leaders like Tito from emerging.

Czech Coup

Against the background of dissension among Communist leaders and growing East-West suspicions, Czechoslovakia became the crucible for developments in the region and a symbol of the direction of global affairs, as it had at the Munich Conference a decade earlier. Czechoslovakia was the least Communist of the regimes that existed in Eastern Europe in early 1948. Before World War II, it had been anti-German, not anti-Soviet. Furthermore, it had been the most industrially advanced and democratic of the interwar Eastern European regimes, and therefore it had special meaning for Western leaders.

In February 1948 a Communist-engineered, Soviet-backed coup seized power in Czechoslovakia. Moscow's heavy-handed action angered the West and convinced many that Stalin had never intended to keep the promises of open elections in Eastern Europe that he had made at the Yalta conference (see Chapter Three). Stalin's moves in Czechoslovakia also failed to intimidate Tito, and the two Communist leaders broke publicly in June 1948. Although the West was slow to grasp the significance of Titoism, this dramatic separation showed that Communist countries were not necessarily part of one monolithic alliance that blindly followed the USSR.

Berlin Blockade

The coup in Czechoslovakia made the United States increasingly concerned with the tightening Soviet grip over Eastern Europe and Germany. As noted in Chapter Three, Germany was divided into four zones of military occupation after World War II, one each for France, the United States, Great Britain, and the USSR. An oddity of the arrangement was that Berlin, the capital of prewar Germany, was also divided among the four powers but was entirely surrounded by the Soviet zone. (See Map 3.5 for occupation zones.) All means of transportation and communication to the Western sectors of the former capital thus had to go through Soviet-occupied territory. In June 1948, ostensibly in response to a currency reform in the Western sectors of Berlin, Stalin ordered the closure of all land-access routes between Berlin and the Western occupation zones. West Berlin was isolated and surrounded by Soviet forces.

The Berlin blockade was a fateful event. Stalin would not allow the transport of food, fuel, or other basic necessities to the Western sectors; if no way could be found to supply West Berlin, the population would soon starve. Truman appeared to be forced to decide between two unpalatable alternatives: The United States could go to war against the huge Soviet army in eastern Germany to reestablish Western rights of access to Berlin, or it could allow the Soviets to control the

Map 4.1 NATO and the Warsaw Pact

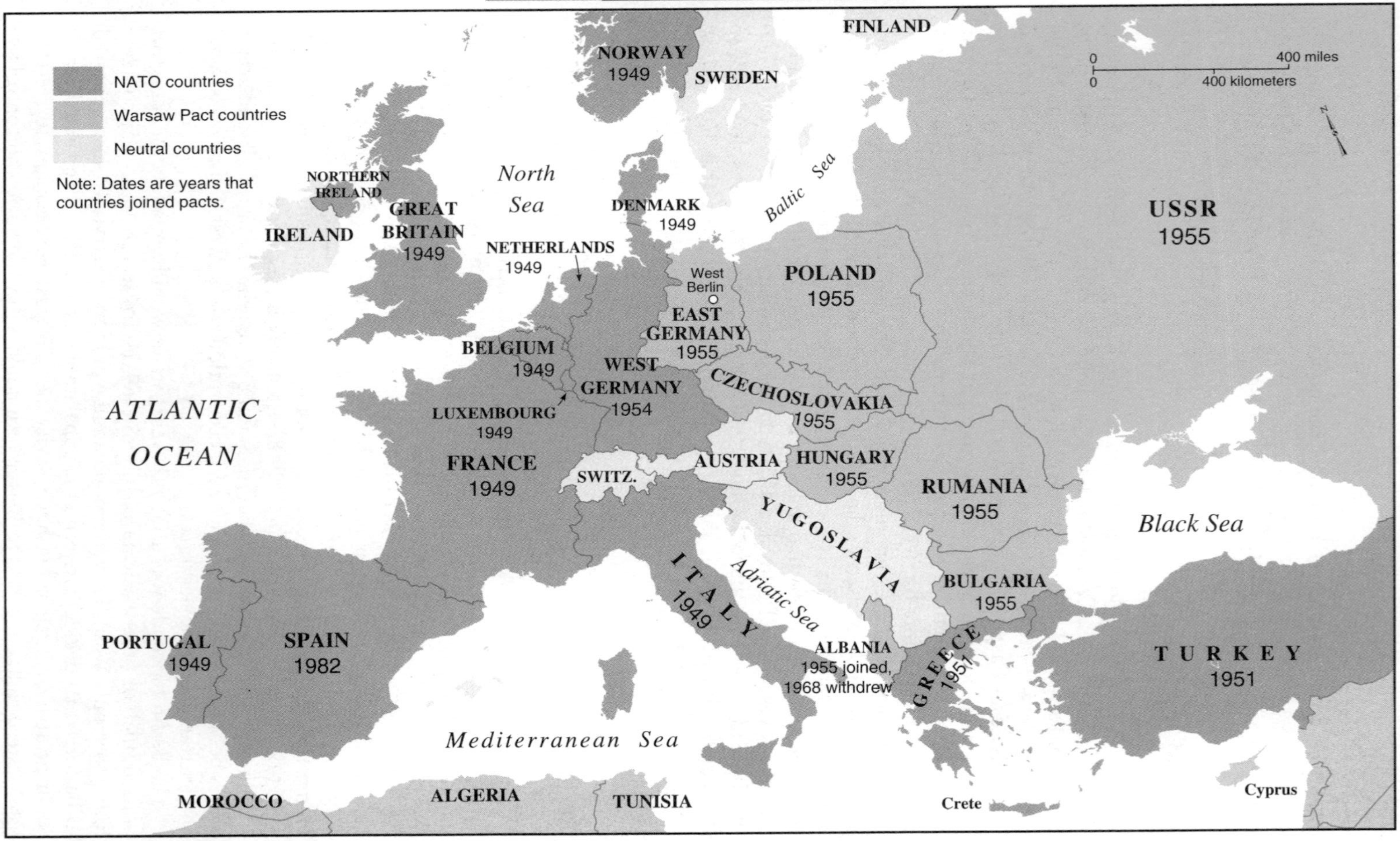

entire city, with horrendous results for West Berliners and a major defeat for the West. Truman and his advisors, however, came up with a third option: initiating a dramatic airlift of supplies to West Berlin. "Operation Vittles," as it was called, was a colossal undertaking to supply the 2.5 million West Berliners. At the height of the airlift, 4500 tons of supplies were flown in each day. At the same time, Truman moved B-29 bombers, the same type of aircraft that had dropped the two nuclear weapons on Japan in 1945, to bases in England. Stalin could have challenged the airlift, but that would have meant war with the Western allies, and he was not prepared to go so far. He halted the blockade in May 1949, though the airlift continued until September.

Stalin's attempt to use military force to gain political concessions failed. A serious crisis had passed without escalating to war. Many in the West believed that the failure of the Berlin blockade verified a prediction by George Kennan (see Spotlight box) that the Soviets would retreat when their efforts were resolutely resisted. Meanwhile, each side proceeded with the consolidation of its parts of occupied Germany. The West backed the formation of the Federal Republic of Germany, with its capital at Bonn, and the USSR formed the Democratic German Republic, with East Berlin as its capital. Each superpower had wanted a single German state on its own terms, but both sides realized after the Berlin blockade that neither could concede all of Germany to the other. Neither side could attain its first preference, so both settled for a divided Germany as their second choice, and the division of Germany thus resulted by default.

NATO Alliance

The Berlin blockade was intended in part to thwart a Western alliance, but actually helped to speed plans for a formal security agreement to counter what the Western countries perceived as Soviet aggression. In April 1949 the North Atlantic Treaty Organization (NATO) was established. The nations of Western Europe banded together with the United States and Canada to commit themselves to resisting Soviet aggression. In joining NATO, the United States effectively renounced isolationism and accepted membership in a peacetime "entangling alliance" for the first time in its history.

THE COLD WAR IN ASIA

Our account of the early Cold War years so far has concentrated on the centers of the conflict to the west and south of the Soviet Union in Europe and the Mediterranean, but conflict was also occurring in Asia. Here, in the early days of the Cold War, the centerpiece of the new competition was China.

By the end of World War II, many Americans had become quite attached to China, and they believed that Asia was actually the center of the conflict with the Soviet Union. The leader of the "Asia Firsters" was the general who had led the Allied war effort against Japan, Douglas MacArthur, who believed that Asia would "determine the course of history in the next ten thousand years" and criticized the Truman administration for concentrating too much on Europe, which he referred to as a "dying system." [15]

America's China policy dilemma became particularly acute after the war's end, when Communist forces led by Mao Zedong and the Nationalist government of Chiang Kai-shek resumed their civil war. Chiang's Nationalist party, the Kuomintang (KMT), had sunk in popularity because of rampant internal corruption and dictatorial practices. In a predicament that would recur throughout the Cold War, the United States found itself caught between the possibility of a future Communist regime viewed as a natural ally to the Soviet Union on the one hand and an unpopular and repressive right-wing government on the other. Predictably, U.S. policy took a middle position: The United States offered just enough economic aid and military assistance to further alienate the Chinese Communists but not enough to have a real chance of saving the KMT. Just as predictably, this strategy failed. In October 1949 the Communists finally won the civil war and established the People's Republic of China, while the Nationalists were driven offshore to the island of Taiwan.

The American government assumed that the victory of the Chinese Communist party would mean automatic alliance with their comrades in the USSR. The Soviets did offer guidance and assistance to Mao's Communist party. However, it is now known that even during the civil war, Stalin had qualms about a Chinese Communist victory and was not averse to doing business with the Nationalists. Stalin and Mao had significant differences of opinion similar to those between Stalin and Tito. A strong China under united Communist control might represent more of a threat to Soviet interests than a weakly divided China under the Nationalists. When presented with a conflict between Communist objectives and Soviet national interests, Stalin chose the latter, establishing a pattern that his successors in the Kremlin would often follow throughout the Cold War. The inherent tensions between Soviet and Chinese interests would eventually lead to hostilities between the two communist giants. In the 1940s, however, Chinese Communists would not have the opportunity to choose between the two superpowers. American antipathy to communism would preclude any possibility of reconciliation.

NSC-68

America enjoyed a monopoly on nuclear weapons until September 1949, when the USSR tested its first atomic bomb. The rapid development of the Soviet bomb (which can be attributed partially to espionage, but also to a massive "crash" program in the USSR) changed the nature of the conflict. Within the American government, key figures were clearly affected by the internal tensions that had been generated by the domestic crisis and by the recent American defeats. Many officials were beginning to think more in military terms rather than concentrating on the political and economic instruments that had been the focus of Kennan's approach adopted in the Truman Doctrine and the Marshall Plan. A document, **NSC-68**, was prepared by the National Security Council (NSC) to address the question of what was to be done to counter the spread of international communism.

NSC-68 called for a major expansion of America's armed forces, adding military instruments to the political and economic means of containment. This approach would significantly alter the form and content of U.S. foreign policy and would eventually lead to direct American military involvement in conflicts in Korea and Vietnam. President Truman, although he agreed with the concept and principles of NSC-68, was not prepared in early 1950 to accept a major escalation in defense spending. He feared that the United States could not afford any such increase and that high military spending would ruin the economy. Unexpected developments, however, soon changed Truman's mind.

Korea: The Turning Point

The escalating pressures on both the international and domestic scenes came to a head in Korea in 1950. After the Japanese surrender that ended World War II, Korea was divided by the victorious allies along the thirty-eighth parallel, with the north occupied by the Soviets and the south occupied by the United States. Despite the desire for union in both halves of Korea, the United States and the USSR were unable to agree to a formula for holding elections under the auspices of the United Nations (UN). The Soviets in particular objected to a national poll and instead held Soviet-style elections in the north, where only the Communist party had any chance of winning. At the head of the new Communist government was Kim Il-Sung, a youthful Korean Communist who had spent many years in the USSR and served as an officer in the Soviet army. (He remained in power until his death in 1994.) Confident in the loyalty of Kim's government, the USSR withdrew its occupation forces by January 1949. The United States was then under pressure to similarly withdraw from the south, which it did by the middle of that year. In early 1950, U.S. Secretary of State Dean Acheson appeared to write off Korea when he proposed a U.S. defense perimeter in Asia that seemed to exclude the country.

An event then occurred that pushed the Cold War past the point of no return. On June 25, 1950, North Korea launched a massive surprise attack against South Korea (see Map 4.2). Although Stalin probably did not instigate the North Korean attack, he undoubtedly acquiesced in it—grossly miscalculating the American reaction. This attack immediately brought to mind the lesson the West had learned at Munich: Aggression had to be checked, or aggressors would become bolder and more ambitious. American leaders saw the North Korean offensive as a major test of U.S. leadership and credibility in the same way that President George Bush, forty years later, would call the Iraqi invasion of Kuwait a threat to world order.

Because Moscow refused to participate in the United Nations Security Council debate on Korea, the Soviets were unable to veto a U.S.–framed initiative to send UN troops to Korea. (As Chapter Nine will explain, one veto by a permanent member is sufficient to reject a UN Security Council initiative. At the time of the debate on Korea, the USSR was boycotting the Security Council to protest the assignment of China's seat on the council to Chiang's KMT government on Taiwan rather than Mao's Communist PRC.) The Security Council authorized a military response to the invasion, and a U.S.–led coalition sent forces to oppose the North Korean offensive. (The pattern would be repeated forty years later, when the UN Security Council authorized another U.S.–led coalition to intervene in Kuwait in 1991 to counteract the Iraqi invasion of that Persian Gulf sheikdom.)

There is no doubt that the intervention of the United States and its allies saved South Korea. The Communists had almost overrun South Korea until, in September, UN forces commanded by MacArthur landed at Inchon behind North Korean lines, trapping and routing the North Korean troops. MacArthur pushed for approval of his plan to liberate North Korea and "unleash" Nationalist forces on Taiwan for an attack on China itself. Truman, however, did not particularly trust MacArthur and was intent on keeping the war limited to South Korean soil. Truman allowed the general to proceed after MacArthur assured him that the Soviets and Chinese would not intervene if the United States invaded North Korea.

MacArthur was wrong. As UN forces approached the Yalu River, on the border separating Korea and China, they were engaged by Chinese armies and forced to retreat. The Chinese had indirectly warned the United States, especially through a message from the Indian ambassador to China, that they would enter the conflict if U.S. forces threatened the Chinese border, but these signals were either not clearly received or were ignored. The Communists quickly pushed the UN forces back into South Korea once again. Continued disagreements between the president and MacArthur prompted Truman to relieve MacArthur of his command in April 1951.

UN forces regained most of Korea south of the thirty-eighth parallel, and UN and Communist forces spent two more years fighting on a line near the original division between North and South Korea. When Dwight D. Eisenhower became the U.S. president in January 1953, he immediately advised the Communists that in the event that the conflict in Korea could not be resolved, the United States "intended to move decisively without inhibition in our use of [nuclear] weapons, and would no longer be responsible for confining hostilities to the Korean Peninsula."[16] This warning, and growing success on the ground by Allied forces, encouraged the Communists to agree to a cease-fire in July 1953.

Korea was a turning point in the Cold War for several reasons. First, the war prompted the expansion of American military forces called for in NSC-68 and a similar buildup of NATO forces in Europe. Second, it stimulated American involvement in Asia and therefore heightened the confrontation with the Soviet Union and China. Third, the Korean War solidified the bipolar competition between the United States and the Soviet Union for clients around the globe, as the United States began to view Communist actions in every part of the world as a threat to U.S. interests. This globalist view of the U.S.–Soviet conflict contrasted with Kennan's original conception of containment, in which only North America, Western and Central Europe, and the Pacific coast of Asia were seen as areas of American vital interest.

Finally, although both the United States and USSR possessed them, nuclear weapons were not used in the war and fighting was restricted to Korean territory.

Map 4.2 **The Korean War**

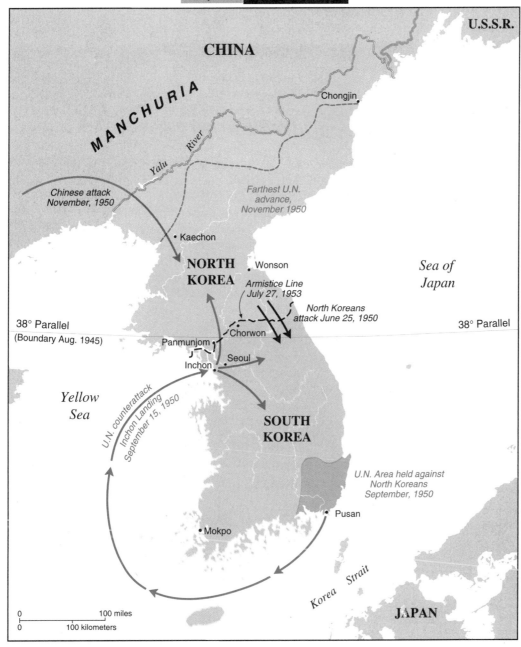

U.S.S.R.

CHINA

MANCHURIA

Chongjin

Yalu River

Chinese attack
November, 1950

Farthest U.N.
advance,
November 1950

• Kaechon

NORTH
KOREA

• Wonson

Sea of
Japan

Armistice Line
July 27, 1953

North Koreans
attack June 25, 1950

38° Parallel
(Boundary Aug. 1945)

Chorwon

38° Parallel

Panmunjom

Seoul

Inchon

Yellow
Sea

U.N. counterattack
Inchon Landing
September 15, 1950

SOUTH
KOREA

U.N. Area held against
North Koreans
September, 1950

• Mokpo

• Pusan

0   100 miles
0   100 kilometers

Korea Strait

JAPAN

The conflict was thus referred to as a **limited war,** fought for limited goals by limited means, which set a pattern for restricted actions throughout the Cold War period. The Korean War thus irrevocably moved the containment effort of the West to the military sphere without escalating into actual military conflict between the superpowers. As the destructive potential of nuclear weapons made total war unthinkable, the superpowers would have to carry on their global conflict by more subtle means.

RELAXATION AND RENEWAL OF TENSIONS, 1953–1957

This new phase began in early 1953, with Stalin's death and the beginning of Dwight D. Eisenhower's first term as president of the United States. As would become the case often throughout the Cold War, the domestic context of the two superpowers moved in opposing directions. In the United States, the new leadership under Eisenhower and his secretary of state, John Foster Dulles, was committed to a continued European-oriented version of American foreign policy (as opposed to the Asia-first strategy of conservative Republicans). Dulles also espoused a highly moralistic and activist view of the confrontation with international communism. He believed that the United States should attempt to "roll back" Communist gains rather than be satisfied simply with containing them in their post–World War II borders.

On the Soviet side, the top officials were preoccupied with resolving the leadership struggle that emerged with Stalin's demise. The Soviet political system lacked a constitutional means for the transfer of political power. Thus, the change from one leader to the next was a major problem in the Soviet Union at a time when the focus was on domestic issues. This was not clearly understood in Washington, leading many critics to argue that the United States missed an opportunity for breaking through the deep hostility between the United States and the USSR.

New Leaders, New Challenges

The official communiqué announcing Stalin's death to the Soviet population stressed the necessity of "prevention of any kind of disorder and panic."[17] This declaration provides a revealing insight into the disarray into which the leader's death had plunged his nation. Stalin's policies, directed toward the relentless mobilization of human and material resources and the forging of a heavy industrial base and superior military strength, to the neglect of consumer goods and agricultural production, exacted a steady toll on the Soviet people. His successors were faced with a difficult domestic agenda of improving the standard of living while departing from the terror tactics employed by Stalin. Foreign-policy issues threatened to divert the energy and resources needed for this ambitious domestic agenda. Reflective of the changes in Soviet policy in the post-Stalin era, an agreement was reached in 1955 between the major powers for the neutralization of

Austria, which had been jointly occupied by the Soviets and the Western Allies after World War II.

Spirit of Geneva

A 1955 summit meeting in Geneva, attended by the leaders of the two superpowers plus Britain and France, raised hope for further relaxation of East-West tensions. At the summit, Eisenhower proposed mutual aerial inspection as a means to build trust and confidence. Although this "Open Skies" proposal was not accepted by the Soviets, a cultural exchange agreement was concluded that seemed to indicate a cooling of tensions. At about the same time, Nikita Khrushchev, the key Kremlin political leader who eventually emerged after Stalin, denounced Stalin's crimes. His "secret" speech before the Twentieth Congress of the Communist party of the Soviet Union in 1956 (the full text of which was not published in the USSR until decades later) indicated potential changes in Soviet foreign and domestic policy.

Regional Tensions Return

Despite these positive developments, a variety of conflictual issues remained around the world. In Eastern Europe, the end of the Stalin era and the promise of liberation through "rollback" by America led to rioting in East Berlin against the Communist regime in 1953, and to growing problems in Poland. As it turned out, however, the Eisenhower administration was wary of intervening in the Soviet Union's "backyard" lest it provoke a major war. This was demonstrated again in 1956, when widespread unrest in Poland brought to power a new Polish Communist regime that strove for a greater degree of autonomy from Moscow. A mass revolt that same year in Hungary also brought about a change in the government. Conceivably, Moscow might have eventually come to tolerate the new regime in Budapest, but when it announced its intention to leave the Warsaw Pact, it was smashed by Soviet forces and a more compliant Hungarian government installed. Despite previous talk of "rollback," the United States and its NATO allies did little but greet refugees streaming into the West.

In Asia the conflict between the Communist People's Republic of China (the PRC or "mainland China") and the Nationalist Republic of China (on Taiwan) after the civil war remained a source of continuing tension. The United States reinforced its relations with the Nationalist Chinese, not only to prevent a forceful Communist attack but also to quell the Nationalists' temptation to challenge the Communists' control on the mainland. In 1954 and 1955, air and naval incidents between the PRC and the American-backed government on Taiwan gradually intensified. After many threats and much posturing on both sides, however, the crisis temporarily abated. Nevertheless, by the mid-1950s, conflicts throughout the world confirmed that the post-Stalin era would not lead to an end to the Cold War. As would happen repeatedly, a promising prospect of relaxation in tensions was followed by renewed antagonism.

Third World

As Chapters Two and Three have outlined, the European empires expanded prodigiously in the eighteenth and nineteenth centuries. By the early twentieth century, however, the spread of nationalism throughout Europe led to calls for independence in the colonial world, and conflicts among the imperial powers further undermined their collective hold on the world outside Europe. The two world wars greatly weakened all the great powers but the United States and the USSR. Particularly in the Middle East and Asia, the two wars strengthened the former colonies that were gaining their independence because the great powers competed for the locals' support against their foes. Finally, the wars demonstrated that the strength of the colonial powers was much weaker than the indigenous peoples had thought. For example, in Indochina the Japanese exposed the weakness of the French when Tokyo was able to defeat them. When the Allies, in turn, defeated the Japanese, they revealed Japan's weakness as well.

In the war's aftermath, native cultures everywhere were emboldened to seek independence, and one by one the weakened imperial powers concluded that these territories were not worth keeping at the military, political, and economic costs they would take to maintain. This conclusion was not an easy one to reach; in some areas, such as Algeria and Vietnam, the decision to retreat from empire was made only after bitter and protracted war between nationalist movements and the colonial power. Ultimately, history had imposed a harsh irony on the imperial powers. From Vietnam to Algeria to India to Palestine to Kenya, European ideas of nationalism and political sovereignty served to undermine the colonial powers' legitimacy throughout the **Third World.** The age of empire was over.

Yet in the wake of imperialism, power vacuums began to emerge as the European powers withdrew their forces and political control. In the zero-sum political environment of the Cold War, the superpowers viewed each newly independent country in what became known as the Third World (belong neither to the East nor the West) as a potential ally or an opportunity for the other side to expand its power and influence. Thus, under Khrushchev's aggressive leadership in the 1950s, Moscow began to expand its influence by establishing political ties with countries that had been previously controlled by European colonial empires, such as India, Egypt, Syria, and Indonesia. Many of these Third World countries emerged on the international scene with serious internal problems. Many were politically unstable and militarily and economically weak. This combination of factors created strategic uncertainties that the superpowers believed they could ignore only at peril to themselves. As a result, Third World countries were drawn into the bipolar conflict of the Cold War, which further globalized the superpower rivalry and multiplied the number of locations where Soviet and American interests collided. (These developments will be discussed in more detail in Chapter Five.)

In the early phases of the Cold War in the Third World, U.S. policy focused on intervening in countries where local nationalists, many of whom were viewed as being agents of the global Soviet Communist regime, were implementing change in their countries. In 1953 the CIA engineered a coup that overthrew Iranian Premier Mohammed Mossadegh, who sought to nationalize British-controlled oil fields in Iran, and restored the Shah, Muhammad Reza Pahlavi, to power. The following year, another CIA-backed coup ousted Guatemalan President Jacobo Arbenz, whom the United States believed to be heavily influenced and supported by Communists, and replaced him with the staunchly anticommunist Castillo Armas.

In other parts of the developing world, the United States became involved in conflicts arising from decolonization. In 1956 Egypt's President Gamal Abdel Nasser nationalized the Suez Canal, which had been owned by an Anglo-French consortium. The American government believed that the matter could be settled by negotiations, but Britain and France saw Nasser's action as directly challenging their continued influence in the Middle East. Without America's knowledge, Britain, France, and Israel secretly colluded to attack and topple Nasser's regime. Israeli forces overran the Sinai, but in order to keep up the pretense that no collusion had occurred, the British and French had to wait to move their forces into place until Egypt had refused their ultimatum. By the time they "intervened" in the conflict, a furious Eisenhower was exerting economic and diplomatic pressure on them to stop. The Soviets backed Egypt with blustering threats against Britain, France, and Israel when the crisis was abating. In the end, Nasser remained in power, the Suez Canal was blocked for many months, Britain and France were humiliated, and the United States replaced them as the major Western influence in the Middle East. (For more on the Suez Crisis and its aftermath, see Chapter Five.)

American involvement in Vietnam began in 1945 and accelerated in 1954, when Communist-led Vietminh rebels besieged and defeated French forces at Dien Bien Phu in northern Vietnam. At one time, the United States might have been tempted to support Ho Chi Minh, the leader of the Communist resistance, because he was a major anticolonialist figure who quoted from the American Declaration of Independence when he proclaimed the end of French rule in his country. But after the Korean War, the United States was preoccupied with stopping communism in Asia, vowing to permit "No More Koreas." Washington also needed France's political support in Europe, and France pressed for American support in Indochina in return. Thus, the United States backed the French, and after their defeat accepted the division of Vietnam into a Communist North and Western-backed South as a transitional measure until nationwide elections could be held. Washington quickly replaced Paris as the key sponsor of the new regime in Saigon, the capital of South Vietnam.

Nonaligned Movement

Moscow and Washington were not always able to gain influence over newly independent Third World states, as their governments often found it beneficial to play one superpower against the other. As a result, the **Nonaligned Movement** emerged in international politics in the mid-1950s, with India's Jawaharlal Nehru, Egyptian President Nasser, and Yugoslavia's Tito in the forefront of its leadership. By playing the United States against the Soviet Union, these countries attempted to gain aid from the competing superpowers. Soviet technological advances impressed many newly independent regimes, and the Soviet model of centralized, state-controlled economic and political development was initially quite attractive to developing countries. In addition to providing an example (for a time) of a successful alternative to capitalism, the Soviets established close relations with a wide variety of Third World states, including Indonesia, Ghana, India, Egypt, Syria, Iraq, and Algeria. Moscow provided aid in the form of weapons, agricultural and industrial machinery, and military and technical advisors. During the Cold War, educational exchange programs allowed an estimated 72,000 students from Third World countries to attend learning institutions in the USSR.

The United States, however, was wary of the Nonaligned Movement, believing that it facilitated the growth of Soviet influence in the developing world. In response, Washington stepped up military and economic assistance to states it considered more reliable as U.S. allies, such as Nicaragua, Iran, and South Vietnam—before anti–U.S. governments came to power in those nations. As a result, a considerable amount of aid flowed from both superpowers to the developing world, but not in the manner the originators of the Nonaligned Movement had intended.

TO THE BRINK AND BACK, 1957–1964

A new phase in the Cold War began with continued escalation of tension between the two superpowers. As before, this wave of confrontation ebbed and flowed as events alternatively strained and improved East-West relations.

Sputnik

After the Suez debacle, the Communist world appeared to the United States to be on the offensive. China's Mao asserted in a 1957 speech that "the international situation has reached a turning point. . . . I think the characteristic of the situation today is the East wind prevailing over the West wind."[18] In addition to gaining new allies in various Third World countries, the Soviet economy and technological progress seemed to be growing. Most spectacularly, the Soviets launched the world's first artificial satellite, Sputnik, which orbited the earth in October 1957. This accomplishment caused many in the West to fear that the Soviets had gained a major technological advantage over the United States that could be exploited for military purposes. Khrushchev deliberately fed those fears, never missing an opportunity to mention the USSR's arsenal of rocket weapons, although the Soviets would not actually deploy missiles capable of striking the United States until 1960.[19]

Nevertheless, the launch of Sputnik signaled to many that the U.S. strategic doctrine of **massive retaliation** against any Communist attack anywhere in the world was no longer viable, because the USSR now seemed able to strike back against American territory. The Eisenhower administration was blamed for allowing a purported "missile gap" to develop, which presidential candidate John F. Kennedy exploited, although it was later proved that such a gap had never existed. The Eisenhower administration had not moved to markedly change its defense policies because it was confident (with good reason) that the threat to the United States was minimal.

The psychological effect of the development of strategic missiles, however, was undeniable. For the first time, Americans were confronted with the possibility that they could become immediate victims in a nuclear war. A peace culture emerged in reaction to these developments, epitomized by the comment by renowned British philosopher Bertrand Russell that civilization was "better red than dead." Among other things, the Gaither Committee report, a presidential commission study, called for the creation of nationwide fallout shelters. This period was famous for a proliferation of antinuclear literature and art warning of the dangers inherent in destructive superpower confrontations. Nevil Shute's novel *On the Beach* tells a morose story about the last survivors of a nuclear war, while Stanley Kubrick's comedy film *Dr. Strangelove* portrays a mad American officer who brings the world to its final disaster with the help of warmongering generals and scientists.

Quemoy and Matsu

Possibly in an attempt to test Soviet and American willingness to intervene militarily in east Asia, the Chinese Communists in 1958 resumed the shelling of two islands off the Taiwanese coast, Quemoy and Matsu. Chiang, the Chinese Nationalist leader, had placed one-third of his armed forces on these two islands in the hopes that the United States would come to their defense and provide backing for his regime. The United States threatened war, but the Soviets disappointed their Chinese allies by withholding strong support, and China eventually ceased the shelling.

Berlin and Cuba

Although fear of the possibility of nuclear war and the political sting of recent Soviet gains spread throughout the West, Khrushchev felt strong enough to press the USSR's advantage. In November 1958 he suddenly announced that the Soviet Union had decided to renounce the remnants of the joint Allied occupation regime in Berlin. In subsequent notes to the United States, Britain, and France, he demanded that they withdraw their occupation forces from West Berlin, declare it a demilitarized "free city," and negotiate directly with the German Democratic Republic (East Germany) on terms of access to the city. He threatened that if the

Western powers did not make an agreement with the East Germans within six months, the Soviet Union would give the German Democratic Republic control of Western military supply routes to Berlin. This action was tantamount to renouncing the post–World War II arrangements for Germany, and it revived memories of the darkest days of the Berlin blockade. With the backing of its NATO allies, the United States refused to accede to Khrushchev's demands, and Dulles replied that NATO would oppose any attempt to change the status of Berlin "if need be by military force." [20]

At the same time, a new arena of East-West conflict was emerging closer to American shores. A revolution brought Fidel Castro (see box) to power in Cuba in January 1959. Castro's forces had overthrown a much-hated dictator, Fulgencio Batista, who had maintained close ties to the United States. Washington reacted strongly to Castro's accession to power, especially when his pro-Communist leanings became apparent. When the United States levied sanctions on Cuba, Castro turned to the USSR for aid. The existence of a Soviet-supported regime just ninety miles off the coast of Florida inflamed U.S. leaders and fomented fears that other countries in Latin America would follow Cuba into the Soviet camp.

▧ Fidel Castro

SOURCE: AP/Wide World

Fidel

Fidel Castro is one of the Cold War's most successful and influential revolutionary leaders. Born the son of a farm laborer and a household servant in 1926, Castro recalled threatening to burn the house down unless he was sent to school. He went on to earn a law degree in his native Cuba, but not before both taking part in an abortive attempt to overthrow the government of the Dominican Republic and playing minor-league baseball as part of the New York Yankees organization.

Castro spent most of his legal career doing pro bono work on behalf of Cuba's poor and attempted to fight corruption by running for political office, but he soon abandoned hope for change by constitutional means. In 1953 he and his brother Raul led an abortive attack on an army barracks in Santiago de Cuba. Castro was imprisoned by Batista's government, but was later released and went to Mexico. In 1956 he set out with eighty-one other rebels on a barely seaworthy boat to land in Cuba and join a revolt against Batista, but the expedition failed miserably, and Castro and his band retreated to the rugged Sierra Maestra to continue the fight. Waging a guerrilla war against Batista, Castro's forces never numbered more than 300, but he steadily gained support among Cuba's peasants. Finally, in late 1958, Batista's forces collapsed and a revolutionary junta led by Castro gained control of Cuba on January 1, 1959.

Once in power, Castro initiated a program of agrarian reforms. He also demanded the nationalization of U.S. property in Cuba, at first expressing willingness to compensate American owners but later confiscating foreign property. These actions and Castro's revolutionary ideology quickly soured relations between Havana and Washington, and the United States became increasingly convinced that Castro's regime was oriented toward communism. When the United States placed economic sanctions on Cuba, Castro turned to the USSR for support and eventually became Moscow's most valuable ally in the Western Hemisphere.

The clumsy attempt to overthrow his government in the Bay of Pigs fiasco in 1961 destroyed any hope of reconciliation with the United States, and there is some evidence suggesting that Castro requested Soviet missiles to defend his regime. For whatever reasons, the USSR subsequently attempted to base missiles in Cuba, which led to the Cuban Missile Crisis in 1962.

Throughout the 1970s Castro became a major proponent of revolution in the Third World, providing arms to Communist insurgents in Central America and sending Cuban troops to fight for leftist regimes in Africa. Meanwhile, the USSR sent huge subsidies to prop up Cuba's economy, donating an estimated $7 billion annually in the 1980s. After Mikhail Gorbachev came to power in Moscow and the USSR adopted less confrontational policies, many Soviets began to see Castro's Cuba as more liability than asset, and subsidies were drastically cut before the collapse of the USSR in 1991.

Unlike Communist leaders in Eastern Europe, however, Castro survived the demise of Soviet communism, and as of 1998 he was still Cuba's leader and a triumphant role model to many Latin American revolutionary socialists. The future of Cuban Communism, however, appears questionable at best, and the unprecedented visit of Pope John Paul II to Cuba in 1998 may have been a signal that even Fidel realizes that major reforms will be required to continue his regime into the twenty-first century.

Summitry

Despite Soviet technological achievements and their confident posture, it is now widely known that the USSR was much weaker in the mid- and late 1950s than it appeared at the time. Though Soviet propaganda emphasized the USSR's achievements in military and space technology, U.S. intelligence, including flights of the secret U-2 spy plane over the Soviet Union, revealed to Eisenhower that American military power was still superior to Soviet capabilities. The Soviet Union and its allies also failed to catch their Western competitors in terms of gross national product, per capita income, consumption, or any other major economic indicator. In many Third World countries, although the Soviets seemed to be gaining at America's expense as they offered aid for major projects, such as Egypt's Aswan Dam, Soviet aid did not always lead to a pro-Soviet political orientation. In the Middle East, bitter disputes between pro- and anti-Nasser Arab states eroded Soviet influence in the region.[21] Additionally, the Sino-Soviet dispute, exacerbated by Moscow's refusal to assist China in developing nuclear weapons, would dominate Communist politics for the next three decades.

In this environment of apparent Communist strength and actual Soviet weakness, Khrushchev took advantage of a diplomatic opening created by the death of staunchly anticommunist Secretary of State Dulles in May 1959 to propose a meeting with Eisenhower. In September 1959 Khrushchev traveled throughout the United States, meeting the president at Camp David, mingling with Hollywood stars such as Marilyn Monroe and Frank Sinatra, and visiting American families in San Francisco. A summit was scheduled to be held in Paris the next year, which was to be followed by a return visit by President Eisenhower to Moscow. It was hoped that major breakthroughs, such as a settlement of the Berlin issue and a nuclear test ban treaty, would be agreed upon at the planned summits.

The U-2 Incident

This interlude of relative harmony between the two superpowers proved short-lived, however. The European allies were alarmed by the possibility that the United States might act on the German question without taking their interests into account. The conservative West German government, under Konrad Adenauer, pressed for a tough American stance at the Paris meeting. Charles de Gaulle, the French president, was also suspicious of American moves.

On May 1, 1960, the Soviets shot down a U-2 spy plane 1200 miles inside the USSR, something that American officials had believed impossible. When Washington initially denied that any overflight of Soviet airspace had occurred, Khrushchev exhibited both the wreckage of the plane and the pilot, Francis Gary Powers, who had been captured alive. (Powers was released in 1962 in exchange for captured Soviet master spy Rudolf Abel.) As the leaders of the United States, USSR, France, and Britain gathered in Paris for the summit meeting, the premier issued threats and demanded that Eisenhower apologize for violating Soviet airspace. He added that whatever the United States did about the U-2 incident, it would be necessary for Eisenhower to cancel his scheduled visit to Russia. The president refused to apologize, and in fact he blamed Soviet actions for necessitating American espionage activities. Khrushchev may have already written off the possibility of a summit before the U-2 incident, but the affair gave him an opportunity to place the blame for its collapse on the United States. In any case, the summit never took place, and the rivalry between the superpowers continued with renewed vehemence.

JFK, Cold Warrior

Eisenhower's vice president, Richard Nixon, narrowly lost the 1960 presidential election, and in 1961 John F. Kennedy (JFK) took office, committed to a more activist American foreign policy. Seeking a wider range of strategic options, the Kennedy administration instituted the doctrine of **flexible response,** which was designed to correct the shortcomings of massive retaliation. Under the new strategy, the United States would be prepared to respond in kind to Soviet moves on a variety of levels, from guerrilla war through conventional challenges to the ultimate stage of nuclear war. Rather than relying solely on nuclear deterrence, flexible response sought to increase America's credibility in dealing with a wide range of security problems by providing a correspondingly wide range of options for dealing with threats.

Committed to taking a new approach to U.S. foreign policy, the new administration had its work cut out for it. The first challenge Kennedy faced involved redressing the supposed "missile gap." Rapid U.S. production of bombers, **intercontinental ballistic missiles** (ICBMs), and **submarine-launched ballistic missiles** (SLBMs) provided a balanced strategic triad of land-, sea-, and air-based weapons (see Chapter Eleven). In a classic example of the security dilemma in action, Khrushchev's bluff that the USSR could outproduce the United States in missiles had been called, because the Soviet Union had actually developed only a minimal missile capability by the early 1960s, and the strategic balance remained in America's favor throughout his tenure in the Kremlin.

Although the "missile gap" proved to be a hoax, the United States nevertheless still appeared weak. In March 1961, the CIA orchestrated an invasion by Cuban exiles at the Bay of Pigs intended to provoke a general rebellion against Castro and topple his government. The invasion, poorly planned and executed, ended in disaster when Castro's forces easily defeated the invaders. This ham-handed attempt to unseat Castro only reinforced the image of declining American power.

Kennedy tried to counteract Soviet influence in developing countries with comprehensive programs of technical assistance (including the Peace Corps, which Kennedy created) and economic and military aid, but the United States continued to face hard choices in its policies in the Third World. Kennedy's comments on the repressive Trujillo regime in the Dominican Republic illustrated the problem:

There are three possibilities in a descending order of preference: a decent democratic regime, a continuation of the Trujillo regime [a right-wing dictatorship], or a

Castro regime. We ought to aim at the first, but we really can't renounce the second until we are sure that we can avoid the third.[22]

Berlin Wall

Meanwhile, back in Europe, tensions in Germany increased steadily. East German refugees, a high proportion of whom were professionals, intellectuals, and skilled workers, continued to flee to the west, creating a serious "brain drain" for East Germany. To stanch the flow of refugees, the East German government suggested the creation of a barrier around West Berlin, and Khrushchev agreed. Without warning, on August 13, 1961, barbed wire barricades were thrown up all around the city and were soon replaced with concrete. The Western sectors were surrounded by the Berlin Wall. The Western Allies would have had to resort to force to remove the wall, but they were unwilling to take that risk, although at one point during the crisis, U.S. and Soviet tanks confronted each other at the Brandenburg Gate on the dividing line between East and West Berlin. The U.S. government portrayed the outcome of this new Berlin crisis as a win for the West, as West Berlin remained in Allied hands, but it was never Khrushchev's intention to take over the Western sectors. Both sides could therefore claim victory, but the fact remained that Kennedy had been unable to respond effectively to a Soviet challenge.

Cuban Missile Crisis

By 1962 the United States was far ahead of the USSR in long-range missile capability, but Khrushchev may still have believed that the young American president lacked the resolve necessary to prevail in a direct confrontation. Sometime in 1962 the Soviet leader ordered offensive missiles to be secretly placed in Cuba. His motives in doing so remain unclear. He may have been trying to exploit a perceived American political weakness, to partially redress the U.S.–Soviet strategic balance, to forestall another attempt to overthrow Castro, or all of the above. Apparently, he assumed that the deployment could be kept secret until the missiles were operational, whereupon Washington would be forced to accept their presence as it had been forced to accept the sudden construction of the Berlin Wall.

Khrushchev's gamble failed, however, when U.S. intelligence discovered the missiles in October 1962, before Soviet crews could make them operational. The resulting confrontation was the most acute crisis of the Cold War. Kennedy had publicly warned Khrushchev that he could never allow the Soviet Union to station offensive weapons on Cuba. The young president, under attack by Republicans for his supposed soft policy on Cuba, could not allow the Soviets to achieve a major political victory by stationing nuclear weapons so close to American shores. (The film *The Missiles of October* dramatizes the dilemma for Kennedy and his advisors.)

In order to compel Khrushchev to withdraw the missiles from Cuba, Kennedy and his advisors decided to impose a blockade on all shipments of weapons to the

LAUNCH POSITION

MISSILE-READY TENTS

MISSILE ERECTORS

▌ Photos like this one, taken from an American U-2 spy plane, proved that the USSR was secretly deploying
▌ nuclear-armed missiles in Cuba in 1962.   SOURCE: AP/Wide World

island. When he revealed the missiles' existence to the world and announced the blockade on Cuba, Kennedy demanded the removal of the missiles, warning that their use against any country in the Western Hemisphere would be regarded as an attack by the USSR against the United States. The possibility of nuclear war seemed closer during the Cuban Missile Crisis than at any other time before or since. If the USSR did not back down, the United States clearly intended to remove the missile sites by military action, which would have involved combat between Soviet and American forces.

Because the United States possessed conventional military superiority in the Caribbean region and held an indisputable advantage in strategic nuclear forces, once Khrushchev's bluff was called, he had no real choice but to back down. In exchange for the removal of the missiles, the United States promised not to invade Cuba again and to withdraw its own short-range Jupiter missiles from Turkey (a withdrawal Kennedy had previously ordered but that had not been implemented). Despite these gestures intended to avoid the humiliation of its adversary, the crisis ended with an embarrassing defeat for Moscow.[23]

The Cuban Missile Crisis had a number of important consequences. First, and paradoxically, one of the initial results of the crisis was a sudden abatement in Cold War tensions. Having confronted each other at the brink of war, both Kennedy and Khrushchev enjoyed the opportunity to reduce hostilities through a series of U.S.–Soviet agreements, including a limited nuclear test ban treaty and the establishment of a telegraphic "Hot Line" that enabled Moscow and Washington to communicate with each other instantly in case of a crisis anywhere in the world. As Kennedy put it, "Relations with the Soviet Union could now be contained within the framework of mutual awareness of the impossibility of achieving any gains through war."[24]

Second, however, Soviet leaders set about challenging America's strategic nuclear superiority with renewed urgency. The Kremlin attempted to catch up with the United States, determined that it would never again be caught in as weak a position as it had been in the Cuban Missile Crisis. The USSR achieved strategic parity with the United States by the late 1960s, but only at tremendous cost. Moscow's strategic programs diverted vast human and material resources away from development of industry, technology, and social welfare, creating hardships and distortions that would eventually lead to the collapse of the Soviet economy and political system.

Finally, after Washington demonstrated its resolve and military strength in the missile crisis, many Americans became overconfident, believing that the United States could accomplish any task in foreign policy to which it was fully committed. Whereas, in the period leading up to the Cuban Missile Crisis, the United States had overestimated Soviet power, it now underestimated the difficulties of containing communism in the Third World.

INTENSIFIED COMPETITION, 1964–1968

Once again, another promising turn in the Cold War was quickly reversed. The assassination of Kennedy in November 1963 and the overthrow of Khrushchev the following year brought new teams of leaders to both capitals. Hostile tendencies that Kennedy and Khrushchev had endeavored to overcome were gradually reinforced. The new Soviet leaders, Leonid Brezhnev and Aleksey Kosygin, increased military spending (especially on strategic weapons), sustained repressive regimes in Eastern Europe, and found themselves in an intensified competition with China.

Much like his predecessor Harry Truman, the new U.S. president, Lyndon B. Johnson (LBJ), had little experience and, initially, not much interest in foreign policy, but he was nevertheless committed to a strong anticommunist position worldwide. His administration saw both China and the USSR as dangerous threats, and these fears were reinforced by China's test of an atomic bomb in October 1964.

What Would You Do ?

You are the leader of the Soviet Union in 1962. Someone in the Politburo has presented you with a risky, yet possibly golden, opportunity to extend your global influence. It involves the secret installation of missiles—capable of striking the United States—in Cuba.

If successful, the ploy could accomplish several important foreign- and domestic-policy objectives simultaneously. First, it could redress the strategic imbalance with the American capitalist ruling class and offer you a bargaining chip by which you could gain the removal of U.S. Jupiter missiles in Turkey. Second, it offers a potential means of deterring another imperialist invasion against Castro; after all, having failed miserably to oust Castro in the Bay of Pigs fiasco, the United States is even less likely to repeat this action against a nuclearized Cuba. Third, it provides a chance to convince the Chinese that "peaceful coexistence" with the U.S. imperialists does not mean you are unwilling to seize opportunities to extend Communist influence in the Third World, thereby pulling China back into your camp. Finally, it could boost your popularity at home.

On the other hand, if the ploy is unsuccessful, it could be prohibitively expensive. First, instead of treating the move as a fait accompli, as it did with the construction of the Berlin Wall, the U.S. imperialists could call your bluff and demand removal of the missiles. You are aware from intelligence reports that the U.S. president is still under tremendous pressure from the opposition Republican party to "get tough" with Castro. The United States might actually remove the missiles and Castro through a full-scale invasion and/or air strike. Second, it could further alienate the PRC leadership and possibly increase Communist China's influence in the Third World. Finally, it could provoke a military or a party coup against you.

This is a risky decision.

What would you do ?

American fears of the spread of Castroism in Latin America reached new heights. As a result, the number of authoritarian dictatorships increased, with implicit or explicit American encouragement and assistance. In April 1965 Johnson sent U.S. Marines to thwart a move that would have returned to power the elected president of the Dominican Republic, Juan Bosch, who had replaced the assassinated dictator Trujillo. Bosch had in turn been ousted by the military, but Johnson feared the instability that was accompanying the attempted return to democracy. He seemed comfortable enough with the junta that had returned that country to authoritarianism, as long as the regime could keep the Caribbean country out of the reach of communism. In Johnson's own words, "We don't propose to sit here in our rocking chair with our hands folded and let the Communists set up any government in the Western Hemisphere."[25] In the end, after American intervention, new elections were held in the Dominican Republic and a conservative president was chosen.

The Cold War had now reached a point of tragic irony. The period after the Cuban Missile Crisis boiled over with U.S. self-confidence and zeal. Rushing about from one trouble spot to another, America almost seemed destined to trip over its own power. It stumbled and fell over Vietnam.

Vietnam

In 1960 a guerrilla movement officially known as the National Liberation Front but commonly referred to as the Vietcong began to attack the American-backed government of South Vietnamese President Ngo Dinh Diem with strong support from North Vietnam. Diem's policies had alienated various sectors of the South Vietnamese population, especially in the countryside, providing opportunities for Communist influence. Kennedy had attempted to use Vietnam to show that it was possible to defeat communist-backed wars of national liberation, and he increased American military and economic aid to the South. Building upon the several hundred advisors sent by Eisenhower, Kennedy increased U.S. military personnel to 16,000 by 1963. Nevertheless, Diem's position continued to deteriorate, and he was killed in 1963 (two weeks before JFK was assassinated) in a military coup to which the United States acquiesced. A succession of generals followed as president, each ousted by a new military figure hoping to pursue the war more effectively and gain the spoils of power for himself.

It became clear by 1965 that stronger American intervention would be required in order to prevent a Vietcong victory in the South. President Johnson was forced to choose between withdrawal, an intermediate level of escalation, or full-scale war. LBJ initially chose the middle option for U.S. intervention, which meant an immediate bombing campaign of the North and deployment of ground forces to protect air bases. As the war progressed, however, the administration repeatedly determined that more troops were required and continued to send more, only to conclude that still more forces were needed.

By mid-1968, 500,000 American troops were fighting in Vietnam, but the United States was no closer than before to achieving the military or political breakthrough necessary to salvage the South Vietnamese regime and permit U.S. withdrawal. American casualties mounted, eventually numbering 58,000 deaths. The seemingly endless and fruitless intervention in Vietnam turned the American public against the war, diminished the public's enthusiasm for the competition with the USSR, and compromised U.S. credibility with many of its allies, especially in Europe. Meanwhile, Moscow sought to capitalize on America's diminished prestige and weakened political will to resist Soviet expansion. In order to compete with China for influence in North Vietnam, Moscow provided Hanoi with military and economic assistance. Thus, the Vietnam War enabled the Soviet Union to increase its standing throughout the Third World while the United States became vilified for conducting an ineffective campaign that resulted in more than 2.5 million military and civilian deaths.[26]

The Six-Day War

While the U.S. focused its attention on Vietnam, the Soviets were concerned that their heavy investment in Arab allies such as Egypt, Syria, and Iraq was being undermined by tensions between the Arab states. The USSR attempted to unite its quarreling clients and secure their allegiance by inflating the threat posed to them by Israel, but when Moscow spread false reports about a purported Israeli invasion of Syria in May 1967, the strategy backfired. Egypt demanded the withdrawal of the UN truce supervision force in the Sinai (which had been in place since the Arab-Israeli war of 1956) and announced a blockade of the approaches to Israel's southern port of Eilat. In the ensuing crisis, Egypt unified the Arab world in preparation for another war with Israel. Encircled by Arab armies, Israel decided that another war was now inevitable, and that a preemptive attack offered the only chance for victory and survival. Israel launched its attack in June and defeated the Arab armies with stunning speed, capturing the Sinai Peninsula and Gaza Strip from Egypt, the Golan Heights from Syria, and East Jerusalem and the West Bank from Jordan in only six days. Israel's occupation of these territories redefined the political and strategic landscape of the Middle East and led both superpowers to increase their involvement in the region and its many conflicts (see Chapter Five).

The Prague Spring

The tense period precipitated by American intervention in Vietnam reached its apex in September 1968. A new leadership in Czechoslovakia had attempted to avoid the mistakes of Hungarian rebels in 1956. Czech reformers under Alexander Dubcek reassured the Soviets of their allegiance to Communist principles, hoping to indicate to the Kremlin that they meant only to liberalize internally and posed no threat to the USSR. But to the entrenched Communist officials in power in Moscow, liberalization, even if limited to domestic affairs, was regarded as a major threat. The Soviet leadership therefore chose to crush this liberal Communist movement and brought a Soviet-backed regime to power. Brezhnev justified the invasion of Czechoslovakia by asserting that the USSR had the right to ensure the survival of any socialist regime on its borders, a formulation that became known in the West as the "Brezhnev Doctrine."

Strategic Parity and the Nonproliferation Treaty

The period that began in the early 1960s with joint Soviet-American moves to limit conflict ended with escalated military activity by both superpowers. Throughout the 1960s the USSR built an arsenal of nuclear weapons and missiles roughly equal to that of the United States. This round of the action-reaction spiral of the nuclear arms race resulted in a situation in which neither superpower could claim military superiority over the other, but both were vulnerable to nuclear attack. Paradoxically, both the U.S. and USSR liked it that way. American strategists, guided by a doctrine known as **mutual assured destruction** (appropriately shortened to MAD) believed that if both sides knew that they had no chance of prevailing in a nuclear war and would be virtually annihilated in a nuclear holocaust, neither would launch a nuclear attack. (See Chapter Eleven for more on MAD.) Soviet leaders, on the other hand, expected that the achievement of strategic parity would finally force the United States to regard it as a political equal and accept their brand of communism as a legitimate force in world politics. Although some believed the time was ripe for mutual disarmament, both sides planned further increases in their nuclear capabilities to prevent the other side from achieving superiority.

The only major breakthrough of the period came in 1968, with the signing of the Nuclear Nonproliferation Treaty. Three of the five nuclear powers, the United States, the USSR, and Britain (China and France initially refused to join), pledged not to employ nuclear weapons against or share nuclear weapons technology with non-nuclear states that signed the treaty. In return, the non-nuclear nations pledged not to develop nuclear weapons. This treaty was a major achievement and certainly slowed the spread of nuclear weapons, but it could not prevent countries such as Israel, India, Pakistan, Iraq, South Africa, and North Korea from proceeding with their nuclear programs (see Chapters Five and Eleven).

ERA OF DÉTENTE, 1969–1979

Although the United States had squandered a portion of its military and political advantages by assisting South Vietnam, the Soviet Union remained vulnerable to American pressure because of its conflict with China and its weak economy. After Johnson declined to run for reelection in 1968, the new administration of Richard Nixon, who had been a staunch anticommunist during the 1940s and 1950s, recognized the depths of the Sino-Soviet dispute and the opportunities it represented for American diplomacy. When border clashes broke out between the USSR and China in April 1969, the Nixon administration used the conflict to gradually improve relations with China. This opening culminated in Nixon's dramatic visit to Beijing in February 1972. This visit increased American flexibility toward both China and the USSR, raised American hopes that Moscow and Beijing could aid the United States in extricating itself from the quagmire in Vietnam, and dramatically enhanced American leverage in dealing with the Soviets.

The new American policy toward China bore fruit for both sides. First, the two leading communist states did facilitate the American withdrawal from Vietnam to some extent. Second, the Communist government in Beijing was finally able to assume China's seat as a permanent member of the UN Security Council, which had been occupied by the Republic of China on Taiwan. Finally, China's image in the United States was transformed from a radical, intractable regime to one with which commercial and diplomatic business was possible.

At the same time, the Nixon team attempted to transform the Soviet Union from a revisionist power to one comfortable with the status quo. In some ways, this was an unexpected course for Nixon to take, as he had begun his political career as a hard-line anticommunist. In particular, Nixon and his chief foreign-policy advisor, Henry Kissinger, sought to pursue three policies vis-à-vis the Soviet Union to augment cooperation.[27] First, they acknowledged that the USSR was a co-equal with the United States, a superpower. By doing so, the United States recognized that the Soviets had achieved nuclear parity and would no longer be treated like a younger sibling. Second, they set out to create a number of institutions in the area of arms control and crisis management that would restrain the security dilemma and define acceptable behavior. Third, they sought to pursue a strategy of linkage politics, intended to prevent the Soviets from seeking cooperation in one area while trying to gain unilateral advantages elsewhere. Instead, it encouraged cooperation and discouraged aggression through a combination of "carrots and sticks," especially economic inducements that could be extended as rewards and withdrawn as punishments. (In this respect, the Nixon-Kissinger policy was very similar to Kennan's original conception of containment discussed earlier in this chapter.)

The Moscow Summit and SALT

After the opening to China and increased diplomatic pressure on the Kremlin, a U.S.–Soviet summit was convened in Moscow in May 1972. Washington was interested in using this opportunity to create a number of mutually supporting relationships with the Soviet Union. Nixon sought not only agreements for controlling the escalating arms race, but also Soviet assistance in ending the Vietnam War. The interests of the two superpowers dovetailed because Brezhnev sought access to Western technology and goods. The Kremlin's defense spending was becoming an increasing burden on the Soviet economy, which was proving increasingly unable to simultaneously maintain the USSR's massive military power and produce enough consumer goods for the population's basic needs.

The Moscow Summit, therefore, set the stage for an unprecedented series of agreements. First, Nixon and Brezhnev signed the first Strategic Arms Limitation Treaty, or SALT I. The two powers agreed to restrict the deployment of **antiballistic missiles** (ABMs, missiles designed to shoot down incoming missiles) and to cap the growth of strategic offensive missiles. Designed to stabilize the arms race, these agreements allowed both countries to continue developing nuclear arms, but placed temporary limitations on the number of weapons they could build. Most importantly, the agreement demonstrated that both sides finally understood that neither would gain from an ever-accelerating arms race. In addition to SALT I, a series of economic agreements were reached that would open the door to expanded trade, including large American grain sales to the USSR. An agreement on the "basic principles of mutual relations" was intended to spell out a "code of conduct" for the superpowers' interactions with each other and their respective allies.

■ Willy Brandt

SOURCE: AP/Wide World

This phase of the Cold War, which seemed again to promise a more cordial superpower relationship, became known as **détente** after the French word for relaxation of tensions. In Europe, these achievements reinforced a growing movement toward less hostile relations with the Soviet Union. Under Chancellor Willy Brandt, who had taken office in 1969, West Germany began to expand political and economic contacts with the USSR and East Germany. Brandt's *ostpolitik* ("eastern policy") signaled that Western aspirations for contact with and more independence for Eastern Europe could be more easily achieved through conciliation rather than confrontation (see Spotlight box). Earlier, de Gaulle had sought to place relations between Paris and Moscow on a less hostile footing. As these European initiatives had preceded the Nixon administration's openings to the USSR and China, the United States could proceed with détente with the confidence that the new American policy would be accepted by its allies in NATO.

Spotlight

Architect of *Ostpolitik*

Willy Brandt (1913–1993) will be remembered as a European leader who made invaluable contributions to his own country, to the European Union, and to East-West relations. From the rise of the Nazi party to power in Germany in 1933 to the end of World War II in 1945, Brandt worked in exile in Norway and Sweden (where he changed his name from Karl Herbert Frahm) as a journalist. He returned to Germany after the war and in 1957 was elected mayor of West Berlin. When the Berlin Wall was thrown up around his city in 1961, Brandt's courage inspired the citizens of the beleaguered city through the ensuing crisis.

As West Germany's foreign minister from 1966 to 1969 and chancellor from 1969 to 1974, Brandt worked to normalize relations with the Communist states of Eastern Europe. His plan for improving ties between the two Germanies and between West Germany and its eastern neighbors became known as *ostpolitik* (eastern policy). Brandt's first step as foreign minister was to reverse previous West German policy by accepting the existence of East Germany and Germany's post-1945 borders.

Although never formally recognizing the East German government, he did recognize the Oder-Neisse Line as the new border between East Germany and Poland. (Following World War II, the Soviet Union moved Poland's western border about 75 miles into what had been German territory to the Oder and Western Neisse rivers.) In 1970 Brandt signed nonaggression treaties with the Soviet Union and Poland, and in 1971 he met with East German leader Walter Ulbricht to open political and trade relations between the estranged Germanies.

For his efforts to bring Eastern and Western Europe closer together, Brandt was awarded the Nobel Peace Prize in 1971. In 1974 Brandt was forced to resign as chancellor after it was revealed that one of his close assistants was an East German spy. Brandt's policies of closer integration of the European Union (EU) and improvement of ties with East Germany were continued by his successors, and ultimately they came to fruition in 1990 with the reunification of Germany as part of the EU.

Tensions in Détente

As détente progressed, however, it became increasingly apparent that both sides' expectations for the new superpower relationship varied significantly and that neither side fully understood the other's perspective. In the United States, détente was intended to transform the nature of superpower relations from one of mortal confrontation to one of limited rivalry by giving the USSR a "stake in the system," which would create incentives for both powers to avoid challenging each other's interests. To the Soviet Union, however, détente meant that Cold War competition would continue, but by new rules. From the Soviet viewpoint, there was no contradiction between détente and support for socialist or Communist "national liberation movements" throughout the Third World. Although the Soviet leaders promised to halt future aggressive actions, they still sought to make gains without directly challenging the United States, as would soon be seen clearly in the Middle East, Southeast Asia, and Africa.

The détente accords of the early 1970s also ignored domestic politics in both countries. Many Americans were uncomfortable with the idea of dealing with the USSR while ignoring its human-rights abuses. In particular, the right of Soviet Jews to emigrate became a salient issue, and the Jackson-Vanik Amendment in 1975 placed limitations on the enhancement of U.S.–Soviet economic ties if the Kremlin continued to disallow Jewish emigration. Soviet leaders, for their part, viewed the linkage of trade and strategic agreements to human-rights issues as unwarranted interference in the USSR's domestic affairs.

American domestic politics were entering a turbulent period as the Vietnam War and the Watergate scandal eroded America's confidence in its leaders. The Vietnam experience made many in the United States wary of getting involved in faraway conflicts. Thus, when South Vietnam was overrun by North Vietnamese forces in the spring of 1975, the United States did not intervene. Halting Communist aggression became a secondary issue, and stopping any further disastrous foreign escapades attained primary importance. "No More Vietnams" became the slogan of the day in the 1970s. This was quite ironic, as the resolve to have "No More Koreas" in the 1950s had led to early U.S. involvement in Vietnam.

Any Soviets who anticipated a variety of gains in Southeast Asia, however, were probably disappointed by the emerging conflicts between Communist states. In 1975, the year of Communist victory in Vietnam, a civil war in Cambodia ended with a Chinese-backed Communist insurgency, the Khmer Rouge, in control of the country. The Khmer Rouge regime, led by Pol Pot, proved to be unspeakably brutal. It turned the country into "killing fields," carrying out a program of genocide that killed as many as 2 million people. The capital city of Phnom Penh was practically depopulated, and anyone who wore glasses risked being summarily executed as a subversive intellectual. This tyrannical regime was not ousted by the West, but was overthrown in 1978 by an invasion by the neighboring Communists in Vietnam, who promptly installed a puppet regime. This action and other conflicts led to a border war between China and Vietnam in 1979. (See Chapter Five for details.)

Escalation of conflict in the Middle East further undermined détente. In October 1973 the Soviet Union did not explicitly warn the United States of an impending attack by Syria and Egypt against Israel. Issuing a clear warning would have entailed significant political costs for the USSR, and an order from Moscow to evacuate the dependents of Soviet personnel in Egypt and Syria just before the attack may have been intended as a tacit warning, but the United States did not perceive it as such. The result was the Yom Kippur War (known also as the October War and described in Chapter Five), in which both the United States and USSR resupplied their clients with massive airlifts of arms. Washington was further antagonized when the USSR encouraged additional Arab states both to join the fray and to impose an oil embargo against the United States. In an effort to pressure the United States to end its support for Israel, Arab members of OPEC (Organization of Petroleum Exporting Countries) joined together in stopping oil shipments to the United States. The OPEC embargo caused a major energy crisis, but U.S. aid to Israel continued. U.S. and Soviet efforts to bring about a cease-fire eventually succeeded, but only after the United States placed its nuclear forces on alert in response to hints that Moscow might send troops to support Egypt.

The United States and the USSR thus continued their global competition despite détente. Moscow expanded its military presence in Cuba, Southeast Asia, and Africa, dispatching military advisors and leasing naval and air bases. In 1976 Cuban troops and Soviet military assistance were sent to aid a Soviet-backed faction in the civil war in newly independent Angola. Both the Nixon and Ford administrations continued their commitment to many Cold War–type policies in order to prevent the emergence of regimes in the Third World that threatened U.S. interests. In 1973, for example, the CIA was complicit in the violent overthrow of Chile's elected Marxist president, Salvador Allende. The United States also attempted to push the Soviets back onto the sidelines in the Middle East in a series of limited accords between Israel and Egypt and Syria in the months that followed the October War. In many ways, détente between the United States and the Soviets more closely resembled the old Cold War than some new form of superpower relationship.

From Dialogue to Discord: The Carter Administration

The next American president, Jimmy Carter, took office in 1977 committed to improving the U.S.–Soviet relationship. Carter sought to undo the conceptual and practical assumptions inherent in American policy that had led to Vietnam in the first place. "We have fought fire with fire, never thinking that fire is better quenched with water," Carter declared.[28] The Carter administration placed more emphasis on economic factors in world politics. The energy crisis that followed the 1973 war in the Middle East led to petroleum shortages and high prices in the West. To Carter, growing international interdependence as epitomized by the energy problem seemed more central to U.S. vital interests than any threat of international communism.

Carter's foreign policy was decidedly more attuned to human-rights questions throughout the world than previous American policy had been. Human-rights issues became an important part of the **Conference on Security and Cooperation in Europe** (CSCE), which first convened in 1975 in Helsinki and later became a permanent international organization. The conference accepted many long-held Soviet positions on political issues in return for Soviet promises to abide by agreements that guaranteed human rights for the citizens of all participating countries. The Kremlin did not take these rights guarantees seriously at first, but many Soviet and East European citizens did, forming "Helsinki Watch" committees to monitor Soviet compliance with human-rights conventions.

Although Carter's policies achieved notable advances in the field of human rights, his less confrontational stance toward the USSR in the early years of his administration may have led some Soviets to believe that the United States would not oppose the further expansion of Moscow's influence, especially in the Third World. Cuban forces intervened in conflicts in Ethiopia and Angola in order to help solidify Soviet positions in those African countries. Cuban actions could not have been taken without Soviet approval, because the USSR was heavily subsidizing Cuba's international military actions (as well as its domestic economy).

Soviet actions and American reactions in the Third World heightened mutual suspicions and thereby threatened progress on arms control. In spite of mutual agreement on the need for another arms-control accord, the United States and USSR squabbled endlessly over the details of a new treaty. An initial agreement between Brezhnev and Ford had been reached in the Soviet city of Vladivostok in 1974, but the talks dragged on, complicated by criticism from American conservatives and by Soviet deployments of new nuclear missiles. In 1979 Carter and Brezhnev finally signed the SALT II treaty, which set a cap on all offensive strategic weapons. Critics argued, however, that the new treaty left American land-based ICBMs vulnerable to destruction by a Soviet surprise attack, reservations that delayed ratification of the new treaty. (As described in Chapter Twelve, the U.S. Senate must approve all treaties signed by the United States before they can come into force.)

By the late 1970s it appeared unlikely that the Soviet Union and the United States could reach a modus vivendi even when both sought means of controlling the competition. Domestic influences in each country and unanticipated developments around the world seemed either to thwart attempts at cooperation or to tempt one or both sides to compromise détente. In 1979, for example, the shah of Iran, one of America's most important and long-standing allies in the Third World, was ousted from power by an Islamic fundamentalist revolution. Many Americans feared that Moscow would capitalize on the revolution to advance its interests in Iran. (In fact, however, the Iranian revolution worried the Soviet Union as well, as many Soviets feared that Islamic radicalism might spread across the border and provoke unrest in the USSR's predominantly Muslim Central Asian republics.)

Also in 1979, in Nicaragua, the forty-year-old dictatorship of the Somoza family was overthrown in a rebellion led by a socialist-oriented alliance, the Sandinista Front. Although Carter attempted to work with the Sandinistas at first, growing consternation over their socialist ideology and support of radical insurgents in neighboring countries increased American opposition to the new government, while the USSR and Cuba extended political and material support to the Sandinista regime.

THE COLD WAR RETURNS, 1979–1985

The Soviet-American disputes arising during the Carter administration might have been resolved in a manner that would have preserved détente, albeit in a diminished form. At the end of 1979, however, the Kremlin took an action that doomed any possibility of a cooperative relationship between Washington and Moscow.

Invasion of Afghanistan

In December 1979 the USSR sent 80,000 troops into Afghanistan to overthrow an unstable fledgling Marxist government and replace it with a stronger pro-Soviet regime in that mountainous nation. The invasion marked the first time the USSR had deployed a large number of troops outside of the Warsaw Pact states of Eastern Europe. The reasons why Soviet leaders felt they could take such a blatantly forceful step without serious international political consequences remain unclear. Perhaps they had become accustomed to the Carter administration's lack of strong resistance to Soviet-sponsored activities in the Third World. Perhaps Moscow believed that the invasion would be quickly successful and forgotten just as rapidly. Or perhaps Brezhnev and other Soviet Communist leaders were hopelessly out of touch with domestic and international political realities and consequently confident that Afghanistan would accept communism without a fight.

The invasion was denounced in the West and much of the Third World as an act of naked aggression. In actuality, the invasion proved disastrous both for Soviet domestic politics and for the morale of Soviet troops. Soviet military resources were seriously depleted when an alliance of Islamic groups established a guerrilla campaign based in neighboring Pakistan that was supported by the United States.

In an effort to coerce the Soviet Union to withdraw, Carter suspended grain sales to the USSR, withdrew the SALT II agreements from consideration by the Senate, increased defense spending, and refused to allow the U.S. Olympic Team to participate in the 1980 Summer Olympics in Moscow. These steps failed to convince Moscow to withdraw its forces, however, and Soviet troops soon became bogged down in a quagmire in Afghanistan just as American troops had become mired in Vietnam fifteen years earlier.

Reagan and the Reagan Doctrine

The war in Afghanistan pushed America toward a revival of Cold War perceptions. The rise of a renewed Cold War in turn contributed to the election of Ronald Reagan as U.S. president in 1980. Although Carter had increased defense spending during the latter part of his term, Reagan expanded defense budgets still further. Through both direct U.S. intervention and indirect support for insurgencies, Reagan abandoned the policy of détente and returned to an assertive form of containment. Like Truman at the outset of the Cold War, Reagan couched his arguments for opposition to Soviet expansion in terms of moral duty, labeling the Soviet Union "the focus of evil in the modern world." [29]

Supporting indigenous anticommunist insurgencies came to be the Reagan administration's specialty. The resulting so-called **Reagan Doctrine** was played out in a variety of locations around the world. Anticommunist insurgents were encouraged in Angola, Cambodia, and, most controversially, in Nicaragua, where assistance was provided to the *Contra* rebels even after Congress prohibited direct military aid. Governments threatened by Soviet- or Cuban-supported insurgencies also received substantial assistance, especially those in Central America such as El Salvador and Guatemala. The United States unsuccessfully intervened in Lebanon in 1982 in an attempt to restore the unity of the country after a long civil war. In 1983 Reagan sent U.S. forces to Grenada to defeat a newly imposed Marxist government supported by Cuban advisors and construction troops. Afghan rebels were supplied with highly effective Stinger missiles that brought down Soviet aircraft in great numbers. The growing successes of the rebels confounded Soviet forces, and the USSR finally abandoned its war effort and withdrew its troops in 1989.

Reagan's policies in the 1980s helped reverse what many had viewed as a decline in U.S. power and influence in the 1970s, but they didn't come cheaply. During his presidency, Reagan authorized more than $2 trillion in defense spending, increasing the size and quality of American nuclear and conventional forces. Critics claimed these defense expenditures wasted American resources that were needed to address domestic problems. Reagan's political popularity, however, enabled him to continue his defense policy. Despite protests from peace activists in the United States and Europe, he carried out the deployment of intermediate-range nuclear missiles to Europe, which NATO had agreed upon during the Carter administration to counter a Soviet buildup of missiles designed for use against European targets.

THE COLD WAR ENDS, 1985–1991

While the Cold War was being fought with renewed vehemence in the international arena in the early 1980s, the Soviet Union began experiencing a series of domestic political upheavals. Brezhnev died in 1982, and both of his successors died in office within a year of acceding to power in the Kremlin. Consequently, Soviet policy entered a period of inertia as the Reagan Doctrine applied pressure to the USSR and its allies. The shooting down of a Korean Airlines flight bound from New York to Seoul in September 1983 symbolized the stagnation of Soviet policies at home and abroad. Although the aircraft had accidentally strayed over Soviet territory, the fact that the Soviets shot down a civilian airliner that was not moving in a suspicious manner indicated either a callous lack of consideration for civilian life, bureaucratic inefficiency, or gross incompetence. By the mid-1980s, many Soviets were convinced that the Communist system in their country was suffering from all three of these ills.

In 1985, when Mikhail Gorbachev assumed leadership of the Soviet Union, Soviet-American relations had reached low ebb, recalling the tense early days of the Cold War, and the Soviet political and economic system was in need of a massive overhaul. Several important changes occurred within the Soviet Union itself as Gorbachev's policies of *glasnost* ("political openness") and *perestroika* ("economic restructuring") promoted democratization and free markets. However, on the whole, the economic reforms did not go far enough to reinvigorate the USSR's economy, while political changes swept forward at a pace that was exhilarating to some and threatening to others. As the 1990s began, the entire Communist system was being challenged and was failing to overcome the obstacles it faced.

The liberalization that began in Soviet society spread to Eastern Europe, culminating in a series of mostly peaceful revolutions in 1989. Regimes that had taken decades to establish were overthrown within months or weeks and even, in Czechoslovakia and Romania, in a matter of days. The deterioration of living standards and the perceived illegitimacy of the governments of these Eastern European countries led to mass uprisings that erupted as soon as the Soviet Union abandoned the Brezhnev Doctrine and declined to use its forces to keep Communist governments in power. Popular movements, such as **Solidarity** in Poland, that had been in perilous existence for years were finally able to assume power in their countries. In an ironic domino effect, the governments of Eastern Europe fell one by one, first Poland, followed by Hungary, East Germany, Czechoslovakia, and Romania. What had seemed impossible for more than a generation finally occurred when the Berlin Wall was dismantled in November 1989, and Germany was reunified in 1990. Thus, appropriately, the Cold War ended where it had begun, in Eastern Europe. An abortive coup in Moscow by hard-line Communists attempting to resurrect the old order in August 1991 resulted in the final discrediting of the old regime and the disintegration of the Soviet Union, bringing the era of U.S.–Soviet antagonism to a close.

WHY DID THE COLD WAR END?

The Cold War between the United States and the Soviet Union lasted for more than four decades and at times took on the appearance of a permanent fixture in international politics. It had arisen gradually and predictably, but it ended abruptly and in a manner that caught the entire world by surprise. As with the Cold War's origins, a variety of possible explanations have been advanced for its end, each corresponding to one of the images of world politics and levels of analysis presented in Chapter One.

The Gorbachev Factor

Many analysts who adopt the "great-man" theory of world politics point to Mikhail Gorbachev and argue that the end of the Cold War could have come about only with someone of his character and stature at the helm. Just as an individual like Stalin or Truman might have been a necessary ingredient in causing the Cold War or influencing its nature, this argument contends that it took someone like Gorbachev to bring it to a close. With initial hesitancy but growing energy, Gorbachev worked to reverse the downward trend in superpower relations. Early in his tenure in office, he stated his intention to put the U.S.–Soviet relationship on a new nonconfrontational footing:

> We certainly do not need an "enemy image" of America, neither for domestic nor foreign-policy interests. An imaginary or real enemy is needed only if one is bent

on maintaining tension, on confrontation with far-reaching and, I might add, un-predictable consequences. . . . It is a sad, tragic fact that Soviet-American relations have been slipping downhill for a long time. Short periods of improvement gave way to protracted spells of tension and a build-up in hostility. I am convinced that we have every opportunity to rectify the situation, and it appears that things are moving that way.[30]

Things were indeed moving that way. Under Gorbachev's leadership, major agreements were reached in the arms-control arena, beginning with an agreement on the elimination of intermediate-range nuclear forces (the INF Treaty) in 1987, continuing on to the Strategic Arms Reduction Treaty (START I) of 1991 by which Soviet and American strategic forces were to be reduced by approximately one-third, and progressing with further unilateral cuts on both sides announced later in 1991 (see Chapter Eleven). Gorbachev also ended the USSR's Afghan debacle by ordering the withdrawal of Soviet forces in 1989. Had Soviet leaders with attitudes similar to those of Brezhnev or Stalin been in power during the late 1980s, the Soviet policies that contributed to the lessening of U.S.–Soviet tensions would probably never have been adopted.

The End of History

A second explanation deemphasizes the role of individual leaders and instead claims that the failures of communism and the spread of democratic ideas to the Eastern bloc account for the waning of the Cold War. According to this domestic-level argument, internal changes within the USSR precipitated a new foreign policy. The most important changes were Gorbachev's policies of *glasnost* and *perestroika,* which encouraged a gradual process of democratization and the attempt to open the country to free markets and foreign investment. Through these reforms, Soviets sought to embrace private property and individual rights such as freedom of religion, assembly, and speech. In fact, the Soviets sought American and Western help and sought out Western advisors to assist in making the transition from a planned to a market economy. The outcome was that in the West, the talk of reform led many to believe that Soviet society would shortly mirror its own and would no longer be foreign or threatening. Incorporating this perspective, Francis Fukuyama contends in his influential book *The End of History and the Last Man* that the victory of capitalism and democracy over communism will result in the end of global ideological conflict.[31]

End of the Evil Empire

A third explanation for the close of the Cold War holds that it ended because the Soviet Union collapsed. The decline of the Soviet Union demonstrated that the Communist system had failed. The Soviet economy was fraught with inherent inefficiencies and outdated technology, particularly after computers and information technology transformed the world economy in the 1980s. The prolonged

Friendly meetings between U.S. President Ronald Reagan and Soviet Premier Mikhail Gorbachev symbolized the improvement of Soviet-American relations as the Cold War came to a close.   SOURCE: AP/Wide World

fiasco tarnished the reputation of Communist party elites. Additionally, with Gorbachev, a new generation came to power in the USSR that had experienced the economic deprivation and political stagnation of the Communist system but had not endured the immense suffering of World War II, which had so often been used as an excuse for continued demands for sacrifice to defend the (increasingly dubious) achievements of communism and to control Eastern Europe. With the USSR no longer able to compete, the superpower competition ended. To this way of thinking, George Kennan's original containment doctrine had finally been proven correct, as American political and economic "counterforce" had prevailed without the need for direct military confrontation.

A variant of this explanation holds that competition with the West was the deciding factor in the political, social, and economic decline of the Soviet system. In part, the laggard nature of the Soviet economy was a result of the huge military expenditures necessary to compete with the United States. It is argued by some that the U.S. defense buildup undertaken during President Reagan's tenure in the 1980s, including the deployment of INF missiles in Europe, conventional and nuclear force modernizations, and research into space-based missile defenses (the **Strategic Defense Initiative** or SDI), convinced many in the Soviet elite that the USSR could no longer compete. The United States thereby won the Cold War through economic and military strength as well as the inherent superiority of capitalism and democracy. From this perspective, Reagan's policies and his unwavering vision of U.S. victory in the Cold War both forced and facilitated Gorbachev's concessions.

A New World Order

A fourth explanation for the Cold War's end considers the changes in the international system in the decades since World War II and concludes that U.S.–Soviet antagonism was bound to lessen because of the decline of bipolarity. As noted in the discussion of the origins of the Cold War, one explanation for the rise of U.S.–Soviet enmity was the advent of a bipolar distribution of power. To be sure, massive military spending exhausted the Soviet Union, but it is also apparent that the arms race took its toll on the United States. The consequence, from this viewpoint, is that in fact the real "winners" of the Cold War were countries like Japan and Germany, which rode on American coattails, allowing the United States to provide for their security while they invested in their domestic industry. The decline of the Soviet Union therefore meant that Moscow was no longer the greatest threat to American security and that the world was moving in the direction of either unipolarity, with the United States as the sole superpower, or multipolarity, with Japan and Germany (or perhaps a unified Europe) as the new economic superpowers confronting the United States. (These ideas will be explored further in Chapter Five; for more on polarity, see Chapter Twelve.)

From this systemic perspective, the Soviet Union posed only a minimal threat even before its final collapse, and a decline in U.S.–Soviet tensions could have been expected even in the absence of ideological change or a reformist leader such as Gorbachev. Many people would dispute this conclusion, but just as the reasons why the Cold War began were argued while U.S.–Soviet competition raged, the reasons why that competition ended are likely to be debated for many years as the structure of world politics assumes a new form.[32]

CONCLUSION: MAJOR "ACHIEVEMENTS" OF THE COLD WAR

A comparison of this chapter with the previous two historical chapters reveals that the Cold War era was a relatively stable one. This is not to say there was no bloodshed during this period or that the respective clients of the two superpowers did

At a Glance

Alternative Causes of the End of the Cold War

Perestroika

Under the new leadership of Mikhail Gorbachev, the USSR determined that in order to overcome internal stagnation, it had to liberalize its political and economic system, adopt a less confrontational posture toward the West, cut back on military expenditures, and stop attempting to maintain exclusive spheres of influence in Eastern Europe and parts of the Third World.

End of History

By the late 1980s, the ideology of communism had demonstrably failed. Any state attempting to remain competitive in the international system, economically or politically, would have to adopt western ideas of democracy and market economics or fall irretrievably behind. The adoption of these ideas also made the USSR appear less threatening to the West, reducing the impetus for conflict.

Collapse of Soviet Power

Burdened by the inefficiencies of communism and excessive military spending, Soviet economic power and technology declined to the point where competition with the West was no longer possible. This decline may have been hastened by Ronald Reagan's assertive American defense and foreign policies in the 1980s.

Decline of Bipolarity

Germany, France, Britain, and Japan regained their economic strength after suffering devastation during World War II and became more competitive in the global marketplace. Their renewed capacity and the growing economic capabilities of some developing states increased the ability of these rising powers to compete with the United States and USSR for political influence. The simple bipolar structure of world politics became complex and multipolar once again, ending the zero-sum competition between the superpowers.

not fight, but that in contrast to previous periods, there were no wars between the great powers. Indeed, for most of the Cold War a total war between the United States and USSR was unthinkable, as it would have meant the nuclear destruction of global civilization. As dangerous as it was, the fact that the two superpowers did not go to war despite their many differences and periodic sharp confrontations makes the Cold War a comparatively peaceful interval in the bloody annals of international politics.

In order to gain some understanding of the Cold War, it is necessary to wrestle with three deceptively simple questions: Why did it start, why did it end, and why did it not turn hot? The reader will not find any simple answers to these questions here and should be suspicious of any analysis that attempts to offer them. Instead, this chapter has sought to present the reader with the basic tools necessary to begin answering these questions, including competing explanations for the Cold War's origins and decline and an outline of its most important events. As noted earlier, the explanations are related to the images and levels of analysis of world politics introduced in Chapter One. Subsequent chapters will explore these concepts in more detail, frequently referring to the events of the Cold War era to illustrate the ways in which individual, state-level, and systemic influences affect international relations. The Cold War offers many striking examples of how personalities, ideology, and the structure of the international system can have a major impact on global politics. For this reason, even if no consensus is ever achieved on the basic questions surrounding the Cold War, attempting to answer them will remain outstanding exercises for anyone desiring a better understanding of the forces that shape the contemporary world.

In the final analysis, the Cold War ended neither with a bang nor a whimper, but with a sigh of relief. The fact that Americans and Soviets resolved the dangerous conflict between their two countries without going to war with each other bodes well for the post–Cold War relationship between America and Russia, even as the uncertain political and economic future of the former Soviet republics clouds the prospects for the emergence of a successful new world order.

Perhaps more than any previous period, the Cold War saw the complete globalization of political conflict. In its wake, political fragmentation coexists with economic globalization, but the peaceful end to the once seemingly intractable U.S.–Soviet rivalry offers hope that local disputes can be kept from escalating into global confrontations and that global conflicts need not be resolved by global war.

PRINCIPAL POINTS OF CHAPTER FOUR

1. With the end of World War II, the United States and the USSR entered into a global political competition that became known as the Cold War.
2. Possible causes of the Cold War include:
   a. Soviet actions.
   b. American actions.
   c. The beliefs and interaction of Stalin and Truman.
   d. The competing ideologies of communism and capitalism.
   e. The fact that the United States and the USSR were the only remaining great powers.
   f. Misperception by each side of the other's actions.
3. The Cold War proceeded through a series of ebbs and flows, in which tensions never escalated into actual warfare between the superpowers, but periods of quiet never resulted in total accommodation.
4. From 1945 to 1953, Moscow and Washington were frequently involved in conflicts on the periphery of the USSR. The sharpest of these were the Berlin blockade in 1948 and the Korean War from 1950 to 1953.
5. In 1953 Stalin died and Eisenhower replaced Truman, but both sides missed or ignored opportunities for reducing tensions.
6. By 1957 the Cold War became globalized as more and more developing states gained independence. The two superpowers began to compete in the Middle East, Africa, Latin America, and Southeast Asia. Hopes for reconciliation were raised at a series of summits but dashed by the U-2 incident in 1960.
7. U.S.–Soviet rivalry, aggravated by a second Berlin crisis, continued at a high level throughout the Kennedy administration. Growing superpower

tensions culminated in the Cuban Missile Crisis, the most dangerous confrontation of the Cold War. Afterward, the superpowers adopted a series of limited confidence-building measures.

8. From 1964 to 1969, the Cold War heated up again as U.S. forces fought in Vietnam and the USSR built up its strategic nuclear arsenal to a level roughly equal to that of the United States, while its dispute with China intensified.

9. From 1969 to 1972, a relationship of relaxed tensions called détente developed. Nixon and Brezhnev signed SALT I and other agreements intended to foster cooperation, but these accords were undermined between 1973 and 1979 by differing understandings of the actions allowable under détente and by domestic politics in both countries.

10. In 1979 the Soviet invasion of Afghanistan ushered in a renewed freezing of the Cold War. American policy became more competitive in the 1980s under Reagan as the USSR faced growing internal political and economic problems.

11. In 1985 Gorbachev came to power in the USSR and presided over a series of reforms collectively known as *glasnost* and *perestroika,* which reduced U.S.–Soviet tensions but were only partially successful in resolving the Soviet domestic crisis.

12. By 1991 continued economic stagnation and social and political upheaval resulted in the collapse of Communist regimes in Eastern Europe and the Soviet Union. The Cold War came to an end with the reunification of Germany and the disintegration of the USSR.

13. Possible explanations for the end of the Cold War include:
    a. Mikhail Gorbachev's reform policies in the Soviet Union.
    b. Globalization of democracy and capitalism.
    c. Collapse of Soviet power, hastened by Reagan's policies and assertive leadership of the U.S.
    d. Decline of bipolarity as other nations gained in economic and political strength.

KEY TERMS

antiballistic missiles
atomic weapons
bipolarity
capitalism
communism
Conference on Security and Cooperation in Europe
containment

détente
flexible response
glasnost
intercontinental ballistic missiles
limited war
massive retaliation
mutual assured destruction

NSC-68
Nonaligned Movement
ostpolitik
perestroika
Reagan Doctrine
realpolitik
security dilemma
Solidarity

Strategic Defense Initiative
submarine-launched ballistic missiles
Third World
Truman Doctrine
zero-sum

SOURCE: Reuters/Dylan Martinez/Archive

Globalism and Regionalism in a New Era

World politics at the end of the twentieth century is a system of paradoxes. On one hand, the end of the Cold War seems to have lain to rest the specter of nuclear holocaust that haunted relations between the superpowers in the nuclear age, leaving the world a safer place free from the fear of another catastrophic world war. On the other hand, regional and ethnic conflicts, the violent collapse of governments, and threats of nuclear proliferation and terrorists armed with weapons of mass destruction lead many to believe that the world is more dangerous than ever. Meanwhile, as multinational states are breaking up, nations are coming together to address common needs for trade, economic development, and environmental protection. Overall, the historic processes of globalization and fragmentation, and cooperation and

laid

conflict, all seem to be running faster than ever, on parallel tracks to an unknown destination.

Comprehending the New Era has been hard enough for world leaders, and world citizens may find it even harder. Not surprisingly, some politicians and analysts have tried to apply old paradigms to help organize their thinking and formulate policy goals. Thus, for some, the world appears to have returned to a classical balance-of-power system, although for others the New Era looks like a transition period between the old Soviet-American Cold War and a new Sino-American confrontation. Others, however, contend that world politics has been fundamentally transformed into a system in which war is obsolete and international organizations or economic and ecological interdependence create opportunities for lasting peace and environmentally sustainable prosperity. As the world has never fit neatly into a single paradigm, the reality of the New Era is likely to be somewhere in between, and leaders and citizens alike face the challenge of making sense of a continuously evolving new system.

To help students of world politics meet that challenge, this chapter adopts a thematic approach to outline a contemporary history of the New Era. It begins by discussing the emerging structure of world politics, showing how international institutions reflect the simultaneous progress of globalization and fragmentation. Next, it outlines what some have identified as a significant trend toward cooperation—renewed international efforts to establish collective security—and examines a reemergent trend toward ethnic conflict. Following this, it surveys three regions of the world which continue to hold great potential for conflict as well as possibilities, or needs, for cooperation: the Middle East, South Asia, and East Asia. Finally, although trying to draw conclusions about a dynamic system is an inherently risky enterprise, we consider how the trends we observe in New Era world politics are linked to one another, and how the tools that will be presented in subsequent chapters can help us grasp them.

A NEW WORLD ORDER?

At the end of the Persian Gulf War (see later in this chapter), U.S. President George Bush spoke of a "new world order" that would replace the superpower rivalry of the Cold War with a system wherein states would cooperate within the framework of international law against aggression and other common threats. The post–Cold War world would therefore be less confrontational and more institutionalized. Subsequent developments have shown Bush to be at least half right: global political confrontation and rivalry have clearly receded, though how long they will remain in the background is far from clear.

Table 5.1, which lists the top ten states in terms of GNP and military spending in 1985 and 1995, tells a story of the international system in transition. In 1985, at the beginning of the end of the Cold War (see Chapter Four), the world was dominated economically and militarily by the two superpowers. Although Japan and some European states approached the United States and USSR economically, none came anywhere near the bipolar rivals in the military arena. By 1995, the Soviet Union had collapsed, and its successor state, Russia, had dropped from second to eighth in world economic rankings. Japan, China, and a reunified Germany were in the same economic league a few steps behind the United States, but militarily the United States was in a league of its own as the world's sole remaining superpower. These marked changes in military and economic rankings over a ten-year period prompt many questions. How long can Russia maintain a relatively high level of military spending without further deepening its economic crisis? How long will it be before China eclipses Japan, and possibly even the United States, in economic power? Would changes in economic rankings lead to new political and military rivalries?

The structure of world politics in the New Era is still emerging, but two trends are clear. The first is that the era of bipolar military competition (see Chapters

Table 5.1	Leading Economic and Military Powers, 1985–1995

Gross National Product

1985

Gross National Product		Military Expenditures	
United States	4,010,000	Soviet Union	275,000
Soviet Union	2,197,000	United States	265,800
Japan	1,361,000	China	24,870
West Germany	649,900	United Kingdom	24,200
France	508,500	Saudi Arabia	22,900
United Kingdom	460,400	France	20,800
China	368,900	West Germany	20,800
Italy	366,400	Iraq	NA
Canada	346,100	Poland	14,610
Poland	245,600	Japan	13,490

1995

Gross National Product		Military Expenditures	
United States	7,247,000	United States	277,800
Japan	5,153,000	Russia	76,000
China	2,759,000	China	63,510
Germany	2,172,000	Japan	50,240
France	1,521,000	France	47,770
United Kingdom	1,110,000	Germany	41,160
Italy	1,082,000	United Kingdom	33,400
Russia	664,000	Italy	19,380
Brazil	656,500	Saudi Arabia	17,210
Spain	553,800	South Korea	14,410

SOURCE: U.S. Arms Control and Disarmament Agency, *World Military Expenditures & Arms Transfers, 1996*
NOTE: Figures are in millions of current U.S. dollars.

Four and Twelve) is over, at least for the time being, and has been replaced by a system in which the United States is unchallenged in global military capability. Although Russia retains a large stockpile of nuclear weapons, China, Britain, and France still possess smaller nuclear arsenals, and many states possess significant military forces in their respective regions, the United States is the only nation with the ability to intervene in any conflict anywhere in the world. Though the size of its military establishment was reduced from the levels built up during the Cold War, the United States remained committed to maintaining the ground, naval, and air forces that would be needed should war again break out in Europe, the Middle East, or East Asia, together with the means to move and supply them, overseas bases to support them, and space-based reconnaissance systems to locate threats and guide weapons to their targets. At the same time, the United States continued its military research and development efforts to keep its technological edge over potential challengers for as long as possible.

These capabilities do not allow the United States to act unilaterally as a "world policeman" or dominate other major states militarily. Conflicts in the Persian Gulf, Bosnia, and elsewhere (see later in this chapter) proved that in most cases the United States must join with regional allies to conduct sustained, large-scale military operations. The United States has also been careful to observe the letter and spirit of international law, seeking the approval of the UN **Security Council** before committing forces to regional conflicts. It is also uncertain how long the United States will be willing to pay the cost of maintaining its global military infrastructure and leadership in defense technology.[1] But until another comparable superpower emerges, the United States remains the only state that can undertake such missions anytime, anywhere, against any aggressor. The U.S. role in the New Era could therefore be likened to that of Britain in the nineteenth century (see Chapters Two and Three). Although not exercising supremacy, the United States may maintain a kind of *Pax Americana*, working with its allies to safeguard strategic stability and contain regional conflicts.

Some states, worried by well-armed regional rivals, welcomed this situation and sought alliances with the United States. Larger, ambitious regional powers such as Russia, China, and India, on the other hand, greeted the prospect of U.S. security leadership with trepidation or reserved judgment. These differing attitudes were brought into sharp focus in 1995–1998, as Poland, Hungary, the Czech Republic, and other Eastern European states sought to join the NATO alliance. Russia viewed the expansion of NATO as an attempt to isolate it from Europe, and considered looking eastward, especially to China, for new security partners. Concurrent U.S. and international efforts to restrict the proliferation of nuclear weapons and ballistic missiles (see Chapter Eleven) similarly produced negative reactions from India, Iran, and other regional powers.

Although the United States is the New Era's only superpower in military terms, in economic terms it may eventually become first among equals. The rise of Europe and Asia to new economic prominence is the second major trend of the New Era. The U.S. economy at the end of the 1990s remained strong, showing impressive gains in productivity with unemployment low and inflation barely noticeable.

However, Japan, the European Union, and the rapidly-developing countries of the Pacific Rim (see Chapter Eight) compete with the United States for export markets and investment opportunities on at least equal terms. Although America maintains advantages in some economic sectors, such as agricultural exports, aircraft, media and entertainment, financial services, and advanced computer technology, other states can match or exceed the United States in productivity and innovations in consumer electronics, automobiles, and other profitable products and services. Still other countries, such as Mexico, China, and the states of Eastern Europe, can compete with the United States by offering cheaper labor. In many ways, the world economy in the New Era reflects the global operation *of comparative advantage,* which allows states to profit from trade by exporting the goods that they produce relatively more efficiently and importing goods that they make relatively less efficiently. (Chapter Six explains trade and comparative advantage in more detail.) The overall result is a more integrated global economy in which every state is interdependent and none is clearly dominant.

The relative economic strength of states inevitably changes, as some exhaust their nonrenewable resources or fail to maintain their infrastructure, while others learn to use their natural and human resources more efficiently. As Table 5.1 indicates, some large nations of the developing world are beginning to equal or exceed the industrialized states in total GNP. Some forecasts conclude that it is only a matter of time before China overtakes both Japan and the United States in overall economic output.[2] The consequences of these economic changes for the political and strategic structure of the New Era will be difficult to predict (though Chapters Twelve and Thirteen suggest how one might try).[3] Regardless of the outcome of the economic competition, it is probable that in the New Era, prosperity and the fulfillment of human needs will depend more than ever before on international cooperation and the smooth operation of global economic and environmental institutions. This will not be easy to achieve, as Chapters Nine and Ten explain.

Just as the industrial revolution changed the relationship between economic and military power in the nineteenth century, the information revolution appears likely to transform the links between material abundance and military might in the twenty-first. Although the advent of mass production after 1848 and its perfection during the world wars emphasized quantity, the Persian Gulf War has shown how the information age puts a premium on precision and quality in military hardware as well as manufacturing and agriculture.[4] The explosive development of computers, robotics, advanced manufacturing processes, and telecommunications has further globalized economic relations, but it also widened the gap between those with and without access to information technology.[5] This gap is easier to close in civilian technology than in the military field, as more economic and scientific data becomes accessible through the Internet although the design secrets of nuclear weapons, stealth bombers, and precision-guided missiles remain jealously guarded. If knowledge truly is power, raw numbers of economic output and military spending may be less reliable indicators of political power in the New Era, as victory may go not to the bigger battalions, but the smarter ones.

INTERDEPENDENCE AND GLOBALIZATION

Although military and economic power will not lose their importance in the fore-seeable future, the outlines of world politics in the New Era cannot be discerned by focusing exclusively on security and economic competition. The preceding chapters have shown how conflicts and rivalries between great powers defined world politics in previous eras, but international relations in the New Era may be shaped by common problems and shared values. To an ever-increasing degree, *interdependence* links together the fate of states. Money, goods, people, infor-mation, pollution, and disease flow across international boundaries, and climate change, drug traffic, and terrorism threaten the well-being of all peoples. Because the security and prosperity of each individual state are increasingly linked to po-litical, economic, and environmental conditions in other states, governments find that they can no longer meet threats or pursue opportunities through unilateral action The result is a true "global village" where states must work together to achieve common goals.

More formally, interdependence may be defined as "a relationship of interests such that if one nation's position changes, other states will be affected by that change."[6] Thus, what happens to one state will have a ripple effect across the oth-ers. (See Chapter Ten for examples of how interdependence affects global issues.) In economic terms, interdependence characterizes any relationship between states that would be costly to break.[7] For example, importers and exporters of oil are interdependent; importers depend on a continued flow of oil, while exporters de-pend on a continued flow of cash. One group or the other may enjoy greater prof-its (depending on supply and demand and other factors that affect the price of oil), but both would suffer if trade in oil were halted. Interdependence has two dimen-sions: **sensitivity** and **vulnerability**.[8] Sensitivity refers to the speed and extent with which changes in one country bring about changes in another. Changes in Ger-man interest rates, for example, usually have an immediate economic impact in the other members of the European Union, but not in the nations of Central America. The other dimension, vulnerability, measures the degree to which a state can suf-fer costs imposed by external events even after policies have been altered in re-sponse to them. Iraq and Syria, for instance, which obtain much of their water from the Tigris and Euphrates rivers, are very vulnerable to changes in those rivers' flow (and thus have been very concerned by Turkish plans to dam them; see Chapter Ten). Sensitivity and vulnerability often go together, but do not necessar-ily correlate. In the case of the 1973 oil embargo and the subsequent rapid increase in the price of oil (see Chapter Seven), the United States was less sensitive than Ja-pan to the external event because a smaller proportion of the U.S. economy was dependent upon foreign imports. However, the United States was also more vul-nerable, because domestic constraints made it more difficult to adjust to changes in oil prices.

Does interdependence foster cooperation? Not necessarily. In fact, interde-pendence sometimes creates tension and even conflict between states. Just as close and continual contact between family members or roommates often illuminates differences of opinion, frequent and long-term interaction between states often creates or exacerbates hostility. Pessimists recognize other dangers associated with interdependence, which can mean economic vulnerability and insecurity. It can leave states vulnerable to economic sanctions, though they may not always react in the ways the sanctioners intend. (As we saw in Chapter Three, the U.S. oil embargo on Japan before World War II was designed to pressure Japan into halting its war in China, but Japan's response to it was an attack on the United States.) Increased interdependence also means less government control over domestic affairs, and less flexibility in addressing domestic problems, as many members of the European Union have learned (see Chapter Seven).

Finally, in cases where interdependence leads to conflict between two states, other nations often feel a ripple effect as well. Heightened economic competition between the United States and Japan serves as a powerful illustration. Despite their interdependence, or more likely because of it, Japan has been concerned about the U.S. debt and its impact on the world economy, while the United States has focused on the imbalance of American-Japanese trade tilted in Tokyo's favor. The deterioration in their relationship in the late 1980s and early 1990s sent chills through the world economy, though by 1996 the two economic giants seemed to resolve many of their differences, or at least paper them over with agreements to lower trade barriers on specific products. Over the long term, U.S.–Japanese interdependence has fostered international cooperation while creating new sources of conflict.

On balance, however, interdependence seems to lead to cooperation more often than it generates conflict once fundamental conflicts (such as disputes over territory) are resolved. The growth of the European Union, which is outlined in Chapter Seven, is the strongest example of the trend toward regional cooperation and integration in the New Era. Outside Europe, groupings such as ASEAN (**Association of South-East Asian Nations**), NAFTA (**North American Free Trade Area**), MERCOSUR (the Southern Cone Common Market), and SAARC (South Asian Association for Regional Cooperation) work toward increased cooperation on regional economic, environmental, and other issues. As Chapter Seven discusses, however, the path toward regional integration has been far from smooth, as states and interest groups often disagree over the costs and benefits of cooperation.

As interdependence, especially in the economic and environmental spheres, requires states to negotiate regulations, resolve disputes, and coordinate policies, how much control will individual nation-states retain over their own affairs? According to some scholars, not much. Richard Rosecrance has argued that just as companies have had to "downsize" to remain competitive in the global marketplace, states have had to downsize as well to maximize their economic potential. While firms have shed employees to become more productive and contracted with production facilities overseas, states have shed control over policies and "contracted" with international institutions to manage global trade. While control over vast tracts of territory and the natural resources they contained was a prerequisite for power in the industrial era, in the information age states will draw their economic power from human capital and intellectual property. Countries

Spotlight

Economic Globalization: GATT and WTO

In 1947, twenty-three of the major trading countries convened in Bretton Woods, New Hampshire, under the auspices of the United Nations and agreed upon a set of basic rules and procedures for reducing tariffs. That charter agreement, which eventually had more than 100 signatories, was the General Agreement on Tariffs and Trade (GATT for short). Central to the GATT was the "most-favored-nation" (MFN) clause, embodying the principle of nondiscrimination, which obligates each signatory to treat all GATT partners equally in terms of tariffs (taxes on imports; see Chapter Six) and other restrictions on trade. Codes of conduct, agreed upon by GATT members, outlined rules on quotas, subsidies, and other unfair trade practices. Special rules for developing countries allowed Third World states to give special protection to their "infant industries."

Since its foundation, several rounds of renegotiation of GATT rules have progressively lowered tariffs and nontariff barriers (such as quotas and discriminatory regulations) to trade among member states. The multilateral nature of GATT, however, allowed many member nations to negotiate exceptions to the GATT rules for some of their export products. Agriculture, in particular, has traditionally received special treatment. In 1955 the United States, supposedly the linchpin of the free-trade system, received a GATT waiver allowing it to limit agricultural (especially cotton-related) imports. This action triggered a chain effect, as many countries resorted to protecting agriculture with nontariff barriers and subsidies, making this sector exempt from most GATT regulations.

The most recent round of GATT negotiations, began in 1986 and known as the Uruguay Round, was especially difficult and sometimes acrimonious. The talks ground to a halt twice over the failure to come to an agreement on eliminating agricultural subsidies. Finally, in December 1993, the round concluded with a compromise agreement covering agriculture, tariff and nontariff barriers, and intel-

need not fear the "export" of manufacturing jobs, and indeed they should welcome the fact that metal is being bashed and plastic poured somewhere else, as the greatest profits will go to the centers of "knowledge work" where products are designed and strategies planned. In the same way that the "virtual corporation" may not own any production facilities—in fact, may own hardly any physical assets—the "virtual state" may control hardly any territory, yet be rich in capital and skilled labor.[9]

Nevertheless, even if states no longer value territory as much as they did in previous eras, the degree to which countries will be willing to give up or share their sovereignty clearly has limits. States will always retain responsibility for the welfare and security of their citizens, and political and cultural values will still define national identity. Moreover, the contentious history of trade talks and environmental negotiations has shown that states will only share or give up their sovereign prerogatives when doing so is clearly in their national interest. Nevertheless, greater interdependence seems likely to impel states toward new levels of cooperation in the New Era. The dispersion of production and capital, the concentration

lectual property (copyrights and patents). Neverthe-less, like the North American Free Trade Agreement (NAFTA), the new GATT rules had considerable trouble gaining ratification, as GATT provided for the removal of many protectionist elements of U.S. trade policy.*

The Uruguay Round also established the World Trade Organization (WTO), which was designed to enforce GATT rules by imposing trade sanctions on violators. WTO has more "teeth" than GATT, pro-viding for faster resolution of trade disputes and a greater likelihood of sanctions for violators. The Uruguay Round also convinced many developing countries that GATT was more than just a club of rich nations, and Southern countries began lining up to join after 1986. Even China and Russia, which had denounced GATT as an imperialist insti-tution during the Cold War, have applied for mem-bership in WTO.

Though WTO has shown steady progress since its founding, many members still regard it, along with other trade forums, as mechanisms for opening others' markets while protecting their own. Al-though WTO rules restrict tariffs and prohibit many nontariff barriers, more than a few states have used negotiations over the "unfinished business" of the Uruguay round (including trade in services, ship-ping, telecommunications, and movement of labor) as excuses to hedge their free trade bets and drag their feet. Some WTO rulings have also upset the United States and other leading members by expos-ing protectionist practices and authorizing correc-tive sanctions, but this is exactly what the organiza-tion was designed to do. The effectiveness of this new organization in regulating world trade will be an important test of the ability of nations to cooper-ate on economic issues in the absence of a hegemonic power to enforce the rules of free trade. Despite GATT's record of success and the WTO's ambitious agenda, the open global trading system envisioned at Bretton Woods clearly has a long way to go.

*For more on the Uruguay Round and the WTO, see Bernard M. Hoekman and Michael M. Kostecki, *The Political Economy of the World Trading System* (New York: Oxford University Press, 1995); and Ernest H. Preeg, *Traders in a Brave New World* (Chicago: University of Chicago Press, 1995).

of specialized skills and knowledge, the global nature of security threats such as terrorism and the proliferation of weapons of mass destruction, and the need to conserve the planet's common environmental heritage will remain strong forces for globalization.

COLLECTIVE SECURITY

Globalization, however, is much easier to talk about in theory than it is to man-age in practice. The contrast between the ideals of globalization and the realities of fragmentation is sharpest when one looks at security. The previous chapters re-late how statesmen have regarded the end of every major war as an opportunity to establish a system of **collective security**—in other words, to move beyond a sys-tem in which each state must build up its own forces to safeguard its security, and peace is maintained through a balance of power (discussed in Chapter Two) to-ward a "one for all and all for one" system of unified response to aggression. The

Concert of Europe, established after the Napoleonic Wars, was an early attempt to set up such a system (with mixed results; see Chapter Two), and the League of Nations and United Nations followed World Wars I and II (see Chapter Three). The end of the Cold War saw a continuation of this pattern. In 1992, the secretary-general of the United Nations, Boutros Boutros-Ghali, called for strengthening the UN's capabilities for peacekeeping and preventive diplomacy. (See Chapter Nine for more on these concepts.) He proposed that member states increase their financial contributions for UN peacekeeping, create a standing stock of vehicles and equipment for UN peacekeepers, and predesignate military forces to be placed at the disposal of the Security Council.[10] Although stopping short of calling for a permanent UN military force, these proposals sought to give the United Nations the ability to act quickly and decisively in a crisis, as its founders had hoped it would, but the history of the Cold War showed it often could not.

During the Cold War, one of the superpowers would almost always veto any action against an ally or any other state aligned with it. (Recall from Chapter Four that the UN approved military action in the Korean War only because the Soviet Union refused to participate in Security Council meetings and therefore could not exercise its veto.) The Gulf War, however, convinced many states that UN-mandated peace enforcement could really work, now that superpower rivalry was a thing of the past. At the same time, the civil war that followed the breakup of Yugoslavia (see box below), the violent disintegration and threat of famine in Somalia, and conflicts elsewhere in Asia and Africa demonstrated an urgent need for international action when diplomatic efforts at conflict resolution failed. The UN was founded on the principle of collective response to aggression and breaches of the peace, and member states had often supported that principle with speeches and rhetoric. The time had come, many argued, for UN members to put their money, and their soldiers, where their mouths had been for almost fifty years.

But although the New Era at first highlighted the prospects for collective security, it quickly demonstrated its limitations as well. The first difficulty that became apparent was the "**free rider**" problem: many countries used the expectation of international action as an excuse to avoid acting themselves. States were understandably reluctant to commit resources and put their troops at risk in conflicts that did not immediately threaten their vital interests. Because all would reap the benefits of collective action whether they joined in or not, many preferred to wait for others to foot the bill. Perhaps the most glaring illustration of the free rider problem came in the former Yugoslavia in 1992–1994, when the United States looked to its European allies to commit troops to reinforce UN peacekeepers, but European states refused to send ground troops unless they were backed up by U.S. air and logistical support. While the United States and Europe waited for each other to act, the fighting, mass killings, and other atrocities in Bosnia continued until NATO took responsibility for military action and the United States brokered an interim settlement (see box under ethnic conflict). In a system with only one military superpower (the United States), it is not difficult to see why other states would wait to follow its lead. However, especially when conflict resolution requires long-term political and economic commitments, even a superpower will be reluctant to take the lead unless it is sure that its allies will follow and stay committed for the long haul.

United Nations actions (or lack thereof) in the former Yugoslavia pointed out another inherent difficulty of collective security, the problem of command and coordination. Before intervention by NATO, which had worked out its military command structures over forty years, the UN commander of peacekeeping forces in Bosnia had to ask UN officials for help whenever peacekeepers came under attack. The UN then had to request additional supplies, assistance with logistics, or supporting air strikes from United States or NATO commanders, who could grant or refuse the requests as they saw fit. Peacekeepers could never be sure that the assistance would arrive, and UN forces and civilians often suffered more casualties until it did. The convoluted chain of command thus contributed to costly delays and gave states an additional means of avoiding commitment and responsibility.

Problems of command and control are almost always soluble, but the confusing relationship between the UN and NATO in Bosnia highlighted what may prove to be the most serious obstacle to collective security. Before the deployment of NATO ground forces in 1995, a UN official could ask a NATO commander to order a supporting air mission, and the NATO commander could oblige, without consulting the U.S. president. This system was completely in accordance with both U.S. and international law, but it left the president "out of the loop" while American forces were committed to combat situations. This reinforced a growing impression that participation in international peacekeeping operations contravened U.S. sovereignty, as American troops would be put at risk under foreign commanders. Although diplomatic circles dismissed this objection, the American public became increasingly concerned that "collective security" would circumvent the constitutional procedures of American foreign policy (see Chapter Eleven) and draw U.S. forces into endless civil or ethnic conflicts that had little impact on American vital interests.

The sovereignty issue cuts both ways, however, because deployment of UN peacekeeping forces requires the consent of the state in which they will operate. If the host country refuses to grant consent or withdraws its consent, international peace operations have no legal basis unless the Security Council takes the drastic step of authorizing military action to counter overt aggression. The UN has done so only twice in its fifty-year history (against North Korea in 1950 and Iraq in 1991), and the political circumstances in each case were extraordinary (see Chapters Four and Eleven). Concerns for sovereignty also frustrated preemptive action in the former Yugoslavia in 1991–1995 and Rwanda in 1994–1995 (see the section on ethnic conflict). The clear message of these efforts to enforce peace is that if states are serious about collective security, they must be prepared to modify or violate the principles of national sovereignty that have been pillars of international law since the seventeenth century (see Chapter Two). States are understandably reluctant to set sovereignty aside, as doing so involves the surrender of some degree of national independence and might someday expose them to international intervention in circumstances they could not control. (See Chapter Nine for more on sovereignty issues.)

Though these problems are formidable, the prospects for collective security in the New Era are not totally bleak. The Gulf War demonstrated that concerted international action against naked aggression is possible, though difficult to arrange and coordinate. Missions to provide food, medicine, and other basic needs to refugees in Iraq, Bosnia, Somalia, Rwanda, and elsewhere have shown that the international community can also carry out humanitarian intervention, if its objectives are well-defined and supported by participating states. Similarly, United Nations efforts to manage peaceful transitions to democracy in Namibia and Cambodia have also achieved marked success against what many believed at the outset to be impossible odds. These missions had political, economic, and military components and involved long-term commitments tantamount to nation-building—commitments that the United States and other states have often shied away from since the 1960s, but that the host countries' neighbors were willing to accept in order to stop internal conflicts from spreading and protect their vital interests in regional stability.

The recent successes and failures of collective security therefore show that like any other form of collective action, collective security requires coordination, enforcement, and self-interested cooperation. Leaders in the New Era have learned through bitter experience that like individuals, governments and national publics will not act in concert out of altruism, idealism, or to uphold principles of international law, but will do so in the pragmatic pursuit of their own security or vital interests. Prince Metternich, chief conductor of the Concert of Europe after the Napoleonic Wars, could have taught them the same lesson.

ETHNIC CONFLICT

Many efforts toward collective security were prompted by ethnic conflict, an ancient phenomenon that has reappeared in an especially violent form in the New Era. No state is ethnically homogenous; although a single group constitutes a majority in most states, every state has at least one ethnic, religious, linguistic, or racial minority, and often a number of different groups inhabit the same state. (Both the United States and Russia, for example, have hundreds of indigenous minorities living within their borders.) Sometimes a group comprising the majority in one state is a minority in a neighboring country, and vice-versa—Hungary and Romania, and Rwanda and Burundi, make up ethnic "pairs" in this pattern. At the same time, many ethnic groups, such as Arabs, Kurds, and Lapps, are split between two or more states. Some form of ethnic tension is therefore practically inevitable in all states, but contrary to widely held opinion in the New Era, the tensions arising from ethnic diversity are usually resolved peacefully through mediating institutions.[11] When these institutions collapse or remain unbuilt, however, fear and mistrust can escalate into violence with frightening speed and intensity.

Ever since the era of European nationalism—the ideology claiming that every major ethnic group or "nation" should have its own independent state—began in the nineteenth century, would-be nation-builders have had to deal with the problems that arise when several ethnic groups live in the same territory. (Chapters Two and Three relate how nationalism contributed to the outbreak of both world wars and other conflicts.) Often, attempts to assert ethnic identity take the form of separatist movements that seek at least a measure of autonomy—if not outright independence—from the central government. For example, many in French-speaking Quebec seek to secede from Canada. Basques and Catalans see themselves as separate from Spain. Some Sikhs want to leave India. Some Scots want to separate from the United Kingdom. Russia is plagued by several movements that seek at least autonomy from Moscow. In the most peaceful, but also starkest case of separatism of the early 1990s, the Czech Republic and Slovakia decided on a peaceful divorce into two distinct states carved out of Czechoslovakia, which had existed since the end of World War I.

Ethnic divisions can contribute to several types of violent conflict. First, ethnic strife within the territory of a single state can lead to civil wars. Though they may spring from other sources, civil wars are often caused by the competition between two or more national groups for control of the state. Sri Lanka, Afghanistan, Rwanda, and the Congo experienced ethnic civil wars in the 1980s and 1990s. Second, **separatism** (a drive for autonomy or independence on the part of a single group) can lead to conflict. Separatist movements do not always result in violent conflict, particularly in democratic states; pressure to separate French-speaking Quebec from the rest of Canada since the 1960s has led to little violence, and Czechoslovakia peacefully separated into the Czech Republic and Slovakia in 1993. However, profound and intractable disagreements, particularly when combined with perceptions of discrimination or oppression, can lead one or more groups to deny the very legitimacy of the state, break away from it, and form a new state, leading to a **war of secession.** An especially brutal war resulted when the nascent state of Biafra tried unsuccessfully to secede from Nigeria in 1967–1970, and an equally brutal conflict followed the attempt by Chechnya to secede from Russia in 1994–1996. Conflicts between states also can be caused by one state claiming territory controlled by another state, whether for historical reasons or because the population of that territory shares the nationality of the aggrieved state. This is **irredentism,** which prompted a war between the former Soviet states of Armenia and Azerbaijan even before the USSR formally broke up. Finally, when ethnic groups are divided between several states, nationalist leaders may attempt to wage a **war of unification** to bring the group together in a single state, as North Vietnam did between 1956 and 1975. Figure 5.1 summarizes these types of ethnic war.

All of these phenomena have been frequent throughout history and remain so in the New Era. The frequency of these conflicts is hardly surprising given the proliferation of states after World War II and, more recently, after the breakup of the Soviet Union. In many cases, state borders were drawn by imperial authorities for their own purposes, often in complete disregard of the ethnic groups that were forced together or split apart. The result was to exacerbate tensions between ethnic groups, sometimes leading to violent conflict.

Figure 5.1

Ethnic Wars

TYPE	CAUSE
Civil War	Violent competition between two or more national groups for control of the state.
War of Secession	When disagreements are so profound and intractable that one or more groups deny the legitimacy of the state, they may try to break away from it and form another state or join with another state.
Irredentist War	Conflicts between states caused by one state claiming territory that is controlled by another state, either for historical reasons or because the population of that territory shares the nationality of the aggrieved state.
War of Unification	Leaders attempt to wage a war in order to create a single nation-state for an ethnic group divided among several different states.

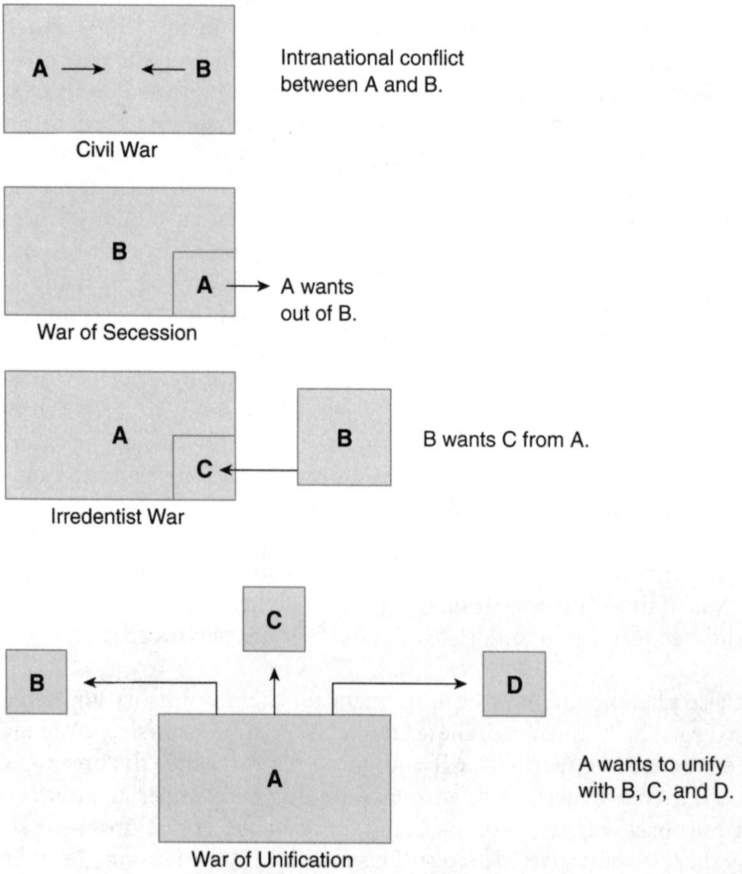

A → ← B

Intranational conflict
between A and B.

Civil War

B

A → A wants
out of B.

War of Secession

A

C ← B   B wants C from A.

Irredentist War

C

B ← → D

A

A wants to unify
with B, C, and D.

War of Unification

Each box represents a nation-state.

The country of Lebanon epitomizes how ethnic conflict can spiral out of control and provoke foreign intervention. From 1943 onward, as a result of a national pact, the president was a Maronite Christian, the premier a Sunni Muslim, and the speaker of the National Assembly a Shiite Muslim. With this balancing act, it is perhaps not surprising that the country has twice in recent decades experienced civil wars fought over the distribution of power, in both instances with external engagement. The 1958 civil war was quickly quelled by American intervention; the civil war that started in 1975, however, lasted sixteen years and was sustained in part by the active involvement of Syria, Israel, the United States, France, Iraq, Iran, and the Palestinians. The complexity of the conflict in Lebanon, exacerbated by foreign power intervention in pursuit of their own objectives, shows why many ethnic conflicts are so stubbornly difficult to disentangle and resolve.

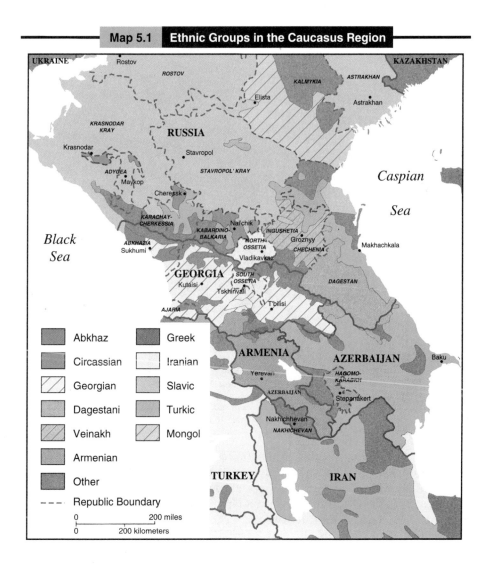

Map 5.1 **Ethnic Groups in the Caucasus Region**

| Map 5.2 | Ethnic Groups in Eastern Europe |

The decline and disintegration of empires often leads to extensive conflict as ethnic groups attempt to stake and enforce their claims over a given territory that is occupied by other ethnic groups as well (see Maps 5.1 and 5.2). For example, as both the Ottoman and Austro-Hungarian empires began to disintegrate in the late nineteenth and early twentieth centuries, fighting broke out between Serbs, Bulgarians, Romanians, and other ethnic groups in the region over the forming of new states (a historical antecedent to the more recent fighting in the Balkans). As we saw in Chapter Three, Serbian support for a secessionist movement in the Austro-Hungarian Empire was the trigger for the beginning of the First World War.

The dismantling of the British Empire after World War II also led to fighting among various ethnic groups. For example, conflict between Hindus and Muslims led to the creation of Islamic Pakistan and secular India, where the Hindus are in the majority. In the turmoil of independence, approximately 7 million Muslims fled to Pakistan and 6 million Hindus to India, and about 1 million people were killed in communal violence. Similarly, fighting erupted between Arabs and Jews in British-controlled Palestine and escalated in 1948 when the surrounding Arab states declared war on the new, Jewish state of Israel. More recently, the disintegration of the Soviet Union led to many conflicting claims over land among ethnic groups in Russia and several other former Soviet republics. In South Africa, the legacy of British imperialism and the policy of apartheid intensified ethnic strife and violence throughout the second half of the twentieth century.

Irredentist claims have frequently created tensions and violence between states. As we saw in Chapter Two, France lost Alsace-Lorraine after the Franco-Prussian War in 1870–1871, and French aspirations for revenge poisoned relations between France and Germany (Prussia's successor) and eventually contributed to World War I. In the late 1930s, Hitler's claim that all Germans should live in one German state led him to annex Austria and then claim the Sudetenland from Czechoslovakia, which was forced by Britain and France to accede to Hitler's

■ UN peacekeepers in Yugoslavia

SOURCE: AP/Wide World

Spotlight

Yugoslavia: A Modern Tragedy

"My apologies to Attila," French Premier Georges Clemenceau once said, "but the art of arranging how men are to live is even more complex than the art of massacring them." Both Attila and Clemenceau would find the tragic events surrounding the dissolution of Yugoslavia all too familiar. During the Cold War, the neutral Communist state of Yugoslavia was often held up as an example of how ethnic groups with long histories of violent conflict could live together peacefully in the same state. However, warning signs of the multiethnic state's impending collapse began to appear shortly after the death in 1980 of Josip Broz Tito, the Communist leader and former anti-Nazi partisan fighter whose legendary reputation and skillful leadership helped hold the country together.

After World War II, Yugoslavia was organized as a federation of ethnically based republics. In the late 1980s, the country became increasingly divided politically, as conflicts appeared between the Belgrade government, dominated by Serbs, and Yugoslavia's other nationalities, including Croats, Slovenes, Albanians, and Muslim Slavs. Following flare-ups of violence in the southern region of Kosovo in 1990, the republics of Slovenia and Croatia seceded from the federation in 1991. Intervention by the federal army did not prevent Slovenian and Croatian independence, but thousands of causalities resulted from the fighting, which ended in an uneasy truce in 1992. The republics of Bosnia and Macedonia seceded shortly afterward.

The most violent act in the tragedy opened in 1992 when a three-sided civil war broke out in Bosnia between Serbian nationalist forces backed by the federal army, Croatian militias receiving support from Croatia, and predominantly Muslim Bosnian forces. The war was fought with a savagery that most modern Europeans would have liked to believe was a thing of the past on their continent. Bosnian Muslims in particular were terrorized by unspeakably brutal policies of "ethnic cleansing," wherein civilians were systematically driven from their homes, put into concentration camps, tortured, raped, or simply slaughtered. An accurate account of casualties from the war may never be made, but estimates of the numbers killed run into the hundreds of thousands.*

The United Nations, the Organization on Security and Cooperation in Europe (OSCE), the European Union, and NATO were slow to coordinate an effective response to the bloodshed. UN peacekeeping forces and relief convoys were deployed early in the conflict, but it was not until 1994 that NATO deployed an Implementation Force, or IFOR (including a sizable contingent of American troops) to guarantee the UN-ordered cease-fire. By that time, well over 70 percent of Bosnia had been carved up by Serbian and Croatian forces. In 1995, after intense pressure from the United States, the three parties signed the Dayton Accords, which provided for an independent multiethnic Bosnia with a collective presidency (in which a Muslim, a Serb, and a Croat serve together as chief executive). NATO deployed a Stabilization Force (SFOR) to police the implementation of the accords, but the agreements were violated in both letter and spirit, and continuing incidents of ethnic violence made the survival of a multiethnic Bosnia appear uncertain.

More acts may yet be added to the tragedy of Yugoslavia, as ethnic conflicts still smolder in Bosnia, Kosovo, and other areas. The halting response of the international community to the war in Bosnia augured poorly for the ability of international institutions to maintain peace, and the human tragedy of the breakup of Yugoslavia proved that ethnic and nationalist conflicts in the New Era could be every bit as bloody as they were in the past.

* For more on the many conflicts in the former Yugoslavia, see Misha Glenny, *The Fall of Yugoslavia* (New York: Penguin, 1992); James Gow, *Triumph of the Lack of Will: International Diplomacy and the Yugoslav War* (New York: Columbia University Press, 1997); Robert Kaplan, *Balkan Ghosts* (New York: St. Martin's, 1993); Sabrina Petra Ramet, *Balkan Babel* (Boulder: Westview, 1996); and Susan Woodward, *Balkan Tragedy* (Washington: Brookings, 1995).

demands at the now infamous 1938 Munich Conference. More recently, Iraq cited irredentist claims against parts of southwestern Iran, inhabited primarily by Arab Sunni Muslims, as justification for its war with Iran in 1980–1988. In the 1990s, Russian claims to the Crimea, which is part of Ukraine, offer another example of political irredentism.

Wars of national unity have also created considerable international conflicts. Perhaps the most prominent example was a series of three wars during the mid-nineteenth century. First, Prussia fought Denmark, then Austria, and finally France, all in order to unify and dominate Germany. Italy was also unified during the mid-nineteenth century, with the Italian state of Piedmont taking the lead and fighting Austria in the process. The Kurds were promised a state by the great powers after World War I. Instead, they were divided into areas that are now in Turkey, Iraq, Syria, and Iran—leading to violent conflicts that have lasted decades and have involved efforts both to secede from some or all of these countries and to achieve unification. Recently, the collapse of the Soviet Union left millions of Russians living in independent former Soviet republics with non-Russian majorities. Many new states have subsequently been rocked by ethnic violence; Russians in Moldova, many hoping to eventually reunify with Russia, created their own secessionist republic in 1992. On the other hand, Abkhazians and South Ossetians tried to secede from Georgia after the collapse of the USSR. Extremist "national-patriotic" movements in Russia have called for the reunification of the great Russian state, and many leaders in Moscow have asserted their country's right to protect the rights of ethnic Russians residing in neighboring states.

The long list of violent ethnic conflicts in the post–World War II period should not prompt the conclusion that ethnic divisions always lead to violence. In many European countries, notably Switzerland, Belgium, and Finland, ethnic groups with long histories of warfare live together peacefully, with the rights of all groups protected by law and constitutional arrangements. It is also not easy to conclude whether some Asian states that have experienced communal conflict, such as Malaysia, Indonesia, and India, represent successes or failures of their regimes in controlling ethnic violence, as the long history of conflict between the ethnic groups in these states might have led one to expect a great deal more violence than has occurred. Nationalism has often been derided by world leaders since the nineteenth century, yet it can be a force that unites as well as divides people, especially when nationalist movements concentrate on building civic institutions based on common values rather than on accentuating ethnic identity and promoting separatism. Thus, although ethnic conflict may very well be a major factor in international relations in the New Era, a number of hopeful examples indicate that governments and international organizations can find ways to moderate ethnic tensions.

REGIONAL CONFLICTS

This chapter now turns to areas that have had frequent international conflict and war since 1945 and are likely to continue to be zones of instability in the New Era.

Unlike the ethnic conflicts in the Balkans or the collapsed African states discussed earlier in this chapter, most of the conflicts in the Middle East, South Asia, and East Asia are not merely domestic disputes writ large. Although domestic politics naturally plays a role in the ways the involved countries deal with the conflicts in which they are embroiled, the regional conflicts examined here are first and foremost disputes between states rather than within them.

Domestic Sources of Regional Conflict

The primary causes of conflicts in the developing world may be divided into the two broad categories of "imported" and "domestic" problems. The domestic sources of disputes lie in **indigenous conflicts,** many of which predated the era of European imperialism and would be just as likely to cause dissension and violence if Europeans had never visited the region. **Imported conflicts,** on the other hand, are generally consequences of integration into the global political and economic system, or essentially extensions of Northern ideas and problems into the South. Despite this distinction, few conflicts are purely imported or domestic in character. For example, ancient animosities between ethnic groups may have been exploited to further a colonial power's imperial ambitions, reinforcing a history of hatred that spills over into the present day. On the other hand, religious conflicts that have persisted for centuries may have originated with the introduction of a faith, such as Christianity or Islam, by an imperial power. Nevertheless, the grouping of sources of regional conflicts into imported and domestic varieties is useful for the analysis of contemporary disputes in the developing world.

As we have described, ethnic conflict is foremost among the domestic sources of regional antagonisms. The withdrawal or collapse of the empires that once ruled over most of Asia and Africa involved the removal of the center's control and often the revival, usually with renewed intensity, of ethnic disputes over territory. Often, these disputes are complicated by the fact that in certain areas ethnic groups have intermingled. For example, the decline of the Ottoman and Austro-Hungarian empires left a vacuum in which the new states of the Balkans fought wars that eventually contributed to the outbreak of World War I. Then, for seventy years the Balkan conflicts remained dormant, as fighting between the ethnic groups was suppressed by monarchical and Communist regimes in Yugoslavia and after World War II by Communist regimes in Romania, Hungary, and Bulgaria. The breakup of the Soviet empire and the subsequent violence in this region clearly showed that these ethnic problems were not solved. This sad pattern has been repeated in many instances throughout the developing world.

Another source of conflict is religion. Before the twentieth century, more blood was shed over religious disputes than any other cause, and this history of violence in the name of faith persists in many nations where norms and institutions of religious tolerance have not taken root. For instance, long-standing religious hatreds exploded into violence after British India was divided into independent India (with a Hindu majority) and Pakistan (where most of the population is Muslim).

In many cases, the line between ethnic and religious conflict is blurred, because concepts of ethnic or national identity sometimes center on religion. In other instances, religious differences reinforce ethnic antipathy, as shown by the recurrent conflicts between Arabs, most of whom adhere to the Sunni branch of Islam, and Iranians, the majority of whom belong to the Shia Islamic sect.

A third domestic source of conflict is economic, having nothing to do with spiritual values and everything to do with material goods. Economic factors alone rarely result in violence, but they can exacerbate political or economic cleavages. In many parts of the developing world, prosperous states border upon desperately poor neighbors with much larger populations. The gap between rich and poor can be particularly painful when the states involved share a common linguistic, ethnic, and cultural identity. This situation is most pronounced in the Arab world, where in 1990 the oil-rich United Arab Emirates enjoyed a per capita GNP of $19,800, compared with a figure of $600 for the most populous Arab state, Egypt.[12] As in the developed North, economic and class differences can generate conflict within as well as between countries, as shown by the violent disputes over land reform in much of Latin America. Few poor states have the resources necessary to make war on their richer neighbors, though Iraq's 1990 invasion of Kuwait, smaller in total GNP but wealthier on a per capita basis, offers a notable exception. Still, in the developing world, as in American cities, the juxtaposition of wealth and poverty can be politically explosive.

Imported Sources of Conflict

Torn as they are by ethnic, religious, and economic conflicts, many developing countries would have more than enough to worry about without any problems brought in from the developed world. But few countries in the developing world are free of imported sources of conflict. One factor mentioned in the previous chapters is the legacy of imperialism, manifested in forms such as arbitrary borders drawn for the convenience of former colonial powers. These borders can separate ethnic groups that would prefer to be united, or unite historically antagonistic groups that have no desire to live together. If one of these groups becomes dominant and carries out policies regarded as unjust (often with very good reason) by the others, violence is the predictable result. This type of conflict has led to bloody struggles in Nigeria, Sudan, Ethiopia, Rwanda, Burundi, Angola, and Congo.

As we read earlier in this chapter and in Chapter Two, the notion that each nationality should ideally live in its own sovereign state with defined borders was originally a European idea. Thus, nationalism may be counted as one of the imported causes of regional conflict. Several of the conflicts just mentioned resulted from attempts by ethnic groups to break away from existing states and create their own nations. Other groups sought instead to unify politically fragmented nations: in the nineteenth century, it was Italy and Germany; in the twentieth, it was Pan-Arabism, an ideology that contends that all Arabs constitute one nation and should be politically united. This chapter's section on the Middle East says more about Pan-Arabism and another nationalist movement that has had a profound impact on the region, **Zionism** (Jewish nationalism). Similarly, China's long-standing goal of reunification with Taiwan, Macao, and Hong Kong (which was returned to China in 1997 after a century and a half of British control) has heightened tensions in East Asia.

Although nationalism and the aftereffects of imperialism are likely to persist for some time, one of the greatest external causes of regional conflict has come to an end. This, of course, was the Cold War, which inexorably brought the developing world into the bipolar confrontation between the United States and the Soviet Union. Both superpowers supported states and insurgencies in developing areas in order to further their political and military objectives and to protect their strategic interests. For example, in Central America in the 1980s, the United States sent generous amounts of military aid and expertise to the government of El Salvador, which was opposed by the Cuban and Soviet-backed Farabundo Marti National Liberation Front (FMLN) movement. Meanwhile, in neighboring Nicaragua, the USSR supported the socialist Sandinista regime in its fight against *Contra* rebels supplied by the United States. The only instances where the Cold War escalated into actual war occurred when the superpowers intervened in such conflicts in the developing world. Tens of thousands of Americans and their allies were killed fighting Communist forces in Korea and Vietnam, thousands of Soviets died in the USSR's attempt to bring Afghanistan into the Soviet orbit, and millions of citizens of those three developing countries lost their lives in those "limited" wars. Several leaders of nonaligned nations, most notably Gamal Abdel Nasser in Egypt and Jawaharlal Nehru in India, attempted to play the USSR and United States off against each other in hopes of receiving largesse from both.

During the Cold War, many people wondered whether the U.S.–Soviet rivalry was intensifying Third World conflicts, or whether the reverse was true—that disputes in developing areas were heating up the Cold War. Much evidence supports both sides of this argument. Many insurgent movements would have had little or no chance of success without U.S. or Soviet support, and so would have "died aborning," but many interstate disputes (particularly the Arab-Israeli conflict) put the interests of both superpowers at risk and so demanded action from Washington or Moscow. This question was the greatest "chicken or egg" controversy of the Cold War: Which came first, the indigenous conflict or superpower involvement?

When the Cold War ended, the debate fizzled out without resolution, but it is worth mentioning because it illustrates an important point regarding regional conflicts. Like the struggles in which the superpowers became entangled, many regional conflicts have been intensified and perpetuated by a vicious cycle of internal and external causes. An ancient ethnic hatred may have been brought to the fore when a colonial power exited, leaving behind borders with no economic or cultural justification and guerrilla forces on both sides of the dispute receiving weapons from the superpowers. Because of the multiplicity of causes and influences that underlie them, subnational conflicts in the developing world often defy simple analyses and solutions. The height of absurdity occurred in Angola, a former Portuguese colony in southern Africa, when troops from Communist Cuba guarded oil fields operated by American companies against attack from UNITA guerrilla forces—which were backed and supplied by the United States!

Contemporary Regional Dynamics

The end of the Cold War transformed the balance of power in all the regions we will discuss. During the period of U.S.–Soviet global rivalry, both superpowers furnished regional allies with arms and technical assistance at low or no cost. However, as the USSR reconsidered its foreign policies under Mikhail Gorbachev, Moscow began to conclude that providing arms and other aid to regional clients effectively free of charge had produced few lasting benefits. After the Soviet Union broke up, Russia continued to sell arms to regional buyers, but on a cash-and-carry basis, and those without cash often found themselves facing hard choices between guns and butter. The United States, meanwhile, continued to sell both guns and butter to most regional powers, though it concentrated outright aid on states participating in the Middle East peace process. Parties with whom the United States refused to deal (including Iran, North Korea, and Iraq after 1990) could shop for arms from emerging suppliers such as China, develop their own weapons programs, or trade with one another. In any event, although global politics often fueled regional conflicts during the Cold War, regional dynamics seems likely to profoundly affect global politics in the New Era.

The complexity of many regional conflicts reflects their multiplicity of causes. The external sources of conflict generally derive from the political and economic globalization, while the indigenous sources typically result from fragmentation, especially within developing nations. Although almost every region has been affected by intrastate violence as a result of these contending forces, wars between (rather than within) states have been concentrated in a few regions of intense conflict, especially the Middle East, South Asia, and East Asia. The following sections will show how regional balances of power have at times prompted attempts to resolve interstate conflicts by war and at other times prolonged disputes in an uneasy state of "no war, no peace." To illustrate these dynamics at work, some review of their recent history is a necessity—in many cases a grim necessity, as these regions have all too often been the locus of bitter and bloody conflict.

The Middle East

Of the three regions we will examine, the Middle East shows in starkest relief the effects of domestic, regional, and global struggles for power. Within the various Middle Eastern states, domestic struggles for power have often led to states that were unstable, frequently governed by the military and intelligence agencies, and prone to use an exterior enemy in order to stifle internal opposition. The intertwined conflicts have created not one but three regional balances of power—Arab-Arab, Arab-Israeli, and Arab-Iranian—that are separate but also interact, with conflict in one frequently spilling over into another. On top of this volatile situation, the Cold War added the struggle between superpowers for allies and clients in the region. The superpowers' provision of economic and, in particular, military assistance to their regional allies helped maintain the regional balances of power but fueled a spiraling regional arms race.[13]

Conflicting nationalist aspirations are the foundation of the three regional balances of power. The conflict between Zionism, or Jewish nationalism, and Arab and Palestinian nationalism forms the core of the Arab-Israel conflict. The Arab world itself has been divided between the tug of Pan-Arab nationalism, which calls for a single Arab state and denies the legitimacy of separate Arab states, and the pull of distinctive statist nationalism (in Egypt, Jordan, Syria, Iraq, and elsewhere), which argues that the independent Arab states are legitimate entities. The ancient rivalry between Arabs and Persians formed one of the bases of tensions between Iraq (both Arab and Islamic) and Iran (Islamic, but not Arab). The religious differences between Sunni Islam, dominant in Iraq, and Shia Islam, dominant in Iran, add yet another dimension of conflict between those states. Thus, although the Middle East is suffused with ancient indigenous hatreds, many of its conflicts are sustained by a concept of nationalism that originated in nineteenth-century Europe (see Chapter Two). Nationalist aspirations in the region draw upon interpretations of history that emphasize periods of national glory but are also to a large extent responses to European events. Zionism was a reaction against the continual persecution of Jews in Europe, culminating in the Holocaust during World War II. It held that Jews would never be safe until they had their own state. Arab nationalism was a reaction to increasing European encroachment on the Middle East; it emphasized the unity and power of the early Arab caliphates. Though Arab-Iranian antagonism has persisted for centuries, Iranian nationalism was partly a response to the indignity of being dominated by Russia and Britain during the nineteenth century and during World War II and to the predominance of American influence after World War II. The shahs who formerly ruled Iran claimed that their dynasties were a continuation of the great Persian empires, while the leaders of the Islamic revolution of 1979 rallied around the struggles and sufferings of Shia Islam.

End of the Ottoman Empire

Prior to 1914 the Middle East was dominated by the Ottoman Empire for four hundred years. As long as the Ottomans, the leading Islamic power, controlled most of the region, peoples' identities were based on family, tribe, occupation, and religion, rather than on nationalism as it was known in Europe (see Chapter Two). By the end of the nineteenth century, however, nationalism was on the rise within the empire, as the Turks "rediscovered" their distinctive ethnicity and sought to exclude Arabs from administrative posts. In turn, the Arabs increasingly "rediscovered" their own ethnic identity and began to press for autonomy and independence. Turks, Arabs, Persians, and Jews were all influenced by European ideas of nationalism and national identity.

Like the Austro-Hungarian Empire, the Ottoman Empire was on the losing side in World War I and relinquished its imperial possessions; the empire itself ceased to exist upon the declaration of the Republic of Turkey in 1923. What to do with its Middle East holdings became a matter of considerable contention in the peace conferences after World War I, in large part because of the contradictory promises Britain had made to various groups during the war. In return for Jewish support, Britain issued the **Balfour Declaration,** which stated in 1917 that Britain supported the establishment of a Jewish "national home" in Palestine, as long as it did not prejudice the civil and religious rights of non-Jewish residents. This promise appeared to conflict with Britain's promises to support Arab independence in exchange for Arab participation in the war against the Ottoman Empire. Conflicting with both of these promises was the arrangement Britain made with France to divide the Middle East into spheres of influence. (Wits remarked that Palestine was truly the Promised Land, as Britain had promised it to both Arabs and Jews.) Trying to reconcile these conflicting promises amounted to squaring a circle; many of the opposing demands were irreconcilable. As it turned out, because they were the most powerful actors in the region after the war, the British and French adhered to their own arrangements and drew the boundaries of their mandated territories to serve their own interests.[14]

This does not mean that the promises to either the Zionists or the Arabs were ignored. The British control of Palestine, Transjordan, and Iraq, and French control of Lebanon and Syria, were mediated through the League of Nations. The Middle Eastern areas were not colonies but mandates to be held until the local peoples were ready for independence and self-government. Arab claims that they were prepared for independence, based in no small measure on their contribution of troops in the war against the Ottomans, were forcefully suppressed, with particularly bloody results in French-controlled Syria. The British and French drew international borders—none had existed previously—to suit their own interests and to the benefit of ethnic or religious communities to whom they were sympathetic. Thus, to the preexisting Maronite Christian areas of Lebanon, France added the predominantly Sunni Muslim north and Shiite south. Britain, to fulfill its promises to Arab leaders, separated Jordan from Palestine.

The new states were not yet independent, but they still faced considerable internal problems in their attempts to consolidate their control. During the Ottoman period many groups had maintained considerable autonomy because of the center's weakness, limitations of communications, and geographic boundaries. The new states, and their British and French overlords, sought to increase their control over such communities. Because the Arab elites' pressure for independence conflicted with the desires of the French and British to maintain control, the latter turned to divide-and-conquer policies. For example, in Syria the French turned to the poorer Alawites and Druze, who were discriminated against by the Sunni majority, as the backbone of the military and internal security apparatus. This would have considerable impact on future developments.

Arab-Israeli Conflict Begins

By the end of World War II, several Arab states had finally become independent, but their weakness was one of the main factors that prevented a coherent and forceful response to the Zionist movement in Palestine. After 6 million Jews were murdered by the Nazi regime in World War II, international support for Zionism increased, as did the pressure for emigration of Jews into Palestine. As fighting intensified there between Arabs and Jews, the British were caught in the middle and decided to withdraw and turn the problem over to the UN. For different reasons both the Soviet Union and the United States supported the UN-proposed partition of Palestine and thus the creation of two independent states, one Jewish, the other Arab; Jerusalem was to become an international city. The Jews accepted the plan, but the Arab Palestinians—backed by the other Arab states—insisted that all of Palestine must become an independent Arab state. When the British departed in May 1948, Israel declared its independence and the surrounding Arab states invaded, beginning the first Arab-Israeli war.

After almost a year of fighting, Israeli forces repulsed the invading Arab armies, and 760,000 Arab refugees fled. Israel conquered lands allotted to the Arab state of Palestine, which never came into being. Territory allocated to the proposed Palestinian Arab state was also conquered by Jordan, whose annexation of the West Bank in 1950 was never internationally recognized as legitimate. Egypt controlled the last portion of Palestine, the Gaza Strip, a small sliver of land onto which were crowded tens of thousands of refugees.

The defeat of the Arab states dealt a considerable blow to the legitimacy and stability of the existing regimes, exacerbating socioeconomic and political divisions. In 1950 King Abdullah of Jordan was assassinated, and in 1952 King Farouk I of Egypt was overthrown by a nationalist revolution led by Gamel Abdel Nasser, who soon became the country's president (see Spotlight box). During the 1950s, Syria experienced several changes of government as military clique replaced military clique, each basing its support on various ethnic groups.

The new Arab regimes in Syria and Egypt were authoritarian. They held the West, including the United States, responsible for Israel's establishment and resented the limitations of arms supplies imposed on the region by Britain, France, and the United States. Egypt's Nasser was especially incensed by the American-British effort to form an alliance against the Soviet Union that would have transformed Egypt's arch-opponent Iraq into the political center of the Middle East. When the United States offered to sell him arms under tight conditions, Nasser rejected the idea and instead approached the Soviet Union for economic and military assistance. The Soviets jumped at the opportunity to play a major role in the Middle East and began to supply Egypt with aid and weapons, thereby destabilizing the balance of power between Egypt and Israel.

Nasser

Within the Arab circle there is a role wandering aimlessly in search of a hero. For some reason it seems to me that this role is beckoning to us—to move, to take up its lines, put on its costumes and give it life. Indeed, we are the only ones who can play it. The role is to spark the tremendous latent strengths in the region surrounding us to create a great power, which will then rise up to a level of dignity and undertake a positive part in building the future of mankind.

This statement by Gamal Abdel Nasser in 1958 exemplified the frustration and hope of the Arab world in the 1950s. Newly independent in the 1930s and 1940s, the Arab world underwent a wave of revolutions after its defeat at the hands of Israel in 1948. A decade later, a new optimism had emerged. Many believed the Arabs—united by culture, religion, and history—should unify and become a major economic and military power on the world scene. Israel would be defeated, prosperity would arrive, the great powers would take the united Arab government seriously, and a major social and intellectual renaissance would occur.

Nasser offered himself as the leader of the Pan-Arab movement. In Egypt, he launched sweeping programs of land reform and economic development, including a project to dam the Nile River at Aswan. But the United States and Britain, concerned over Nasser's ties with the Soviet bloc, withdrew funding for the dam in July 1956; five days later, Nasser announced the nationalization of the Suez Canal. A subsequent invasion by Israeli, British, and French forces failed to topple his government, and Nasser emerged more popular than ever. His most dramatic step toward unifying the Arab states was the joining of Egypt and Syria in the United Arab Republic in 1958. Another victory for Nasser occurred when the pro-Western Iraqi gov-

ernment he opposed was toppled by the Baghdad regime's radical adversaries.

Yet many of his gains were illusory. Although many Arab leaders supported Pan-Arabism, they were not prepared to relinquish their regime or their rule to others. Thus, Nasser soon found that the radical Iraqi regime caused him as much trouble as the old pro-Western rulers. Syria withdrew in disgust from the union with Cairo in 1961. After Nasser ordered Egyptian troops to intervene in the 1962 civil war in Yemen, the Saudi monarchy put a $1 million price on his head.

Facing growing problems at home as his development plans foundered, Nasser tried to rally support by railing against Egypt's main enemy, Israel. His remilitarization of the Sinai and blockade of the Strait of Tiran prompted Israel to strike preemptively in 1967, and Egypt suffered another devastating defeat. Although Nasser remained in office, his power was irretrievably diminished. He died of a heart attack in September 1970 after working furiously to bring about a settlement of the civil war in Jordan.

Nasser's dream of a unified, secular Arab state died with him, but his example as a leader who defied colonialism and the superpowers lives on throughout the Arab world. His frustrations and failures symbolize the underlying divisions that remain among Arab countries. A quarter century later, Islamic fundamentalism has replaced secular radicalism as the central threat to Western interests. In the wake of the new divisions in the Arab world created by the Persian Gulf War of 1991, Pan-Arabism is now weaker than ever. An Arab world of individual rulers and regimes has for now won out over the Pan-Arab vision.

Conflicts of the 1950s and 1960s

Nasser was also angered by the American rejection of economic assistance to construct the Aswan High Dam, which was designed to control the Nile River and was seen as crucial to Egypt's economic development. In retaliation, in July 1956 he nationalized the Suez Canal, which was under the jurisdiction of an Anglo-French company. Nasser's moves infuriated the British and French, the latter already angered by his support for the Arab rebellion against French control of Algeria.

Britain and France began to coordinate policy with Israel, which was concerned about Egypt's growing military strength, and the three states agreed on a secret plan to attack Egypt. The plan was set in motion when Israel invaded Egypt's Sinai Desert in October 1956, and shortly afterward Britain and France intervened, ostensibly to separate the two sides and protect the Suez Canal. Although Israel gained a military victory, Egypt scored a political knockout when both the United States and the USSR, each for its own reasons, forced Britain, France, and eventually Israel, to withdraw. President Eisenhower, infuriated by the secrecy of the attack, believed that it undermined American efforts to build good relations with the Arab states. The Soviets, seeing an opportunity to demonstrate their importance in the fight against imperialism, ostentatiously threatened Britain and France with missile attacks and Israel with destruction. After Britain, France, and Israel backed down, Nasser's prestige in the Arab world rose dramatically.

Nasser's appeal increased the attractiveness of his call for Arab unity, the central goal of Pan-Arabism, and his cries for the overthrow of Arab regimes viewed as puppets of the imperialist West. (See Chapter Twelve for more on Nasser's goals and style of leadership.) During the late 1950s there was considerable domestic unrest throughout the Middle East, and 1958 proved to be a fateful year for many Arab countries. Lebanon experienced a civil war, which led to American intervention. (The U.S. forces landed with no opposition; sunbathers on Beirut beaches, surprised by American landing craft, asked the Marines if they had come to start a war and resumed sunbathing when told that the Marines were a peace-keeping force.) King Hussein of Jordan was threatened at home by supporters of Nasser. Meanwhile, in Iraq the monarchy was overthrown by radicals, who were in turn overthrown in 1963 in a coup executed by the Ba'ath (Arab Socialist Renaissance) party. In Syria the internal upheaval was so severe that the ruling clique united the country with Nasser's Egypt, thus forming the United Arab Republic.

The domestic unrest was eventually quelled with the assistance of U.S. intervention in Lebanon and British intervention in Jordan. In 1961 the United Arab Republic dissolved when Syria seceded from Egypt. With his standing in the region now diminished, Nasser increased political propaganda and subversion efforts against the regimes he saw as opponents. In 1962 Egypt intervened in North Yemen on the side of socialist-oriented republicans, who were fighting a civil war against the Saudi-supported monarchists. The Egyptian intervention in Yemen has been called "Nasser's Vietnam," and his economic and political costs, including the antagonism of Saudi Arabia and the United States, were considerable. In 1966 the radical left wing of the Ba'ath party took control of Syria and supported military and terrorist attacks against Israel. Syria was militarily weak, however, and was consistently defeated in skirmishes with the Jewish state. The government in Damascus, joined by Jordan and Saudi Arabia, accused Nasser's Egypt of failing to confront Israel, which they contended was their primary threat.

Six-Day War and Its Aftermath

The charge of failing to confront Israel embarrassed Nasser, and when Syria and Israel engaged in border clashes during the spring of 1967, he intensified his rhetoric against Israel. In May 1967 the Soviets, fearing for the survival of the Syrian regime, falsely told Nasser that Israel was planning to invade Syria. Nasser moved Egyptian troops into the Sinai Peninsula in order to deter Israel from such an attack. If this policy had been successful, it would have brought Egypt considerable prestige. Instead, the move initiated a crisis that led inexorably toward war.

The UN acceded to Nasser's demand that its peacekeeping forces already in Sinai withdraw, removing a buffer between Egyptian and Israeli troops. Nasser promptly blockaded the important Israeli port of Eilat. Significantly, Jordan and Syria then placed their armies under Egyptian command; this formation of a coalition against Israel represented a dramatic shift in the Arab-Israeli balance of power. Fearing encirclement and an imminent Arab attack, Israel launched a preemptive war on June 5. In the course of six days, Israeli ground and air forces routed the armies of Egypt, Jordan, and Syria. The Soviets, who had contributed to provoking the crisis, were stunned by the rapid Israeli defeat of their Arab allies. Fearing that Israel might drive for total victory, Moscow decided to break diplomatic relations with the Jewish state and to pressure the United States to restrain Israel.

The 1967 war, known as the Six-Day War, was the definitive event in contemporary Middle East history. Israel captured the Sinai Peninsula and the Gaza Strip from Egypt, the West Bank from Jordan, and the Golan Heights from Syria (see Map 5.3). The defeat severely weakened Nasser, and he was forced to rely on economic aid from the oil-producing gulf states, especially Saudi Arabia (in exchange for Egyptian withdrawal from Yemen). The inability of the superpowers to control events, and the possibility that a Middle East crisis could lead to a superpower confrontation, increased the desire of the United States and the USSR to attain some sort of settlement.[15]

Although Washington and Moscow engaged in diplomatic efforts to achieve a negotiated settlement, their positions generally reflected those of their combative allies fairly closely. The early result of the diplomacy was UN Security Council Resolution 242, which enshrined the principle of "land for peace." The resolution called upon Israel to return "territories occupied" in 1967 in exchange for recognition of its right to exist within secure borders. (The resolution was very carefully worded and deliberately ambiguous; it did not explicitly call for Israel to return all territories occupied in the war.)

Meanwhile, the superpowers rearmed their regional clients. The result was the 1969–1970 War of Attrition that Egypt initiated in frustration when it did not regain the Sinai. Initially the fighting consisted of artillery duels across the Suez Canal, but it soon escalated as Israel launched deep-penetration air attacks against Egypt. Placed on the defensive, Nasser sought and received direct military support from the Soviets, who sent in advisors and pilots. Because it was preoccupied with events in Vietnam, America's response to this unprecedented Soviet intervention was initially subdued, but Washington's diplomatic efforts brought about a cease-fire in August 1970.

If one of the effects of the 1967 war was to demonstrate the weakness of the Arab states, another was to increase the importance of the Palestinian national movement. Prior to 1967 the Palestine Liberation Organization (PLO) was poorly led and was a tool of various Arab states, especially Nasser's Egypt. After 1967 this organization, an umbrella for various Palestinian groups with different ideologies, became more independent under its dominant faction, Yasser Arafat's al-Fatah. As the PLO launched terrorist attacks against Israel, it increasingly came into conflict with the Arab states, which were suffering from Israeli military retaliation. In Jordan the PLO's strength made it resemble a state within a state, and its power was seen as a challenge to King Hussein. After numerous skirmishes, in September 1970 a full-fledged civil war broke out between the PLO and the Jordanian army. Serious Palestinian setbacks led to Syrian intervention. This move initiated an international crisis, in which the United States and Israel put pressure on Syria to withdraw its forces from Jordan. As the Jordanian army drove the Syrians out and routed the PLO forces, Nasser engaged in diplomacy aimed at saving the PLO's position in Jordan. The PLO survived the civil war but was forced to shift its base to Lebanon. Upon completing his mediation efforts, Nasser suffered a heart attack and died, marking the end of an era.

Petroleum, Power, and Politics

The 1950s and 1960s were decades of revolutionary nationalism in the Arab world, but the 1970s was a decade of oil wealth. In the years immediately after Nasser's death, Egypt's new president, Anwar el-Sadat, moderated Cairo's foreign policy by improving relations with the rich oil-producing states. Not surprisingly, Egypt's relations with the Soviet Union grew cooler, and in 1972 Sadat expelled the Soviet military advisors Nasser had invited. In an attempt to improve relations, the Soviets subsequently sold considerable quantities of arms to Egypt, paid for in part with Saudi money. At the same time, the United States and other Western countries became increasingly dependent on Middle Eastern oil, due to the rapid economic growth of the 1960s and the correspondingly rapid depletion of U.S. oil reserves.[16] Unable to gain support for their demands that Israel return the territories it conquered in 1967, Egypt and Syria grew progressively resentful and came to believe that only another war would enable them to create favorable political conditions. The two countries thus began to coordinate their strategies in another

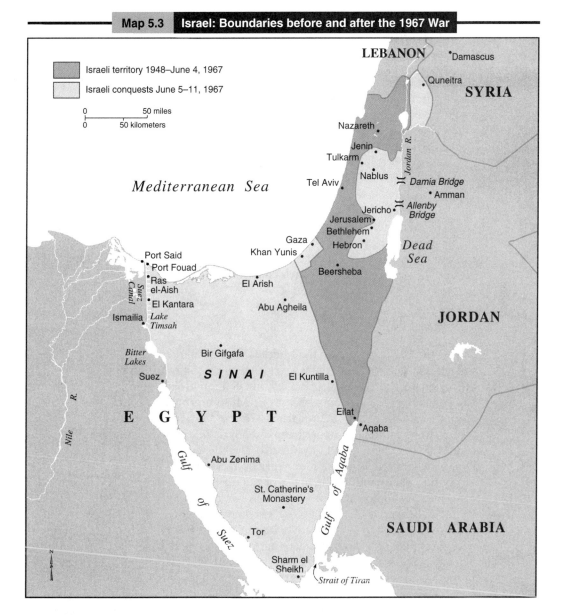

Map 5.3 **Israel: Boundaries before and after the 1967 War**

Israeli territory 1948–June 4, 1967

Israeli conquests June 5–11, 1967

attempt to turn the Arab-Israeli balance of power to their advantage. They also received assurances from Saudi Arabia that in the event of war, it would impose an oil embargo against Israel's supporters among Western countries.

Their strategy was implemented in October 1973 when Egypt and Syria launched a surprise attack against Israel known as the October War (or the Yom Kippur War, because the attack began on that Jewish holiday). Israel's forces in the Sinai and Golan Heights were initially thrown on the defensive, but after suffering heavy losses took the offensive. Because of the intensity and length of the fighting, both the USSR and the United States conducted emergency airlifts of weapons and supplies to their allies. After a brief cease-fire arranged by the superpowers, fighting resumed, and Israel was positioned to annihilate the portion of the Egyptian army trapped in the Sinai. Fearing the complete defeat of its ally, the Soviet Union mobilized airborne troops and threatened to intervene directly. In response, the United States put its military forces, including its nuclear weapons, on heightened alert. The risk of a direct superpower confrontation was exaggerated, but American pressure convinced Israel to accept a cease-fire.[17]

During the war, Saudi Arabia and the other Arab oil-producing states imposed an oil embargo on the United States and the Netherlands for their support of Israel. The price of oil, a vital resource for industrial economies, increased dramatically, and the startling rise in the price and disruption of the availability of gasoline sent shock waves throughout the industrialized states. This use of the "oil weapon" prompted the United States to redouble its efforts to bring about a political settlement of the Arab-Israeli conflict.[18]

Land for Peace

During the 1970s, politics in the Middle East was marked by two contrasting tendencies. On the one hand, there was growing instability within many countries in the region. In one example, a civil war in Lebanon broke out in 1975 as Maronite Christians opposed attempts by various Muslim groups to change the country's political balance of power. In early 1976 the Muslims, supported by the PLO, seemed to be gaining the upper hand until Syria intervened on the side of the Maronites. Meanwhile, the PLO remained an independent force in southern Lebanon, which it used as a base for terrorist attacks against Israel.

On the other hand, in the midst of the turmoil in Lebanon, the United States continued its diplomatic efforts to resolve the region's seemingly intractable conflicts. Between 1973 and 1976, Secretary of State Henry Kissinger sought to bypass the Soviets to deal directly with the Middle Eastern states. U.S. diplomatic efforts resulted in a disengagement agreement between Israel and Syria and two agreements between Israel and Egypt, in both of which Israel pulled back its forces in the Sinai. Believing that Kissinger's step-by-step approach had achieved all it could, in 1977 the new Carter administration sought to reengage the Soviets in an effort to achieve a comprehensive peace. Although the operation was a failure, the patient's health improved: fearing that a peace process including the Soviets and the Syrians would go nowhere, Egypt's President Sadat astounded the world in 1977 by visiting Jerusalem, Israel's capital. As the Egyptian-Israeli peace process proceeded with active American involvement, other Arab states vilified Sadat. The next year, with President Jimmy Carter's mediation, Egypt and Israel agreed to a "framework for peace" outlined in the Camp David Accords and concluded a peace treaty in 1979.[19] The other Arab nations expelled Egypt from the Arab League and stopped providing Cairo with economic aid.

Conflicts of the 1980s

If 1979 was a year of peace, it was also a year of revolution. The repressive shah of Iran, a close American ally who was regarded as a stabilizing influence in the Persian Gulf, was overthrown by a radical Islamic revolution. The new government in Teheran was anti-American to the core, led by the Ayatollah Ruhollah Khomeini (whose own regime was also brutally repressive). In part the revolution was a legacy of the profound social disruption caused by the vast wealth derived from oil exports. The fact that many of the Arab Gulf states, including Iraq, Kuwait, Saudi Arabia, and the United Arab Emirates, were also experiencing considerable social change meant that Khomeini's call for the overthrow of these regimes generated deep concern. Although many Arab regimes feared that the spread of Islamic radicalism would lead to further instability, it was clear that the balance of power that had existed in the Persian Gulf region had been disturbed. Worries over instability in the Gulf raised oil prices in developed countries; Americans waited in long lines for gasoline, and industrialized economies slumped into recession.

In 1980 Iraq invaded Iran. The attack was motivated in part to forestall the threat of Khomeini's revolution spreading across the border, in part to take advantage of Iran's preoccupation with its confrontation with the United States over American hostages being held in Teheran, and in part to gain revenge for previous Iranian territorial gains. Iran put up a surprisingly stiff fight, not only halting the Iraqi attack but also going on the offensive. Fearing that Iraq might lose the war and that Iran might subsequently come to dominate the Persian Gulf, the wealthy oil-producing Arab states provided Baghdad with substantial economic aid. As the war bogged down into an eight-year struggle of attrition, the United States began to back Iraq, although it secretly attempted to trade arms to Teheran in hopes of securing the release of American hostages. In the mid-1980s Iran appeared to have the upper hand and even to be on the verge of victory. In response the United States supplied Iraq with military intelligence and provided naval escorts for oil tankers in the Persian Gulf. By 1988 both sides were exhausted and agreed to a cease-fire, which was viewed as a victory for Iraq at the time. The Iran-Iraq war and the Israel-Egypt peace created great unease in the Arab world. Arab countries were not only more divided than ever, but their financial and political fortunes were declining as well. Although the price of oil rose dramatically in the wake of the Iranian revolution, it gradually declined as oil-importing states cut back on their use of oil and developed domestic energy resources. Some Arab oil-producing states, particularly Saudi Arabia, undermined OPEC's efforts to maintain high prices by increasing production in an effort to gain a greater share of the world market for oil.

In 1982 Israel invaded Lebanon to eliminate the PLO and in the process dealt a devastating blow to the Syrian forces in Lebanon. The absence of Arab support for either the PLO or Syria during the war demonstrated how divided and weakened the Arab world had become. Israel's success was soon overshadowed by debilitating guerrilla attacks on its troops, and Lebanon began to be called "Israel's

Vietnam." Israel eventually withdrew most of its forces, but maintained a "security zone" in southern Lebanon. The Lebanese civil war dragged on, until after the Iraqi invasion of Kuwait. In the light of Syria's support of the American-sponsored coalition against Iraqi leader Saddam Hussein, the United States looked on quietly as Syria solidified its dominance over most of Lebanon.

New World Order, Old Regional Conflicts

As the 1980s came to a close, three trends developed that would have considerable impact on the balance of power within the region. The first was the gradual decline and then demise of the Soviet Union. In practical terms, Russian weakness meant that it was both less able to provide support to its Arab allies and less willing to back them if such support came at the expense of relations with the United States.[20] The second development was the Palestinian uprising, or **intifada,** in the Israeli-occupied Gaza Strip and West Bank. Beginning with spontaneous riots in late 1987, the uprising spread without the direction of the PLO, reflecting the frustration and despair of Palestinians over the absence of any diplomatic progress that promised to meet their goals. The intifada put considerable strains on U.S.–Israeli relations and contributed to a brief American willingness to talk directly with the PLO in 1989. Talks were broken off soon, however, in the wake of a PLO terrorist attack against Israel.

The third development was a disturbance of the regional balance of power caused by the continued weakness of Iran and the growing strength of Iraq. After the Iran-Iraq war, the Gulf Arab states put pressure on Iraq to repay its debts. Faced with economic problems and possessing a huge military machine, Iraq invaded Kuwait in 1990, and in so doing threatened to gain a dominant position in the Persian Gulf. (Iraq's move was encouraged by a huge imbalance of power between the two Arab countries, as the size of Iraq's army was roughly equal to that of Kuwait's total population.) This act of naked aggression—the first attempt by one Arab state to conquer another—shocked the world. In an equally unprecedented move, the United States spearheaded an international coalition, diplomatically supported by the Soviet Union, that sent troops to defend Saudi Arabia. The following year, in the face of Iraq's refusal to accept UN demands to withdraw, the coalition launched an offensive to evict Iraqi forces from Kuwait. The American-led coalition drove Iraq from Kuwait and severely damaged Iraq's military capabilities and economic infrastructure.

Whether the new order will be more peaceful than the old, however, remains a question. The collapse of the Soviet Union has removed the U.S.–Soviet rivalry that fanned the flames of the region's many conflicts, but the conflicts themselves remain. Despite the overwhelming victory won by the coalition forces in the Gulf War, the terms for a final political settlement have yet to be determined, and Saddam Hussein survived in office. None of Iraq's neighbors want it to reemerge as the dominant power in the region, but most feel that a counterweight to Iran is still needed to prevent Teheran from dominating the Gulf, and several are skeptical that America's policy of containing both Iran and Iraq will work. Moreover, the stability of many Arab governments is illusory—the departure of President Hafez al-Assad of Syria or King Hussein of Jordan from the political scene could easily lead to violent succession struggles within those states.

Nevertheless, the American-led victory in the Gulf War, along with the decline of the USSR, also reinvigorated the Arab-Israeli peace process. After the Madrid Conference in October 1991, Israel and its Arab neighbors began direct bilateral negotiations for the first time, supplemented by multilateral talks that included other Arab states. After more than four decades of violence, the possibility of a new order in this war-torn region had finally emerged. The primary process, parallel bilateral negotiations between Israel, Jordan, the Palestinians, Syria, and Lebanon, also made little progress until secret contacts in Oslo, Norway, resulted in a breakthrough in September 1993, when the PLO and Israel recognized each other's legitimacy for the first time. Subsequent talks led to the withdrawal of Israeli forces from Gaza, as well as other cities in the West Bank, and the turning over of these areas to the Palestinian Authority between 1994 and 1997. The Israel-PLO agreement broke up a diplomatic logjam on the Israeli-Jordanian front, and a peace treaty between those two countries followed in 1994.

For a time, bilateral and multilateral contacts between Arabs and Israelis increased, and it appeared that an end to the conflict might be in sight. However,

Israeli Prime Minister Yitzak Rabin and PLO Chairman Yasser Arafat, encouraged by President Bill Clinton, shake hands on the White House lawn after signing the Oslo Accords in 1993.   SOURCE: AP/Wide World

extremists on both sides, bent on destroying the peace process, began to counter-attack. Arab opponents intensified terrorist attacks against Israel, and in November 1995, an extremist Jewish student assassinated Israeli Prime Minister Yitzhak Rabin. A new wave of terrorism in 1996 resulted in the election of a conservative Israeli government. Conflicts over the implementation of Israeli withdrawals followed, and unresolved fundamental differences over Jerusalem and the possibility of a Palestinian state soon threatened to derail the process.[21]

Thus, many fundamental conflicts in the region remain unresolved, but uneven progress has been made. The regional balances of power in the Middle East may offer the primary guarantee against the outbreak of war, but the region's violent history shows how often that guarantee has failed in the past. The spread of weapons of mass destruction in the region, exemplified by Iraq's ability to maintain stocks of chemical and biological weapons despite ongoing UN inspections (see Chapter Eleven), is testimony to continuing dangers. Yet, agreements achieved since the Persian Gulf War show that progress is possible, but further progress will require the support of the international community, good faith, imagination, and no small amount of courage from all the involved parties.

SOUTH ASIA

Like the Middle East, post–World War II South Asia has been marked by continual tensions with occasional outbreaks of violence, both within and between states. Instead of three distinct but interacting balances of power, as in the Middle East, the international relations of South Asia have been dominated by the antagonism between India and Pakistan. Here, too, the sources of instability stem from the colonial legacy, the efforts of the regional states to consolidate control, and ethnic and religious hatreds. Both superpowers were actively involved in South Asia, and their involvement exacerbated the indigenous tensions. But the direct involvement of China, through its border disputes with India and its ties with Pakistan, distinguishes South Asia from the Middle East.

As noted in Chapter Five, Britain had imperial control over virtually all of the Indian subcontinent prior to World War II. As pressure for independence became stronger between the two world wars, the Indians themselves increasingly became divided along religious lines—that is, between the Hindu majority and Muslim minority. The bases of these differences were in part ethnic, in part religious, in part historical (Hindus resented the past Muslim domination of India), and in part political. As independence appeared increasingly likely, both sought to ensure that their economic, political, and social interests would be protected. When suitable provisions for their interests could not be agreed to, Muslims demanded independence for the areas in which they constituted a majority. In 1947 these two areas, in the northwest and northeast corners of India, separated by 1000 miles of Indian territory, became the nation of Pakistan (see Map 5.4).

Severely weakened by World War II, Britain sought to eliminate the burden of controlling India as quickly as possible. In the hasty withdrawal, the British tried

Map 5.4 South and East Asian Independence since 1945

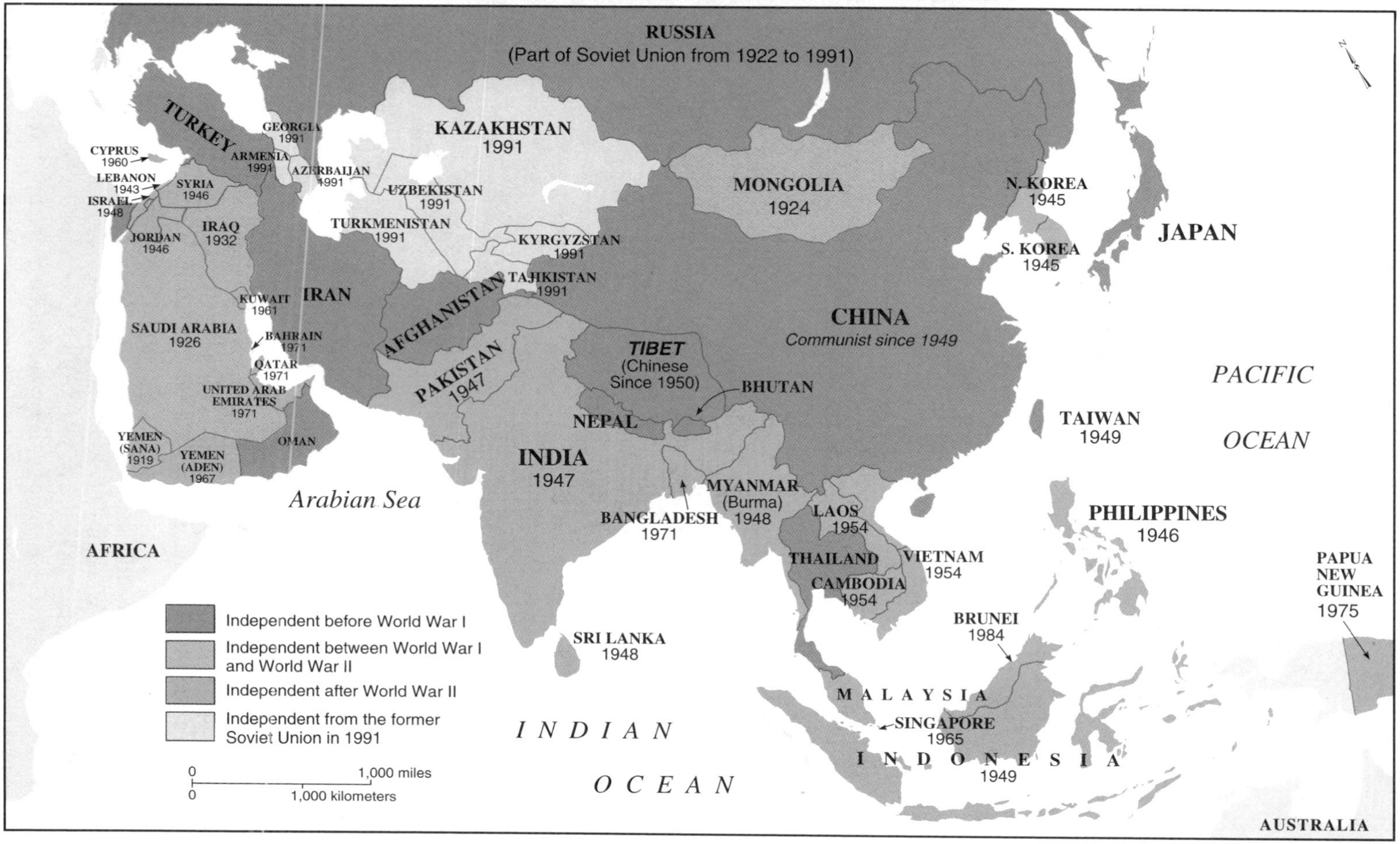

RUSSIA
(Part of Soviet Union from 1922 to 1991)

JAPAN

PACIFIC

OCEAN

PAPUA
NEW
GUINEA
1975

AUSTRALIA

N. KOREA
1945

S. KOREA
1945

TAIWAN
1949

PHILIPPINES
1946

MONGOLIA
1924

CHINA
Communist since 1949

BRUNEI
1984

VIETNAM
1954

LAOS
1954

THAILAND
1954

CAMBODIA
1954

MALAYSIA

SINGAPORE
1965

INDONESIA
1949

BHUTAN

MYANMAR
(Burma)
1948

TIBET
(Chinese
Since 1950)

NEPAL

BANGLADESH
1971

KAZAKHSTAN
1991

KYRGYZSTAN
1991

TAJIKISTAN
1991

UZBEKISTAN
1991

TURKMENISTAN
1991

AFGHANISTAN
1947

PAKISTAN
1947

INDIA
1947

SRI LANKA
1948

INDIAN

OCEAN

GEORGIA
1991

ARMENIA
1991

AZERBAIJAN
1991

TURKEY

IRAN

BAHRAIN
1971

KUWAIT
1961

QATAR
1971

UNITED ARAB
EMIRATES
1971

OMAN

Arabian Sea

CYPRUS
1960

LEBANON
1943

ISRAEL
1948

SYRIA
1946

IRAQ
1932

JORDAN
1946

SAUDI ARABIA
1926

YEMEN
(SANA)
1919

YEMEN
(ADEN)
1967

AFRICA

Independent before World War I

Independent between World War I
and World War II

Independent after World War II

Independent from the former
Soviet Union in 1991

0   1,000 miles

0   1,000 kilometers

■ Gandhi

SOURCE: AP/Wide World

to draw borders that were generally acceptable; nevertheless, the final demarca-
tion left many Muslims in India and Hindus in Pakistan. Independence thus created a massive refugee problem, as more than 12 million Muslims and Hindus fled
to their new "homelands." The migration of refugees was accompanied by widespread violence; 1 million people died as a result of massacres, other hate crimes,
and starvation.

The most contentious area was and is Kashmir, where the population is primarily Muslim. When in 1947 the Hindu prince of Kashmir was given the choice
of joining Pakistan or India, he procrastinated and even contemplated declaring
independence, because joining either would mean giving up power, and becoming
part of India risked popular rebellion. Because the majority of the population was

Spotlight

The Mahatma

Mohandas Karamchand Gandhi is one of the greatest heroes in the annals of the human spirit. Born to a Hindu family in Bombay in 1869, Gandhi initially pursued a career in law, studying for the bar in London and practicing in India and South Africa. As a young barrister, he affected the dress and mannerisms of an affluent English gentleman, working within the colonial legal system to fight discrimination against Indians. But as his struggle for political and civil rights continued, he set his sights higher and devoted himself to the abolition of the colonial system in his home country. He returned to India in 1915, renounced all material possessions, and adopted a life of voluntary poverty, vegetarianism, celibacy, and nonviolent opposition to colonial oppression. (After his vow of poverty, Gandhi always dressed in homespun clothes, usually only a loincloth. When someone commented on his scanty attire during a meeting with King George V at Buckingham Palace in 1931, he replied, "The king was wearing enough for us both.")

Campaigning tirelessly against British rule, Gandhi developed the resistance strategy of *satyagraha*, "holding to the truth," which sought to expose the immorality of oppression through peaceful civil disobedience. He used personal fasts and hunger strikes as nonviolent weapons against the colonial authorities, and was repeatedly jailed for his protests against the British. Realizing that philosophy alone could not effect political change, he proved to be a brilliant political tactician, organizing strikes, boycotts, and, in 1930, a 200-mile march from Ahmadabad to the sea to gather salt crystals in defiance of the government monopoly on the sale of that basic necessity of life. This demonstration electrified India and precipitated a wave of peaceful protests throughout the subcontinent. Gandhi was arrested, as he had been many times before, but knew that his movement had scored a major victory. As he put it, "The honor of India has been symbolized by a fistful of salt in the hand of a man of nonviolence."

Gandhi's methods and infinite patience got results. His "Quit India" campaign persuaded London that British control of India could not be maintained, and in 1947 the colonial Raj was dismantled. The two new nations of India and Pakistan were immediately wracked by bloody fighting between Hindus and Muslims, and in 1948 the aged, frail philosopher fasted until Hindu and Muslim leaders signed a peace agreement. He was not able to enjoy the fruits of his lifelong struggle for independence, however; he was fatally shot by a Hindu extremist that same year.

Throughout his long fight against colonialism, Gandhi displayed a rare combination of enlightened spirituality and political canniness. Journalist William Shirer said of him, "I never knew a more deeply religious man, nor a subtler politician." The most fitting tribute to Gandhi, however, is the sobriquet he was granted by his followers and by which he will be remembered throughout the world as an example of nonviolent resistance: Mahatma, or Great Soul.

Muslim, and Pakistan's *raison d'etre* was to be a Muslim state, Pakistan naturally felt strongly that Kashmir should accede to it. When the prince's temporizing led to revolts among the Muslim population of Kashmir, Pakistani tribesmen infiltrated to give support. Facing a revolution, the prince joined India, which sent troops to put down the rebellion and repulse the Pakistani tribesmen. In December 1947, India appealed to the United Nations, which called for a cease-fire and a vote to determine the wishes of the people. Instead Pakistani troops intervened in early 1948 and occupied parts of western Kashmir; a cease-fire was finally agreed to in 1949. The vote has yet to be held.[22]

Era of Nonalignment

During the 1950s the Kashmir dispute receded into the background as India and Pakistan sought to address internal demands. Under the leadership of Jawaharlal Nehru, India claimed to base its foreign policy on a set of principles known as *panchsheel:* respect for other countries' sovereignty and territorial integrity; non-aggression; noninterference in the internal affairs of others; equality and mutual benefit; and peaceful coexistence. India sought to remain neutral, staying outside the Cold War alliances then forming, and to keep the superpowers out of South Asia. India's neutral stance and moralistic attitude rankled the United States in particular. Meanwhile, the weaker countries of South Asia saw India's neutralism as an attempt to dominate the region and its moralism as pure hypocrisy, given India's sometimes heavy-handed policies toward them.

As the weaker state, and fearing impending Indian domination, Pakistan sought external allies for help. In 1954 it obtained U.S. military assistance and then joined both the Baghdad Pact and the Southeast Asia Treaty Organization (SEATO), becoming a crucial hinge in the U.S. containment policy. In 1959 the United States pledged to protect Pakistan's independence and territorial integrity, with force if necessary. These developments angered India, which increasingly turned to the Soviet Union for political backing and military assistance. Both India and Pakistan received economic aid from the two superpowers.

In addition to its border problems with Pakistan, India also had territorial disputes with China. One disputed area was the Aksai Chin, to India's northwest, while the other was in its northeast, bordering Tibet. As China's relations deteriorated with the Soviet Union in the late 1950s, Beijing began to build a road through the Aksai Chin to link Tibet with the western province of Xinjiang, which it feared the Soviets might try to destabilize. At about the same time, China faced internal unrest in Tibet, which it had forcibly occupied in 1950, and greatly resented India's grant of asylum to Tibet's spiritual leader, the Dalai Lama, in 1959. Disgusted by India's recalcitrance in resolving their border disputes and angered at the encroachment of Indian forces in Tibet, China invaded the disputed area in 1962 and dealt India a sharp, though indecisive, blow.

Indo-Pakistani Hostilities

The 1962 Sino-Indian war created great concern in the United States and the Soviet Union, both of which saw China as an increasingly aggressive and unpredictable power. New Delhi called for both American and Soviet assistance, and both moved to support India. Pakistan saw these developments as detrimental to its balance of power with India. Superpower support for India thus brought Pakistan and China closer together, and Beijing backed Pakistan's claim to Kashmir.

Convinced that India's poor performance in the 1962 war meant that it was for the moment weak, and fearing that the American and Soviet assistance would make India stronger soon, Pakistan began to contemplate launching a war over Kashmir. India in turn increased its own military spending and turned to the Soviet Union for military assistance, having first been rebuffed by the United States.[23]

The Pakistani government came to believe that India was consolidating its control of Kashmir, but that in the short term the balance favored Pakistan. Religious conflict soon created a spark in the region's volatile atmosphere. In 1963 the theft from a Muslim shrine in Kashmir of a holy relic, a hair from the Prophet Mohammed, led to rioting there and in Pakistan. This development strengthened the belief of Pakistani leaders that they could gain the support of Kashmir's Muslims and that they had a short-term advantage—a conclusion reinforced in 1964 by the death of Nehru, India's popular, charismatic leader.

In April 1965 Pakistani tank forces defeated Indian troops at the Rann of Kutch, a sparsely inhabited area of salt flats on the Indian-Pakistani border. After the British and the UN intervened diplomatically, both sides agreed to a cease-fire and a partial withdrawal of forces. The victory emboldened Pakistan, which now believed it had military superiority. Consequently, in August 1965, Pakistan sent agents into Kashmir in the expectation that they would generate a rebellion among Kashmir's Muslims, a rebellion in which Pakistan could intervene in their support. Although a broad uprising never occurred, Pakistan still invaded, seeking to cut Kashmir off from India. To Pakistan's surprise, India did not counterattack in Kashmir, but instead launched an offensive across the Indian-Pakistani border and drove for the important Pakistani city of Lahore. The United States slapped an arms embargo on both sides and secured a cease-fire. Both India and Pakistan accepted a Soviet invitation to mediate, which led to an agreement to return to the status quo ante bellum.[24]

Neither side gained from the 1965 war; to the contrary, both India and Pakistan suffered economically and politically. Pakistan suffered more, as an economic downturn exacerbated long-standing differences between the western and eastern sections of the country. Although the eastern sector, East Bengal, had the majority of the population, the west was dominant politically and economically. Even before 1965 there had been growing resentment in East Pakistan against West Pakistan, and when elections were held in 1970, the east overwhelmingly elected a party that favored increased autonomy. When negotiations broke down between the Pakistani government and the victorious party, riots erupted in East Pakistan, only to be ruthlessly suppressed by the Pakistani military. The East Pakistani leadership now declared its independence as Bangladesh in March 1971, and a civil war ensued. As perhaps 10 million refugees flowed into India, New Delhi moved its forces to the border.

Pakistan feared that it was about to lose the eastern half of the country, but it knew that if it tried to restore order in East Pakistan by force, India would inevitably intervene. Faced with the prospect of a war it could not win in the long run, Pakistan thought that if it attempted a preemptive attack against India, it could defeat the larger Indian forces, just as Israel had defeated the Arabs by striking first in 1967. When Pakistan finally declared war on India in December 1971, things did not work out that way. India was ready for the conflict after years of military preparations and rapidly defeated the Pakistani forces. The new state of Bangladesh replaced the old eastern sector of Pakistan. India also retook parts of the Rann of Kutch and a portion of Kashmir, lost in Indian-Pakistani clashes in 1947 and 1965.[25]

Pakistan had little choice but to accept India's de facto control of Kashmir. But the war did not shift the balance of power in the subcontinent decisively in India's favor. In spite of its victory over Pakistan and its closer relations with the USSR, represented by the 1971 Treaty of Mutual Friendship and Cooperation, India still felt threatened. Ironically, despite India's democratic regime, the United States frequently tilted toward Pakistan during the Cold War because of the close ties between New Delhi and Moscow. Pakistani governments, even though they were usually run by dictators, were often seen in Washington as more compliant with American interests.

India also became concerned in the early 1970s that its security was being threatened by nuclear weapons. During the 1971 war, the United States had dispatched a nuclear-armed aircraft carrier to the Bay of Bengal as a sign of support for Pakistan. China, a previous and potential adversary, was developing its nuclear forces, and USSR already possessed a huge nuclear arsenal. In response to these perceived threats and in an effort to demonstrate its military and technical potential, India began a program to develop nuclear weapons in 1972. Two years later, India conducted what it called a "peaceful nuclear explosion," declaring to the world that it had nuclear capabilities. Pakistan's fear that India could someday use nuclear threats to blackmail it accelerated efforts to gain the capacity to produce nuclear weapons, and in February 1992 Islamabad admitted that it had the capacity to produce at least five nuclear weapons. Pakistan's efforts to produce nuclear weaponry has strained relations with its neighbors, as well as the United States.

Global Tensions and Internal Conflicts

The 1979 Soviet invasion of Afghanistan proved fortuitous for Pakistan. The United States began to pour large amounts of economic and military aid into Pakistan, which became the bulwark against further Soviet expansion into South Asia. The United States also muted its public concern over Pakistan's nuclear program. Through the 1980s, U.S. relations with Pakistan improved dramatically, as Pakistan provided a crucial base of support to the Afghan rebels fighting against the Soviet occupation. After the Soviet withdrawal from Afghanistan in 1989, U.S. relations with Pakistan cooled, with the nuclear issue returning to the fore. Pakistan's recent tentative return to democracy has done little to improve relations with the United States, as the army still plays too large a role in Pakistani politics to allow democratic institutions to take root. The nuclear issue also remains important.

During the 1970s and 1980s India increasingly came to dominate the international politics of South Asia, but it also experienced heightened domestic turmoil. These domestic problems stemmed from the tensions between various ethnic groups and increased demands for autonomy. In the northeastern state of Assam, the Hindu population increasingly resented the influx of Muslim Bengalis, and communal violence began anew. Continued ethnic and religious violence prompted the suspension of the country's democracy and the declaration of a state of emergency in 1975, but the emergency was suspended and democracy restored in 1977. An explosive situation remained in the northwest state of Punjab, where the Sikhs, a slight majority, progressively pressed for increased autonomy and possibly independence. In 1984, after Indian forces assaulted rebels holed up in the Sikhs' holiest shrine, the Golden Temple in Amritsar, Prime Minister Indira Gandhi, who had ruled almost without interruption since 1966, was assassinated by two of her own Sikh guards.

These internal problems have not prevented India from assuming a dominant, even hegemonic, role in the international relations of South Asia. India has been quick to show its displeasure at the attempts of smaller states to conduct foreign policies that are not to its liking, going so far as to blockade Nepal in 1989–1990. In the 1980s, Sri Lanka (formerly Ceylon) was convulsed by a civil war pitting the majority Sinhalese against the minority Tamils. India came to the support of the Tamils, whose ethnic brethren were preeminent in a southern Indian state. In 1987 the Sri Lankan government launched a major attack against Tamil rebels, and in response to domestic demands the Indian government sent relief supplies to Tamil-controlled areas.

Enraged, but recognizing that India might intervene, the Sri Lankan government reached an agreement with India in which autonomy was given to the Tamil areas in exchange for India's commitment to prevent its territory from being used as a rebel base. More to the point, India also agreed to send a peacekeeping force to disarm the Tamil rebels in Sri Lanka; in effect, Sri Lanka got India to do its dirty work. The Indians were no more successful at this task than Sri Lankan forces had been, however, and in 1990 India's troops withdrew. The following year, Indira Gandhi's son Rajiv Gandhi was assassinated as he campaigned in the southern Indian state of Tamil Nadu to again become prime minister of India; the assassin allegedly was a Sri Lankan Tamil.

Thus, half a century after the British withdrawal, South Asia again has a dominant power, but India faces many serious challenges to this role. It is increasingly torn by internal dissension and opposed by a tacit alliance between China and Pakistan. The collapse of the Soviet Union has deprived India of its major ally and has offered Pakistan new opportunities for influence among the Muslim former Soviet republics of Central Asia. But the end of the Cold War also meant that the United States had less reason to align with Pakistan, and India's recent economic reforms and greater openness to trade created the possibility of closer relations between India and the United States. At the same time, a strategic partnership between India and Russia also appeared possible, as Russia looks southward for new allies and markets for its nuclear and military technology.

The end of both the colonial era and the Cold War have left South Asia with an imbalance of power in India's favor, but the region's frequently violent indigenous conflicts continue to cast doubt on India's capacity for leadership. After several years without official talks, negotiations between India and Pakistan over Kashmir and other issues resumed in 1997, but neither side expected rapid progress. Local conflicts have repeatedly pushed international tensions in South Asia to the brink of war and beyond. If this pattern is repeated, the next such confrontation may be between regional powers beset by ancient quarrels but wielding modern nuclear weapons.[26]

EAST ASIA

The post–World War II balance of power in East Asia is a complex relationship between global powers (the United States and, before its collapse, the USSR), major regional powers with global aspirations (China, Japan, and now Russia), and smaller regional powers that nonetheless possess significant economic and/or military strength (North and South Korea, Taiwan, Vietnam, and others). Because most states with interests in this region have been weak in one or more of the basic forms of power—military, economic, and political—the history of the region has been one of shifting alliances as the regional powers try to compensate for their weaknesses and protect their interests. Throughout all of the military posturing and diplomatic maneuvering, however, a central goal has usually been the containment of China, which dominated the region before the mid-nineteenth century and could easily do so again. Because of its large number of strong independent actors, East Asia since 1945 has resembled eighteenth- and nineteenth-century Europe in many respects, including the frequent occurrence of limited but nevertheless destructive warfare.

Three main features characterized post–World War II international relations in East Asia: the emergence of a powerful Communist China and its support of Communist insurgent activities in its neighboring states, the independence of formerly colonized Asian countries, and the global rivalry between the two superpowers.

Early Cold War Tensions

Although Asia was not the top priority on America's foreign policy agenda, the conflicts between the superpowers in this region did not wait long to surface after 1945. From the advent of the Cold War, the United States and the Soviet Union were at odds over the former Japanese colony of Korea. Their division and occupation of the Korean Peninsula in 1945 anticipated the future instability and conflicts of the area. Furthermore, the civil war in China between Nationalist and Communist forces reinforced a widespread perception that conflicts in East Asia could easily kindle a new global conflagration.

After the establishment of the People's Republic of China in 1949 and the conclusion of a Sino-Soviet Treaty of Friendship and Alliance in 1950, the United States adopted its policy of containing China as part of its global strategy. Though some U.S. officials realized that potential fissures in the Sino-Soviet relationship were already apparent, many Americans regarded Moscow and Beijing as part of a monolithic Communist bloc that was bent on world revolution. Fiery rhetoric from the Communist capitals reinforced this perception.

In this atmosphere of suspicion, many regarded the outbreak of the Korean War in 1950 as the first step in a global confrontation. The conflict, which dragged on for three years before it became clear that the United States would not permit Communist forces to gain control of the South, set off a new round of balancing and counterbalancing in Northeast Asia. The fighting between Chinese and American forces in Korea had terrible consequences for the relations between these two countries for the next two decades. Both countries perceived each other as a major threat to their vital interests. The United States believed that the Chinese were intent on overrunning all of East Asia, and China vehemently denounced American "hegemonism" in the region.[27]

The American policy of containing Chinese expansion manifested itself in a series of bilateral treaties with several of China's neighboring countries. The U.S.–Japanese and U.S.–Philippine security treaties were signed in 1951. Following the signing of a mutual defense treaty between the United States and South Korea in late 1953, a similar treaty was concluded in 1954 between the United States and the Republic of China on Taiwan, where Nationalist forces had fled after the Communist victory in China. These actions reinforced the Chinese view that the United States was determined to encircle it with hostile forces (which was half correct; the United States was attempting to encircle China, but for defensive—not offensive—purposes). Meanwhile, Beijing's stated determination to capture Taiwan and its continued bellicose posture toward countries aligned with the United States heightened American fears.

The containment of China had become an inseparable part of America's global response to the possibility of Communist expansion. Washington's system of alliances in East Asia succeeded in protecting the areas it regarded as vital to its security and economic interests, namely Japan, South Korea, Taiwan, and the Philippines. To counter the encirclement created by the United States and its Asian allies, China was prompted to develop closer relations with the Soviet Union. Thus, in the 1950s, when East-West tensions were at their height, East Asia was the military focal point of the Cold War.

Sino-Soviet Split

This rigid balance of forces began to change as Sino-Soviet relations deteriorated. The ideological and policy differences between the two Communist giants broke into the open in 1958 over the USSR's weak support for China's attempt to capture Taiwan, an endeavor Moscow regarded as dangerously reckless. Moscow's retraction of its promised support for the Chinese nuclear weapons program was also a point of contention, though this dispute was less publicized. The United States was slow to realize the implications of the Sino-Soviet split. The stalemate of antagonism between China and the United States (and its Asian allies) was reinforced by China's explosion of a nuclear bomb in 1964, by its bellicose support for revolutionary **guerrilla warfare** ("peoples' wars," as Beijing called them), and by its self-imposed isolation during the Great Proletarian Cultural Revolution of 1966–1969. At the same time, the competition between Moscow and Beijing for the leadership of the Communist bloc was strengthened by continued ideological disputes and unrest along their long common border.[28]

Ironically, because of the Sino-Soviet split in the 1960s, Northeast Asia proceeded through a relatively stable period, as neither Communist power wanted a renewed conflict between the Koreas to complicate an already tense situation. In the meantime, the primary focus of U.S. policy shifted to Indochina. After the victory of the Vietminh over French forces and the interim partition of Vietnam in 1954, Southeast Asian nations' fears of Chinese expansion grew. As a result, in the 1950s and 1960s Washington not only contained China in Northeast Asia, but also built military alliances in Southeast Asia, establishing a limited military presence in South Vietnam and Thailand. In an attempt to break out of the U.S. containment along its southern flank, China sought better relations with its neighbors in Southeast Asia, but most remained alienated from Beijing because of its continuing support of Communist insurgencies within their countries. Their suspicions were reinforced by the strong Chinese backing of North Vietnam and Communist forces in South Vietnam fighting against American "imperial aggression." By 1965 the fighting between South Vietnamese government troops and the Vietcong in South Vietnam drove the United States to intervene with substantial ground and air forces, and the Vietnam War began in earnest (see Chapter Four).

Chinese-American Rapprochement

Three events changed the outlines of international politics in East Asia near the end of the 1960s. First, China gradually recovered from its self-imposed diplomatic isolation and began to seek improved relations with the outside world. Second, border clashes between Chinese and Soviet troops in 1969 (during which Moscow hinted that it could employ its nuclear weapons) contributed to the Chinese regime's willingness to consider a closer relationship with the United States. Third, the new American president, Richard Nixon, belied his past record as a fierce anticommunist by being much more receptive than his predecessors to the mending of fences between the United States and China.

During Nixon's first term, a series of small steps and signals from both sides suggested a possible improvement in Sino-American relations. (One of these signals was Beijing's granting of permission for a Chinese table tennis team to compete in the United States, which might today look like a trivial gesture but at the time was a startling departure from China's venomous anti-American rhetoric and isolation from the outside world. The U.S. government reciprocated by officially referring to China as the People's Republic of China rather than "Red China.") The nervous and halting Sino-American courtship culminated in Nixon's dramatic visit to China in February 1972, which constituted a profound breakthrough in relations. Both China and the United States had gained powerful leverage with respect to the USSR. For Beijing, the opening made it harder for Moscow to threaten to wage war along their common frontier. Washington, for its part, hoped that the rivalry between Moscow and Beijing would increase American leverage and that both Communist powers would help the United States end its long Vietnam nightmare without a total defeat for the South Vietnamese.

The rapprochement between Washington and Beijing revolutionized the balance of power in East Asia. Hostility between China and Japan had reached high levels during the Cultural Revolution, but following the "Nixon shock" Tokyo quickly readjusted its posture toward Beijing, seizing the opportunity to establish a profitable trade relationship. After twenty-two years of Cold War confrontation, full diplomatic relations between the two most powerful Asian countries was established after Japanese Prime Minister Kakuei Tanaka's visit to Beijing in September 1972. China also established diplomatic ties with U.S. allies Australia and New Zealand. Meanwhile, the USSR attempted, clumsily and unsuccessfully, to lure Japan away from China.

The only ally that the Soviets could now rely upon in East Asia was Vietnam, which was brought into closer alignment with Moscow by yet another series of dramatic developments.[29] In 1973 a cease-fire between the warring parties in Vietnam cleared the way for an American withdrawal. However, fighting between the North and South Vietnamese soon resumed, but American disillusionment with the war eliminated any possibility of U.S. reentry into the conflict. Saigon fell to North Vietnamese forces by April 1975, and by the end of that year Communist forces had gained power in the three Indochina states of Vietnam, Laos, and Cambodia. After its victory in Indochina, Hanoi, the capital of reunified Vietnam, emerged as a potential regional power, but its war-torn economy urgently needed outside assistance. Because China was still recovering from the disastrous Cultural Revolution, the Soviet Union became the only available contributor to Vietnam's economic reconstruction. The entente that developed between Hanoi and Moscow caused anxiety in both China and the United States. Although it tried hard to maintain the friendly relations with both Moscow and Beijing that existed during the war, Hanoi soon realized that the Sino-Soviet split had made this policy impossible.

New Asian Cold War

By 1978 the antagonism between China and the Soviet Union in the region had acquired the outlines of a regional cold war. The withdrawal of U.S. troops from Indochina in 1973 created a power vacuum that the USSR was happy to fill. As Hanoi began to develop its own regional ambitions and aligned itself closer to Moscow, the Chinese leaders became concerned that Vietnam would become an "Asian Cuba" for Russian expansion into Southeast Asia. The chance of a Sino-Soviet conflict through their proxies in Indochina increased as the tension between the Soviet Union and China over Indochina escalated.

The state of the Sino-Soviet-American triangular relationship illustrated the fluidity of alliances in the East Asian region. In the early stages of the Cold War in Asia, the United States had used its regional allies to contain China, while China

President Richard Nixon's historic February 1972 visit to Beijing broke more than thirty years of Chinese-American hostility. Here Nixon and Chinese Premier Zhou Enlai toast each other at a banquet hosted by the visiting Americans.   SOURCE: © UPI/Bettmann Newsphotos

and the USSR built friendly relations. By the late 1970s, however, the Soviet Union was endeavoring to contain China with its own regional allies, while U.S.–Chinese ties gradually improved.

Emboldened by an alliance treaty with the USSR, Vietnam invaded Cambodia in 1978 and replaced the pro-Chinese Khmer Rouge regime with a Communist government friendly to Moscow and Hanoi. Though they had no sympathy for the brutal Khmer Rouge, the United States, Japan, and the Association of South-East Asian Nations (ASEAN)—Indonesia, Malaysia, Singapore, Thailand, Brunei, and the Philippines—joined China in condemning Vietnam's invasion of Cambodia and demanding the withdrawal of foreign troops from that country. A UN resolution to that effect was vetoed by the Soviet Union, however. Chinese leaders undoubtedly felt uneasy about a possible two-front confrontation with the Soviet Union on their mutual frontier in the north and with pro-Soviet Vietnam in the south.

To reduce the possibility of a two-front war, Chinese party leader Deng Xiaoping strove to gain the support of the United States and Japan. Although he failed to elicit any explicit backing from these two countries, he was confident that the international community would not oppose his efforts to block Soviet expansion in Southeast Asia. Convinced that Vietnam wanted to increase its power and influence not only in Indochina, but also in the whole of Southeast Asia, Deng was now ready to move. Charging that Vietnam had violated China's borders, he launched a massive "punitive measure," sending his troops into Vietnam for seventeen days in February 1979 to "teach Vietnam a lesson." China's incursion into Vietnam helped to solidify ties between Moscow and Hanoi: Vietnam now needed outside assistance more than ever, because ASEAN nations had refused to help.

Yet Sino-Soviet relations took another plunge after the Soviet invasion of Afghanistan in December 1979. Beijing perceived this development as a serious threat, because a pro-Moscow regime in Afghanistan could become a Soviet surrogate on China's western border, just as Vietnam was on its southern frontier. In response, the Chinese Communist party announced in 1980 that Beijing would not continue the Sino-Soviet negotiations on the "normalization" of their relations. When the talks between the two countries were finally resumed in 1982, Beijing insisted on three preconditions for the normalization of relations: (1) the USSR should remove its massive military deployment along the Sino-Soviet border and in outer Mongolia, (2) Moscow should stop aiding Vietnam's aggression in Indochina, and (3) the Soviet Union should withdraw all its troops from Afghanistan.

The shock waves created by the invasion of Afghanistan were also felt in Japan. For most of the postwar era, Japan felt quite secure under the U.S. commitment to Japan's defense, codified originally in the Mutual Security Treaty of 1951. The Soviet invasion of Afghanistan made some Japanese worry about what might also happen to their own country, which had territorial disputes with Moscow over the Kuril Islands, which the USSR occupied at the end of World War II. Accordingly, in 1980 the Japanese government for the first time explicitly identified the Soviet Union as a major threat to its security. China, reversing other long-standing Cold War policies, not only endorsed the U.S.–Japan Mutual Security Treaty but also made public pronouncements advocating a Japanese military buildup to oppose Soviet hegemonism. In short, Soviet moves in Afghanistan prompted an alignment of Washington, Beijing, and Tokyo against Soviet expansion in Asia.[30]

Anti-Soviet sentiment was also widely shared among the ASEAN countries of Thailand, Singapore, and Malaysia during the Afghan crisis, which came just one year after the Vietnamese invasion of Cambodia. ASEAN anxiety was further aroused by Vietnam's armed incursion into Thailand in 1980 and by a summit of Soviet, Vietnamese, and Cambodian leaders in Moscow. The new perception of a Soviet threat worked dramatically in favor of China's relations with the ASEAN countries, enabling a new cooperative relationship between them to take shape gradually. Thus, by the early 1980s the balance of power in East Asia took an essentially bipolar form, as a tacit alliance between the United States, China, Japan, and the ASEAN countries coalesced to contain expansion by the Soviet Union and Vietnam.

Global Confrontation Recedes, Regional Powers Emerge

This new strategic alignment proved to be short-lived. However, it was not broken up by diplomatic maneuvering, but rather by domestic political developments.

In March 1985 Mikhail Gorbachev became the leader of the USSR and soon began pursuing a rapprochement with both China and the United States. As recounted in Chapter Four, the new Soviet leadership hoped to create a favorable international environment for Soviet economic reconstruction. It therefore sought to cut back costly, wasteful, and counterproductive commitments abroad. When foreign leaders became convinced that Gorbachev was intent on carrying out this reform, Moscow's relationship with China, Japan, and the United States improved markedly.

In a 1986 speech in Vladivostok, on the USSR's Pacific coast, Gorbachev outlined the main principles of a new Soviet Asian-Pacific policy. These included the recognition of the Soviet Union as an Asian country, the acknowledgment of the United States as a partner in many Asian-Pacific issues, the improvement of relations with Japan and China, the reduction of Soviet military forces in East Asia, and the call for an Asian-Pacific regional organization similar to the Conference on Security and Cooperation in Europe.

Gorbachev's new policy was not all talk. In 1989 Moscow began to withdraw its troops from Afghanistan and to reduce its military presence in Mongolia. In response, the Chinese government invited Gorbachev to visit Beijing in May 1989. This summit completed the prolonged process of normalizing relations between Moscow and Beijing, and it had a direct impact on relations between Vietnam and the Soviet Union. First, Moscow started to withdraw its military equipment and personnel from Vietnam. Second, in late September 1989, Vietnam withdrew its troops from Cambodia. These actions led to a more receptive attitude toward Moscow on the part of the ASEAN countries. The development of a rapprochement between Moscow and its two regional rivals, Beijing and Washington, facilitated other bilateral interactions among the major powers in East Asia. For example, Japan and Moscow entered into extended discussions over the Kuril Islands after 1988, although the dispute remained unresolved as of 1998.

Although the Soviet Union's reputation in the international arena was rising, China's took a dramatic turn downward. China had been liberalizing its economic policies throughout the 1980s but resisted change in its political system. When in 1989 thousands of protesters camped for months in Tiananmen Square in Beijing to demand democratic reforms, the government sent soldiers and tanks to clear the square. The brutal repression, publicized by live television reports, forcibly demonstrated that Beijing was not interested in political change. As the USSR adopted new policies, shed its socialist empire, and finally began to disintegrate, China's value to the United States as a counterweight to Soviet power diminished, and Sino-American relations cooled once more.[31]

The end of the Cold War between the superpowers and rapprochement between the two Communist giants created a favorable environment for a solution to many troublesome regional conflicts. In January 1991 a peace conference was held in Paris to discuss solutions to Cambodian issues, and by October an agreement was reached among representatives from eighteen nations to end the war in Cambodia and carry out elections under UN supervision. The agreement proved difficult to implement, and although a new government was finally established two and a half years later, violence broke out again in 1997 and the Khmer Rouge refused to participate. In Northeast Asia, the possibility of another North Korean attack against the South was reduced by the establishment of full diplomatic relations between the USSR and South Korea in 1990 and between China and South Korea in 1992. Direct talks between the two Koreas and their entry into the UN in 1991 as member states further muted tensions on the Korean Peninsula, though talk of the possible development of nuclear weapons and missiles by North Korea rekindled tensions. The death of North Korea's leader Kim Il-Sung in the summer of 1994 added further confusion. A crisis nearly erupted later that year when Pyongyang refused international inspectors access to its plutonium reprocessing plant and threatened to withdraw from the nuclear nonproliferation treaty (NPT). The situation was defused when North Korea agreed to cease some suspicious nuclear activities in return for assistance with its civilian nuclear power program from the United States, Japan, and South Korea. Flooding and food shortages in North Korea in 1995–1997 further increased instability in the North and anxiety throughout the region, with many people in South Korea fearing that a desperate North Korea might attack across the demilitarized zone in a reckless attempt to reverse its fortunes. Although talks on a formal peace treaty began in 1997, tensions in Northeast Asia continued to run high, with the Korean Peninsula delicately poised between a breakdown toward war and a breakthrough toward peace.[32]

After the collapse of the Soviet Union, the United States reoriented its Asian-Pacific policy by reducing its commitments in East Asia, including the reduction of military forces in South Korea, the Philippines, Japan, and Thailand. However, the increasing economic ties between the United States and the Asian countries ensures that America will remain actively engaged in the region. Since the mid-1980s, bilateral trade between the United States and Asian countries has exceeded trade between the United States and Europe. Although the level of technological and investment interchange with Europe remains greater, the importance of Asian trade is still growing. The volume of American exports to Asia is the highest in the world, and imports from that region account for most of the U.S. trade deficit. Therefore, despite pressure in Washington to further reduce U.S. force levels in order to cut the defense budget, it remains clear that America will continue to maintain a military presence to protect its interests in East Asia.

The reduction of Russian and American military forces in Asia significantly reduced the threat to China posed by the former Cold War antagonists. As the balance of power in the region shifted yet again, China began to perceive Japan as the major potential threat to its security. This was indicated by Beijing's opposition to Japan's 1991 decision to allow the deployment of noncombat troops overseas as part of UN peacekeeping forces. On the other hand, China itself experienced remarkable economic growth in the late 1980s and early 1990s. Hoping to take advantage of its growing economic strength and military capabilities, Beijing continues to claim the oil-rich Spratly Islands in the South China Sea (which are also claimed by Vietnam and the Philippines), and in 1996 tried unsuccessfully to persuade Taiwan to call off presidential elections, firing missiles into the crowded sea lanes around the island. China's economic power was further enhanced by its

■ Aung San Suu Kyi   SOURCE: AP/Wide World

acquisition of Hong Kong in 1997. These developments prompt the conclusion that China, even more than Japan, has both the will and the means to emerge as a global power.

To prevent China, Japan, or India from dominating Southeast Asia, the members of ASEAN (which in 1998 were Brunei, Indonesia, Malaysia, Philippines, Singapore, Thailand, and Vietnam) have recognized the necessity of creating new mechanisms to maintain a balance of power. Many ASEAN nations have strengthened their own defenses and some (notably Singapore) have allowed the United States to use military facilities in their territories should a crisis arise. In keeping with the multipolar character of the region, in 1994 ASEAN members met in Bangkok with representatives of the United States, the European Union, Japan, China, Russia, Australia, South Korea, and other Pacific Rim states to inaugurate the ASEAN Regional Forum, which meets annually to discuss regional security and cooperation.

As the twentieth century draws to a close, ASEAN seems ready to play even greater roles in regional politics and the global economy. Other regional forums are also beginning to emerge. Recognizing the growing importance of economic

A Peaceful Tiger

Aung San Suu Kyi's long and often lonely struggle for democracy in Myanmar offers a story of unsurpassed moral courage in the face of overwhelming odds and shocking brutality. Born in 1945 in what was then the British colony of Burma, she was only two years old when her father, the de facto prime minister, was assassinated. In 1960, she went to India with her mother, who was appointed Burma's ambassador to New Delhi. In India, she studied the political philosophies of Mahatma Gandhi and acquired a special admiration for Gandhi's nonviolenct principles. After pursuing advanced studies at Oxford (where here classmates called her "Burmese Suu" because she usually attend classes dressed in a traditional Burmese sarong), she married, had two children, and lived an inconspicuous life until she returned permanently to Myanmar in 1988 to care for her ailing mother.

Immediately after her return, she witnessed the flagrant cruelty and mass torture of civilians by the military government of Ne Win. In a series of upheavals (depicted in John Boorman's film *Beyond Rangoon*), thousands of protesters were killed and opposition leaders were jailed or punished indiscriminately. She tried at first to remain neutral, but when protesters began carrying portraits of her father during their demonstrations as a symbol of Burmese pride and independence, she felt she had no choice but to take an active role in the protests. Angered but undaunted by the military regime's blatant displays of force, she began speaking out against its leaders' corruption and disrespect for human rights. Before her emergence as an opposition figure, the pro-democracy movement had lacked competent, charismatic, and decisive leadership. Her ability to inspire admiration and command support (dramatically demonstrated in her famous address to a mass rally at Rangoon's Shwedagon Pagoda in August 1988) and her principles of nonviolence appealed to millions of Burmese and were instrumental in transforming the pro-democracy movement from a spontaneous uprising into a sustained force for what she called "the second struggle for independence."

Although women played an important role in the nationalist movement during the colonial period and greatly contributed to Burmese independence, many observers viewed Aung San Suu Kyi's emergence in Burmese politics as a rare development, given the strict military dictatorship and its lack of respect for women's rights. In 1990, her National League for Democracy won more than 80 percent of the parliamentary seats contested in that years' elections, but the military government ignored and then nullified the election results, and she was soon arrested and held in isolation. Later, under international pressure, she was given the opportunity to leave the country quietly without further harassment, but she refused to do so and instead continued to denounce the military government's dictatorial rule. Although she was awarded the Nobel Peace Prize in 1991, she was kept under house arrest until 1995. After her release, she founded a health and education trust with her Nobel Prize money and continued to work for freedom, democracy, and women's rights in Myanmar. Though her tireless efforts have as yet brought few reforms in her native country, her defiance of dictatorship flies in the face of many who argue that "Asian values" demand silent deference to authority, and she has inspired millions of activists throughout the world through the courage of her convictions.

ties across the Pacific, the Asia-Pacific Economic Cooperation (APEC), a loose organization of Pacific Rim states, began promoting trade and investment through summit conferences and other activities in 1993. Despite steady increases in trade, Malaysia, Thailand, Indonesia, and other Southeast Asian states experienced serious recessions in 1997–1998, caused by a number of factors including currency crises, sharp drops in regional real estate and stock markets and consequent reductions in foreign investment, and the exposure of corruption and cronyism. The International Monetary Fund (the IMF, discussed further in Chapters Six and Eight) and other international lenders quickly arranged emergency loans and other aid to stabilize the situation, and the long-term prospects for ASEAN may depend on the successful implementation of economic and financial reforms.

With the disappearance of the U.S.–Soviet Cold War rivalry, East Asia resembles a classical multipolar system. The key relationship in future regional balances of power may well be between Japan and China, with Russia, the Koreas (which may not remain plural), Vietnam, Taiwan, and Indonesia as secondary but nonetheless important regional powers. As long as the United States has vital interests in the region and the political will to protect them, it will continue to hold the balance of power, but America's level of involvement may be determined by economic factors rather than strategic considerations. The region's economic ties

ASEAN foreign ministers shake hands after a ceremony in Jakarta, Indonesia, marking the entry of Burma and Laos into the regional association in July 1997.   SOURCE: © Associated Press

may eventually lead to increased roles for APEC, ASEAN, and other multilateral organizations as institutions for political dialogue and conflict management. If strong regional institutions do not emerge, however, East Asia in the early twenty-first century may become the world's foremost example of a classic multipolar, balance-of-power system, with changes in the strengths and aims of the leading states producing shifts in alignment and struggles to contain regional conflicts.[33]

CONCLUSIONS: COMING TOGETHER OR FALLING APART?

The enthusiastic attempts by many states to cooperate with their regional neighbors furnish a hopeful image of world politics in the New Era. In Europe, the former great powers and states that were at one another's throats decades ago have engaged in a slow but steady process of integration, building up networks of cooperation and policy coordination culminating in a European Union with a common parliament, plans for a common currency, and a commitment to strive for "ever-closer Union" (see Chapter Seven). North and South America have forged regional free trade agreements, and some leaders promote a vision of a common market for the Western Hemisphere. In Asia and the Pacific, APEC and ASEAN facilitate regional cooperation grounded in economic interaction despite the many differences among their members. Recognition of the benefits of working together on health, food supplies, and disaster relief have spurred further global and regional cooperation through a plethora of official and nongovernmental organizations (discussed in Chapter Nine). Particularly in the two areas of trade and the environment (which are intimately connected), a global web of interdependence has taken international cooperation to new heights in the New Era.

Turn on the television, however, and you are likely to see a very different image of world politics. A new ethnic conflict or civil war seems to break out every week. Warring groups resort to famine and even genocide to destroy each other, and terrorism literally explodes onto the screen. Experts warn of the threat of dictators or lunatics armed with missiles, chemical or biological weapons, or stolen nuclear bombs. Multiethnic states like the USSR, Yugoslavia, and Ethiopia have fallen apart, and even Quebec and Scotland talk about leaving long-established unions. States such as Somalia and Liberia, their resources and institutional capacities strained beyond the breaking point, have gone through periods of complete collapse, requiring international intervention to control their armed mobs and starving refugees. The UN and other international organizations seem to try their best to stem the tide of chaos, but many observers suggest that the political, economic, ecological, and social fragmentation will get worse before it gets better—*if* it ever gets better.[34]

Which vision is more accurate? In many ways, both are equally true, and equally false. International cooperation on trade, collective security, and economic integration has progressed, but citizens of many states are increasingly nervous about loss of sovereignty and the impact of faceless or biased international institutions on their lives. Governments themselves have proven reluctant to commit their own resources to goals that do not directly relate to their vital interests, and many international forums produce far more rhetoric than positive action. At the same time, while weak states built on inadequate foundations crumble, new formal and informal networks are being constructed to achieve common goals and provide for basic human needs, encouraging participants to "think globally and act locally." Interdependence has accelerated both cooperation and conflict in the New Era, and the failure of old institutions has prompted the creation (albeit slowly and haltingly in some cases) of new ones.

If one finds it difficult to make sense of the New Era, one must remember that the world has never "made sense"—leaders, scholars, and citizens make sense *of* it by applying intellectual tools to comprehend changing conditions, dynamic processes, recurring themes, and new phenomena. A review of the preceding history chapters reminds us that many of the developments we encounter today are not so new. Trade, ethnic conflict, shifting alliances, and the rise and fall of institutions and empires have been part of history for thousands of years. Although some technological developments, such as computers and nuclear weapons, really are new, the need of political, economic, and social structures to adapt to new elements is not (recall the changes wrought by the Industrial Revolution). One reason why the Peace of Westphalia acknowledged the principle of national sovereignty is that nation-states proved to be the most effective structures at the time for containing conflict and promoting cooperation. In the New Era, as some states fail and others voluntarily "pool" their sovereignty to create regional associations, the state may gradually lose its primacy as the fundamental unit of the international system, and may eventually cease to exist as we know it.[35]

Does this possibility worry you? Maybe it should, but don't panic. The international system is undergoing a process of creative destruction. All of us are "present at the creation" of new global political, economic, and environmental systems, and all of us have a part to play in their construction. We as individuals may take an active part in the process of change or accept a passive role, but the effects on our own lives will be profound whatever we choose. The chapters that follow will introduce many concepts that can be used to understand or to shape the coming changes, but none of them will be of any value unless we know what changes have been attempted in the past and what influences contributed to their success and failure. We must also appreciate the capabilities and limitations of international bodies, national governments, corporations, military forces, and other organizations, and their past performance is a valuable though not completely reliable indicator of their potential for success. We may want to emulate the success of some institutions (perhaps the Concert of Europe) and seek to avoid the mistakes made by others (such as the League of Nations), but our attempts will achieve little unless we understand how those institutions functioned and why they failed. Even those who regard the history of world politics as little more than a tragedy of hatred, greed, and error will still profit from studying how reason and tolerance can overcome these inherent human frailties. In short, we must know our past in order to grasp our present, and we have no other foundation upon which to build our future.

PRINCIPAL POINTS OF CHAPTER FIVE

1. The linked processes of globalization, fragmentation, cooperation, and conflict are proceeding together at an accelerated pace in the New Era.

2. The end of the Cold War has left the United States as the only military superpower in the international system, but the United States does not dominate militarily, as its actions are constrained by international law and the need to act with regional allies.

3. Economically, the playing field of world politics is much more level, as the European Union, Japan, China, and many developing states can compete effectively in world markets. Despite continued strength in the U.S. economy, China may eventually overtake Japan and the United States in total economic output. The advantages of quality over quantity in the information age make it unclear how this will change the balance of political and military power.

4. Efforts to establish international mechanisms for collective security were renewed after the Cold War. These efforts have met with some success, but they remain constrained by national interests and problems of coordination.

5. Ethnic conflict has reemerged as a major cause of war and fragmentation in the New Era as multinational states have broken apart and persistent civil wars (exemplified by Rwanda, Congo, and the former Yugoslavia) have resulted in many cases.

6. Regional conflicts and balances of power are likely to be increasingly important dynamics of world politics in the New Era.

7. Domestic causes of conflict have included ethnic, religious, and economic hostilities—usually examples of fragmentation. Imported causes of conflict from outside particular regions and as a legacy of imperialism include arbitrary borders, nationalism, and struggles between great powers—the latter typically a consequence of globalization.

8. In the Middle East, three balances of power have dominated: Arab-Arab, Arab-Israeli, and Arab-Iranian.

9. By contrast, South Asia has been dominated by the antagonism between India and Pakistan.

10. The balance of power in East Asia remains the most complex, consisting of one global power (the United States), regional powers with global aspirations (China, Japan, and Russia), and smaller regional powers (such as North and South Korea, Taiwan, and Vietnam) that nonetheless possess significant economic and/or military strength.

11. The international system of the New Era may seem to be simultaneously coming together and falling apart, as old states and institutions disintegrate while new ones are being created. Nevertheless, the history of world politics can help us understand how these process are occurring, how we may try to shape them, and how they will affect our lives.

KEY TERMS

Association of
  South-East
  Asian Nations
Balfour
  Declaration
collective
  security

free rider
guerrilla
  warfare
imported
  conflicts
indigenous
  conflicts

intifada
irredentism
North American
  Free Trade
  Area
panchsheel
Security Council

sensitivity
vulnerability
war of secession
war of
  unification
Zionism

PART

III

The Economic Dimension in World Politics

SOURCE: David Turnley/Detroit Free Press/Black Star

CHAPTER

6

▫ ▫ ▫ ▫

Introduction
to
International
Economics

Thus far, the reader may feel that our examination of international relations has emphasized war and conflict. Indeed, most studies of world politics focus on conflict for the same reason that public affairs broadcasts seem to devote most of their time to scandals, crime, earthquakes, and plane crashes: these developments are out-of-the-ordinary, dramatic events—they are "news." But just as most neighbors don't fight each other and most planes don't crash, most states interact with each other peacefully most of the time. Trade and economic exchange have always accompanied the ongoing struggle for national power and security. While economic concerns have therefore influenced the rarefied realms of **international law** and diplomacy, trade also is the aspect of international relations that has the greatest impact on our individual lives. For proof of this, look down at your shoes: they were probably made in a country different from the one in which you are reading this book, whatever country that happens to be.

With this in mind, this chapter presents an overview of the history and operation of the global economy. Like any other field of human relations, economic exchange can involve conflict as well as cooperation. Many scholars contend that rising economic interdependence—the mutual dependence of national economies—has facilitated cooperation among nations. At the same time, however, this interdependence has produced its own set of international and domestic political tensions, especially for the advanced industrialized states. To see why these tensions occur and how they may be resolved, the first three sections of this chapter introduce the basic economic concepts required for an understanding of the global economy. This introduction is necessarily theoretical, as a basic appreciation of economic theory is essential for understanding the structure and operation of the global economy. Readers who have a strong background in economics should regard these sections as a quick review of basic concepts. Readers unfamiliar with economic theory shouldn't worry, as the theoretical sections are relatively quick and painless.[1] Even readers who feel that economics truly deserves to be called "the dismal science" should not despair, because the chapter then turns to a pragmatic discussion of economic power: what it is, how it can be measured, and how it is acquired.

The demonstrable impact of economic power on world politics raises some extremely important questions. If it is in the interest of states to maximize their individual economic strength, and other states are potential rivals in world markets, should they try to cooperate with one another? What are the barriers to economic cooperation between states, and how can they be overcome to realize the maximum potential benefits from trade? The final sections of the chapter therefore examine the problems and prospects for economic cooperation, returning briefly to theory to examine how states can try to make trade a "win-win" proposition. Taken as a whole, this chapter will help students of international relations understand how economic concerns can promote cooperation and foster conflict, and how interdependence intensifies both cooperation and conflict in the globalized economy of the New Era.

TO TRADE OR NOT TO TRADE?

Although some states have tried, none has ever achieved total economic self-sufficiency. Most states need goods and services that other states produce, and most produce goods and services that other states need. Thus, the only way for states to get all the goods and services they need (short of conquering other countries, which is usually very expensive if not morally repugnant) is to trade for them.

This is especially true for certain natural resources that are unevenly distributed across states. For instance, just a few countries such as Saudi Arabia and Iran produce large quantities of oil, but virtually all countries use oil in their economies for industrial processes, heating, generating electricity, and as fuel for automobiles.

This is also true for many agricultural products. For instance, coffee grows best in highland tropical climates, so if Americans want to have a cup of coffee, it has to be imported from countries like Colombia, Brazil, or Kenya (although the United States does produce a small amount of coffee in Hawaii). Similarly, bananas do not grow well in the United States (though some farmers have tried) and must be traded for with tropical countries like Ecuador or Honduras. This works both ways, of course. If Brazilians want apples or maple syrup, they must trade with temperate agricultural countries like the United States or Canada.

Even when countries can produce the same goods or services, trade may occur because states have different allocations of resources. Trade theory usually identifies three categories of resources: land, labor, and capital. A nation is land-abundant if it has a lot of land (agriculture and resources) relative to its population, while it is labor-abundant if wages are relatively low, usually caused by a large population. Similarly, capital-abundant means that a nation is relatively rich, both in terms of money and industrial plant and equipment.

Because nations have different allocations of resources, each enjoys a **comparative advantage** in producing those goods that use its abundant factor.[2] Some specialize in labor-intensive industries like textiles because they are abundant in labor. Others specialize in capital-intensive industries like airplane manufacturing because they are wealthy and can build factories and develop technology. And still others produce agriculture because their land is inexpensive. Comparative advantage is thus an explanation for why countries with different resources and skills engage in trade.

It is logical to expect that a country will produce the goods it can make more efficiently than other countries. When a country is more efficient than others in producing a certain good, it is said to have an **absolute advantage** in that good's production. However, mutual gains from trade are still possible even if one party has an absolute advantage in all goods. David Ricardo (1772–1823), an English economist who contributed to the development of both economics and political economy, proved why this is so. Although his simplified model only took into account how labor productivity differs across nations, it provided a stepping stone for the theoretical developments of a century later.[3]

Ricardo's Model of Trade

Ricardo showed that even if one nation has an absolute advantage in the production of all goods, trade can still be mutually beneficial if the less efficient nation has a comparative advantage in one good over another. To see why this is so, consider two imaginary countries, Fredonia and Sylvania. (The imagination in this case is that of the Marx Brothers, from their film *Duck Soup*, a classic satire on international politics.) Both countries produce only two goods, wine and cloth. Figure 6.1 shows the amount of labor (a cost of production) required to produce one bottle of wine and one bolt of cloth in each country.

The figures indicate that Sylvania has an absolute advantage in both wine and cloth; each is more costly to produce in Fredonia. Nevertheless, mutual gains from

Figure 6.1	Comparative Advantage	
Country	Worker-hours needed to produce one unit of:	
	Wine	Cloth
Fredonia	12	6
Sylvania	2	4

trade are still possible because of comparative advantage. The ratio of production costs for the two goods differ in the two countries. In Sylvania, one bottle of wine will exchange for one-half bolt of cloth (because the ratio of labor costs per unit of output of the two goods is 2:4), while in Fredonia, one bottle of wine will exchange for two bolts of cloth (because the ratio of labor costs for the two goods is 12:6). These ratios reflect the labor input to produce each item. Cloth is relatively cheaper in Fredonia than in Sylvania; because one bottle of wine earns more cloth (12:6 versus 2:4), Fredonia has a comparative advantage in cloth-making. Wine is relatively cheaper in Sylvania; because one bolt of cloth garners more wine (4:2 versus 6:12), it has a comparative advantage in wine-making. Therefore, because of these relative prices, trade between these two countries will be mutually advantageous. Fredonia can sell one bolt of cloth for one-half bottle of wine domestically—or it can sell it for two bottles in Sylvania. Clearly, Fredonia will choose to trade with Sylvania. Sylvania can get one-half bolt of cloth per bottle of wine domestically, but it can trade with Fredonia for two bolts.

Each country gains by exporting the good in which it has a comparative advantage and by importing the good in which it has a comparative disadvantage. Mutual gains will lead to specialization within each country, making goods less expensive and production more efficient for both. But the gains are not necessarily equal; because Fredonia has higher production costs for both goods, it gains more through trade and specialization. This is because trade and specialization allow nations to concentrate on the production of the goods they produce most efficiently. When goods are produced efficiently, they are produced at minimum cost. As Fredonia's costs decrease, so should the prices charged to consumers for those products. Of course, the same pattern occurs in Sylvania, but because it was more efficient to begin with, its gain from trade is less than Fredonia. Nevertheless, consumers in both countries benefit from trade.

Trade Barriers

Given the preceding discussion, it might seem counterintuitive for states to implement barriers to free trade. Yet, governments often attempt to protect their domestic markets from international competition. Why? The trade theory just presented shows that national welfare improves when consumers purchase goods from the most efficient (least expensive) producer, whether it is foreign or domestic. However, competition may force domestic producers to go out of business if they become less efficient than foreign producers. Oftentimes, governments will not stand idly by while companies or entire industries go bankrupt. This is especially true if those industries employ many workers and/or have tremendous political influence (like the U.S. automotive industry). States may therefore impose trade barriers to protect domestic industries.[4]

Barriers to free trade result from the conflict of two interests: consumers who want inexpensive products versus industries who want to stay in business. Because protection benefits a concentrated group of industrialists and workers and hurts a large group of unorganized consumers, political support for protection can usually penetrate even the most ardent free-trade governments. This section presents various kinds of trade barriers, citing examples of their use in the U.S. economy.

One common form of protection is the **tariff,** a tax imposed on a good entering a country from abroad. This additional cost makes the foreign good more expensive than it was before. If domestic consumers are relatively price conscious, they will curb their consumption of foreign goods in exchange for locally produced goods. Thus, tariffs aid local producers who compete against foreign-produced goods. One negative consequence of a tariff is that consumers pay higher prices because they no longer have access to cheaper foreign products. Also, local firms have less incentive to become more efficient because they are subject to less international competition. Nevertheless, in the short term, the domestic economy might improve because the tariff encourages domestic production, albeit at the cost of higher consumer prices and less efficient production.

One famous example of a tax on imports is the **Smoot-Hawley Tariff.** After the stock market crash of 1929 (described later in Chapter Seven), many in the United States feared that foreign competition would destroy even more U.S. jobs than had been lost as a result of the crash. In an attempt to protect remaining jobs, Congress in 1930 raised prices on all imports by 19 percent; by 1932 the average tariff reached 59 percent. Foreign countries responded to the Smoot-Hawley tariff by raising tariffs of their own. Such a course of action is called a **beggar-thy-neighbor policy.** The United States succeeded in raising import prices and making foreign goods less competitive domestically, but once other states responded with tariffs of their own, U.S. exports became more expensive abroad. As a result of these countervailing tariffs, export industries collapsed worldwide because they were increasingly shut out of the international market. Ultimately, this cycle of protection had a devastating impact on the world economy by accelerating and deepening the Great Depression.[5]

In addition to tariffs, there are other impediments to free trade, collectively known as "nontariff barriers." The first is called an import quota. A state can put a limit on the number of imports it receives from the rest of the world. This is an explicitly protectionist barrier. However, sometimes a state will compel another nation to "voluntarily" limit its exports. These are called **voluntary export restrictions** (VERs). The importer might threaten to impose tariffs if the exporter does not comply. A government can demand VERs in order to protect its own industries from being pushed out of its own market. Since 1980 the United States

These French farmers, destroying imported Spanish produce in 1997, exemplify the continued political support for trade protection in many countries.

SOURCE: AP/Wide World

has demanded that the Japanese restrict car exports to the American market in order to protect local automobile producers. Japan has complied, but it is interesting to note that Japanese automakers have responded to VERs by building factories in the United States and exporting higher-value Japanese luxury cars to meet the VER quota. This helped soften the blow of export restrictions.

States can also impose regulations on imports, ostensibly to protect consumers but that essentially inhibit or prohibit those goods from competing with domestic products. Agricultural products, in particular, are often hit with these kinds of nontariff barriers. The European Union, for example, tried in the 1980s to prohibit imports of beef from the United States on the grounds that American ranchers fed their livestock too many hormones. In the same decade, trade officials in Japan restricted imports of skis on grounds of consumer safety, citing the purportedly unique character of Japanese snow. Labor and environmental regulations, while they may be well-intentioned, can also be used to block imports.

Finally, governments can use **subsidies** to support domestic industries. These government payments allow producers to price their goods below the cost of production without going out of business. While the ostensible purpose of **internal subsidies** (called price supports in the United States) is to allow producers to compete against imports in the home market, and that of **external subsidies** is to allow these producers to compete in the international market, both in effect aid domestic producers. In the international system, it may be hard to distinguish between external subsidies and **dumping,** in which one country sells (or "dumps") its products in a foreign market so far below the costs of production that it causes other producers in that market to go out of business. In the last two decades, U.S. steel producers, for instance, have frequently brought antidumping suits against foreign steel producers before the Department of Commerce (to determine whether the products were "dumped" or unfairly subsidized) and the International Trade Commission (ITC) (to determine, if dumping has occurred, whether it resulted in "material harm" to domestic producers). One of the problems with dumping is that after a domestic producer has been driven out of business, the foreign company may increase the price, so both domestic producers and consumers lose.

MONEY MAKES THE WORLD GO ROUND

Our simplified discussion of international trade has focused on goods and services, but as we all know, almost all trade involves money in some form. Prior to the development of money, trade was conducted by barter, the mutual exchange of goods and services. This system was inefficient because, in the first place, it was difficult to establish rates of exchange between goods and services. Second, in a barter system there must be a coincidence of wants—every party must want exactly what the other has to offer. If you have a cow and want apples, then you need to find someone with apples who wants a cow; otherwise, you need a third person or another commodity to trade. Third, many commodities are perishable and may not last long enough to trade. Money solves all these inconveniences as a medium of exchange, unit of account for contracts, and store of value. Within countries, authorities have been established to ensure the legitimacy and stability of the currency and to deter counterfeiting and fraud; in the United States, for example, the Treasury Department has exclusive authority to issue paper and coin currency and to ensure that no one else does.

At a Glance

Trade Barriers

Tariffs

- Definition: A tax imposed on a good entering a country from abroad. This additional cost makes the foreign good more expensive than it was before. If domestic consumers are relatively price conscious, they will curb their consumption of foreign goods in exchange for locally produced goods. Thus, tariffs aid local producers who compete against foreign-produced goods.

Example: The Smoot-Hawley Tariff was passed in Congress in 1930, raising prices on all imports by 19 percent. By 1932, the average tariff reached 59 percent. Many foreign nations responded by raising their own tariffs. This led to a collapse of export industries worldwide and accelerated and deepened the Great Depression.

Import Quotas

- Definition: A limit on the number of imports a state receives from the rest of the world. This is an explicit protectionist barrier.

Example: The Japanese government has import quotas on the amount of foreign rice that it will allow into the country. It does this to protect the domestic producers of rice by keeping prices artificially high.

Voluntary Export Restrictions

- Definition: A state compels another nation to "voluntarily" limit its exports. The importer might threaten to impose tariffs if the exporter does not comply. A government can demand these restrictions in order to protect its industries from being pushed out of its own market.

Example: Since 1980, the United States has demanded that the Japanese restrict auto exports to the American market in order to protect local domestic manufacturers.

Subsidies

- Definition: Government payments that allow producers to price their goods below the cost of production without going out of business. Although the ostensible purpose of internal subsidies is to allow producers to compete against imports in the home market, and that of external subsidies is to allow producers to compete in the international market, both in effect aid domestic producers.

Example: Several nations subsidize the European conglomerate Airbus in order to help keep it competitive in the international airplane manufacturing business.

Dumping

- Definition: A process in which one country or firm sells (or "dumps") its products in a foreign market so far below the costs of production that it causes other producers in that market to go out of business.

Example: U.S. steel producers have frequently sought antidumping protection against foreign steel producers before the Department of Commerce and the International Trade Commission.

Exchange Rates

Of course, each state has its own currency: the U.S. dollar, the German mark, the British pound sterling, the Japanese yen, the French franc, the Italian lira, and so on. A way must always be found to exchange these equitably. As those who have traveled abroad know only too well, rates change constantly; so, for example, the exchange rate between the dollar and franc may be altered daily. For the individual traveler, this is enormously inconvenient and potentially expensive. Such has not always been the case, however. Between 1870–1914 and 1945–1973, as we will discuss in Chapter Seven, countries agreed to fix their currencies' value so that they would not fluctuate daily. Although this might seem like a worthwhile system, there are benefits and costs to both fixed and floating exchange-rate systems.

Fixed exchange-rate systems arise when nations agree to establish a set of currency rules. Two examples of such a system are the **gold standard** (1870–1914) and the **Bretton Woods system** (1945–1973). During each period, all currencies were valued at fixed rates against one another. Aside from the benefits to travelers, it also encouraged international trade. Let's examine why this should be so. Suppose an American restaurant owner wants to buy fifty bottles of wine from a French vineyard next month. In order to do so, she must make the purchase in francs. One bottle costs 5 francs, and today's exchange rate is $1/10 francs. If the American makes the purchase today, she pays $25. Under a fixed system, she will also pay $25 next month.

But what if a **floating exchange-rate system** is in effect? If the franc fluctuates during the month so that when she actually purchases the wine, $1 equals 5 francs, she would then owe $50, twice as much as before. Because prices can fluctuate, people might be less likely to trade because of its inherent risks. This problem, of course, is alleviated with fixed exchange rates because everyone can be confident about future currency values.

Given this problem, why would countries choose to have floating exchange rates, as the United States does today? There are surprising advantages to floating rates. Exchange rates are supposed to reflect the general health of an economy. If a nation goes into a prolonged recession, people expect its currency to weaken as well. In a fixed arrangement, however, exchange-rate values cannot change. If a recession does occur, a government has two choices. First, it can pursue policies, like raising interest rates, that inflate the exchange rate in order to maintain its fixed value. Officials might choose to do this because they have made agreements with other nations to defend their currency. As will be discussed in Chapter Seven, the United States made this sort of agreement during the Bretton Woods period between 1945 and 1973.

However, artificially inflating a currency can worsen a country's domestic economy. For example, if a government attempts to shore up its exchange rate by raising interest rates, then foreign nationals will increase their demand for domestic investments, like savings accounts and certificates of deposit (CDs), because they will receive a good rate of return on their money. If interest rates are 10 percent in one country and 8 percent in another, money is likely to flow to the country giving a better deal. Citizens of the country with the 10 percent rate will also deposit their money at home. Thus, when domestic investments become more attractive (especially relative to foreign investments), people demand more local currency, increasing its value.

What Would You Do ?

You are the U.S. secretary of the Treasury. The year is 1890, and the U.S. economy is in what we today would call a serious recession. The United States, along with all the major countries of Europe, participates in a fixed exchange rate system, the gold standard—the currencies of the largest U.S. trading partners are fixed against one another and to the value of gold. This standard eliminates the risk of currency fluctuations and facilitates transatlantic trade. However, because the U.S. economy is weak, the major banks on Wall Street and in the financial centers of London and Paris are reluctant to invest in the United States and are considering moving their capital (which the U.S. economy badly needs) to the emerging markets of Russia and South America. Loans and bonds denominated in dollars are beginning to be discounted; the value of the dollar is beginning to fall.

In order to maintain the dollar's value under the gold standard and continue to attract foreign capital, U.S. banks must raise interest rates. But if U.S. interest rates rise, it will become more difficult for Americans to borrow money to finance farms and factories and to purchase consumer goods. Prices will rise, even more jobs will be lost, and the recovery from the depression will be even more prolonged and painful. The United States will fulfill its international obligations, and by doing so improve its long-term trade and investment picture, but the short-term costs could be high—and politically unpopular.

To complicate matters, populists are calling for the United States to abandon the gold standard entirely and switch to a standard based on silver, which is abundant in the Western states. This would provide relief to debtors, who would be able to repay their loans with devalued silver dollars rather than dollars backed by gold. Many banks and other creditors would suffer serious losses, however, and the United States would no longer be part of the international fixed exchange rate system, increasing the risks of trade and possibly panicking foreign investors. A shift from the gold standard to "Free Silver" would thus be popular on Main Street but unpopular on Wall Street, and it could have significant long-term costs to the economy.

You face a difficult choice. On the one hand, your friends on Wall Street encourage you to stay on the gold standard and raise interest rates, to maintain trade and competitiveness over the long term. One the other hand, Free Silver members of Congress harangue you to abandon the gold standard and give badly needed debt relief to farmers, small businesses, and consumers. You could adopt a middle course and stay on the gold standard, but refuse to raise interest rates, but that will satisfy no one politically, make the United States a poor investment risk in international financial markets, and harm the balance of trade. There is, at this point in history, no Federal Reserve board to make the controversial decision for you; you must make your recommendation to Congress and the president.

What would you do ?

What are the drawbacks of this policy? While high interest rates might help preserve a country's fixed currency rate, this policy decision also makes borrowing money more expensive. To the extent that borrowed funds help us buy goods like homes and cars, higher interest rates reduce the number of these purchases. When people choose to reduce their own spending on goods and services, it hurts the national economy. Therefore, in order to defend its currency's value, a state often has to jeopardize its national economy.

A second option for policy-makers is to stop defending their currency. This action reduces the exchange rate's value and does not have the same negative consequences on the economy that defending the currency might have. In fact, it might improve economic conditions by making exports less expensive (see the discussion on trade deficit and exchange rates later in this chapter). Under a fixed exchange-rate system, however, if a weakened currency is not bolstered, a country will have to renege on an agreement it made with other countries, potentially harming its reputation. This can become important because states have to interact in the future, on currency issues and others as well. If animosity develops, it can affect trade relations, security arrangements, and other related issues. Floating exchange rates thus have an advantage over fixed rates in that they accurately reflect a state's economic health and allow governments to pursue economic policies independent of exchange-rate requirements.

This explanation of the benefits and costs of fixed and floating exchange rates has revealed two important points. First, fixed exchange rates make the international economy more stable and predictable, but they can also force governments to pursue harmful policies when the currency's value goes in one direction and the economy's health in the other. Second, floating exchange rates accurately reflect an economy's well-being, but they create additional uncertainty in the world economy. This uncertainty can develop into an international crisis if individual governments—especially leaders of powerful economies—try to raise or lower their own currency in relation to their trading partners, most of whom will resist this action if they fear it will adversely affect their own economies. This maneuvering can itself create tensions, as it did between the United States and Japan in the 1980s and 1990s, which can produce bitterness and severe economic problems for one or both countries.

Balance of Payments

Another important concept for understanding international economic relations is the **balance of payments.** Much like companies, states keep "balance sheets" that present its transactions with the rest of the world. These national accounts tell us a country's trade balance (exports of goods and services minus imports of goods and services), how much money locals earned overseas, the amount of foreign currency invested in the domestic economy, the level of official foreign aid given to other countries, as well as the amount of foreign currency held by the central bank (the Federal Reserve in the United States, for example, or the Bundesbank in Germany).[6]

The sum total of a nation's imports, exports, foreign aid and other government transactions, and investment income and payments is referred to as the **current-account balance**. This is the figure usually cited in news reports about a country's "balance of trade." If the current-account balance is positive, the country enjoys a **trade surplus**—or a "net profit" from trade. If it is negative, the state has a "net loss," or **trade deficit**—though consumers in the state may still be better off as a result of trade, because they are able to buy less expensive and/or higher quality imported goods.

Accounting procedures guarantee that the balance of payments always equals zero. This is due to double-entry bookkeeping. For example, if an American purchases a foreign good, the import's value is recorded as a reduction from the balance of payments. However, once that foreign producer obtains U.S. dollars in exchange for his good, he usually deposits it in a bank, the same way most people deposit paychecks. If he does a lot of business in the United States, he might deposit it in an American bank. Once he deposits his money in the United States, his account's value is added to the plus side of the balance of payments. Even if the foreign producer deposits it in his own bank abroad, that foreign bank must eventually deposit it in a U.S. bank in order to redeem its value—that is, in order to get paid back. This has the effect of an addition to the balance of payments. For accounting purposes, this transaction's net effect is zero, in much the same way that assets always equal liabilities plus equity on a company's balance sheet. However, as we are about to see, the balance of payments can tell us something about a nation's trade balance, which has important ramifications for the state's economy. Although accounting procedures might make the balance of payments appear to be in equilibrium, the potential problems suffered through a trade deficit cannot be overcome by sleight of hand on the accountant's ledger.

Exchange Rates and Trade Deficits

Thus far we have discussed exchange rates and the balance of payments, but no direct link has been established. For our purposes, the most important tie is between the exchange rate and trade deficit. To see how this works, let's go back to our American restaurateur who wants to purchase French wine. In that case, using floating exchange rates, as the dollar depreciated (became less valuable relative to the franc), the wine's price increased. This occurred because, even though the bottle's price remained constant at 5 francs, it took more dollars to purchase the same number of francs; the price of 5 francs rose from 50 cents to $1. This fluctuation automatically doubled the price of a bottle of wine to a foreign purchaser.

Now, what effect might this price doubling have on the restaurant owner? First, she might decide to purchase the wine anyway, causing her to reduce her spending on other matters or go into debt. Second, she could choose to purchase a California wine whose price (for instance, $30 per bottle) is now cheaper than French wine. In general, we assume that if the California wine is relatively similar to the

French wine, then the owner will probably increase her consumption of the local product relative to the foreign one.

This situation can easily be extrapolated to the national economy. If the dollar weakens relative to foreign currencies, foreign goods tend to become more expensive than domestic goods. In most instances, this leads to a relative decline in the consumption of foreign goods and an increase in the consumption of domestic goods. Conversely, the opposite occurs abroad. As the dollar becomes cheaper, American exports become less expensive in foreign countries, increasing consumption of U.S. goods. Both of these effects improve the U.S. trade balance by reducing imports and increasing exports. Of course, the opposite occurs when the dollar strengthens against foreign currencies. Under those circumstances, the U.S. trade balance worsens as Americans consume more imports and export less abroad.

Figure 6.2 shows that this relationship between the exchange rate and trade balance does exist, albeit imperfectly. For example, in both 1980 and 1991, the dollar exchange rates were roughly equal. Why was the American trade deficit so much worse in 1991? As the graphs shows, the dollar strengthened (and the trade deficit worsened) dramatically during this period, only to revert back to its original level. Many reasons can explain why the trade deficit did not improve as much as one would expect after the dollar weakened. For example, consumer behavior might have lagged. If American consumers believed that foreign products were better than domestic ones, they might have been unwilling to change brands, even if their favorite items' prices increased. Second, once importers got a foothold in the U.S. market, they might have been willing to risk profits to maintain their presence. Therefore, even when the exchange rate forced their goods' prices higher, they did not pass this cost along to the consumer so that they could remain competitive.

Finally, Americans' demand for foreign goods might have become **price inelastic,** meaning they bought the good regardless of its price. This could be true for some goods, like oil, that the United States imported in larger amounts in the late 1980s than it did in the 1970s. All three effects played a role in enlarging the trade deficit in 1991 despite the dollar's reversion to 1980 levels. In spite of these deviations, the relationship between the exchange rate and trade balance, as the graph suggests, remains generally intact.

ECONOMICS AND POLITICS

Our brief discussion of free trade and **protectionism** reminds us that governments often make economic decisions for political reasons, and vice versa. The discipline of international political economy explores the many ways in which politics and economics interact at the national and global levels. This section outlines three major schools of thought on the complex web of relationships between the world economy and national and international politics. These three perspectives are commonly referred to as liberalism, realism, and Marxism.[7]

Figure 6.2	U.S. Trade Balance and Exchange Rate

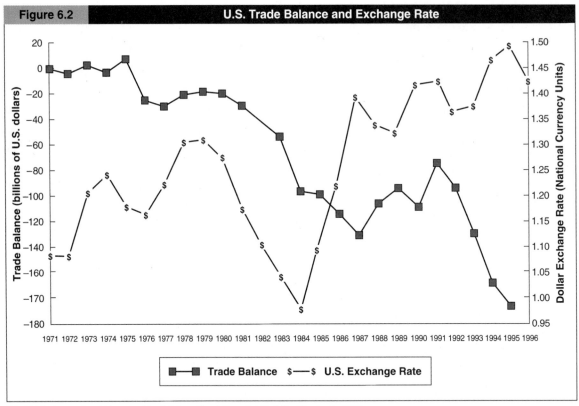

SOURCE: International Monetary Fund, *International Financial Statistics Yearbook, 1997*

Liberalism

In the late eighteenth and early nineteenth centuries, many economists (particularly David Ricardo) who studied international trade concluded that trade barriers were an impediment to economic growth. Influenced by the economic theories of Adam Smith (see box), they theorized that if states allowed the market to function autonomously and removed as many barriers to trade as possible, states would make maximum use of their comparative advantages and trade would evolve to the benefit of all concerned. As the Industrial Revolution led to an expansion of production in Europe, leading to an explosion in demand for both manufactured and agricultural goods, their arguments inspired governments, especially Britain's, to reduce their intervention in trade and other economic activity. Their perspective on trade ultimately became known as **liberalism.**

Economic liberals make three assumptions: First, that individuals are the principal actors in the political economy. Thus, in order to understand the world economy, we must focus on individuals within society and how they interact with the market. Second, individuals are rational. They have certain preferences that are consistent and stable over time. Finally, individuals maximize their utility by making trade-offs between costs and benefits. Under these assumptions, liberals argue that the market best allocates the world's scarce resources in the most efficient manner possible. They view trade as a positive-sum game, meaning that when nations develop their own comparative advantage, trading benefits every actor involved. According to this theory, governments need not involve themselves with the market mechanism—indeed, government intervention only frustrates the most efficient outcome. Liberals thus conclude that states should practice **laissez-faire, or "leave well enough alone," in their economic policies.** (This terminology may be somewhat confusing to students of American politics, where conservatives support laissez-faire and liberals often advocate government intervention. As Newt Gingrich would be quick to explain, when the principles of free trade and laissez-faire were first advocated they were called "liberal" because they promoted individual freedom and liberty.[8])

Liberal theory is useful because it helps us understand how economic incentives would guide states if all they were concerned about was maximizing their national income. However, states are not only wealth maximizers. National policies are implemented by leaders interested as much in the state's survival and security as their own job security. For both purposes, a country's wealth may matter less than its relative strength.

Realism

While liberals argue that economics should be independent of politics, realists look at power relations among nations to determine economic outcomes. They contend that because relative levels of power matter in the international system, economics must follow politics. The more powerful one country is compared with another, the more capable it is of coercing other states in trade and economic dealings as well as political issues.

The three basic assumptions of realists are that nation-states, rather than individuals, are the appropriate units of analysis in the international political economy; that these nation-states are rational actors; and that they seek to maximize power. States act in a manner that they feel will promote their military prominence, even if it means that economic factors are compromised. Realists think states often have no choice but to sacrifice maximum economic growth for national security. Consequently, while classic liberals contend that the search for individual wealth is at the heart of the international economy, for realists the world economy pivots on the quest for national power.

The realist perspective dominated international trade policies prior to the late eighteenth century. Before economists developed theories of the market and comparative advantage, most states followed policies of mercantilism, an economic philosophy that regards trade primarily as an instrument of power politics. As one author writes:

> [During the era of mercantilism] the economic realm became the main arena for political conflict. The pursuit of state power was carried out through the pursuit of

■ Adam Smith

SOURCE: Culver Pictures

national economic power and wealth. . . . All international economic transactions were regulated for the purpose of state power.[9]

Mercantilists thus argued that states should exercise strict control over trade, protect domestic industries through tariff barriers and subsidies, and obtain and monopolize trade with overseas colonies. European governments and an emerging class of merchants gained the most from these policies, reaping tremendous profits. During this period, the European powers established colonies in the New World, Asia, and Africa and sought to control trade. Their goal was to expand their own export markets to these new areas, prohibit rival states from doing the same, and import inexpensive commodities at artificially low prices. (As noted in Chapter Two, these policies, when applied to Britain's colonies in America, were major causes of the American Revolution.)

Spotlight

Adam Smith and the Free Market

Two events occurred in 1776 that were destined to transform the world. One was the writing of the Declaration of Independence by Britain's American colonies; the other was the publication of *An Inquiry into the Nature and Causes of the Wealth of Nations* by the Scottish economist Adam Smith (1723–1790). Smith, considered to be the founder of the study of political economy, outlined the classical model of economics that laid the foundations for capitalism as we know it today. Before he developed his theories, most states thought trade was a zero-sum game—that is, one party to an exchange (either the buyer or the seller) would gain, but the other would lose, so the objective of trade was basically to gain profits by cheating one's trading partners. This view of trade, known as **mercantilism**, led many countries to put up economic walls (such as the Navigation Acts, which restricted trade with and caused much political dissension in the American colonies) to protect themselves from the supposedly predatory practices of foreign traders. Under mercantilism, many European nations sought to colonize and dominate many areas outside Europe in order to monopolize trade in goods that could not be produced in Europe, such as spices from Indonesia and silk and tea from China.

Smith, however, endorsed the idea of the free market. He believed strongly in the effectiveness of market forces and proved that trade could benefit both the buyer and the seller, enriching everyone.

Moreover, he argued that Britain and the other European powers should abandon their mercantalist trade policies in favor of a policy of laissez-faire (essentially "leave well enough alone") on trade and business. The idea that interference in the markets by government benefited the economy, Smith argued, was a destructive illusion; the market would bring the best outcome for all.

Smith also believed that persons had natural rights with which governments should not interfere. *The Wealth of Nations* not only argued for free trade, but also contended that states should confine themselves to providing national defense, a judicial system for property rights and contracts, and maintaining public works and an infrastructure (roads, post offices, and so on). People would not invest unless property was secure, Smith held, so governments must protect property rights. The free play of market forces is beneficial to all, Smith concluded, as in the long run markets are the most efficient and productive means of allocating resources.

Smith's arguments gained credence as his economic predictions proved accurate. First Britain and later many other nations came to favor the free-trade policies he advocated. Many point to the collapse of the Communist political and economic systems in Eastern Europe and the former USSR in the late 1980s and early 1990s as further proof of his conviction that the free market is superior to state management of the economy.

If trade barriers help states to maximize their power, however, why have there been various periods in history when world trade was relatively free from barriers? Some realists explain this apparent contradiction with the theory of **hegemonic stability.** According to this theory, if one major state becomes the leading economic and military power in the international system, and that state perceives advantages in maintaining an open trading system, it will use its power to set and enforce rules of free trade. As Chapter Seven details, Britain pursued such a policy in the mid-nineteenth century, as did the United States in the years following World War II. When there is no single hegemon, an alliance of leading economic states can attempt to enforce trade agreements and otherwise promote cooperation multilaterally, through organizations such as the General Agreement on Tariffs and Trade (GATT) and its successor, the World Trade Organization (WTO). This cooperation can be difficult to achieve, however, because in an anarchic world, it can be difficult to punish a recalcitrant state for breaking a trade agreement. Despite this difficulty, cooperation can emerge if states acknowledge that they will need one another's help in the long run.[10] If the major trading states do not cooperate, however, realists warn that they are likely to form trade blocs and set up trade barriers to promote their exports and protect their domestic markets from foreign competition. Many analysts thus fear that regional trading areas such as the European Union and North America under the North American Free Trade Agreement (NAFTA) could become "fortresses" closed to imports from outside. (See Chapter Seven for more on the GATT, WTO, EU, and NAFTA.)

Marxism

While liberals view the international political economy from the level of the individual and realists from the nation-state level, Marxists see it at a class level. Class

■ Karl Marx   SOURCE: Culver Pictures

Karl Marx

The thoughts of Karl Marx (1818–1883) have had sweeping effects on the politics, economics, and history of the twentieth century. Dubbed Marxism, his theories of socialism and revolution have been a powerful ideological force in the modern world.

Marx's central work, *The Communist Manifesto* (1848), has become the cornerstone of socialist thought. This pamphlet, written in collaboration with Friedrich Engels, called on the workers of the world to unite against the exploitation inherent in the capitalist system. He argued for revolution as the mechanism to instill communism, a societal framework wherein workers benefit equally from their labor. The main problem with capitalism, Marx argued, is that the workers do not own the means of production and thus do not reap the rewards. Workers toil in factories, which are owned by capitalists.

Marx's other major work, *Das Kapital* (1867), is representative of this position. In it, he writes that misery for the worker will continue until "the knell of capitalist private property sounds. The expropriators are expropriated."

In short, the essential assertion by Marx is that the *proletariat*, or working class, must unite globally and revolt against the *bourgeoisie*—the beneficiaries of the capitalist system, those who own property of any kind—in order for the proletariat to receive the full benefits of its labor. Marx advocated central (government) ownership of the means of production to ensure equal distribution.

interests, for Marx and his followers, determine economic policy. Indeed, Marxists believe that the state itself is the expression of the preferences of the dominant class. In industrial democracies, the dominant class, the bourgeoisie, is the owner of capital. These capitalists control the means of production while the working class, or proletariat, provides the labor to fuel the capitalist system. Marxists foresee alienation on the part of the exploited proletariat. The working classes will unite, both domestically and internationally, to revolt against capitalism. The final result will be communism, in which the state, on behalf of all the people, controls the means of production and ensures that everyone benefits equally.[11]

Although Marxism might seem out of date today after the collapse of communism worldwide, it is still a tool that some scholars use to analyze the role of labor in our increasingly global economy, as well as the plight of the less developed world. Regarding the role of labor, Marxists believe that multinationalism—the advent of international capital mobility through multinational corporations—has undermined labor's ability to negotiate an equitable division of profit. Researchers analyze how labor should respond to this growing division. Also, as we will see in Chapter Eight, a branch of Marxist-inspired thought known as **dependency theory** studies how the world system has divided between industrialized "core" countries and underdeveloped "periphery" countries. From this perspective, core countries exploit the periphery for their own ends and stunt industrialization.

Dependency theorists thus focus on strategies for ending this dependency. (For much more on dependency theory and the role of developing countries in the global economy, see Chapter Eight.)

International Conditions and the Domestic Political Economy

Regardless of whether one adopts a liberal, realist, or Marxist perspective on international political economy, it is clear that leaders have both economics and politics in mind when making trade policy. How does increased exposure to international trade affect domestic politics? Do domestic actors prefer fixed or floating exchange-rate systems? In order to answer these types of questions, one needs an analytical framework for understanding how conditions in the international economy affect domestic politics. Two methods will be discussed here: one called the **factor approach,** the other the **sector approach.** These approaches can help us to better understand the domestic conflicts over international trade that, as national economies become progressively globalized, are becoming increasingly prominent features of the political landscape.

The factor approach hypothesizes that every society has three basic interest groups: landholders, capital owners (shareholders in corporations, investors, and so on), and workers.[12] Conflicts arise between those groups that benefit from international conditions and those that are harmed. For example, increased exposure to free trade will benefit those people associated with factors that have a comparative advantage domestically (because they can sell their products abroad); it will hurt those who are associated with scarce factors. This might explain why American organized labor opposed the North American Free Trade Agreement, while factory owners supported it. Unskilled Mexican labor is cheaper than unskilled American labor, giving Mexico a comparative advantage. U.S. workers feared that free trade would encourage United States factories to go south to take advantage of these lower costs. Because the United States has a comparative advantage in capital, capital owners have an incentive to export (this includes exporting factories) if they can earn higher profits overseas. In this case industrialists will make more money if they employ cheaper labor in Mexico than if they use the more expensive workers in the United States. Therefore, in this example, a natural conflict emerges between capital and labor.

The sector approach focuses on sectors of the economy rather than factors of production.[13] A sector is a group of related industries within a nation; oil, coal, natural gas, and nuclear power, for example, make up the "energy sector." The sector approach assumes that capital is fixed in a particular industrial sector, at least in the short term. This means that increased foreign competition might hurt some capital owners more than others. Let's say there is an economy in which capital is specific to either the production of clothing or computers. If international trade hurts clothing manufacturers but helps computer manufacturers (because the latter are more competitive internationally), then cloth producers might

At a Glance

Three Perspectives on Political Economy

Liberalism	Realism	Marxism

- States should allow the market to function autonomously.

Assumptions: First, individuals are the principal actors in the political economy. Second, individuals are rational. They have certain preferences that are consistent and stable over time. Third, individuals maximize their utility by making trade-offs between costs and benefits.

Argument: The market best allocates the world's scarce resources in the most efficient manner possible. Trade is a positive-sum, win-win game. Government need not involve itself by interfering with the market mechanism—indeed, government intervention only frustrates the most efficient outcome. Therefore, states should practice laissez-faire.

Usefulness: It helps individuals understand how economic incentives would guide states if all they were concerned about was maximizing their national incomes.

- Because relative levels of power matter in the international system, economics must follow politics. The more powerful one country is relative to another, the more capable it is of coercing other states in trade and economic dealings, as well as on political issues.

Assumptions: First, nation-states—rather than individuals—are the appropriate units of analysis in the international political economy. Second, these nation-states are rational actors. Third, each seeks to maximize power.

Arguments: States act in a manner that they feel will promote their military prominence, even if it means that economic factors are compromised. States often have no choice but to sacrifice maximum economic growth for national security. The world revolves around the quest for national power.

Usefulness: It helps us to understand how leaders evaluate their nation's military power and their relation to other states in the international arena.

- Class interests determine economic policy. Adherents believe that the state itself is the expression of the interests of the dominant class.

Assumptions: In industrial states, the dominant class, the bourgeoisie, is the owner of capital. These capitalists control the means of production while the working class, or proletariat, provides the labor to fuel the capitalist system.

Argument: Marxists foresee alienation on the part of the exploited proletariat. The working classes will unite, both domestically and internationally, to revolt against capitalism. The final result will be communism, where the state—on behalf of all the people—controls the means of production and ensures that everyone benefits equally.

Usefulness: It helps to analyze the role of labor in our increasingly global economy, as well as the plight of the lesser-developed world.

begin lobbying for protectionism against the wishes of computer makers. This model suggests that a rivalry will develop between these sectors, with one being for and the other against free trade.

The sector approach is useful for understanding why, at any given time, some industries will support free trade while others favor protectionist policies. In the United States, the automobile industry has consistently sought protection from foreign competition, particularly through the use of voluntary export restrictions, as discussed earlier. On the other hand, pharmaceutical companies, which are very competitive internationally, have lobbied against any protectionist provisions, fearing that foreign reprisals would affect their industry. In this circumstance, sector divisions transcend other divisions between factors that might exist in society.

Are these models contradictory? Not always. Some argue that the sector approach is useful for predicting short-term cleavages while the factor model better explains long-term political divisions. In the short term, it is reasonable to believe that capital is fixed—a computer manufacturer cannot become a cloth producer quickly and cheaply. Yet, in the long term, capital tends to be mobile. Capital owners, like the investors in the clothing industry, might find that in the long term they can earn higher profits in other industries or abroad. If this situation materializes, divisions between capital owners and labor could easily become the dominant division, just as they did in the case of NAFTA.

Effect of Domestic Politics on the International Arena

Just as international trade can affect domestic politics, domestic politics can have an impact on the global economy. One approach to the study of international political economy concentrates on the fact that the trade policies of a state are often shaped by the domestic interest groups that exert the most influence nationally. (For more on the role of interest groups in the making of foreign policy, see Chapter Twelve.) International cooperation can arise when a group of states' domestic coalitions all agree on specific policy goals. For example, some analysts argue that fixed rates succeeded prior to World War I because influential domestic interests in each state supported a cooperative international monetary system. This was due to the fact that export-oriented industries had a tremendous amount of political clout in most of the dominant states at the time.

As we suggested earlier in this chapter, exporters will often prefer fixed rates over floating rates because they reduce the risks involved with international trade. In general, these dominant interests can be represented by landowners, laborers, and capital owners, or various economic sectors. Regardless of which it is, these interests will have to be more powerful than their competitors in order to succeed. The main point of this approach is that preferences for free trade or protection do not rely directly on the relationships among states in the international system, but on the preferences of domestic coalitions. According to this view, coalitions of interest groups within and between the major trading states will be more important than diplomacy in determining the basic conditions of the international economy.

ECONOMIC POWER

Cynics often argue that like domestic politics, international politics follows the Golden Rule: Whoever has the gold makes the rules. One does not have to be a cynic to realize that regardless of one's perspective on international trade, control of resources, capital, and other productive assets usually translates into influence in the international system. At the same time, as economic realists emphasize, economic power forms the material basis for military power. A state's raw materials, population, industrial capacity, technology, and geography all contribute to its strategic strengths and vulnerabilities. For all these reasons, liberals, realists, and Marxists alike all counsel their countries to develop economic power, though the policies they advocate in pursuit of economic strength often differ widely.

Some elements of economic strength, such as **gross national product** (GNP), oil reserves, and balance of trade, are relatively easy to calculate to allow comparison with other states. Other components of material power, such as the skills of a nation's labor force and the creative potential of its research and development establishment, are equally important but more difficult to quantify. In all its aspects, economic power forms the physical basis of a nation's political strength. For our survey of the sources of power it is convenient to divide economic power into the three categories of territory, population, and trade and industry. Though states can be competitive in world markets by maximizing their comparative advantage in specific economic "niches," a state must usually be strong in all three categories to remain a major player in the global economy over the long haul.

Territory: Geography and Natural Resources

A nation's most important territorial assets include its geography (size, location, climate, and physical features) and its natural resources. A glance at the globe shows how geography benefits the United States and Russia. The United States is separated from both Europe and Asia by oceans, which provide convenient trade routes but make invasion more difficult. Russia's vast land area straddling these two continents gives it a strong strategic position in both. The territorial expanse of Russia and the United States (the world's largest and fourth largest nations in terms of land area, at 6.59 and 3.68 million square miles, respectively) gives them control over abundant natural resources, an advantage shared by other large nations such as Canada (second largest at 3.85 million square miles), China (third, at 3.69 million square miles), Brazil (fifth, at 3.29 million square miles), and Australia (sixth, at 2.97 million square miles).

Size is not all that matters, however. In geopolitics, as in real estate, the three most important factors are location, location, and location. While the areas of Japan and the United Kingdom do not even rank in the top thirty, both countries are island powers whose positions provide them with a strong buffer against invasion (Britain has not been successfully invaded since the year 1066), as well as a strong orientation toward maritime trade. Because neither nation has needed a large army since World War II, both have concentrated on building strong navies for the twin purposes of defense and protection of trade. Location on an island is no guarantee of safety or political influence, though; island nations such as Madagascar, Sri Lanka, Indonesia, and the Philippines have been colonized or occupied by more powerful states at various times.

Proximity to major trade routes is also a key economic and strategic advantage, one that has helped Britain, the Netherlands, and Singapore become major trading centers. Similarly, serviceable deep-water ports are some of the most important "amenities" in global economic real estate. Fine harbors give port cities like Rotterdam, New York, San Francisco, and Tokyo major economic advantages. On the other hand, Russia has traditionally lacked conveniently located ports that are free of ice year-round and cannot easily be blockaded. For this reason, control of the Turkish Straits linking the Mediterranean with the Black Sea was for centuries a major objective of Russian foreign policy, and shipment of oil and hazardous cargoes through the narrow straits remains a contentious issue.

A second and equally important set of territorial assets are natural resources, such as iron, coal, oil, timber, and **arable land** (land usable for agriculture). In considering the short-term value of a nation's natural resources, both production and reserves must be taken into account, while in the long term, renewability and sustainability (see Chapter Ten) must be considered as well. Since the Industrial Revolution, the most important natural resources have been metals and **fossil fuels,** and many wars have been fought over the possession of both. In the years following World War I, oil became the source of energy most important to the world economy, and to the world's military forces. Petroleum remains critically important, providing the classic example of how resources affect power in international politics.

Figure 6.3 shows that among the world's leading oil producers, only the United States, Russia, China, and the United Kingdom are among the world's leading economic powers. They also have large proven reserves, which mean they have clear advantages over other major economic powers. Russia, having inherited most of the former USSR's oil reserves, should find its energy resources to be a major advantage in its economic development. Japan, on the other hand, is poor in oil reserves and must rely heavily on oil imports to meet its energy needs. A consequence of Japan's dependency on imported oil is its economic vulnerability to any threat against its energy supply. The oil price rises of 1973–1974 and 1979 dealt sharp jolts to Japan's economy; to avoid such shocks in the future, a main objective of Tokyo's foreign policy is to ensure a steady flow of oil from the Middle East. Although Britain, with its relatively large North Sea reserves, enjoys a good measure of energy security, the other leading industrial nations of the EU (Germany, France, and Italy) have inadequate oil reserves and depend heavily on Middle Eastern oil to satisfy their energy requirements. This dependence has often affected European policies toward Middle Eastern nations, especially in times of conflict.[14]

While the protection of energy supplies has been a salient issue in recent decades, the supply of food is even more important. As with oil, any state that is self-sufficient in its basic food requirements enjoys significantly greater flexibility in

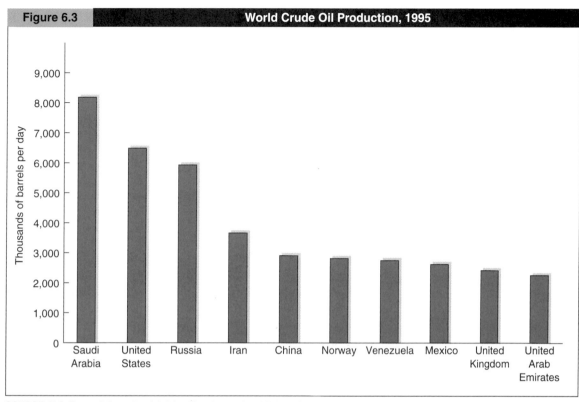

Figure 6.3   **World Crude Oil Production, 1995**

SOURCE: U.S. Energy Information Administration, *International Energy Annual,* 1995

economic and foreign policies than those states unable to feed their people from domestic agricultural production. Japan and the United Kingdom, both lacking in arable land, have traditionally had to rely on imports of food. This caused serious problems for both countries during World War II, when their import lifelines were attacked by submarines. In recent times, Tokyo has continued to heavily subsidize its politically powerful but highly inefficient rice farmers in order to prevent Japanese dependence on other states for this dietary staple. The United States, by contrast, has been called the "breadbasket" of the world because of its abundant arable land and continues to be a major exporter of agricultural products. Although the Soviet Union possessed vast expanses of rich farmland, the inherent inefficiencies of its overcentralized planned economy created chronic grain shortages that had to be made up with imports.[15] (Soviet farms consistently produced more than enough food for the USSR's population, but an inadequate transportation network was usually unable to deliver food supplies in time to prevent spoilage.)

Again, as with oil, dependence on imported food makes states vulnerable to interruption of supplies. Following the Soviet invasion of Afghanistan in 1979, the United States halted all grain sales to the Soviets in the hope that the embargo would press them to withdraw their forces. However, as Washington soon discovered, economic sanctions are effective only when the embargoed good is unavailable elsewhere; the USSR simply bought grain from other suppliers and did not alter its policy toward Afghanistan. (The United States canceled the embargo in 1981.)

Population

In determining the extent to which population will be a factor in material power, what matters most is size, demographic structure, and the educational and skill levels of the labor force. A sufficiently large population is a prerequisite for great-power status, but it is not sufficient in itself. Too large a population might create a drain on resources, while one too small might prevent economic growth and limit military capabilities.

As shown in Table 6.1, in 1977 the ten most populous countries included six major economic powers—China, the Soviet Union, the United States, Japan, West Germany, and the United Kingdom. By 1997 Indonesia and Bangladesh had supplanted united Germany and the United Kingdom on the list of the world's top ten countries in terms of population. Despite their size, China, Bangladesh, India, Indonesia, Pakistan, and Nigeria are developing countries that must devote large shares of their resources to basic food production, often at the expense of industrial development. On the other hand, Israel's population of about 5 million is so small that it cannot become a major power, despite its military and economic strength. Similarly, the highly industrialized countries of Finland and Switzerland have been prevented from becoming major economic powers by their small populations.

Table 6.1	Ten Most Populous Countries, 1977 and 1997		
1977		**1997**	
China	982,531,000	China	1,160,045,000
India	643,040,000	India	856,303,000
USSR	258,900,000	United States	248,710,000
United States	216,817,000	Indonesia	179,379,000
Indonesia	141,462,000	Russia	147,022,000
Brazil	117,685,000	Brazil	146,825,000
Japan	113,860,000	Japan	125,570,000
Bangladesh	85,511,000	Bangladesh	104,766,000
Pakistan	75,472,000	Nigeria	88,992,000
Nigeria	66,628,000	Pakistan	84,254,000

SOURCES: 1997: "Population and Vital Statistics Report," UN Department for Economic and Social Information and Policy Analysis, *Statistical Papers*, Series A, vol. XLIX, no. 3. 1977: U.S. Bureau of the Census, *Statistical Abstract of the United States, 1979*, Washington, DC

In addition to size of population, the demographic structure of a state's population can have a major impact on its economic power. A nation that has a relatively large proportion of children and teenagers, typically due to high birthrates and short life expectancies, will face greater challenges in developing a highly skilled labor force and must devote substantial resources to child education and welfare. On the other hand, states fortunate enough to have a low birthrate and long life expectancies will face the problem of caring for senior citizens, especially if a pronounced "baby boom" is followed by a "baby bust," as is the case with Japan and the United States. Both these conditions can constrain the resources available to conduct an activist foreign policy.

The size and quality of a nation's labor force is crucial to its economic strength. The overall skill level of a country's working population is difficult to measure, but some indices offer a rough idea of the education and skills possessed by a nation's workers. The percentage of the labor force employed in agriculture is a useful indicator of economic advancement; as a rule, as industrialization increases, the percentage of workers engaged in farming drops. This is because of two factors: (1) the increased availability of jobs in manufacturing and services and (2) the greater agricultural productivity made possible by scientific and technological development. In 1990, China had 67.5 percent of its labor force in agriculture, Brazil, 24.3 percent, and the Soviet Union, 13 percent—a sign of continuing weaknesses in the economies of all three countries. By contrast, the United States had only 2.3 percent of its population engaged in agriculture, despite its position as one of the world's major agricultural producers—an indication of enduring strength for the American economy.[16]

A country's literacy rate roughly indicates the educational and skill level of its labor force. For example, more developed nations, such as EU members Italy (97 percent) and Greece (93 percent), tend to have a higher rate of adult literacy than developing countries such as India (48 percent) and Nigeria (51 percent). China's literacy rate of 73 percent reflects a potential for enhancement of its workers' productivity, while countries such as Nigeria and India face a more difficult task in developing a well-educated, skilled labor force. Somalia's very low adult literacy rate (24 percent) reflects the enormous economic challenges that contributed to that state's near-total collapse in 1992–1993.[17]

Trade and Industry

Regardless of its geographic or demographic advantages, a nation's economic power depends on its ability to use its human and natural resources through domestic production and foreign trade. Economic strength is readily quantifiable through such measures as gross national product (GNP), per capita income, growth rate, and trade balance, although such numbers do not tell the whole story. A state's industrial capacity also depends on qualitative factors like technology.

GNP serves as a crude but convenient means of comparing the economic strength of various countries. GNP measures the market value of goods and services produced during a particular time period (usually a year) and provides an estimate of a nation's total agricultural, industrial, and commercial output. GNP differs from **gross domestic product** (GDP) in that the latter does not take into account income earned by a nation's citizens and corporations that operate outside its borders. GNP also is a useful way to compare the growth rates of states in both absolute and relative terms. For example, during the 1980s, while the U.S. economy was growing larger in terms of total output, its share of world production was declining relative to both Japan and Germany. Because power in international politics is relative, the relative size of national economies has more political significance than their absolute size. Table 6.2 lists the ten nations with highest GNPs in 1975, 1985, and 1995 in order to give an indication of the changes in the balance of economic power over that twenty-year period.

As noted in Chapter Five, the GNP tables show that while the United States has remained the world's principal economic power throughout the period, the relative margin between it and its economic rivals has been steadily narrowing. If Japan and Germany increase their economic strength, they could continue to improve their economic positions, perhaps even enough to challenge the United States for political leadership. However, in the early 1990s they both suffered from recessions, exacerbated for Germany by the difficulties encountered in the absorption of the former Communist East. At the same time, China has grown by about 9 percent a year since 1978 and now ranks as one of the world's three largest economies. Meanwhile, the American economy improved, and it began to move ahead again.

The Soviet Union's decline in relative economic strength, which contributed to its political collapse, is also apparent from this rough comparison of total output. The USSR's economy remained about half the size of the United States' from the 1970s to the end of the 1980s, but other nations' economies grew faster, and by the end of this period Moscow had been eclipsed by Japan as the second-ranked economic power. Since the breakup of the USSR at the end of 1991, Russia has

Table 6.2	Gross National Product of Top Ten Countries, 1974–1995				
1974		**1985**		**1995**	
United States	1,413,530	United States	4,010,000	United States	7,247,000
Soviet Union	598,640	Soviet Union	2,197,000	Japan	5,153,000
Japan	446,026	Japan	1,361,000	China	2,759,000
West Germany	388,670	West Germany	649,900	Germany	2,172,000
France	285,780	France	508,500	France	1,521,000
China	224,640	United Kingdom	460,400	United Kingdom	1,110,000
United Kingdom	200,830	China	368,900	Italy	1,082,000
Italy	156,510	Italy	366,400	Russia	664,000
Canada	139,260	Canada	346,100	Brazil	656,500
Brazil	95,920	Poland	245,600	Spain	553,800

SOURCES: *World Bank Atlas 1975;* U.S. Arms Control and Disarmament Agency, *World Military Expenditures and Arms Transfers 1986, 1996*
NOTE: Figures are in millions of U.S. dollars.

fallen even further behind because of reduced size and economic performance and now requires heavy doses of economic aid from its former adversaries. Map 6.1, a cartogram showing states sized according their gross domestic product, provides a graphic representation of the balance of economic power in the New Era.

Another measure of economic wealth is per capita income (GNP divided by population). Although the most economically advanced states will generally have the highest per capita incomes, the statistic does not provide a measure of a state's total economic capability, nor does it show how equally income is shared throughout a society. Nations with high per capita incomes have an advantage in that a higher percentage of their national income is likely to be available for investment in further growth, for spending on military forces, or for increasing the state's political influence worldwide through channels such as foreign aid. Table 6.3 lists the top ten nations in terms of per capita income in 1974, 1985, and 1995. Comparison with the tables for GNP shows immediately that the nations with the greatest total production do not necessarily have the highest standards of living.

The figures for 1985 illustrate the impact of the energy crises of the 1970s on the world economy as OPEC's cutbacks in petroleum production caused oil prices to quadruple in the 1970s. As a result, per capita incomes of oil-exporting countries soared. In the 1980s, however, oil prices declined, as oil-importing states substituted other energy sources (such as coal, hydroelectric power, and nuclear energy) for oil, took steps to conserve energy, and developed previously unexploited oil fields (like those in Alaska and the North Sea). Table 6.3 reflects the impact of the rise and fall of oil prices on the fortunes of OPEC. The per capita GNPs of OPEC member countries the United Arab Emirates (UAE), Qatar, and Kuwait, ranked first, second, and fourth, respectively, in 1984, but none made the top ten in 1995.

The figures on per capita income show the relative economic positions of the superpowers as well. While the United States' 1974 per capita GNP of $6,670 was surpassed only by the much smaller Sweden and Switzerland, its 1984 per capita GNP had slipped to fifth behind the oil-rich United Arab Emirates, Qatar, and Kuwait. By 1995 the United States' per capita income of $27,550 trailed Japan's as well of that of several small industrialized European states, and the oil sheikdoms were out of the running. Meanwhile, though the Soviet Union's total GNP was among the world's largest, its per capita GNP consistently fell below all the developed Western states. (Note that it never appears in the top ten per capita income rankings.) This meant that Moscow had few resources to spare to enhance its military power or political status; by spending extensively in these categories nonetheless, Soviet leaders hastened their nation's economic decline and political disintegration.

To measure how fast a nation's relative economic power rises or declines, it is helpful to look at rates of growth. A state that maintains higher annual growth rates than its partners or adversaries is gaining on its rivals; a state with comparatively lower growth rates is falling behind. For example, although the American economy grew faster in 1980–1990 than it did in the previous fifteen years, Japan's economic growth outstripped that of the United States in both periods.

Map 6.1   Countries According to Gross Domestic Product, 1994

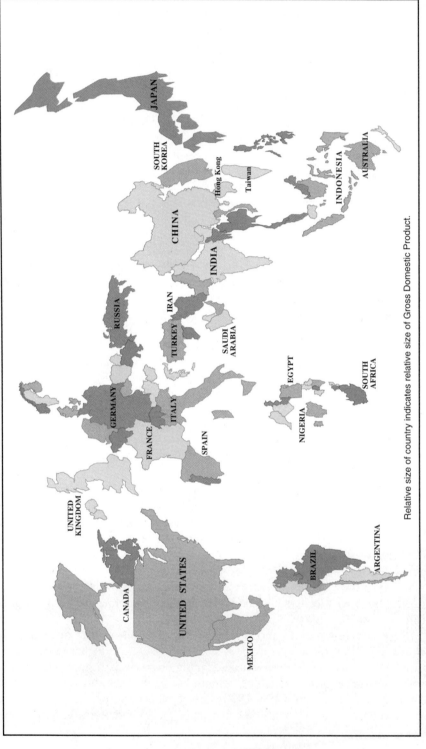

Relative size of country indicates relative size of Gross Domestic Product.

SOURCE: *Handbook of International Economic Statistics*, 1995

Table 6.3	Gross National Product Per Capita, Top Ten Countries, 1974–1995				
1974		**1984**		**1995**	
Switzerland	7,780	United Arab Emirates	20,300	Luxembourg	46,370
Sweden	7,240	Qatar	19,570	Switzerland	44,070
United States	6,670	Switzerland	16,220	Japan	41,160
Denmark	6,430	Kuwait	15,980	Denmark	32,540
West Germany	6,260	United States	15,380	Norway	29,350
Canada	6,190	Norway	13,400	Austria	28,860
Norway	5,860	Canada	13,100	United States	27,550
Belgium	5,670	Luxembourg	13,030	Belgium	26,550
France	5,440	Sweden	11,050	France	26,290
Australia	5,330	West Germany	11,020	Germany	26,190

SOURCES: *World Bank Atlas 1975; World Military Expenditures and Arms Transfers* 1986, 1996
NOTE: Countries with populations of 1 million or more; figures are in rounded U.S. dollars.

West Germany's GDP growth slowed in the 1980s, and the costs of German re-unification continued to slow growth into the 1990s.[18] In the early 1990s, America's ability to emerge from recession earlier than Japan or Europe gave the United States a relative boost, high growth rates accelerated China's emergence, and a declining economy deepened Russia's woes.

While total output, per capita income, and growth rates are important indicators of economic strength, so is a nation's ability to trade effectively with other states. With the disappearance of the ideological and military threat posed by the former Soviet Union, competition for global markets is likely to become even more important. Accordingly, a nation's trade balance is likely to become an increasingly useful indicator of its relative economic power. A positive current-account balance indicates a trade surplus; a negative balance shows a trade deficit. Between 1970 and 1990, the shifts from trade surplus to deficit (experienced by the United States and the United Kingdom) and from trade deficit to surplus (Japan and Germany) indicate a dramatic change in the flow of world trade during the twenty-year period.[19]

In 1970 most of the leading economic powers enjoyed a trade surplus, but in 1990 most had a trade deficit. The glaring exceptions are Germany and Japan. Both nations emerged from the rubble of World War II to become trade power-houses. For numerous reasons, Japan often has been singled out for special criticism of its trade policies. Even before U.S.–Soviet tensions diminished, many Americans began to complain that "unfair" Japanese trading practices were helping to fuel Japan's economic growth while hurting the welfare of the United States, and by implication, the viability of the liberal trading order. They called for the establishment of a "level playing field" through equalization of trade barriers, either by lowering those around Japan or raising those around the United States. Today many Americans are concerned that Europe as well as Japan might soon wrest economic leadership from the United States. As Chapter Seven will discuss, the question of trade barriers is an issue of both historical importance and growing prominence.

Research, Development, and Technology

Another factor that plays a major role in the creation and use of a nation's economic power is technology. However, because a state's overall level of technology is made up of a plethora of products, techniques, and ideas, a nation's relative technological capability is difficult to measure. A rough approximation of scientific and technical capacity may be arrived at by examining a nation's spending on technological research and development (R&D). Such a figure will not reveal how well a nation is succeeding at advancing its military and civilian technology, but it will at least provide an idea of how hard it is trying.

A comparison of R&D spending from 1986 to 1989 among the three largest Western industrial countries suggests the strengths and weaknesses of each party at the end of the Cold War. On the surface, the United States appears to have the clear lead. While America spent $100 billion on R&D, Japan spent $39 billion, and West Germany $19 billion. America has a similar lead in terms of numbers of scientists and engineers.[20] On the other hand, in terms of percentages of GNP spent on R&D, the three were nearly identical (2.6 percent for the United States, 2.9 percent for Japan, and 2.8 percent for West Germany). Moreover, the United States spends a greater percentage of its total scientific and technical resources on the defense industry than either Japan or Germany, as suggested by their comparative defense burdens. In 1987 the United States spent 6.3 percent of its GNP on defense; the West Germans 3.1 percent; and the Japanese, 1 percent. Targeting a higher percentage of R&D expenditures directly at civilian industry gives Germany and Japan an advantage in developing industrial technology. With the end of the Cold War, the ability of the United States to convert its concentration on defense R&D to civilian pursuits will help determine its future competitiveness relative to Japan, Germany, and other leading economic powers.

Technological development became a major economic and strategic concern for nations during the Industrial Revolution (see Chapter Two). In the Information Age, technology promises to become an even more important determinant of economic power. Recognizing this, the United States and other countries have made significant efforts to develop their technological and communications infrastructure, building "information superhighways" that allow information to flow faster and at higher volume then previously imaginable. Just as railroads and ports were the arteries of a nation's economic lifeblood in the nineteenth century, a nation's ability to use the Internet and other information networks will be vital to its economic health and growth in the twenty-first. While geography, natural resources, and population will continue to be major sources of economic power, knowledge, information, and communications will become increasingly important. The need for specialized data and skills is likely to result in increased specialization on the part of both firms and nations, which in turn may make economic alliances and unions more important as interdependence enables states to further maximize their comparative advantages.

These trends are not without disadvantages, ranging from the availability of objectionable material on Internet to issues of sovereignty and policy coordination (discussed in Chapters Seven and Nine). The ability to promote cooperation and manage conflict among international economic actors will therefore become increasingly critical in the New Era. In a competitive economic environment, states will have powerful incentives to support their own industries at the expense of others, and they may use trade barriers and industrial espionage as instruments to protect their technological edge and other economic advantages while preventing others from pulling ahead. As noted in previous sections, economic realists will often be wary of foreign investment in or ownership of firms and will push for high trade barriers to protect domestic industries, while economic liberals usually advocate the benefits of free trade and international partnerships. Overall, although the possibility of cooperation almost always exists, the incentives to compete and seek unilateral advantages will remain strong, and coordination will be extremely difficult without the consensus and active leadership of the major trading states. But these problems are not unique features of the New Era. As the following section outlines, overcoming the barriers to economic cooperation among states has been a difficult ever since the "information superhighway" consisted of smoke signals and carrier pigeons.

BARRIERS TO COOPERATION

The mention of international trade usually calls forth two sets of images. One is of leaders getting together in exotic places like Davos or Jakarta and signing trade agreements with much fanfare, conviviality, and talk of ever-expanding cooperation. The other is of businesses shutting down and factories closing because of overseas competition, while farmers block roads in protest against imported food and lobbyists and labor activists warn that jobs are being shipped overseas and that foreign goods are being "dumped" on the home market. Both of these images, crafted to put the desired "spin" on economic news, contain an element of truth about the world economy. The global market is highly competitive, but rewards of cooperation between states and companies can be great for all concerned. There are, in short, incentives for both conflict and cooperation in world trade. Is it possible for states to overcome the incentives for conflict and realize the mutual benefits of cooperation? The realist and liberal perspectives on trade give different answers to this question. (Because the Marxist perspective on trade has lost influence in most industrialized countries, it is not treated in detail here, but see Chapter Seven for the Marxist view of trade between the developed North and developing South.)

For realists, the answer is "not really," as all states are in competition for bigger slices of the global economic pie. Because states seek to maximize their power to ensure their chances of survival, they are sensitive to any decline or loss in their relative capabilities. When also guided by the assumption that today's ally may well be tomorrow's enemy, states become reluctant to cooperate because they fear that they might be helping to strengthen a potential rival. The barrier, then, is that states are more concerned about any loss in their relative ranking in the international system of states. The question is not "will both of us gain?" but "who will gain more?" from cooperation. The implication is that in some instances, even when both states will obtain absolute gains, they will still fail to cooperate because one state fears that the other might disproportionately benefit from collaboration. Accordingly, states may give up increases in their absolute gains if doing so prevents others from achieving even greater gains. Additionally, in a world of dog-eat-dog competition, states have a natural distrust of one another. Because there is no world government or supranational body to guarantee that agreements are honored, states are reluctant to cooperate, because they fear getting duped by a partner who defects from an agreement.

From the realist perspective, therefore, an individual state seeking to maximize its own economic power and security may trade with others for things that it cannot produce itself (if it has no oil, for example, it has no choice but to import it). However, national security is more important than trade, and economic policy should be a tool of power politics. Thus, states should be reluctant to trade with other states—even if trade would allow both to profit—because potential rivals might use the profits from trade to gain advantages over them. For example, realists would argue that states should not trade potato chips for computer chips even if they enjoy a huge comparative advantage in potato chips and are at a disadvantage in making microchips, because they cannot afford to let another country's microchip industry become dominant in the world market. That outcome, they fear, would not only "destroy jobs" in their own microchip industry, but would give foreign microchip-producers control over the supply of a good upon which their national economy and defense both depend. Plus, if they do agree to trade, there is no means to prevent the other side from dumping computer chips at prices lower than their cost of production, because there is no effective world body that can prohibit this practice (and no state would agree to create one, for fear of losing its own sovereignty). From the realist perspective, cooperation may be possible, but it is likely to be limited and is often a bad idea in the long run. Tariffs and other trade barriers will be the order of the day, as states seek to protect their own markets and shield industries from foreign competition.

Trade liberals, on the other hand, answer that cooperation is both possible and beneficial, but not easy to arrange.[21] The liberal perspective on trade accepts many of the assumptions of realism, such as the supremacy of the nation-state and the anarchic character of the international system. But for liberals, trade is not a zero-sum game in which one state's gain translates into another's loss (that is, both actors cannot mutually benefit), but it is instead a variable-sum game—that is, through cooperation, all states can simultaneously and mutually benefit. (For more on zero-sum versus variable-sum games, see Chapter Twelve.) Cooperation allows states to benefit because the size of the pie is not fixed; it continues to grow. The greatest barrier to cooperation is not self-interest, but the difficulty of coordination and enforcement of cooperative agreements.

Liberals further argue that even though there is no world government to enforce agreements, international institutions can act as mediators when disputes occur. While trade barriers may have some value from the liberal perspective (such as to protect infant industries), all parties will be better off in the long run if trade barriers are removed on a reciprocal basis. Go ahead and trade potato chips for microchips, liberals argue; both sides will benefit as each exports what it produces more efficiently and imports what the other produces more efficiently. Even though one side may become a little richer from trading either potato chips or microchips, the differing profits should not be a concern. Both sides profit from trade and can sit happily at their computers, munching on potato chips while making deals over the Internet.

Realists respond that regardless of agreements or institutions, states are still motivated by self-interest, and any incentives for cooperation are likely to be ignored whenever the cooperative action involved is inconvenient or costly. Thus, cooperative behavior will reflect only a state's temporary interest. Primary issues of state survival or security will take precedence, say the realists, over any incentives to cooperate on trade. For both realists and liberals, therefore, the barriers to economic cooperation are formidable. Not surprisingly, as both sides see the problem differently, the prescriptions they offer for overcoming these barriers differ as well.

Overcoming Barriers

Thomas Hobbes, in his classic work of political philosophy *Leviathan,* described the natural state of humankind as a "war of all against all," a no-holds-barred competition driven by vulnerability and fear. Anyone who has studied or worked in international trade will find this image all too familiar. While states may fight wars with guns and rockets, they fight economic battles with tariffs and subsidies, weapons that can be as destructive to prosperity as their military counterparts.

Nevertheless, some degree of economic cooperation among states has always occurred, and trade negotiators and business people have worked out many innovative ways of managing competition and promoting mutually profitable exchange. Success in these efforts depends on the choice of an appropriate strategy for overcoming the barriers to cooperation discussed in the previous section. Trade liberals, generally more optimistic about the prospects for cooperation, offer four basic options for surmounting the problems of cheating and relative gains: **reciprocity,** international **regimes,** international law, and interdependence. Realists, pessimistic as they are about trade cooperation, still offer one strategy for creating cooperative order out of the **anarchy** of international competition. Like Hobbes (himself a realist *par excellence*), they contend that if a state strong enough to be the world's economic leader can enforce cooperative agreements, a stable **hegemonic** order can enable self-interested states to overcome their fears of cooperation. This section examines each of these strategies in turn and offers examples of how they have been applied, with varying degrees of success, in the international trading arena.

Reciprocity

If two parties expect to deal with each other only once, and they believe they can profit by cheating or deceiving each other, they will probably do so if they think can get away with it. (Anyone who doubts this hasn't shopped for a used car lately.) However, if they expect to deal with each other on a regular basis (as supplier and manufacturer, for example, or family shopper and corner grocer), they can benefit from building a relationship of mutual trust, *if* they both demonstrate that they are going to play fairly. In economists terms, if their transaction is repeated over and over again, and if they value future gains from cooperation, it is possible to achieve a mutually beneficial outcome by employing a **tit-for-tat** (TFT) strategy. This is accomplished by cooperating on the first round no matter what the other party does, to demonstrate good faith, and then mimicking that party's moves on subsequent rounds—cooperating when it cooperates, cheating when it cheats. The purpose of this strategy is to convince the other side that you are willing to cooperate if it does, but are also ready to cheat if it acts dishonestly. You show your willingness to take a chance on the first round by cooperating unconditionally, but you also demonstrate that you will not be taken for a sucker. This strategy shows that cooperation is possible, even in a decentralized and anarchic system, through a self-enforcing strategy of reciprocity.

Tit-for-tat can be an effective strategy for reducing trade barriers. While trade friction between the United States and Japan heated up in the early 1990s, with each side accusing the other of dumping, using import inspections and other bureaucratic delays as trade barriers, and other unfair trade practices, some of these tensions were eased through bilateral negotiations. Japan agreed to open its domestic market to U.S. exports of beef, citrus fruit, and other products, while the United States dropped plans to set **import quotas** and other restrictions on Japanese produces. Though these measures did not resolve all issues outstanding between the two trading giants, they did use tit-for-tat reciprocity to prevent economic competition from escalating into a full-scale trade war.

International Regimes

A second solution to the problems of cooperation is to set up voluntary rules or institutions to detect and punish cheating. Many theorists advocate the creation of strong international institutions to help states work together in an otherwise anarchic world.[22] These institutions, more broadly termed *regimes,* can range from informal customs to negotiated agreements to international organizations like the International Monetary Fund (IMF) and World Trade Organization (WTO). (See Chapters Five and Seven for more on IMF and WTO, and Chapter Nine for more on regimes in general.) Trade liberals contend that regimes influence and change the costs and benefits of individual state actions. More specifically, they alter states' interests or preferences by reducing the attractiveness of cheating, thereby allowing states to cooperate without fear of being taken advantage of. In exchange, states become willing to relinquish at least some independent decision-making and instead agree to act according to established international **norms.**

International regimes establish the general rules and principles, or norms, of state behavior that facilitate cooperation. These norms are usually formalized in treaties, which in turn establish institutions and/or organizations to provide states with opportunities to meet and discuss their common problems. In the international system, institutions can emerge as a result of traditional international customs, such as freedom of the seas, or through a more specific process of bargaining and negotiation over a set of issues. For example, since the end of World War II, a large group of countries negotiated GATT as a means to gradually lower trade barriers, and in 1994 adopted an even more liberal trade regime that provided for the World Trade Organization for resolution of trade disputes. Members of another loose economic grouping, the **Organization for Economic Cooperation and Development** (OECD) often try to coordinate their monetary policies to stabilize the exchange rates between their national currencies, with some success. Regimes, not limited to formal institutions, may include informal cooperative programs by which governments abide. Before the 1967 Arab-Israeli War (see Chapter Five), Israel and Jordan followed a tacit agreement to share the waters of the Jordan River even though they had no formal diplomatic relations and were technically at war.

In contrast to national, state, or local governments, however, international regimes often lack any mechanism to enforce compliance. As a result, states seem unlikely to comply with regimes when they find it particularly inconvenient or costly.[23] Many theorists argue that this lack of enforcement power means that regimes reflect only a state's temporary interest and are thus unable to constrain national behavior. OPEC, lacking any enforcement mechanism, is frequently unable to force overproducers (that is, cheaters) to comply with their quotas. Iraq's invasion of Kuwait in 1990 was in part caused by Kuwait's continued overproduction, which kept international oil prices down and thereby hurt Iraq, which needed prices to remain high to earn more income. In this case, the failure of an international regime to enforce its agreements prevented it from overcoming the barriers to cooperation.

International Law

International law is a third strategy for overcoming barriers to economic cooperation. Much more will be said about international law in Chapter Nine, but for now it is important to know that like domestic law, international law discourages states from selfishly acting against the common good or unfairly maximizing their individual gains at the expense of others. In particular, international law encourages all states to forgo short-term advantages gained by cheating and instead concentrate on the long-term benefits gained from cooperation.

Before 1945, international law focused on resolving disputes over navigation and shipping, abolishing the slave trade, and regulating the conduct of states in wars. In recent years, many attempts have been made to use international law to regulate the environmental consequences of international trade. The Montreal Protocol, signed in 1987, restricts the production and trade of chlorofluorocarbons (CFCs), chemicals that can damage Earth's ozone layer. Other international conventions prohibit trade in endangered species and regulate the shipment of nuclear and hazardous waste. These conventions include provisions for determining violations, resolving disputes, and penalizing states for noncompliance (usually through trade sanctions). Again, just like domestic laws, these international laws are not always obeyed, but they do set standards for proper behavior and create incentives for compliance.

There is no international sovereign authority to enforce international law. Thus, international law cannot stop states from, say, whaling or overfishing in defiance of international convention. The overall result, many realists argue, is that international law has the same advantages and disadvantages of international regimes as a strategy for facilitating cooperation. Both establish rules or norms of desirable state behavior, but neither provides an adequate enforcement mechanism to ensure compliance.

Hegemonic Stability

Not to be outdone by trade liberals, realists have their own explanation for the prevalence of economic cooperation during certain periods. In an anarchic trading system, they argue, the only way to establish some level of order is to establish some level of authority. This can occur only, according to realists, when one major state becomes the dominant military and economic power in the international system. This dominant power, or hegemon, sets and enforces the rules for the global economy. The United States, for example, was often considered a hegemon from 1945 to 1973. It assumed the responsibility of guaranteeing the free flow of international goods, providing international security arrangements (such as NATO), and stabilizing world currencies (through the Bretton Woods system, discussed in Chapter Seven).

During a hegemonic period, the international economic system works well because a dominant state pays the costs of providing these economic stabilizers. Why is it prepared to do that? Because the hegemon, as the world's economic and military giant, furthers its own interests by creating a stable economy and expanding its sphere of influence. By pursuing its interests, it effectively guarantees that many of its smaller allies will be able to take advantage of a stable economic and military environment without paying any of the costs.

But uneasy is the head that wears a crown. There is a problem with hegemony: It is ultimately self-defeating. While in the short run all trading partners gain because the hegemonic influence helps open markets and increases trade, the costs of hegemony tend to grow over time. As the hegemon's trading partners become more competitive relative to the hegemon, the hegemon becomes increasingly less capable of maintaining open markets for its partners' products, policing the open seas, and protecting access to crucial resources (such as oil) without its partners' help. As the hegemon begins to decline relative to its trading partners, it will be more willing to use its residual economic clout in coercive ways to get growing partners to pay for their share of the benefits they receive. For example, beginning in the 1970s, the United States began to demand that its European and Japanese allies help maintain a stable economic system and international security. By the time the Gulf War occurred in 1991, however, America's allies were paying much of the cost of sending U.S. troops into combat in order to protect oil supplies from the Middle East.[24]

Hegemonic-stability theory also contends that there is a link between the provision of certain public goods or "services" and the degree of openness and stability of the international trading system.[25] These global services are provided by the hegemon, with little or no assistance from other states. They include making loans to countries in need, providing markets for various commodities, and defending the seas to make them safe for international trade. According to the theory, the hegemon's rationale for unilaterally providing these services is that since it has the largest economy, it has the most to gain from free trade, even if the other states elect to free-ride. Likewise, it also has the most to lose if all other states impose tariffs and other trade barriers. Both realists and liberals would argue that since these global services are public goods, other states are tempted to free-ride, hoping that the hegemon alone will provide the service. However, if no state provides them, or if the hegemon cannot do it alone, then the international system will decline into disorder.

Proponents of this theory contend that Britain provided hegemonic leadership in the nineteenth century and that the United States played a similar role following World War II. During the interwar period, Britain, exhausted after World War I, was unable to provide these services. The United States, adhering to an isolationist strategy, was also unwilling to provide them. The consequence was increased protectionism, economic chaos, an accentuation of the Great Depression, and ultimately political and military upheaval.[26] The consequence is that periods of free trade tend to correspond with periods of hegemony, while economic protectionism and chaos often correspond with periods of hegemonic decline. For hegemonic stability theorists, America's economic decline relative to other trading powers in the New Era is a preview of global instability, until and unless a new hegemon, or a coalition of states that can play a hegemonic role, emerges. Both trade liberals and realists would probably agree that if the major economic powers agree to reduce trade barriers, expansion of global trade and economic interdependence will continue, and conflicts over trade will be easier to resolve. However, if they do not, global competition for markets and capital will intensify, efforts at cooperation and policy coordination will be hampered, and the world economy of the New Era may be in for a rough ride.

CONCLUSION: A WORLD THRIVING ON CHAOS?

After considering the prevalence of barriers to economic cooperation and the difficulties inherent in overcoming them, readers may conclude that the prospects for cooperation are bleak and that it is a wonder that states trade with one another at all unless motivated by absolute necessity. While the world economy can look shaky in theory, however, it is thriving in practice. International trade continues to grow annually, and markets and investment opportunities stubbornly expand despite the best efforts of governments to erect trade barriers. While policy coordination remains difficult at the international level, trade flourishes at the level of the multinational corporation, if only among units of the same company operating in different countries. Even small local firms and entrepreneurs can buy and sell products all over the world, placing orders over the Internet and receiving goods via international air express. Individual businesses may expand or fail, and government policies may lead to sustainable development and growth, or to stagnation and near-total collapse. The globalized economy of the New Era seems to press on regardless, rushing forward at ever-increasing speed.

Adam Smith, for one, would not be surprised. Over two centuries ago, he argued that states were steered toward prosperity not by the firm hand of government, but by the "invisible hand" of enlightened self-interest and individual enterprise. Governments, he was quick to point out, set the rules of economic interaction both within and between states, regulated currencies, enforced contracts and other agreements, and provided for public goods like law and order and defense. But even when economic policy is planned centrally, as Karl Marx argued for and Adam Smith argued against, it must be executed locally, by individuals seeking to increase their welfare within their national economies and the global economic system. The rules imposed by states and international organizations may change, resources may be scarce or plentiful, and markets boom or crash, but individuals, at once interdependent and self-reliant, adapt and prosper as best they can. Smith would probably nod in approval of this simultaneous globalization and fragmentation, while Marx might shake his head in dismay.

The same process will continue in the New Era, with the pace of change accelerating and the web of interdependence growing ever tighter. Greater economic interdependence is likely to increase both the incentives and the risks of cooperation among states. The theories outlined in this chapter are basic tools for understanding how those incentives operate and how their attendant risks can be managed. Students may use them to understand how global economic forces affect their lives, and for formulating informed opinions on national and international economic policy. For economic realists, free-trade liberals, and Marxists alike, knowledge equals economic power, and individuals have the responsibility to use that power to increase both individual wealth and social welfare. On that point, Marx and Adam Smith would finally agree.

PRINCIPAL POINTS OF CHAPTER SIX

1. The operation of the global economy has a tremendous political and economic impact on all states. This impact is greater on states that trade more, but international economic relations affect even states that strive for self-sufficiency.

2. States that produce specific goods more efficiently than other states can clearly profit from trade. However, comparative advantage can make mutual gains from trade possible even if one trading partner has an absolute advantage in the production of all goods.

3. Free trade (open access to markets for all goods, regardless of country of origin) maximizes economic efficiency and benefits to consumers. Because domestic industries often find it difficult to compete with more efficient foreign producers, however, governments often impose trade barriers favoring domestically produced goods and services. Because these barriers seek to "protect" domestic producers from foreign competition, their imposition is referred to as protectionism.

4. There are two basic types of trade barriers:
   a. Tariffs, or taxes on imports; and
   b. Nontariff barriers, including
      i. Subsidies for domestic producers, including price supports,
      ii. Quotas, or limits on the quantity of goods that may be imported, and
      iii. Structural barriers, such as discriminatory safety and inspection standards or distribution systems.

5. Unless it is conducted through barter (direct exchange of goods for goods), trade involves money. Because different states have their own currencies, a system of exchange rates must be established to determine the relative value of national currencies.

6. Exchange-rate systems may be fixed, like the gold standard and Bretton Woods system, or floating, in which currencies are allowed to fluctuate. Both systems have advantages and disadvantages.

7. A nation's balance of payments summarizes all of its international trade and financial transactions, including exports, imports, foreign-aid transfers, and investments.

8. The most commonly cited component of the balance of payments is the current-account balance, which is the sum of a country's imports, exports, government payments and receipts, and investment income and payments. If the current-account balance is positive, the state has a trade surplus; if it is negative, it has a trade deficit.

9. There are many links between domestic and international politics and the world economy; international political economy is the study of how these links function.

10. There are three basic schools of thought on the relationship between global politics and economics:

    a. Liberalism contends that the purpose of economic activity is to maximize national and individual wealth. According to liberals, free markets allocate scarce resources in the most efficient manner possible, giving maximum benefit to consumers. Therefore, liberals usually argue for free trade and against trade barriers.

    b. Realism views the accumulation of state power as the purpose of economic activity. Realists thus often contend that trade barriers can be used to increase a nation's economic, military, and political power.

    Marxism perceives economic activity as a political class struggle between workers and capital owners and rich and poor nations. Many Marxists contend that developed countries and multinational corporations exploit developing nations in order to exact excessive profits.

11. The main determinants of a state's economic power are:

    a. Territory, comprising geography (including defensive terrain and proximity to trade routes) and natural resources (arable land, minerals, oil, and so on).

    b. Population—preferably neither too large nor too small—including educational level and skilled labor force.

    c. Trade and industry (measured by GNP per capita income, growth rate, and industrial technology).

12. While states can often realize many benefits from trade and economic cooperation, concerns over relative gains, the possibility of cheating, and the difficulty of coordination and enforcement create barriers to cooperation.

13. Liberals argue that economic cooperation can be maintained even in the absence of a central authority or world government. Potential means for overcoming barriers to cooperation include reciprocity, international regimes, and international law.

14. Theories of hegemonic stability seek to explain economic cooperation from a realist perspective. According to this theory, the world economy is most stable when a global dominant power (the hegemon) sets and enforces rules of free trade, from which it derives great benefits, but the hegemon will eventually decline as the costs of hegemony grow over time and trade enriches rival powers.

KEY TERMS

absolute advantage	Bretton Woods system	external subsidies	gold standard
anarchy	comparative advantage	factor approach	gross domestic product
arable land	current-account balance	fixed exchange-rate systems	gross national product
balance of payments	dependency theory	floating exchange-rate system	hegemonic
beggar-thy-neighbor policy	dumping	fossil fuels	hegemonic stability
			import quotas

internal
  subsidies
international
  law
laissez-faire
liberalism
mercantilism

norms
Organization
  for Economic
  Cooperation
  and Devel-
  opment
price inelastic

protectionism
reciprocity
regimes
sector approach
Smoot-Hawley
  Tariff
subsidies

tariff
tit-for-tat
trade deficit
trade surplus
voluntary
  export
  restrictions

SOURCE: Mansell Collection/Time, Inc.

CHAPTER 7

Evolution of the Global Economy

The concepts and approaches outlined in Chapter Six were intended to provide the reader with the basic economic and theoretical tools necessary to analyze the world economy. The goal of Chapter Seven is to outline the history of global economic relations. As there is an economic dimension to almost any major development in world politics, some aspects of that history, such as the industrial revolution, were covered in Part I, while others focusing on relations between the industrialized North and the developing South will be examined in the following chapter. Therefore, rather than attempting a detailed, all-inclusive economic history of the world, this chapter surveys how the global trading system has evolved from a poorly regulated hegemonic system in the early nineteenth century to a multilateral system of global and regional institutions at the dawn of the twenty-first century. The reader should continue to think about how the tools and theories outlined in Chapter Six connect with the history presented in this chapter, keeping in mind that the prevalent theme throughout is the interconnection between politics and economics.

ORIGINS OF THE WORLD ECONOMY

Since ancient times, societies have engaged in exchange and trade.[1] Nations have traded for goods, ranging from olive oil to silk, which they do not produce at home. However, before the expansion of the European empires in the eighteenth century and the industrial revolution in the early 1800s, many factors limited the growth of world trade. The prevalence of high tariff barriers and other mercantilist policies in the European empires (see Chapters Two and Six, and remember how the mercantilist Navigation Acts helped push Britain's American colonies away from the mother country), the difficulty of moving goods over land, and underdeveloped systems of international banking and finance made it difficult for people, goods, capital, and ideas to cross national and imperial boundaries.

Not until the Industrial Revolution and the concomitant rise of British manufacturing and trade in the late eighteenth century did a truly global economy begin to emerge. The Industrial Revolution prompted an expansion of trade, capital flows, and population movements unlike any that had come before. The explosion of industrial and agricultural production, the growth in demand spurred by expanding populations, and the incentives to specialize in order to maximize comparative advantage (see Chapter Six) increased interdependence dramatically and distinguished international economic relations in the industrial era from those of earlier periods. The consequence of technological developments and increased understanding of the advantages of trade prompted the development of a truly international economy.[2]

Rise of Britain

As the first industrialized nation, Britain enjoyed the advantages of economic and technological leadership, achieving what many analysts consider to be hegemonic status. In Britain, already a highly commercialized economy with the largest market in Europe by the late eighteenth century, population growth and rising agricultural productivity laid the basis for rapid industrialization.[3] Britain's long and successful experience with international trade, a relatively unrestricted labor market (facilitating the internal migration of workers from rural to urban areas), and availability of capital paved the way for the development of industry, wool-spinning (later textile-weaving) and iron-making in particular. Within this context, British entrepreneurs developed more productive techniques of production (such as the use of fertilizer in agriculture and the steam engine and coal in manufacturing) to drastically reduce the costs of production. As a result, the country enjoyed an explosion of exports.

British exports, dominated by cotton products (mainly textiles), increased sharply from the 1780s to 1814, becoming for the first time a powerful engine of growth.[4] By 1801, sales abroad approached 18 percent of national income, with the cotton industry alone representing almost 7 percent of national product.[5] To meet the increasing demand for industrial goods at home and abroad, British entrepreneurs turned to alternative sources of supply outside the British Empire (see Chapter Two). The expanding United States became one such source, providing cheap and abundant cotton to Britain and in return absorbing a large portion of British exports.[6] This growth of trade between sovereign states, as opposed to that within the British Empire, presented statesmen with tremendous opportunities to capture gains from trade. By the mid-1800s, Britain's industrial capacity, financial strength, political influence, and worldwide network of colonies and military bases made it the first industrialized global superpower.

Although British economic and social innovations set the stage for the creation of a truly global economy, the initial spread of industrialization occurred very unevenly across the world. The French Revolution and the Napoleonic Wars delayed economic development and trade on the European continent and allowed Britain, on the basis of its naval superiority, to extend its imperial reach. Only after the Congress of Vienna restored order on the Continent and British political and economic leaders began to recognize that mercantilism blocked further economic growth and development, however, could the leap to an interdependent world economy be made.

BRITISH HEGEMONY

In the wake of the Napoleonic Wars, Britain moved away from a protectionist foreign economic policy and promoted a more open international economy, one based upon the liberal approach to trade embodied in the writings of such early economists as Adam Smith and David Ricardo (discussed in Chapter Six). Convinced that trade and exchange were "a source of peaceful relations among nations because the mutual benefits of trade and expanding interdependence among national economies tended to foster cooperative relations,"[7] British policy-makers turned toward free trade.

The movement toward free trade in Britain, however, was not without political difficulty. After the initial burst of free trade following the Congress of Vienna (refer again to Chapter Two), Britain began to experience a growing urban population and falling export prices, necessitating the search for a means to counter growing unemployment and economic troubles at home while reestablishing competitiveness abroad. Exports no longer acted as "the engine of growth," falling from 18 percent of the national income in 1801 to 11 percent in 1841.[8] Initially, Britain experienced a decline in exports of its comparatively disadvantaged agricultural sector, as countries with a comparative advantage in agricultural production, such as Russia and the United States, developed this potential more fully and deprived Britain of a large segment of its market.

The loss of export markets for agricultural products, mainly wheat, threatened politically powerful landed interests. In the late eighteenth and early nineteenth centuries, British landowners were accustomed to trade protection through the set of tariffs and other restrictions on agricultural imports collectively known as the **Corn Laws.** Along with the growing working class, British manufacturing and financial interests—based in Manchester and London and imbued with the ideals of economic liberalism—came to regard these agricultural restraints as barriers to solving Britain's problems. Proponents of freer trade hoped that a unilateral reduction in British tariffs would induce other countries to adopt freer trade policies as well, leading to an international division of labor. This division would lead those countries with abundant labor to exploit their comparative advantage in agriculture while other countries (Britain in particular) would specialize in the production of capital-intensive manufactured goods. Britain's landed elites ultimately recognized that they could not defend the Corn Laws any longer. By 1846 these laws were repealed, facilitating a boom in international trade.

We see here the operation of several of the trends discussed earlier. On the one hand, Britain was acting as the classic hegemon, using its advantages to promote a free-trade system. Then, too, the system it promoted encouraged competition from others, in this case American agriculture. On the other hand, we also see the influence of domestic pressures and influences, and the reflex reaction of a threatened group to cry out for protection, in this case agricultural interests. Only when these internal conflicts were resolved in favor of free trade could Britain resume its hegemonic role.

Thus, Britain coupled its unilateral move toward openness with persistent diplomatic efforts to promote free trade abroad. Negotiations between Britain and France in the 1850s, culminating in the Cobden-Chevalier Treaty of 1860, were significant in this respect. France, traditionally protectionist under Napoléon III, used trade policy to improve relations with Britain, an ally during the recent Crimean War (see Chapter Two). This treaty removed tariffs on British imports of French goods, such as wine and perfume, and opened the French market to British textiles and other commodities. Richard Cobden, who negotiated the treaty on the British side, was an almost messianic advocate of free trade, and his belief that removal of trade barriers would lead to both peace and prosperity was unshakable. As he wrote in 1857, "Free trade is God's diplomacy, and there is no other certain way of uniting people in the bonds of peace."

An important feature of the treaty was the inclusion of a **most-favored-nation** (MFN) clause. Even today, the MFN principle symbolizes the cordiality of bilateral relations, as the debate in the United States over revoking Communist China's MFN status attests (see Chapter Eight). In the Cobden-Chevalier accord, the MFN clause meant that if Britain (or France) signed a tariff agreement with a third party, the goods of France (or Britain) were entitled to enter British (French) markets on terms "no less favorable" than those of the third party. In other words, both France and Britain promised each other that they would both receive the best deal available in their respective markets. Subsequent British and French trade agreements, all of which contained the MFN clause, hastened the spread of free trade

What Would You Do ?

You are the British prime minister in 1846. As head of the parliamentary ruling party, you are aware of the growing support among the Manchester manufacturers and toiling classes for the idea of international free trade, and of the growing discomfort of the landed nobility over such an idea. The debate centers on whether to repeal the Corn Laws, a set of tariffs on grain imports.

Repeal of the Corn Laws would probably result in an influx of cheap grain imports, which would decrease the costs of food for the lower classes. This would have several results. First, it would allow for the lowering of wages at no real cost to the workers. Second, it would allow British manufacturers to reduce the price of their wares on the world market. Third, it might also persuade other countries to repeal their own tariffs and thus open up their markets to British manufactured goods.

On the other hand, repeal of the Corn Laws does not necessarily mean other countries will purchase a greater amount of Britain's exports. Many of these countries tax imported goods in the hope that they too can build a manufacturing economy that will be the envy of the world. Britain could also become dependent on foreign countries for its food supply, leaving it vulnerable to blockades in time of war. Finally, repeal of the grain tariffs might increase social blight by destroying what is left of Britain's farming past, forcing even more people into crowded and squalid city slums and eroding the economic privileges of many members of your party.

Will you choose to support repeal of the Corn Laws ?

throughout Europe. As one scholar recounts, "For a decade or so, in the 1860s and 1870s, Europe came as close as ever to complete free trade until after World War II." [9]

A number of other developments between 1850 and 1875 further expedited the growth of trade and the world economy. As industrialization proceeded apace on the European continent and in North America, a number of new industrial powers, notably the United States, France, and Germany, rose to challenge Britain's industrial preeminence, the upshot of which was a tremendous expansion of the international economy. Technical innovations in textile and iron production, and later in the manufacturing of steel, machine tools, and chemicals, resulted in a flood of new goods, including railway equipment, steamships, steel and electrical products, machinery of all kinds, and a variety of other manufactured products. In addition, many items already traded on the world market, especially cotton products, became substantially cheaper, resulting in the rapid expansion of foreign trade in manufactures. Although it is difficult to convey the dramatic growth of industry at the close of the 1800s, Tables 7.1 through 7.3 offer some insight into the productive and trading capacities of the great powers at the close of the nineteenth century.

Technological developments, especially steam-powered industrial machinery, railroads, and the telegraph, played a vital role in the growth of the world economy. As one author describes it,

> By promoting the exchange of a growing volume of goods; by expanding markets, as well as opening up new sources of supply of many products; by permitting the concentration of certain types of production in fewer centers, thereby encouraging specialization and assisting the realization of economies of scale; and by allowing a greater interregional flow of men and capital, the new forms of transport and communications made possible that growing economic interdependence of the whole world which is so remarkable a feature of nineteenth-century economic development.[10]

Challenges to British Hegemony

The growth of railways, in particular, paved the way for greater German participation in international affairs. Aware of the economic changes in Britain and elsewhere on the continent, the leaders of Prussia (the most powerful German state) enacted reforms resulting in the formation of the *Zollverein* (customs union). The *Zollverein* abolished internal tolls and customs barriers between the various German states, in effect creating a German "common market," characterized by a uniform external tariff and creating an economic basis for subsequent German unification (see Chapter Two). This tariff was relatively low, allowing Germany to participate in the world economy.[11] An influx of foreign capital, technology, and enterprise in the 1850s contributed to Germany's development, but railroad construction played the key role in setting the stage for unification and industrial growth.

Ironically, British trade in the Continent, particularly in manufactured goods, facilitated continental industrialization because these exports were necessary for

Table 7.1	**Distribution of World Industrial Production, 1820–1913**					
	Percentage of global industrial production in:					
Country	1820	1840	1860	1881–1885	1896–1900	1913
Britain	24	21	21	27	20	14
France	20	18	16	9	7	6
Germany	15	17	15	14	17	16
Russia	—	—	—	3	5	6
Italy	—	—	—	2	3	3
United States	4	5	14	29	30	36

SOURCE: Walt W. Rostow, *The World Economy: History & Prospect* (Austin, TX: University of Texas Press, 1978), pp. 52–53

Table 7.2	Distribution of World Trade, 1840–1913				
	Percentage of world trade production in:				
Country	1840	1860	1880	1901–1905	1913
Britain	25	25	23	16	16
France	11	11	11	7	7
Germany	8	9	10	12	12
Russia	5	3	4	4	—
Italy	5	3	3	3	3
United States	7	9	10	11	11

SOURCE: Rostow, *The World Economy*, pp. 70–73

Table 7.3	Gross National Products of European Great Powers		
	GNP		
Country	1840	1870	1890
Austria/Hungary	8.3	11.3	15.3
Britain	10.4	19.6	29.4
France	10.3	16.8	19.7
Germany	8.3	16.6	26.4
Italy	5.9	8.2	9.4

SOURCE: Paul Kennedy, *The Rise and Fall of the Great Powers* (New York: Vintage, 1987), p. 171
NOTE: GNP is expressed in billions of 1960 U.S. dollars.

economic development, and they reduced the gap between Britain and other European powers.[12] Britain had played the classic hegemonic role, leading eventually to the creation of its own competitors. In fact, rival industrial states, namely the United States and Germany, had begun to eclipse Britain. Although quantitative indicators of economic power do not capture the whole picture (as we noted in Chapter Six), it is clear that Britain's standing among the great powers had suffered. In particular, the United States and Germany, as Figure 7.1 indicates, emerged as significant economic and potential military rivals. The implications of this change in the international distribution of power reverberated throughout the international economy from the 1870s to World War I and beyond.

Protectionism and Discord

The international economy continued to expand in the years from 1873 to 1914. Industrialization even spread to a limited extent to the Third World (see Chapter Eight). The continuing expansion of production promoted a greater degree of interdependence among national economies. At the same time, however, this

Figure 7.1	GNP of the United States, Great Britain, and Germany, 1870 and 1913

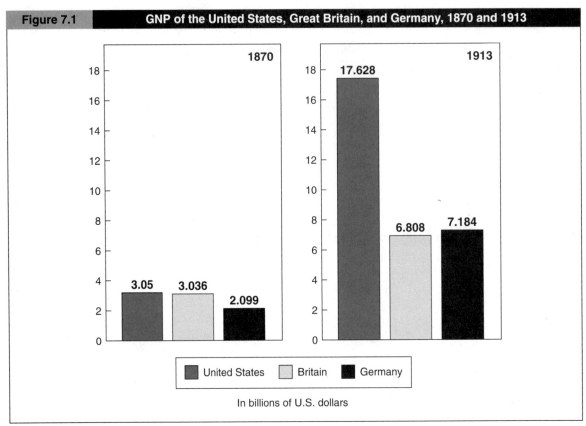

SOURCE: Albert Chandler, *Scale and Scope: The Dynamics of Industrial Capitalism* (Cambridge, MA: Harvard University Press, 1990), p. 52

growing interdependence became increasingly difficult to manage, as manifest in the return to protectionism beginning in the 1880s.

Why did interdependence create problems for various nations? Free trade pressured economies to cease producing goods for which they did not have a comparative advantage. This inevitably hurt many capital owners and laborers who relied on these industries for their livelihood. Many of these sectors were politically powerful and lobbied governments for protection from foreign competition. Even in those states that maintained open trading policies, these political cleavages made jobs of policy makers significantly more difficult. Thus, one of the great problems of free trade was operating again—the constant pressure by industries disadvantaged by competition for protection.

The growing dislocations of domestic economies was brought about by two concurring phenomena. First, the increasing volume of world trade intensified competition for international markets. Governments wanted to increase their wealth and stay on the road toward industrial development. Many feared that international competition would hinder their prospects for growth. Their response was to increase protectionism at home in order to help domestic industries develop into world competitors. They felt that protecting industries would reduce the inevitable time lag between industrialization and domestic development.

The second phenomenon associated with protectionism was the revival of nationalism, particularly in Germany and Italy (see Chapter Two). All states were sensitive in this period to the promotion of their industries as a matter of national honor. In some sense, economic power was seen as an achievement worthy of national pride. Taken together, as one scholar argues, "nationalism and the lag in industrialization made protection inevitable."[13] Related to nationalism was the rise of security concerns stemming from the fears of military aggression that accompanied the changing balance of power in Europe. This also prompted states to employ tariffs (the direct income tax was not yet known) as a means to raise funds in order to pay for military expenditures.

Through it all, Britain remained the center of world trade and finance, commanding 31 percent of world trade in manufactured goods, with Germany at 27.5 percent and the United States at 13 percent, even as late as 1913.[14] Britain also remained the dominant financial power of the time, possessing 44 percent of the great powers' overseas investment, compared to France's 19.9 percent and Germany's 12.8 percent in 1914. Yet the great powers' ability to manage the increasingly interdependent world economy proved more and more difficult after 1870, beginning with two unforeseen economic developments: the huge influx of cheap U.S. and Russian grain into European markets and the depression of 1873–1879.

By the 1870s the growth of railroads enabled the United States to export its surplus wheat more rapidly from the fields of the Great Plains states to markets in Europe. As more wheat entered the world market, the price of wheat began to fall. As other commodity producers began to sell their goods internationally, this pattern repeated itself. Regional commodity markets broke down and developed into international markets, increasing world supply and reducing prices. Although this was good for consumers, it was bad for many countries that relied on commodity sales for national wealth. In combination with an economic depression during 1873–1879, falling commodity prices resulted in a shuffling of traditional political and economic alignments throughout Europe and the world, especially on the tariff issue, and an intense lobbying effort for protection by those industrial and agricultural producers whose livelihoods were threatened by cheaper imports. Many governments, notably those of Germany and France, accommodated the rising demands for protection. Pressure for protectionism was particularly strong in Germany, where the protectionist coalition of heavy industry and the landed aristocracy—which controlled much of the nation's agriculture—became known as the "marriage of iron and rye."

The Calm before the Storm

By the close of the 1880s, much of the free-trade system had begun to collapse. However, these events manifested themselves slowly over time. As we saw in

Chapters Two and Three, the period between 1870 and 1914 was still one of relative stability, especially when compared to the period between World War I and World War II. Storm clouds were gathering over Europe, especially in the Balkans, but there were no great totalitarian ideologies or blatantly aggressive moves of one European state against another as would occur in the 1930s.[15]

One reason relative stability prevailed as long as it did before World War I was the existence of a strong international monetary (exchange rate) system. The gold standard, as it was called, lasted between 1870 and 1914 and was reintroduced again after World War I. In this fixed exchange-rate system, each nation set its currency's value to gold. For example, if one ounce of gold was worth ten U.S. dollars and five British pounds, then the dollar/pound exchange rate would be 2:1, and it remained at the same rate regardless of particular economic developments. Moreover, traders did not have to worry that changes in exchange rates might destroy their profits or that the currency of the countries they hoped to trade with was not convertible on the international market. An entrepreneur could board a boat train in London with British pounds sterling in his pockets, cross over to Calais in France, and get off a train in Russia's capital, St. Petersburg, knowing that his money would be freely convertible into gold at a constant rate anywhere along his route.

The pre–World War I gold standard's success was due largely to England's devotion to stable exchange rates as well as to France's and Germany's active participation in monitoring the system. These states were able to cooperate because each one of them agreed to pursue economic policies that guaranteed exchange-rate stability, even if it caused temporary domestic economic hardship (see the section on fixed and floating exchange rates in Chapter Six). One example of cooperative behavior occurred during a currency crisis in 1907. England began to experience a severe drain on its gold reserves, which translated into international pressure on its currency to devalue. However, because of England's premier position in the world economy at the time, a devaluation of the pound sterling would have led to an immediate crisis internationally. The crisis was not contained until France and Germany reduced their own gold reserves and transferred some gold to Britain. A reduction in gold reserves affects the economy in the same way that a rise in interest rate does. Although higher interest rates dampened economic activity in Germany and France, their leaders believed that global stability benefited them more in the long run, because it encouraged trade and international investment.

Another reason that these countries chose to emphasize international over domestic concerns was that labor and import-competing firms (domestic firms producing goods that competed with foreign imports) were either underrepresented in legislatures or placated with tariff protection. As noted earlier, different groups benefit and lose from the existence of a fixed exchange-rate system. At the time, labor feared that it would lose jobs as firms were forced to become more competitive by laying off workers. However, its views were usually marginalized, mainly because few workers were organized into labor unions (in many states unions were illegal). Import competitors had a greater voice in government but did not oppose the gold standard as long as other policies, like tariff protection, were implemented on their behalf. Tariff protection for the coalition of iron and rye in Germany is one example of such a policy.

Governments at the time felt that the trade-off between international currency stability and moderate tariff protection was worthwhile. Although tariff protection and international monetary cooperation might seem to contradict each other, the world economy has never been completely free from economic nationalism. Trade-offs always exist, and managing those inherent in free trade and protection is a major task of any national government. Because these trade-offs were successfully managed at the national and international levels, the world economy was relatively stable in the first decade of the twentieth century.

As World War I approached, Britain remained staunchly committed to an open international economy, but the failure of France and Germany to follow suit doomed efforts to manage the effects of **economic interdependence.** Protectionism became more popular as domestic groups who had opposed the gold standard, like labor and import competitors, increased their political power. In the United States, for example, proponents of abandoning the gold standard were led by the charismatic William Jennings Bryan, who argued passionately that by continuing under the gold standard, America's economy would be controlled by foreign capital and American workers and farmers would be "crucified on a cross of gold." His beliefs, and his passion, would be echoed by subsequent generations of economic nationalists in the debates over trade policy covered later in this chapter and in Chapter Eight.

In many ways, the growing tide of protectionism, fed by nationalistic fervor, helped to create the spiral of insecurity that led to World War I (see Chapter Three). The economic interdependence of the European powers failed to prevent the four bitter years of military struggle that disrupted the world economy and redistributed international economic power. Thus, the international coalition that had functioned to preserve Britain's hegemony broke down, leaving few vestiges of either hegemony or multilateral cooperation. After World War I, the situation would only get worse.

WORLD WAR AND GLOBAL DEPRESSION

By collapsing trade within Europe and forcing economies onto a war footing, World War I disrupted the international economy. However, proving that it's an ill wind that blows no good, the war was a boon to producers and exporters outside of Europe. The United States, in particular, quickly emerged as the chief supplier of war-related materiel to the Allied powers. By war's end, Britain and France had accumulated over $10 billion in war debts to the United States, which became the world's largest creditor as a result. (Britain's debt to U.S. banks was secretly secured by its shares in the vital Suez Canal Company.) Other states benefited from the war's disruption of traditional export markets and created significant export sectors of their own. Japan, for example, experienced dramatic industrial improvements in the course of meeting the various needs of open markets in Europe and Asia.[16]

The impact of the war on the European participants, however, was not nearly as benign. Besides huge war debts, the victors of World War I inherited a devastated production base (Britain and France, in particular, lost almost an entire generation of young men), inflation, and the loss of traditional export markets. As the vanquished power, Germany faced punitive demands for reparations, which Britain and France forced on that country in order to pay off their debts to the United States. This state of affairs produced a precarious situation for the world economy, a situation exacerbated by the inability of the world's leading industrial economies to cooperate in order to manage the ensuing economic turmoil.

This sequence of events deserves some more attention, largely because the most important diplomatic negotiations throughout the 1920s centered on the issue of war debts and reparations.[17] Two things proved constant over the decade—the United States insisted upon being paid back for its war loans to France and England, and these Allies were determined to extract reparations from Germany, both for punitive reasons and in order to pay back their war debts. By 1924 it became apparent that Germany would be unable to meet its obligations. It was forced to print money in order to pay its debts. Printing money, however, led to the condition known as **hyperinflation,** which made German prices rise as much as 500 percent or more each month.

Hyperinflation savaged the German economy and made its currency worthless (the U.S./German exchange rate exceeded 1 million marks to the dollar). Clearly, something had to be done to alleviate the pressure caused by reparations. In 1924 the **Dawes Plan** was signed by the Allies, Germany, and the United States. Under the agreement, the United States (primarily American private investors) would lend money to Germany, which it could use to pay its reparations to the Allies. These reparations payments could then be transferred to the U.S. government from the Allies in order to service war loans.

Why would the United States lend money to Germany only to have it return as Allied debt repayment? It is important to note that the American private sector was primarily investing in Germany, not the U.S. government. The German government was willing to pay an attractive interest rate, much like a bank pays interest on a savings account, so American investors invested in Germany out of self-interest, not for humanitarian reasons. When this money was recycled to the U.S. government as debt service, all parties, including the U.S. government and investors, seemed to be made better off by the Dawes Plan. In fact, this system stabilized the international economy for the next few years. The economies of many countries, including that of the United States, began to grow rapidly.

Boom and Bust

By 1928 America's economic expansion was at its peak. One particular manifestation of this was a stock-market boom. Investors continued to pump significant amounts of money into speculative investments, pushing the stock market to record heights. The Federal Reserve (the American institution responsible for guiding U.S. monetary policy) began to fear that this speculation was getting out of control. Its response was to raise U.S. interest rates. The Federal Reserve's economists believed that raising interest rates would dampen economic activity just enough to slow down this speculative investment.

Let's analyze what the effect of rising U.S. interest rates would have on the international economy. As an analogy, pretend that you have $100 to invest in a savings account. You have a choice between two banks, both of which pay an interest rate. If they pay the same rate, you will be relatively indifferent as to which bank receives your money. But what if one bank decides to raise its interest rate? If you are a smart investor, you will choose to invest your money in the bank with the higher interest rate.

How does this relate to U.S. monetary policy in 1928? When the Federal Reserve raised interest rates in the United States, many investors in Germany decided to switch their investments into U.S. interest-bearing accounts. This essentially broke the cycle of capital that flowed through the international economy. Without foreign capital, Germany was forced to delay its reparations payments, and the Allies ultimately did the same regarding their debts to the United States. Even though U.S. domestic policy instigated this hardship, the United States was unwilling to renegotiate war debts because the American public, as isolationist as ever, did not want to acquiesce to European demands. This pushed the Allies into remaining steadfast on reparations payments. As a result, Germany's economy collapsed altogether. (As Chapter Three relates, this collapse occasioned the rise to power of Adolf Hitler's Nazi party.)

The inability to cooperate on debt and reparations led to increased tension and further economic nationalism. The gold standard, which had been reintroduced after World War I, collapsed in 1931 because states were unwilling to cooperate on monetary policy. Additionally, protectionist trade policies, like the Smoot-Hawley tariff (discussed in Chapter Six), appeared throughout the globe. The Great Depression, initiated by the crash of the overvalued U.S. stock market in 1929, would prove unmanageable until the great powers could agree to pursue cooperative economic policies.

Thus, the interwar period proved to be a model for the disasters that can arise when there is no hegemon (the isolationist United States refused to play this role in the interwar period), the major industrial states do not cooperate, and protection reigns supreme. For the post–1945 generation of leaders after World War II, the nationalism that had led to the global economy's collapse proved to be as important a lesson of what not to do as the appeasement of Hitler that had led to Munich.

TRANSFORMATION OF THE WORLD ECONOMY

World War II and the subsequent rise of the United States to global preeminence heralded a new age of global economic interdependence and growth. The Second World War fundamentally altered the distribution of power in the international

How bad was German inflation in the 1920s? Here a man papers his wall with worthless German marks.

SOURCE: © UPI/Bettmann

system, ultimately set the stage for Cold War polarization between the communist and capitalist blocs of nations (see Chapter Four), and brought about great changes in the international political economy.

Foremost among these changes was the emergence of U.S. hegemony. The events of 1939–1945 both revealed and underscored the dominance of the U.S. economy. The United States dominated the world in terms of production. The supply of war materiel and finance, largely through the Lend-Lease program to the Allies during the war, and the vast destruction of European physical and capital stock, ensured a prominent role for U.S. finance following the war. By war's end, the United States was producing 40 percent of the world's armaments, and its productivity (output per unit of input, usually labor) far surpassed that of its nearest competitors. The result was a massive increase in U.S. gross national product (GNP), from $88.6 billion in 1939 to $135.0 billion in 1944.[18]

This rise of American hegemony coincided with a rapid resumption of growth in the world economy as shown in Figure 7.2. Bolstered by the outbreak of the

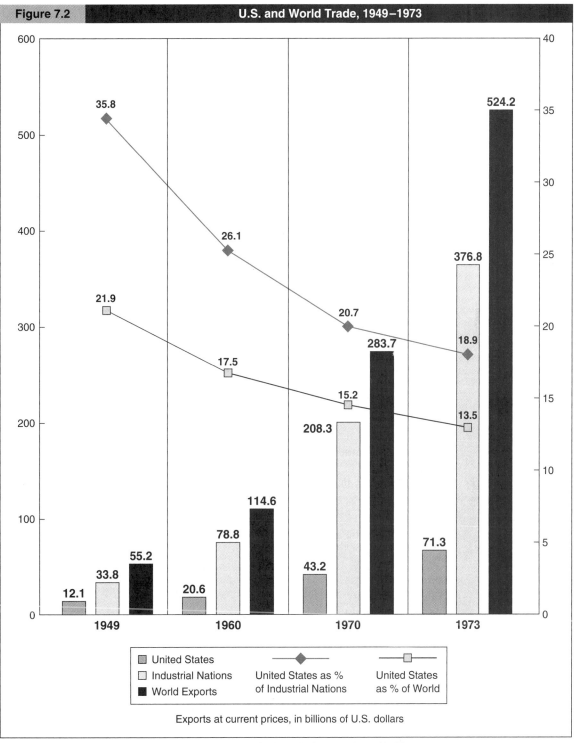

Exports at current prices, in billions of U.S. dollars

SOURCE: International Monetary Fund, *International Financial Statistics Yearbook, 1979,* pp. 62–67

Cold War and the desire to preserve economic stability and peace, international trade and investment grew within the American sphere of influence. The 1950s and 1960s were decades of rapidly rising living standards throughout much of the industrial world. From 1950 to 1973, production of the major industrial countries in Europe rose at an average annual rate of 4.8 percent, while the rate of productivity increased dramatically as well.[19] Economic growth, fueled by newly accessible Middle Eastern oil, a relatively cheap source of energy, solidified the recovery of Western Europe and Japan.

The Bretton Woods System

Unlike the disarray characteristic of the international economy during the interwar period, the growth of the world economy after 1945 took place within the context of an institutionalized economic system, known as the Bretton Woods system, led by the United States but premised on cooperation between the major Allied powers. The foundations for the postwar liberal economic system, one designed to avert economic nationalism and the mistakes of the interwar period by fostering free trade and a high level of interdependence, were laid at a 1944 conference held at Bretton Woods, New Hampshire. Here policy-makers attempted to tackle the difficult tasks of creating an international monetary system, a prerequisite for the smooth operation of international economic transactions, and more specifically, an international lending mechanism to help nations get back on a secure economic footing. To realize these ends, the conferees at Bretton Woods established the **International Monetary Fund** (IMF) and the **International Bank for Reconstruction and Development** (IBRD, more commonly known as the **World Bank**), to assist in the recovery effort.[20]

The IMF coordinated national currencies by establishing fixed exchange rates and helping to settle international accounts by advancing credit to countries with balance-of-payments deficits. On the basis of rosy recollections of how the nineteenth-century gold standard worked, the IMF established fixed exchange rates in the belief that they would best promote economic stability. The Bretton Woods monetary system fixed the dollar's value in gold at $35 per ounce and pegged the value of other currencies to that of the dollar (that is, governments were committed to intervene in the currency exchange market to keep the value of their currencies within the permissible bounds of the fixed rate). As the largest holder of the world's gold at the time and the primary contributor of funds to the IMF, the United States exercised a preponderant influence in the institution.

One of the primary purposes of the IMF was to provide short-term loans so that countries could rebuild their war-torn economies (the Marshall Plan, discussed in Chapter Four, was one such vehicle for doing this) and rectify balance-of-payment deficits. In the case of very serious imbalances, the IMF permitted countries to devalue their currency relative to the value of other currencies, with the intention of increasing export revenue and reducing international debts.

Also established at Bretton Woods was the World Bank. Created to help finance reconstruction after the war, the World Bank played only a marginal role to that end. As interest grew in developing the newly independent nations of the Third World in the 1950s and 1960s, however, the bank found a new purpose, lending billions of dollars annually to these lesser developed countries. (See Chapter Eight for more on financing development in the Third World.)

Creating institutions designed to manage international trade proved to be somewhat more complicated.[21] The U.S. government originally hoped to create an international organization, the International Trade Organization (ITO), to serve as the equivalent of the IMF in the area of international trade. Opposition in the U.S. Congress, however, derailed the ITO. An alternative arose in 1947 called the **General Agreement on Tariffs and Trade,** or GATT (see the box in Chapter Five), which formed one section of the ITO's proposed charter. GATT's emergence as a practical replacement for the doomed ITO reflected the political consensus that a liberal trading regime containing certain safeguards for disadvantaged domestic social groups would promote both peace and prosperity.

AMERICAN HEGEMONY

The Bretton Woods institutions, bolstered by U.S. leadership, functioned relatively smoothly throughout the 1950s. By 1949 the formation of the North Atlantic Treaty Organization (NATO), which signaled a clear commitment on the part of the United States to defend its allies and trading partners in Europe, had helped to quell fears of the Communist expansion into Western Europe (see Chapter Four). Aid to Western Europe, through the Marshall Plan in 1948–1952 and additional military aid, further enshrined the dollar as the key international currency and, together with easy access to vital energy resources such as oil (which the U.S. government's military and political protection of the conservative monarchies of the oil-rich Middle East helped to secure), ensured a rapid European recovery. In short, the system functioned as most policy-makers had hoped. The developed world grew at a dramatic pace, and the United States benefited through its own export promotion.

Yet the Bretton Woods system created its own set of problems for the United States. The role of the dollar as the key international currency gave the United States considerable leeway in managing the international economy—for instance, by granting it the prerogative of printing money to cover its balance-of-payments accounts (other states had to earn money through exporting in order to pay for their debts). But the tremendous outflow of dollars required to finance the postwar recovery eventually undermined foreign confidence in the dollar. The Bretton Woods agreement guaranteed that the United States could convert dollars into gold on demand. As the number of dollars increased faster than the American gold stock, it became difficult for the United States to cover this obligation. The United States was caught in a catch-22; mitigating this problem would require limiting the number of dollars abroad, but these overseas dollars were necessary in order to maintain a sufficient level of cash flow in the global economy.

By the late 1950s, U.S. policy-makers tried to respond to this dilemma. Although imbalances in countries' balance of payments often occurred during the

1950s and were usually restored by increasing or lowering the exchange value of their currencies, the U.S. government could not employ such an option. Because the United States was committed to defend the Bretton Woods system, whose cornerstone was the convertibility of the dollar to gold at $35 per ounce, dollars held abroad had to be redeemed at that price. As stated earlier, if the amount of dollars held abroad exceeded U.S. gold supplies, all potential claimants could not be paid without raising the dollar price of gold—that is, devaluing the dollar. Devaluing the dollar, however, was politically problematic, because it might adversely affect the economies of allies who held large amounts of dollars as a reserve currency and provided political and military support in the struggle against communism. (Devaluing reduced the amount of gold their dollars were worth.)

Furthermore, the possibility of devaluation fueled currency speculation and fears of a "run" on the dollar, meaning that if countries speculated that a currency was about to decline in value, they might try to hedge their bets by reducing the supply of that currency in their overall basket of currency holdings. Because confidence in the dollar, or the belief that the dollar's value was secure, represented the key to international monetary management, U.S. efforts to resolve its balance-of-payments problem dominated international economic relations in the 1960s.

As early as 1960, the amount of foreign-held dollars exceeded the U.S. supply of gold, and U.S. liabilities continued to grow throughout the 1960s and 1970s. After the first run on the dollar in November 1960, the U.S. government abandoned unilateral management of the monetary system and moved toward multilateral management. Together with other Western industrialized countries, the United States developed a number of new institutional arrangements to help resolve problems of monetary coordination and stability. The IMF became more active in lending funds to European countries to help finance temporary payment imbalances. Cooperation among central banks (such as the U.S. Federal Reserve Bank and Germany's Bundesbank) emerged as a form of multilateral management. Cooperation was further institutionalized through regular meetings of the finance ministers of the United States, Japan, Germany, France, Britain, Italy, and Canada, collectively known as the **Group of Seven** (G7) because they are the seven leading member nations of the Organization for Economic Cooperation and Development (OECD).

Yet, despite the efforts of the Western industrialized nations to hold the Bretton Woods system together, economic and political developments in the 1960s and 1970s proved too debilitating to the already unraveling system. The growth of monetary interdependence accompanying the revitalization of Western Europe and Japan complicated efforts to manage the international economy. Multinational banks and corporations arose as vehicles for large international financial flows. By 1974 the assets of foreign branches of U.S. banks totaled over $125 billion, and those of foreign banks operating in the United States totaled roughly $56 billion. **Multinational corporations** (MNCs)—that is, corporations headquartered in one country but with production facilities and assets in more than one country—also became significant players in the world economy. Although the overall costs and benefits of these MNCs is controversial (see Chapter Eight), they did show up on the otherwise unfavorable U.S. balance-of-payments ledger in the assets column.

The tremendous growth of international capital markets further complicated the increasingly difficult task of international monetary management. Consequently, multilateral and individual efforts to support international economic practices notwithstanding, international economic relations between the United States and other Western nations continued to worsen. With the economic recovery of Europe and Japan complete by the 1960s, U.S. economic dominance and the prerogatives of unilateral leadership were no longer politically sustainable either at home or abroad.

Decline of U.S. Hegemony

The Bretton Woods system ultimately fostered two concurrent outcomes: the rise of Western European and Japanese economic power and the development of U.S. trade imbalances. These conditions, along with greater fluidity in international financial markets, destabilized the international economic order. In order to understand its eventual demise, however, one must focus on the actual decline of U.S. hegemony. While the United States was still the dominant player in the international economy, other industrialized nations, as Table 7.4 reveals, became increasingly important.

Although U.S. export volume increased throughout the 1960s, exports of West Germany, France, and Japan increased much more rapidly. Moreover, these countries, in contrast to the United States, captured an increasingly greater share of the world export market throughout the decade. By 1972 West Germany nearly rivaled the United States in terms of volume and percent of world exports.

Associated with these divergent export growth paths were adverse trends in the U.S. economy. A glance at some data reveals an inflating trade deficit by the early 1970s. In 1960 the United States had a current-account surplus equal to $1.8 billion. By 1972 the balance spiraled into a deficit of over $8.4 billion.[22] In addition to the deteriorating U.S. trade balance, budget deficits were increasing rapidly and the economy was slowing down at home. Fueled in large part by

Table 7.4	World Exports, 1960–1972							
Country	1960	%	1965	%	1970	%	1972	%
United States	20.6	18.0	27.5	16.5	43.2	15.2	49.8	13.2
Great Britain	10.6	9.3	13.8	8.2	19.6	6.9	24.7	6.6
West Germany	11.4	9.9	17.9	10.7	34.2	12.1	46.7	12.4
France	6.9	6.0	10.2	6.1	18.1	6.4	26.5	7.0
Japan	4.1	3.6	8.5	5.1	19.3	6.8	29.1	7.7
World Exports	114.6		167.1		283.7		376.8	

SOURCE: Adapted from International Monetary Fund, *International Financial Statistics Yearbook, 1979,* pp. 62–63
NOTE: Figures are in billions of U.S. dollars, with percent of world total.

excessive domestic expenditures on new antipoverty and social welfare programs, the rising costs of financing the Vietnam War, and the refusal to either raise taxes or cut spending, budget deficits and inflation on the home front contributed to a crisis in the international economic arena. Another look at Table 7.4 illustrates the declining U.S. position in world trade by 1973.

In 1971, after several years of seeing its share of the world export market decline, the United States began to register a persistent trade deficit. This deficit added to the costs of the war effort and shortfalls in domestic revenue, ultimately proving detrimental to the international monetary system. Continued "benign neglect" in the area of monetary policy proved untenable in the face of rising foreign pressure, and on August 15, 1971, President Richard Nixon announced that the United States would no longer bear a disproportionate share of the burden of maintaining the international monetary system. The United States suspended its commitment to convert dollars to gold, imposed domestic wage and price controls, demanded dollar depreciation, and imposed a 10 percent tariff on imports. Collectively, these actions amounted to a rejection of the basic rules of international monetary relations and a demand for greater "burden-sharing" by U.S. military and economic allies.

The "Nixon shock" of 1971 was indicative of the problems inherent in a hegemonic system. For decades the United States had been the preeminent state in the world economy, forging a united front with its allies against the Soviets and augmenting the economic development of those allies. Yet, this process ultimately created a tremendous amount of instability, as disagreements arose between the United States and its now powerful allies over how to fix the international system. The French and the Japanese governments resisted U.S. pressure most strenuously, with France insisting that the United States honor its commitment to convert dollars into gold, and Japan demanding that the United States fix its domestic economic problems. Negotiations continued for thirteen months over how to salvage the Bretton Woods regime. Ultimately they failed, and the leading industrial powers agreed to eliminate the fixed exchange-rate system. By March 1973 most major currencies floated in financial markets.

The eclipse of U.S. predominance contributed to the decline of international economic order. In the past, the United States had been welcomed as a necessary stabilizer for the international economy. By the 1970s American leadership was viewed more suspiciously, especially as other Western industrial powers grew. Accordingly, efforts to restore order in international economic relations after the collapse of the Bretton Woods system took on a decidedly more multilateral cast. Just as the United States and Western industrial powers began the arduous task of restoring international monetary order, however, unexpected crises made an already difficult endeavor even more so.

OPEC and the Oil Crisis

Although negotiations to reform the international monetary system continued, developments in the Middle East threatened the supply of cheap oil upon which the

Western industrial nations had come to rely by the early 1970s. The U.S. case exemplifies this growing dependence. Its share of world oil production between 1957 and 1972 declined from 43.1 percent to 21.1 percent. A concomitant rise in Middle East oil production increased its world share from 19 to 41 percent. During the same period, U.S. oil imports also rose dramatically, from 11 to 35.5 percent of total U.S. consumption. Other Western industrialized states were similarly dependent upon foreign oil. By the early 1970s, as demand began to outstrip supply worldwide, the price of oil began to increase.[23]

As noted in Chapter Five, in October 1973 Egypt and Syria attacked Israel. U.S. support of Israel in the resulting Yom Kippur War prompted several Arab members of the **Organization of Petroleum Exporting Countries** (OPEC) to impose an oil embargo. This involved reductions in total oil production and a ban on shipments to the United States and the Netherlands (both supporters of Israel). By January 1974 crude oil prices had risen from $3.01 a barrel at the outset of the crisis to $11.65, a near fourfold increase, and prices for gasoline and heating oil more than doubled. The steep climb in oil prices confronted the United States with a shift in economic power that, according to Henry Kissinger, "altered irrevocably the world as it had grown up in the postwar period."[24]

FROM HEGEMONY TO MULTILATERALISM

With the demise of the Bretton Woods system in 1971 and the sudden shock of the oil crisis of 1973, the postwar international economic order lay in partial disarray. Despite the relative decline of the United States, however, international economic activity continued to thrive. Rather than shrinking, trade and finance expanded markedly after 1973. Spurred by the need to recycle the OPEC states' surplus "petrodollars" (see Chapter Eight), finance became truly international, with worldwide financial markets inseparably linked. Trade levels, although subject to marked fluctuations, also increased dramatically, fueling spectacular growth in Japan and Southeast Asia. As Figure 7.3 shows, although trade increased worldwide, it increased at a faster rate for industrialized countries.

The expansion of trade and financial flows prompted the advanced industrial states to renew their efforts to manage the international economy in a cooperative manner. Nations developed common interests in managing interdependence to minimize its conflictive aspects. These interests have given rise to many new arrangements, perhaps the most important of which include recurrent efforts to manage floating exchange rates and coordinate macroeconomic policies (which use taxation, spending, and money supply to regulate aggregate national economies). The state of the economy is no longer the province of "low politics" that it once was: Presidents and prime ministers, finance ministers and their staffs, and central bankers have become deeply involved in these matters for national security reasons.[25]

Despite the cooperative trends, conflict is never far behind. The international economy still generates powerful competitive incentives. Those actors able to set

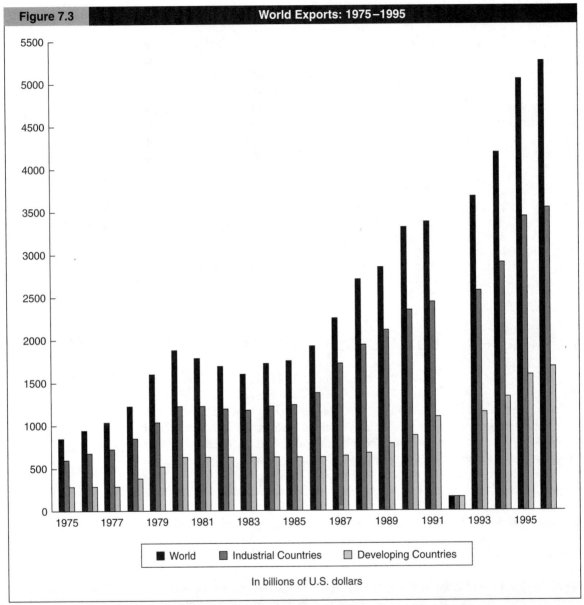

Figure 7.3 **World Exports: 1975–1995**

In billions of U.S. dollars

Legend: ■ World ■ Industrial Countries □ Developing Countries

SOURCE: International Monetary Fund, *International Financial Statistics Yearbook, 1996,* p. 7

the world economic agenda will benefit, while others will lag behind. Thus, the need for international cooperation is often mitigated by a countervailing need for institutions and national strategies capable of adapting to and prospering in an intensely competitive environment. The growth of world trade, the declining dominance of the United States, and the extraordinary success of Japan have intensified concerns about competitiveness as markets for goods and services became increasingly globalized.[26]

From Shock to Recovery

Cooperation and conflict in the international political economy developed within the tumult of events and policy shifts after 1973. The unprecedented increase in oil prices in 1973–1974 forced dramatic adjustments on industrial nations already highly dependent on oil. Largely unable to lessen their demand for oil despite the dramatic price increase, the developed countries experienced severe economic dislocations, including reduced purchases of many goods, long lines at the gas pumps, and inflation. Throughout 1974 and 1975, many countries in the developed world experienced **stagflation,** a combination of low, or stagnant, economic growth and a high rate of inflation. According to classical economic theory—the history of business cycles up to this time had confirmed this point— unemployment and inflation were thought to correct each other, with unemployment dampening consumer demand and putting downward pressure on prices, and inflation increasing production and employment levels. Economic recovery and relatively stable crude oil prices (at a new level of $11 to $13 per barrel) set in during the mid-1970s, but came to an abrupt end once again in 1979 with the Iranian revolution and overthrow of the shah. Already tight oil supplies were reduced by the loss of production in Iran; as a result, oil prices again skyrocketed. By 1980 oil prices had reached about $35 per barrel, and the world economy, unable to adjust, once again entered the throes of stagflation.

Efforts within the United States to overcome these shocks to the world economy had only limited success. The Federal Reserve, in order to eradicate inflation, chose to raise interest rates dramatically. This led to a severe recession in the United States in 1981–1982 that spread worldwide. The economic doldrums caused the advanced industrial nations to consider radical shock therapy. Brought to power in part to provide this shock treatment, American President Ronald Reagan and British Prime Minister Margaret Thatcher implemented deregulatory policies and tax cuts, which they felt would facilitate a return to strong economic growth. At the same time, these leaders were elected to combat growing Soviet military power, heightened by the 1979 Soviet invasion of Afghanistan (see Chapter Four). The combination of increased defense spending and tax cuts led to record U.S. peacetime budget deficits.

Although U.S. budget deficits increased, the rise in government spending and reduction in taxes spurred a strong economic recovery in the country. The United States ultimately became the world's engine for growth, as its prosperity filtered worldwide. One consequence of these policies, however, was to push American interest rates above those in other countries. As was discussed in the beginning of this chapter, higher interest rates have two effects on the domestic economy: they appreciate the currency and increase the price of domestic goods abroad. In fact, both phenomena occurred in the United States during the 1980s. The result was a persistent, massive trade deficit. The Reagan administration's effort to revitalize the national and world economy worked in the short term, but this growth came at a price. Trade and budget deficits grew out of control, manufacturers of exports and domestic goods could not compete with foreign firms, and U.S. savings and investment rates declined dramatically.

Imbalances in the world economy since the 1970s are shown in Figure 7.4, which details the current-account balances of the three major trading states: the United States, Germany, and Japan. All were basically balanced until the early 1980s, when the U.S. figures began to show a deficit and German and Japanese figures began to show surpluses until Germany began to dip in 1991 with reunification.

Ultimately, interdependence has brought nations closer together, increasing their reliance on one another for economic prosperity. In the postwar era, particularly since the 1970s, trade has increased substantially, capital flows between nations have ballooned, and foreign exchange transactions have reached tremendous proportions. The consequences of these forces have been significant for the world economy and its major participants in many ways. First, multilateralism has increased, as nations are forced to coordinate in order to succeed economically. Unlike the periods of British and American hegemony, today the great powers cannot afford to go it alone. Unilateral pursuit of economic policy often yields tremendous trade imbalances and unwanted exchange-rate fluctuations.

Second, and in direct contrast to the previous point, as the number of powerful states has increased, so has the probability for conflict. With more and more nations vying for market share and profits, competition has become intense, and failure to keep up with one's competitors has serious consequences.[27]

Eastern Europe and Russia: From Communism to the Free Market?

The collapse of Communist regimes in the former Soviet bloc nations (see Chapter Four) has profoundly affected European economies, and its potential impact on the world economy is much greater.[28] The complete transformation from communism to capitalism in Russia, Eastern Europe, and Central Asia will probably take a generation to occur, require a coordinated effort along many fronts, and take place at different rates among the former Soviet bloc countries. Specifically, economic reform entails ending fiscal deficits and establishing monetary stability, eliminating price controls and state subsidies, creating a convertible currency, and eliminating trade barriers.

These economic reforms required sweeping institutional changes, including privatization of state firms and the banking system, provisions to protect private property, revamping of the tax system, and establishment of a social safety net for pensioners, the unemployed, and other vulnerable groups. Moreover, in many formerly Communist states, all these reforms had to be carried out in a political climate in which many government officials and political parties are reluctant to give up Soviet-style state control of the economy.

The countries that have been most successful are the ones that pursued eco-

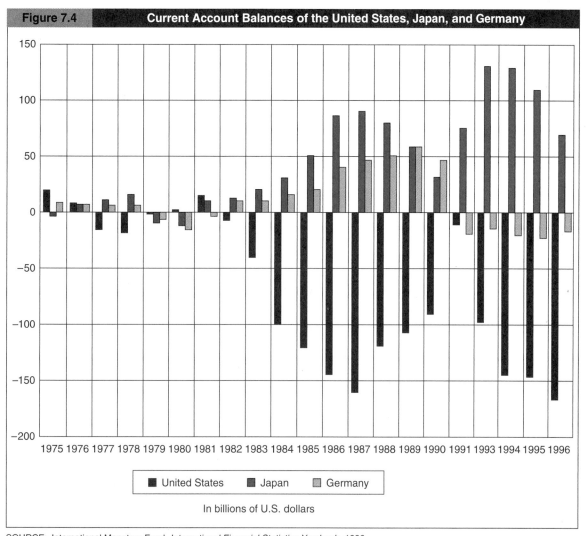

Figure 7.4 — Current Account Balances of the United States, Japan, and Germany

■ United States   ■ Japan   ▨ Germany

In billions of U.S. dollars

SOURCE: International Monetary Fund, *International Financial Statistics Yearbook, 1996*

nomic liberalism most fervently. Poland, the Czech Republic, and Hungary each implemented privatization policies along with democratic reforms that protect and encourage private ownership. The former East Germany was fortunate in this respect, as German unification allowed integration into strong West German economic and political institutions—but the social and financial costs of unification have proven higher than anticipated. Other countries, including Russia, Romania, and Bulgaria, have been less successful, largely because electorates have been unable or unwilling to remove former Communist bureaucrats.

In many respects, a state's ability to achieve reform depends on the political will to accept economic hardship. This transition requires a tremendous amount of pain, including high inflation, unemployment, and a scarcity of basic goods and services. In some states, particularly Hungary and the Czech Republic, the public was willing to support political parties that sought to liberalize the economy. In other states, including Russia and Ukraine, the hardship has been extremely severe, and the public's support for reformers has waned. Even in Poland, by 1997 many voters supported reformed socialists and former Communists in response to the economic pain imposed by new liberal programs. Only the future will tell how successful many of these states will be at integrating into the world economy.

The West has more than an academic interest in the former Soviet bloc's success. Throughout the Cold War, East-West trade was minimal. U.S.–led institutions like GATT and the Bretton Woods system helped integrate the economies of the capitalist world, while Soviet-led institutions, particularly the **Council of Mutual Economic Assistance** (CMEA or COMECON), solidified trade relations in the East. Now that political tensions have eased and these Communist institutions have collapsed, most capitalist nations see this region as an untapped market. Yet, there are more general reasons why the West hopes reform will continue. Their leaders believe that a capitalist and democratic Russia and Eastern Europe will eliminate the need for massive military budgets. The less money needed for weapons, the more money that can be spent on creating economic wealth or managing social and environmental problems.

Despite these concerns, the West has only tentatively helped these states, providing modest amounts of economic aid and only partial acceptance into their institutions. The **European Union** (EU), for example, has refused to establish a free-trade area between itself and Eastern Europe. Why would the United States, Japan, and the EU respond in such a manner? The answer points to the inherent tensions present in an interdependent world. Although no one wants these states to revert to Soviet communism or other forms of authoritarianism, many powerful interest groups are worried about increased economic competition from the East. Economic integration might lead Western firms to move to the East, because many former Communist states have cheaper labor and lax environmental laws. The European debate over economic integration with Eastern Europe thus closely resembles the debate in the United States over NAFTA.

Both East and West have thus far been unable to solve this puzzle: How can they guarantee that capitalism will take hold within the former Soviet bloc without infringing upon their own economic position? In the short run, the puzzle may be insoluble, but accepting pain now in return for gain later could make both Eastern and Western Europe more secure and prosperous in the long term.[29]

The Need for Cooperation

Increasing interdependence has taught policy-makers that it often pays to cooperate to manage international economic relations. Yet, it is often difficult to predict when cooperation between states will emerge or how it will manifest itself. What we do know is that cooperation results from strategic bargaining between two or more states; it does not connote that states work together in perfect harmony.

States often have different preferences, but situations can arise in which compromise can be beneficial for all. The goal, of course, is to give up as little as possible, while achieving an outcome that benefits all states involved. This balance between national autonomy and international cooperation is tenuous and suggests why states often cannot agree on a set of policy outcomes.

Since the breakdown of the Bretton Woods system, economic summits among the Group of 7 have tried to restore a degree of international economic stability. There have been many instances of great success. Four summits were arranged between 1975 and 1978 in order to facilitate a world recovery from recession. An agreement materialized whereby the major powers agreed to coordinate their fiscal policies and reduce their reliance on foreign oil. In 1985 the G7 nations agreed to alter their currencies' values in order to eliminate the tremendous trade imbalances that appeared worldwide. The resulting policy changes had a tremendous effect, with the dollar depreciating 67 percent in three years, just as the states had hoped. Since the 1980s, G7 summits have marked growing if unsteady progress in global economic cooperation, but have sometimes been little more than photo opportunities for the participating leaders. In recognition of its post–Cold War economic progress, Russia was invited to participate in the 1997 summit, but it was not given the same formal status as the G7 powers.

The uneven results of the G7 summits, however, suggests that international cooperation can be muddled if one or more states decide not to cooperate. A prime example of this can be seen by analyzing U.S. economic policy during the early 1980s. Suffering from high inflation rates, the United States decided to raise interest rates in order to squelch inflationary pressure. Because the United States was such an important factor in the world economy, its unilateral policy decision had a momentous impact both within the nation and on its trading partners. Higher interest rates led to a deep global recession in 1981–1982, broadsiding the efforts of other states that were trying to manage their own economies. Additional effects were an appreciated dollar and an enlarged U.S. trade deficit. Even though the recession ended in 1982, the resulting trade imbalances led to a degree of conflict between the United States and its trading partners. Although the 1985 economic summit alleviated some of this diplomatic pressure, the unilateral rise in interest rates hindered international coordination.[30]

These examples show that even though most states claim to be in favor of international economic cooperation, domestic considerations can mitigate policy coordination. The overall success of GATT, its successor, the World Trade Organization (WTO) and agreements adopted at the annual G7 summits have demonstrated that states can collaborate. The prospects for sustained cooperation, however, are far from certain. Domestic considerations can change a state's proclivity for international coordination. In order to counterbalance this uncertainty, states have begun to form additional relationships that parallel global summitry. The formation of **economic blocs,** such as the European Union and the North American Free Trade Agreement (NAFTA), have simultaneously and somewhat contradictorily increased the possibility for both free trade and protectionism in the world economy, and they will conceivably alter the nature of global economic relations.

ECONOMIC BLOCS: THE SHAPE OF THE FUTURE?

An economic bloc is a political or economic organization designed to promote high levels of internal cooperation as well as enhance competitiveness with the rest of the world.[31] The two most common types of economic blocs are **common markets,** which are characterized by common external trade barriers and uniform (or nonexistent) internal trade barriers, and **free-trade areas,** which provide for the removal of internal trade barriers without coordination of external trade policy. One of the greatest concerns about economic blocs is that they might promote internal cooperation by increasing trade levels among bloc members but create conflict between different blocs. Also, by discriminating against imports from non-bloc countries, economic blocs may function as protectionist "fortresses" for member countries. In fact, some critics of economic blocs believe that by concentrating more of their regional economic activity, the advanced industrialized states might undo the accomplishments of international institutions such as the World Trade Organization in reducing global tariff levels and increasing global trade.

In spite of their importance in the contemporary world economy, it is too early to tell what impact trade blocs will have. If the world divided into different blocs, some suggest it might become easier to negotiate international economic agreements. Why? Today, many countries acting individually negotiate agreements like the WTO. If they were organized into blocs, there would be fewer actors at the negotiating table, conceivably making it easier to compromise. Others say that regions will never become self-sufficient and that interregional trade will increase further. The bottom line is that although no one can be sure what the future holds, regional trade blocs seem likely to become increasingly important.

European Union (EU)

The European Union is the world's largest economic bloc (comprising over 400 million people) and the most highly integrated. The foundations of the EU were laid in 1951, when France's foreign minister, Robert Schuman, initiated the European Coal and Steel Community (ECSC) to create a common market in coal and steel as a means of guaranteeing peace, especially between France and Germany. By 1955 this organization had contributed to a 23 percent increase in coal production and a 150 percent increase in iron and steel production. In the 1957 Treaty of Rome, the six members of the ECSC (France, West Germany, Italy, Belgium, the Netherlands, and Luxembourg) inaugurated the European Economic Community (EEC). The members envisaged the EEC to be much more than just a free-trade union: They sought the eventual elimination of internal tariffs, a free flow of capital and labor, and similar wage and social benefits in all the participating countries.[32]

The EEC proved so successful at increasing trade and prosperity levels among its members that in 1973 members of the **European Free Trade Association** (EFTA)—comprising Britain, Norway, Sweden, Switzerland, Austria, and Portugal, and formed in 1959 as a British-dominated counterweight against the French-dominated EEC—entered into a free-trade agreement with the Common Market. Great Britain, Ireland, and Denmark became EEC members in 1973, Greece in 1981, Spain and Portugal in 1986, and Austria, Finland, and Sweden by 1996. Further applications from Turkey, Cyprus, former Soviet-bloc countries, such as Estonia, Poland, Hungary, and the Czech Republic, are being considered as well, but the entry of many of these states may be blocked by politics as well as economic considerations.

Progress toward the full economic integration of European Community members entered a new stage when they signed the Single European Act in December 1985. This act entailed 282 new laws that all members agreed to implement by January 1993, including the elimination of customs checks, the creation of a single banking market among these states, and a uniform value-added tax (the European equivalent of sales taxes). At their meeting in December 1991 at Maastricht in the Netherlands, the EC nations agreed to the Treaty of European Union

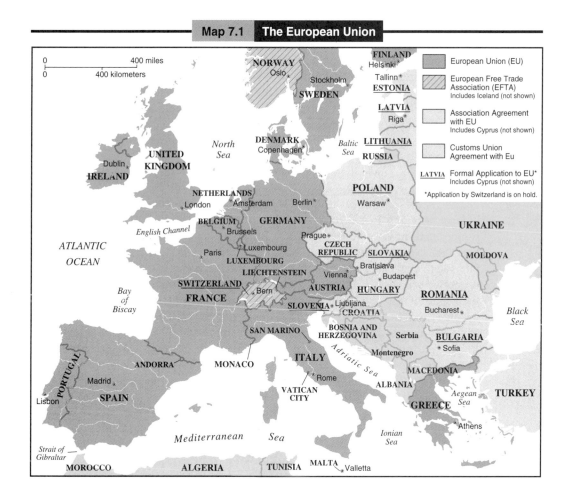

Map 7.1   The European Union

to finalize their political and monetary union (symbolized in their new collective name, the European Union). They further agreed to establish an economic and monetary union (EMU), with a single currency, the euro. Banks and stock exchanges in eleven EU countries (Austria, Belgium, Finland, France, Germany, Ireland, Italy, Luxembourg, Netherlands, Portugal, and Spain) will begin using the euro in 1999, and euro bank notes and coins are scheduled to go into circulation in 2002. EMU also provides for an independent European central bank governed by a twelve-person board, with members representing each state.

Continuing controversies over EMU, however, illustrate the political difficulties of economic integration. Britain and Denmark were skeptical of EMU from the start, questioning the wisdom of handing over control over their currencies to a European bank, and retained the option to "opt out" of EMU (though a Labour-led British government elected in 1997 may well choose to participate after all). Other states, especially Italy and Greece, worried that the Maastricht criteria for inflation, budget deficits, and public debt, which states must keep within limits in order to join EMU, would be difficult to meet. Even in Germany and France, bullish on EMU from the start, the measures necessary to bring their public finances within the Maastricht criteria have caused economic stringency and political controversy. Postwar Europeans had become accustomed to high spending on social welfare and old-age pensions, and EMU would force many governments to cut corners in order to fulfill their social promises as their populations aged (and, in some cases, grew with refugees and immigrants from Eastern Europe and North Africa). In France, a wave of major strikes in 1994 and the electoral beating taken by the governing conservative coalition in 1997 exemplified how many workers, grown accustomed to solid job security and generous benefits, bitterly resented the cuts in public spending necessary for monetary union. Many European voters similarly questioned whether, given Europe's persistently high levels of unemployment, monetary union would be worth the price of restricting social spending.

Moreover, some critics doubted that the European central bank would be truly independent and insulated from political concerns (as the rock-ribbed German Bundesbank has been). Though most EU members expected to join EMU (if not by 1999, then later as they get their financial houses in order), the institution will face tough challenges to maintain a stable European currency despite political and economic pressures.[33] It certainly remains to be seen whether the euro will replace the U.S. dollar as the leading currency of international trade and finance, or will become too unstable to suit either European financiers or world markets. The controversies over EMU show how greater economic and political cooperation within Europe is based on an often tenuous convergence of interests. Germany would like to see its major continental trading partners follow its own low-inflation policies, and it is willing to relinquish some autonomy over the German economy in return for a powerful European central bank independent of political control and capable of managing European inflation. Other EU states, especially France and Italy, are willing to surrender a measure of sovereignty over inflation rates and budget deficits in return for an additional role in European policy-making.

Despite its steady progress since 1951, European economic integration has been neither smooth nor easy. Referenda in Denmark and France ratified the

Maastricht treaty by slim margins, indicating the level of popular apprehension about integration in much of the Union. Though the Norwegian government had applied for membership, a referendum there rejected joining the EU in 1994. Disagreements over trade and monetary policy still divide EU members. France would like monetary union, but it fears being dominated by Germany. Other states, in particular Britain, fear losing sovereignty to a continental institution and have resisted certain aspects of the plan, in addition to demanding a clause for their departure if they see fit. Germany has also been uncooperative at times. Attempting to cope with unification (see Chapter Four), Germany pursued economic policies that threw the entire continent into a deep recession.

The admission of new members raises additional concerns, both economic (such as the effect of new Eastern European on labor markets) and political (Greece, in particular, opposes the admission of Turkey, at least until resolution of the contentious Cyprus question). Despite these problems and setbacks, it seems that European integration is moving forward, albeit slowly and with much trepidation. Though this may encourage Eurosceptics, proponents of "ever-closer union" are not discouraged, as the founders of the EEC were under no illusions that integration would be either smooth or easy.

North American Free Trade Agreement (NAFTA)

The movement toward European integration, as well as Japan's increasing assertiveness in Asia and the world, led the United States to develop its own regional response. The **North American Free Trade Agreement** (NAFTA) between Canada, the United States, and Mexico created a free-trade area within North America that went into effect January 1, 1994. It does not go nearly as far as the EU regarding integration. NAFTA eliminates only internal trade barriers between these three countries. It does not set barriers with other states, nor does it create supranational economic or political institutions (except panels to resolve disputes over tariffs and dumping). Nevertheless, it was an important step for the United States in its attempt to remain competitive in the world economy.

The history of NAFTA began in January 1989, when the U.S.–Canadian free-trade agreement took effect. Its objective was to eliminate virtually all tariffs and duties between the United States and Canada by 1999.[34] Incorporating Mexico into this free-trade pact encountered significant political opposition from environmental groups, some industries (mainly low-tech and low-skill), and labor organizations in the United States because of the substantial economic differences between the United States and Mexico. Environmental groups feared that more U.S. industries would set up *maquiladoras* (factories that assemble inputs produced in the United States into goods reexported to the U.S. market) in Mexico to take advantage of poorly enforced environmental laws. Labor unions were alarmed by the prospect of job flight to Mexico, where the wage rates for unskilled labor are roughly one-seventh of those in the United States.

Supporters of the trade accord argued that freer trade would create jobs and lower consumer prices in all three countries, and that as Mexico grew more pros-

perous, environmental regulations would become more popular and more effectively enforced. After an acrimonious debate (see Chapter Eight), and after the
Clinton administration added side agreements to make the transition to freer
trade more palatable to labor, farm, and environmental groups, NAFTA was
ratified by the U.S. Congress in November 1993. Detractors attributed Clinton's
success in getting NAFTA passed to the side deals (bribes, to some) given to pressure groups and crucial industries, but it was clear that an important step had been
taken toward free trade with America's northern and southern neighbors.

Free-trade advocates soon pushed for further reduction of hemispheric trade
barriers, calling for the eventual creation of a Free Trade Area of the Americas
(FTAA). Looking forward to this, Chile announced in 1994 its intention to join
NAFTA. Canada and Mexico quickly supported Chilean membership, but the
U.S. Congress again expressed reservations. Opponents of NAFTA kept the controversy alive after its ratification. Protectionists trumpeted that NAFTA had "destroyed" about 80,000 American jobs by 1997, citing the certification of job losses
required by one of the side deals mentioned above. (Certification of jobs created
by NAFTA was not required.) By way of comparison, however, the U.S. economy
created 7 million jobs in the same period, so NAFTA "destroyed" only about as

Barrels full of chemicals, abandoned by a U.S.–owned business in Juarez, Mexico, rust in
the Mexican desert. Scenes like this inspired many opponents of NAFTA, who believe that
U.S. companies exploit lower environmental standards across the border.

SOURCE: © Richard Perry/Sygma

many U.S. jobs as are created in ten working days.[35] U.S. trade deficits with Mexico in 1995 and 1996 were cited as an additional negative effect of NAFTA, but the United States ran a surplus with Mexico in 1994, before Mexico's economy went into recession. Mexico's financial crisis in 1995, which was contained only by an unprecedented U.S.-backed bailout of the peso, and continuing controversy over lax labor and environmental standards in Mexican industry engendered further criticism of the agreement.

Nevertheless, trade among the NAFTA partners has continued to grow rapidly (U.S.–Canada trade reached almost $1 billion *per day* in 1996), and manufacturing of automobiles, electronics, and other goods has become more efficient as the pact promoted specialization and trade in components. Overall, the effect of freer trade has been marginally positive, as economic theory would lead one to expect. Thus, the benefits of NAFTA have not been as great as its proponents had hoped, nor its costs as high as its opponents had feared. (Some have argued that this was not true for Mexico, however. For more on the effects of NAFTA on its southern trading partner, see Chapter Eight.)

MERCOSUR

Prompted by the movement toward free trade to their north, Brazil, Argentina, and Uruguay formed the Southern Cone Common Market (known by its Spanish acronym **MERCOSUR**) with the Treaty of Asuncion in 1991. Later joined by Paraguay and with Chile as an associate member, the MERCOSUR countries have lowered tariff barriers among themselves, achieving the status of a free-trade area similar to NAFTA. Further integration to a European-style common market, however, has proved more difficult, though progress has been made on harmonizing external trade barriers. Trade within MERCOSUR (which grew about 30 percent annually from 1990 to 1994) has burgeoned even faster than trade within NAFTA (which rose about 10 percent per year during the same period).[36] However, the next steps in forming a true common market—providing for free movement of labor and capital, coordination of monetary policy, and standardization of labor and environmental laws and other practices and standards envisioned for the bloc—will pose significant challenges, as they have in Europe.

The relationship of MERCOSUR to NAFTA and the proposed Free Trade Area of the Americas has also been controversial. Some analysts believe that it would have been easier for member countries to join NAFTA individually (taking the route Chile adopted) rather than to arrange a merger of the MERCOSUR countries as a whole with the northern free-trade area. Integrating other South American countries into MERCOSUR will also pose problems, leading some to argue that the MERCOSUR partners should have first created a free-trade area, then added other countries or joined NAFTA en bloc, before attempting to move onto a common market. These issues and others raised by the fitful progress of economic reform in Latin America (see Chapter Eight) must be dealt with if the hemispheric free-trade area envisioned by many supporters of NAFTA and MERCOSUR is to be realized, but the overall outlook for further reduction of trade barriers in the Americas appears cautiously optimistic as the twentieth century draws to a close.

Free-Trade Areas of the Pacific Rim

The movement toward economic integration in Europe and North America accelerated the movement toward a free-trade area or common market in Asia. In 1992 the member states of ASEAN (Association of Southeast Asian Nations; see Chapter Five), concerned that the single European market and NAFTA would divert global investment to Europe and North America, launched the **ASEAN Free-Trade Area** (AFTA), a fifteen-year plan for reducing tariffs on products in fifteen major categories. Asian leaders also formed the **East Asian Economic Caucus** (EAEC), which is devoted to rapid economic growth. It includes the six ASEAN nations, Japan, China, and other Asian countries, but not the so-called Anglo-Saxon states of Australia, New Zealand, Canada, and the United States.

Concerned by an apparent desire to keep these states out of the fastest growing economic region in the world, President Bill Clinton convened the first meeting of the **Asia-Pacific Economic Cooperation** (APEC) organization in 1993. Originally proposed by Australia, APEC is a loose conglomeration of more than a dozen Pacific Rim states (including Australia, Brunei, Canada, Chile, China, Hong Kong, Indonesia, Japan, Malaysia, New Zealand, the Philippines, Singapore, South Korea, Taiwan, Thailand, and the United States) with a combined GNP of over $14 trillion. Like other economic blocs, APEC embodies a mix of cooperative and conflictive interests. The U.S. government desires APEC to ensure a foothold for the United States in Asian markets, and it sees APEC as a way to pressure European governments to open their markets and make concessions in world trade talks or else be shunned by the United States. On the other hand, the export-oriented Asian states seek to preserve their share of the U.S. market and prevent NAFTA member Mexico from replacing Asia as the United States' source of electronics and semiprocessed goods.

Are Trade Blocs Examples of Cooperation or Conflict?

In many ways, regional integration and trade blocs have arisen in response to the decline of U.S. economic hegemony. Their emergence makes clear two themes that underlie foreign economic relations since 1973. First, the major industrialized states have repeatedly attempted to cooperate in order to manage the world economy. Through G7 meetings, these states have avoided an economic collapse that many feared would materialize without a hegemon at the center of the international system. There has also been an upsurge in regional cooperation, as economic blocs formed in order to deal with intensified global competition.

A parallel trend, however, has been the resurgence of economic conflict and uncertainty. Although G7 meetings were successful forums for discussion, they were no substitute for strong international institutions to regulate trade and finance. The summit meetings often failed to accomplish their goals and left world markets wondering what would happen next. Additionally, the emergence of economic blocs makes it unclear whether regional cooperation will lead to greater global tension. Trade blocs have unquestionably spurred the growth of regional trade and the institutionalization of regional cooperation; whether they will heighten cooperation, or conflict, at the global level remains an open question.[37]

CONCLUSION: THE GLOBAL ECONOMY IN THE NEW ERA

More than any other aspect of international relations, the changing world economy exemplifies the intertwining trends of cooperation and conflict, globalization and fragmentation. The explosive growth of world trade since 1945 has made nations more interdependent than ever, as states have come to depend on one another for markets, capital, natural resources, and financial stability. This interdependence has fostered the growth of international institutions, such as the G7 and WTO, and of regional organizations like the EU, ASEAN, and NAFTA. These cooperative institutions have made conflicts over trade less intense, but their myriad rules, regulations, and panels for resolving disputes indicate how economic conflicts have become more frequent as trade has expanded. As economic activity inherently involves both cooperation (between partners in an exchange) and conflict (between buyers and sellers over prices, and between competitors for customers), this should not be too surprising.

What is perhaps more surprising is how the world economy has simultaneously become more globalized and more fragmented. Air transportation and satellite communications and the Internet have given small firms and individuals routine access to global markets; TV commercials for air express services trumpet how easy it now is for a corner store in Moscow, Idaho, to reach customers in Moscow, Russia. At the same time, some economists warn that the world may be dividing into antagonistic trading blocs, as Europe, Japan, and the United States break down barriers to regional trade while setting up barriers to imports from other regions. National leaders demand that their governments "get tough" in pressuring others to lower tariffs and nontariff barriers (conveniently ignoring the barriers that protect their own industries), while regions within nations, from Siberia to Scotland to Chiapas (in Mexico), demand more autonomy and worry about the effects that regional integration may have on their local economies. Overall, the twin processes of globalization and fragmentation are weakening the economic sovereignty of the nation-state and transferring it to supranational institutions and subnational groups. Marx predicted in the nineteenth century that communism would make nation-states obsolete, but the contemporary global economy shows that the triumph of capitalism, rather than communism, is causing the state to wither away.

This chapter has outlined how the structure of the world economic system changed from British hegemony in the mid-nineteenth and early twentieth centuries to conflicting trade blocs between the World Wars, U.S. hegemony after World War II, and cooperative multilateralism since the 1970s. Throughout all these periods, some governments and industries have called for freer trade, although other interests have demanded barriers against international competition. Whatever structure the world economy takes on in the New Era, the struggle between free-traders and protectionists is almost certain to continue. This political conflict will continue to be played out in the economic sphere, and vice versa.

Nevertheless, since the Industrial Revolution and Adam Smith's theories of free trade began the decline of mercantilism, the world economy has moved definitively, if not steadily, toward openness and multilateralism. This movement, which has been interrupted by periods of conflict and depression, may now be sidetracked onto a path toward regional rather than global integration. But the fits and starts with which the global trading system has liberalized over the past two centuries may exemplify a "punctuated equilibrium" in the evolution of world trade, wherein major shocks (such as the world wars and the oil crisis) produce new structures and adaptations (such as the WTO and coordination among the G7). The fittest, most productive states and corporations are most likely to survive in a system of freer trade, but the interaction between global economics and local politics periodically produces protectionist "throwbacks." Because the liberal, realist, and Marxist perspectives on trade (outlined in the previous chapter) each have different views of prosperity and fairness, the system that finally emerges from economic competition and political compromise may not be the best of all possible worlds.

This chapter's review of the history of the world economy was designed to help readers to better understand those aspects of international relations that will have the greatest impact on their personal lives and careers. Regardless of whether the future of the world economy belongs to global institutions, multinational corporations, regional blocs, or economic nationalism, its influence on our lives can only increase. Those who doubt that this is so—who think that economic globalization, fragmentation, cooperation, and conflict are of purely academic interest—should turn off their televisions (made in Taiwan, showing news live via satellite from South Africa), put on their running shoes (made in South Korea), get in their cars (built at a Japanese-owned factory in Ohio), drive (using gasoline made from Saudi oil) to McDonald's (a multinational corporation), and order a hamburger (made from Australian beef) to remind themselves that as the world economy gets bigger, the world gets ever smaller.

PRINCIPAL POINTS OF CHAPTER SEVEN

1. Although states have traded for thousands of years, the origins of the modern global economy lie in the Industrial Revolution, which began in the late eighteenth century and led to the explosive growth of world trade.
2. Britain, as the first industrialized nation and the leading naval power, established hegemony in the mid-nineteenth century and encouraged free trade.
3. As the nineteenth century progressed, the economies of other states (especially Germany and the United States) grew rapidly, and Britain faced challengers for hegemonic status. Nevertheless, the world economy remained relatively stable from the establishment of the gold standard in 1870 until World War I.

4. Between the two world wars, the world economy lacked a clear hegemon. After 1929, war debts, German reparations, a stock-market crash in the United States, and a wave of protectionism launched by the Smoot-Hawley tariff created a global depression.

5. After World War II, the United States emerged as the global economy's hegemon. The Bretton Woods system was set up to provide fixed exchange rates and financial stability, and the General Agreement on Tariffs and Trade (GATT) sought to promote free trade and resolve trade disputes.

6. As the economic strength of Europe and Japan grew in the 1950s, 1960s, and 1970s, the United States found it difficult to maintain its hegemonic status. The collapse of the Bretton Woods system in 1971 and the oil crisis of 1973 inaugurated a period of cooperative multilateralism, during which the leading industrial states attempted to cooperate to regulate international trade and finance (not always successfully).

7. In the late twentieth century, the formation of the World Trade Organization (WTO) as a successor to GATT demonstrated continued commitment to the reduction of trade barriers. At the same time, many states increasingly integrated their economies into regional trade blocs, such as the European Union, the Southern Cone Common Market (MERCOSUR), and the North American Free Trade Agreement (NAFTA). It remains to be seen, however, whether these blocs will cooperate to promote freer trade and financial stability or will become protectionist "fortresses" against imports from other regions.

8. There has been movement toward greater openness in the world economy over the past two centuries, but this movement has been gradual and uneven, and how far it will continue is uncertain. In any case, economic interdependence, technology, international institutions, and demands for regional and local autonomy are eroding the economic sovereignty of the nation-state.

KEY TERMS

ASEAN Free-Trade Area
Asia-Pacific Economic Cooperation
common markets
Corn Laws
Council of Mutual Economic Assistance
Dawes Plan
economic blocs
economic interdependence
East Asian Economic Caucus
European Free Trade Area
European Union
free-trade areas
General Agreement on Tariffs and Trade
Group of Seven
hyperinflation
International Bank for Reconstruction and Development
International Monetary Fund
maquiladoras
MERCOSUR
most-favored-nation
multinational corporations
North American Free Trade Agreement
Organization of Petroleum Exporting Countries
stagflation
World Bank
Zollverein

SOURCE: Stephanie Maze/Woodfin Camp

North-South Economic Relations: The Challenge of Development

THE CONTEMPORARY SOUTH

The economic problems facing the developing countries of the South (chiefly Latin America, South and Southeast Asia, the Middle East, Africa, and the Pacific) are very different from those confronting the industrialized states of the North (North America, Western Europe, and Japan). Many Southern countries are very poor, and large segments of their population have minimal access to education, medical care, and employment opportunities. Economic development is the first priority all governments of the South claim to have on their agenda. Indeed, development is the central topic of negotiation, if not a preoccupation, in contemporary relationships between South and North. It is, however, a nebulous concept subject to radically different interpretations. To the U.S. Agency for International Development (USAID), development may mean increasing agricultural productivity or opening up Southern markets to American exports. Development to the World Health Organization (WHO) may mean expanding rural health clinics to stop babies from dying from dysentery. Development to environmentalists may mean creating a sustainable economy that generates minimal waste and pollution. Development to Iraq's Saddam Hussein may mean producing a nuclear bomb or other weapons of mass destruction. Thus, development is one of the most ambiguous terms in contemporary social science.

One thing clear about development is that it is a constantly moving goal. This is because the "standard" for development is "what developed countries have," and the developed countries are themselves continuing the development process. In the mid-nineteenth century, the "high-tech" industries were textiles and railroads, which were the foundation of Britain's industrial might. By the 1930s one critical standard of development was the capacity to produce steel and heavy machinery; consequently, Joseph Stalin sacrificed enormous human and material resources to construct the Soviet Union's massive metallurgical complexes to defend "socialism in one country." Today, of course, textiles and steel are increasingly produced in developing and newly industrialized countries, such as South Korea, while many factories in the English midlands, where the Industrial Revolution began, and the Ural Mountains, where Soviet Russia built the tanks to defeat the Nazi invasion, are obsolete by most international standards. Instead, most developed countries compete against one another in the electronics, computer, and aviation industries and scramble to develop biotechnology, supercomputers, and optical computer systems to gain a competitive edge in the information age.

Because the development standard is a constantly moving target, countries that do not sustain economic growth find themselves rapidly falling behind. Many Southern countries, particularly in Africa, have not achieved significant economic development in the post–World War II era, meaning that the gap between the "haves" in the North and the "have-nots" in the South has widened dramatically. For instance, between 1950 and 1990, the gross national product (GNP) of the United States tripled while its population increased by only two-thirds. America's per capita income therefore more than doubled. For Japan and the countries of Western Europe, which were devastated by World War II but today have standards of living roughly equivalent (if not superior) to that of the United States, the increase in per capita GNP has been even greater. By contrast, some African countries produce less total economic output in the 1990s than they did in the 1960s because of civil wars or political instability, while the population in these countries has been increasing at rapid rates (see boxed feature on "One Planet, Many Worlds"). Imagine a car traveling along a road at 25 mph while a jet aircraft soars overhead at the speed of sound, and you begin to get the picture. There are also great disparities in growth rates among the developing countries. In Israel and the East Asian "Tigers" of Hong Kong, South Korea, Taiwan, and Singapore, per capita incomes have risen quickly enough to begin catching up with the advanced industrial countries. Thailand, Indonesia, and South Africa have also achieved impressive advances despite formidable economic and political problems. Countries such as Sudan, Somalia, Liberia, and Haiti, however, have fallen even further behind their Southern neighbors, while others, like Mexico and Algeria, seem almost perpetually poised at the crossroads between economic takeoff and stagnation.

Some believe that the increasing disparity between North and South makes the development process much more difficult for late developers by demanding ever larger inputs of capital to make the leap from underdeveloped to developed. This is, of course, disputed by others.[1] Development may be more like a learning process, in which all countries have to begin with low-technology industries and then gradually acquire the skills and capital to expand and upgrade their international competitiveness. What is clear, however, is that in the age of instantaneous global communications that reach the most remote areas of the planet, even the poorest rural residents of Asia and Africa know that they live far below the standard of living achieved by the average American, European, or Japanese. Thus, a "revolution of rising expectations" is likely to increase the demand for faster economic development.

Development in Theory and Practice

Although it is difficult to predict the precise development path of any country, development in all countries is similar in some important respects. Virtually all countries start the development process as rural societies in which the vast majority of the population engages in **subsistence agriculture** (hand-to-mouth farming for direct consumption by one's own family). As development occurs, fewer and fewer people work in the agricultural sector and more people find employment in the manufacturing and service industries, which are typically located in urban areas. Development has therefore meant a huge migration of labor from farms to cities. With fewer farmers to grow food (and other agricultural products like cotton) and with more urban dwellers to feed, the productivity of agriculture must increase (as it has, exponentially, in the United States and Western Europe) if food shortages and widespread hunger are to be avoided.

Moreover, when people first enter the urban labor market, they usually lack skills and must take low-wage jobs. As a large percentage of their wages must be spent on food, the price of food typically becomes a major political problem in countries just beginning to industrialize. If food prices are too high, urban unrest and riots become likely. If food prices are kept artificially low (through subsidies), however, farmers will not produce enough to supply urbanites, and the impoverished countryside may become fertile ground for rebellion. The initial stages of development thus often generate intense rural-urban conflicts as the economy shifts away from subsistence agriculture and toward industry.

Clearly, raising both agricultural and industrial productivity is as critical to development in the South today as it was in the North over the past two centuries. The major question facing Southern governments is, therefore, not whether to modernize their traditional agricultural economies, but how to do so. The main challenge they face is determining the economic development strategy that will

One Planet, Many Worlds

In discussions of economic development, states have typically been categorized into a tripartite classification: the First, Second, and Third Worlds. The **First World** was the industrialized West, the **Second World** was the Communist East, and the **Third World** was the developing South. However, with the rapid industrialization of several Southern states and the end of the Cold War, this rough classification of states has become outdated, and the World Bank now uses several classifications for developing countries, as shown in the following table.

First World

The First World consists of the industrialized countries and includes the states of Western Europe, North America, and Japan (see Chapter Seven). Although comprising only a quarter of the world's population, the First World accounts for over four-fifths of the world's GNP. In 1995 the overall GNP per capita of the states ranked by the World Bank as high-income countries was $24,930.* Topping the list were Switzerland at $40,630, Japan at $39,640, Norway at $31,250, Denmark at $29,890, Germany at $27,510, and the United States at $26,980. Besides a high per capita GNP, the First World is characterized by the export of services and manufactured goods. Other important characteristics include a low infant mortality rate, low illiteracy rate, long life span, and low population-growth levels (0.6 percent since 1990).

Second World

The Second World consists of the former Communist nations of the USSR and Eastern Europe. Although economic data on these states have been scarce and unreliable, the Second World has roughly matched the First in some indicators of development, such as physicians per capita, literacy, and life expectancy. In other respects, however, such as percent of workers in agriculture and per-capita GNP, Second World countries have mirrored the level of development characterized by the wealthier Third World countries. Even though these states no longer have centrally planned economies, most now share serious problems associated with the transition from communism to a market-oriented economic system, often including high under- or unemployment and rapid inflation coupled with declining real wages.

Third World

Finally, the Third World includes over 160 underdeveloped and developing nations in the Middle East, Asia, Africa, and Latin America. The Third World accounts for three-fourths of the world's population but less than one-fifth of the world's production of goods and services. In contrast to industrialized countries, which usually have a diversified economic base, many Third World countries depend heavily on the export of a single commodity or raw material, such as cocoa, coffee, copper, timber, or petroleum. Most Third World states also have a high percentage of workers in agriculture (often in subsistence farming), a highly skewed distribution of wealth between the rich and poor, low levels of literacy, shorter life expectancy, a high level of infant mortality, and a high rate of population growth. However, the Third World is far from uniform in its level of economic development, and several additional classifications have evolved to more precisely categorize Southern states.

The *low-income countries*, sometimes called the **least developed countries** (LDCs), are the poorest of the poor. These states have a much lower standard of living in comparison to other states in the Third World. In 1995, their per-capita income averaged $430. (The poorest states for which reliable data are available in 1995 included Mozambique, with a per capita GNP of $80; Ethiopia, with $100; Tanzania, with $120; Burundi, with $160; and Malawi, with $170.) Two-fifths of the adult population is illiterate, life expectancy is roughly fifty years, and many farmers are subsistence farmers, producing only enough for their family's consumption. India is included in this group of countries, as is China, which despite its rapid industrial growth had a per capita GNP of only $620 in 1995. In between the low income and developed countries are *lower-middle-income* economies, such as Ecuador and Turkey, with per-capita GNPs averaging $1,670 in 1995, and *upper-middle-income* countries, such as Mexico and Malaysia, with an average per capita GNP of $4,260.

A group of Third World states consisting of *oil-exporting countries,* including the member states of OPEC (Organization of Petroleum Exporting Countries), stands out from other developing nations. Although sharing many similarities with low income countries, such as the reliance on the export of a single product, the most notable difference is their comparatively high average per capita income—over $2,000 in 1995. Some smaller members of this group have per-capita GNPs that are quite high; in 1995 that of Kuwait and the United Arab Emirates was more than $17,000. However, like all states that rely on the production of a single good, these countries are very vulnerable to fluctuations in the price of their primary export. The oil exporters often resemble other developing states in other aspects, such as adult illiteracy.

The **newly industrialized countries** (NICs) comprise another group of developing states. NICs are generally characterized by rapid growth in the export of manufactured goods. They include such states as Brazil and the four Asian "Tigers" (Hong Kong, Singapore, South Korea, and Taiwan). The Asian NICs share a number of features, including great success at promoting the export of manufactured goods (which will be discussed later in this chapter), a Confucian cultural heritage, strong regimes that have made economic development their highest priority, and finally, a high level of foreign investment, particularly from Japan. With a relatively high GNP per capita ($9,700 for South Korea and $26,730 for Singapore in 1995), low infant mortality, and high literacy levels, the Asian NICs come closest to bridging the gap between the First and Third Worlds.

Problems with Classification

Although it provides a convenient verbal shorthand, the division of states into First, Second, and Third World categories based on their income levels has a number of problems. As noted, a number of NICs traditionally classified as Third World states now have little in common with their less developed neighbors. With a high GNP per capita, rapid industrialization, low illiteracy levels, and long life spans, they share many of the characteristics of the industrialized North. By contrast, the oil exporters have high per-capita incomes, but lack a diversified industrial base, and their prospects for sustained growth are problematical at best. Any attempt to divide the countries of the North and South into convenient categories shows how difficult it is to come up with a single standard of "development" that all states can aspire to, given their differing strengths and problems.

*All figures in this box are from World Bank, *World Development Report 1997,* pp. 188–189.

Category	Total Population (millions)	GNP per Capita	Life Expectancy at Birth	Adult Literacy (%)
Low Income	3,179.9	$430	66	66
Lower Middle	1,152.6	$1,670	67	82
Upper Middle	438.3	$4,260	69	86
High Income	902.2	$24,930	77	95

SOURCE: World Bank, *World Development Report 1997,* pp. 188–189

best redeploy their human resources into more productive endeavors. In making this determination, Southern countries must keep in mind two sets of variables that will influence their chances for successful development: domestic political and social factors and the international environment in which development must occur.

With this in mind, the first part of this chapter presents two contending schools of thought, **modernization theory** and **dependency theory**. These theories hold differing views on the ways in which domestic and international factors create opportunities and challenges to development. In a nutshell, modernization theory contends that the global trading system can be a great help to development, while dependency theory argues that it has been a great hindrance. The second part of this chapter examines the successes and failures of some development strategies that Southern countries have followed in their quest for economic growth and social progress. The chapter's final section uses the debates over extension of most-favored-nation status (see Chapter Seven) to China and the North American Free Trade Act (NAFTA) as examples to consider how trade between North and South presents dilemmas and opportunities to both developing and developed countries.

CONTENDING THEORIES OF DEVELOPMENT

Modernization Theory

Modernization theory contends that the most important factors contributing to development, and the primary causes of underdevelopment, are the economic, political, and cultural conditions within the Southern states themselves.[2] In reaching this conclusion, the founders of modernization theory studied the experience of Europe and North America, long-established developing states such as Iran and Turkey, and the newly independent nations of Asia and Africa, including India, Pakistan, Côte d'Ivoire (Ivory Coast), Myanmar (Burma), Ghana, and many others.

Modernization theory draws a sharp distinction between "traditional" and "modern" societies. A traditional society is usually depicted as a peasant village where generations pass on their customs, rituals, and folkways to each new generation. Modern societies, in contrast, are more urban, dynamic, flexible, and innovative, and willing to adapt. To develop, modernization theorists contend, Southern societies must undergo the same process of transition from traditionalism to modernity previously experienced by the states of the North.

From this perspective, the fundamental obstacle to development is traditional culture, which blocks the societal transformations necessary for rapid economic growth. Traditional societies are dominated by religious or aristocratic authority, are based on rural life, and are characterized by rigid social structures, such as the Indian caste system. Although replacing traditional customs with a more modern outlook is essential to development, traditional culture is resistant to change. Thus, getting from traditional to modern values can take generations, as well as produce enormous social tensions, as Europe experienced as a result of the Industrial Revolution (see Chapter Two).

Guided by the Western experience of development, modernization theorists contend that less developed states will develop only by shedding their traditional social, political, and economic institutions. Socially, this requires the ability to achieve status through merit or success (rather than birth or caste) and tolerance of social and intellectual diversity. Politically, this translates into the emergence of democracy, the rule of law, political opposition, human rights, and basic freedoms. Economically, development means the creation of a market-based economy, though some level of state intervention for social reasons (to relieve poverty, care for the elderly, or cushion the shock of unemployment, for example) is possible and desirable. From the modernization perspective, therefore, economic growth and democratization form a virtuous circle, each strengthening the other as both progress. Industrialization, increased incomes, education, and **urbanization** all increase the likelihood of political democracy—which, in turn, protects and reinforces the market economy that is necessary for continued economic development.

For many modernization theorists, trade is the engine of economic growth. Accordingly, they call for free trade and open markets. In this relationship, Northern multinational corporations and international investment play an important role in disseminating capital, managerial and technical skills, and technology necessary for the emergence of a modern industrial sector. Aid from the developed countries will help fill the resource gaps in underdeveloped states. At the same time, developing countries can "pull themselves up by their own bootstraps" by saving to accumulate financial capital, buying equipment and improving infrastructure to increase physical capital, and investing in education and training to improve human capital. One U.S. program for economic development in Puerto Rico was even called "Operation Bootstrap."

Social Impact of Modernization   At first glance, the path to development as prescribed by modernization theory may appear straightforward. In practice, however, modernization creates wrenching changes in a society. These changes lead to political, social, and economic problems that must be addressed in order for development to continue. The opportunities and challenges presented by development are illustrated by two trends characteristic of modernization: **demographic transition** and urbanization. (These trends occur in all developing societies, not just those where development is guided by modernization theory. They are discussed here because modernization theory regards them as "growing pains" that societies must work through in the modernization process.)

Underdeveloped, traditional societies generally have very high birth and death rates, whereas in modern societies these rates are much lower. This change between high and low rates is termed *demographic transition*. In many underdeveloped countries, the number of children who die prior to reaching one year of age—the **infant mortality rate**—exceeds 100 per 1000 live births. In high-income countries, by contrast, infant mortality averaged 7 per 1000 live births in 1994.[3] High infant mortality, poor sanitation, and inadequate medical care combine to make life expectancy shorter in most preindustrial societies—an average of 56 years for most low-income countries, compared to an average of 77 years in the developed world.[4]

In most traditional societies, a high death rate leads to a high birthrate. In order to ensure that enough children will survive to help with the back-breaking labor of subsistence agriculture, women in many underdeveloped areas are compelled by social conventions to marry young (often at age fourteen or fifteen, or as soon as puberty is reached) and bear as many children as possible. Children are also expected to support their parents in their old age, serving as a kind of social security system. Consequently, the fertility rate (the average number of children born per woman) is very high in most low-income countries; in 1994 an average woman in most developing countries could expect to bear more than six children in her lifetime.[5] (See Map 8.1.)

A real dilemma, then, arises when the introduction of modern medicine causes the death rate to fall dramatically. The infant mortality rate may fall from more than 200 to less than 40 within twenty or thirty years in even the most impoverished of traditional societies, and life expectancy may rise from forty to sixty-five years or more in the same period. The traditional emphasis on having many children often persists long after the death rates fall, resulting in a population explosion. As countries industrialize, however, fertility rates tend to decline as more women go to work and pursue higher education, death rates tend to decline as nutrition and medical care improve, and population growth slows markedly. Table 8.1 compares annual rates of population growth in representative countries of the North and South. Many sub-Saharan African countries experience annual population growth of over 3 percent, meaning that the country's population could double in twenty years. Accordingly, the OECD countries have the lowest population-growth rates, followed by the rapidly industrializing East Asian Tigers.

In Southern countries, with so many new mouths to feed, clothe, shelter, and educate, the economy and society are put under enormous strain, and there is little left over for investment. In order to keep population growth from overwhelming the resources of the country, the birthrate must be brought down, which means that overall health standards must be improved so that infant mortality is lessened. However, traditional social values concerning the necessity to marry young and have many children are often difficult to change. Additionally, some Northern development agencies such as the Population Council that promote family planning and contraception are often accused of racial or ethnic discrimination in their attempts to reduce population growth, despite the fact that they spend the vast majority of their resources on maternal and infant health care in order to reduce infant morality and thus save lives.

The net result of rapid population growth in the early stages of demographic transition is that half or more of the population consists of children and teenagers. Figure 8.1 compares the "population pyramids" of developed, newly industrialized, and developing countries to illustrate the balance between age groups in states going through different stages of development. Note how the population pyramid of established industrialized states is relatively tall and thin, indicating a long life expectancy and a population relatively balanced between youths, adults

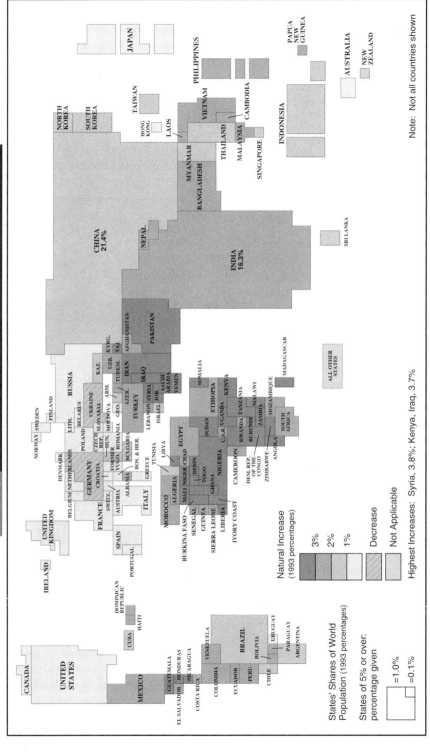

Map 8.1 States Sized according to Population, 1996

CANADA

UNITED STATES

IRELAND

UNITED KINGDOM

DOMINICAN REPUBLIC

HAITI

CUBA

SPAIN

PORTUGAL

NORWAY | SWEDEN

FINLAND

DENMARK

BELGIUM | NETHERLANDS

GERMANY

FRANCE

SWITZ.

AUSTRIA

ITALY

GREECE

ALBANIA

CROATIA

FORMER YUGO.

BOS. & HER.

BULGARIA

ROMANIA

HUN. | SLOVAKIA

CZECH REP.

POLAND

LITH.

BELARUS

UKRAINE

RUSSIA

KAZ.

KYRG.

UZB.

ARM.

GEO.

AZER.

TURKM.

TAJ.

AFGHANISTAN

PAKISTAN

MOLDOVA

TURKEY

LEBANON | SYRIA

ISRAEL | JOR.

IRAN

IRAQ

SAUDI ARABIA

YEMEN

JAPAN

TAIWAN

HONG KONG

LAOS

NORTH KOREA

SOUTH KOREA

CHINA 21.4%

NEPAL

INDIA 16.3%

BANGLADESH

MYANMAR

VIETNAM

CAMBODIA

THAILAND

MALAYSIA

SINGAPORE

PHILIPPINES

INDONESIA

PAPUA NEW GUINEA

AUSTRALIA

NEW ZEALAND

SRI LANKA

MOROCCO

ALGERIA

LIBYA

TUNISIA

EGYPT

BURKINA FASO

MALI | NIGER | CHAD

SENEGAL

GUINEA

SIERRA LEONE

LIBERIA

IVORY COAST

GHANA

TOGO

BENIN

NIGERIA

CAMEROON

DEM. REP. OF THE CONGO

C.A.R.

SUDAN

ETHIOPIA

SOMALIA

UGANDA

KENYA

RWANDA | TANZANIA

BURUNDI

MALAWI

ZAMBIA

MOZAMBIQUE

ANGOLA

ZIMBABWE

SOUTH AFRICA

MADAGASCAR

ALL OTHER STATES

MEXICO

GUATEMALA

EL SALVADOR | HONDURAS

NICARAGUA

COSTA RICA

VENEZUELA

COLOMBIA

ECUADOR

PERU

BRAZIL

BOLIVIA

CHILE

PARAGUAY

URUGUAY

ARGENTINA

States' Shares of World Population (1993 percentages)

States of 5% or over: percentage given

☐ = 1.0%

▫ = 0.1%

Natural Increase (1993 percentages)

3%

2%

1%

Decrease

Not Applicable

Highest Increases: Syria, 3.8%; Kenya, Iraq, 3.7%

Note: Not all countries shown

SOURCE: Michael Kidron and Ronald Segal, *State of the World Atlas*, 5th ed. (New York: Penguin, 1995)

Table 8.1	Population-Growth Rates in Selected Countries			
	Annual Average Population-Growth Rate (%)		Population (millions)	
Country	*1980–1985*	*1990–1995*	*1950*	*1995*
Tanzania	3.2	3.0	7.89	29.69
Zimbabwe	3.3	2.6	2.73	11.26
Egypt	2.6	2.2	21.83	62.93
Cameroon	2.8	2.8	4.47	13.23
Ecuador	2.7	2.2	3.39	11.46
Mexico	2.4	2.1	27.74	93.67
South Korea	1.4	1.0	20.36	44.99
Denmark	0.0	0.2	4.27	5.18

SOURCE: World Resources Institute, *World Resources 1996–97*, pp. 190–191

in their prime productive years, and senior citizens. Although states with such a population structure will have to devote a significant portion of their incomes to caring for children and pensioners, the number of workers in mid-life is relatively large and fairly constant.

In developing countries, however, the population pyramid is broad and flat, indicating a lower life expectancy and a preponderance of children and teenagers. Not only will these young people require significant long-term investments in education and training if they are going to gain the skills necessary for the further development of the country, but they also will need jobs when they reach working age. This is true of young people everywhere, but rapid population growth in developing countries also means a rapid increase in the number of new jobs demanded every year by young workers who are ready to enter the labor force. If large numbers of new jobs for young adults are not available, massive unemployment and underemployment will cause serious social problems, and resources for child and senior care will be even scarcer. However, poor countries typically do not have the means to educate all their children, and so a cycle of grinding poverty perpetuating high birthrates and resulting in more poverty is established. Few economies can generate jobs fast enough to employ all the workers available when population is growing at 3 percent or greater per year. Consequently, very rapid population growth can overwhelm the capacity of an economy to prosper and a society to develop, and it is one of the principal reasons why several African and Asian countries have failed to raise their per-capita incomes since their independence in the 1960s. Conversely, the success of China and newly industrialized countries (NICs) in East Asia in reducing their population growth and managing demographic transition has been an important feature of their relative economic success.

A major consequence of demographic transition and industrialization is urbanization. One way that many families in traditional societies attempt to cope with the pressure of chronic overpopulation and the resulting unemployment is to

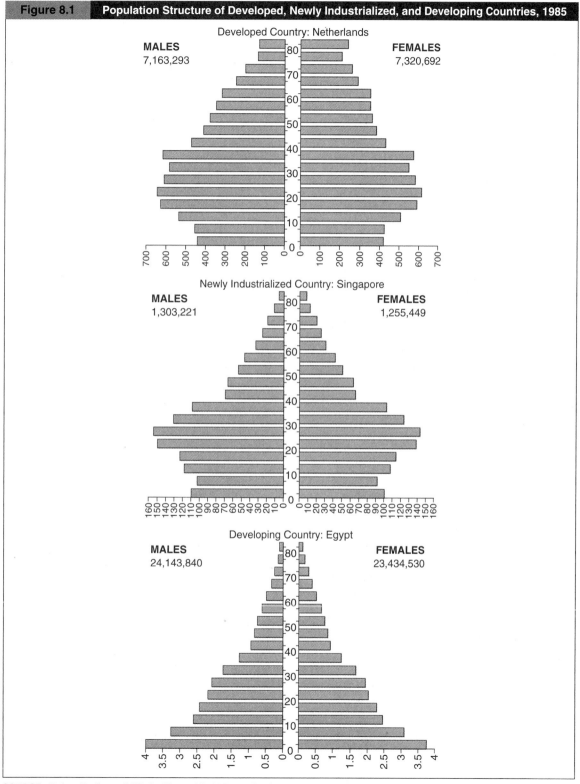

Figure 8.1 | Population Structure of Developed, Newly Industrialized, and Developing Countries, 1985

Developed Country: Netherlands

MALES
7,163,293

FEMALES
7,320,692

Newly Industrialized Country: Singapore

MALES
1,303,221

FEMALES
1,255,449

Developing Country: Egypt

MALES
24,143,840

FEMALES
23,434,530

SOURCE: Nathan Keyfitz and Wilhelm Flieger, *World Population Growth and Aging* (Chicago: University of Chicago Press, 1990)

send some children to urban areas to find cash employment. If work can be found, the proceeds can be sent back to the family to be used to educate younger siblings or support parents in their old age. There is no social security for the elderly in most Southern countries, so parents often rely on their children for support. However, in many cases, work cannot be found, yet rural migrants nevertheless settle in urban areas, becoming part of the vast shantytowns that have grown up around virtually all cities of the contemporary South, such as São Paulo, Calcutta, Soweto, Cairo, and Jakarta.

The rate of urban population growth in the South during the 1960s and the 1970s was typically between 3.5 and 5 percent, and in some countries even higher, sometimes reaching twice the rate of population growth. Obviously, these newly burgeoning cities do not have the resources to provide services such as fire, police, and sanitation that residents in Northern cities take for granted. Whatever infrastructure that was built by Europeans in the colonial era in the way of sanitation, electricity, and water was quickly overwhelmed in postcolonial Asia and Africa. Therefore, shantytowns are often overcrowded, acutely poor, and persistently crime-prone.

Despite these hardships, the modernization perspective generally views urbanization as an essential step in the development process away from subsistence agriculture and toward a modern economy. The newly urbanized migrant is undergoing a difficult but necessary shift away from traditional superstitions and beliefs and toward a more flexible and adaptive view of the world. This process of urbanization is never easy, but it may be a necessary stage in creating a modern society—the Industrial Revolution produced vast slums in nineteenth-century Britain. Additionally, from the perspective of modernization theory, the city becomes the focus of the diffusion of new ideas, of science and technology, of social mobility based on productivity and the rise of a professional and middle class, the development of a division of labor within society, and perhaps most importantly, the center of an industrial manufacturing and service-based economy.

Critiques of Modernization Theory　Modernization theory has been criticized on a number of fronts. First, its critics question whether the North's path of development can be duplicated by the South.[6] Countries modernizing in the late twentieth century, they contend, are likely to face different kinds of problems (such as global environmental degradation and resource shortages—see Chapter Ten) from those faced by the Northern countries that developed in the nineteenth century. In addition, although in the nineteenth century countries like Britain, the United States, and Japan could borrow from other **First World** states and sell their goods either to one another or to their colonial empires, the **Third World** today is dependent on industrialized nations for markets and capital.[7] Finally, industrializing countries in Europe faced little competition from already developed rivals, while today Southern countries must compete with industrialized states with well-developed manufacturing sectors.

Second, critics of modernization theory stress that traditional social and political institutions are often difficult to change. As one author notes, "We have learned that in much of the Third World, so-called traditional institutions have, first of all, proved remarkably resilient, persistent, and long-lasting; rather than fading, crushed under the impact of change, they have instead proved flexible, accommodative, and adaptive, blending to the currents of modernization but not being replaced by them."[8] The survival of these traditional institutions can force Southern societies into paths of development very different from those taken by Northern industrialized states.

Third, many theorists and policy-makers contend that modernization theory is Eurocentric. That is, this pattern of development is grounded essentially on the singular experience of Western Europe. Similarly, some contend that modernization theory was a product of the Cold War mentality that sought to keep the Third World out of the Soviet sphere by tying Third World nations into a Western and liberal development pattern.

Finally, some political economists and many Third World states contend that the structure of the international trading system is biased against the South, and that, historically, wealth has not flowed from the rich states to the poor states through trade and aid, but in fact the opposite has occurred. This perspective on trade and development contends that, at first through colonialism and later through multinational corporations and foreign lending, Northern countries have kept the South in a perpetual state of underdevelopment. This criticism is the heart of the alternate school of thought on development known as dependency theory.

Dependency Theory

Dependency theory rejects the modernization theory premise that the source of Third World problems is domestic in nature.[9] Instead, it emphasizes the international context, contending that international institutions, multinational corporations, and the states of the First World have deliberately kept the Third World in a dependent condition. In contrast to modernization theory, which has its roots in classical economics and the liberal perspective on world trade (refer to Chapter Six), dependency theory draws many of its insights on the relations between the North and South from a branch of Marxist thought.

Dependency theorists argue that the existing international economic system is inherently biased against the South. The roots of this unequal relationship between the periphery (the Third World) and the core (the First World) can be traced to the sixteenth century, when European countries began to colonize the Southern Hemisphere.[10] In this relationship, the periphery exported raw materials to the industrializing states in Europe (and later to the United States and Japan), and in turn the North exported manufactured goods to the periphery. More recently, multinational corporations based in the North have replaced the colonial powers in sustaining this relationship. According to *dependencistas* (adherents of dependency theory), this unequal relationship has ensured that Third World states remain the global economy's "hewers of wood and drawers of water." This fundamental inequality of the economic relationship between North and South, dependency theorists contend, fueled development in the North and stifled it in the South.

Primary-Product Exports   In dependency theory, the disadvantaged position of the South stems from the fact that most Southern countries' economies depend heavily on the export of **primary products**—that is, raw materials such as timber, oil, and metals, and agricultural goods such as coffee and bananas. Beginning in the sixteenth century, the "periphery" supplied the raw materials and foods for the economies of Europe, and then for the Industrial Revolution in Europe and later the United States. In turn the periphery imported manufactured goods from the industrialized countries. Capitalist economists view this relationship as the operation of comparative advantage (see Chapter Seven), but dependency theorists view it as an international division of labor wherein the South does the "dirty work" of producing raw materials while the North gets the "good jobs" in manufacturing and services. They contend that this division of labor encourages the Third World to remain exporters of primary goods and discourages the development of a modern manufacturing sector.

Table 8.2 compares the exports of typical less developed, developing, and industrialized countries. Primary products make up a very high percentage of the exports of developing countries like Nigeria, which exports oil, and Côte d'Ivoire, which produces cocoa. Middle-income countries like Malaysia and Brazil have much more diversified economies, and therefore export a higher percentage of manufactured goods, while exports from more developed states like Singapore and Japan consist primarily of manufactures. Note how Malaysia, Brazil, and Singapore increased the share of manufactured goods in their exports as their development strategies succeeded over the two decades from 1970 to 1991.

To make matters worse, the exports of many Southern countries are dominated by a single commodity. These countries lack the diversity of goods and services that most Northern countries have achieved in their exports and are thus vulnerable to fluctuations in the demand for or price of their main export. Perhaps the best examples of one-commodity countries are the oil-exporting states. Petroleum in its various forms accounts for virtually all of the exports of Saudi Arabia, Kuwait, Iraq, Iran, the Persian Gulf states, Libya, Nigeria, Gabon, Angola, and

Table 8.2	Percentage Share of Merchandise Exports by Product Category, 1970–1991									
	Fuels, Minerals, Metals		Other Primary Goods		Machinery and Transport Equipment		Other Manufactured Goods		Textiles and Clothing	
	1970	1991	1970	1991	1970	1991	1970	1991	1970	1991
Nigeria	62	96	36	3	n/a	0	1	1	0	0
Côte d'Ivoire	2	11	92	79	1	2	5	9	1	2
Malaysia	30	17	63	22	2	38	6	23	1	6
Brazil	11	16	75	28	4	18	11	38	1	4
Singapore	25	18	45	8	11	48	20	26	5	5
Japan	2	1	5	1	41	66	53	31	11	2

SOURCE: World Bank, *World Development Report 1993*, pp. 268–269

Brunei, and it is the most important export of Venezuela, Mexico, and Indonesia. When the world price for oil is high, these countries reap large rewards, but a drop in the oil price can lead to economic disaster. Many other developing countries depend on exports of a single commodity. Sugar dominates the exports of Cuba, Fiji, Mauritius, and, to a lesser degree, the Philippines. Coffee is the principal export of Colombia, El Salvador, Burundi, Rwanda, Uganda, Costa Rica, Kenya, and Ethiopia. Copper is the major export of Zaire, Zambia, and Chile. Jamaica, Guinea, and Surinam export bauxite, Honduras produces bananas, Niger mines uranium ore, Liberia exports iron ore, and Peru's main export is an illegal drug—cocaine.

Dependency theorists argue that this international division of labor—primary products in the South, manufactured goods in the North—perpetuates the Third World's backward position. As long as the South remains the exporter of primary products for the world, they contend, Southern countries will not develop their own indigenous industries and will remain dependent upon the North for manufactured goods and technology.

According to the dependency school, fluctuations in the prices of primary goods perpetuate the dependency of Southern countries. Countries that depend heavily on primary product exports are very sensitive to sudden changes in the world prices for those commodities. Fluctuations in price can create externally induced boom-and-bust cycles. Random events may allow the producers of a specific commodity to enjoy a short period of excellent prices—such as when a freeze ravaged Brazilian coffee production in the mid-1970s and sent coffee prices to all-time highs. Though the Brazilian industry took a loss, all other coffee producers reaped great profits. This boom lured growers to switch to coffee, and the next year, when Brazilian coffee returned to the global marketplace, the glutted market led to a bust as prices—and profits—plummeted.

Commodity industries may also enjoy a period of boom that prompts the development of substitutes or replacements, or of compensatory measures leading to a collapse in prices. The rubber boom of the 1920s (which resulted from the rise of the automobile) fell apart when synthetic rubber was introduced during World War II. Similarly, the oil-price boom of the 1970s was followed by the oil glut of the 1980s as new oil fields were tapped, alternative energy sources were developed, and consumers began using less oil.

Boom times typically result in overinvestment in speculative ventures that, when they go bust, create disastrous ripples throughout the economy and cause a depression. Moreover, boom-and-bust cycles make long-term planning difficult, especially for government expenditures in such areas as education, health, and infrastructure. Price fluctuations hit especially hard in countries that rely extensively on the export of a single commodity, such as oil, coffee, or rubber, and are at the mercy of the world market. In contrast, in industrialized states with large and diversified economies, fluctuations in the price of a few primary or finished products usually have little impact on the economy as a whole.

Unequal Terms of Trade Dependency theory also argues that disadvantageous **terms of trade**—that is, the ratio of export prices to import prices—further impoverish the Third World.[11] If the prices of a country's exports are rising faster than the prices of the goods it imports, its terms of trade are increasing; conversely, if import prices are increasing faster than export prices, its terms of trade are declining. For most developing countries, this means that if the prices of primary products decline while the prices of manufactured goods from the North increase, the Southern nation's terms of trade will worsen. Dependency theorists contend that prices of primary goods tend to decline over the long run relative to the price of manufactured goods. (Whether or not this is actually occurring will be discussed later.)

At the same time, many *dependencistas* contend that in the global market, because there are often many sellers of raw materials and few buyers (a condition known as **monopsony**), it is easier for the buyers to impose artificially low prices. According to dependency theory, this "monopsony power" creates a buyers' market in which Northern buyers can hold down the prices of Southern primary goods. To give one example, sales of bananas in the United States, Western Europe, and Japan are dominated by three corporations. When banana-producing countries formed the Union of Banana Exporting Countries (UBEC) and tried to impose an export tax in 1974, the buyers refused to purchase bananas from participating countries, stopped production at their plantations, and destroyed crates of bananas at the ports. Eventually, the banana-exporting countries backed down and the taxes were withdrawn.[12]

Multinational Corporations Typically, multinational corporations (MNCs), large corporations that have branches in many countries (see Chapter Nine), have their headquarters in the North, but many invest in, own, and/or operate factories and subsidiaries in the South as well. MNCs and foreign investment are nothing new. European firms made huge investments in the developing United States in the nineteenth century, and by the early 1890s several American manufacturers, such as Singer, American Bell, and Standard Oil, had manufacturing investments and plants overseas.[13] Some MNCs, such as General Motors, IBM, Toyota, British Petroleum, and Siemens, are corporate giants, with total sales rivaling or surpassing the GNP of many countries. In 1988, forty-one of the world's one hundred largest economic units were MNCs, and General Motors' sales amounted to more than the GNPs of such countries as Finland, Denmark, Indonesia, Argentina, or South Africa.[14] MNCs also wield a tremendous amount of power within developing countries, particularly because of their control over manufacturing in the Third World. At one time, for example, MNCs controlled 70 percent of the manufacturing industry in Nigeria, 50 percent in Ghana, and 44 percent in Malaysia.[15]

Modernization theorists contend that MNCs promote development in the South, providing capital, technology, training, and managerial know-how to Southern states. Dependency theorists, however, challenge this benevolent view of MNCs. They contend that MNCs exploit the South, hinder its development, and contribute to the widening of the gap between rich and poor. According to dependency theory, MNCs have replaced the colonial system as the primary means of penetrating the South and extracting wealth from the Third World. Three primary complaints are as follows:

First, MNCs avoid paying their share of taxes by bookkeeping and accounting tricks devised to increase profits and minimize tax burdens. Because they have subsidiaries throughout the world, MNCs are able to use transfer-pricing mechanisms to transfer profits to countries where taxes are lower. Here is one author's description of a transfer-pricing scheme:

> A U.S. manufacturer, for instance, might produce parts in a factory located in Texas but ship these parts to a plant in Mexico for assembly. In turn, the assembled product is transported back to the United States for final sale. The price that the home firm charges the Mexican subsidiary for the parts or that the subsidiary charges the home firm for the assembled product is essentially arbitrary since these transactions take place within the same company and are not exposed to market forces. If, let us say, Mexico imposes a higher tax on corporate profits than does the United States, then the MNC can lower its overall tax bill by overpricing the parts shipped to Mexico while underpricing the assembled products that are "sold" back to the home firm in the United States. By manipulating the prices on intra-firm trade in this way, the Mexican subsidiary will show little profit on its books, thus avoiding the high Mexican tax rate, while the profit of the home firm will be artificially boosted—allowing it to be taxed at the low U.S. rate.[16]

Of course, MNCs use **transfer pricing** to avoid taxes in industrialized countries as well. In addition, dependency theorists claim, MNCs remove scarce capital from the South by charging royalties and licensing fees for manufacturing products on which they hold copyrights and patents (as they do in the North). Finally, through bribery and lobbying, MNCs prevail upon Third World legislators to give them special tax breaks. For instance, when Honduras imposed a tax on the export of bananas, United Brands (formerly United Fruit) bribed a government official to reduce the tax.[17] In short, *dependencistas* claim that many business practices—legal and illegal—carried out by MNCs all over the globe cause more harm when they are applied in the resource-poor developing world.

Second, the technology that MNCs transfer to the South is often not appropriate for the region. In many instances, it is **capital-intensive** technology, which relies on expensive equipment and highly skilled workers and therefore does little to lower the often very high Southern unemployment rates. In addition, imported technology may stunt the development of local technology, discourage local research and development, and drive out local entrepreneurs. Developing areas, according to the dependency school, often don't need high technology—instead, they need appropriate technology that can be produced locally, run and maintained by local workers, and adapted to Third World conditions.

Thirds, MNCs do not bring capital into the Third World, but instead often set up businesses that use up the limited supply of local capital. Bank loans to MNCs mean less money is available for local entrepreneurs to borrow. By using local capital, MNCs crowd out local entrepreneurs, and competition from MNCs often destroys existing domestic industries.[18] In addition, top managers of MNC

In the post–Cold War era, investment has replaced aid and military intervention as the prime source of great-power interest in the Third World.

SOURCE: Efeu/Nebelspalter/Rorschach, Switzerland

operations are often brought from the parent country, not recruited in the host country.

In general, dependency theorists allege that MNCs can control and manipulate the production of primary commodities in developing countries; in so doing, they act as the North's instruments of control and subjugation over the South. This "neocolonial" exploitation of the developing world is actually more efficient and more profitable than the colonial system under which the United States and the European powers dominated most of Asia, Africa, and Latin America before World War II. Dependency theory concludes that although Third World states may have achieved political independence, they cannot achieve economic sovereignty because they are kept in a dependent state by the capitalist world economy.

Critiques of Dependency Theory Dependency theory has been criticized on a number of fronts.[19] The foremost criticism is that it has been proven false by the fact that a number of Southern states have managed to industrialize and have done so with the help of Northern investment and trade with developed states. These NICs, particularly the East Asian Tigers, have large, vibrant, and diversified industrial sectors and improving standards of living. By pursuing a strategy promoting the export of manufactured goods instead of isolating themselves from the global economic system, they have embraced international trade as a means of growth. (For more on their strategy, see the discussion on export-led growth in the next section.)

Second, the plight of primary product exporters may not be as bad as dependency theorists claim. Although world prices for primary commodities (except oil) have tended to decline since 1973, many developing countries that have improved productivity in their primary product industries have achieved substantial economic growth. Commodity producers that boosted agricultural productivity and lowered barriers to foreign trade and investment, such as Malaysia, Thailand, and Chile, have used primary product exports as a springboard to diversified economic development. By contrast, countries that raised barriers to imports of agricultural machinery and imposed export taxes on farm products (as have many in Africa) have remained dependent on primary products and lost market share to more efficient producers.[20]

Moreover, although dependency theory contends that the terms of trade are declining for the South, the data do not clearly support this contention. Table 8.3 shows the changes in the terms of trade for low- and middle-income countries in developing regions, oil-exporting countries, and the developed OECD states from 1965 to 1986. Although some regions or categories of countries have gone through periods of sharp declines in terms of trade (such as sub-Saharan Africa in 1965–1973 and the oil exporters in 1980–1986), the table shows that both developing and developed countries have experienced periods of declining terms of trade.

The table does indicate, however, that the terms of trade for developing countries generally tend to fluctuate more than those of the developed North. (Notice the sharp drop in the terms of trade of oil exporters between 1973–1980 and 1980–1986, reflecting the global oil boom of the 1970s and bust of the 1980s.) Once more, this may be attributed to greater reliance on primary products (with prices often subject to change without notice) in the South, while most industrialized Northern countries have diversified economies less vulnerable to sudden changes in prices. Apparently, economic downturns and business cycles hurt both industrializing and developed states alike, though underdeveloped Southern countries may be hurt more.

Third, dependency theory lays the blame for the South's poverty squarely on the North, with little if any discussion of factors within the developing world

Table 8.3	Average Annual Percentage Change in Terms of Trade, 1965–1986		
Country Group	1965–1973	1973–1980	1980–1986
Sub-Saharan Africa	−8.5	4.8	−4.0
East Asia	−0.6	1.2	−1.3
South Asia	3.7	−3.4	1.5
Latin America	3.8	2.3	−3.3
Oil exporters	0.3	11.5	−7.3
OECD members	−1.0	−3.3	1.1

SOURCE: World Bank, *World Development Report 1990* (New York: Oxford University Press, 1990), p. 165

At a Glance

Contending Theories of Development

Modernization Theory

Definition
Contends that the most important factors contributing to development, and the primary causes of underdevelopment, can be found within the Southern states themselves. A traditional society is depicted as a peasant village where generations pass on their customs, rituals, and folkways to each new generation. Modern societies, in contrast, are more urban, dynamic, flexible, and innovative, and ready and willing to adapt. To develop, Southern societies must undergo the same process of transition from traditionalism to modernity previously experienced by the states of the North.

Obstacles
The fundamental obstacle to development is traditional culture, which can block the societal transformations necessary for rapid economic growth. Religion, aristocratic authority, and the rural lifestyle are more prominent in traditional societies and are difficult to change because of their resistance to change itself.

Necessary Changes
Politically, the emergence of democracy, the rule of law, political opposition, human rights, and basic freedoms are vital. Socially, this requires the ability to achieve status through merit or success (rather than birth or caste) and the tolerance of social and intellectual diversity. Economically, development means the creation of a market-based economy, in which some degree of state intervention for social reasons is possible and desirable. Trade is vital for economic growth.

Problems
A high death rate leads to a high birthrate. Women in many underdeveloped areas are compelled by social conventions to marry young and bear as many children as possible to help with the labor of farming. These children are also expected to care for their elderly parents. When new drugs reduce infant mortality, a population explosion results. With so many new mouths to feed, clothe, shelter, and educate, the economy and society are put under enormous strain, with little left over for investment. Many children are sent to the urban area to find work, which leads to urbanization. As a result, the cities are overwhelmed and overcrowded; and acutely poor and persistently crime-prone shantytowns evolve. Although difficult, this process is seen as necessary.

Critiques
Its critics question whether the North's path of development can be duplicated by the South. Also, critics suggest that because traditional social and political institutions are so difficult to change, perhaps the attempt to change them is misguided. Others contend that modernization theory is Eurocentric. Finally, some believe that the structure of the international trading system is biased against the South, and that historically wealth has not flowed from the rich states to the poor states through trade and aid, but in fact the opposite has occurred.

itself that contribute to economic stagnation and poverty. There can be little doubt that domestic factors such as rapid population growth, high rates of illiteracy, and corruption are partly responsible for persistent poverty and underdevelopment.

Critics of the dependency school do not seek to "blame the victims" for underdevelopment. They recognize the disadvantages of heavy dependence on primary-

Dependency Theory

Definition

It emphasizes the international context, contending that international institutions, multinational corporations, and the states of the First World have deliberately kept the Third World in a dependent condition. Dependency theory draws many of its insights on the relations between the North and South from a branch of Marxist thought.

Obstacles

It argues that the existing international economic system is inherently biased against the South. This fundamental inequality of the economic relationship between the North and South fueled development in the North and stifled it in the South.

Necessary Changes

Southern nations need to diversify their product lines. Although some products are booming on the international market, others are not. As a result, those nations that produce a primary product that is not in high demand face difficult times. Theorists believe that the nations of the South need to produce manufactured goods and diversify their export products. The unequal terms of trade will thus be altered and must continue to change. Governments must limit the amount of exploitation that multinational corporations commit.

Problems

The disadvantaged position of the South stems from the fact that most Southern countries' economies depend heavily on the export of primary products. These include raw materials such as timber, oil, and metals, and agricultural goods such as coffee and bananas. Dependency theorists view this as the **international division of labor,** in which the South does the "dirty work." Furthermore, the economies of many of these primary-product producers are dominated by a single commodity. Thus, they lack diversity in the goods and services that they can export. These economies can easily go through periods of booms and busts. Theorists also argue that the terms of trade are against the South—the value of the products that they import is greater than the value of the products that they export. Consequently, they will lose money. These situations must be changed. Dependency theorists believe that multinational corporations exploit the South, hinder its development, and contribute to the widening of the gap between rich and poor.

Critiques

Critics of dependency theory argue that a number of Southern states have managed to industrialize and have done so with the help of Northern investment and trade with developed states. Furthermore, it is unclear whether a number of dependency theory's assumptions can be substantiated. Specifically, while dependency theory contends that the terms of trade are declining for the South, the data do not clearly support this contention. Critics also believe that dependency theorists lay the blame for the South's poverty squarely on the North, with little if any discussion of factors within the developing world itself that contribute to economic stagnation and poverty.

product exports and realize the extent of poverty and suffering in the developing world. They also offer a ready solution to the problems of underdevelopment: develop! As we have seen, however, this is far more easily said than done. The next part of this chapter discusses how Southern countries have tried to tackle the problem of development, with varying degrees of success.

DEVELOPMENT STRATEGIES

Our discussion of theories of development has highlighted the daunting internal and external obstacles Southern states must overcome in order to achieve their development goals. Given the geographic, ethnic, and political diversity of developing countries, it should come as no surprise that they have adopted a variety of development strategies. The sources of ideas for development have been numerous. Many developed countries, such as the United States, Britain, France, Sweden, and Japan, have offered examples, recommendations, and aid for various development programs. China and the now defunct Soviet Union also extended advice and assistance to the South, particularly in the 1950s, 1960s, and 1970s. There has thus been no lack of ideas or experimentation in the field of development. Four decades of experience have made the costs and benefits of various models of development relatively clear, but have not made the economic, environmental, and social tradeoffs associated with each model any easier. This section describes and evaluates how development strategies have fared in practice.

Alternative Strategies

There are three general trading strategies that Third World states have used to pursue their development goals: **import-substitution industrialization, export-led industrialization,** and collective bargaining among Southern states. Import-substitution industrialization (ISI), a strategy followed by numerous developing states after World War II, seeks to promote domestic industries by reducing imports from the North. Some of the states that initially adopted this strategy later turned toward export-led industrialization (ELI), which promotes growth through trade in the global market. Finally, during the 1970s a number of Third World states sought to coordinate their efforts to change the international trading system, improve the terms of trade for primary product exporters, and establish the **New International Economic Order** (NIEO) through collective bargaining. Although each of these strategies has its merits and drawbacks, ELI has emerged as the strategy of choice for most successful developing states at the end of the twentieth century. This section will survey the positive and negative aspects of all three development strategies to see how this came about.

Import-Substitution Industrialization (ISI)

The global market is highly competitive, and industries struggling to get off the ground in the developing world often find it difficult to compete with established industries in the industrialized North. For this reason, many developing countries have at various times chosen to protect their infant industries from foreign competition and promote domestic production of goods that had formerly been imported. This import-substitution industrialization (ISI) strategy aims at greater economic self-sufficiency. To a large extent, the young United States pursued this policy throughout the nineteenth century; the high tariffs that protected Northern manufacturers were a major source of the antagonism between North and South that led to the Civil War. Many Latin American states were pressed to adopt de facto import substitution because of the collapse of international trade between the beginning of World War I and the end of World War II (see Chapters Three and Seven). Many of these countries continued to pursue such policies in the 1950s and 1960s.

ISI is a strategy of economic isolation intended to encourage domestic entrepreneurs to manufacture products otherwise imported from abroad. First, the exchange rate is overvalued, meaning that the rate at which currencies are exchanged makes imported goods relatively cheaper and exported goods relatively more expensive. Second, high tariff barriers are erected on consumer goods to block foreign competition. The intention is to make imports of capital goods (such as manufacturing equipment and spare parts) cheap while making imported consumer goods (such as automobiles and appliances) expensive, so that consumers will buy from domestic producers.

Most countries pursuing an ISI strategy initially experience growth in domestic industries that produce consumer goods, just as planned. The next stage of the strategy, sometimes called "deepening," is the development of manufacturing capabilities in intermediate industries such as steel. However, investments in these industries require more capital and more sophisticated technology from the North, and an overvalued exchange rate hurts exports, which are necessary to earn foreign capital. Consequently, in practice ISI has often led to massive borrowing from foreign banks and growing external debt, resulting in even greater dependence upon Northern states for capital.

The trouble with ISI is that it typically requires a great deal of foreign capital to create and subsidize domestic industries. Because ISI undermines the profitable export sector, it tends to lead to a balance-of-payments deficit (that is, the nation's economy cannot earn enough through exports to pay for the imports it needs—see Chapter Six.) This makes it difficult to purchase capital goods from industrialized countries, a problem that may defeat the whole purpose of the strategy.

Latin America offers the best examples of the successes and limitations of the ISI strategy.[21] The rapid decline in world trade that was a cause and effect of the Great Depression prompted Argentina, Brazil, and Chile to pursue de facto strategies of import substitution. In the years following World War II, ISI was formally adopted as a strategy of economic development and a way to reduce economic and political dependence. High tariffs were established to protect infant industries, and currencies were overvalued. The short-run impact was a shortage of foreign capital and a steep decline in the profitable export-oriented sector. Around 1960, through import and exchange controls, the initial, easy stage of industrialization characterized by the substitution of locally produced for imported consumer goods was successfully completed. In some cases, notably in Brazil, great strides were made in the domestic production of more durable consumer goods and some intermediate goods, including transportation and electronic equipment, metal fabrication, and chemicals.

The next stage of industrialization called for the development of capital goods, but as noted previously, these goods require substantial foreign investment and technical know-how. Because their export-oriented industries had declined as a result of the ISI strategy, Latin American countries lacked the foreign exchange necessary for the import of the appropriate technology from the North. This led to heavy foreign borrowing and severe indebtedness, which contributed to the "stalling out" of their industrial development.

In Africa, one country closely associated with import substitution was Tanzania, whose policies of *ujamaa* ("unity") and *kujitegamea* ("self-reliance") received great attention in the late 1960s. However, by the early 1980s Tanzania's economy was in severe crisis. Many of its state-owned industries were operating at roughly 10 percent capacity, and because farmers were taxed so heavily to pay for critical imports, agricultural exports fell. Essentially, after a period of initial success, ISI had stalled and failed once again.

In short, ISI has not been very successful at either emancipating the South from economic dependence or providing a basis for long-term economic development. In most instances, it has resulted in greater dependence upon capital and imports from the Northern industrialized states without raising the general standard of living in Southern countries.[22]

Export-Led Industrialization (ELI)

The second principal strategy of growth promotes industrialization through trade. Export-led industrialization (ELI) seeks to promote development by working within, rather than against, the global economic system. Its advice to developing countries on their relationship to the industrialized North is simple: "If you can't beat 'em, join 'em."

In the 1960s and 1970s, several developing countries, particularly Brazil and the newly industrialized countries of East Asia, adopted an ELI strategy by giving substantial economic incentives to firms to export their products, particularly by undervaluing their foreign exchange rates, which made their exports cheap and their imports expensive.[23] For Japan, South Korea, Taiwan, Hong Kong, and Singapore, export promotion has proven to be a major impetus for exceptionally rapid economic development. The results of this strategy are especially impressive in the East Asian Tigers (Hong Kong, Singapore, South Korea, and Taiwan). In the course of less than two generations, these countries have been transformed into industrialized nations poised to produce the high-tech products of the twenty-first century. Their tremendous growth rates have been accomplished through intensive state intervention in the economy and society, borrowing of technology from the industrialized North, and the promotion of research and development.

Figure 8.2 summarizes the results of this development strategy in economic terms, showing the high growth of trade and GNP in the Four Tigers since 1970. Although some average growth rates appear to dip during the 1980s, they remained higher than average OECD growth rates, let alone most other developing

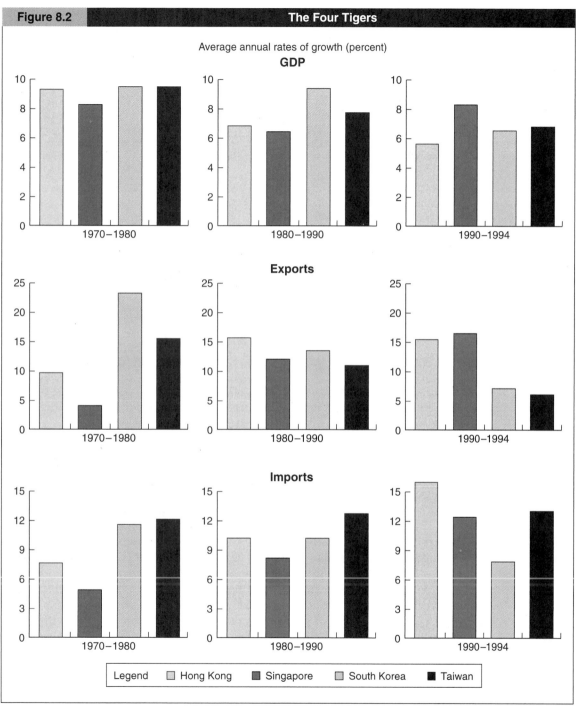

Figure 8.2 The Four Tigers

Average annual rates of growth (percent)

GDP

1970–1980　　1980–1990　　1990–1994

Exports

1970–1980　　1980–1990　　1990–1994

Imports

1970–1980　　1980–1990　　1990–1994

Legend　☐ Hong Kong　■ Singapore　☐ South Korea　■ Taiwan

SOURCE: *World Development Report 1996: From Plan to Market;* Republic of China Council for Economic Planning and Development, *Taiwan Statistical Data Book, 1997*

Spotlight

Rise and Fall of OPEC

OPEC, the Organization of Petroleum Exporting Countries, was formed in August 1960 with the purpose of gaining higher prices and greater control over production of member states' petroleum resources. OPEC's thirteen members were Algeria, Ecuador, Gabon, Indonesia, Iran, Iraq, Kuwait, Libya, Nigeria, Qatar, Saudi Arabia, the United Arab Emirates, and Venezuela. (However, in 1992 Ecuador withdrew from the organization.) The potency of the OPEC cartel was demonstrated to the world in 1973 when, in response to the Yom Kippur War, the Arab members of OPEC reduced production and embargoed oil to the United States and the Netherlands, countries considered pro-Israeli; then OPEC raised prices fourfold. OPEC's success encouraged other developing states to believe that they, too, could achieve control over their natural resources by forming similar cartels.

OPEC's pride, in many ways, led to its fall. In response to skyrocketing oil prices in the 1970s and the possibility of another embargo, industrialized countries reduced their demand for OPEC oil. This was accomplished by a combination of energy conservation efforts, the discovery of other sources of oil (in the North Sea and Mexico, for example) and the switch to alternative sources of energy (France, in particular, increased its reliance on nuclear power). In large part, these conditions were of OPEC's own making, as the price increases arranged by the cartel made the development of remote oil fields and alternative energy techniques more economically viable. Disagreements among OPEC members themselves also undermined OPEC's influence. Difficulties intensified over questions of pricing and production levels between states that had immense reserves (Saudi Arabia) and those with fewer reserves, and between those with larger and smaller populations. Political disagreements, as well, led to tensions, and in some cases open hostilities, most dramatically exemplified by the Iran-Iraq War of the 1980s and the long-term dispute between Iraq and Kuwait over oil fields that contributed to the Persian Gulf War in 1991. Although still a potentially powerful actor because of the continued importance of oil, OPEC has lost the prominent position it enjoyed in the mid-1970s.

countries. The standards of living, life expectancy, health, literacy, and educational levels in these countries have shown equally impressive improvement.[24]

Some theorists have argued that the success of the NICs cannot be duplicated elsewhere in the South, as those East Asian nations have saturated trading opportunities with the North to such an extent that other Southern countries have been squeezed out.[25] In essence, this perspective argues that trading opportunities with the North are a fixed sum, and thus the gain in trade by one developing country forecloses openings for other developing countries. This view has some merit; as prices rise, international primary-product markets can become glutted from increased production in other Southern countries. But global demand for most products is not static—as economies grow, they typically generate more demand for raw materials, consumer and capital goods, and services. It must also be noted that industrial development in the Four Tigers has had significant social and environmental costs, just as it has everywhere else.[26] (Chapter Ten discusses these problems in more detail.) The ELI strategy is therefore not a panacea for development by any means. Nevertheless, although the striking success of the Asian

---

What Would You Do ?

You are the king of Saudi Arabia in mid-October 1973. You desire a leading role in the Arab states' collective effort to punish the backers of Israel after the current war ends. Your energy minister has suggested a plan whereby the Arab members of the Organization of Petroleum Exporting Countries could impose an embargo on the shipment of oil to Israel's Western supporters (especially the United States and the Netherlands) to drive up the "true" costs of their support for Israel.

Collectively, OPEC controls 50 percent of the world's oil reserves. An oil embargo would dramatically increase the short-run price of oil, leading to higher energy costs and inflation in the Western industrialized economies (especially in Japan and in most of the European countries) and forcing the most vulnerable Western states to distance themselves from Israel, further isolating it. By raising the price of oil, the embargo could increase your own prosperity and allow you to demonstrate the international magnanimity of your royal house toward poorer Third World countries. This would augment the political influence of your conservative regime within the more radical nonaligned movement.

Conversely, by leading the oil embargo, your government would have to act as a "swing producer" (adjusting your own oil production levels to accommodate the desire of the more desperate OPEC nations for larger production quotas). In the short run, a desperate United States might decide to take military action if the pinch becomes too painful. In the long run, as your Western-educated economic advisors have also warned, an oil embargo could lead Western countries to develop their own sources of oil or other substitute energy sources. This would depress the price of oil and lead OPEC members to cheat by exceeding their production quotas. Still, Saudi Arabia would have to decrease its own production quota to maintain the ceiling on overall OPEC supply.

You want to balance these short-run and long-run considerations.

What would you do ?

NICs was slowed by currency crises and recession in 1998, opportunities for export-led growth are likely to exist for Southern countries as long as they have access to global markets.

New International Economic Order (NIEO)

In the early 1970s many Southern countries tried to pool their resources in order to press for changes in the international economic system. It was hoped that through collective bargaining, developing states could gain higher prices for primary-product exports and greater access to Northern markets. Proposals for

At a Glance

Strategies of Development

Import-Substitution Industrialization (ISI)

Definition

Many developing countries at various times choose to protect their "infant industries" from foreign competition and promote domestic production of goods that are imported. This strategy aims at greater economic self-sufficiency.

Process

First, high tariff barriers are erected on some goods to block foreign competition. Second, the exchange rate is overvalued, meaning that the rate at which currencies are exchanged make imports cheap and exports expensive. Tariffs are manipulated so that foreign consumer goods become expensive and capital goods become cheap. The next stage is the development of manufacturing capabilities in intermediate industries such as steel. The following stage calls for the development of capital goods, but as noted above these goods require substantial foreign investment and technical know-how.

Evaluation

In short, import substitution has not been very successful at either emancipating the South from eco-

nomic dependence or in providing a basis for long-term economic development. In most instances, ISI has resulted in greater dependence upon capital and imports from the Northern industrialized states without raising the general standard of living in Southern countries.

Export-Led Industrialization (ELI)

Definition

Development is promoted by working within, rather than against, the global economic agenda. This strategy's advice to developing countries on their relationship to the industrialized North is simple: "If you can't beat 'em, join 'em."

Process

In the 1960s and 1970s, several developing countries adopted an export promotion strategy by giving substantial economic incentives to firms to export their products, particularly by undervaluing their foreign exchange rates, which made their exports cheap and their imports expensive. The results of this strategy are especially impressive in the East Asian Tigers (Hong Kong, Singapore, South Korea, and Taiwan). In less than two generations, these countries have

solidarity among Southern nations culminated in the call for a New International Economic Order (NIEO) issued by a group of developing states (the Group of 77) at a special session of the United Nations in 1974.[27] The NIEO movement was inspired by dependency theory, which (as we saw earlier in this chapter) contends that declining terms of trade for primary-product exporters and control of industries in developing countries by multinational corporations keeps the developing South subordinate to and dependent upon the industrialized North. NIEO advocates sought to exploit industrialized countries' dependence upon primary goods from the South and thus turn the tables on the North.

During the 1960s and 1970s, many Southern countries nationalized their mineral and agricultural export sectors, wresting control of these industries from multinational corporations. Although no single Third World country controlled enough of any primary commodity to restrict supplies, many Southern countries hoped to increase their collective-bargaining power by forming **commodity**

been transformed into industrialized nations poised to produce the high-tech products of the twenty-first century. Their tremendous growth (until the late 1990s) was accomplished through intensive state intervention in the economy and society, borrowing of technology from the industrialized North, and the promotion of research and development.

Evaluation

Some theorists have argued that the success of the NICs cannot be duplicated elsewhere in the South, as East Asian NICs have saturated trading opportunities with the North to such an extent that other Southern countries have been squeezed out. But global demand for most products is not static—as economies grow, they typically generate more demand for raw materials, consumer and capital goods, and services. Opportunities are likely to exist as long as markets remain open.

Collective Bargaining (NIEO)

Definition

Using this process, many Southern countries tried to pool their resources in order to press for changes in the international economic system in the early 1970s. It was hoped that the developing states could gain higher prices for primary product exports and greater access to Northern markets.

Process

Proposals for solidarity among Southern nations culminated in the call for a New International Economic Order (NIEO), issued by a group of developing states (the Group of 77) at a special session of the United Nations in 1974. The NIEO movement was inspired by dependency theory, which contends that declining terms of trade for primary product exporters—and control of industries in developing countries by multinational corporations—keep the developing South subordinate to and dependent upon the industrialized North. NIEO advocates sought to exploit industrialized countries' dependence upon primary goods from the South and thus "turn the tables" on the North.

Evaluation

By the end of the 1980s, repeated failures to improve primary product exporters' terms of trade prompted most countries to conclude that collective bargaining was no substitute for the development of a diversified economy. The problem of exactly how to achieve economic growth, however, remained.

cartels. The members of these cartels hoped to duplicate the success of the Organization of Petroleum Exporting Countries (OPEC) in raising the price of oil and achieving control over their own natural resources by reducing the power of multinational oil companies (see the boxed feature on OPEC). If collective action by oil exporters could be effective, why not try collective action by exporters of coffee, copper, bauxite, or bananas?

However, many would-be cartelizers soon found that other primary materials did not lend themselves to similar results. OPEC's success was due to the pivotal role petroleum plays in the world economy and the geographic accident of the distribution of oil reserves. By the late twentieth century, the supply of oil was concentrated in the hands of a few states. In 1970, for example, OPEC members accounted for 90 percent of world oil exports.[28] Oil also was, and remains, a resource of critical importance to industrialized nations. Coffee, sugar, rubber, and so forth, are not as critical as oil, and alternative sources or substitutes are more easily found. Also, controlling production and coordinating policy are much more difficult when there are many producers. Therefore, the commodity cartels' bargaining position was far weaker than OPEC's.

The Group of 77 (which never changed its name, though it grew to over 120 members) called for other measures, including **buffer stocks** and compensatory pricing mechanisms, to stabilize commodity prices.[29] By the end of the 1980s, however, repeated failures to improve primary-product exporters' terms of trade prompted most countries to conclude that collective bargaining was no substitute for the development of a diversified economy. The problem of exactly how to achieve economic growth, however, remained, which led analysts in both North and South to reconsider the roles of trade and international assistance in promoting growth and development.

AID AND DEVELOPMENT

In the late 1940s the United States recognized the need to jump-start the reconstruction of war-torn Europe in order to forestall political extremism. The Marshall Plan provided billions of dollars in assistance, and by the 1950s Western Europe was enjoying an "economic miracle." The success of the Marshall Plan led many people in and out of government around the world to believe that international aid might be a critical means by which development could be initiated or accelerated in many Southern countries. Since World War II, international aid has been provided in essentially three forms: bilateral, multilateral, and private.

In the 1950s, 1960s, and 1970s, the United States, as well as many other countries in the North, extended significant economic assistance directly to many developing countries—a process called **bilateral aid.** Moreover, the United Nations agencies that were set up to facilitate the rebuilding of Europe—the International Bank of Reconstruction and Development (the World Bank) and the International Monetary Fund (IMF)—gradually turned their focus from war reconstruction to the problems of development in the South and thus have become the principal distributors of **multilateral aid.** Finally, outside official government channels, **private aid** has been provided by nongovernmental organizations (NGOs) such as the Red Cross, Save the Children, Oxfam, and CARE. In short, an entire infrastructure of international development assistance sprang up after World War II. Each form of assistance, however, has its own agenda and problems.

Bilateral Aid

In the case of bilateral aid, direct aid in the form of grants or loans from a single developed country is provided to a specific developing state, especially when it is a victim of natural disaster or it suffers from severe defense burdens. Today the importance of bilateral aid to development has been downgraded, primarily because the success of the Marshall Plan has not been replicated in developing countries despite the transfer of billions of dollars of resources. Indeed, foreign aid is often harshly criticized for becoming something like an international form of welfare that inhibits economic initiative and encourages corruption within the South. Often, it seems that the more aid a country receives, the worse it does.

For many low-income countries, aid has become a significant percentage of GNP. A glance at some data shows that in extreme cases, foreign-aid receipts can account for more than one-half of a poor nation's GNP. Some of the most extreme cases are Guinea-Bissau, where in 1994 official development assistance equaled 74 percent of GNP, and Mozambique and Rwanda, where development aid that same year actually exceeded GNP.[30] In the long run, such huge infusions of aid are unhealthy for a country's economy, as recipient states come to depend on foreign assistance and lack incentives to develop local production. Too much aid can also allow countries to delay necessary reforms (such as breaking up huge plantations into smaller farmer-owned plots, selling state-owned enterprises to private investors—**privatization**—and allowing prices to reflect supply and demand) by subsidizing bureaucracies or elites who look after their own narrow interests. By contrast, the end of significant direct American aid to South Korea in the late 1950s induced the government to initiate economic reforms that became the basis for South Korea's spectacular economic success.

Bilateral aid has other drawbacks from the points of view of both donors and recipients. Many citizens of developed countries question whether development assistance is a worthwhile use of tax money. Most opinion polls in the United States indicate that foreign aid is the least popular of the federal government's expenditures, and consequently, American aid in terms of a percentage of GNP has steadily decreased. In 1965, for instance, the United States spent 0.26 percent of its GNP on development assistance to low-income countries, while in 1995 it spent only 0.1 percent of GNP on such endeavors, ranking last among the 21 member states of the OECD Development Assistance Committee. (Denmark ranked first, spending 0.97 percent of its GNP on development aid.) The United States remains one of the largest donors, however. In 1995, the U.S. provided $7.3 billion in development assistance, ranking fourth among OECD countries behind Japan (which gave $15.5 billion), France ($8.4 billion) and Germany ($7.5 billion).[31] America's economic leadership also enables it to act quickly to alleviate acute financial crises in Southern countries, as it did when the Mexican peso was threatened with collapse in 1995. The end of the Cold War may increase demands to redirect American foreign aid resources from security assistance to economic and humanitarian aid, but U.S. leaders will have to make this case before Congress and the American public (see Chapter Twelve).

Multilateral Aid

The drawbacks of bilateral aid have led to a rise in multilateral aid, in which aid is channeled to many countries through international organizations. **Multilateral** aid is still official, or public, assistance because the providing agencies are funded and supervised by two or more governments pooling their resources.

Two UN agencies in particular, the World Bank and the International Monetary Fund, have become the chief sources of development assistance and technical economic advice for most Southern countries, as well as for Eastern Europe and the former Soviet Union. (See Chapter Nine for more on the World Bank and IMF.) These organizations provide billions of dollars worth of financial assistance (mostly long-term loans at favorable interest rates) every year, but that is only one aspect of their influence. The financial contributions of their member states determine voting rights, and given that virtually all the capital is provided by the United States, Western Europe, and Japan, these two agencies generally reflect the economic policy preferences of the industrialized North. However, because they are independent of any single government and are affiliated with the UN, they are perceived as being more politically neutral by many Southern states, and they also provide a forum for Southern concerns. Importantly, the World Bank and the IMF do not lend money directly for military purposes, but instead focus exclusively on economic development. (Of course, providing funds for economic projects frees up resources for other purposes.)

The Debt Crisis

In the early 1970s, multinational banks were awash with huge sums of "petrodollars" deposited by the newly rich nations of OPEC. The banks "recycled" the petrodollars by making loans to developing countries on generous terms, thereby providing Third World states with badly needed capital while earning substantial profits for themselves. When oil prices soared again after 1979, however, the resulting worldwide recession prompted banks to tighten up their terms for loans to developing states and, simultaneously, reduced the demand for many exports from the developing world.

By the 1980s, therefore, many Third World countries found themselves with an enormous debt burden piled up during the "easy money" years of the petrodollar period. In many of these states, foreign debt totaled 400 to 3000 percent of annual export earnings, and a large proportion of their foreign exchange earnings went for the repayment of old loans.[32] As private investment began to dry up, heavily indebted nations were caught in a ruinous financial trap. They were faced with three basic options, all of them bad: squeeze domestic consumption and investment to pay their foreign creditors, borrow new money to pay off old debts, or default on their loans. In a sense, their "credit cards" were "maxed out"—they had reached the limits of their allowable debt, and needed to borrow more money just to make the payments. The situation was precarious for lenders as well, because if big Third World debtors such as Mexico, Argentina, and Brazil had defaulted on their loans, multinational banks could have lost billions of dollars, which might have precipitated a global financial panic.[33]

The IMF and World Bank stepped in by providing short- and long-term loans to developing countries to get them out of their debt fix. However, debt relief came with strings attached, in an arrangement referred to as **conditionality.** As a condition of receiving financial assistance, the debtor countries had to undertake structural-adjustment policies approved by the lending institutions. Usually, these policies included the opening of markets to imports, devaluation of overvalued currencies, cutting government spending, reducing price controls and subsidies, and reducing direct state ownership of industries. These free-market-oriented reforms are often unpopular when they are first instituted, as they frequently require cutting government jobs and reducing the subsidies on food that keep the prices of staple foods low for urban consumers.

In 1989, the IMF began brokering packages of payment rescheduling and partial debt forgiveness for countries that agreed to carry out programs of **structural adjustment.** This arrangement, known as the Brady Plan, was named after its chief proponent, U.S. Treasury Secretary Nicholas Brady. Five years later, roughly 80 percent of the money lent by commercial banks to developing countries had been restructured. By working with Northern lenders and Southern borrowers, the IMF and the World Bank helped prevent the debt crisis of the 1980s from turning into a global financial disaster.

The IMF and World Bank recognize the hardships that structural adjustment often entails, but they see them as necessary changes to make it possible for debtor countries to pay back the loans, attract private investment in the future, and reorient economies for long-term growth. However, many debtor governments resent these policies and view conditionality as foreign meddling. In some cases, structural-adjustment policies have led to violent protests, as in Venezuela in 1989 when rising food prices sparked off riots that killed 300 people and injured more than 1000. Some countries attempt to unilaterally "cap" payments, or simply default on their loans, but when Peru tried this in the 1980s, it quickly ran out of foreign exchange and was forced to borrow more money under even more restrictive conditions to pay for essential imports. Similarly, popular resentment of IMF conditions, and official reluctance to implement them, contributed to widespread unrest in Indonesia in 1998.

Like it or not, many debt-strapped countries have little recourse but to accede to conditionality because of their great need for foreign capital. Private investment often shuns Southern countries that do not meet IMF- and World Bank–conditioned targets on policy reform. Moreover, the World Bank in particular has specialized in the analysis of development, carrying out studies and collecting economic information that few countries would have provided to any single other country or private concern. (That is why so much of the data used in this chapter comes from World Bank development reports.) Technical expertise coupled with financial resources have given the World Bank and IMF enormous political clout in their own right; most contemporary development debates, for instance, are centered on how swiftly and how far "structural adjustment" should go, not on whether the changes are essential. Of course, many Southern countries would prefer to set their own development agendas and avoid borrowing from the IMF and the World Bank. As they are often essentially bankrupt, however, they must negotiate with the North for assistance, and that job has been taken on by these agencies.

Private Aid

There is one other major means by which development assistance is transferred to the South: private organizations and other nongovernmental organizations (NGOs) (see Chapter Nine for more on NGOs). This type of assistance is not tied to any particular government directly and thus is considered private. Unlike governments or the IMF or World Bank, which usually seek to promote economic development with their major development projects and loans, NGOs typically emphasize humanitarian aid. Moreover, unlike official assistance, which generally comes in the form of loans, private assistance usually is given as grants that need not be paid back directly.

Private aid is hardly a new idea. Throughout the era of European imperialism, religious missionaries often provided what now would be considered development assistance, particularly in the fields of health and education by building schools and hospitals. Since World War II, a wide variety of humanitarian private organizations have established international aid programs. Some organizations, like *Medecins sans Frontiers* ("Doctors without Borders") and the Red Cross, move from one crisis area to another, attempting to distribute food and medical supplies to victims and refugees of famine, floods, and wars, while others, like CARE and Save the Children, attempt to alleviate chronic problems in many countries.

NGOs rely mostly on private donations from individual citizens in the North and distribute their aid directly to individuals in the South, thus bypassing official channels at both ends. With the rising global concern about overpopulation, the global environment, and the spread of diseases like AIDS, these humanitarian, health, and environmental organizations translate the concerns of their memberships and donors into pragmatic action. In many cases, they are seeking to fill voids left by lack of official action by governments in both the North and South. Their efforts are largely stop-gap in nature, although some would argue that this is all that ever can be expected of international aid.

Evaluating Aid

Developing countries often complain that the largest problem with bilateral aid is that it is almost always driven more by political concerns than by any humanitarian or economic criteria. Typically, military assistance forms a major aspect of bilateral aid. During the Cold War, the United States and the USSR both used development assistance to further their geopolitical and strategic interests. Though some of its interests have changed, the United States continues this practice in the post–Cold War era, sending large amounts of aid to Egypt and Israel for the sake of political and strategic stability in the Middle East. Similarly, Pakistan received generous amounts of American aid in the 1980s, largely because of its permission to use Pakistani bases to funnel U.S. military supplies to the Afghan guerrillas— the *mujahideen*—in their struggle against the Soviet Union (see Chapter Four). After the Soviets withdrew, aid to Pakistan was suspended because of the country's nuclear program. Turkey, because of its close proximity to the Soviet Union at a critical strategic crossroads was likewise a major recipient of U.S. aid, as were the Philippines, mostly because of the huge naval and air bases that the United States established there during its period of colonial rule and maintained as a means of projecting American military might toward East Asia. These bases were shut down in late 1992, when the U.S. and Philippine governments could not agree on the amount of aid the United States would provide in exchange for permission to continue using the bases.

Other developed countries have displayed similar political objectives in their aid programs. Virtually all French development assistance goes to former French colonies in West and Central Africa in what some have referred to as a neocolonial relationship. Britain sends most of its development aid to poorer countries in the Commonwealth of Nations, which is composed of most of the countries that once made up the British Empire. Of course, when political and strategic objectives override any economic concern, such assistance is not likely to spur economic growth.

A second complaint by the Third World is that bilateral aid is often tied to the purchase of products from the donor country, even in instances in which aid takes the form of a loan. This requirement forces Third World countries to purchase goods that might not be the most appropriate or the cheapest available. This policy benefits manufacturers in the donor country and promotes future orders for spare parts and other equipment. One source calculates that over two-thirds of bilateral aid is tied.[34] Of Germany's $1.4 billion in bilateral aid in 1986, for instance, 86 percent was earmarked for the purchase of German goods, and 80 percent of Japanese aid was tied in this way.[35] Strings can be tied to bilateral aid in other ways. Many Japanese-funded road-building projects in Latin America, for example, are designed to open forest areas to logging in order to ensure a steady supply of logs to Japanese industries.

A third problem in foreign aid has been the North's preference for big projects over smaller ones.[36] Large, visible projects such as dams or port facilities often win over less visible projects such as health care, schools, and agricultural programs, because they are more easily identified with the donor, and the donor therefore receives more credit and publicity. In many cases, the unfortunate result has been the construction of huge "white elephants" of dubious value. Perhaps the biggest white elephant of all was the Aswan Dam on the Nile in southern Egypt. Egyptian President Nasser (see Chapter Five) played the Soviet Union and the United States off against each other in attempting to finance the dam. In so doing, Egypt got the dam financed and built by the Soviets, but along the way the project increased U.S.–Soviet competition, setting the stage for the Suez Crisis of 1956. And, the dam itself may be doing more long-term harm than good to Egypt's economy and environment, as it has reduced the productivity of downstream farms and accelerated the erosion of scarce arable land.[37]

As the 1990s have progressed, the white-elephant syndrome has lessened as environmental concerns have been raised about big projects like dams and highways being constructed through sensitive rain forests (see Chapter Ten). Indeed, there now seems to be growing coordination among aid donors as bilateral and UN donors increasingly channel aid through NGOs and local development groups in Southern countries. The watchword for development aid in the next century may be "small is beautiful" as Southern governments, private donors, and international organizations work with communities in the developing world on projects designed to fulfill local needs rather than national ambitions. Official and private aid to developing countries will clearly continue to play a vital role, but disenchanting experiences with aid in both the North and South seem likely to prompt the exploration of other alternatives.

DEVELOPMENT DEBATES OF THE 1990S AND BEYOND

It has been said that "success has many fathers, while failure is an orphan." In the field of development, success typically generates many imitators in a kind of bandwagon effect. The East Asian NICs, who have pursued an ELI strategy, have been the most successful developers (see Figure 8.2). In the late 1980s and early 1990s, many diverse developing countries adopted trading policies remarkably similar to the policies of the Four Tigers in the 1960s and 1970s. China eased its dogmatic Maoist opposition to capitalism and opened up many areas to foreign investment. Turkey sought membership in the EU, hoping that this would expand its trading opportunities. Even India, formerly committed to economic self-sufficiency, reduced its legendary bureaucratic barriers to imports and exports, and its new openness has contributed to substantial economic gains in the 1980s and 1990s.

Though many countries thus agreed that ELI offers good prospects for development, many developing states face serious problems of market access. Without open markets, particularly in developed states, exports cannot flourish. Indeed, one of the arguments for ISI in the interwar period was rampant protectionism in many of the major trading states (see Chapter Seven). Getting some countries, especially Japan and the members of the EU, to open their domestic markets to the exports of developing states has been far from easy. To date, only the United States has allowed truly open access to the exports of many developing nations. Consequently, the success of Taiwan, South Korea, Singapore, Thailand, Malaysia, and many other successful developers was based in large part on their ability to export to the American market.

One of the critical reasons why the United States allowed the East Asian NICs access to its huge domestic market was that they were perceived as "bulwarks against communism" in Asia. With the end of the Cold War, this political rationale for open markets is no longer pertinent. Instead, the debate in the United States has shifted to the domestic consequences of free trade, which effectively integrates First World economies with Third World economies. Recent controversies over the U.S. extension of most-favored-nation status (see Chapter Seven) to China and the North American Free Trade Agreement highlight the problems and opportunities of North-South trade. In both cases, the debate has centered on whether the economic benefits of increased trade outweigh the social costs and political dilemmas.

China: Should Free Trade Require Freedom?

During the 1980s the People's Republic of China, for the first time since the Communists seized power in 1949, opened many of its coastal regions to significant foreign investment. In the process, many profitable trading relationships were established, and the United States extended most-favored-nation (MFN) tariff rates to Chinese exports. It looked as if China and the United States had turned the corner on what had been a very hostile relationship (see Chapters Four and Six).

However, in May 1989 many Chinese students demonstrated in Tiananmen Square, in the heart of Beijing, for greater democratization in China's political system. The Chinese government responded by sending in soldiers and tanks to massacre hundreds of peaceful demonstrators. After the massacre, many in the United States called for the end of MFN status for China because of the Tiananmen incident and other human rights abuses. It was further pointed out that some Chinese exports were made by prison labor and thus could not be legally imported into the United States. China's repression of ethnic Tibetans was also offered as proof of Chinese political intransigence. Why, many Americans asked, should the United States extend the benefits of free trade to a nation governed by a repressive Communist regime?

The Bush and Clinton administrations, however, opposed the end of MFN status for China and resisted congressional efforts to revoke it. Many U.S. interest groups also favored continued extension of MFN to China. The Boeing corporation, for example, sells dozens of airplanes worth hundreds of millions of dollars to China's growing airline industry. Since 1993, the Clinton administration has separated MFN from human rights, but under continuing pressure from Congress, that it will promise try to convince China to improve its human rights record. When elections on Taiwan raised tensions with the mainland to near-crisis levels in 1996, critics of China's policies redoubled their efforts to block MFN status, but it was renewed yet again in 1997.

China's authoritarianism, growing strategic power, and increasing political influence in East Asia (see Chapter Five) almost ensure that some level of political conflict over MFN will continue for the foreseeable future. Its rapidly expanding economy, however, is likely to attract foreign investment and increase demand for imports. Balancing the benefits of increased trade with China's abysmal human rights record will be far from easy for the United States, especially because many countries are prepared to simply ignore human rights violations in favor of profits.

Controversy over NAFTA

Like many other developing countries, Mexico in the 1980s radically changed the direction of its economic policies from heavy protectionism to more open economic links with the developed world—especially the United States. Mexico joined the General Agreement on Tariffs and Trade (GATT) in 1986 (see Chapter Seven), and since then has lowered tariffs and dramatically increased trade

Spotlight

Where Credit Is Due

The Grameen Bank, established in 1976, is considered by many to be the most successful program in eradicating poverty and promoting human rights in a developing country. The success of this program is attributed to the innovative approach to banking and credit taken by Muhammad Yunus, the creator of the Grameen project. Yunus challenged the "anti-poor, anti-landless, anti-illiterate, and anti-women" standards of other banks. The Grameen ("village") bank, which targets the poorest 50 percent of the population in Bangladesh, does not require collateral, credit history, or a co-signer or guarantor from the villagers. In lieu of these items, a member is required to join a five-member group and attend

Grameen Bank founder Mohammed Yunus visits a village benefiting from the bank's microloans.   SOURCE: Courtesy Muhammad Yunus/Grameen Bank, photo Salahuddin Azizee

with its northern neighbor. In the 1990s the United States, Canada, and Mexico negotiated the sweeping free trade pact known as the North American Free Trade Agreement. As well as an ambitious attempt to create a free-trade area, this agreement is an unprecedented experiment in integrating First and Third World economies.

The debate in the U.S. Congress and among the American people over NAFTA highlighted the difficulties of the agreement. Detractors pointed out that Mexican labor unions are controlled by the government, that Mexican wages are much

weekly meetings. Money is lent out on the basis of "social collateral," as each villager must assume the collective responsibility of all the loans extended to each member of her group.

The Grameen Bank works at an unconventional level of economic theory as well. Rather than pumping funds into the highest levels of the economy (the government or major corporations) the bank injects money at the foundations of the economic system—the poorest segment of the population. This "bubble-up" approach enables villagers to vastly improve their standards of living in the short run and provides hope for the future through investment within a limited range. In the past twenty years, the Bangladesh-based bank has extended loans in excess of $1.5 billion (half that amount has been lent in just the past two years) and instituted more than 1050 branches. The vast majority of its loans are very small, typically $100 or less, and are designed to finance home- or village-based businesses. The program serves over 2 million clients and maintains a loan repayment rate of over 97 percent. Significantly, 94 percent of the clients are women.

In a nation where women's rights are severely circumscribed by law and custom, the bank has been a torchbearer in improving basic human rights for women. The Grameen Bank, dedicated to serving the poor, could not ignore the fact that the poorest people in Bangladesh were landless women. Yunus thus began arranging workshops and center schools in an attempt to facilitate improvements in the living standards of women, and through them, the entire population. Today, the bank conducts approximately 3000 workshops a year, addressing the problems of health care, family planning, business opportunities, and other social issues.

As a result of the bank's bold economic approach and much-needed programs of social awareness, the status of women and the living standards of those affected by their ascent have improved at an astonishing rate. Although nonmembers contribute only 25 percent of a household's overall earnings, Grameen women contribute close to 55 percent. As studies have concluded that Bengali women are more likely to invest their earnings in their children than men are, the increase in contribution has led to a higher child immunization rate and improvements in the general health of their children that exceed the national standard. The financial resourcefulness promoted by Grameen loans also helps women resist spousal abuse, maintain their personal dignity and assert other basic rights. Most profoundly, 58 percent of Grameen borrowers crossed over the poverty line, while only 18 percent of nonmembers were able to accomplish such advancement.

However, Yunus' bold approach to economic and social reform has not been free of criticism. Many question whether helping people stay in their villages represents economic progress or contend that it fosters socioeconomic stalemate and discourages industrialization or technological advancement. Nevertheless, by extending credit where it will do a great deal of both economic and social good, the Grameen Bank has demonstrated that "micro-lending" offers an imaginative and effective approach for promoting human development where it is most needed.

lower than American wages, and Mexican health, safety, and environmental standards, although similar on paper to those in the United States, are sparsely enforced. In the United States, labor and environmental groups lobbied strenuously to defeat NAFTA, fearing that American jobs, wages, and environmental standards would "go south." However, advocates of free trade argued that in the long run, the pact would create more American jobs (through increased trade) and improve Mexican environmental standards (because as countries become richer, they tend to be more concerned about environmental quality).[38] After impassioned speeches, media blitzes, and political pressure and logrolling from both sides, Congress voted to ratify the agreement in November 1993.

Most analysts agree that the overall economic impact of NAFTA has been modest, but generally positive, though protectionist critics continue to decry its effects on the U.S. labor market.[39] Whatever costs and/or benefits NAFTA will have for the United States and Canada, the agreement will almost certainly have a much greater impact on Mexico. NAFTA guarantees Mexico a huge market for its ELI strategy, but it also is likely to bring Mexico much greater scrutiny from the United States. With NAFTA, the United States is likely to look at antidemocratic practices and abuses of government power in Mexico much more closely than in the past, and Mexico is likely to resent the resultant criticism and potential interference in its sovereignty. On the other hand, many NAFTA supporters argue that the free-trade agreement will create pressure and incentives for more real democracy. This may in turn allay the fears of labor unions and environmentalist groups that NAFTA will be a means by which American corporations will be able to avoid labor and environmental standards by moving their plants and facilities to Mexico. In any case, as these concerns may prompt lawmakers to add "killer amendments" (changes unacceptable to one or more of the trading partners) to future trade pacts, Congressional ratification of agreements to expand NAFTA into a Free Trade Area of the Americas (FTAA) may depend on renewal of the president's "fast-track" negotiating authority—the ability to present specified treaties to the Senate for a straight up-or-down vote, with no amendments allowed.

Other critics of NAFTA will be much harder to convince. In the mid-1990s, insurgent movements in Chiapas and elsewhere in Mexico cited NAFTA as the reason for growing economic disparities in that country. However, many Latin American states that did not join free-trade areas experienced uneven economic development and consequent social unrest in the 1990s in spite of structural adjustment and political reform.[40] In any event, as Chile advances its application for membership, NAFTA seems certain to attract further controversy over the environmental, political, and social costs of development and between supporters of free trade and protectionism.

Political Aspects of Economic Interdependence

Considering that export-led industrialization is now the preferred development strategy for many Southern countries, the debates over NAFTA and MFN for China are likely to be repeated many times over. As trade between the North and South grows, greater economic interdependence between developed and developing countries will pose many questions with both political and economic implications. Will increased trade between the First and Third Worlds undermine employment and wages for low-skilled workers in developed countries? Will multinational corporations take advantage of lax environmental laws in developing nations to avoid pollution-control measures? Will increased trade help entrenched authoritarian regimes hold on to power, or will it instead give impetus to the spread of democracy and human rights? Will multinational corporations employ vulnerable women and children in "sweatshops" in developing states at a fraction of the wages prevailing in industrialized countries? Will differences in economic opportunity, political freedom, or social welfare prompt ever-increasing waves of migration from South to North?

At the core of all these questions is an enduring political dilemma: As the global economy leads to greater interdependence among all nations, what standards should be adopted to govern the disputes that inevitably arise from higher levels of trade—the minimal standards of many developing countries, or the exacting standards of developed countries? It is far too early to speculate on how this question or any of the other dilemmas of interdependence (see Chapter Ten) will be resolved. All that can be said with any confidence at the present time is that parts of the developed and developing worlds are becoming more closely linked economically, that growing trade and interdependence will create greater prosperity for many but will pose some challenges to all, and that solutions to the dilemmas of economic globalization will not be found quickly or easily.

CONCLUSION: THE DEVELOPMENT IMPERATIVE

Throughout this chapter, we have referred to the relationship between the "First World" and the "Third World," or the "developed world" and the "developing world," almost as if industrialized and nonindustrialized states were located on different planets. In reality, of course, developed and developing states share the same small world, which is being made smaller every day by the globalization of trade and communications. At the same time, however, a process of fragmentation is also occurring, as rapidly growing NICs pull further and further ahead of the low-income countries and primary-product exporters struggle to achieve the stability and prosperity enjoyed by developed states with diversified economies.

The concurrent processes of globalization and fragmentation lead some authors to conclude that in the near future, the contrasts between the "zones of turmoil" in developing areas and the "zones of peace" in industrialized regions will become even greater, but the two zones will nevertheless become increasingly interdependent.[41] As trade flows increase, the channels through which the problems of one zone spread into the other will widen (see Chapters Six and Ten). As nations become more closely tied together, and thus more affected by one another's problems, demands for development can only increase, because diversified economies become less vulnerable to both domestic crises and external shocks.

Although modernization theorists and adherents of the dependency school disagree on the causes of underdevelopment, both agree that industrialization, with all its attendant drawbacks, is the only cure for the poverty and misery that billions of people in the developing world experience every day. This cure does not come without costs; as this chapter has noted, industrialization creates social and environmental problems as developing states "graduate" from the dilemmas of poverty, through the dilemmas of transition, to the dilemmas of affluence. (See Chapter Ten for more details.) The environmental costs of development, in particular, have led some to contend that curbing population growth and reducing consumption of resources, rather than expanding production, are the only long-term solutions to the economic, health, and environmental problems that affect both industrialized and nonindustrialized countries. These environmentalists therefore counsel programs of development that are ecologically sustainable—but they still call for development, recognizing that people who lack food, shelter, and safe water can't afford to worry too much about the ozone layer.

For Southern countries, therefore, development is not an option, but an imperative. Disagreements exist not over the need for development, but over the means to that end. Each of the development strategies discussed in this chapter has been tried by a number of developing states. Each has succeeded in some cases and failed in others. The varied track records of the ISI, ELI, and NIEO strategies have led some development theorists to contend that no single strategy offers all Southern states the best chance to achieve their development goals. Rather, developing states must consider many factors, including their resources and the conditions prevailing in the global marketplace, when they formulate their development programs.[42]

In many ways, a country's choice of a development strategy is similar to an individual's career. Just as most people must either get a job or go on welfare, most states must either adopt a strategy for development or resign themselves to the fact that the vast majority of their citizens will continue to live in miserable poverty. Also, like a student trying to decide what career or course of study to pursue, a nation attempting to develop its economy must take into account its own strengths, weaknesses, and values, and must make a careful survey of the global "job market." Success is never ensured for either individuals or nations, but in both cases industriousness, innovation, flexibility, the availability of leadership and role models, and perseverance all increase one's chances.

PRINCIPAL POINTS OF CHAPTER EIGHT

1. It is difficult to derive a precise definition for development, as the international standard for development is a constantly moving target. By any definition, however, development includes economic diversification; transition away from subsistence agriculture toward manufacturing, services, and modern farming; and improvements in health and in standards of living.

2. Development in any form typically results in social changes that can cause serious political problems in developing states. Two of the most important changes brought about by development are demographic transition and urbanization.

   a. Demographic transition refers to the change from the high birth and death rates characteristic of traditional societies to the low birth and death rates usually found in industrialized countries. It is typically accompanied by rapid population growth until the decline in the birthrate matches the decline in the death rate.

b. Urbanization, or the rapid growth of cities, is often accompanied by overcrowding, unemployment, and crime.

3. There are two major schools of thought on the root causes of development and underdevelopment: modernization theory and dependency theory.

4. Modernization theory holds that domestic social and political structures are the key factors for development. Grounded in the liberal perspective on international political economy (see Chapter Seven), modernization theory views development as a transition from a "traditional" agrarian economy to a "modern" capitalist economy. This school contends that development may be achieved through open markets and investment in physical, financial, and human capital.

5. Dependency theory, based on Marxist ideas, focuses on a country's assigned role in the global economic system. Dependency theorists contend that the global economy operates to keep primary-product exporters (countries that produce commodities such as copper, petroleum, and bananas) dependent on industrialized countries and multinational corporations for manufactured goods, thereby hindering their development. From this perspective, development can be achieved only if primary-product exporters improve their terms of trade (the ratio of export prices to import prices) so that capital will flow from developed to developing countries rather than vice versa.

6. Developing countries may attempt to achieve development through aid, trade, or some combination of both. The course a country adopts in its pursuit of development is termed its development strategy.

7. Three basic trading strategies are available to developing countries, each having its own record of success and failure:
   a. Import-substitution industrialization (ISI) attempts to replace imports from developed countries with domestically produced goods.
   b. Collective bargaining attempts to change primary-product exporters' terms of trade through commodity cartels (such as OPEC).
   c. Export-led industrialization (ELI) promotes production of goods for the global market. The newly industrialized countries (NICs) of East Asia (Hong Kong, South Korea, Singapore, and Taiwan) have achieved spectacular growth with this strategy.

8. Three types of development aid, each with its own advantages and disadvantages, may be extended to developing countries:
   a. Bilateral aid is direct aid from one developed state to one developing state, typically handled by the donor's and recipient's governments.
   b. Private aid is donated by individuals and groups through nongovernmental organizations (NGOs). This type of aid usually bypasses the recipient's government and goes directly for humanitarian purposes or economic-development projects.
   c. Multilateral aid is aid channeled through international organizations, most often the World Bank and the IMF. This type of aid usually (but not always) comes in the form of loans from the international organization to the recipient government.

9. In the 1970s, many developing countries borrowed heavily from multinational banks to raise capital for development. This led to a debt crisis in the 1980s when many Third World states became unable to repay their loans. The IMF arranged for debt relief and rescheduling for many debtor nations, but made debt relief conditional upon the adoption of free-market economic reforms, or structural adjustment. Some governments regard conditionality as foreign interference, however, and contend that structural adjustment imposes unnecessary economic hardships.

10. Though ELI has become the strategy of choice for many of the more successful developing states, the experiences of various Southern countries prove that there is no single strategy for development that works best in every situation. Countries must carefully assess their own resources and respond to conditions in the global market in order to achieve their development goals.

11. The increasingly close economic relationships between developed and developing countries have lead to political dilemmas. For example, labor unions often complain that trade with Third World states destroys lower-skilled jobs in industrialized states, human rights advocates oppose trade with Southern states ruled by authoritarian regimes, and environmentalists worry that multinational corporations will set up operations in developing areas to circumvent environmental standards in industrial states.

12. Although development has drawbacks, often including social upheaval and environmental pollution, there is no real alternative to development if global standards of living are to be improved. (Some of these drawbacks may be alleviated or avoided by sustainable development, which stresses the need to conserve natural resources over the long term; see Chapter Ten.)

13. Increased trade and communications are likely to continue to make developed and developing countries more interdependent—and therefore more susceptible to one another's problems.

KEY TERMS

bilateral aid
buffer stocks
capital-intensive
commodity cartels
conditionality
demographic transition
dependencistas
dependency theory

export-led industrialization
First World
import-substitution industrialization
infant mortality rate
international division of labor
least developed countries

modernization theory
monopsony
multilateral aid
New International Economic Order
newly industrialized countries
primary products
private aid

privatization
Second World
structural adjustment
subsistence agriculture
terms of trade
Third World
transfer pricing
urbanization

□ □ □ □

PART

IV

Issues and Institutions in World Politics

SOURCE: Reuters/Eric Miller/Archive

International Law and Organization

The previous chapters have shown how the New Era has been characterized by the simultaneous yet contradictory trends of globalization and fragmentation. Two recent events illustrate the uncertainty as to whether international law and organizations will be able to bring about increased global cooperation and at the same time reduce the fragmentation that has marred the "new world order" since the end of the Cold War. In 1991, for instance, the global community showed that it was capable of exerting its collective might to oust the forces of Iraqi leader Saddam Hussein from neighboring Kuwait. Because of the favorable battlefield terrain, high economic stakes, clearly defined objectives, and an agreed-upon division of the war's costs, enough countries believed that fulfilling their collective obligation under the **United Nations** (UN) to defend a fellow UN member from outside aggression would be a worthwhile endeavor. On the other hand, the international community's defense of

UN member Bosnia-Herzegovina's territorial integrity and Muslim population has taken years to become effective, and the final results of the UN's efforts are still very much in doubt. In this case, unfavorable battlefield terrain, low economic stakes, and uncertainty and disagreements over the objectives of any UN armed intervention in Bosnia made it difficult for the great powers to seriously stem the unfortunate course of that country's fragmentation and disintegration.

These two different international responses to crises illustrate the fundamental difference between international and domestic politics introduced in Chapter One: that although domestic politics functions under a system of authority, global politics is anarchic. There is no central authority to determine how nations should act toward one another and unilaterally enforce rules for such interactions. Chapter One likened domestic politics to a soccer field and international politics to a jungle: Both are competitive environments, but on the field there are rules and referees, while the "law of the jungle" is "every creature for itself." Not surprisingly, in this environment, states often follow the principles of "kill or be killed" and "do unto others before they can do unto you," and the result has been frequent violent conflict and war.

Throughout history, many people have been profoundly disturbed by this state of affairs, and it is easy to understand why. The death, destruction, and suffering caused by war over the centuries are powerful arguments for making the international system less anarchic. From the seventeenth century onward, systematic efforts have been made to establish some form of authority in the international system in the hope that doing so might facilitate peace and cooperation among nations. International law and organizations are manifestations of this hope, and this chapter looks at how they attempt to make the international system less anarchic.

The chapter begins with a definition of international law, an overview of how it is established, and an assessment of how effective it is in the absence of a global authority to ensure compliance with it. Special attention will be given to global conventions on human rights, which are among the most worthwhile and admirable components of international law, but are also the most frequently violated and difficult to enforce. Following this, the chapter turns to international organizations, especially those that have attempted to replace international anarchy with systems of collective security. The most recent of these is the United Nations, whose structure, function, successes, and failures will all be discussed in detail. Finally, the chapter looks at how other international groups, from the Organization for Economic Cooperation and Development (OECD) to **Amnesty International**, attempt to exert varying degrees of influence on international politics.

Not all international organizations seek to promote international cooperation. Some, such as the terrorist organizations discussed in Chapter Ten, carry on acts of violence to pursue their objectives. But all of the organizations and agreements examined here have one thing in common. In one way or another, intentionally or not, they are all forces for globalization. Humanitarian relief agencies and terrorist groups alike attempt to mobilize opinion and gather resources for solving problems across state boundaries. Some treaties and organizations try to solve global problems at the global level, while other groups strive to globalize a local conflict in the hope that other nations will intervene. It is clear, therefore, that although the successes attained by international law and organizations in making the world less anarchic are debatable, the increasing ability of various groups to voice their concerns on the world stage must be acknowledged. Though many have been slow to take hold, international institutions have become an integral part of global politics.

INTERNATIONAL LAW

International law, also referred to as the law of nations, may be defined as "a body of rules which binds states and other agents in world politics in their relations with one another."[1] International law has evolved in tandem with the nation-state system, from the Peace of Westphalia (see Chapter Two) to the present. It conforms to the decentralized nature of the international system and differs from domestic law in two fundamental ways. First, the law of nations reflects the lack of an international sovereign, or single institution possessing a monopoly on coercive force. Because the international system lacks such a central authority, international law can be enforced only through reciprocity (doing unto other states as you would have them do unto you), individual or collective sanctions (such as freezing assets or imposing trade embargoes), or, when all else fails, reprisals (retaliation or response in kind).

Second, international law differs from domestic law in that there is no global legislature, or lawmaking body, to set down laws for all nations. International law is therefore ultimately based on consent—states must accept its provisions, explicitly or implicitly, in order to be bound by them.[2]

The array of issues addressed by international law are diverse and wide-ranging. These areas include, but are not limited to, rules regarding human rights, warfare and aggression, the law of the sea, outer space, Antarctica, the environment, and international trade. (Chapter Ten addresses several of these global issues in more detail.) Before looking at how international law attempts to promote cooperative solutions to these problems, it is necessary to examine the origins of international law and to ask why states bother to obey it at all in a largely anarchic world.

Sources of International Law

Without a world legislature, who puts international law "on the books"? There are two primary sources of international law: **treaties** and **customary practices.** Essentially, signing a treaty constitutes explicit consent to be bound by international law, while customary practices establish international law through implied consent. (Similar principles apply in some aspects of domestic law: A person who signs a contract explicitly agrees to its provisions, while everyone who applies for a driver's license gives implied consent for a police officer to pull them over if they are suspected of driving while intoxicated.) In addition to treaties and customary

Spotlight

The First International Lawyer

Dutch jurist Hugo Grotius (1583–1645) is considered the "father" of international law. Grotius began life as a very gifted child—he wrote poetry in Latin at age eight and enrolled at Leiden University at eleven. Grotius gained firsthand experience in what would now be called human rights law when he was sentenced to life imprisonment for his political activities in 1618. He escaped to Paris in 1621, however, hidden in a box of books. In Paris, during the calamitous Thirty Years' War, he published *De Jure Belli ac Pacis (On the Law of War and Peace)*, an ambitious study of the rules of conduct applying to nations. This work publicized many of the emerging practices of customary law, especially attempts to humanize the conduct of war.

In his further writings, Grotius also formulated the legal basis for the principle of national sovereignty, which would later be codified in the Peace of Westphalia. When not devoting his energy to legal scholarship, he wrote works on history, linguistics, and theology as well as a prodigious amount of poetry. He served as the Swedish ambassador to France from 1634 until his death in a shipwreck in 1645, three years before the treaty ending the Thirty Years' War incorporated into its terms many of the concepts he developed. Though he achieved little fame during his lifetime, many of the ideas he espoused later became the guiding principles of the Concert of Europe and the United Nations.

practices, the writings of legal scholars, rulings of courts such as the International Court of Justice, and decisions of international organizations such as the UN help to refine, enrich, and expand upon international law.

Customary Practices   International custom, or customary practices, refers to established and consistent practices of states in international relations. The notion of custom as a source of law has its origins in the ancient Roman concept of *jus gentium,* the "law of the tribes," which were the common features Roman jurists identified among the subject peoples of their empire. Later, when states' adherence to unwritten rules of conduct or multilateral declarations became commonplace and widespread—that is to say, customary—they were regarded as binding on all states, even those that never expressly consented to them. The most prominent aspects of customary international law include **diplomatic immunity** and many provisions of human rights law, including the prohibition of slavery (later codified in the 1926 Slavery Convention), genocide (codified in the 1948 Genocide Convention), racial discrimination, and torture.

The concept of diplomatic immunity illustrates how international law develops from customary practice. For centuries in Europe, diplomats representing foreign states were accorded freedom of movement without fear of molestation from the governments they were sent to negotiate with. UN Resolution 43/167 and the Vienna Convention on Diplomatic Relations codified what had by the nineteenth century become the practice of diplomatic immunity, or extending freedom from arrest and prosecution to accredited diplomats. This practice has become crucial to the stability of interstate relations, as negotiators must be able to conduct diplomatic business without worrying about being harassed or arrested on trumped-up charges. (Members of Congress enjoy similar freedom from arrest in the United States.)

States violating this custom usually receive immediate international condemnation and political sanctions, as Iran did in 1979 when U.S. embassy personnel were kidnapped and held hostage. Controversy over this custom arises when embassy personnel fail to adhere to the provision of the 1961 Vienna Convention, which states that diplomats must abide by the laws of the host country. The inability of host countries to prosecute protected diplomats accused of serious crimes raises the question of how far the protection afforded by this custom should extend. Usually, abuses of diplomatic immunity involve personal misconduct, as in a 1996 case in which a Georgian diplomat in New York, even though he was involved in an accident in which a pedestrian was killed, could not be arrested for driving drunk until his government voluntarily withdrew his diplomatic immunity. However, some countries, notably Libya, have been accused of sending terrorists abroad under cover of diplomatic passports. If a foreign diplomat is suspected of committing an offense, all a nation may do according to customary law is declare that individual *persona non grata* (an "unwelcome person") and expel him or her. To curb abuse of this practice, it is customary for the home country of the expelled diplomats to make a similar declaration regarding an equal number of the other country's envoys and order them out as well.

Treaties   Also known as charters, pacts, conventions, or covenants, treaties represent the second main source of international law. Forming a large part of modern international law, treaties are similar to written contracts in that they impose obligations only on the parties that sign them. However, if the provisions of a particular treaty become customary practice, it can be argued that it has become a general law binding on all states. International law takes treaties very seriously; in practice it is assumed that agreements must be kept (*pacta sunt servanda*) and performed in good faith (*bona fide*). Also, a state's internal laws cannot exempt it from compliance with international laws and often must be amended to comply with international agreements, particularly on trade and the environment.

Some treaties become part of international law in a process quite similar to that of domestic legislation. UN conventions, for instance, become law in a three-stage process. Delegates from a member state must sign the treaty, the state's national legislature must then ratify it, and domestic legislation must finally be enacted to bring the nation into compliance. Article 18 of the 1969 Convention on the Law of Treaties stipulates that a state that has signed a treaty subject to ratification must refrain from acts that would defeat the object and purpose of the treaty.

Not all treaties are enacted through the United Nations, of course. Some are bilateral, or agreed upon by two countries. Unless it later entered into that agreement between those two countries, a third country would not be bound by its provisions. For example, when the United States and the Soviet Union signed the bilateral START arms reduction agreement in 1991, it was binding on these two countries only. Problems arose when the Soviet Union broke up at the end of the same year, leaving four Soviet successor states with nuclear weapons deployed on their territory—Russia, Ukraine, Belarus, and Kazakhstan. Russia, the USSR's legal successor, was automatically bound by the treaty, but separate agreements, including offers of economic aid to defray the costs of transferring weapons to Russia, had to be concluded to bring the others into compliance.

As the volume of international transactions increases through the growth of global trade and communications, treaty-making has tended to become multilateral, or conducted between more than two parties at the same time. Many multilateral treaties are now hammered out in common forums, such as special conferences, such as the 1992 UN Conference on Environment and Development (the Earth Summit; see box), or in **intergovernmental organizations,** such as the UN or **Organization of American States** (OAS).

The New Era promises an accelerating trend toward multilateral treaty-making, as global issues such as population growth, environmental degradation, resource depletion, and migration come to dominate the attention of governments. Treaty negotiations can strengthen customary practices by creating new organizational venues to disseminate information and foster international cooperation. Or, like the ill-starred **Mutual and Balanced Force Reductions** (MBFR) talks, which strove fruitlessly for over twenty years to reduce the North Atlantic Treaty Organization (NATO) and Warsaw Pact conventional forces, they can produce mountains of verbiage with no appreciable effect. (This constitutes another similarity between domestic and international lawmaking.) Overall, it appears that the trend toward globalization and greater cooperation among nations will become more pronounced as global issues continue to dominate domestic agendas.

Violation and Compliance

Considering that there is no world legislature to make international law and no global authority to enforce it, it comes as no surprise that many states regularly flout international law when it runs counter to their national interests. In 1984, for instance, the government of Nicaragua (then ruled by the Soviet-backed Sandinista regime) won a unanimous decision from the International Court of Justice supporting its contention that the U.S. government's support of anti-Sandinista *Contra* rebels and mining of Nicaraguan harbors violated international law. But the United States simply ignored the ruling. When Nicaragua took its claim to the UN Security Council, the United States vetoed its consideration.[3] Such flagrant disregard for international law reinforces the widespread notion that it rarely works.

As with domestic law, however, violations regularly make the headlines, whereas adherence to the law is much more common—and therefore isn't news. A wide variety of actors, including governments, private companies, and individuals, adhere to international law on a regular basis. For example, freedom of the seas is observed as a customary principle of international law. Thousands of ships with millions of dollars worth of goods sail to hundreds of ports every day, un-molested by pirates of other governments, and kidnapping or abuse of embassy personnel by host-country governments is rare. Although international law may not always work as well as it is intended, it works better than is often realized.

Today, most governments justify what they do in terms of international law, even when their actions are questionable. For instance, when the Bush adminis-tration sent 24,000 U.S. soldiers to Panama in December 1989 to oust and arrest Panamanian dictator Manuel Noriega (who refused to relinquish the presidency of Panama despite having been defeated in an earlier election), the deployment was justified as "an exercise of the right of self-defense recognized in Article 51 of the United Nations charter" and "to fulfill our responsibilities under the Panama Canal Treaties."[4] Noriega, however, disputed the legality of this action, claiming to be a prisoner of war rather than a common criminal. The incident illustrates how the legality of an action under international law often depends on one's point of view—another effect of the lack of an internationally sovereign authority.

There are a number of reasons other than moral principle why states obey in-ternational law. First, international law provides a framework for the orderly conduct of international affairs. If norms of behavior such as the granting of diplo-matic immunity were not followed, states would quickly find themselves unable to do business with one another. Nations adhere to international law because it is in their interest to preserve international order, just as most automobile drivers prob-ably follow the convention of driving on the right side of the road for the sake of their own safety, even without a highway patrol to enforce regulations.

Second, states may adhere to the law of nations for fear of sanction or reprisal. For example, the use of chemical weapons in war was outlawed by the Geneva Protocol of 1925. Although both Germany and Britain possessed stockpiles of chemical weapons during World War II, both elected not to use poison gas against each other because both feared retaliation with potentially dire consequences to civilian populations and industry. (Hitler had no qualms, however, about using poison gas to exterminate concentration camp inmates, who lacked the capability to respond in kind.)

Third, international law may be enforced by reciprocity. In many cases, the long-term benefits of observing international law outweigh the short-term advan-tages of violating it. If states expect to interact with one another in the future and value their future relations highly enough, they will be more likely to follow laws and conventions as long as other states respond in good faith. This behavior is re-ferred to as tit for tat, or doing as the other side does as long as the other side keeps doing it.[5] As discussed in Chapter Six, many trade agreements are conducted on a tit-for-tat basis. The General Agreement on Tariffs and Trade (GATT), for ex-ample, specifies that if a country raises discriminatory tariffs on goods coming in from another, the second country has the right to respond with "countervailing" tariffs.

Reciprocity in adhering to international law promotes an international envi-ronment in which, in the long run, "cheaters never prosper." If a state routinely violates international norms, it may acquire a general reputation for lawbreaking that could result in international ignominy and erode opportunities for trade and cooperation with other nations. States that consistently prove they cannot be trusted at their word may become **"pariah states"** and be ostracized. Although North Korea initially signed the Nuclear Nonproliferation Treaty (see Chapter Eleven), it withdrew from the agreement in early 1993 and refused to allow international inspections of its nuclear facilities, despite mounting evidence of attempts to develop nuclear weapons, until the United States offered assistance with civilian energy programs in 1994 (see Chapter Five). The North Korean government's reputation for untrustworthiness and unpredictability gave rise to serious doubts as to whether Pyongyang would live up to its end of the deal.

AREAS OF INTERNATIONAL LAW

The Principle of Sovereignty

One of the fundamental principles of international law is national sovereignty. Deriving from, though not explicitly defined in, the Peace of Westphalia signed in 1648 (see Chapter Two), this principle holds that individual states are the ultimate authorities within their own countries. Before Westphalia, under the feudal system, two or more rulers often held joint or competing jurisdiction over various territories, which predictably caused frequent conflict. For example, from the eleventh to the fifteenth century the kings of England held land in France as vassals of the French kings; this overlapping of jurisdictions provoked a long series of conflicts that culminated in the Hundred Years' War. A sovereign state has complete freedom of action in international law to deal with its own nationals ("personal sovereignty") and its own territory ("territorial sovereignty"), to make use of the public domain (the high seas, the atmosphere, and outer space), to enter into legal relationships with other sovereign states, to become a member of international organizations, to fight wars in self-defense, and to remain neutral when others are at war.[6] Sovereignty also implies that, in all matters falling within the domestic jurisdiction of any state, any interference by another state is outside the scope of international law.[7]

Even though national sovereignty makes only one country sovereign over a given territory, other countries may claim the right to rule over that territory. Before the establishment of the League of Nations (see Chapter Three), attempts to seize territory by force were common. The practice continued when the League proved unable to contain expansionist ambitions; in the 1930s Japan conquered Manchuria, Italy invaded Ethiopia, and Germany stormed into Austria and Czechoslovakia. During the Cold War, territorial aggression across international boundaries became less frequent, but still occurred. In the 1970s Vietnam occupied Cambodia, and Soviet tanks rolled into Afghanistan; in the late 1970s and 1980s Israel and Syria invaded parts of Lebanon; Argentina attempted to seize the

Falkland (Malvinas) Islands from Britain in 1982; and in 1990 Iraq occupied Kuwait. Although few such transgressions against the rule of sovereignty go unprotested, many go unpunished. The League of Nations applied sanctions against Italy for attacking Ethiopia, protests were lodged at the UN against the Vietnamese invasion of Cambodia, and the United States placed a grain embargo against the USSR for its invasion of Afghanistan, but none of these measures convinced the invaders to pull out. Each departed years later through a combination of diplomatic and military pressure. The UN applied economic sanctions against the Iraqi invasion of Kuwait, but stronger measures were needed to restore Kuwait's sovereignty: military force applied by a UN-sponsored and U.S.–led multinational coalition.

Although armed intervention to redress transgressions of sovereignty can be effective, its legality is often subjective. Invaders frequently claim that failure to intervene in the transgressed territory would have lead to threats to their own or another country's sovereignty. For instance, in the years after civil war broke out in Lebanon in 1975, the United States, France, Israel, Syria, and the UN stationed troops in that country at various times, ostensibly to restore internal order. (U.S. troops withdrew after a terrorist's car bomb killed 241 U.S. Marines in 1983, and after earlier withdrawls, Israel began actively exploring options for the withdrawal of its troops from the southern sector, its remaining "security zone," in 1998.) At the same time, Syria—with 30,000 troops and a remaining dominant role in most of the country—showed no inclination to depart. The Vietnamese and Soviet governments used similar justifications for invading and occupying Cambodia and Afghanistan, respectively. Detractors argue that such military interventions are really opportunistic seizures of territory or attempts to set up regimes friendly to the invaders. As these examples illustrate, the actual conditions vary, depending on the situation.

Another problem with national sovereignty is that some countries believe that it allows them to flout their international commitments. As mentioned earlier, although North Korea signed the Nuclear Nonproliferation treaty and an additional pact obligating its plants to inspection by the UN International Atomic Energy Agency (IAEA), it has not always permitted the inspections to take place. One North Korean newspaper warned that forcing inspections "on us and the inviolable soil of our country . . . would result in plunging the whole land of the north and south into the holocaust of war."[8] Then North Korea simply withdrew from the treaty and later indefinitely suspended its withdrawal, raising international concerns over its nuclear program to even higher levels. By the same token, countries frequently attempt to restrict imports in defiance of GATT, citing environmental concerns or the need to protect domestic industries and jobs. The World Trade Organization's streamlined grievance procedures and enhanced regulatory powers were designed to curb this practice, but it is too early to tell if they will be effective (see Chapter Seven).

The thorniest issue pertaining to national sovereignty is the notion of "personal sovereignty," which implies that because a sovereign government has exclusive control over its subjects, individuals cannot be the targets of international law or claim any rights under that system for themselves.[9] This aspect of national sovereignty has allowed governments that do not face democratic constraints on their power to run roughshod over human rights. Dictators such as Hitler in Germany and Pol Pot in Cambodia committed unspeakable crimes against humanity while they were in power; Hitler committed suicide and Pol Pot died under suspicious circumstances before he could be brought to justice. Globalization, however, has been able to bring recent human rights abuses to the world's attention. Although Hitler and Pol Pot carried out their extermination programs in secret, China's 1989 crackdown on the student demonstrations at Tiananmen Square was broadcast throughout the world on television.

Human Rights under International Law

The idea that sovereign governments should be subject to some form of international legal constraints to prevent them from abusing the rights of their citizens is a relatively new phenomenon, although the idea that human beings have certain inalienable rights is not new. In eleventh- and twelfth-century Europe, Christian canon lawyers debated the legal maxim that "an unjust law is not a law," which implies that even though a law has been enacted through due process, it may not be in accordance with accepted standards of justice. This developed from Roman and Greek philosophical principles that human beings have inherent rights regardless of the laws enacted by governments. These conceptions of human rights are grounded in the doctrine of **natural law,** which holds that certain human rights derive from a "higher law" rather than from the actions of rulers or governments. After the Reformation (see Chapter Two), philosophers like Thomas Hobbes, John Locke, and Jean Jacques Rousseau promoted the idea of a social contract that conferred rights as well as obligations on citizens and their rulers. The English Bill of Rights (1689), the American Declaration of Independence (1776) and Bill of Rights (1789), and the French Declaration of the Rights of Man (1789) offered lists of fundamental rights and freedoms regarded as both inherent in all human individuals, by the sole virtue of their humanity, and as inalienable, not capable of being taken away.

In the nineteenth century international law began to develop a doctrine of humanitarian intervention when states committed shocking atrocities against their own subjects. For example, international collaboration pushed for the abolition of the slave trade (at the 1884 Berlin Conference on Africa) and then slavery (at the 1926 League of Nations' Slavery Convention), set regulations for the conduct of war and treatment of prisoners (at The Hague and Geneva Conventions in the years before World War I), and offered protection from gross exploitation of workers (through the League of Nations' International Labor Organization, founded in 1919).

Efforts to extend international law to cover human rights were hindered, however, by the doctrine of **positive law,** which held that rights could not derive from some unwritten "higher law," which the doctrine held to be a meaningless concept, but could originate only from human action, including the lawful acts of nation states. Therefore, according to positivists, international law stems from the tacit or specific actions of states, and any law is meaningless without a sovereign authority to enforce it. Many positivists even denied the very existence of international law, contending that states could act however they wished in domestic affairs. The doctrine of positive law was taken to its cruel extreme in the National Socialist laws, enacted by the German Nazi government in 1936 at Nuremberg, which legalized first the persecution and then the wholesale murder of Germany's Jews.

During World War II, the Allies served notice on the Axis that trials for violations of international law would be held after the war. The St. James's Palace Declaration of 1942 stated, "There will be punishment of those guilty or responsible for the crimes, whether they have ordered them, perpetrated them or participated in them." After the Allied victory, Nuremberg was chosen in 1946 as the site of trials for Nazi officials accused of "crimes against humanity" in the Holocaust and other atrocities (see Chapter Three). The Charter of the International Military Tribunal of Nuremberg was endorsed by the fledgling UN in 1946. The charter defines crimes against humanity as "murder, extermination, enslavement, deportation, and other inhuman acts committed against any civilian population before or during the war, or prosecutions on political, racial or religious grounds . . . whether or not violation of the domestic law of the country were perpetrated." The document thus asserts the superiority of international law over national law in questions of the grievous violation of human rights.

Twenty-one of the top Nazi leaders were convicted and sentenced to death or to life imprisonment, and ninety-eight lower-ranking defendants were also convicted. (The proceedings and many issues surrounding them are dramatized in the classic courtroom drama film *Judgment at Nuremberg*.) Analogous trials were held in Tokyo for Japanese officials arraigned on similar charges. Two legal and moral principles became part of international law at Nuremberg: orders given by one's superiors do not justify transgressions against human rights, and individuals as well as governments may be held accountable for war crimes.

After the Holocaust and Nuremberg trials of 1946, the UN took the lead in codifying principles of human rights into international law. An early result was the 1948 Universal Declaration of Human Rights, a comprehensive statement of principles not binding on UN member states, but generally recognized as customary law. In 1966 the UN General Assembly strengthened the declaration's provisions with three covenants: the International Covenant on Civil and Political Rights; the International Covenant on Economic, Social, and Cultural Rights; and the Optional Protocol, which allows citizens to sue governments for redress of human rights violations. The covenants received the required number of ratifications (thirty-five nations) and went into effect in 1976.

The UN has refined some of the basic principles through recent, more specific agreements. These include an agreement outlawing racial discrimination (1969), a convention on eliminating discrimination against women (1981), an accord forbidding torture (1984), and a convention on children's rights (1990). Not surprisingly, these and other agreements have not escaped controversy. Western, industrial countries have tended to focus on individual civil rights and freedoms (reflecting Lockean tradition), while non-Western countries frequently stress collective economic rights (consistent with Marxist thought).

In recent decades, the rights of women have acquired a special place in international human rights law. Gender equality in civil and political rights, equal access to education, economic opportunities, and health care, and prevention of violence against women have become international norms, though as with many other aspects of human rights these principles are often violated in practice. Cultural ignorance of or indifference to women's concerns, and strong political resistance in many countries, have made it difficult to abolish even the most egregious abuses of women's rights. Despite international condemnation, mass rape was used to terrorize women and children in the civil war in the former Yugoslavia, and abhorrent practices such as female genital mutilation and the selling of women and girls into prostitution are still common in parts of Asia and Africa.[10] Growing empowerment of women has made the rights, welfare, and status of women matters of global concern, but action on women's concerns within the framework of international law has been hampered by disputes over abortion, divorce, and other social controversies (see the box on the World Conference on Women).

Can Human Rights Conventions Be Enforced?

Historically, when principles of human rights have clashed with the principle of state sovereignty, sovereignty has usually won out. Torture, imprisonment for political activity, and other abuses of human rights are practiced by governments in many parts of the world, despite protests from the UN and human rights organizations like Amnesty International (a nongovernmental organization dedicated to the release of all political prisoners).

During the Cold War, the issue of human rights became politicized along East-West lines, as UN member states disagreed fiercely over who was in violation of human rights law. When the United States accused Communist and nonaligned regimes of human right abuses, those regimes countered that such charges masked an "imperialistic" desire to interfere in their internal affairs and cited examples of human rights abuses in the West. In the late 1970s, for instance, the United States repeatedly accused the USSR of violating the human rights provisions of the 1975 Helsinki Accords, citing Soviet restraints on Jewish emigration and imprisonment of dissidents in psychiatric hospitals. In response, the Soviet Union maintained for years that Leonard Peltier, a Native American rights activist convicted in the deaths of two FBI agents in a June 1975 shoot-out at Wounded Knee, South Dakota, was a political prisoner. Peltier's attorney even visited the Soviet Union in 1988 to seek aid on behalf of the jailed militant.[11] Recent controversies over alleged U.S. violations of human rights include the 1991 police beating of Los Angeles motorist Rodney King and Amnesty International's condemnations of U.S.

death penalty policies. China and several African countries charged the United States with hypocrisy in citing other countries for human rights violations given its own problems at home. With the demise of the Cold War, countries have been more willing to consider enforcing human rights guarantees with multilateral intervention, at least in principle. In practice, however, the UN has been reluctant to commit troops to potential combat situations in order to safeguard human rights. The peacekeeping mission in the former Yugoslavia illustrates the difficulties inherent in preventing violations of human rights and bringing their perpetrators to justice. Since fighting broke out over the secession of Croatia in 1991 and Bosnia in 1992, hundreds of thousands have lost their lives, and millions have been driven from their homes.[12] Military, police, and militia forces have carried out a policy of "ethnic cleansing," entailing the forcible eviction, imprisonment, torture, rape, and murder of thousands of civilians. Although most of the reported incidents involved Serbian forces, Croatian and Muslim forces have been accused of similar atrocities. Although the UN Security Council established an international court in The Hague to investigate and punish war crimes committed in the former Yugoslav republics, little was done to stop the massive human rights abuses or apprehend those accused of ordering them until NATO forces intervened in 1995 (see Chapter Six). However, arrests of suspected war criminals have often been fraught with political trouble, as one sides' "war criminal" is often another's nationalist hero. The problems encountered in brining war criminals to justice in the former Yugoslavia testify to the political and legal difficulties of enforcing international human rights law.

Warfare and Aggression

Another important area of international law concerns states' conduct during periods of warfare and aggression. Efforts to regulate the conduct of warfare have evolved from the task of articulating the legal obligations of belligerents to the relatively more difficult one of securing protection for individual noncombatants during wartime. An early agreement on the conduct of warfare was the 1856 Declaration of Paris, which clarified the rights of neutral vessels. However, it is the 1945 UN charter that contains the most universally accepted rules of warfare. The charter allows states to use force or other coercive methods (including economic sanctions) against other states in self-defense or as part of an organized peacekeeping organization. In an anarchic environment, however, aggression is still too often justified as self-defense when it is perceived as furthering a state's national interests.

Another set of conventions sets limits on the methods of warfare. The 1899 Hague Convention and the 1925 Geneva Protocol, in particular, prohibit the use of poisonous or asphyxiating gases. As of 1986, 105 nations had signed the 1925 accord, although the U.S. Senate did not ratify it until December 1974. In January 1993, 125 nations signed the Chemical Weapons Convention, which is much stronger—banning the possession, acquisition, production, stockpiling, transfer, and use of chemical weapons—and came into force in 1997. There is also an accord banning the use of biological weapons. Saddam Hussein violated the accord on poisonous gas use during the 1980s in his war with Iran and against Iraq's own Kurdish citizens, but the world community was slow to respond.

A third set of agreements seeks to protect human rights during warfare. Rules to protect sick and wounded combatants are laid out in the 1864 Geneva Convention. The rights of prisoners of conventional war were refined most recently in 1977, which extended protection to those involved in guerrilla warfare.

As can be surmised by the violations mentioned in the preceding paragraphs, efforts to regulate the conduct of warfare, protect combatants and noncombatants alike, and punish those who violate the rules have been only partially successful. The reasons for this limited success stem not only from the enforcement of international law in an anarchic environment, but also from the inherent contradiction of trying to establish rules of "conduct" for violent, aggressive, and often desperate acts. Such rules work only when both sides fear retaliation should they violate them.

The Environment

Concerns about the global environment are truly international, as greenhouse gases, acid rain, and other environmental problems have no respect for national borders. Protection of the environment has become a focal point on several continents for international cooperation and conflict, especially between the economically advanced and developing countries.

In 1972 delegates at the Stockholm Conference on the Human Environment issued and approved the Declaration of the Human Environment, which stresses that poor countries cannot and should not bear the largest burden of cleaning up the environment, and that countries should cooperate in establishing rules for reducing pollution that crosses political borders. The Stockholm Declaration's twenty-six principles have formed the basis for further cooperative effort in areas such as marine and air pollution, depletion of the ozone layer, and global warming and the so-called greenhouse effect. Recently established, the UN Commission on Sustainable Development has been charged with monitoring progress in implementing "Agenda 21," an environmental action program adopted at the 1992 "Earth Summit" (see box) that covers these various issue areas in a comprehensive and systematic manner. One of the most significant results this undertaking, the UN Framework Convention on Climate Change, entered into force in 1994. Designed to achieve stabilization of atmospheric greenhouse gases so as to limit the impact of human activity on climate change, this convention remains controversial in many of the signatory states (including the United States), and as a result its implementation has been disappointingly sporadic. A revised Convention, signed in 1997 in Kyoto, Japan, calls for more stringent limits on carbon emissions from the industrialized states, but serious domestic opposition in many signatory states could delay or prevent its entry into force and continue to frustrate compliance.

Meanwhile, several other agreements that relate to the environment have been enacted. Many of the conventions pertaining to marine pollution have been formulated under the auspices of a UN subsidiary organization, the International Maritime Organization. These agreements include the 1975 Convention, which held liable ships from which polluting oil escaped for any pollution damage caused. Specific accords on air pollution include the 1979 Convention and Resolution on Long-range Transboundary Air Pollution and a 1985 protocol (signed by Canada, but not by the United Kingdom or the United States) to this agreement on reducing sulfur emissions and their transboundary movement. In 1986 Canada and the United States agreed on a plan to combat the effect of acid rain, which falls on the United States and Canada alike but is chiefly caused by pollution from power plants and factories in the United States. However, the plan stalled in the U.S. Congressional legislative process until the passage of the Clean Air Act in 1990. Measures to combat acid rain have been taken in the European Union as well, but political difficulties inhibit similar action in Northeast Asia, where the problem is exacerbated by the burning of many tons of high-sulfur coal in China.

Another set of important environmental treaties pertains to preservation of the ozone layer (the belt of rarefied gas above the earth's surface that protects us from the sun's harmful rays). Building on the 1985 Vienna convention on the ozone layer, the 1987 Montreal protocol called for a freeze in the production of **chlorofluorocarbons,** or CFCs (a primary agent of ozone depletion found in aerosol spray cans and refrigerants), and a nonbinding 1989 Helsinki declaration (signed by seventy-nine countries) that proposed halting production and use of CFCs completely by the year 2000. This set of treaties, in particular has divided the advanced and developing countries. The European Union countries, Canada, the United States, and Australia all announced dramatic unilateral cuts, but several developing countries, including China and India, have protested the enormous cost of adapting to environmentally friendly technologies. The arguments of those developing nations that have opposed international environmental law are quite controversial, but nonetheless interesting: Since the industrialized nations took over 100 years to develop their economies, contaminating much of the world's environment along the way and depleting the natural resources of their colonies, shouldn't the newly independent, developing countries have an equal opportunity to modernize their economies without costly environmental regulations imposed on them by the already developed nations?

Antarctica

One issue related to the environment that has produced more cooperation than conflict is the use of Antarctica. Since the late 1950s, the uses of the resources of the South Pole, especially for scientific purposes, have become increasingly subject to international regulation. In 1959 twelve nations signed the thirty-year Antarctic Treaty, which declared that Antarctica shall be used for peaceful purposes only. The treaty also prohibited new territorial claims to the continent and outlawed nuclear explosions and the storage of radioactive waste there. Later, twenty

The Earth Summit

The 1992 Earth Summit in Rio de Janeiro captured the world's imagination, but quickly gave rise to misunderstandings and disputes over the role international organizations should play in environmental protection. The two years of preparation for the conference were marked by conflict, especially between the industrialized Northern states and the developing South, and between the United States and other states in the North. The conference did produce a weak treaty on global warming and a stronger treaty intended to preserve the world's biodiversity. However, it remains to be seen whether these actions will lead to the kind of detailed environmental action plan that conference organizers desired.

The conference had its roots in the 1972 UN Stockholm Conference on the Human Environment, which elevated environmental issues to the international level by urging states to cooperate in their resolution. Then, in 1983, the UN-created World Commission on Environment and Development warned that patterns of contemporary economic growth were not environmentally sustainable. The 1990s brought additional international environmental concerns, such as global warming (caused by the buildup of carbon dioxide and methane in the atmosphere) and rapid loss of plant and animal species (a result of industrialization).

The central question at the Earth Summit was how to protect the environment and still maintain development. This question pitted North against South with respect to financial aid and transfers of technology. Industrialized states feared that issues of aid and debt relief would simply take on an environmental label, which would make it more difficult for Northern nations to negotiate foreign-aid agreements, because domestic environmental groups also would want their concerns accounted for. Developing states argued that although they supported protection of the environment, they would be unable to implement programs without financial and technical assistance.

How to balance environmental and economic concerns was also the basis for a more specific dispute at Rio: whether to include reductions of carbon dioxide in the World Climate Convention. Western European states, most of which had already agreed as members of the European Union to limits on emissions of carbon dioxide and other pollutants, called for stringent international reductions. As the state with the highest levels of carbon dioxide emissions, the United States charged that these demands were too costly to undertake, especially when the effects of global warming remained uncertain.

In 1997, a special General Assembly session titled "Earth Summit+5" was held to review the progress made on the goals adopted at the Rio conference. Although the session could report that a number of conventions and treaties had been signed since the original Earth Summit, most delegates concluded that overall progress on controlling greenhouse gases and other pollution, preserving biodiversity, conserving habitats and natural resources, and other environmental goals has been disappointing. The reasons why this was so were painfully obvious: disagreements remained between

additional states became parties to the treaty, as well as states from the former Soviet Union.

Other efforts to impose international regulations on that icy land mass have not escaped controversy, however. In 1989 France and Australia, backed by Belgium, Italy, and a coalition of 200 environmental organizations in thirty-five countries,

North and South and within developed and developing countries on the best approach to balancing sustainability and development. Individual states continued to use the international forum as a means for pursuing their specific environmental and economic goals.

The UN Convention on Climate Change, committing industrialized states to reduce their emissions of greenhouse gases to 1990 levels by 2010, was opened for signature in December 1997, but differing standards for developed and developing countries reflected a continuing North-South division on environmental issues and prompted opponents of the treaty to lobby harder against its ratification. All in all, the Earth Summit and the efforts at international action which followed from it offer a vivid illustration of the difficulty of reconciling divergent needs and interests with the overarching objective of safeguarding the global environment.

U.S. Senator Albert Gore speaks at the first UN Conference on Environment and Development (the Earth Summit) in 1992. SOURCE: Carlos Humberto/Contact/Woodfin Camp

launched a proposal to ban all mining on the South Pole and establish a nature reserve there. The United States, Great Britain, Japan, New Zealand, and Chile opposed the ban, contending that it would be too detrimental to business and economic development. An additional protocol, drafted and signed in 1991 by representatives from twenty-four nations, banned mining and oil exploration in

Antarctica for a period of fifty years and extended the original treaty's ban on use of the continent for military purposes. Some issues remain to be resolved, and the 1991 protocol has not yet come into force.[13]

Law of the Sea

The Law of the Sea is an international treaty that governs uses of the oceans. Initially drafted by the UN in 1958, the comprehensive **UN Convention on the Law of the Sea** (UNCLOS) was not approved until April 1982, following years of often volatile multilateral negotiations. In simple terms, the convention divides the world's oceans into public (free-access) and private (regulated-access) property zones for the purpose of regulating competition over the oceans' finite resources. For example, the area of water extending twelve miles from a state's coastline is defined as that state's "territorial waters." Each state is also permitted exclusive rights to exploit natural resources lying within 200 miles of its shorelines.

What to do with the remaining, undivided part of the ocean has proven to be more controversial. Lacking the sophisticated mining technology of the major industrial states, the less developed countries suggested that an International Seabed Authority (ISA) be established to manage ocean resources beyond the 200-mile limit, including the mining of ocean-floor materials. The advanced, industrialized countries, however, want to enjoy continued free access. Such concerns over business interests prevented the United States and Great Britain, among others, from initially signing the 1982 UNCLOS Treaty. In the 1980s, the Reagan administration complained that the treaty's regulation of deep-seabed mining was in opposition to the economic interests of U.S. companies, although the administration did agree to abide by other provisions in UNCLOS. The Clinton administration, favoring most of the conventions' provisions on environmental protection, finally joined most industrial countries in signing the treaty in 1994, and it came into force that same year.

Clearly, the issues surrounding UNCLOS illustrate the obstacles in formulating international law. What appears to be in accordance with most nations' interest might run counter to those of a few, and if the few are powerful, they may count for more than the majority. It usually takes at least minimal support by key states to sign and implement an agreement in international law. As is the case with many other multilateral treaties, extensive negotiations were necessary to bring about an agreement on the Law of the Sea that all interested parties were willing to sign, and UNCLOS supporters had to wait over three decades before their efforts came to fruition.

The Verdict on International Law

The successes and failures of international law over the centuries suggest that the same attitudes toward law that prevail among individuals are shared by states. Some persons obey the law because they believe it is their moral duty to do so; others disregard it whenever possible, and still others are swayed by circumstances.

Similarly, some governments have taken great pains to abide by international law; others have repeatedly and flagrantly ignored it; while still others weigh the advantages of breaking the law against the risk and costs of enforcement sanctions in a given situation before deciding whether or not to obey. The vital role that effective enforcement plays in keeping honest people honest and making dishonest ones think twice before breaking the law thus has implications for international law. Generally speaking, elements of international law that have been readily enforced, such as diplomatic immunity, the prohibition of slavery, and the General Agreement on Tariffs and Trade, are less frequently violated than those provisions that nations have been unwilling or unable to enforce, such as the Kellogg-Briand Pact (which outlawed war except in self-defense) or conventions against torture.

As this section has shown, the international system is not a totally anarchic environment. The world may perhaps best be likened to a town in the American Old West that lacks a competent sheriff or marshal. Laws are on the books, and there may even be a courthouse and jail, but catching suspected criminals and bringing them to trial is a chancy business. Because the authorities cannot keep order, many citizens carry guns, and violent and sometimes deadly fights break out all too often. Persons who are wronged may resort to vigilante justice, taking the law into their own hands, often without regard for the rights of the accused. Even the most dangerous criminals can be brought to justice, however, when a posse is organized and sets out to catch the desperadoes.

The "Wild West" analogy suggests that good organization is the key to effective law enforcement in a society without a sovereign authority. This thought occurred to international jurists generations ago, prompting many to give first priority to the establishment and strengthening of international organizations. The next section will examine how well their efforts have succeeded.

INTERNATIONAL ORGANIZATIONS

States may be the most important actors in the international system, but they are not the most numerous. The Yearbook of International Organizations lists more than 24,000 entries, as compared to about 200 nation-states.[14] Despite the proliferation of international organizations (IOs) in the last few decades, a debate continues over whether they are in fact manipulated and controlled by governments. In either case, it is clear that international organizations try to make the world a less anarchic place by assuming tasks states cannot or will not undertake themselves, from humanitarian efforts to peacekeeping. They are both a cause and an effect of globalization in the contemporary era, and they are called upon to deal with an increasingly wide array of political, social, and economic issues.

IOs may be divided into two broad categories, intergovernmental organizations and nongovernmental organizations. Intergovernmental organizations (IGOs) are associations of sovereign states that are established through formal agreements. IGOs include the United Nations, the North Atlantic Treaty Organization, and the European Union (EU). Nongovernmental organizations (NGOs) are groups of institutions and individuals established through more informal means. Greenpeace,

At a Glance

International organizations: Intergovernmental (IGOs) and Nongovernmental (NGOs)

Specialized IGOs with Global Membership

Promote international mutual assistance between members of a specific field (for example, Interpol provides assistance to law enforcement)

Examples: Interpol, World Health Organization, International Civil Aviation Organization, International Atomic Energy Agency

Notes: Sometimes become involved in political controversies related to where they are situated (for example, Interpol, in 1938, moved to Berlin and came under Nazi control)

General-Purpose Regional IGOs

Promote regional security and provide forum for resolving regional disputes

Examples: League of Arab States (Arab League), Organization of American States, Commonwealth of Independent States, European Union, and Association of South-East Asian Nations

Notes: The European Union is the most successful general-purpose regional IGO. It began in 1957 as primarily an economic union.

Specialized Regional or Limited-Membership IGOs

Promote collective defense, human rights, or political issues

Examples: North Atlantic Treaty Organization, Organization on Security and Cooperation in Europe

Notes: Limited membership. IGOs are not always effective in promoting local security (for example, OSCE was unable to take effective action in Yugoslavia).

Other Specialized IGOs

Oversee primarily economic matters

Examples: Organization for Economic Cooperation and Development, European Free Trade Area, and Organization of Petroleum-Exporting Countries

Notes: OPEC was created in 1960 by oil producers to increase their profits from oil exports.

Humanitarian Organizations (NGOs)

Work toward ameliorating pain and suffering or otherwise forwarding the welfare of humanity

Examples: International Red Cross, Amnesty International, Doctors without Borders, International Child Care USA, Save the Children, International Community for the Relief of Starving and Suffering

Notes: Many of the most famous NGOs are humanitarian organizations.

Multinational Corporations (MNCs)

Exist for financial reasons: seek worldwide profits, promote needs of the home country

Examples: Credit Suisse, General Motors, AT&T, IBM, Mitsubishi, and Shell Oil

Notes: MNCs are seen by some as having inhibited Third World development and by others as having promoted it. They are also NGOs.

Amnesty International, and the International Olympic Committee are familiar examples. Even though NGOs do not include states in their membership, and so lie outside the structure of traditional international politics, many have exerted a significant impact on world affairs. Groups such as Amnesty International have influenced governments' policies through public pressure and lobbying, while organizations like *Medicins sans Frontiers* ("Doctors without Borders") have acted directly to provide humanitarian relief.

IOs can be further categorized by their membership base and intended purpose. Some, such as the **International Committee of the Red Cross,** seek members throughout the world, while others are oriented towards a particular region, like the Economic Community of West African States. Multipurpose organizations such as the Organization of American States (OAS) handle a broad range of tasks, while specialized organizations like the International Criminal Police Organization (**Interpol**) perform more specific functions. The charts in the "At a Glance" box indicate the wide range and diversity of contemporary IOs, many of which could fill entire books with their endeavors and accomplishments.

The primary reason why IOs have taken on increasingly important roles in the nineteenth and twentieth centuries is that sovereign nation-states gradually came to the realization that they could not address all problems that plague the international system by themselves. They came to acknowledge that institutions promoting and facilitating international cooperation are required in order to deal more effectively with problems that affect them all.

By now, the reader has become familiar with IOs that address a variety of issues. For example, the World Trade Organization (WTO) is the premier international economic organization, while the European Union is a regional organization that addresses a variety of economic, social, and political concerns to links its member states in an "ever-closer union." Both were established with the primary purpose of promoting cooperation in day-to-day matters as well as resolving specific conflicts. Although various IOs frequently propose solutions for problems that confront states, states often ignore or fail to abide by the IOs' recommendations and decisions for fear of losing their sovereign powers. Because one of the most vital sovereign rights of a nation-state is that of self-defense, organizations formed to promote collective security as an improvement over the anarchic "every state for itself" security environment have found it difficult to achieve their objectives despite centuries of effort. The sections that follow reveal the constant tension that exists between sovereignty and cooperation, especially within IOs designed to provide collective security.

GENEOLOGY OF THE UNITED NATIONS

The Concert of Europe

As discussed in Chapter Two, the Treaty of Paris (1814–1815) and the Congress of Vienna (1814–1815) established the Concert of Europe to restore the European balance of power after the Napoleonic Wars. As the Quadruple Alliance (Austria, Britain, Prussia, and Russia), the Concert fulfilled its immediate purpose by defeating Napoleon once and for all at Waterloo in 1815. The Congress of Vienna revealed, however, that the Concert was not an autonomous organization that could make rules for sovereign nation-states in a disinterested manner. The Congress disposed of much European territory in a way that reflected the existing power relationships among the European great powers. Once the monarchy under Louis XVIII had been restored, France was confined to its somewhat expanded

1792 borders. As for the rest of Europe, to the victors went the spoils: Austria gained parts of Italy, Prussia gained parts of Austria, Russia gained most of Poland and Finland, Britain gained overseas territories seized from France and the Dutch, and the Netherlands regained its independence. The world's first collective-security organization did not start life in an unselfish spirit of international cooperation.

Although the Concert system at first dampened nationalist and liberal aspirations of many European peoples (including those of Belgium, Greece, Italy, and the German Confederation, among others), it did keep the peace among ideologically opposed great powers. Nevertheless, the excessively elitist orientation of the Concert's concept of balance power made it incapable of responding to the desire on the part of many subject people in Europe for national self-determination, and this elitism proved to be its Achilles' heel. As Chapter Three recounts, the Concert deteriorated in the latter part of the nineteenth century, and the unstable peace it kept collapsed with the outbreak of World War I.

The League of Nations

The successor of the Concert of Europe was the League of Nations, created by the Treaty of Versailles at the end of World War I in order to prevent another catastrophic global war (see Chapter Three).[15] The Geneva-based organization lasted from 1919 until 1946, although for all practical purposes it was moribund by 1939. Many would argue that the League was in fact stillborn, because the isolationist United States did not ratify the Versailles Treaty, which incorporated the League's charter. Without the support of the most powerful country, the organization could do little to prevent the instances of military aggression that led to World War II.

Unlike the Concert of Europe, which operated informally, the League was specifically chartered as a formal international organization dedicated to arbitration of international disputes, disarmament, and open diplomacy. Its founders were convinced that the nineteenth-century doctrine of the "balance of power," loosely maintained by the Concert, failed to prevent World War I because that doctrine was in disharmony with the ideals of national self-determination. As a result, a more active form of collective security, an "international police force," was deemed necessary for preventing future war. Collective security is an attempt to replace the "every state for itself" of the anarchic international system with a "one for all, and all for one" mentality; in other words, "the organizing principle of collective security is the respect for the moral and legal obligation to consider an attack by any nation upon a member of the alliance as an attack upon all members of the alliance."[16] By ostensibly guaranteeing the security of all states in the international system regardless of their size or power, it was hoped that collective security would be a mechanism to pull states away from the brink of war in the nick of time.

In reality, collective security proved difficult to organize. To begin with, states such as Britain and France continued to practice balance-of-power politics, as demonstrated by the way they handled the Italian invasion of Ethiopia in 1935 (see Chapter Three for details). Additionally, the League did not include key global players in its membership. Original members Japan and Italy quit in 1933 and 1937, respectively. After having failed to gain a reversal of the provisions of the Versailles Treaty, Germany also withdrew from the League in 1933. A few months after the Soviets signed the Nazi-Soviet Pact and Hitler invaded Poland in 1939, a League council resolution revoked the USSR's five-year-old membership. And, as mentioned before, the United States never joined the League and thus missed many opportunities to exert its influence to avert the events that escalated into World War II.

The League of Nations' decision-making structure also hampered the organization's political power. There were four main components to the League: the Assembly, composed of representatives from all member states; the Council, consisting of permanent seats held by the most powerful states as well as rotating members chosen by the Assembly; the Secretariat, a primarily administrative organ; and the World Court, an international tribunal of judges to which nations could appeal for rulings in international law. The Council, which during the history of the League ranged from eight to fourteen members, handled mainly political matters. These included major disputes likely to lead to war, as well as minor problems such as frontier adjustments. All decisions of substance required a unanimous vote of all Council members, except for those directly involved in the dispute in question (whose votes did not count). However, any members of the League Assembly whose interests were concerned in the decision's outcome also had the right to veto League action.

Thus, the League was doubly constrained in taking action against belligerents. In the first place, the negative vote of any member (including one in the Assembly, not just the Council) sufficed to block any decision to authorize sanctions. Few of the Council's decisions were vetoed, if only because they tended to be watered down to near-meaninglessness. Second, even when the Council could manage to get a unanimous decision to use force, the League found it almost impossible to enforce the sanctions available to it, which ranged from trade embargoes to air and naval strikes against offending nations. The League's deficiencies rendered it powerless to stop Italy from invading Corfu (a Greek island) in 1923 and Ethiopia in 1935, to stop Bolivia and Paraguay from fighting over possession of the Chaco region in a war that claimed 200,000 lives (1932–1935), to stop Japan from invading Manchuria in 1931, to stop Germany from its host of treaty violations and aggressive acts in the years before World War II, or to stop the Spanish Civil War.

In many respects, the structure of the League was an overreaction to the great-power politics that plagued the Concert of Europe. The feebleness of the League's collective-security provisions reflected a forlorn hope that these measures could work through moral force alone, without the backing of the most powerful states. But without the tangible support and concerted effort of the great powers, the organization's vacillations and meek declarations merely aggravated expansionist dictators, inviting further aggression. After such aggression led to a war even more horrible than the First World War, world leaders attempted to construct an organization that could ensure the widest possible respect for and adherence to its decisions.

THE UNITED NATIONS IS BORN

President Franklin D. Roosevelt and Secretary of State Cordell Hull coined the name of the League of Nations' successor organization in the 1942 Declaration of the United Nations. (British Prime Minister Churchill liked Roosevelt's proposed name "United Nations" better than his own suggestion of "Associated Powers.") The new organization was officially established in June 1945 when fifty-one founding members signed the charter of the United Nations, which came into effect that October, after the surrender of Germany and Japan ended World War II. The League of Nations quietly voted itself out of existence and transferred its assets to the UN in April 1946.

Thus, the UN supplanted the League of Nations as the preeminent collective-security organization in the international system. Its primary purpose was and still is to maintain international peace and security. It is also dedicated to developing friendly relations between peoples, cooperating internationally in solving international economic, social, cultural, and humanitarian problems, and promoting respect for human rights. The UN charter established six primary organs of the United Nations, headquartered in New York City: the General Assembly, the Security Council, the Economic and Social Council, the Secretariat, the Trusteeship Council, and the International Court of Justice (ICJ), or World Court. (The Trusteeship Council, organized to oversee the administration of non-self-governing areas assigned to member states for temporary administration before graduating to full independence, suspended operations in 1994 because all such territories had become independent.) Although these organs and their auxiliary and subsidiary bodies are supposed to promote the widest possible cooperation among member states in the areas of collective security and peacekeeping, in practice states have traditionally hewn to narrow definitions of their national interests in determining the desirability of international cooperation. This has often transformed the UN into an arena for political grandstanding and competition.

Although the UN thus has a distinguished pedigree, it has not always performed like a thoroughbred. The next section will assess the effectiveness of the UN's primary organs, looking at the effect of politics on decision-making, and at the nature of the political and economic difficulties that each body faces.

THE UNITED NATIONS: STRUCTURE, FUNCTIONS, AND POLITICS

General Assembly

From 51 original members, the UN General Assembly (GA) has expanded to include 185 nation-states as of 1997. Figure 9.1 shows its organization and scope.

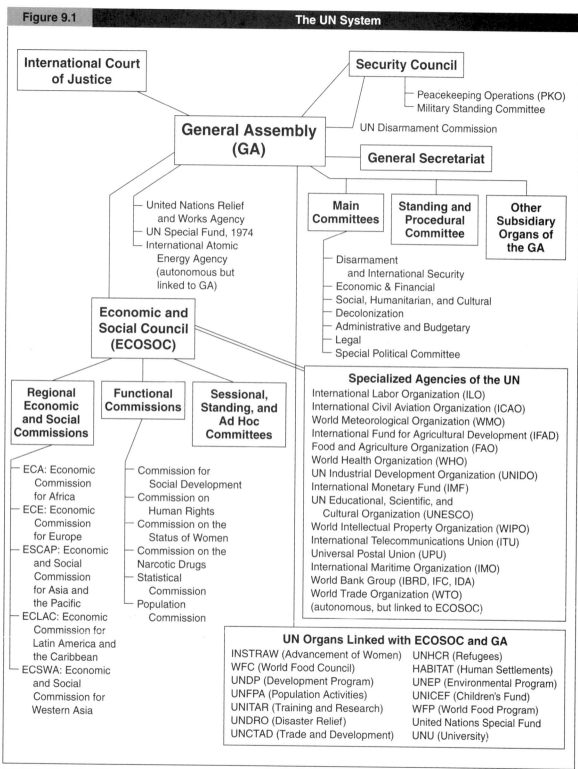

Figure 9.1 **The UN System**

International Court of Justice

Security Council
— Peacekeeping Operations (PKO)
— Military Standing Committee

UN Disarmament Commission

General Assembly (GA)

General Secretariat

— United Nations Relief and Works Agency
— UN Special Fund, 1974
— International Atomic Energy Agency (autonomous but linked to GA)

Main Committees
— Disarmament and International Security
— Economic & Financial
— Social, Humanitarian, and Cultural
— Decolonization
— Administrative and Budgetary
— Legal
— Special Political Committee

Standing and Procedural Committee

Other Subsidiary Organs of the GA

Economic and Social Council (ECOSOC)

Regional Economic and Social Commissions
— ECA: Economic Commission for Africa
— ECE: Economic Commission for Europe
— ESCAP: Economic and Social Commission for Asia and the Pacific
— ECLAC: Economic Commission for Latin America and the Caribbean
— ECSWA: Economic and Social Commission for Western Asia

Functional Commissions
— Commission for Social Development
— Commission on Human Rights
— Commission on the Status of Women
— Commission on the Narcotic Drugs
— Statistical Commission
— Population Commission

Sessional, Standing, and Ad Hoc Committees

Specialized Agencies of the UN
International Labor Organization (ILO)
International Civil Aviation Organization (ICAO)
World Meteorological Organization (WMO)
International Fund for Agricultural Development (IFAD)
Food and Agriculture Organization (FAO)
World Health Organization (WHO)
UN Industrial Development Organization (UNIDO)
International Monetary Fund (IMF)
UN Educational, Scientific, and Cultural Organization (UNESCO)
World Intellectual Property Organization (WIPO)
International Telecommunications Union (ITU)
Universal Postal Union (UPU)
International Maritime Organization (IMO)
World Bank Group (IBRD, IFC, IDA)
World Trade Organization (WTO)
(autonomous, but linked to ECOSOC)

UN Organs Linked with ECOSOC and GA
INSTRAW (Advancement of Women)
WFC (World Food Council)
UNDP (Development Program)
UNFPA (Population Activities)
UNITAR (Training and Research)
UNDRO (Disaster Relief)
UNCTAD (Trade and Development)
UNHCR (Refugees)
HABITAT (Human Settlements)
UNEP (Environmental Program)
UNICEF (Children's Fund)
WFP (World Food Program)
United Nations Special Fund
UNU (University)

SOURCE: International Monetary Fund, *International Financial Statistics Yearbook, 1997*

All UN members have a seat in the GA, and almost all independent nations are members of the UN. Those that are not include Switzerland, because of its long-standing tradition of strict neutrality, and Taiwan, because Beijing will veto its claims to be the rightful government of all of mainland China. A few other states have not been permitted to join: North and South Korea were denied membership until both joined simultaneously in 1991, and Monaco was denied membership because its foreign policy is controlled by France.

The GA is the UN's primary forum for the discussion of global issues. Operating according to the "one state, one vote" principle, it embodies the idea that the United Nations is based on the sovereign equality of all its members. Dominance of the GA, defined as the ability to get one's resolutions passed by the required two-thirds vote, was first held by the United States, whose supremacy continued up until the 1960s, at which point the United States found itself at odds with the assembly majority on a number of issues involving decolonization and development. (The USSR exploited this rupture to its advantage by taking the opposite stance.) The decline in U.S. influence began in 1960, when seventeen new nations, most of them African, joined the GA. Many of these states identified the United States as the prime patron of their colonial oppression, because of its alliance with all of the former colonial European powers.

By the 1980s well over half of the 160 members of the GA were either Asian or African, and these developing countries continued to use the UN as a forum to espouse their preferences and aims. For many smaller countries of the developing world, the GA remains their most important channel to international diplomacy. However, since the breakup of the Soviet Union and the Persian Gulf War, there has been a marked increase in the American success rate, mirroring the end of the Cold War and America's status as "first among equals" in a new international environment (see Chapter Five).

Although East-West and North-South disagreements have inhibited the effectiveness of the General Assembly, budget disputes have been even more detrimental. Members are often delinquent in their payments; in 1992 over 80 percent of member nations owed money. At other times, nations have threatened to withhold money because of developments within the UN itself. In 1980, for example, the United States withheld over $100 million in contributions, primarily because of its perceptions of anti-Western bias and repeated incidents of wasteful spending. By 1998, United States assessments to the UN were in arrears by over $1.3 billion, or roughly half of the total owed to the UN by member states. Plans for the United States to pay its arrears are hampered by the continuing argument between those who believe the country should fulfill its financial obligations immediately and others (especially in Congress) who hold that the UN should reform its organization and financial practices first.

Still another concern affecting GA effectiveness is the overloading of the assembly agenda when it convenes every September. Some feel that the GA is losing its focus. In a recent year, the GA agenda contained over 140 items, some of which are also on the agenda of the Security Council (which, by the charter, has precedence). Some proposals to limit the bloating of the GA agenda and thereby enhance its effectiveness include creating a specific "steering group" that would set and refine agenda items; a cessation of annual discussions of intractable questions, discussing them instead at greater intervals, such as every couple of years; a time limit on speakers whose windy ramblings distort the proceedings; and more meetings between the support staffs of major powers before GA sessions, in order to become aware of their key positions earlier on and thus save time.[17]

Security Council

The Security Council (SC) was designed to be the sword beside the UN's olive branch. It is charged with organizing collective-security operations and dispatching observer missions and peacekeeping troops (defined later in this chapter) around the world at the request of one or more of the combatants involved. This body has the right to investigate any dispute or situation that might lead to international friction and to recommend methods of settlement. On all resolutions and proposals for action the rule of **great-power unanimity** holds: a veto by any one of its five permanent members (China, France, the United Kingdom, Russia, and the United States) will kill any proposal. Every permanent SC member has used its veto power to protect what it has seen as its vital interests. An example was Moscow's veto of the SC resolution condemning the Soviet downing of a South Korean passenger jet in September 1983. Another example from that same year was the U.S. veto of the SC vote against the American intervention on the Caribbean island of Grenada.

Over the past five decades, the SC has employed a wide variety of ways to maintain international peace. These have ranged from resolutions condemning violence to the establishment of peacekeeping forces and the implementation of sanctions.

Through its debates, the SC has reflected the sentiment of the international community. Simply by allowing grievances to be aired, debates have often diffused tension. On the other hand, bitter debates in public view sometimes intensify disputes, to the detriment of private negotiation. When such disputes result in resolutions that are perceived by member nations as biased, the status of the Council is undermined, along with its ability to act (see box).

The SC also serves as a forum for negotiation. By arranging cease-fires or disengagements and by setting up fact-finding missions, the SC can "buy time" in crucial situations to allow participants in a given conflict to reconsider their positions. Even more so, resolutions passed by the SC can provide the framework for dispute settlement. The "land for peace" provisions in UN Resolutions 242 and 338 have served as a basis for settling the Arab-Israeli conflict.

If peaceful means fail, the SC also can impose harsh sanctions on a nation or even launch military actions. Prior to the UN's authorization of the U.S.–led intervention to forcibly expel the Iraqi army from Kuwait in 1990, the only significant military action on which the SC was able to achieve a consensus was intervention in the Korean War. The United Nations intervened in Korea because the Soviet Union had been boycotting SC meetings as a protest against the continuing presence of nationalist China (Taiwan) as a permanent member, rather than the Communist People's Republic of China (PRC), which controlled the

Conflict and Cooperation in the Security Council

In hindsight, it appears that the UN Security Council (SC) was not designed with a bipolar world in mind. Throughout the Cold War, the SC served as a forum in which the Soviet Union and the United States fought to influence world opinion in favor of their respective positions.

For nearly the first two decades of the UN's existence, the USSR had no allies in the SC and few in the General Assembly (GA). As a result, the Soviet Union had to lean heavily on its veto power to kill recommendations on peace and security matters with which it did not agree. In the first five years of the SC's existence, the USSR used the veto forty-seven times; the United States, zero. In fact, the United States did not veto a single SC resolution until 1970.

In the 1960s and 1970s, however, many newly independent African and Asian countries leaned toward the Communist bloc or Non-aligned Movement because they resented the West for its colonial past. They began to pack the GA and fill some of the two-year seats in the SC. As a result, fortunes began to reverse themselves in favor of the Soviet Union. By the mid-1980s, the votes of the GA and the Soviet delegation were in agreement 79 percent of the time; during the same period, the U.S. figure had plummeted to 14 percent. In the early 1980s, the USSR used its veto power only twice, while the United States resorted to it twenty-eight times.* In the 1990s, however, the collapse of communism in the USSR broke the bipolar deadlock. The USSR did not veto the U.S.–led peace enforcement operation in the Persian Gulf War, and the United States

and Russia accommodated each other's plans for peacekeeping in the Caucasus and Haiti in 1994. Finally, it seemed, the Security Council began to function more or less as its founders intended.

In the New Era, debate over whether the membership composition of the SC reflects the current global power structure (see Chapter 12) has been renewed. Serious consideration has been given recently to whether the SC should be expanded to include Japan and reunited Germany, especially because other countries have become increasingly dependent on them to fund expanded UN programs. Reluctance to give Japan and Germany permanent seats both within and outside those countries is a reaction to their legacies of aggression, their post-war constitutional prohibitions against fielding large standing military organizations, and a general feeling that both nations are not (or should not be) wholeheartedly committed to active participation in international politics. Additionally, the United States has anticipated that new admissions to the SC would reduce U.S. leverage, renew Third World countries' demands for an end to the permanent members' veto power, and invite other large Third World nations such as India and Brazil to seek permanent SC membership.†

*Robert E. Riggs and Jack C. Plano, *The United Nations: International Organization and World Politics* (Chicago: Dorsey, 1988).
†For discussions of these issues, see James Weish, "The Partnership to Remember," *Time*, March 11, 1991, pp. 49–50; and *New York Times*, September 27, 1992, and January 12, 1993.

mainland. With the USSR out of the picture, the pro-Western SC was easily persuaded by the United States to authorize the Korean "police action" under its leadership. The assembled military forces were dispatched by President Harry Truman to drive North Korean forces back across the thirty-eighth parallel. After a three-year struggle, the conflict ended in a stalemate and frustration for both sides (see Chapter Four). However, because it was a successful collective effort to block aggression and limit its consequences, the Korean War was the first instance where the UN acted as a "world policeman," just as its founders intended. U.S.–Soviet antagonism during the Cold War ensured that it would not do so again until the Persian Gulf War, forty years later.

Secretariat and Secretary-General

Headed by the secretary-general, who serves a five-year term and reports to the General Assembly, the Secretariat is the UN's chief administrative body. The secretary-general is thus the "chief executive" of the UN, but he or she has little power to act independently of the SC or GA. However, the secretary-general can bring any matter that threatens world peace to the SC's attention and can call special sessions of the GA. In keeping with the tradition established by the League of Nations covenant, the UN Charter pledges the secretaries-general to strict impartiality in the discharge of their responsibilities.

The Secretariat contains a 16,000-member international civil service staff, 11,000 of whom are located throughout the world, with 5000 remaining at UN headquarters in New York City. Despite the large size of the staff, this administrative body has been hindered in the past by the limited resources available. The secretary-general is not authorized to engage in certain types of activities that might be perceived as violations of national sovereignty. One such example is that the secretary-general cannot order intelligence-gathering activities. If member states are not willing to provide sufficient information when a crisis erupts, the danger increases that the secretary-general's effectiveness as an impartial arbitrator will suffer. This problem became particularly acute when the UN Special Commission on Iraq (UNSCOM) was charged with verifying that Iraq had destroyed its weapons of mass destruction after the Gulf War. Iraq's attitude toward UNSCOM's efforts to gather information on its weapons and research facilities ranged from obstinacy to hostility, and safeguards had to be taken to ensure that secret information sent to UNSCOM by other member states did not leak out. Some analysts suggest ways to get around these types of restrictions. For example, to accomplish intelligence-gathering the Secretariat could push for the development of UN satellite-gathering equipment capabilities, purchase commercially available satellite images, or perhaps just send special UN ambassadors to global capitals on a regular basis to gather information for the secretary-general.

These proposals would improve the resources available to the secretary-general but would not necessarily safeguard the desired impartiality of the office itself. Indeed, the process of selecting the security-general can be an especially political undertaking. Starting in 1956, the UN undertook an obligation to consider geographic origins when selecting a secretary-general. This was to ensure that no one particular region of the world was more "represented" than others, although geographic distribution was still supposed to remain subordinate to questions of merit when selecting the most desirable candidate.

Of the seven individuals who have served as secretary-general, all have made significant contributions to the peaceful resolution of conflicts in many parts of the world. Some have been more activist than others in terms of leadership style, some more controversial than others, but all have been political figures dependent upon the cooperation (and influence) of member nations (especially the five permanent SC members) and all have sought to wield influence over the membership as well as over the UN bureaucracy.

Norway's Trygve Lie (1946–1953) called the new and poorly defined position of secretary-general "the most impossible job in the world." Despite a broadly recognized talent for negotiating, he was forced to leave office in April 1953, a political victim of the Cold War. Communist countries accused Lie of serving Western imperialism and boycotted him after he recommended UN intervention in the Korean War, causing him to depend more on the West. At the time of his resignation, however, he was having problems with the FBI over questions of staff loyalty; sixty American citizens employed under Lie were being investigated for alleged Communist subversion.

Sweden's Dag Hammarskjöld (1953–1961) lost his life in the line of duty, as he was killed in a plane crash in the Congo while directing UN attempts to end fighting there. He was posthumously awarded the 1961 Nobel Peace Prize for his efforts (see box). Hammarskjöld believed that the chief executive of a body that represents so many nations must play a large role, and he did. He established the precedent of inserting the UN into troubled areas and made the secretary-general the leading political officer of the organization. In his first years, he restored confidence in the secretary-general and turned his role into chief negotiator of the UN, often in the face of vague and unhelpful directives from the SC and the GA. He also clashed with Nikita Khrushchev repeatedly; the Soviet premier first demanded Hammarskjöld's ouster in 1960 because he was perceived to be a Western puppet.

U Thant (1961–1972) was a Burmese diplomat and civil servant before taking the position of secretary-general. He believed that the secretary-general "must be impartial, but not necessarily neutral." In other words, he believed that the secretary-general must make decisions on his own in moments of crisis. He was nonaligned in every sense of the word, so that he maintained the support of both Moscow and Washington, which helped him to be unanimously reelected for a second term.

Kurt Waldheim's (1972–1982) polished, nonideological style was acceptable to both superpowers, making him a desirable candidate for secretary-general. He faced the difficult task of reconciling the superpowers and also the developing states at a time when the latter were increasing their power as a voting bloc. His strategy was to lead by consensus. Although Waldheim's tenure was relatively uncontroversial, the Austrian-born secretary-general became embroiled in a bitter controversy over his World War II service during his successful 1986 bid for the Austrian presidency. Accused of being a former Nazi, Waldheim claimed that he had served in the Balkans with the German Army but not in any decision-making capacity. Nevertheless, the World Jewish Congress revealed that he had served as an intelligence officer and alleged that he had a direct role in Nazi activities. Overall, the controversy tarnished his reputation as well as that of Austria, which elected him to office despite international condemnation.

The UN's Hands-On Leader

The role of UN secretary-general was still poorly defined when Dag Hammarskjöld (1905–1961) got the job in 1953. The son of one of Sweden's prime ministers and a professor of economics at the University of Stockholm before he became a diplomat, Hammarskjöld began his term as the UN's chief executive as an advocate of quiet diplomacy, as befitted the prevailing notion of international civil service. He usually adopted a posture of strict neutrality and negotiated behind the scenes, believing that unpublicized and undramatic talks were the best way to resolve conflicts. In 1955, for example, he traveled secretly to Beijing to secure the release of U.S. airmen captured by the Chinese government; the prisoners were released later that year without fanfare or incident.

Later in his term of office, however, Hammarskjöld enhanced the importance of the secretary-general's position by advocating more freedom for the Secretariat to take action in emergencies without the prior approval of the Security Council or the General Assembly. He believed that this ability to act independently was essential for defusing conflicts quickly, especially when the superpowers were at odds with each other (which was usually the case during the Cold War). He was particularly sensitive to the concerns of developing countries that the UN would be dominated by the Security Council powers to the exclusion of other members. His decisiveness often contrasted with the Security Council and General Assembly's indecision. In the Suez Crisis of 1956, Hammarskjöld dispatched the UN Emergency Force (UNEF) to the Sinai immediately after a cease-fire was reached, and he sent UN peacekeepers to Lebanon and Jordan in 1958 on his own authority. Hammarskjöld's actions to establish a UN presence in conflict regions paved the way for expanded use of UN peacekeeping forces in the coming decades.

In addition to the Middle East, Hammarskjöld directed the UN's attention to conflicts in the newly independent states of Africa, especially in the Congo. In contrast to his early emphasis on conflict resolution by quiet diplomacy through the secretary-general's good offices, he came to believe that the UN must be prepared to undertake peace

■ Dag Hammarskjöld   SOURCE: Corbis/Bettmann

enforcement operations to prevent civil wars from escalating and spreading. In 1960, establishing a pattern that would be repeated in many future conflicts, he organized a UN military force of 19,000 Blue Helmets from twenty-one countries, none of which came from Security Council members, to intervene in the Congo. Although his actions were denounced by the Soviet Union (which demanded his resignation), Hammarskjöld proceeded with the controversial intervention. Although the peace enforcement mission in the Congo was successful, he would not live to see his efforts come to fruition; he died in a plane crash in 1961 en route to help negotiate a final settlement. In recognition of his unflagging efforts to make the UN an active force for collective security, and in tribute to his bold, hands-on, yet nonconfrontational style of leadership, he was posthumously awarded the Nobel Peace Prize that year.

Like his immediate predecessors, Javier Perez de Cuellar (1982–1992) showed little in the way of activism as secretary-general. The former Peruvian diplomat was elected to the position as a dark-horse, compromise candidate. He was acceptable to many states because he was perceived as a man of caution who would not upset the status quo.

Boutros Boutros-Ghali (1992–1997), the first African and first Arab to head the UN, returned to the activist precedents set by Hammarskjöld. An Egyptian, Boutros-Ghali assumed office shortly after the end of the Cold War. The UN was therefore expected by many to play a more dominant role in global politics, and he responded to the challenge with a vigorous administration, attempting to revitalize the UN, overseeing the expansion of peacekeeping, and pushing for democratization of the international community. Not all UN members agreed with his assertive style of leadership or his objectives, especially his call for a permanent armed peacekeeping force under UN control, and other critics held him responsible for wasteful spending and financial difficulties. Largely because of U.S. objections, he was not reinstated for a second term.

Boutros-Ghali was replaced in 1997 by fellow African Kofi Anan, a Ghanaian diplomat who had served as undersecretary-general for peacekeeping operations. The first UN bureaucrat to take on the role of secretary-general, Anan displayed his nonconfrontational leadership style by negotiating an agreement with Iraq's President Saddam Hussein to resume UN inspections of suspected Iraqi nuclear and biological weapons facilities in 1998, defusing or at least delaying the potential for renewed conflict in the Persian Gulf. Anan's mission to Baghdad illustrated the daunting challenges of leading a UN committed to new responsibilities with limited resources in an uncertain political environment. His responses to these challenges will do much to define the Secretariat's role in the early twenty-first century.

International Court of Justice

Headquartered in The Hague, Netherlands, and permanently in session, the International Court of Justice (also known as the World Court, like its League of Nations predecessor) is the principal judicial organ of the UN. Its fifteen judges are elected by the GA and SC for nine-year terms. All questions brought before the court are decided by majority vote.

The court hears cases brought to it by the state involved. It also provides advisory opinions to the GA and SC at their request. Although its decisions are formally binding between the parties concerned, there are no formal mechanisms to enforce its rulings. However, the UN charter provides that if a party fails to perform its obligations under a judgment, the other party may go to the SC, which may apply more pressure on the offending party to enforce the ruling.

The notion of state sovereignty also limits the effectiveness of court decisions. Because there is no formal obligation to accept the rulings, those that are perceived as violating state sovereignty are often brushed aside. Iran, for example, ignored the court's order to release the hostages held after the takeover of the U.S. embassy in Teheran in 1979, and the United States similarly dismissed an order to halt the mining of Nicaraguan harbors in the 1980s.

The election of the fifteen judges to the International Court is one of individuals, not of states. Individuals are chosen on the basis of their high moral character and their expert legal qualifications. No two judges are to be from the same nation, in order to ensure that most of the world's principal judicial and legal systems are represented on the court. The composition of the court, though not free of political influences, changes periodically to ensure that the justices are drawn from leading states whose legal systems and institutions are well-established, legitimate, and stable.

Economic and Social Council

The **Economic and Social Council** (ECOSOC), responsible for coordinating the work of the UN "family" of more specialized agencies and organizations, has been the most controversial organ of the UN. Most of the UN's humanitarian organizations fall under the ECOSOC umbrella, such as the Universal Postal Union (UPU), **International Children's Emergency Fund** (UNICEF), the World Meteorological Organization (WMO), and the **World Health Organization** (WHO). As examples of how these organizations function, we can examine two of the more successful UN family members, the **Food and Agriculture Organization** (FAO) and the International Labor Organization (ILO).

The principal goals of the FAO, established in 1945 and based in Rome, include combating famine and hunger, raising nutritional levels of the world's population, securing efficiency improvements in the production and distribution of all agricultural products, and bettering conditions for the world's rural population. To attain these objectives, the FAO undertakes various agricultural-related research, subsidizes technical assistance to individual nations, distributes information through educational projects, and publishes a variety of periodicals and yearbooks about the production, trade, and consumption of agricultural commodities. The FAO is governed by the biennial FAO Conference, in which each member nation is represented and has one vote. The Council, which supervises the work of the FAO, is composed of representatives of twenty-four member governments and is elected by the Conference.

The International Labor Organization established in 1919 by the Treaty of Versailles, transferred its affiliation from the League of Nations to the UN after World War II. To achieve its principal aim of enhancing living standards and conditions of labor throughout the world, the ILO promotes international standards for working conditions and wages, provides assistance in social policy and administration, fosters cooperation between workers and employers, and compiles labor statistics. The executive authority of the ILO, the Governing Body, is elected during the annual International Labor Conference, which has representatives from trade unions, employers, and national governments. Daily ILO operation is handled by the International Labor Office in Geneva, which is under the direction of an appointed director general. During its affiliation with the League of Nations, the ILO was principally concerned with the economic development of its European members. Since 1945, the ILO gradually shifted its attention to the states of the Third World. Because of its far-flung and constructive activities in these states, the ILO was awarded the Nobel Peace Prize in 1969.

Other specialized agencies under ECOSOC concentrate on environmental issues and sustainable development—that is, the achievement of economic growth sustainable for the benefit of future generations, without substantially damaging the environment or exhausting natural resources. The United Nations Environmental Program (UNEP) promotes environmental protection and conservation by providing technical assistance to member states and coordinating international environmental projects. Major areas of UNEP activity are protection of the marine environment (including international efforts against ocean pollution and promoting fisheries and coastal zone management) and fighting desertification, especially in Africa and East and South Asia. Similarly, the United Nations Development Program (UNDP) assists member states in striking the balance between industrial growth, basic human needs, resource conservation, and environmental protection. These goals are not incompatible, but as Chapter Ten will point out, pursuing all of them simultaneously entails tradeoffs and compromises, and UNDP studies and technical assistance help developing countries make policies and investments for sustainable growth and development.

In contrast to the UNEP, UNDP, FAO, ILO, and WHO (which was instrumental in essentially wiping out smallpox, formerly one of the world's most deadly diseases), the specific tasks that other specialized agencies have sought to accomplish have drawn widespread criticism. Again, disputes between member states and ECOSOC specialized agencies seem to erupt most often when the question of state sovereignty becomes prominent. In 1992, for example, inspectors from the Vienna-based International Atomic Energy Agency (IAEA) endured verbal and physical harassment when trying to inspect alleged nuclear weapons production facilities inside Iraq. Inspectors were to determine whether Saddam Hussein was complying with UN prohibitions against such facilities there. Hussein opposed the holding of inspections, claiming they violated Iraqi sovereignty. In response, President George Bush, in August 1992, threatened to bomb the Iraqi Ministry of Military Industrialization, largely responsible for Baghdad's nuclear programs, if inspections were not permitted. The confrontation fizzled as the IAEA team was allowed to complete its inspection without attempting to enter the national security ministry itself.

A second set of controversies over ECOSOC centers on the Paris-based **UN Educational, Scientific, and Cultural Organization** (UNESCO). UNESCO promotes international collaboration among states in education, scholarship in the humanities and social sciences, and the arts. In 1984 the Reagan administration withdrew the United States from UNESCO, charging it with anti-Western bias and economic mismanagement. Lack of American funding greatly reduced the effectiveness of the organization, although the recent end of the Cold War has led

At a Glance

UN Bodies: Structure and Function

General Assembly (GA)

Contents: 181 members

Qualifications for Membership: All UN members are part of the GA

Voting Requirements for Resolutions: Two-thirds majority on "important issues"; simple majority on "ordinary issues"

Activities: UN's primary forum for discussion of global issues; makes recommendations on all matters within scope of the UN charter; determines membership of other UN organs; approves UN budget

Security Council (SC)

Contents: five permanent members (China, France, Russia, United Kingdom, United States), ten nonpermanent members

Qualifications for Membership: GA elects nonpermanent members to two-year terms

Voting Requirements for Resolutions: nine members for "procedural" matters and nine, including unanimity of permanent members, for "substantive" issues

Activities: Organizing collective-security operations; dispatching observer missions and peacekeeping troops; investigating disputes that might cause international friction. Every permanent member has used veto power to protect what it views as its national interest.

Economic and Social Council (ECOSOC)

Contents: UN specialized agencies, and World Bank Group (WTO)

Qualifications for Membership: GA elects ECOSOC's fifty-four members to three-year terms

Voting Requirements for Resolutions: Not applicable

Activities: Coordinates work for the "UN family" of organizations. Many organizations under ECOSOC umbrella are humanitarian, including the World Health Organization (WHO); some focus on environmental issues (United Nations Environment Program, UNEP), while others concentrate on striking a balance between human needs and sustainable development (Food and Agriculture Organization, FAO, and United Nations Development Program, UNDP). WTO, while linked to ECOSOC by agreement, is an autonomous organization.

Secretariat

Contents: Secretary-general, his or her aides and other officials

Qualifications for Membership: Officials appointed by secretary-general, who is elected to a five-year term

Voting Requirements for Resolutions: Not applicable

Activities: Chief administrative body; can bring any matter threatening world peace to SC's attention; can call special GA sessions

International Court of Justice

Contents: Fifteen judges

Qualifications for Membership: Elected by the GA and SC for nine-year terms

Voting Requirements for Resolutions: Majority vote

Activities: Principal judicial organ of the UN. State sovereignty limits effectiveness of court's decisions.

to renewed calls for the United States to rejoin UNESCO. Britain, which dropped out along with the United States, already has taken steps to rejoin the organization. Meanwhile, the United States has expressed its approval of a set of Japanese proposals to streamline and reform UNESCO's bureaucratic apparatus. Overall, much like their primary organs, UN cultural and educational agencies have not always lived up to the lofty goals proclaimed by their founders.

UN MISSIONS: EXPECTATIONS AND EXPERIENCE

When UN collective-security operations involve the use of force against a belligerent, UN peacekeeping and truce-supervision forces serve as armed sentries. Known as the "Blue Berets" and **"Blue Helmets"** because they retain their national uniforms but wear UN headgear, they are dispatched only at the invitation of parties to a local conflict (sometimes with great-power prodding), with their primary mission to separate armed combatants in order to make violation of a peace agreement more difficult. Peacekeeping forces are assigned to the UN by member states; the UN does not maintain a standing army, although this has been suggested. Since 1948 the SC has authorized forty-two peacekeeping operations, involving 600,000 troops, more than 1400 of whom have died in the line of duty. The Blue Helmets collectively received a Nobel Peace Prize in 1988 in recognition of their efforts.

There are three types of missions that the UN undertakes: **observer, peacekeeping**, and **peace enforcement**. The observer missions are international forces sent to observe a cease-fire that has been organized by the two opposing sides of a dispute. These forces are not usually large enough to make the cease-fire effective. Peacekeeping missions not only observe the cease-fire but also act as a buffer between the two sides. Peace-enforcement missions observe, act as a buffer, and, as a last resort, are allowed to use military force to keep the peace. Thus, peacekeeping operations differ from peace-enforcement actions in that peacekeepers are dispatched to prevent combat, not take part in it. UN-approved military operations in Korea and the Persian Gulf, classified as "peace-enforcement" according to the UN charter, did not require the permission of the countries where UN forces operated. (It would have been difficult to imagine Iraq's President Saddam Hussein giving "permission" for UN forces to enter Kuwait to reverse the gains made by the Iraqi invasion of that country.) Like the Wild West, these military actions represent cases where a "sheriff's posse" was organized to act against blatant aggression that violated the law of nations.

The end of the Cold War has allowed ethnic conflicts to resurface in various regions of the world, just as the decline of Cold War politics within the UN has encouraged the wider use of UN missions to mitigate these conflicts. However, expectations of what peacekeepers can now accomplish in a post–Cold War world frequently outpace what they can in fact achieve. The mixed success of UN missions in the former Yugoslavia, Cambodia, and Somalia provide illuminating examples.

Ethnic tensions in Yugoslavia between Serbs, Croats, and the Bosnia Muslims were unleashed following the collapse of that Communist state. The UN set up a mission in Bosnia and Croatia in 1992 to help ease, if not prevent, civilian illnesses, lack of supplies, and in some cases, starvation. Although the UN was for the most part been successful in distributing and ensuring access to humanitarian relief supplies, it has not been able to serve as a buffer between the warring factions. More fundamentally, it was unable to find a solution to the root problem of ethnic hatred in that region. Despite higher expectations, its 45,000 troops in the former Yugoslavia were limited to assisting civilians whenever possible, even though it faced blockades, inspections, and snipers from every side of the war. Only NATO intervention in 1995, following an agreement among the warring parties, was able to provide effective peacekeeping.

Another ambitious UN project was the peacekeeping operation in Cambodia, initiated in 1991. Costing $2.6 billion in a single year and involving over 22,000 troops and civilian officials, the mission achieved noteworthy successes but did not prove fully adequate to the huge task demanded of it. It managed to register 4.64 million voters (96 percent of the eligible population) and supervise elections for a constituent assembly. Yet the peacekeepers were not able to convince the forces of the Khmer Rouge (the deadliest of four major guerrilla factions) to demobilize and disarm, and a new wave of political violence crested in 1997 in a coup led by the country's former Communist leader, Hun Sen.[18]

The UN intervention in Somalia was even more painful. It began initially as a humanitarian mission in late 1992 to alleviate mass starvation and widespread suffering. By mid-1993 it deteriorated as UN peacekeepers were gradually drawn into local politics. Fighting and casualties began affecting both local militias and UN forces. For a time UN troops, led by the United States, sought to arrest faction leader Mohammed Farah Aidid for his guerrillas' attacks on UN soldiers and to assist in the organization of a viable government. In the end, however, Aidid was not captured, and the United States completed the withdrawal of its troops at the end of March 1994. The remaining UN mission was left understrength and overcommitted. Meanwhile, the UN attempted to come to terms with the requirements for continued humanitarian assistance and the need to confront local political factions—including Aidid's.

Perhaps the biggest challenge facing UN peacekeeping missions in the future rests not on the field of battle, but rather in the pocketbooks of member states. An independent advisory group concluded in 1993 that the UN still lacks the funding necessary for most effective peacekeeping and enforcement operations. International demands on the UN for peacekeeping grew dramatically in the 1990s. In 1991 about 15,000 UN peacekeepers were deployed around the world; by 1995 the number peaked at 60,000 in seventeen countries.[19] To manage the ongoing problems of funding operations on such a scale, the report recommended the creation of a unified peacekeeping budget, annual assessments from member governments, and the establishment of a $400 million revolving fund for peacekeeping, to be financed by all member states.[20]

Overall, despite the ongoing problem of inadequate funding, UN missions have played a vital role in bringing many conflicts to an end, especially in Africa,

Map 9.1   United Nations Peacekeeping Missions

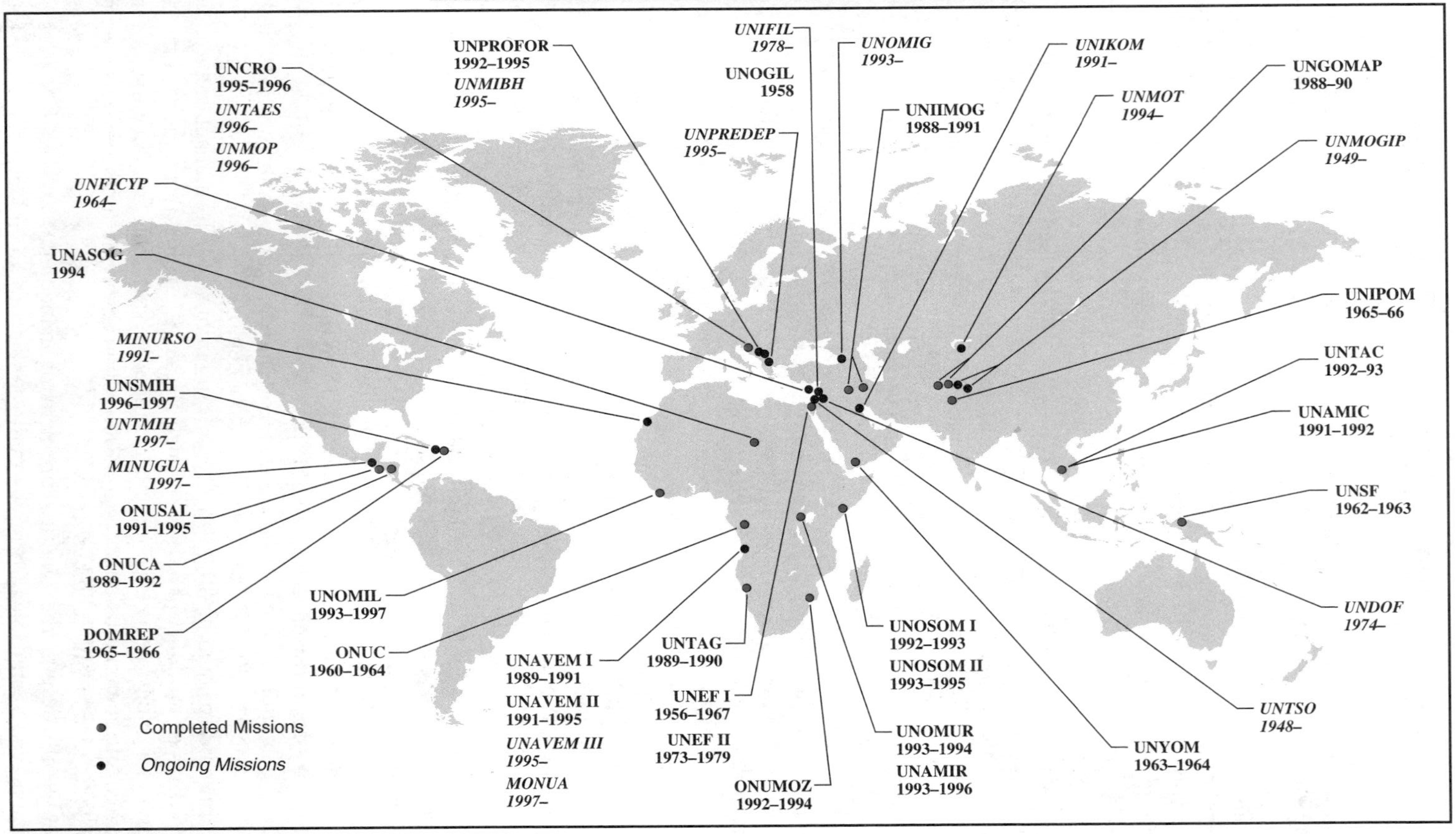

UNGOMAP 1988–90
UNMOGIP 1949–
UNIPOM 1965–66
UNTAC 1992–93
UNAMIC 1991–1992
UNSF 1962–1963
UNDOF 1974–
UNTSO 1948–
UNYOM 1963–1964

UNIKOM 1991–
UNMOT 1994–
UNMIG 1993–
UNIIMOG 1988–1991

UNOSOM I 1992–1993
UNOSOM II 1993–1995
UNOMUR 1993–1994
UNAMIR 1993–1996
ONUMOZ 1992–1994

UNIFIL 1978–
UNOGIL 1958
UNPREDEP 1995–

UNTAG 1989–1990
UNEF I 1956–1967
UNEF II 1973–1979

UNPROFOR 1992–1995
UNMIBH 1995–

UNAVEM I 1989–1991
UNAVEM II 1991–1995
UNAVEM III 1995–
MONUA 1997–

UNCRO 1995–1996
UNTAES 1996–
UNMOP 1996–

UNOMIL 1993–1997
ONUC 1960–1964

UNFICYP 1964–

UNASOG 1994

MINURSO 1991–
UNSMIH 1996–1997
UNTMIH 1997–
MINUGUA 1997–
ONUSAL 1991–1995
ONUCA 1989–1992
DOMREP 1965–1966

• Completed Missions
• Ongoing Missions

SOURCE: UN Office of Peace Information

UNTSO
United Nations Truce Supervision Organization (Israel, Occupied Territory)
June 1948–

UNMOGIP
United Nations Military Observer Group in India and Pakistan
January 1949–

UNEF I
First United Nations Emergency Force (Egypt)
November 1956–June 1967

UNOGIL
United Nations Observation Group in Lebanon
June 1958–December 1958

ONUC
United Nations Operation in the Congo
July 1960–June 1964

UNSF
United Nations Security Force in West New Guinea (West Irian)
October 1962–April 1963

UNYOM
United Nations Yemen Observation Mission
July 1963–September 1964

UNFICYP
United Nations Peace-keeping Force in Cyprus
March 1964–

DOMREP
Mission of the Representative of the Secretary-General in the Dominican Republic
May 1965–October 1966

UNIPOM
United Nations India-Pakistan Observation Mission
September 1965–March 1966

UNEF II
Second United Nations Emergency Force (Egypt)
October 1973–July 1979

UNDOF
United Nations Disengagement Observer Force (Israel, Occupied Territory, Syria)
June 1974–

UNIFIL
United Nations Interim Force in Lebanon
March 1978–

UNGOMAP
United Nations Good Offices Mission in Afghanistan and Pakistan
May 1988–March 1990

UNIIMOG
United Nations Iran-Iraq Military Observer Group
August 1988–February 1991

UNAVEM I
United Nations Angola Verification Mission I
January 1989–May 1991

UNTAG
United Nations Transition Assistance Group (Namibia)
April 1989–March 1990

ONUCA
United Nations Observer Group in Central America
November 1989–January 1992

UNIKOM
United Nations Iraq-Kuwait Observation Mission
April 1991–

UNAVEM II
United Nations Angola Verification Mission II
May 1991–February 1995

ONUSAL
United Nations Observer Mission in El Salvador
July 1991–April 1995

MINURSO
United Nations Mission for the Referendum in Western Sahara (Morocco)
April 1991–

UNAMIC
United Nations Advance Mission in Cambodia
October 1991–March 1992

UNPROFOR
United Nations Protection Force (Croatia, Bosnia-Herzegovina)
March 1992–December 1995

UNTAC
United Nations Transitional Authority in Cambodia
March 1992–September 1993

UNOSOM I
United Nations Operation in Somalia I
April 1992–March 1993

UNOMOZ
United Nations Operation in Mozambique
December 1992–December 1994

UNOSOM II
United Nations Operation in Somalia II
March 1993–March 1995

UNOMUR
United Nations Observer Mission Uganda-Rwanda
June 1993–September 1994

UNOMIG
United Nations Observer Mission in Georgia
August 1993–

UNOMIL
United Nations Observer Mission in Liberia
September 1993–

UNMIH
United Nations Mission in Haiti
September 1993–June 1996

UNAMIR
United Nations Assistance Mission for Rwanda
October 1993–March 1996

UNASOG
United Nations Aouzou Strip Observer Group (Chad)
May 1994–June 1994

UNMOT
United Nations Mission of Observers in Tajikistan
December 1994–

UNAVEM III
United Nations Angola Verification Mission III
February 1995–

UNCRO
United Nations Confidence Restoration Operation in Croatia
March 1995–January 1996

UNPREDEP
United Nations Preventive Deployment Force (Macedonia)
March 1995–

UNMIBH
United Nations Mission in Bosnia and Herzegovina
December 1995–

UNTAES
United Nations Transitional Administration for Eastern Slavonia, Baranja and Western Sirmium
January 1996–

UNMOP
United Nations Mission of Observers in Prevlaka
January 1996–

MONUA
United Nations Observer Mission in Angola
July 1997–

MIPONUH
United Nations Civilian Police Mission in Haiti
December 1997–

What Would You Do ?

You are the secretary-general of the United Nations in the late 1990s. Despite a broad international effort earlier in the decade to end the civil war and establish democracy in Cambodia, the country is seized by a wave of violence as political factions begin fighting once again. Civilian casualties are mounting, and images of reported atrocities flash across television screens every night. Some UN observers, along with relief workers from many countries, are still in place, but they are increasingly threatened by the escalating conflict, and the head of the UN mission reports that their position may soon become untenable. The government in Phnom Penh is prepared to allow an expanded UN presence, but only if the government believes this will increase its chances of survival, which are uncertain. The United States is prepared to use its military forces to evacuate American civilians, and Japan has indicated that it would be willing to partially finance expanded humanitarian relief, but no other member states have made commitments. The Security Council has passed several resolutions calling for an end to the violence, but they have been essentially ignored by the warring factions.

You have no permanent forces under your command, so if you believe urgent action is necessary you must rely on the Security Council and the member states. You cannot force member states to take action, but you can try to persuade them to act and explain why expanded UN intervention would be in their own interest and in the interest of international security. But most members of the Security Council regard Cambodia as an area of peripheral interest, at best, and will be very reluctant to spend money and risk lives in a conflict that does not directly affect them. The sole exception is China, but it lacks the logistical capability to transport large numbers of troops or quantities of supplies for humanitarian relief. Moreover,

Central America, and the Middle East. Because the end of the Cold War has led to a proliferation of regional and ethnic conflicts all over the world, it is clear that UN forces will continue to be called upon to play a major role in the resolution of these conflicts. The question remains whether UN forces should help settle conflicts, build new governments, protect personnel providing humanitarian relief, or just separate the combatants. These tasks have proven difficult to separate in practice, and the linkages between them have often resulted in "mission creep," as peacekeepers find that their initially modest objectives cannot become accomplished without undertaking more ambitious tasks such as disarming warring factions. The commitment of the Blue Helmets to their missions has never been in question, but the negative response to former Secretary-General Boutros-Ghali's call for a predesignated reserve of peacekeeping forces, and the UN's bitter experiences in Yugoslavia, Somalia, Rwanda, and elsewhere, have cast further doubt on the extent to which UN member states will be willing to commit more troops and funds for their efforts.[21]

the other SC members would almost certainly veto a major operation in which China had the leading role, and even suggesting such a move would provoke strenuous opposition from Japan, South Korea, and the ASEAN states. Thus, a truly international effort is the only option for a renewed UN presence.

But should the UN try again where it has failed before? It will not be easy to justify another major UN effort at peace-keeping and nation-building even if all sides in the conflict agree to participate. The SC and other member states may find it difficult to justify spending more money and risking more troops in what they may now perceive as a lost cause. It may be better to evacuate the military and civilian observers now in place and use your influence to try to achieve a negotiated truce. This will take time, however, as long as one or more of the factions believes that they can gain something by fighting. If action is not taken soon, the death toll could rise, and a repeat of the horrors of the "killing fields" of the 1970s may not be out of the question.

Therefore, you are faced with some difficult choices. Should you ask for an expanded international commitment to stop the fighting, or should you withdraw UN personnel from this dangerous situation? If you ask for intervention, should you justify your request on the grounds of peacekeeping, humanitarian aid, or both? What precedents will your decision set for future UN peacekeeping? How could the actions you call for affect demands for political and financial reform of the UN—or should these even be considered at this time of urgent need?

The decisions you make and the actions you support could define the role of the United Nations at the start of the twenty-first century, but the potential victims of violence in Cambodia are your immediate concern.

What would you do ?

United Nations' Effectiveness

Like the Concert of Europe, the basic idea for the UN was forged by the "Big Three" allies (Great Britain, the United States, and the Soviet Union) in the crucible of war. The wartime participants met in San Francisco (April–June 1945) to create an organization whose primary purpose, like the League of Nations, would be maintaining collective security against military aggression. To this effect, they established the Security Council, whose permanent members were recognized and expected to act as the "world's policemen."

Mindful, however, of how the lofty expectations for the League of Nations had quickly been dashed, the founders of the UN sought to dampen expectations about what the new organization could accomplish. They believed that only the concerted will and strength of the great powers, reflected in agreement between the five permanent SC members, could rebuff aggression. Although it would seem that the veto power exercised by any permanent SC member could prevent the United Nations from taking any action and thus limit its effectiveness, the veto was intended to ensure that the UN would undertake only those actions that all the great powers would support.

It was hoped that this "great power government" would be adequate to meet any challenge presented to the postwar international system. In recognizing that the power of all nations was not created equal, the UN's founders demonstrated a more realistic grasp of global power politics than the idealistic founders of the League of Nations.

Thus far, the UN appears to be the only existing organization with a chance of countering aggression in a legitimate and impartial manner. As we will see in the next chapter, its activities transcend those of the collective-security organizations that preceded it, as its various agencies deal with a wide array of global issues. The power and effectiveness of the UN is still hamstrung, however, by its inability to claim sovereign authority over all nations engaged in international affairs. Action by the UN usually requires consent of the countries involved.

This need for consent creates an obstacle to UN resolution of conflicts, especially in the developing world. It is not surprising that the developing states are reluctant to give up even a modicum of sovereignty to an international organization, because most have gained independence recently and are thus extremely sensitive to interference in their internal affairs. Just as individuals usually resent searches of their persons and property by the police, so countries regard intervention by outside agencies, however well-intentioned, as an unwelcome intrusion.

As was the case with the League of Nations, the UN cannot force any state to comply with its resolutions if the major powers are not committed to enforcing those resolutions with military might when necessary. Many argue that UN sanctions per se against Iraq for its invasion of Kuwait in 1990 would not have sufficed to compel Iraq to withdraw. Rather, a coalition of great powers (especially Britain, France, and the United States) was necessary to achieve that goal in the Persian Gulf, and would similarly have been required to put an end to the fighting in Bosnia in an expeditious manner. Might may not make right, but right is often impotent without might.

Lack of sovereign authority does not mean that UN sanctions are condemned to futility. In some cases, a UN sanctions resolution alone can inflict considerable costs on a state that is transgressing international law if the resolution's goals are shared by other states. Although many states find ways around sanctions, a state facing a UN-sanctioned embargo carries the stigma of being an international troublemaker, and few states wish their good standing tarnished by being associated with a stigmatized state. Arguably, for example, the governments of Rhodesia (now Zimbabwe) and South Africa were pressured to change their racist domestic policies by UN-sponsored sanctions.[22]

The UN's five decades of existence have proven that the objectives and expectations of the organization's founders were essentially correct. The UN was not designed to be all things to all nations. It was created as a forum for the discussion of global issues, as a coordinating body for development aid and humanitarian relief, and as a means to facilitate collective security when the world's major powers agreed on what should be done to meet specific threats. Overall, it has performed these functions remarkably well, though it has been a target of justifiable criticism as mentioned in this section. It has not brought about world peace; it cannot do so, and it was never intended to.

The UN is capable of doing more if its member states provide it with more resources, but its efforts will always be subject to the limitations imposed by national sovereignty as long as sovereignty remains a fundamental principle of international relations. Sovereignty constrains international organizations just as civil rights constrain national governments. In both cases, the governed cannot be blamed for thinking carefully before conceding more power to the government, even in the interest of law and order.

The UN's greatest challenge in the twenty-first century will be to adapt its structure and mission to the changing international system. It has risen to this challenge in some areas, placing new emphasis on sustainable development, famine relief, and programs to fight diseases such as AIDS and ebola (see Chapter Ten). In other areas, particularly peacekeeping, the need for further reform, division of responsibilities with other IOs and national governments, and finding a better balance between goals and resources is clear. Changing the UN charter to reflect the realities of the New Era will be difficult, but the United States and other countries continue to call for organizational and financial reforms. The UN has furthest to

■ Bejing Women's Summit

SOURCE: M. Atlan/Sygma

Spotlight

The World Conference on Women

More than 50,000 people, over two-thirds of them women, attended the UN-sponsored fourth World Conference on Women held at Beijing in 1995. The conference focused on convincing the international community that women's rights are synonymous with human rights. Building on previous UN conferences on women (held in 1975 in Mexico City, 1980 in Copenhagen, and 1985 in Nairobi), representatives of 189 governments and a host of interest groups and NGOs put together a declaration and a platform for action on the empowerment of women, the removal of obstacles preventing women from equal participation in the economic, social, and political sphere, and the promotion of equality, development, and peace.

The Beijing Declaration recognized that the status of women had advanced in many ways in recent years, but it emphasized that deeply rooted inequalities between men and women have yet to be addressed, that women's participation in society continues to be stifled by cultural bias and that, in many countries, the basic human rights of women are routinely ignored. The action platform identified twelve critical areas of concern for women: poverty, education, health, violence, armed conflicts, economic disparity, decision-making and power-sharing, institutional mechanisms, human rights, the media, the environment, and the girl child. More specific goals of the platform called for action to assure women equal access to affordable housing and land, enact laws calling for the equal pay of women and men, and encourage ratification of existing human rights treaties.

Despite the widespread agreement on these goals, political and ideological conflicts engendered a great deal of frustration and conflict at the conference. The platform section on health, in particular, led to heated debate, as the section reiterated and expanded on many of the goals for population control and reproductive rights adopted at the International Conference on Population and Development held in Cairo in 1994. Representatives of the Vatican and many Islamic States challenged the language on sexual and reproductive health, especially birth control and abortion. Paragraphs referring to the right of women to "control all aspects of their health, in particular their own fertility" as basic to women's empowerment, and another asking all countries to reconsider laws against abortion, were staunchly resisted by conservative delegations. Despite their opposition, the sections on reproductive health and abortion remained in the declaration.

In the end, despite the expressed reservations of forty countries on specific provisions, again mostly dealing with health, the Platform for Action was adopted by consensus. The controversies at the Beijing conference did not prevent it from sending a unified and powerful message: governments, NGOs, and the private sector must work together to remove all elements of discrimination, coercion, and violence from the lives of women and girls. Though the conference made no attempt to conceal the conflicts and difficulties inherent in the realization of its goals, it confirmed that the human rights of women must remain a high priority on the global agenda.

go in reforming its political structure. Some reform proposals advocate expanding the Security Council, adding permanent seats for Germany, Japan, and major developing countries like Brazil and India, and/or changing the rules regarding vetoes. Such measures may help make the UN more effective, but like its member states, the UN must find ways to adapt to economic globalization, regional integration, political fragmentation, and reemerging threats to security such as terrorism and ethnic conflict. Otherwise, like its ancestors the Concert of Europe and the League of Nations, it may soon discover that the world it was designed to serve has left it far behind.

OTHER INTERGOVERNMENTAL ORGANIZATIONS

The UN is a multipurpose intergovernmental organization with a global membership base. Other important IGOs operate worldwide but confine their activities to a few specific functions; others undertake a wide range of activities in a particular geographic region; still others are specialized both in membership and in purpose. Regardless of their objectives or scope of membership, most of these IGOs are affiliated with the UN in one way or another. And like the UN, most are constrained by the will and resources of their members.

General-Purpose IGOs

The leading general-purpose IGOs confine their membership to specific regions or categories of states. These include many associations of states that promote regional security and act as forums for resolving regional disputes. The League of Arab States (commonly called the Arab League) includes among its membership twenty-one Arab states, as well as the Palestinian Liberation Organization (PLO). It was created in 1945 to "safeguard the independence and integrity" of the member states and unsuccessfully tried to mediate in the dispute that led to the Iraqi invasion of Kuwait in 1990.[23] The Organization of American States (OAS), which includes most of the nations of the Western Hemisphere, is another example of an organization that attempts to address a number of regional concerns.

Other general-purpose regional IGOs include the **Organization of African Unity** (OAU), which promoted decolonization and now focuses on regional development and cooperation, and the Association of South-East Asian Nations (see Chapter Five), which encourages peaceful cooperation and economic development among its members. The **Commonwealth of Independent States** (CIS), the organization of successor states to the former Soviet Union, could also be considered a general regional IGO, although its primary goals and the extent of its authority remain unclear. The most successful general-purpose regional IGO is the European Union, which began life in 1957 as a primarily economic organization but has made halting progress in the direction of becoming a regional "superstate" with a common European citizenship, currency, and other features associated with sovereign states (see Chapter Seven).

Overall, the record of general-purpose regional IGOs in fostering international cooperation and reducing anarchy is mixed. They have by no means stopped or prevented all regional conflicts, but what is more certain is that such organizations at the very least serve as effective forums for debate among member nations. Because debate and public discussion in themselves increase the likelihood for peaceful dispute resolutions, these IGOs have at times made important contributions to regional cooperation. Basically, like any clubs, regional IGOs are what their members decide to make of them.

Specialized IGOs

One of the most famous specialized IGOs with a global membership base is the International Criminal Police Organization (Interpol), based in Lyons, France. Created in 1923 and now composed of more than 150 members, Interpol's purpose is to promote the widest possible mutual assistance between all police authorities within the limits of the law existing in the different countries and in the spirit of the universal Declaration of Human Rights. Perhaps because of its limited objective—it is forbidden to undertake any intervention or activities of a political, military, religious, or racial character—Interpol serves as an example of how IGOs can effectively foster cooperation between states. Once focused on terrorism, almost half of Interpol's activities are now dedicated to countering drug trafficking and money laundering.

Specialized regional or limited-membership IGOs include several groups of states designed to promote collective defense. Prominent among these is the North Atlantic Treaty Organization, which during the Cold War comprised fourteen European states as well as the United States and Canada. As Chapter Four describes, NATO was created in 1949 to promote defense cooperation in Western European and repel any armed aggression directed against a member state. The main threat that led to NATO's creation came from the Soviet Union (and later the Soviet bloc countered with a military alliance of its own, the Warsaw Treaty Organization). Though it has not been free of controversy and organizational difficulties, NATO was a definite success in bringing a sense of order, purpose, and focus to Western defense efforts during the Cold War. The end of the Cold War has not robbed NATO of its collective defense role, as it has proven effective (at least more effective than the UN and other organizations) in carrying out peacekeeping operations in the former Yugoslavia. Worried by potential instabilities in the regions once dominated by the USSR, former Warsaw Pact members Poland, Hungary, and the Czech Republic sought membership in NATO and were invited to join in 1997. They may be joined by Slovenia, Romania, and other states of Central and Eastern Europe. Russia, however, strenuously objected to this expansion of NATO's membership, fearing that NATO's military strength might once again be directed against it despite the end of Cold War–era superpower rivalry. Though Russia and NATO signed an understanding in 1997 designed to alleviate this concern, many Russian leaders continue to believe that the exclusion of Russia from European politics and regional relations, and an attempt to relegate Russia to the status of a second-class power, were hidden agendas behind NATO's westward expansion.

Collective security throughout all of post–Cold War Europe is the province of the Organization on Security and Cooperation in Europe (OSCE). Originally created as the Conference on Security and Cooperation in Europe (CSCE) in 1975 as part of the Helsinki negotiations, the OSCE includes most European states, the states of the former USSR, plus the United States and Canada. The end of the Cold War has given the CSCE the opportunity to come into its own as a new Concert of Europe designed to manage regional crises. Its record has not been promising, as it proved unable to take effective action against the fighting following the breakup of Yugoslavia.[24] Russia prefers that the OSCE assume primary responsibility for collective security in Europe, but its consensus decision rules and questionable track record lead many other states to doubt its potential effectiveness.

Other specialized IGOs are concerned with economic matters. The twenty-four-member Organization of Economic Cooperation and Development (OECD), composed of mostly advanced industrial states, was formed in 1961 to promote economic and social welfare in member countries and to stimulate and harmonize efforts on behalf of developing nations. As we saw in Chapter Seven, a smaller subset of the OECD countries, the Group of Seven (G-7)—comprising Canada, France, Germany, Italy, Japan, the United Kingdom, and the United States—is an organization of the world's major industrial countries whose leaders meet periodically to discuss global economic issues.

As noted in Chapter 7, common markets and free-trade areas have been established in many regions with varying degrees of success. These include the Economic Community of West African States (ECOWAS), the Caribbean Community and Common Market (CARICOM), the North American Free Trade Area (NAFTA), Asia-Pacific Economic Cooperation (APEC), and the Southern Cone Common Market (MERCOSUR). None of these come close to the achievements of the European Union (EU), and without an equivalent degree of political commitment from their members, none is likely to soon. Whatever their focus or accomplishments, economic IGOs strive to bring order to the global or regional economy for common benefit, thus making the world a less anarchic place.

NONGOVERNMENTAL ORGANIZATIONS

Not all organizations taking an active part in international politics are directly affiliated with governments. These nongovernmental organizations (NGOs) operate across national boundaries independent of governments. Like IGOs, they can be widely or narrowly focused, with either more broadly based or narrowly restricted memberships. The Roman Catholic Church, the International Red Cross, Amnesty International, Greenpeace, and many multinational corporations are examples of NGOs with broad-based memberships (the Roman Catholic Church has 800 million members). Because most NGOs cannot command resources as easily as states or IGOs, they tend to focus their efforts on specific projects in order to maximize their effectiveness. Through these projects or through global public support, they can exercise a profound influence on the conduct of states.

A Hero of Peace

A few years after the founding of the International Committee of the Red Cross, the international businessman and philanthropist who set up the organization was living in poverty in his native Switzerland. Jean-Henri Dunant (1828–1910) was introduced to the horrors of war in 1859 as a neutral observer at the Battle of Solferino, which resulted in 40,000 French and Austrian casualties. Dunant organized emergency medical attention for the wounded on both sides, and a few years later he proposed the formation of voluntary societies in all countries dedicated to humanitarian relief, regardless of nationality, religion, or ethnicity. His vision for an international humanitarian organization became a reality in 1864, when Dunant founded the International Red Cross in Geneva. That same year, the first Geneva Convention on the conduct of war and the treatment of prisoners of war was convened at his initiative.

Dunant soon became one of the promoters of another well-known charitable organization, the World Alliance of Young Men's Christian Associations (YMCA). By 1867, though, he was bankrupt, having spent most of his time on charity work rather than on his business. Dunant left Geneva for an austere life in the Swiss countryside, but he continued to promote disarmament, settlement of international disputes by arbitration, the foundation of a Jewish homeland, and the abolition of slavery. He was not destined to end his life as an unsung hero, however. After a chance encounter with a newspaper reporter in 1895, Dunant was finally brought out of seclusion and awarded many honors. In 1901 he was the co-recipient of the first Nobel Peace Prize.

Humanitarian NGOs

NGOs vary widely in terms of their stated purpose. Many of the most famous NGOs engage in humanitarian activities. The International Red Cross (called the Red Crescent in Muslim countries) acts as an international relief agency and maintains strict neutrality in order to alleviate suffering without becoming involved in politics. Its many activities include disaster and famine relief, immunization and public health programs, and efforts to ensure humane treatment of prisoners of war. Amnesty International works on the behalf of prisoners of conscience around the world. It seeks the release of political prisoners and the abolition of torture, investigating abuses of human rights and organizing campaigns for the release of persons jailed for political activity.

Multinational Corporations

Some NGOs are just in it for the money. Multinational corporations (MNCs), based in a specific home country, have branches that conduct business all over the

■ Jean-Henri Dunant   SOURCE: AP/Wide World

world. Banks, such as Credit Suisse and Mitsubishi, and industrial giants such as IBM and General Motors, tend to be the largest MNCs in terms of capitalization and sales, but the most familiar and pervasive multinational corporation is McDonald's. The Golden Arches can be found in almost every country in the world, and when the huge Moscow franchise opened in 1990, it was not only the most popular restaurant in the city for several months, but also the only place in Moscow to find fresh lettuce. Although MNCs seek profits worldwide, many promote the interests of their home countries directly or indirectly, and a few have even developed reputations for meddling in the politics of developing countries. (see Chapter Eight).

Other NGOs

A wide variety of NGOs that do not fit in any of the preceding categories seek to promote global cooperation on specific global issues. Many of these groups will be discussed along with the issues they address in the following chapter, so only a few will be mentioned here. Greenpeace and the World Wide Fund for Nature (WWF) focus on environmental issues, and the International Olympic Organizing Committee (IOOC) stages the winter and summer Olympic Games in the hope of enhancing ties between nations through sport. Finally, persons who believe that these undertakings should be pursued by a global government can join the World Federalist Association.

CONCLUSION: LESS ANARCHY, OR MORE?

In this chapter, we have seen how international law and organizations constitute both a source of conflict and cooperation in the international system. Although usually designed to promote cooperation or end conflict on some set of issues, international law and organizations sometimes generate new controversies. These unintended effects of attempts to reduce anarchy, coupled with the failures of international security organizations to prevent conflict and war, lead many people to question the whole enterprise of international law and organizations. It cannot be said that international law has worked perfectly or that the functioning of the UN and other global organizations has been above reproach. Still, these drawbacks are often apparent in domestic law and government as well, and few reasonable people would conclude that laws and governments in general should be abandoned. Sometimes both domestic and international institutions fail because they are poorly designed; at other times the laws and organizations are not themselves faulty, but failures result from weaknesses in the ethics or leadership of the individuals charged with running them. Many efforts to make the world less anarchic have failed for either reason, and sometimes both, but much good has come from their efforts nonetheless. If nothing else, international law sets ethical standards for the conduct of nations, and facilitates the coordinating of action on various matters.

Like domestic law and government, international law and organizations tell us how we should act, and why. Sovereign authority can give us powerful incentives to comply, but the decision to obey or disobey is ultimately ours, as is the responsibility for paying the penalty if we choose to break the law. Constrained as they are by national sovereignty, international law and organizations have weak enforcement mechanisms, but they can still give nations and leaders incentives to behave in ways that benefit the global community without sacrificing vital national interests.[25]

In his pivotal book *Leviathan,* the seventeenth-century philosopher Thomas Hobbes argues that all-powerful sovereign authority is the only possible way to raise society above its "natural" state of "war of every one against every one."[26] As long as international relations are based on national sovereignty, the effectiveness of international law and organizations will be inherently limited. Nevertheless, through example and the threat of sanctions, international institutions have helped to advance the world a few steps beyond the near-anarchy that prevailed before the Peace of Westphalia set the foundations for the modern international system. In the coming century, the world may face a new kind of anarchy, as interdependence promotes cooperation among regions, corporations, municipalities, individuals, and other nonstate actors outside the framework of the of nation-states and traditional international organizations. Ironically, the decline of the nation-state may lead to the rise of international law, as groups establish mutually advantageous rules and regimes for economic and environmental cooperation. The model for future international organizations may be the Internet, which has no central controlling authority, but has rules and conventions enforced by reciprocity and common practice which enable it to function well despite exponential growth. This kind of "governance without government" may become an important part of the international system's adaptation to globalization and fragmentation. For Hobbes, "anarchy" connoted "chaos," and in the preindustrial and industrial eras the two generally went hand in hand. One of the paradoxes of the information age, however, may be that the world is becoming both more anarchic and more orderly.

PRINCIPAL POINTS OF CHAPTER NINE

1. International law and organizations are efforts to make the international system less anarchic.

2. International law attempts to set rules for interactions among nations and to safeguard human rights. Its fundamental principle is that of national sovereignty, set forth in the Peace of Westphalia in 1638. There is no global legislature to make laws that are binding on all nations. Instead, international law is established through formal treaties (bilateral, multilateral, or negotiated through international organizations) or through customary practice (such as diplomatic immunity).

3. In the absence of a global sovereign authority or police force, international law may be enforced through reciprocity (mutual adherence), sanctions (such as trade embargoes), or responses in kind to transgressions (such as retaliation for aggression).

4. International organizations are of two kinds: intergovernmental organizations (IGOs) and nongovernmental organizations (NGOs). Both have multiplied in recent years as groups of states and individuals have come to regard these organizations as the best forums for coordinating action on various issues.

5. The world's most important IGO is the United Nations, established after World War II by the victorious Allies to further collective security, sponsor cooperation to address global problems, and promote human rights. (Previous collective-security institutions, the Concert of Europe and the League of Nations, had failed to prevent destructive global wars.)

6. The UN's central organizations are the General Assembly (in which all UN members are represented), the Security Council (which has five permanent members with veto power—the United States, the United Kingdom, Russia, France, and China—and ten other rotating members), and the Secretariat, headed by the secretary-general.

7. In addition, the "UN family" of IGOs (including WHO, IAEA, UNEP, UNDP, and UNICEF) promote cooperation on a wide variety of global issues.

8. Other IGOs include specialized global institutions (such as Interpol), general-purpose regional organizations (such as the Arab League and ASEAN), and specialized organizations with limited or restricted memberships (such as OSCE and OPEC).

9. Groups that operate across national boundaries independent of governments are nongovernmental organizations. The most effective NGOs are focused on specific economic, environmental, or other well-defined goals. Examples include Amnesty International, the International Committee of the Red Cross (ICRC), the World Wide Fund for Nature (WWF), and multinational corporations (MNCs).

10. As the international system becomes simultaneously more globalized and more fragmented, the roles of international law and organizations are changing. Traditional organizations and conventions designed to regulate relations between states may give way to "governance without government" driven by the need to establish rules for interactions between nonstate actors in an interdependent world.

KEY TERMS

Amnesty
  International
Blue Helmets
chlorofluoro-
  carbons
Commonwealth
  of Independent
  States

Contras
customary
  practices
diplomatic
  immunity
Economic and
  Social Council

Food and
  Agriculture
  Organization
great-power
  unanimity
intergovernment
  al organizations

International
  Children's
  Emergency
  Fund
International
  Committee of
  the Red Cross

Interpol
Mutual and
  Balanced Force
  Reductions
natural law
observer

Organization of
  African Unity
Organization of
  American States
pariah states
peace enforcement
peacekeeping

positive law
treaties
UN Educational,
  Scientific,
  and Cultural
  Organization

UN Convention
  on the Law of
  the Sea
United Nations
World Health
  Organization

SOURCE: AP/Chris Tomlinson/Wide World

Global Issues

WHAT MAKES AN ISSUE GLOBAL?

"No man is an island, entire of itself; every man is a piece of the continent, a part of the main," the English poet John Donne wrote in 1623. What Donne said about individuals applies even more to states in the New Era. Nations are becoming tied together ever more closely, through communications, trade, population movements, changes in the environment, and other manifestations of globalization. In an era when news is transmitted by satellite, nuclear bombs can be delivered by missile, and narcotics are smuggled in the stomachs of airline passengers, no country can remain isolated from the world beyond its borders.

As nations have become more interconnected, however, they have not become noticeably less argumentative. Indeed, as the ties that bind countries become more numerous and stronger, countries seem to have found more to disagree about, not less. In many ways, although greater interdependence has become a defining factor of the New Era, it has led to as much conflict as cooperation. The need to rely on other states for markets and resources, and to cooperate to solve common problems, has created friction and frustration. Like high school friends who become college roommates, nations must learn to share their living space, and sometimes their friendship breaks under the accumulated weight of disputes and quarrels.

This chapter will survey some problems and controversies that cross national boundaries and figure prominently on the agendas of decision-makers around the world. Global issues that will be covered include the world's increasing population, population movements (migration), food and hunger, energy and natural resources, concerns about the environment, health issues, drug traffic, and terrorism. It is impossible to examine any one of these issues in depth in a single chapter, and this book does not attempt to do so. Instead, it introduces the reader to the most salient issues in the community of nations and offers an overview of how the community is attempting to address them. In many cases, these problems are closely interrelated; an increase in population, for example, frequently leads to migration and environmental degradation.

Before examining each issue, it is necessary to identify what makes a common problem a global issue. A number of serious problems affect millions of people worldwide but do not become international political issues. The simple fact that a problem is widespread does not qualify it as a global issue, because it does not automatically demand the attention of all nations, though persons and governments throughout the world may care about the problem and try to alleviate it. Issues become global only when there is transnationality of cause and effect— a fancy way of describing a problem that originates in one country but is felt in others. Muggings in New York's Central Park do not lead to increased crime in Toronto, but pollution from American factories can kill Canadian trees. The international links between causes and effects may be either unintentional (as they are in the spread of tuberculosis) or deliberate (as in the case of terrorism), while other problems (such as global warming) arise in and affect all countries simultaneously. This chapter will not examine every problem that each nation faces, but it will show how pressing problems that cross national boundaries affect international politics, and vice versa.

POPULATION

The rapid growth of the world's population is the root cause of many global problems. It took two centuries (1650–1850) for world population to double from 550 million to 1.18 billion, but a second doubling took only 100 years (1850–1950, from 1.18 billion to 2.56 billion), and a third doubling occurred in only 41 years (1950–1991, from 2.56 to 5.42 billion). The 1997 world population of 5.8 billion people is projected to increase to almost 8 billion by 2020. About 95 percent of the increase is expected to come from developing countries (see Figure 10.1).[1]

Why is the world's population increasing so fast? Chapter Eight discussed the phenomenon of the demographic transition that accompanies technological and economic development. To review, once a population gains access to rudimentary

Figure 10.1

World Population Growth

Population by region, in billions

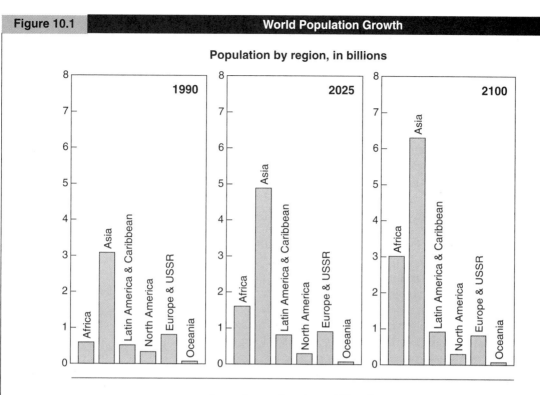

Annual growth rate and time for the population to double, 1990 data

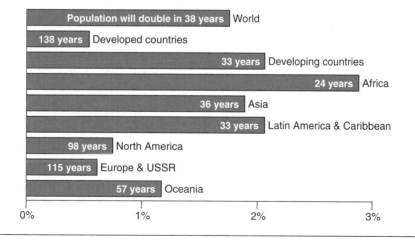

sanitation and medical services, the fertility (birth) rate quickly overtakes the mortality (death) rate, life expectancy increases, and the size of the population begins to increase steadily. In industrialized nations, population growth then levels off; the developed regions of Europe, the former USSR, and North America are growing very slowly or not at all. In these areas, increased life expectancy and participation in the workplace has led many couples to postpone marriage and have fewer children.[2] In the less developed countries of Asia, Africa, and Latin America, by contrast, medical advances such as vaccination have reduced death rates, but families often remain large and birthrates remain high, mainly because children are needed to provide labor and income for the family. As a result, developed countries generally have older and stable, slowly growing, or declining populations, while the populations of many Third World states remain younger and faster-growing. In 1950 the less developed countries (LDCs) had double the population of the more developed countries (MDCs); at the present time, they have almost four times as many people, and by 2020 they are expected to have more than four and one-half times as many.[3]

Alarmingly, by the time you finish reading this paragraph about fifty people will have been born around the world (a rate of three people per second, or a quarter of a million people a day). The world's fastest growing regions continue to be its poorest, and most of the growth is occurring in already overburdened, heavily polluted urban regions. Mexico City and São Paulo, Brazil, already the world's most populous metropolitan areas, are expected to be home to about 30 million and 25 million inhabitants, respectively, by the year 2000.[4]

The crowding in many Third World cities is made even worse by high population density (number of people per square mile): enormous numbers of people are squeezed into comparatively small areas. The population density of Lagos, Nigeria, is thirteen times that of New York City.[5] The emergence of such "megacities" has exacerbated already acute difficulties in providing basic services in developing countries. Affordable housing is difficult to find, crime rates are on the rise, transportation and communication infrastructures are increasingly strained, and social tensions are more pronounced.

International Responses to Overpopulation

Reducing overall population growth is linked to achieving the international goal of "replacement-level fertility," where two parents are replaced by two children. Even though the results of their efforts will not be evident for a few generations, international organizations, such as the United Nations Fund for Population Assistance (UNFPA) and International Planned Parenthood (IPP), have concentrated on trying to create the social, economic, and political conditions necessary for reducing the birthrate. The challenges are daunting. Achieving replacement-level fertility where it is most urgently needed—the least developed countries—will require an increase in investments in human resource developments, such as improvements in women's status and access to education on health and the means of family planning.

The level of fertility is strongly related to contraceptive use. According to most estimates, a 10 percent increase in contraceptive use results in roughly a 70 percent drop in the fertility rate. To keep the world's population at a more acceptable level of 8.5 billion in 2025, the proportion of couples using contraception must increase from today's 45 percent to at least 56 percent by 2000, an increase from 326 to 535 million.[6] Thus, the mission of international organizations such as the UN's IPP is clear: design and implement effective family-planning programs throughout the world.

Family-planning programs have succeeded in fits and starts. Information provided by programs such as the UN-sponsored African Census Program in the 1970s illustrated to many governments the full dimensions of the population problem, and thus won their support for population programs. However, government support does not automatically lead to successful program implementation. Between 1982 and 1986, for example, the Mexican government cut its national health budget by two-thirds, resulting in slowed rates of growth in the number of women using modern birth-control methods.[7] And in Africa, according to one estimate, an average of only 14 percent of women use contraceptives, a figure that must be more than doubled if desired projections are to be met. Contraceptive use, however, is not the only factor in fertility; improving educational and economic opportunities for women also tends to lower birthrates. Overall, because many developing countries are chronically strapped for funds, they often have difficulty in fully staffing and funding family-planning programs.

According to one UN estimate, the world's population may increase to 14 billion by 2025 if there is no increase in the use of family-planning measures. To prevent this from happening, women in developing countries will have to steadily reduce the average number of children they bear from a high of 4.2 (1980–1985) to a low of 1.9 by 2025. In response to estimates like these, in 1994 nearly 180 nations participating in the UN Conference on Population and Development reached an agreement to limit the world's population to 7.2 billion over the following two decades. The plan passed despite reservations regarding abortion and family planning raised by many Islamic and Catholic representatives.

Clearly, continued population growth will result only in increased strains on the world economy and the global ecosystem. Huge increases in Third World populations will continue to lead to increased numbers of emigrants to the hard-pressed developed countries of the world, more demand on the world's available supplies of food and energy resources, and greater stresses on the environment. Although the developing countries of the South are affected most by the population explosion, the industrialized North must either cooperate in solving the problem now or join in suffering its effects later.

The Abortion Debate and Family-Planning Assistance

Although they have their detractors, government family-planning programs do reduce the rate of population growth. One widely quoted study found that at any level of social development, the stronger the family-planning effort, the greater the decline in the birthrate. In developed countries, for example, the birthrate decline between 1965 and 1980 in countries with a strong family-planning program was three times faster than those with a very weak or nonexistent program.[8]

Most people support the goals of family planning—to reduce poverty, overcrowding, and other harmful effects of unrestrained population growth—but many object to some of the means employed. Religious objections to contraception restrict or prohibit the use of birth control in many countries, particularly those where a majority of the population is Roman Catholic or Muslim. The most controversial aspect of family-planning programs, however, is abortion. China's draconian (but effective) family-planning laws, for example, restrict couples to a single child, and officials pressure or compel many women to have abortions in observance of this requirement.

President Ronald Reagan, a staunch supporter of the American right-to-life movement, in 1984 ordered a cutoff of funding for all international organizations, including the United Nations Population Fund, that supported abortion as a birth control means of last resort. Because at the time no U.S. funds went to the support of abortion in other countries, Reagan's decision did not have much direct impact on the provision of abortion services abroad. Criticism of family-planning programs by opponents of abortion, however, may have led to decreased levels of overall funding. The controversy returned during the Clinton administration, though this time the administration favored full funding of family-planning programs that included abortion while many lawmakers in Congress objected. Although the net impact of the debate over abortion in the U.S. on population control in developing countries is difficult to assess, the controversy illustrates how cultural factors and domestic political disputes can affect international efforts to address global issues.

MIGRATION

An imbalance between population and economic resources often leads to movements of population, or migration. In general, migration brings people from regions that suffer from a dearth of land or capital resources, such as Central America or Eastern Europe, to those that are richer, like the United States and the European Union. In recent years, however, many developed countries have gone through cycles of economic recession and thus are becoming more reluctant to accept more immigrants. Additionally, migration is not a purely economic phenomenon. It emerges out of a complex mix of economic scarcity, warfare, ethnic conflict, religious persecution, political repression, and environmental degradation. Migration has always played a major role in the history of the human species (and, indeed, that of its hominid ancestors). This section will focus on patterns and problems of migration at the end of the twentieth century and the start of the twenty-first.

Economic Migration

With rare exceptions (such as the African slaves brought to the Americas before the nineteenth century), most people who have immigrated to the richer countries of the world have done so in search of a higher standard of living. This is hardly surprising, as higher birthrates in the developing world have produced an enormous population that has sought work in the industrialized world, with its comparative wealth, lower birthrates, and aging citizenry. It is estimated that more than 70 million people now work legally or illegally in countries other than those in which they were born, a number increasing by almost 2 million annually (see Figure 10.2) Despite attempts in many countries to restrict immigration, this influx of immigrants is surpassed in terms of the rate of migration only by the two

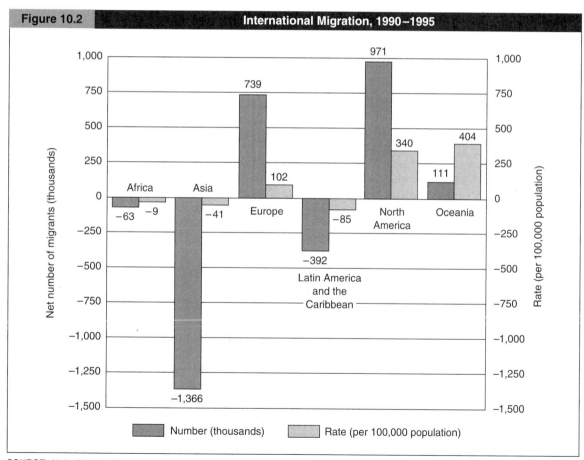

Figure 10.2 — **International Migration, 1990–1995**

SOURCE: United Nations Department for Economic and Social Information and Policy Analysis, Population Division

surges of European immigration into the United States during the first two decades of the twentieth century, when the U.S. imposed very few immigration
restrictions.[9]

Contrary to the popular belief that most migrant workers are male "bread-
winners," women constitute a high proportion of economic migrants. Social, environmental, and economic factors often affect women more strongly than men in
poor countries and can create a different set of incentives for migration. Women
in rural areas who do not have the right to own land or who face a life a virtual
servitude after marriage may try to escape poverty by moving to cities. In addition
to poor and unsafe working conditions, female migrants also typically face a dis-
parate burden of child care, and many are subjected to violence or forced into
prostitution. Nevertheless, thousands of women emigrate each year to find jobs in
other countries, and just as with male migrants, many remit a substantial portion
of their wages to their home countries.[10]

Refugees

In addition to those seeking economic opportunity, migrants today also flee from
war and oppressive dictatorships. These persons are collectively referred to as refugees, because they are forced to flee their home countries for reasons not related
to their economic standard of living. The UN High Commissioner for Refugees
(UNHCR) defines a refugee in its 1967 protocol as a person who, "owing to well-
founded fear of persecution for reasons of race, religion, nationality, membership
of a particular social group or political opinion, is outside of the country of his nationality and is unable or, owing to such fear, is unwilling to avail himself of the
protection of that country."[11] However, many countries suspect that new arrivals
may be claiming some sort of persecution in order to enter a country for the purpose of securing a better job. These countries, including the United States and Germany, tend to accept refugees who are fleeing persecution but refuse to admit
economic migrants.

Most refugees are displaced within their own countries, or flee to neighboring states or regions. As an indication of the dimension of the problem, there were
2.5 million refugees in 1970; 8 million in 1980; and more than 13 million in
1995—with the number growing by 10,000 a day. Not surprisingly, refugees tend
to be from poorer parts of the world. In 1994, Iran alone had more than 4 million
refugees, Pakistan 1.6 million, and Malawi, where more than 10 percent of the
population are refugees, more than 1 million. As indicated in the first part of
Map 10.1, most of these people fled from horrid conflicts within countries, especially Afghanistan, Rwanda, and Bosnia. Conflict in recent years in the former
Yugoslavia, Burundi, Liberia, Somalia, and Eritrea—among others—have added
to refugee statistics. Ethnic conflict and genocide in Rwanda drove hundreds of
thousands of refugees to flee to Congo and Tanzania in 1994; perhaps 600,000 returned by 1996, but huge numbers remain in neighboring countries.

The UN estimates that over 13 million refugees lived outside of their home
countries in 1996, in addition to almost 10 million who were refugees or displaced

within their own states. In the 1990s, African countries were particularly prominent as sources of internal refugees (South Africa, Sudan, Mozambique, Angola, and Liberia). The former Yugoslavia, Iraq, Myanmar (formerly Burma), the Philippines, and parts of the former Soviet Union were also identified as places where those who left or lost their homes remained, voluntarily or not, within their own country. In many other developing countries, hundreds of thousands of people leave their home regions because of soil exhaustion, chemical contamination, lack of access to clean water, or inundation of towns and farms, becoming environmental refugees.

The refugee problem is therefore growing at an alarming rate both within and between states. By one estimate, the total number of uprooted people in the world in 1996 was 26 million.[12] Clearly, the New Era is a period characterized by increased movement and, disturbingly, increased dislocation.

Consequences of Migration

The influx of immigrants, whatever their reasons for coming, have periodically provoked backlashes by the host-country population. Reactions are often racially motivated; nativist movements (political movements favoring the native-born and discriminating against immigrants) arise and gain strength during economic downturns, when immigrants are often blamed for unemployment and rising crime rates. Nativist pressure in the United States prompted the passage of the Immigration Act of 1924, which discriminated against potential immigrants from Southern and Eastern European countries and tightened already existing restrictions against Asians. The economic recession of the early 1990s in Europe and North America similarly prompted calls for limiting foreign immigration.

Although the European Union has declared that citizens of EU member states should be able to move freely from one country to another, negative reactions to immigrants have spread throughout Europe. EU member states are particularly worried about the possibility of a flood tide of immigration resulting from the collapse of the Soviet Union and the Communist regimes in Eastern Europe. However, faced with waves of immigrants from Eastern Europe and North Africa, EU member states have begun to close their national borders, at least symbolically. In France, increasingly strict controls on immigration have been enacted since Algeria became independent in 1962, partly as a result of the belief that immigrants from North Africa were not being assimilated into French society. More recently in France, nativist forces such as Jean-Marie Le Pen's National Front have used the immigration issue as a means of gaining political power, creating pressure on the French government to take further action against immigration.

Germany's situation is becoming similar. With some of the most liberal asylum provisions in the world, the German government's review of an individual's request for asylum may take years, during which time each asylum-seeker is given housing, food, clothing, and medical expenses. Even though only 5 percent ultimately qualify, the UNHCR reported that Germany harbored 350,000 asylum-seekers in 1996, in addition to 430,000 recognized refugees and family members,

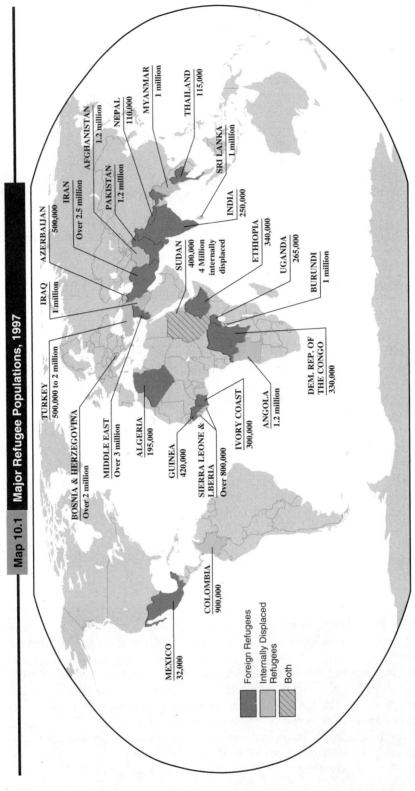

Map 10.1   Major Refugee Populations, 1997

MEXICO
32,000

COLOMBIA
900,000

BOSNIA & HERZEGOVINA
Over 2 million

MIDDLE EAST
Over 3 million

ALGERIA
195,000

GUINEA
420,000

SIERRA LEONE &
LIBERIA
Over 800,000

IVORY COAST
300,000

ANGOLA
1.2 million

DEM. REP. OF
THE CONGO
330,000

TURKEY
500,000 to 2 million

IRAQ
1 million

AZERBAIJAN
500,000

IRAN
Over 2.5 million

AFGHANISTAN
1.2 million

PAKISTAN
1.2 million

NEPAL
110,000

MYANMAR
1 million

THAILAND
115,000

SRI LANKA
1 million

INDIA
250,000

SUDAN
400,000
4 Million
internally
displaced

ETHIOPIA
340,000

UGANDA
265,000

BURUNDI
1 million

Foreign Refugees

Internally Displaced
Refugees

Both

SOURCE: *The New York Times International*, December 9, 1997; United Nations Comissioner for Refugees

Having fled the chaos in their country, Albanian refugees are detained in October 1991 by Italian authorities at the port city of Bari.

SOURCE: © P. Durand/Sygma

500,000 "de facto" refugees who have been refused asylum but are allowed to stay for legal or humanitarian reasons, and 320,000 "temporary" refugees from the conflict in Bosnia. With unemployment persistently high, especially in the formerly Communist East, the climate was conducive to racist violence against foreigners. "Guest workers" and their families, residing legally in Germany but not possessing full German citizenship, are frequent targets of ethnic hate crimes. Although this violence aroused protests at home and abroad, it had its effect: Germany revised its generous asylum laws in the mid-1990s.

Even in the United States, where the Statue of Liberty beckons to immigrants, political pressure to restrict immigration is rising. It is not so much political refugees that Americans mind, as the United States has historically granted asylum to people fleeing countries with which the United States has less than friendly relations. Between 1975 and 1992, the United States admitted about 1.7 million political refugees, most from East Asia (particularly Vietnam) and the Soviet Union.[13] The United States has not extended the same welcome, however, to people fleeing from non-Communist countries. Although almost 97 percent of Soviet and former Soviet asylum-seekers and 95 percent of Vietnamese refugees were admitted from 1975 to 1992, only 1.2 percent of persons attempting to flee from impoverished, politically repressed Haiti were granted asylum. In 1992 hundreds of Haitian refugees, attempting to escape poverty and political violence by sailing to Florida in homemade rafts, were detained at sea and sent to the U.S. naval station at Guantanamo Bay, Cuba.[14] President Bill Clinton criticized this policy as inhumane during his 1992 campaign, but later he resumed the detention of Haitian refugees until 1994, when U.S. forces intervened to restore an elected government in Haiti. In contrast, virtually all those fleeing the Communist island of Cuba interdicted at sea en route to Florida were granted asylum in the United States as political refugees. This policy changed, however, in 1994 when the United States refused to grant asylum to Cubans attempting to flee, instead sending them to havens in Guantanamo Bay and Panama. This exodus led to an agreement between Washington and Havana for controlled immigration from Cuba.

Many U.S. citizens, like their counterparts in other industrialized countries, are becoming less receptive to economic migrants, fearing that immigrants are taking jobs away from native-born Americans (even though great numbers of immigrants accept low-paying jobs that few native-born citizens are willing to take). Nativists claim that new immigrants consume government services (such as Medicare and welfare) in excess of what they contribute in taxes, but these contentions are hotly disputed. Anti-immigrant sentiment contributed to the passage of a ban on welfare payments and Medicaid (low-income health insurance) coverage for immigrants in 1996, but these benefits were restored in 1997. Fear and resentment of immigrants and the inevitable friction caused by cultural diversity have taken other forms, ranging from "English-only" ballot initiatives in many areas to the 1992 presidential candidacy of David Duke, a reactionary former grand wizard of the Ku Klux Klan.

International Solutions to Problems of Migration

Several international organizations have attempted to address the issues and problems surrounding economic migration. For instance, an international convention approved by the UN's General Assembly in December 1990 seeks to protect the human rights of migrant workers. The convention recognizes that migration results in the scattering of the family; illegal, often secret movements; trafficking in human cargo (such as the smuggling of Mexican and Chinese people into the United States for exorbitant fees); and the exploitative employment of undocumented workers. More importantly, it also codifies a series of rights to which migrant workers and their families are entitled. Countries such as Morocco and Mexico, both of which have many citizens who work abroad, have supported the convention, while many richer countries such as Oman, Japan, and Australia, worried about an influx of economic migrants, have expressed reservations about adopting it.[15]

The UN High Commissioner for Refugees has carried out a number of programs designed to protect, resettle, and repatriate political refugees. The UN-sponsored 1989 International Conference on Central American Refugees, for example, obtained pledges of $156 million for aid and resettlement of over 440,000 persons displaced in that region.[16] The United Nations Relief and Works

Administration also operates a number of programs of relief and humanitarian assistance for Palestinian refugees, spending over $250 million on these efforts in 1996. In recent years, many states also have cooperated to promote efforts for voluntary repatriation of political refugees, and these attempts have achieved some notable successes. After the Iraqi invasion of Kuwait in August 1990 displaced 5 million people from several countries of origin, an April 1991 Memorandum of Understanding between the UN and Iraq initiated a mass voluntary repatriation effort involving 1.5 million refugees. Most of these were Iraqi Kurds who had been displaced to squalid camps along the border with Turkey and Iran. While there, up to 800 people reportedly fell victim to disease and malnutrition every day.[17] Another international voluntary repatriation effort, the 1989 Comprehensive Plan of Action for Indochinese refugees, has aided in repatriating thousands to their homelands in Cambodia, Laos, and Vietnam.[18]

Recent international efforts have made substantial progress in assisting refugees. In many other cases, however, displaced persons find themselves with no place to go. Although many Kurdish and Vietnamese refugees returned voluntarily to their homelands in 1991, the United States sent almost 2000 Haitians back to Haiti, Italy returned 17,000 Albanians, and Turkey expelled almost 450,000 Kurds.[19] Indeed, long-term refugees continue to pose major problems for their host countries and the international community. Although many economic migrants achieve the prosperity for which they came to their new homelands, thousands of others face discrimination and anti-immigrant violence. Until democracy, economic progress, and environmental protection catch up with population growth in the developing world, great numbers of people will continue to leave developing countries in search of political freedom and economic opportunity in the developed world. Industrialized nations can choose between turning away immigrants or welcoming them, and can decide how and how much to promote economic development abroad, but they cannot ignore the crowds outside their gates forever.

FOOD AND HUNGER

Population increases have resulted in more than just migration. A second, perhaps more fundamental challenge is that of adequately feeding the more than 5.8 billion people that inhabit the planet. Contrary to widespread belief, the problem is not a worldwide shortage of food, but rather the difficulty getting food to those who need it most, before hunger, malnutrition, and ultimately death result. The rest of this section will show that distribution generally differs from developed to developing countries. Although developed countries are easily able to feed their populations, many developing states are not.

Daily per capita caloric intake (that is, how many calories each person, on average, consumes every day) serves as a rough indicator of the adequacy of a nation's food supply. Although the global per capita availability of food has increased despite population growth, great disparities exist between developed and developing regions in terms of daily caloric intake. According to the UN Food and Agriculture Organization (FAO), average daily calorie consumption in the developed countries grew from 3190 in 1971 to 3350 in 1992, while consumption in developing countries grew from 2140 calories to 2520 in the same period.[20]

These figures do not consider quality of diet; many people in Third World countries have inadequate supplies of protein and other nutritional necessities. It will come as no surprise that the richer nations consume diets vastly superior in quantity and quality from those of the developing nations. It has been estimated that the average North American consumes five times as many agricultural resources as the average person in India, and that average American consumption exceeds by two to four times the quantity of protein that the human body can use.[21] As developing countries become richer, their citizens typically want to eat more meat, leading some agricultural experts to question whether the world could produce enough meat if Southern appetites demanded Northern levels of consumption.[22]

Despite these differences in average consumption, food supplies in the developing world as a whole are adequate—few people will starve on an average of 2000 calories per day. Nevertheless, the grave consequences of inadequate nutrition are readily apparent. It is currently estimated that more than 800 million people suffer from chronic malnutrition and that each year hundreds of thousands die from hunger-related diseases.[23] In 1998, with world agricultural production adversely affected by the infamous "El Niño" weather pattern, FAO estimated that thirty-seven countries countries would require emergency food assistance.

Why are people suffering in the midst of such plenty? The answer is that although the quantity of food produced is generally adequate, its distribution is not. The major reason for chronic shortages of food is poverty—the lack of sufficient income to buy food or means to grow it. Soil exhaustion, depletion of water supplies, and other environmental problems can also lead to persistent shortfalls in food production. Flooding, drought, warfare, and misguided economic programs are the major causes of acute food shortages and famine. Areas prone to drought are especially vulnerable to drastic temporary shortages of food. If drought-stricken regions have poorly developed transportation systems and lack the cash to buy food from nearby sources, the result can be mass starvation. This is what occurred during the famines in the Sahel (the semiarid region of Africa just south of the Sahara) in the late 1960s and mid-1980s. In other cases, hunger results from man-made disasters, such as political chaos and intranational warfare. During the civil wars in Ethiopia in the 1980s, government forces often blocked food supplies to rebellious regions and hampered international relief efforts, in effect using famine as a weapon against separatist uprisings. In 1994–1997, two years of catastrophic floods followed by a severe drought led to widespread famine in North Korea, and an estimated 5 million people suffered from serious malnutrition or starvation. Although the U.S. and other countries together pledged more 650,000 tons of food aid for North Korea, the socialist regime's mismanagement, tight control over the economy, closure to foreign trade, pervasive secrecy, and unwillingness to admit the extent of the problem hampered international relief efforts.

The situation in Somalia prior to the arrival of U.S. troops in 1992 to augment a UN relief effort provides another example of tragically inadequate food distribution. In 1991 and 1992 Somalia suffered a famine that threatened more than 4 million people with starvation. The cause was not only a severe drought, but also the factional fighting and violent disputes over farmland that followed the collapse of the Somali government. Consequently, less food was grown, and much of the food that had been produced was hoarded by people afraid that they would not have enough to eat in the future and by those eager to get a higher price for their foodstuffs in the short term. A tragic irony for Somalia was that there was food in the markets, but the prices were prohibitive for most people. Local strongmen and armed gangs took what they needed by force, while children, the aged, and those who couldn't steal succumbed to hunger. At the start of 1993 Somalia relied on foreign aid for its food supply, and, despite the efforts of U.S. forces and the UN, more than one-sixth of the country's population still faced starvation. By the time that the last of the U.S. troops departed in March 1994, leaving a weaker UN presence, these conditions had improved but the country still suffered from a serious economic and health crisis.

International Food Aid and Famine-Relief Efforts

Efforts to get food to countries that cannot feed themselves have been relatively successful, even though donating governments sometimes resort to using food as a weapon to try to get recipient countries to change their policies. Many states have acted independently to redress the balance between food production and consumption. The United States, rich in agricultural resources, has been active in fighting hunger and starvation on its own, as well as through contributions to UN relief agencies and other international relief efforts. However, the United States has also tried to use food as a political tool, most obviously in the grain embargo directed against the Soviet Union in 1980 as punishment for its invasion of Afghanistan. This attempt to use food for political purposes failed, chiefly because the Soviet Union was able to purchase grain from other countries such as Canada and Argentina, and the embargo was lifted in 1981 after fifteen months (much to the relief of American farmers, who had profited from the sale of grain to the USSR throughout the Cold War). An embargo on trade with Iraq instituted during the Persian Gulf War, intended to convince the regime to fully dismantle its capabilities to develop weapons of mass destruction, also had discouraging results because the ruling elite found ways to treat itself to an extravagant lifestyle while the masses suffered (see Chapter Eleven).

International organizations have taken a number of approaches to alleviate the problems of hunger and malnutrition. Several nongovernmental organizations (NGOs) such as Oxfam (Britain's largest overseas charity) and the United Support of Artists for Africa (best known for its recording of the song "We Are the World" in 1985) concentrate on short-term relief of acute food shortages. Other groups, such as the UN Food and Agriculture Organization, work toward long-term solutions to problems of food production and distribution, providing technical and financial assistance for agricultural projects in developing countries.

Though all are well-intentioned, some famine relief and agricultural development efforts generate a great deal of controversy. The UN's relief effort in Somalia, for example, was widely criticized for failing to create the necessary infrastructure for food distribution, primarily because of its difficulties in persuading Somalia's warlords to cooperate. Other famine-relief efforts have been criticized for their shortsighted solutions. In Rwanda, for example, a high proportion of food aid intended for refugees went directly into the hands of corrupt officials and even suspected perpetrators of genocide. Often, because debt-ridden developing countries do not have adequate export earnings to pay for food imports, they are encouraged by international organizations to increase domestic food production. Bringing more land under cultivation, however, often entails clearing ecologically valuable forests for farming and ranching. The use of traditional farming and ranching methods on these lands leads to further deforestation or gradually turns arable lands into desert, thus paradoxically leaving countries more vulnerable to drought and famine. The ecological balance of the Brazilian Amazon, for example, has been upset by clear-cutting and the introduction of agricultural techniques to farm the land. Such land is unable to sustain itself for food-growing over time, leaving the country more vulnerable than ever in the long term, with even less usable land.

Despite the many difficulties relief efforts have encountered, the problem of world hunger appears to be the least contentious and most easily soluble global issue, because world capabilities for food production continue to increase and both governments and private donors are usually quick to support famine relief. However, the longer that states and international organizations wait to adopt solutions, the more urgent the problem becomes, because the world's population continues to expand. Both short- and long-term solutions to world hunger are relatively straightforward, but each has its costs. In the short term, the best solution to the food and hunger problem is to improve distribution networks and the type of aid given. Developed countries, which produce more than enough food to feed themselves and their less developed neighbors, usually prefer to donate surplus food (bulky, difficult to transport, and quick to spoil) instead of money (easy to transport and not perishable, but often subject to theft by corrupt officials or speculators). At the same time, free distribution of food aid to famine-ravaged areas undercuts the efforts of local farmers to increase production and improve long-term food security.[24] In the long term, economic development is the best solution to hunger and malnutrition, but as noted earlier, economic development must proceed in such a way as to minimize environmental costs. Especially in developing countries, plans for sustainable agriculture must take soil exhaustion, renewable supplies of water, the potential harm of clearing forest lands for cropland, and other environmental factors into account to ensure a bountiful, reliable, and affordable food supply for future generations. In the future, a global food crisis seems unlikely, but the world may still have to learn how to eat within its means.

THE ENVIRONMENT

Environmental issues vividly demonstrate global interdependence. The spread of radioactive fallout from an accident at a nuclear reactor at Chernobyl (then in the Soviet Union, now in Ukraine) in 1986, the plumes of smoke from burning oil fields in Kuwait in 1991, and the deadly smog created by catastrophic forest fires in Indonesia in 1997–1998 give striking examples of how environmental disasters can quickly cross national boundaries.[25] Less dramatic but equally damaging environmental problems, such as **deforestation, desertification,** and acid rain, have pronounced effects on regional ecosystems but may also have global impact. Although the international scope of environmental hazards is now well-known, individual states have historically addressed environmental concerns mainly through domestic laws and regulations. Only recently have nations begun to use international forums to address global environmental issues and promote collective solutions. We will examine these some of these solutions after a brief survey of two key global environmental issues.

Representative Environmental Problems: Deforestation and Pollution

The old joke—that a developer is someone who wants to build a house in the woods, while an environmentalist is someone who already has a house in the woods—illuminates one of the reasons why environmental problems can be difficult to solve: Few people pollute deliberately, but most cause some form of environmental damage in the pursuit of their material needs. This section will briefly examine two ways in which economic activity causes environmental degradation, namely through deforestation and **industrial pollution.**

Deforestation occurs when people cut down trees without planting enough new ones to replace them. Although popular belief often holds that greedy lumber companies are responsible for denuding the earth of trees for wood profits, commercial logging is not the primary cause of deforestation. The real culprit has been the clearing of forests for human settlement, cattle pasture, and farmland, which resulted in the loss of two acres of forest for every one acre of arable farmland added between 1971 and 1986. According to reliable estimates, by 1995 about 25 million acres of forests and wooded lands, equivalent to 0.2 percent of the global total, were being stripped of trees each year.[26] (That works out to over forty-five acres deforested every minute.)

The traditional slash-and-burn technique for clearing land for crop rotation can also contribute to deforestation and desertification, as well as a host of additional environmental concerns, including topsoil erosion and increased emissions of nitrous oxide, methane, and carbon dioxide.[27] War and other unnatural disasters can also result in deforestation. It has been estimated that between 1955 and 1975, the Vietnam War leveled 2.5 million acres of forest and rendered at least

■ Brazilian homesteaders clear burned rain forest debris to prepare the soil for cultivation. This family has cleared 50 of their 123 acres in such a manner.   SOURCE: © AP/Wide World Photos

5 million acres unproductive because of the use of the defoliant Agent Orange and other chemical pollutants.[28]

Deforestation does not just mean the loss of trees. It also contributes to a loss of wildlife. More than 34,000 plant species and at least 700,000 animal species live in only 3.5 percent of the earth's remaining primary forests. Loss of the forest cover in these wooded areas, occupying a mere 0.2 percent of the earth's surface, could mean the extinction of almost 7 percent of all plant and animal species on land. It is difficult to know exactly how fast species are disappearing, but some estimates hold that 500,000 to 600,000 species could become extinct in the next twenty years.[29] Additionally, the burning of forests produces carbon dioxide, which many ecologists fear is causing global warming (see the boxed feature, Is the Earth Getting Warmer?). Some studies suggest that halting deforestation could cut worldwide emissions of carbon dioxide by 25 percent.[30]

Although deforestation has become an increasing global concern in recent years, most people traditionally associate environmental damage with industrial pollution. After all, urbanization and industrialization create such familiar and readily noticeable environmental ills as smog, acid rain, and elevated levels of carbon dioxide and chlorofluorocarbons (CFCs). This air pollution is glaringly evident in smog-blanketed cities all over the world, from Mexico City to Los Angeles to Warsaw to Bangkok. The six countries emitting the most carbon dioxide (in descending order) are the United States, China, Russia, Japan, Germany, and India. Moreover, all seven members of the G-7 economic group are among the top eleven nations in CO_2 emissions.[31] Such pollution not only worsens the problems of global warming and the depletion of the ozone layer (which shields the earth from harmful ultraviolet radiation), but creates other health problems as well. One estimate concludes that 70 percent of urban dwellers breathe unhealthy air, and another 10 percent breathe air of questionable quality.[32]

Airborne pollutants can affect areas far from the cities and factories where they are emitted. For example, the burning of fossil fuels (coal, oil, and gasoline) spew sulfur oxides into the air, which eventually fall back to earth in the form of acid rain. This combination of toxic chemicals and atmospheric moisture kills trees, erodes the surfaces of buildings, and acidifies bodies of water, making them inhospitable to the life therein and even creating a threat to safe drinking supplies. Tension between the Canadian and U.S. governments over acid rain flares up periodically. The Canadian government insists that American industries, which produce most of the acid rain that falls on both sides of the U.S.–Canadian border, clean up their manufacturing processes. Attempts at doing so have run into political obstacles, however, as companies ordered to reduce sulfur-dioxide emissions contend that the increased costs would result in the elimination of many jobs. By the late 1990s, the United States and Canada made progress on the acid rain issue, but a similar problem exists in Northeast Asia, where political tensions (see Chapter Five) make environmental cooperation much more difficult.

Efforts by the developed nations to get the issue of atmospheric pollution on the agenda have not always been accepted by the developing nations, whose concern for preserving forests, wetlands, and the ozone layer pales in comparison to their desire to industrialize. As a whole, the major industrialized countries account for most of the emissions of greenhouse gases in the world and burn 75 percent of the fossil fuel used each year. Developing countries, however, are closing the pollution gap. The annual carbon dioxide output in Third World nations grew almost 2.4 percent per year between 1960 and 1990 (with emissions from industrial sources increasing almost sixteen-fold from 1950 to 1985), and energy consumption grew at 4 percent per year between 1980 and 1986, ten times faster than in industrialized countries. If past trends continue, by 2015 the developing world will emit as much carbon into the atmosphere as the industrialized states, and by 2025 developing countries could be emitting over four times as much as developed countries today, leading to a total world output per year of three times the present level.[33] Much of the rapid rise in pollution in developing countries is attributable to the fact that industries in poorer states often tend to use dirtier fuels. China, for instance, relies on cheap, abundant high-sulfur coal, which is among the most polluting energy sources known.

Development that produces more pollution will in the long run damage the global ecosystem, with potentially severe repercussions for international politics. For example, if significant changes in the climate were to occur, creating increased precipitation in some areas and desertification in others, the ability of many states to produce enough food for their people could be drastically reduced. In turn, this could cause huge population movements with potentially disruptive consequences, as discussed in the previous section.[34]

International Cooperation for Saving the Environment

International organizations began to focus their attention on environmental issues in the mid-twentieth century. The objectives of the Council of Europe (1949) included preservation of the environment and responsible uses of natural resources, goals the European Union continues to advocate today. In 1949 the UN hosted the Scientific Conference on the Conservation and Utilization of Resources to discuss problems relating to natural resources. This was the first international forum convened to address the problem of resource conservation, although no major recommendations were issued.

During the late 1960s and early 1970s, the issue of the environment moved closer to the top of the UN's agenda. In 1968 the UN Economic and Social Council adopted an initiative calling for legislation to address the "human environment." The first result of this initiative was the Founex Report of 1971, which recognized the important relationship between development and the environment in the Third World and suggested that the poverty found in the developing world was directly related to environmental degradation. The 1972 Stockholm Conference helped to establish the UN Environmental Program, whose main purpose was to promote international environmental cooperation. In 1974, the third UN Conference on the Law of the Sea (UNCLOS) established a new law for protecting the marine environment. (See Chapter Nine for more on UNCLOS.) Overall, these international reports and conferences did much to raise awareness of environmental concerns, although very little progress was made in terms of finding practical solutions to the problems at hand.

International efforts in the 1980s and 1990s continued to link environmental concerns to issues of trade and economic development. Environmental programs sponsored by the United Nations, the World Bank, and other international organizations focused primarily on sustainable development—that is, strategies for increasing economic growth and raising standards of living in the developing world without exhausting natural resources or causing irreparable environmental damage (see Chapters Eight and Nine). UN treaties such as the Framework Convention on Climate Change (signed in 1992 and reviewed in 1997) and the Convention to Combat Desertification (signed in 1994) pointed the way toward increased international cooperation on environmental concerns. These cooperative endeavors have greatly increased awareness of these issues, but their attempts at practical problem solving have yielded mixed results. A typical example is the 1987 Montreal Protocol, which required signatory states to phase out the use of CFCs (ozone-depleting chemicals) over a period of time and obligated them to prohibit importation of all products containing the offending chemicals. The protocol contained a loophole, however, which permitted developing countries to increase their per capita use of CFCs, which could allow a 70 percent rise in CFC

IS THE EARTH GETTING WARMER?

A well-publicized, and controversial, global environmental concern is the emission of gases such as carbon dioxide (CO_2) and methane, which can trap heat in the earth's atmosphere. In the 1990s, industry, transportation, and other human activities emitted over six billion metric tons of carbon dioxide into the atmosphere each year, and total emissions of CO_2 continue to rise.* The source of carbon dioxide that has attracted the greatest environmental concern is the burning of fossil fuels (including coal, oil, and gasoline) for energy. The UN's Intergovernmental Panel on Climate Change (IPCC) estimates that the concentration of carbon dioxide in the atmosphere has risen from 280 parts per million by volume (ppmv) in preindustrial times to 360 ppmv today.**

This statistic has many people worried. Many scientists have argued that continued emission of greenhouse gases has increased the earth's average temperature, a phenomenon known as the **greenhouse effect.** Most climatologists agree that greenhouse gas emissions are probably responsible for at least part of a rise of about half a degree Celsius, or one degree Fahrenheit, in the average global temperature over the last century. The IPCC predicts that if production of greenhouse gases is not slowed, average world temperatures will rise by 1 to 3.5 degrees Celsius (about 2 to 6.5 degrees Fahrenheit) by 2100. (By way of comparison, the world has warmed by 5 to 9 degrees since the last Ice Age). This may not sound like much, but it would be enough to cause persistent droughts in many areas, seriously affecting global food production, and could cause enough melting of the polar ice caps to raise the world's sea level by half a meter or more, causing serious flooding in low areas. (Some small island states, such as the Maldives, are worried that they could be inundated if serious global warming occurs.) Climate change could hurt more than real estate values; for example, an average warming of just 2 degrees Fahrenheit could melt enough Hud-

son Bay ice to wipe out the local polar bear population, because they need ice as a platform for hunting seals, a main source of food.

There is some evidence of recent global warming. The part of the Northern Hemisphere covered by snow has been shrinking, sea ice in the Arctic Ocean is receding toward the North Pole, expanses of the sea ice north of Greenland have thinned by about 15 percent, and the Canadian and Alaskan permafrost has warmed by about 3.7 percent over the past 100 years. However, other evidence, such as measurements of changes in the earth's temperature taken from satellites, show little or no warming trend. The effects of climate change would also be uneven; some areas would probably become warmer or dryer, but others could become wetter or cooler.

Some experts therefore remain skeptical that a greenhouse effect even exists, or that if it does, that it is as dangerous as environmentalists contend. Although scientists agree that levels of carbon dioxide in the atmosphere have increased over the last century, some point out that the earth has gone through other warm spells, none of them brought on by human activity. Variations in solar radiation, for example, have a much greater effect on global temperatures than that exerted by industrial emissions. As reliable records of temperatures have existed for little more than 100 years, and there is still much disagreement over models used to predict climate change, proving whether or not a greenhouse effect exists and poses a threat is likely to remain a difficult task. Persuading individuals to change their priorities and behavior, and getting governments to agree on environmentally sustainable energy and industrial policies will be harder still.

* Estimate by the Energy Information Administration in *International Energy Annual 1995* (Washington: U.S. Department of Energy/EIA, December 1996)

** Figures from the *Second Assessment Report of the Intergovernmental Panel on Climate Change,* 1996.

emissions by 2040.[35] Amendments to the Protocol in 1990 and 1992 helped address the problem, but CFC production remains a contentious issue between North and South.

Some of the most effective efforts to preserve the environment have been carried out by nongovernmental organizations (NGOs), through independent projects and through the pressure they apply on states and intergovernmental organizations. In the United States, one of the earliest environmental organizations, the American Forestry Association (founded in 1875), is still active in trying to preserve and manage natural resources. Another well-known environmental organization, the Sierra Club, was founded in 1892 to promote the conservation of public lands in the form of national parks. Environmental concerns took a back seat during the Great Depression, but after World War II a renewed interest in the environment emerged because of pollution resulting from industrialization and a perceived serious reduction in available natural resources.

The year 1948 saw the creation of the International Union for the Protection of Nature, now the World Conservation Union. This organization consists of both governmental and nongovernmental actors and focuses on the use of science to work toward environmental goals, including the preservation of biodiversity, the creation of national parks, and the promotion of environmentally safe economic development. Other environmental NGOs emerged in the 1960s, including the World Wildlife Fund (now called the World Wide Fund for Nature, but still abbreviated WWF), which is primarily concerned with the conservation of biodiversity.

Today NGOs and other private groups are engaged in efforts to save all sorts of natural treasures, especially tropical rain forests. Rock musicians and bands such as Sting, REM, and the Grateful Dead have lent their names to campaigns to preserve the Brazilian rain forest and halt deforestation. Businesses such as Ben & Jerry's Ice Cream and The Body Shop have purchased products grown in rain forests to show that these areas do not have to be converted to farmland in order to have economic value. By using trade, rather than aid, to promote conservation of biological resources, these companies try to convince governments that the long-term economic benefits of environmental protection can exceed the short-run profits from environmentally destructive activities.

A Green and Pleasant Globe?

Many states and international organizations are convinced that economic incentives are the best way to address the problems of pollution and deforestation. Few incentives are great enough, however, to convince poorer countries to cease environmentally harmful development efforts, and a strategy of relying on the social consciousness of governments, private companies, and individuals is questionable at best. For these reasons, sustainable development is one of the most urgent items on the global economic and environmental agenda. At the same time, developed countries have a long way to go to put their own environmental houses in order, as shown by the problems with acid rain and carbon emissions.

The world's track record on the environment illustrates how awareness of a global problem does not necessarily lead to global changes in behavior. The costs of environmental damage usually accumulate over the long term, although the benefits from production and consumption can be enjoyed quickly. Adoption of the long-term perspective on the ecosystem is the only way that environmental movements within states have been able to make their countries cleaner and greener. Despite the best of intentions, international environmental preservation efforts cannot succeed until both developed and developing countries adopt a long-term perspective in both global vision and local action.

HEALTH AND DISEASE

The Global Health Picture

Previous sections have touched on some of the consequences of overpopulation, environmental degradation, and malnutrition on human health. This section takes a closer look at global health issues, examining some of the problems and prospects for improving health and eradicating epidemics across international boundaries.

At almost every stage of life, people in developing countries are more susceptible to health problems than those in richer nations, because poverty, malnutrition, and poor sanitation contribute to the spread of disease. One broad measure of general health, life expectancy, is now about sixty-two years for the world as a whole, but on average, people in developed regions can expect to live fourteen years longer than those in poorer nations.[36] Over 95 percent of child and infant deaths occur in the Third World.[37] Although the rate of death from complications during pregnancy is only 5 out of 100,000 live births in some parts of Europe, the rate soars to 1000 per 100,000 live births in parts of Africa and Asia.[38]

The prevalence of infectious diseases, which kill more than 17 million people per year worldwide (11 million of them children under five years old), remains a serious global health problem and illustrates the distressing health conditions in much of the developing world. Every year 8 million children in developing countries die or are disabled from six vaccine-preventable diseases: measles, poliomyelitis, tuberculosis, diphtheria, whooping cough, and tetanus. One authority estimates that without immunization, virtually 100 percent of the children in developing countries would contract measles between the ages of six months to three years.[39] It has also been estimated that 300 million people, almost 80 percent of them in Asia, are infected with hepatitis B, which can develop into serious liver disease and cancer in persons forty years of age and up.

Many developing countries face especially serious problems with tropical diseases such as malaria. In 1997, for example, the World Health Organization (WHO) estimated that malaria killed up to 5 million African children each year.[40] The risk of infection with malaria is particularly high where antimalaria programs are weak or nonexistent, such as in "frontier areas" of economic development, farming and mining projects in newly cleared jungle, and areas suffering the effects of warfare, smuggling, and refugee migration.

Cholera, a deadly disease primarily transmitted by contaminated water, also claims a significant number of victims in developing areas. A major outbreak in 1992 led to 600,000 recorded cholera cases worldwide, two-thirds of which occurred in Central and South America, and more than 200,000 cases were reported in 1995.[41] Besides malaria and cholera, other tropical diseases claim a substantial number of victims: leprosy, schistosomiasis, river blindness, Chagas' disease, and African sleeping sickness.[42]

Although it has thus far claimed far fewer victims than these tropical diseases, acquired immune deficiency syndrome (AIDS) has become one of the world's most serious health problems. Caused by the human immunodeficiency virus (HIV), it is actually a complex interaction between impairment of the immune system and opportunistic infections such as pneumonia, tuberculosis, syphilis, or other conditions. It is transmitted through blood (via intravenous drug use or, rarely, transfusion of infected blood), sexual contact, and from pregnant women to the fetuses they carry. Although intravenous drug use is said to carry the highest risk of HIV transmission, most recorded cases of AIDS are the result of unprotected sexual contact. The global AIDS epidemic began in the early 1980s; by 1996, an estimated 23 million people had become infected with HIV, of whom more than 4.5 million had developed AIDS, and 6000 new infections occurred every day.[43]

As with the diseases just discussed, patterns of HIV infection differ between developed and developing countries. In the United States, over 80 percent of AIDS cases occur in urban areas, and most cases involve homosexuals, bisexuals, or intravenous drug users.[44] In developing regions, by contrast, the primary means of HIV transmission is through heterosexual contact. In Zaire, for example, an estimated 1 percent of the sexually active population in the countryside and 8 percent of the population in towns may suffer from AIDS.[45] Africa has been hit especially hard by this insidious disease; some estimates conclude that in 1995, 70 percent of the global total of AIDS cases occurred in sub-Saharan Africa (which has 10 percent of the world's population) and that region had 11 million people living with AIDS.[46] The spread of AIDS is increasing in Asia as well. According to WHO, HIV is spreading most rapidly in South and Southeast Asia, where 3 million adults had the virus in 1996—double the number estimated in 1993.[47]

Although therapies involving multidrug "cocktails" and recent experimental vaccines for HIV offer hope, the prospects for curing AIDS or curbing its spread still appear discouraging, especially in some developing regions. WHO has projected that by the year 2000, 30 million to 40 million people may be living with HIV, and there may be an additional 12 million to 18 million cases of full-blown AIDS.[48] According to even more pessimistic estimates, as many as 30 percent of the overall population of sub-Saharan Africa, and 40 percent of urban populations there, may become HIV carriers.[49] For sexually active adults in this region's urban areas, the figure could eventually reach 70 percent.[50]

Emerging diseases such as hantavirus and hepatitis C present special global health concerns because, though they are much less prevalent than widespread diseases like malaria and AIDS, their spread and treatment are still poorly understood. Perhaps the most frightening emerging disease is ebola, a hemorrhagic fever that killed 244 people in central Africa in a single outbreak in 1995.[51]

Responses to Global Health Problems

Most global responses to international problems depend upon the individual reactions of single states, many of whom are constrained by domestic financial considerations. Global health problems present no exceptions. AIDS is only the most recent of many deadly diseases to which the world community has tried to formulate a unified response. The ways in which the international community has dealt with these problems, ranging from immunization to attempts at eradication, illustrate the difficulties in securing international cooperation, even on the most deadly issues.

Immunization is one of the most cost-effective weapons for disease prevention in developing countries. Since its foundation in 1948, the UN-affiliated World Health Organization has done much to control diseases through immunization. In 1980, for example, WHO announced that it had reached its 1965 goal of eradicating smallpox, a malady that killed millions worldwide for centuries. WHO is also making progress on eradicating polio, and projects that leprosy and the tropical maladies Chagas' disease, river blindness, and filariasis can be eliminated as public health problems within ten years.[52] WHO's Expanded Program on Immunization (EPI) has achieved great success in expanding its immunization coverage of the world's children. In 1989, the EPI was credited with preventing the deaths of 2.2 million children. By the 1990s, EPI sponsored the immunization of over 70 percent of the world's children less than one year of age against the six vaccine-preventable diseases mentioned previously.[53]

Other diseases, such as malaria and AIDS, have been more resistant to eradication. The malaria virus, for instance, has proven resistant to a variety of treatments. One observer believes that the statement of the second Report of the Malarial Commission of the League of Nations in 1927 is still substantially valid today: "The history of special antimalarial campaigns is chiefly a record of exaggerated expectations followed sooner or later by disappointment and the abandonment of work."[54] WHO, which has abandoned its goal of eradicating malaria by 2000, warns that drug-resistant tuberculosis and other infectious diseases could become increasing public health threats.[55]

Because multidrug treatments are still prohibitively expensive for developing countries, and no vaccine is yet available, WHO has concentrated on promoting awareness of the high-risk behaviors associated with HIV infection (namely, unprotected sex with multiple partners and shared use of needles among intravenous drug users). In 1987 WHO established the Global Program on AIDS, whose goals include the prevention of HIV transmission, care for HIV-infected people, and unification of national and international efforts against AIDS. Together with its scientific advisory body, the Global Commission on AIDS, the program supports national AIDS-control plans, which use education to try to curb the spread of the disease. By 1996 the Global Program on AIDS had achieved its primary goal of helping developing countries to fight the epidemic, creating more than 160 national programs with WHO financial and technical support.

As with most global issues, the problem of AIDS has exacerbated international tensions as often as it has contributed to cooperation. Many national governments have reacted to the spread of AIDS in their countries by denying it is "their" problem. In the United States, AIDS was initially perceived as a Haitian and gay disease. In Europe, it was first considered a disease of African and Caribbean people, while in many Asian countries AIDS was commonly regarded as a disease primarily afflicting "foreigners." As a result of these perceptions, governments have enacted more stringent travel restrictions and screening procedures. The United States, for example, has a law prohibiting entry to people with a "deadly, infectious or contagious disease," a prohibition that was extended to cover HIV in 1987 and upheld in 1993. It may be hoped that the stigma associated with AIDS will fade over time, but the initial difficulties in securing international cooperation to fight this devastating disease show how governments remain reluctant to combat diseases that they perceive to be somebody else's problem.

DRUGS

Some Third World nations charge that their terms of trade with the developed world are unfair, because the prices industrialized nations pay for their exports of commodities (such as copper and coffee) are too low (see Chapter Eight). There is one category of products from the developing world that has made fabulous fortunes for their producers, though few citizens of developing nations share in these profits: narcotics and other illegal drugs. According to one UN estimate, international trade in illicit drugs totals more than $400 billion each year, equal to eight percent of total world trade and exceeding the value of trade in iron, steel, or motor vehicles.

As with population, health, and environmental concerns, the problem of drugs at times has fostered admirable international cooperation. In other instances, disputes over the method employed to combat the movement of drugs across international boundaries has severely strained relations between states. Historically, efforts to reduce or stop the drug trade have focused on curbing the supply of illegal drugs moving from developing regions to richer countries, where the bulk of demand for drugs has always been located. Only since the late 1980s have international efforts begun to focus on curbing demand for drugs. This section examines the roots of the drug problem, the effectiveness of supply-side programs, and the emergence of more comprehensive measures in the war on drugs.

Drug Production

World narcotics production is concentrated in four areas: Southeast Asia, the Middle East, Central America, and South America. Each region has its own specialty product, with Southeast Asia concentrating on opium and its derivatives (including heroin), the Middle East on hashish, Central America on marijuana, and South America on cocaine. In many cases, drug production in these regions is sustained or encouraged by insurgencies, civil war, and other violent internal conflicts.

The vast majority of the world's opium is produced in two regions: Myanmar, Laos, and Thailand, known collectively as the Golden Triangle, and Afghanistan, Iran, and Pakistan, together referred to as the Golden Crescent. These nations taken together produced more than two and a half tons of opium, ninety percent of the world total, in 1995.[56] The lack of international influence over the isolationist regime in Myanmar is demonstrated by the continued increases in opium production and the acreage devoted to growing the opium poppy there. Those increases can be attributed to the fact that the government in Rangoon, the capital, has allied with major traffickers and permitted trafficker-affiliated insurgent groups to produce narcotics, and even to exercise security and police functions in the areas under their control.[57]

The Eastern Mediterranean is the hub of the world's production of hashish, a drug made from a plant related to marijuana. Before its civil war began in 1975, Lebanon was one of the principal trading states of the Middle East and also was a leading center of the drug trade. In the 1960s Lebanon's Maronite Christian community became involved in shipping hashish from Lebanon's Bekaa Valley and Asian heroin from ports run and protected by Christian militias. In the early 1980s Turkish poppy-growers introduced opium and heroin to the Bekaa Valley, which also became home to cocaine refiners who obtained their coca paste from Lebanese merchant communities in South America. During its civil war, Lebanon's hostile factions, including elements of the Palestine Liberation Organization (PLO) and the Popular Front for the Liberation of Palestine (PFLP), exported hashish, opium, heroin, and cocaine to Europe and the United States in return for cash and armaments. There also is substantial evidence that the Syrian government has become engaged in the Lebanese drug trade.[58]

According to U.S. estimates, in 1994 Mexico produced more than 3,400 tons of marijuana, accounting for more than 42 percent of world marijuana production. This nevertheless represented a substantial decrease from previous levels, as Mexico's marijuana eradication programs had nearly halved the amount of land devoted to growing the crop the year before. During this same period, Mexico also reduced its opium cultivation and production by nearly one-third of its 1990 levels, even though opium production and land devoted to opium cultivation in Guatemala, the other significant Central American opium-grower, each increased by over 30 percent. Mexico serves as not only a major producer of the world's marijuana crop, but also as a key transporter of a more deadly drug, cocaine. It has been estimated, for example, that Mexico transports about 70 percent of the Colombian cocaine consumed in the United States.[59]

Four South American countries—Peru, Bolivia, Colombia, and Ecuador—grow more than 98 percent of the world's coca leaf, from which cocaine is derived. Peru's Upper Huallaga Valley accounts for over 50 percent of total world cultivation, and over half of the cocaine used in the United States comes from

Peruvian coca.[60] The cocaine trade brings in much of these countries' export revenues: one study estimated that Peru's drug trade was equivalent to about 20 percent to 25 percent of the country's legal exports, and that Bolivian cocaine earned an amount equal to 60 percent to 90 percent of its exports and employed 4.3 percent of its 7 million people.[61]

Growth of International Drug Trafficking

Because cocaine, heroin, marijuana, and other drugs are illegal in most countries, drug trafficking, the transportation of drugs from producers to consumers, has become a major international criminal enterprise. As official efforts to curb drug supply and abuse have attained moderate success, many traffickers have responded by expanding the geographical scope of their production and distribution channels. The complex operations mounted by drug cartels to purvey their illicit goods rival major multinational corporations in scope and sales volume (see Figure 10.3).

Colombian traffickers headquartered in the cities of Medellín and Cali, for instance, have forged extensive international production and distribution networks. When the Colombian government began cracking down on domestic drug operations, the drug rings moved some of their operational centers to Brazil, where they could more easily obtain chemical processors, and some of their coca processing laboratories to Ecuador. As cocaine abuse stabilized somewhat in the United

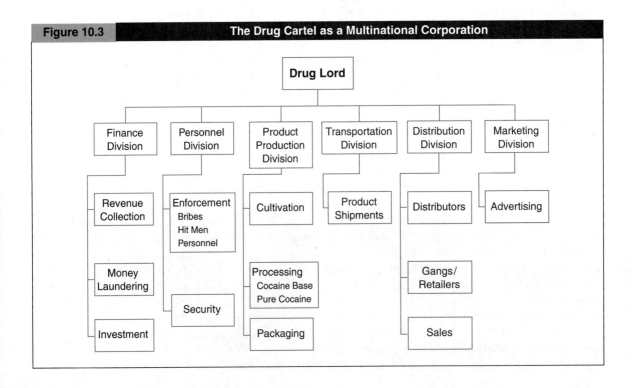

Figure 10.3 — **The Drug Cartel as a Multinational Corporation**

States but expanded in Europe and elsewhere, the Colombian cartels have offered cocaine-smuggling networks into the United States to the heroin traffickers of West and Southwest Asia in return for access to more of the world's illegal drug-distribution avenues. After the 1992 arrest of Colombian drug lord José Duran in Rome, Italian investigators found that the Colombians were working out a deal to grant to the Sicilian Mafia the entire cocaine-dealing franchise for all of Europe, in return for a share of the Mafia's global heroin market as well as assistance in laundering profits through legitimate businesses.[62]

Africa has also become a major locus of drug traffic. Transshipment of South American cocaine through Africa has soared, and cocaine has been seized in almost every region in Africa.[63] Africa now has its own cocaine producers and distributors, which emulate Colombian operations. Nigeria and Cameroon grow coca crops, and increasing amounts of heroin are being shipped through Ghana and Nigeria to Europe and the United States.[64]

Middle Eastern drug rings have also expanded their worldwide operations, primarily to purchase more weapons.[65] European criminal networks have assisted Middle Eastern drug traffickers and terrorist groups. In one complex arrangement, Palestinian drug traffickers traded hashish, heroin, and morphine (another opiate) produced by Palestinian and Syrian-controlled labs in Syria or Lebanon's Bekaa Valley to Bulgarian connections in return for light infantry weapons. The Bulgarian smugglers then sold the heroin to the Sicilian Mafia for hard currency. Italian law enforcement authorities also believed at one time that a member of a ranking Italian crime family administered Syrian drug-running operations worldwide.[66] Asian traffickers have also expanded or shifted their distribution networks in response to changing patterns of demand and enforcement. Russian authorities regularly seize tons of Afghan hashish, along with marijuana and opium grown in Central Asia. Some Southeast Asian heroin producers have begun routing their goods through China, contributing to new addiction problems and the spread of AIDS through the use of contaminated hypodermic needles.[67]

The United States is not free of responsibility for the international drug trade. In 1991, the International Narcotics Trafficking & Money Laundering Task Force found that the United States protected many international drug barons during the Cold War in exchange for their support in covert operations and other foreign policy objectives. Such alliances between drug syndicates and American operatives played a key role in the movement of drugs into the United States.[68]

Bilateral and Multilateral Drug-Control Efforts

The world's largest consumer of illegal drugs, by a wide margin, is the United States. Figures for 1995 estimate the number of habitual cocaine users in the United States at 3.6 million, regular users of marijuana at 17.8 million, and users of heroin at more than 400,000. (A substantial amount of the marijuana consumed in the United States is domestically produced, whereas cocaine, opium, and their derivatives are imported.) Authorities estimate that users in the United States spent $50 billion on illegal drugs annually between 1988 and 1993.[69]

This staggering total of drug money provides U.S. officials with a large incentive to take the initiative in combating the international drug trade. Common American rhetoric, both within and outside of Washington, holds that primary responsibility for the drug problem lies with pushers and criminal gangs who prey upon vulnerable citizens. (This was the same line taken during the Prohibition in the 1920s and the marijuana scare of the 1930s, depicted in the films *The Untouchables* and *Reefer Madness*.)

Accordingly, the United States has traditionally concentrated on restricting the supply of drugs rather than reducing demand for them. This may be done through **interdiction** (stopping drugs from coming into the country, primarily through customs inspection) or **eradication** (destruction of the crops that are processed into illegal drugs). Dissatisfied with the inability of interdiction alone to prevent importation of drugs, the United States has recently shifted the focus of bilateral drug-control efforts to eradication of crops. Many U.S.–led eradication programs involve attempts to use military means to crack down on the drug trade. Most of these projects have been controversial bilateral programs over which the United States can generally exercise more operational control.

The countries of the Western Hemisphere have also organized multilateral programs, such as the thirty-nation International Drug Enforcement Conference (IDEC) put into operation in 1988.[70] The Bush administration's Andean Initiative, launched in 1990, was designed to foster cooperation between the United States and South American nations to disrupt drug production at the processing stage.[71] The Clinton administration has continued efforts to work with Latin American countries to fight the drug trade, and in 1998, the OAS announced the formation of a new hemispheric organization, the Alliance Against Drugs, designed to strengthen multilateral drug control efforts.

However, attempts by the United States to try to reduce drug production in cooperation with South American countries have frequently been stymied by four factors. First, as noted earlier, the drug trade is a major source of employment and export revenues in many Latin American countries. Their governments have attempted to impress upon the United States that one of the ultimate solutions to the drug trade is for the United States to import more of the legal goods of their countries. At a meeting with George Bush in Washington in September 1989, President Virgilio Barco of Colombia implicitly reminded Bush that the Colombian drug economy flourished because Colombia could not earn the foreign exchange it needed through legitimate exports.[72]

Second, efforts at drug eradication that do not provide for a transition to legal alternative employment for coca and marijuana growers, or balance-of-payments support for drug-producing countries, encounter a great deal of resistance. The United States, with a dwindling pool of dollars to spend on international aid, has been reluctant to commit funds for agricultural and industrial development designed to supplant drug cultivation. Although the 1990 Cartagena Declaration committed the United States to financially support alternative development strategies in the Andean countries of South America, the U.S. government has been slow to fulfill those commitments. In early 1993 a group of Central American countries issued the Declaration of Belize, which promised cooperation with the United

States in introducing drug-abuse programs, drug eradication, development of alternative crops, and relieving foreign debt. U.S. assistance to anti-drug programs in developing countries has often come in the form of equipment and training for the military and law enforcement agencies that combat drug cartels.[73]

Third, domestic resistance to what is perceived as Yankee imperialism has been exploited by drug traffickers to undermine joint U.S.–South American antidrug action. In Bolivia and Peru, coca-growing families are organized into associations that can be mobilized to shut down eradication efforts. As is the case with many Latin American governments, U.S. pressure on the Mexican government to stamp out drug-related corruption has often offended anti-imperialistic sensitivities in Mexico. U.S.–Mexican tension came to a head in 1985, when U.S. drug enforcement agent Enrique Camarena was tortured and murdered, reputedly by associates of a Mexican drug lord. A diplomatic furor subsequently erupted over the Drug Enforcement Agency–arranged abduction, for trial in the United States, of a Mexican doctor who was suspected of keeping Camarena alive during torture. The doctor was subsequently acquitted, but Mexican authorities warned their American counterparts that such infringements on Mexican sovereignty would not be permitted in the future.[74]

Finally, and perhaps most seriously, corruption, violence, and intimidation of political and judicial authorities within drug-producing nations continue to frustrate cooperative drug control programs. In Peru's Upper Huallaga Valley, for example, the government limited its crop-eradication efforts in the 1980s for fear of increasing support for the Sendero Luminoso (Shining Path) or Tupac Amaru guerrilla movements.[75] Drug-related corruption can reach to the highest levels in many drug-producing and transit countries. In December 1996, after scoring great successes against a major gang of Mexican drug smugglers, General Jesus Gutierrez Rebollo was named Mexico's top antidrug official. Two months later, he was arrested on charges of conspiring with another drug gang. In Colombia, kingpins rarely hesitate to use kidnapping and assassination to undermine government attempts to curb their activities. By the 1990s the drug war in Colombia had claimed the lives of thousands of public officials, including three presidential candidates, an attorney general, twelve supreme court justices, over forty judges, more than 170 other judicial employees, dozens of journalists, and more than 3000 police and soldiers.[76] By 1996, corruption and intimidation had become so pervasive in Colombia that the Clinton administration "decertified" Colombia's compliance with drug control agreements and withheld a portion of the development aid it would ordinarily receive under U.S. law. These sanctions were waived for Colombia and three other decertified countries (Pakistan, Paraguay, and Cambodia) in 1998, but decertification penalties were applied to Afghanistan, Burma, Nigeria, and Iran, and Mexico was certified only after heated debate.

An Expanding Global Problem, an Emerging Global Solution

In the past few years, an international consensus about how to deal with the drug problem has begun to emerge. On one hand, the advanced industrial nations, especially the United States, have slowly come to realize that as long as their demand for illegal drugs does not drop appreciably, their crop-eradication and anti-smuggling programs merely prompt traffickers to move their operations to areas outside the programs' geographic compass. In other words, until there is a substantial change of strategy, the industrial nations will continue to lose the war on drugs. The industrialized nations have started to approach the problem of curtailing demand in a variety of ways, ranging from mandating tougher penalties for convicted drug kingpins to expanded education and treatment programs to decriminalization and legalization of some drugs.[77]

On the other hand, the expansion of drug production has also brought the concomitant ills of addiction to more developing nations. The Central and South American countries have also had to deal with the money laundering, drug abuse, and corruption associated with the drug trade.[78] Thai authorities calculate that the 1 percent of the population that is addicted to heroin has greatly contributed to the spread of AIDS in that country.[79] Of the estimated 2.5 million drug users in Pakistan, more than 1 million were reported to be heroin abusers, and heroin use is on the rise in many Indian cities.[80] In the Middle East, heroin abuse is spreading in conjunction with hashish abuse.[81]

The drug trade has also had unforeseen effects on the environment. Drug producers, using slash-and-burn techniques, are responsible for significant destruction of forests and the erosion of topsoil, as well as the pollution of waterways through the dumping of chemicals used to process cocaine and heroin.[82]

Efforts coordinated by the United Nations International Drug Control Program (UNDCP) to fight drug abuse and trafficking intensified in the early 1990s. At a special session of the General Assembly held in February 1990, the United Nations, as mentioned earlier, proclaimed a UN Decade against Drug Abuse (1991–2000) and unanimously adopted a thirty-point Political Declaration and Global Program of Action against illegal drugs. The declaration recognized that the drug problem in all its dimensions is linked to economic, social, and cultural conditions in affected countries and acknowledges links between drug abuse and the spread of AIDS, as well as the connection between drug trafficking and terrorism. Among its main recommendations, the Global Program suggested giving higher priority to drug-abuse prevention programs, especially those directed at children.[83] The UN-sponsored London Declaration, concluded later that same year, called for drug-abuse education, prevention, and treatment programs, improved living conditions for those affected by drug abuse, and alternatives to prison for drug-abuse offenders who wish to undertake treatment.[84]

Only some of the recommendations made by less developed countries on the supply side of the drug equation have been carried out. For example, although the London Declaration was successful in devising strategies to reduce demand for drugs in the industrial nations, the drug-producing developing nations failed to win more than a general pledge of help in supporting crop-substitution programs.[85] On the other hand, a number of developed countries have joined the Financial Action Task Force, which studies measures to cooperatively prevent laundering of drug money through financial institutions. Additionally, more than twenty countries now belong to the Chemical Action Task Force, an organization dedicated to controlling the "precursor" chemicals used to manufacture illicit drugs.[86]

In contrast to supply-side programs, which have been largely ineffectual, the demand-side provisions of the UN programs have met with some success. The U.S. Bureau of International Narcotics Matters, for instance, has provided demand-reduction training and technical assistance to private and public officials in twenty-eight countries and has pursued joint education and training activities with governments in Southeast Asia and Latin America.[87] A UN Special Assembly on Drugs, which will review both supply- and demand-side programs, was scheduled for June 1998.

Drug control experts argue that the global economy of the New Era makes multilateral cooperation more important than ever because it relies heavily on the free exchange of goods, services, labor, and capital across sovereign borders. As one author concluded in 1991, no unilateral customs effort "could conduct detailed inspections of the 430 million people, 120 million automobiles, 8 million containers, 720,000 jets and small planes, and 290,000 ships and small boats that cross U.S. borders in a single year. But somewhere amidst that traffic is all the cocaine needed to satisfy the American coke habit for a year—enough to fill thirteen tractor trailer trucks."[88] And the problem has worsened since then.

Disagreements between the United States and Latin American countries over drug-control strategy show how the drug trade exerts different effects on drug-producing and drug-consuming nations. Rich, drug-importing countries experience the health problems, crime, and economic harm attributable to addiction, while corruption and narco-terrorism become endemic in the poorer states that produce the narcotics. Because no nation is immune to some of the ills created by drug abuse and trafficking, almost all states now regard the international war on drugs as an important and urgent cause. But unlike hunger or disease, the drug trade is a hugely lucrative business, and traffickers have a strong motivation to match supply to demand. Unless individual states and the international community take further steps to reduce both the supply and demand sides of the drug equation, the global narcotics industry will continue to find ways to turn coca, hemp, and poppies into gold.

TERRORISM

Terrorism is bound to be one of the most contentious global issues in the New Era. Terrorism has a long history; in first-century Judea, religious zealots revolted against Roman rule by creating an atmosphere where "no one was to be trusted and everyone was to be feared."[89] Many terrorist groups seek to create the same effect in the contemporary international system, but despite widespread condemnation of terrorism, effective international action to deal with the problem remains an elusive goal.

International terrorism may be defined as the use of violence across international boundaries, intended to coerce a target group into meeting political demands.[90] Unlike war or simple murder, terrorism is violence directed at an

What Would You Do ?

You are the president of the United States. The time is the present. Even though past drug-interdiction and demand-reduction efforts have achieved some successes in reducing illegal drug availability and abuse in the United States, these successes have been modest. Shipments of drugs into the United States continue unabated, and drug abuse remains stubbornly high in many inner cities. Because the federal budget for fighting the drug war is limited, you must decide whether to concentrate these dollars on attempts to reduce demand through education and treatment programs, or on efforts to reduce supply through drug-interdiction efforts. These interdiction efforts include the sending of U.S. troops to the source countries, an action that has proved unpopular in countries where it has been tried.

Suppose you invest drug-fighting dollars in education and treatment programs. Because drugs go to where the demand is located, this strategy could have numerous benefits. It would reduce demand at home, convincing drug producers and traffickers to get out of the business or move their operations elsewhere. It would also be more effective than border-control efforts (for example, stationing radar balloons and AWACS surveillance planes at the border, or beefing up customs personnel), and less intrusive than sending U.S. troops to source countries. But demand-reduction programs work slowly and uncertainly (no one can be positive that these programs are getting to the hard-core addicts who commit much of the drug-related crime). Meanwhile, drug shipments continue to come into the country, increasing the pressure on you to produce quicker and more visible results.

Suppose you put drug-fighting dollars in continued efforts to interdict supply, either at the border or to work on the source countries. Interdiction efforts give the politically popular impression that you are actually doing something (shipments halted, traffickers arrested), and sometimes they produce real results in terms of curbing availability. However, if demand remains high, drug traffickers usually find a way of designing their routes around these barriers, often by transshipping the drugs through third countries.

Sending U.S. troops to source countries is risky. Although it can give the impression that you are tackling the source of the problem, it can also antagonize the populations of the source countries, who would accuse the United States of imperialism. And it can harm the legitimacy of source-country governments, many of which are already facing severe political difficulties. These governments often wink at drug production because it provides employment and income for many poor peasants, employment that otherwise would not exist, in part because of the failure of the wealthier drug-consuming nations to purchase the legitimate products of the source countries.

You face a dilemma: You need to decide which strategy will be most effective in solving the drug problem.

What would you do ?

audience beyond those directly victimized. Though the practice is widespread, the ultimate effectiveness of terrorism is questionable. Although some claim that systematic campaigns of violence succeed in promoting the terrorists' message, others contend that negative reactions in the international community and the success of anti-terrorism policies limits the ability of terrorists to achieve their aims.[91]

The distinction between atrocious acts of terrorism and "legitimate" violence in support of a political cause or national goal is often blurred. One side's heroic revolutionaries are another's murderous thugs. The *Contras*, U.S.–backed insurgents against the socialist Sandinista regime in Nicaragua in the 1980s, exemplify this difference in perspective. Although the Sandinistas perceived the *Contras* as criminal terrorists bent on the overthrow of a legitimate government, President Ronald Reagan viewed the Nicaraguan "freedom fighters" as "the moral equivalent of our Founding Fathers."

Contemporary Terrorism around the World

Though most terrorist organizations have a regional base and political outlook, many have global reach, possessing capabilities to strike at targets far from their bases of operation. As a result, as demonstrated by the 1993 bombing at New York's World Trade Center, no region is immune to international terrorism. Political and economic globalization, coupled with rapid improvements in technology, increase the fear created by terrorists in the New Era. Developments in transportation (especially international aviation) create new vulnerabilities and give terrorists access to new targets. Improvements in communications, such as satellite broadcasting and the Internet, enable terrorists to publicize their motives and magnify the element of fear in regions far beyond their area of activity. Modern weapons technology, such as plastic explosives and small submachine guns, allow terrorists the use of less conspicuous and more destructive means of dealing in death. The possibility of terrorists obtaining weapons of mass destruction, such as nuclear, biological, or chemical weapons, is one of the most frightening threats to international security in the New Era.

According to counter-terrorism specialists in the U.S. Department of State, more than 10,000 acts of international terror were committed between 1976 and 1996. The highest number of incidents (665) occurred in 1987, while in 1996 terror incidents reached a twenty-five-year low of 296.[92] Although there has been a general downward trend in terrorist activities in the 1990s, the overall threat remains extremely serious. The death toll attributed to international terrorism expanded from 163 fatalities in 1995 to 311 victims in 1996.

Although terrorists can strive virtually anywhere, some areas of the world experience terrorist attacks more frequently than others. An estimated 40 percent of international terrorism occurs in the Middle East or is motivated by the many conflicts in that region, and 35 percent of the fatalities from terrorism are suffered there.[93] Terrorism in Europe reached its peak in the 1970s, but many European-based terrorist organizations still remain active. Although the collapse of the Soviet Union has decreased the number of incidents perpetrated by ideological terrorists such as the Red Brigades in Italy, the Red Army Faction in Germany, and Action Direct in France, groups like these continue to carry out terror attacks.

In the developing South, most international terror attacks are the work of ideological or separatist guerrillas. Leftist revolutionary groups such as the Sendero Luminoso or Tupac Amaru in Peru, and ethnic insurgents such as the Tamil Tigers in Sri Lanka, may continue engaging in terrorism until their political goals of overthrowing the government or creating a separate state are achieved or until their organizations are wiped out.

The extent and variety of terrorism across the globe shows that although terrorist organizations may use similar tactics, they have widely varying objectives and political orientations. Categorizing terrorist groups according to these characteristics is a useful first step in understanding terrorism, but it must be noted that many groups fall into more than one category. For example, Hamas, a separatist group dedicated to the eradication of Israel and the creation of an Islamic Palestinian state, has both ideological and nationalist motivations. At the same time, Hamas wages its struggle by peaceful means as well as violent methods, providing humanitarian relief for Palestinian refugees to further its cause and increase its political support (which in turn makes its terror campaign more effective).

State-Sponsored Terrorism

National governments engage in terror by subduing opposition within their own countries by cruel and violent means (a practice known as **enforcement terror**) and by sponsoring nonstate actors to carry out acts of violence abroad. The use of fear and violence against a state's own citizens has a long and bloody history. In the sixteenth century, Russia's Tsar Ivan the Terrible employed terror not only to punish offenders, but simply to instill fear among his subjects. The French Revolution (see Chapter Two) was followed by the Great Terror, when an estimated 30,000 real and imagined opponents of the revolution were executed, many by guillotine.[94] In the twentieth century, the ruling regimes of Nazi Germany, Soviet Russia and Communist China carried out state-sponsored terror on a massive scale. During the Cold War, both the United States and the USSR authorized covert operations involving the use of terror against unfriendly regimes (see Chapter Four). Military governments in Argentina and Brazil, Shah Mohammed Reza Pahlavi's regime in Iran, and the apartheid regime in South Africa were other notorious users of enforcement terror.

Some states regularly support terrorism in other countries. In 1997, the U.S. Department of State listed Cuba, Iran, Iraq, Libya, North Korea, Sudan, and Syria as sponsors of terrorism.[95] Although Cuba has few resources for financial support of international terror, it provides refuge and training for terrorist groups ranging from the Revolutionary Armed Forces of Columbia to Basque separatists in Spain. The Islamist government of Iran remains an active sponsor of terror, supporting insurgent groups including the Kurdish Workers' Party (PKK), Hezbollah, Hamas, and Islamic Jihad. The Iraqi regime, which has a long record of practicing enforcement terror against perceived domestic opponents, also supports the PKK and Islamic terror groups including the Abu Nidal organization (see box). Libya continues to defy international sanctions, including a ban on international air service, by failing to cooperate with the investigation of the bombings of international flights in 1988 and 1989. The government of Sudan, in addition to harboring international terrorists, also exercises enforcement terror, and is suspected of hiring the Islamic Group to attempt to assassinate Egyptian President Hosni Mubarak in 1995. North Korea and Syria have decreased their sponsorship of international terrorism in recent years, but both nations continue to provide funding, weapons, training, and other assistance to terrorist groups.

Nationalist Separatists

Terrorist groups in this category have political objectives of national liberation or self-determination. Because nationalism gains momentum from the bond of a shared identity (see Chapters Two and Five), terrorism instigated by separatist groups tends to have clear ethnic, cultural, or religious overtones. Conflicts between nations over autonomy can continue for generations. By some definitions, the antagonism between Britain and Ireland goes back over 800 years, and some scholars trace the Palestinian-Israeli dispute back to 1400 B.C.[96] Although separatists typically claim to be freedom fighters crusading for a separate homeland, their violent means and often indiscriminate targets can earn them reputations as terrorists of the most malicious nature. Notably, however, not everyone belonging to radical nationalist organizations espouses random violence, and many such groups are umbrella organizations for movements that include elements that support nationalist causes by peaceful means.

The conflict in Northern Ireland has given rise to some of the most feared nationalist terrorists. The Provisional wing of the Irish Republican Army (IRA) and Irish National Liberation Army have carried out campaigns of bombing, assassination, and other attacks to achieve their goals of a British withdrawal from Northern Ireland. (Some radical groups of Unionists, who oppose this goal in the name of Northern Ireland's Protestant majority, also resort to terrorist violence.) After decades of terrorist activity, the IRA declared a cease-fire in 1994, but this respite lasted only seventeen months. In 1997, a new IRA cease-fire, the renunciation of violence by Sinn Fein (the legal political party associated with the IRA), and the start of formal multilateral negotiations offered new hopes for peace. In April 1998, these negotiations culminated in an accord between the British and Irish governments and leading Catholic and Protestant groups that was overwhelmingly ratified by voters in both Northern Ireland and the Irish Republic. Widely regarded as an important step toward peace, the agreement ends Ireland's constitutional claims on the northern counties, replaces direct British rule in Northern Ireland with an autonomous assembly, and establishes cooperative links between north and south.

Terrorism also continues to play a role in the Palestinian-Israeli conflict. Before the creation of the state of Israel in 1948, both Jewish and Muslim terrorist groups operated in the mandated territory of Palestine. After 1967, when Israel occupied the West Bank and Gaza in the Six Day War, militant units of the Palestine Liberation Organization stepped up their activities against Israeli targets and Palestinian "collaborators." Although the PLO officially renounced terrorism after signing the Oslo accords in 1993 (see Chapter Five), renegade groups including the Popular Front for the Liberation of Palestine and the Democratic Front for the Liberation of Palestine continue to conduct terrorist attacks.

In Europe, the separatist group Basque Fatherland and Liberty conducts terrorist operations, including attacks on tourists and an attempt to assassinate King Juan Carlos in 1995, in order to obtain independence for the Basque country of northern Spain. The Kurdish Workers' Party in Turkey, Sikh nationalists in India, and Tamil guerrillas also conduct separatist terrorism.

Terrorism as a means to attain a national homeland remains as problematic as it was centuries ago. (Recall from Chapter Two that World War I was sparked off by the assassination of the Austrian Archduke Franz Ferdinand by a Serbian nationalist.) Feeding upon ethnic tensions, this class of terrorism threatens the integrity and security of multinational states by perpetuating and rekindling old animosities. At the same time, nationalist groups are frequently used by rival states to further their own ends, thus combining separatist and state-sponsored terror. Especially in the Middle East, many states support rebel terrorists in neighboring countries in a deadly game of regional politics and nationalist ambitions.

■ Victims of a suicide bomb attack in Israel
SOURCE: AP/Wide World

Profile of a Terrorist

Abu Nidal is the assumed name of Sabri Khalil al-Banna and also the name of his group—the Abu Nidal Organization (ANO). Known at times as the Fatah Revolutionary Council, the Arab Revolutionary Council, the Arab Revolutionary Brigade, Black September, and the Revolutionary Organization of Socialist Muslims, the ANO opposes all efforts toward political reconciliation of the Arab-Israeli conflict. It believes that both inter-Arab and intra-Palestinian terrorism is needed to lead to an all-embracing Arab revolution that will liberate occupied Palestine, or, in other words, destroy Israel. Abu Nidal began his independent efforts after the October 1973 Arab-Israeli War, when Yasir Arafat decided to restrict the PLO's terrorism to Israeli targets in Israel and the occupied territories. He broke with Arafat and decided to fight all moderates, committing terrorist acts against Israeli targets, pro-Arafat Palestinians, moderate Arab states, and countries (usually European) that had imprisoned ANO members, as well as other Western nations like the United States, United Kingdom, and France.

The Arafat–Abu Nidal rift intensified in the mid-1970s, when the PLO chairman sentenced the renegade Nidal to death. In response, in 1978 the ANO assassinated three prominent PLO officials allied with Arafat, yet this act was followed by a temporary rapprochement between the two adversaries.

Abu Nidal's vicious attacks have been felt worldwide. In more than 90 terrorist incidents in 20 countries, more than 900 people have been killed or injured. The most infamous attacks were the 1985 shootings of civilians at the Rome and Vienna airports, the 1986 bombing of the Neve Shalom synagogue in Istanbul, the 1986 hijacking of a Pan Am jet in Karachi, and a July 1988 attack on an excursion ship off the coast of Greece.

The ANO maintains its own political agenda, despite the government aid it has received. Nidal headquarters were in Iraq from 1974 to 1983, in Syria from 1983 to 1987, and in Libya since then. It is possibly the most economically stable terrorist group in the world. One-third of its income comes from patron states; one-third is from graft and blackmail; and one-third is from its network of business companies and front organizations. Reports have circulated that Abu Nidal is ill or even dead; however, the ANO is said to be so strong that his demise would affect the group's operations minimally, if at all.*

Abu Nidal   SOURCE: Reuters/Archive Photos

* Compiled from *Patterns of Global Terrorism 1992*, U.S. Department of State, released April 1993; and *Terrorist Group Profiles*, U.S. Department of Defense, 1989.

Ideological Terrorism

Ideological terrorism refers to violence committed by groups influenced by extremist or revolutionary doctrines such as Marxism-Leninism or anarchism. These radical opposition groups work to overthrow a regime or political system. The rage that animates violent insurgencies often stems from the desire to overthrow oppressive governments or express anti-imperialist sentiments. Although the collapse of the Soviet Union has decreased the support and motivation of many communist-inspired terrorists, the disappearance of ideological terror remains a far-distant prospect.

Notable perpetrators of communist ideological terror include groups such as Action Direct in France, the Baader-Meinhof Gang in Germany, and the Japanese Red Army. The Red Brigades, an Italian organization notorious in the 1970s and 1980s, in its heyday not only attempted a coup intended to spark a communist revolution, but directly targeted representatives of what they termed the "multinational army of imperialist counter-revolution," exemplified by the kidnapping of U.S. General James Dozier in 1981 and the murder of former Prime Minister Aldo Morro in 1978. One of the most persistent and violent opposition groups in Latin America, the Sendero Luminoso guerrillas of Peru also espouse a Marxist ideology. The organization attempts to cultivate the support of farmers and impoverished rural residents for its antigovernment insurgency, but the strength of the group declined after the imprisonment of many top leaders in the 1990s.

In general, revolutionary terrorism based on Marxist or anarchist ideologies appears to be on the wane following the end of Soviet support for Marxist rebels in Europe and developing countries. It has been argued, however, that the discrediting of these groups due to the collapse of communism will give rise to a sense of isolation and powerlessness among disenfranchised groups, which will ultimately provoke a new wave of ideological terror.[97] The Tupac Amaru revolutionary movement in Peru was believed to have weakened because of defections and the success of law enforcement, but it rose again to prominence in 1996 when the group took over the Japanese ambassador's residence in Lima, holding attendees of a diplomatic reception hostage for weeks until the insurgents were wiped out by a commando raid.

Religious Terrorism

With the decline of Marxist terrorist groups, religious radicalism has overshadowed Marxism as the prime ideological generator of international terrorism. Islamic radical groups such as Hamas in the West Bank and Gaza and Hezbollah (the "Party of God") in Lebanon embody a deadly combination of ethnic nationalism and religious fanaticism directed primarily against Israel, demonstrated with tragic effects by waves of suicide bombings since 1994. Other Islamist terrorists, such as the Armed Islamic Group in Algeria seek to overthrow secular regimes and forcibly institute Islamic government and law, murdering secularist teachers, journalists, women wearing Western dress, and other victims. In Egypt, Islamic extremists strike foreign tourists (killing sixty-two people in a single attack at Luxor in November 1997) as well as Egyptian citizens in order to discredit and weaken the government. A radical Japanese religious sect, Aum Shinrikyo, used homemade nerve gas in an attack on the Tokyo subway in 1995. Other religiously motivated terrorists include Sikh separatists in India and Jewish extremists in Israel.

Religious terrorism can attain especially frightening dimensions because religious terrorists typically regard violence as a morally justified, and even spiritually sanctified, means for the attainment of goals inspired by tenets of their faith. Islamic radicals do not consider the killing of nonbelievers to be murder, and they assert that fighters killed while committing terror strikes are assured of a place in heaven. Countering religious terror groups can be especially difficult because of the fervent commitment of their believers and the support these groups often receive from disaffected religious or ethnic groups.

Combating International Terrorism

Although almost all states publicly condemn terrorism, nations differ greatly in the actual stance toward it. Although some governments actively combat terrorism, others just as actively support international terror or engage in it themselves, and still others do both as suits their political objectives. Nevertheless, the United States, the European Union, and many governments and international organizations have attempted to cooperate to locate, thwart, and apprehend terrorists.

Efforts to coordinate action against terrorism can be organized at the bilateral, regional, and international levels. Bilateral cooperation involves collaboration between two countries in areas ranging from exchange of intelligence information to joint police operations and border controls. Although bilateral cooperation can be effective between states that share political objectives, problems often arise when two states differ in their ideological or strategic outlook. Jordan and Israel, for example, agreed to cooperate against terrorism in their 1994 peace treaty, but cooperation was strained for several months after Israeli security services acknowledged responsibility for an attempt to assassinate Hamas leader Khaled Meshal in Amman in 1997.

Bilateral cooperation can also encounter legal difficulties, such as tortuous procedures for **extradition** (turning over suspects to another country for trial). In an infamous incident in 1978, an agreement was underway to extradite four leading terrorists captured in Yugoslavia in exchange for the extradition of Yugoslav suspects held in Germany. The exchange was bungled, however, and Yugoslavia released the German terrorists instead of handing them over to German authorities.[98] The efforts of some law enforcement and intelligence agencies to nab terrorists can also raise serious questions of national sovereignty. Because so many nations offer freedom from extradition or other forms of "safe haven" for terrorists, the techniques used to apprehend suspected terrorists have been likened to kidnapping.

Major Terrorist Organizations

Abu Nidal Organization (ANO)

- Split from PLO in 1974
- International terrorist organization led by Sabri al-Banna (better known as Abu Nidal)
- Several hundred-plus "militia" members in Lebanon and overseas support structure
- Believed to be based in the Bekaa Valley and in several Palestinian refugee camps in Lebanon. Operates in the Middle East, Asia, and Europe

Activities: Has carried out more than 90 terrorist attacks in 20 countries since 1974, killing or injuring almost 900 people. Targets vary depending on who is sponsoring the attacks. Major attacks include Rome and Vienna airports in December 1985 and the September 1986 Pam Am Flight 73 hijacking in Karachi, Pakistan. Continues to assassinate Palestinian and Jordanian officials connected with the Arab-Israeli peace process, but has not attacked Western targets since the late 1980s.

External Aid: Received aid from Iraq (1973–1974) and Syria (1983–1987). Supported by Libya afterward

Basque Fatherland and Liberty (ETA)

- Founded in 1959
- Has the aim of creating an independent homeland in Spain's Basque region
- Divided into political wing, the Herri Batasuna Party, and military wing, which carries out terrorist actions
- Strength unknown. Could be in the hundreds
- Operates primarily in Spain and France and to a limited degree in Italy and Germany

Activities: Carries out bombing, kidnapping, and assassinations of Spanish government targets, especially security forces. Has killed nearly 800 people in last 30 years. More than 40 people were killed and 200 injured in ETA attacks in 1991. Obtains funds by extorting "revolution taxes" from companies and wealthy individuals. Attempted to assassinate King Juan Carlos of Spain in 1995.

External Aid: Has received training from Libya, Lebanon, and Sandinista-controlled Nicaragua. Has close ties to to the Provisional Irish Republic Army.

Hamas (Islamic Resistance Movement)

- Founded in 1987 as an outgrowth of the Palestinian branch of the Muslim Brotherhood
- Uses both political and violent means to pursue the goal of establishing an Islamic Palestinian state in place of Israel
- Loosely structured, with some elements working openly through mosques and social service institutions to raise money, organize activities, and distribute propaganda
- Strength is concentrated in the West Bank and Gaza
- Unknown number of hard-core members; tens of thousands of supporters and sympathizers in the occupied territories and Jordan

Activities: Militant elements have conducted many attacks including suicide bombings against Israeli civilians and military targets, suspected Palestinian "collaborators," and rivals in the Palestinian Liberation Organization. Claimed responsibility for bombings that killed more than 60 people in 1996. Has increased public and political support through sponsorship of social and medical programs, appealing to Palestinians disaffected by the sporadic progress of the Israeli-Palestinian peace process. Spiritual leader Sheik Ahmed Yassin was released from Israeli prison in 1997.

External Aid: Receives funding from Palestinian expatriates, Iran, and donors in Saudi Arabia and other Arab states. Some fundraising and propaganda activity in Europe and North America.

Hizbollah ("Party of God")

- Radical Shia group formed in Lebanon under the guidance of the Ayatollah Ruhollah Khomeini in 1982. Dedicated to the creation of an Iranian-style Islamic republic in Lebanon and the removal of all non-Islamic influences from the area. Strongly anti-West and anti-Israel

- Numbers 700 to 4000
- Operates in Lebanon and has established cells in Europe, Africa, and South America
- Linked to Islamic Jihad

Activities: Known or suspected to have been involved in numerous anti-U.S. and anti-Israel terrorist attacks, including the October 1988 suicide attack that killed eight Israeli soldiers and a wave of bombings in July 1994 of Jewish community centers in Buenos Aires and London and the Israeli Embassy in London. Responsible for taking many Western hostages in Lebanon in the 1980s. Operates with relative impunity in Lebanon's Bekaa Valley. Also sponsors public welfare programs including schools and hospitals.

External Aid: Receives financial support, weapons, explosives, political, diplomatic, and organizational aid and training from Iran

Japanese Red Army (JRA)

- An international terrorist organization formed in 1971
- Stated goals are to overthrow the Japanese government and monarchy and to help foment world revolution. Is closely associated with the Popular Front for the Liberation of Palestine and is heavily dependent upon that organization for financial support
- Includes about 15 core members and unknown number of sympathizers
- Based in Lebanon; may have organized cells in Manila, Singapore, and other cities in Asia.

Activities: Before 1977, JRA carried out a series of brutal attacks, including the massacre of passengers at Lod airport in Israel in 1972. Since the mid-1980s, the JRA has carried out several crude rocket and mortar attacks against a number of U.S. embassies.

External Aid: Receives aid from radical Palestinian terrorists and possibly from Libya

Kurdistan Workers Party (PKK)

- Established in the mid-1970s
- Seeks to set up a Marxist state in southeastern Turkey, which has a large population of Kurds
- Includes 10,000 to 15,000 guerrilla fighters plus thousands of sympathizers in Turkey and Europe
- Operates in Turkey and Western Europe with training grounds in Lebanon and strongholds in Iraq and Syria

Activities: Primary targets include the Turkish government and civilians in southeastern Turkey but is becoming increasingly active in Western Europe against Turkish targets and rival Kurdish groups. Conducted attacks on Turkish diplomatic and commercial facilities in dozens of European cities in 1993 and 1995. Declared a yearlong unilateral cease-fire in 1995, but in 1996 resumed attacks on military and civilian targets, including suicide bombings.

External Aid: Receives haven and some aid from Syria, Iran, and Iraq

Liberation Tigers of Tamil Eelam (LTTE, Tamil Tigers)

- Founded in 1976
- Goal is establishment of independent Tamil state in Sri Lanka
- Most powerful Tamil group in Sri Lanka; led by Velupillai Prabhakaran
- Approximately 10,000 armed combatants
- Controls most of the northern and eastern coastal areas of Sri Lanka, but has significant overseas support base and has conducted acts of terrorism throughout the world

Activities: Carries out major campaign of guerrilla warfare in Sri Lanka's countryside and bombings in the capital, Colombo. Has assassinated military and political leaders in Sri Lanka and India, including Indian Prime Minister Rajiv Gandhi in 1991 and Sri Lankan President Ranasinghe Premadasa in 1993. Also engages in drug trafficking in Europe.

continued

At a Glance (continued)

External Aid: Uses international contacts to procure funds, weapons, and communications equipment

Palestine Islamic Jihad (PIJ)

- Originated in Gaza in the 1970s
- A series of loosely affiliated factions rather than a cohesive group
- Committed to the creation of an Islamic Palestinian state and destruction of Israel through holy war (*jihad*). Also attacks United States personnel in the Middle East because of U.S. support for Israel.
- Strength unknown
- Operates in Israel, Israeli-occupied territories, Jordan, Lebanon, and other areas of the Middle East. Largest faction is based in Syria.
- Linked to Hezbollah

Activities: Carries out cross-border raids against Israeli and Western targets. Responsible for the 1983 attack on the U.S. Marine barracks at Beirut Airport that killed 241. Also carried out several other bombings of French, U.S., and Israeli installations in Lebanon, the downing of a French airliner in September 1989, and suicide bombings in Jerusalem in 1994–1996.

External Aid: Receives aid from Iran and possibly Syria

Popular Front for the Liberation of Palestine— General Command (PFLP-GC)

- Split from the Popular Front for the Liberation of Palestine in 1968, intending to focus more on violence and less on politics
- Expresses violent opposition to Palestine Liberation Organization
- Numbers several hundred
- Led by Ahmad Jibril, former captain in the Syrian Army
- Headquarters in Damascus, with bases in Lebanon and cells in Europe

Activities: Has carried out numerous cross-border attacks into Israel using unusual means such as hot air balloons and motorized hang gliders

External Aid: Receives logistic and military support, along with safe haven, from its chief sponsor, Syria; also receives funds from Libya and support from Iran

Provisional Irish Republic Army (PIRA)

- Formed from radical elements in Irish Republican Army (IRA) in 1969
- Closely connected to Sinn Fein, IRA's legal political movement, which is dedicated to removing British forces from Northern Ireland and then to unification of Ireland. PIRA is Marxist in orientation.
- Includes several hundred members, plus thousands of sympathizers
- Based in Northern Ireland, Irish Republic, Great Britain, and Western Europe

Activities: Carried out bombings, assassinations, kidnappings, extortion, and robberies. Targeted British government and private-sector interests along with Northern Irish Protestant paramilitary organizations. In the autumn of 1992, PIRA launched a major bombing campaign in London against train stations, hotels, and shopping areas, resulting in casualties and major property damage. These activities were suspended when a cease-fire was called in 1994, but resumed in 1996 until a second cease-fire was declared in 1997. Sinn Fein subsequently entered negotiations with British and Irish governments, but some acts of violence continue, possibly perpetrated by splinter groups such as Continuity Army Council and Irish National Liberation Army.

External Aid: Has received aid from a variety of countries and sympathizers, including Libya, and

Recognizing their common interests in countering terror, the Organization of American States and the South Asian Association for Regional Cooperation (SAARC) have attempted to organize regional responses to terrorism. Although these efforts have facilitated some police and intelligence cooperation and prompted dialogue on important issues, they have generally done little to suppress

private U.S. citizens. Also linked to the Basque ETA.

Revolutionary Armed Forces of Colombia (FARC)

- Established in 1966
- The military wing of the Colombian Communist Party. Goal is to overthrow the government and ruling class and eliminate U.S. influence.
- More than 7000 armed combatants and unknown number of supporters, mostly in rural areas

Activities: Carries out armed attacks against Colombian targets, bombings of U.S. businesses, kidnappings of Colombians and foreigners for ransom, and assassinations. Has disrupted local elections in attempts to demonstrate de facto control over large areas of country. Often attacks oil pipelines jointly operated by Colombian and foreign companies. Also traffics in drugs.

External Aid: FARC has ties to Cuba

Sendero Luminoso ("Shining Path," SL)

- Formed in 1970
- Peru's largest subversive organization, it is among the world's most dangerous and ruthless terrorist groups. Its goal is to destroy existing Peruvian institutions and replace them with a peasant revolutionary regime as well as to rid Peru of foreign influences.
- Includes 1500 to 2500 armed combatants and receives strong rural support
- Draws inspiration from Maoist political theories

Activities: Specializes in the assassination of government officials, but has attacked diplomatic missions of nearly every country represented in Peru, foreign businesses, and humanitarian aid projects in addition to Peruvian government and private-sector targets. Has concentrated on drug traffick-

ing, kidnapping, extortion, and other common criminal activities since the collapse of communism and Marxist ideologies. Uses earnings from drug traffic and kidnapping to buy weapons and pay fighters (sometimes more than the Peruvian army pays its soldiers). Although the arrest of its primary leader, Abimael Guzman, significantly weakened the organization in 1992, it has continued to carry out bombings and assassinations.

External Aid: Has no known foreign sponsors, but receives money from Colombian narcotics traffickers

Tupac Amaru Revolutionary Movement (MRTA)

- Formed in 1983
- Based in Peru
- Traditional Marxist-Leninist revolutionary movement in Peru, seeking to establish a Marxist regime in Peru
- Strength unknown

Activities: MRTA is responsible for more anti-U.S. attacks than any other group in Latin America. Acts include the burning of several Kentucky Fried Chicken restaurants in 1985 and a car bombing outside the U.S. ambassador's residence in Lima. In 1996, twenty-three MTRA members took over the Japanese ambassador's residence in Lima during a diplomatic reception, capturing hundreds of hostages. A raid by Peruvian army special forces four months later ended the hostage situation and killed fourteen guerrillas, including MTRA leader Nestor Cerpa Cartolini.

External Aid: Has received training from Cuba and possibly from Libya

SOURCES: U.S. Department of State, *Patterns of Global Terrorism, 1996*; Stephen E. Atkins, *Terrorism: A Reference Handbook* (Santa Barbara, CA: Contemporary World Issues, 1992); Jay M. Shafritz, E. F. Gibbons, Jr., and Gregory E. J. Scott, *Almanac of Modern Terrorism* (New York: Facts on File, 1991).

terrorist violence. Some SAARC countries were even suspected of commissioning terrorist attacks on their regional neighbors even while they ostensibly cooperated in antiterrorist programs.[99] The region that could benefit most from regional cooperation against terrorism, the Middle East, seems unlikely to achieve or even attempt it soon.

The success of international cooperation in combating terrorism depends on the efficacy of international law and organizations. Police and security agencies have attempted to coordinate their antiterrorist efforts at the international level, with modest success. Interpol, the International Criminal Police Organization, has fostered cooperation among national police forces for decades. Although the United Nations has passed many resolutions unanimously condemning terrorism, these declarations have had essentially zero impact.

All states, whether they recognize it or not, have an interest in curbing terrorism. National, ethnic, ideological, and religious conflicts spill across state borders so easily that no state can consider itself immune from the pestilence of terrorism. Many of the mechanisms for cooperation against terrorism by police and security agencies are already in place; however, to take full advantage of these existing organizations, or to build new avenues for cooperation against terrorism, states will have to abandon the support of terrorism as a component of their foreign policies. Nations cannot completely prevent the victimization of innocent civilians by killers who want to publicize their causes. But governments, international organizations, and nonstate actors can come together to seek better ways of preventing terrorist attacks, apprehending suspected terrorists, and denying modern weapons to fanatics willing to kill and die for ancient hatreds and contemporary animosities.

ENERGY AND NATURAL RESOURCES

As populations grow and economies industrialize, the world's available supplies of nonrenewable energy and natural resources become increasingly scarce. International forums such as the 1992 Earth Summit have sought, with varying degrees of success, to promote widespread commitment to sustainable economic development (see the environment section of this chapter and Chapter Nine). In the absence of an international agency to enforce accords that deal with energy use, states do not face many incentives to use resources in a manner that takes into account the needs of other countries and future generations.

This chapter has already noted the inherent tension between conservation and use of resources in its discussions of conflicts over farmland (in the section on food) and rain forests (in the environment section). As with all the global problems considered in this book, it would be impossible to explain fully the complexity and urgency of natural-resource issues in the space available here. This section, therefore, will present "snapshots" of the conflicts over two vital resources that have sparked conflicts in the past and may cause more in the future: energy and water.

The Need for Energy

Societies need energy to survive just as human beings do. In a sense, the course of technological progress is the story of the discovery, use, and conservation of new sources of energy. All societies consume energy in some form; before the Industrial Revolution, demand for wood fuel was a major reason for deforestation on every continent (as it still is today in many developing countries). As states attain higher levels of economic and technological development, they "graduate" to dependence on different sources of energy—from animal power to wood, to coal, to oil, to nuclear power, and so on. Although a significant amount of the energy used by the developed world comes from nuclear fission and **hydroelectricity** (electricity generated by water power in dams), the main sources of energy for developed and developing countries alike are fossil fuels (oil, coal, and natural gas).

World energy consumption increased by 3 percent in 1996, double the average increase in the previous ten years.[100] Because there is a close relationship between economic growth and growth in consumption of energy resources, much of the increased demand for energy resources in recent years has come from the developing countries. In fact, consumption in countries outside of the Organization of Economic Cooperation and Development (OECD), which includes most of the developed countries of the world, is expected to increase significantly from 45 percent in 1993 to just over 50 percent in 2010.[101] Although the 1973 OPEC oil crisis and the 1990 Persian Gulf War reinforced the importance of securing energy supplies in the developed world, economic growth in the developing world poses the possibility of a new struggle over supplies, especially among those countries that rely heavily on imports to meet their energy requirements.

Oil's Critical Role

Since the invention of the automobile, oil has been the Western world's most important source of energy. However, the greater the reliance on oil to fuel the developed countries' economic (and automotive) engines, the greater is the danger they face to their economies if the oil stops flowing. This was illustrated by the long lines at gas stations following the energy crises of 1973 and 1979. After the OPEC oil embargo of 1973, the OECD countries progressively reduced their dependence on oil. In 1996, though total world demand for oil increased to record levels (more than 71 million barrels per day), it accounted for only 40 percent of total primary energy supplies, compared with 1973 when oil represented almost 55 percent of global energy demand. This decreased reliance on petroleum, combined with the glut on the world market, has lessened OPEC's power over the price of global oil supplies since the early 1980s (see Chapters Six and Eight).

In general, demand for oil rises and falls with total economic activity. The recession of the early 1990s led to decreased demand for oil in North America and Europe (by 2 percent in 1990–1991 in North America). As soon as economic activity picked up, demand for oil did as well (by 1.5 percent in 1992 in North America). In Eastern Europe and the former Soviet Union, by contrast, the convulsions caused by the collapse of the Soviet Union and the Communist system have led to a precipitous decline in oil use.

In the developing countries, demand for oil is rising with economic growth, especially in Asia, and consequently the demand for oil in the Third World is increasing much faster than in the industrialized countries. Between 1986 and 1995, overall demand for petroleum in the member states of the Organization for Economic Cooperation and Development (OECD) increased by 13.2 percent, to an estimated total of 40.4 million barrels per day in 1995. The states of the former Soviet Union experienced a 46.7 percent decrease in oil demand in those years, reflecting their severe economic disruption, but energy demand in that region is expected to grow steadily over the next decade along with economic recovery. However, demand for oil in developing countries during the same period increased by 52.6 percent. The most rapid increase in oil use occurred in South and East Asia, where demand increased 105.1 percent.[102] Estimated demand for oil in developing countries (including the former Soviet states) exceeded 29 million barrels per day by 1995, and further increases seem almost certain in the twenty-first century.

Energy Crises and Global Responses

Since the early 1970s, there have been three major oil crises—in 1973, 1979, and 1980—and a relatively minor crisis in 1990. The first involved an approximately 7 percent reduction in world oil supplies following the decision of the Arab members of OPEC to impose embargoes on the United States and Netherlands for their support of Israel during the 1973 Arab-Israeli war (see Chapter Five). The response of oil-consuming countries to the embargo was uncoordinated and competitive. Many countries sought to position themselves favorably by imposing restrictions on petroleum exports and by issuing pro-Arab statements in hopes of winning preferential treatment for their oil companies. This cacaphony of national responses contributed to the quadrupling of official prices (from $3 to almost $12 per barrel) between the beginning of October 1973 and January 1974.

Concerned with the effects of the embargo on its economy, the United States led an initiative to establish the International Energy Agency (IEA) in 1974. The initial objectives of this agency were to develop an emergency system for sharing oil, establish an information system to monitor the oil market, facilitate long-term measures to reduce net demand for oil on world markets, and set up multinational energy research and development activities. The IEA program is designed to protect member states from the economic difficulties that would result if their access to oil was significantly reduced. For example, if any member of the IEA suffers an oil-supply shortfall exceeding 7 percent, it can ask the IEA secretariat to put into effect the emergency sharing system.

The IEA was put to its first test in 1979, when the Iranian revolution resulted in a virtual cessation of Iranian oil exports. Oil-consuming nations responded by scrambling to ensure supplies (usually by stockpiling) for themselves at whatever price had to be paid, and as a result, prices doubled, even though production outmatched consumption for 1979 as a whole. When Sweden, suffering from an oil-supply shortfall of more than 7 percent, requested that the emergency sharing system be activated in the winter of 1979, the IEA's governing board declined the request. In this case the IEA did not come through when it was needed.

The third oil crisis resulted from the onset of the Iran-Iraq war in September 1980. This time, prices did not rise precipitously. In July 1981 they were only 5 percent higher than prewar levels. Oil prices remained stable, due mostly to weakness in demand and to the Saudis' willingness to increase production, and also to the IEA's efforts to persuade oil companies to sell oil inventories rather than stockpile them.[103]

Although no major oil shortage developed from the UN embargo on Iraq following its invasion of Kuwait in 1990, it did remove 4 million to 4.3 million barrels per day from the world's supply of crude oil. Initial uncertainties surrounding the invasion and fears of previous crises caused a temporary "spike" in oil prices. This complicated economic problems in Eastern Europe and the Third World and damaged aviation and automobile industries in the industrialized nations. However, a more serious crisis was avoided by Saudi Arabia's willingness to increase production, reduced worldwide demand, and the IEA countries decision to release oil from their strategic stocks.[104] After the collapse of the Soviet Union, Western oil companies scrambled to develop the vast energy resources of Russia, Azerbaijan, and the Central Asian states, which many companies welcomed as a guarantee against future oil crises. However, political disputes, an uncertain economic climate in many former Soviet countries, and the need to build long pipelines to transport petroleum for export has slowed the arrival of post-Soviet oil on the world market.

Coal and Natural Gas

Although petroleum is the energy resource that receives the most attention, other fossil fuels are also extremely important. Natural gas, for example, is used for cooking, and for the heating of homes and offices. North America accounts for two-thirds of total gas consumption among members of the Organization for Economic Cooperation and Development (OECD), but 40 percent of the world's natural gas reserves are located on the territory of the former Soviet Union. Exports from the former Soviet states constitute one-third of all internationally traded volumes. Natural gas is difficult to transport by sea and can be expensive to transport over long distances by land, and as a result, internationally traded gas still accounts for only 15 percent of total global gas consumption.[105] But because of its many uses, relatively low emissions, and low cost when available nearby, natural gas will remain a significant source of energy.

Another primary energy source is coal, especially for generating electricity. In 1994 coal contributed 38.5 percent of electricity generation in the OECD, while nuclear power and oil contributed only 24.4 and 7.7 percent, respectively.[106] Coal is also the dirtiest fossil fuel, and the fact that a large percentage of electric power is generated by burning coal has caused some environmentalists to question the wisdom of encouraging the development of electric cars. If the batteries on electric vehicles are charged with coal-generated electric power, the overall pollution produced by each car could be higher than that produced by gasoline-powered vehicles.

Spotlight

The Chernobyl Syndrome

Nuclear power is another way to generate electricity. Nuclear power plants can often produce electricity at lower cost than plants burning coal or oil, pollute the air much less, and offer countries with limited petroleum reserves a reliable alternative to imported oil. Although extensive research on nuclear energy began in the late 1940s, the oil crises of the 1970s gave states additional impetus to diversify their sources of energy and resulted in increased funding for nuclear power research. For many years, however, there were suspicions about the potential environmental side effects of nuclear power. These suspicions were heightened by a nuclear accident at Three Mile Island, Pennsylvania, in 1979, but an accident at Chernobyl, Ukraine (then part of the Soviet Union) in 1986 confirmed some of the world's worst fears of nuclear power.

Three explosions occurred on April 26, 1986, in the Chernobyl plant's No. 4 reactor. The first two explosions blew the lid off the reactor, and the third scattered fragments that caused local fires. This reactor was entombed in concrete to prevent further radiation contamination, while the three remaining reactors continued in operation. (Reactor No. 2 was closed in 1991 following a turbine fire, and No. 1 was shut down in 1997.) Thirty-two fatalities, mostly firefighters and plant emergency personnel, were immediately reported, and approximately 500 people were hospitalized with injuries.

But the most serious effects of the Chernobyl disaster came from the release of radioactive substances. Within a few days, 135,000 people were evacuated from an area of nineteen square miles surrounding the plant. Within this contaminated area, there have been excessively high cancer rates, especially thyroid cancer, leukemia, and other radiation-related diseases. Radioactivity from the force of the explosion was spread across the Northern Hemisphere, with the heaviest radioactive fallout in the western Soviet Union and parts of Europe. The Belorussian, Ukrainian, and Russian republics experienced the worst plumes of contaminated air. The contamination affected buildings, transportation facilities, roads, water, forests, and other vegetation. Radioactive material entered the food chain, particularly in milk, vegetables, and fruit. In Ukraine, panic resulted. Orders were issued not to swim in reservoirs or eat leafy vegetables. Radiation checks on people leaving the contaminated areas were mandatory. The sale of ice cream, cakes, and drinks on the street was banned.*

By early 1994, Ukrainian authorities had listed up to 8000 deaths from illnesses caused by the explosion. The No. 4 reactor was leaking and deteri-

Renewable Energy

Not all sources of energy pollute the environment as much as fossil fuel does, but more environmentally friendly alternative energy sources remain a small part of global energy consumption. Renewable energy sources contributed only 6 percent of total OECD energy supply in 1994. They make their greatest contribution in electricity generation, with hydroelectric power accounting for 15.3 percent and other sources (wind, solar, and so on) only 3.6 percent of total IEA electricity generation.[107] North America is the leader in the development and use of alternative energy sources.

Every alternative to fossil fuels has drawbacks, however. Most of the time, nuclear power is relatively clean and safe, but nuclear plants are expensive to build,

orating rapidly and was in danger of collapsing. The International Atomic Energy Agency (IAEA), in a report filed in March 1994, also listed "numerous safety deficiencies at the plant." Ukraine has promised to shut down the remaining operational reactor by 2000.

The Chernobyl experience and fear of future accidents and contamination led to protests worldwide over the continued construction of nuclear power reactors. However, the most pressing environmental concerns regarding nuclear power do not arise from the remote but frightening possibility of accidents, but from the need for safe disposal of radioactive waste, both high-level (highly radioactive material such as spent reactor fuel) and low-level (slightly radioactive material such as used pipes and containers). International controversies often arise over the transport and storage of radioactive waste. In 1997, an agreement to ship low-level nuclear wastes from Taiwan to storage sites in North Korea caused considerable consternation in South Korea, Japan, and other Pacific Rim countries.

Despite these concerns,, nuclear power generators remain fairly numerous today, and many states remain committed to nuclear power. By 1996, according to the IAEA, almost 400 reactors were operating or being built in 32 countries, supplying about 6 percent of global energy and 17 percent of the global electricity supply.** The nations that currently use nuclear power the most are the United States, France, Japan, Great Britain, Russia, Canada, Germany, Ukraine, and Sweden. Of these countries, the United States and France are the largest users. In 1993 the United States had 109 reactors in operation, with the capacity to supply over one-fifth of national energy needs. And by the end of the 1990s, U.S. dependence on nuclear energy may increase to about 25 percent. France, with its fifty-six operational reactors, relies even more heavily on nuclear energy, and Russia plans to increase its use of nuclear power, particularly in Siberia and the Russian Far East, where many towns have poor access to or cannot afford other sources of energy. Nevertheless, the U.S. Department of Energy forecasts that the global share of electricity produced by nuclear plants will decline from 17 percent in 1997 to about 11 percent by 2015.† In the final analysis, although solar power and other alternative sources of energy are promising, no source of energy is without drawbacks, and governments and consumers in the New Era will continue to face economic and environmental tradeoffs on energy policy.

* Richard F. Mould, *Chernobyl: The Real Story* (Oxford: Pergamon Press, 1988).
** Victor M. Mourogov, "Nuclear Power Development: Global Challenges and Strategies," *IAEA Bulletin* 39/2, pp. 2–8.
† U.S. Department of Energy forecast reported by Associated Press, November 4, 1997.

and the possibility of spectacular accidents such as those that occurred at Three Mile Island in Pennsylvania in 1979 and Chernobyl in Ukraine in 1986 makes many people nervous about reliance on nuclear energy (see box). Solar and wind power are unreliable in many areas and, though their cost is steadily decreasing, still too expensive to compete on price with fossil fuels. Hydroelectric power is available only near major rivers and has significant environmental side effects, such as killing aquatic wildlife, reducing water quality, and inundating land under their reservoirs. Almost all energy sources apart from fossil fuels are prohibitively expensive for developing countries, making coal and oil the most affordable energy options in most of the South. Indeed, despite efforts to make the world more reliant on renewable energy, fossil based fuels are projected to account for almost 90 percent of primary energy supplies in 2010 because of continuing growth in

OECD transport demand, the lack of substitution possibilities in other sectors and rapid economic growth in the developing countries.[108]

In the long run, states will have to learn to do more with less energy in order to sustain economic growth without dangerously depleting world energy resources and causing further damage to the environment. In the short term, however, states have no choice but to use all means to conserve and safeguard their supplies of energy. For some, this has meant shedding blood for oil.[109]

Water

Though oil is a crucial commodity in the modern world, only one fluid is literally vital: without water, life itself is impossible. A growing global population places strains on available fresh-water supplies, for industrial and agricultural use as well as for basic household consumption. An estimated 1.2 billion people lack clean and safe water, and almost 1.8 billion live without adequate sanitation. Nearly 80 percent of all cases of disease in developing countries have been linked to contaminated water.[110] In areas where fresh water is plentiful, disputes over water are usually limited to arguments between farmers over water rights. In many dry regions, however, water is a scarce resource, lending more than a ring of truth to Mark Twain's adage, "Whiskey is for drinking, water is for fighting."

In the mostly arid Middle East, serious concerns over water supplies add to the potential for international conflict. With population growth of 3 percent per year, inadequate rainfall, and boundaries of important water resources (rivers, lakes, aquifers, subterranean canals) shared by more than one state, some experts believe that the next war in the Middle East will be fought not for land, but for water.[111] Table 10.1 indicates how rapid population increases have put serious strains on the region's water resources and may lead to critical shortages in many countries by 2025.

Three Middle Eastern river basins, the Jordan, the Tigris-Euphrates, and the Nile, have been scenes of recurring conflict over water among neighboring states for thousands of years. Cooperation among states in the Jordan River basin has been closely tied to the overall Arab-Israeli peace process. Although the Johnston Plan for assigning Jordan River water rights played a constructive role in providing a basis for water sharing between Israel and its Arab adversaries, that 1950s-era plan did not stop the various states, especially Israel and Jordan, from bitterly arguing over transboundary water resources.[112] Access to important water sources reinforces Israel's reluctance to relinquish the Golan Heights captured from Syria in 1967.[113] The 1993 PLO-Israel agreement has also forced the Palestinians and Israelis to confront more directly their differences over water resources, especially rights to groundwater in the West Bank.[114] The 1994 Jordan–Israel peace treaty, which included a protocol on water, may lead to new technical solutions that may help resolve differences over water issues between the two countries.[115]

Equally complex has been recurring conflict over the resources of the Tigris and Euphrates, which rise in Turkey and flow through Iraq and Syria before converging at the Shatt-al-Arab, where Iraq borders Iran. Turkey's goal of developing its

Table 10.1	Middle East Water Availability	

Country	Water availability per capita (cubic meters)	
	1990	2025 (projected)
Algeria	750	380
Egypt	1070	620
Iran	2080	960
Israel	470	310
Jordan	260	80
Kuwait	<10	<10
Lebanon	1600	860
Libya	160	60
Morocco	1200	680
Oman	1330	470
Qatar	50	20
Saudi Arabia	160	50
Tunisia	530	330
United Arab Emirates	190	110
Yemen	240	80

NOTE: Some hydrologists have identified 1000 cubic meters per person per year as a minimum water requirement for an efficient, moderately industrialized nation. The countries of the Middle East listed here are those that either in 1990 failed or in 2025 will fail to meet this level of fresh water availability. The change between 1990 and 2025 is due solely to increases in population.

SOURCES: Computed from United Nations population data and estimates. Population and water availability data come from World Resources Institute, *World Resources 1991–92* (New York: Oxford University Press, 1991). Adapted from Peter H. Gleick, "Water and Conflict: Fresh Water Resources and International Security," *International Security* 18, no. 1 (Summer 1993), p. 101.

southeastern Anatolian region (near its border with Syria) has brought it into conflict with its downstream neighbors. In the mid-1970s, the lakes behind the newly completed Keban Dam in Turkey and Ath-Thawrah Dam in Syria began filling at the same time, reducing the flow of water running through Iraq by about 75 percent. This brought Syria and Iraq almost to the brink of war, which was averted by Saudi mediation.[116]

The upstream position of Turkey provides it with a lever of power in the Tigris-Euphrates basin. In 1987 Turkey imposed a water embargo on Syria over the latter's support for Kurdish terrorists in Turkey. In late 1989, Syria and Iraq were alarmed when the Turkish president announced that his country would temporarily block the flow of the Euphrates in order to fill Turkey's just completed Ataturk Dam, a mammoth project designed to turn the country into a food exporter.[117] Turkish "water pressure" is particularly feared by Syria, which has few water resources under its own control. In turn, Damascus has blocked World Bank funding for Turkey's $23 billion, thirteen-part Anatolia project until Turkey signs a new agreement to share water, and in June 1996 Syria began massing armored units on its border with Turkey, declaring that the sharing of the water of the Euphrates was its "main quarrel" with Ankara. Turkey, however, remains determined to proceed with the project, which threatens to bring further disputes with its downstream neighbors.[118]

Conflict over water among the Nilotic countries (the states of the Nile River basin), especially Sudan and Egypt, has stimulated efforts to achieve lasting cooperation. Ever since Sudan and Egypt squared off over Egypt's plans to build the Aswan Dam in 1958, use of the Nile has been loosely regulated by a 1959 Sudanese-Egyptian water-sharing agreement.[119] Still under discussion is an Egyptian proposal to tap the Nile to generate electric power for export to other regions (including Syria, Turkey, Jordan and the European Union) in exchange for hard currency, which would be used in turn for water and irrigation projects in the Nile countries, as Egypt plans a canal project that has been likened to a "second Nile" in its western desert regions.[120]

Conflict and Cooperation on Resource Issues

Mahatma Gandhi once remarked, "There is enough in the world for everyone's need, but there is not enough in the world for anyone's greed." The supply of all resources is limited, and therefore they must be allocated in some manner among all the parties that require them. The mechanisms for allocation may be economic (like the global market for oil) or political (like the agreements governing the use of water from the Rhine, Jordan, Ganges, and Colorado rivers). When the means of allocation are regarded as fair, states have been able to cooperate in sharing resources equitably. When they are not, governments in some cases have gone to the brink of war and beyond to protect their access to crucial resources.

Since the end of World War II, states have gained a great deal of experience in resolving resource issues peacefully. Perhaps the best example is the European Coal and Steel Community, which originally coordinated the use of energy resources but gradually evolved into a supranational political entity, the EU. Indeed, the international system has come a long way from the days of the War of the Pacific, 1879–1883, when Chile, Bolivia, and Peru fought one another over nitrate deposits (essentially, petrified bird droppings), which were used to make explosives. But scarcity still has great potential to provoke conflict, and if markets and negotiations fail to provide countries with adequate access to vital resources, nations will still find conflict an acceptable alternative to freezing, starvation, or thirst.

CONCLUSION: GLOBAL ISSUES—SOURCE OF COOPERATION; SCENE OF CONFLICT

In the New Era, pressing global issues are the source of both cooperation and conflict among nations. All states have common interests in each of the issue areas discussed in this chapter; all countries want to control the spread of AIDS, for example, and no state wants terrorism to occur on its own territory. At the same time, interests between and within states can conflict sharply. Farmers in the

Peruvian highlands may view the cultivation of the coca leaf as the only feasible means of earning money to feed their families, although the Peruvian government may agree with drug-enforcement agencies in Europe and the United States that cocaine traffic must be curtailed.

Like hawkers and shoppers in a street bazaar, countries attempting to address global issues have objectives that are simultaneously complementary (buyers and sellers both want to strike a bargain) and competing (buyers want low prices while sellers want high ones). Unlike the street vendors and shoppers, however, nations have no global police force to call upon when brawls break out because of heated arguments and accusations of cheating. Instead, they must work out agreements among themselves to enforce rules and strive for fairness in their transactions. In regard to some global issues, such as the eradication of smallpox, international organizations have formed to facilitate cooperation, and many have performed remarkably well. In regard to other issues, like combating drug traffic, they have failed dismally. Despite this mixed record, the growing urgency of the problems discussed in this chapter makes it imperative for the international community to continue its coordinated efforts to tackle the related problems of population, migration, environmental protection, food, health, drugs, terrorism, and resource conservation.

Many specific issues appear to place developed and developing countries in opposing camps. Rich countries tend to support restrictions on the use of chlorofluorocarbons (CFCs) and the preservation of tropical rain forests, for example, while many developing countries regard CFC use and clearing rain forests for farmland as economic necessities. In part, these differences suggest that although world politics in the mid-twentieth century was dominated by the conflict between the democratic West and Communist East, global affairs in the New Era may see increasing contentiousness between the developed North and the developing South. Conflict may not be limited to the North-South divide, however, because there are as many opposing interests and perspectives on global issues within both North and South as there are differences of opinion between them.

Despite (or because of) this conflict potential, industrial and developing countries alike are increasingly coming to the realization that collaborative efforts between them will be necessary, and unavoidable, in order to control problems that cross national and regional boundaries. In the New Era, as North-South conflicts become more frequent, they will likely be balanced by attempts at cooperation.

In the final analysis, there is only one world, and it appears to be shrinking. More people, faster transportation, new technologies, and heightened awareness of transnational problems all promise to make interdependence a defining characteristic of world politics. But, as repeatedly shown in this chapter, interdependence does not guarantee cooperation. Leaders and citizens will be faced with difficult decisions as nations are drawn closer together and interact more frequently (and on more levels) than previous generations would have thought possible, or even desirable. It is far too early to tell whether such globalization will make world politics more or less conflictual. What is abundantly clear, however, is that successful resolution of global issues requires states to recognize their responsibilities toward their neighbors. To deal successfully with the problems that confront them all, the nations of an increasingly interdependent world must develop and practice a code of global citizenship. John Donne described interdependence in the language of the seventeenth century, but the international community would do well to recall his words in the New Era: "Any man's death diminishes me, for I am involved in mankind; and therefore never send to know for whom the bell tolls; it tolls for thee."

PRINCIPAL POINTS OF CHAPTER TEN

1. The world's nations are becoming increasingly interdependent. As a result, transnational problems—those with origins in one state but affecting others—are becoming issues of growing salience and urgency in world politics.
2. Although population growth has tapered off in the developed countries, it continues strong in the developing states. This growth has severe consequences for immigration into the developed countries; the world's supply of food, energy, and natural resources; and the health of the world's people and environment.
3. The number of migrants and refugees throughout the world is at a record high. Because many economic migrants are attracted to countries with higher standards of living, many developed countries have received more immigrants than they can absorb. As a result, pressures to close borders and tighten requirements for political asylum have increased, particularly in North America and Western Europe.
4. The world overall has an abundance of food, and food supplies are likely to remain adequate in the future. Food is especially plentiful in the developed world, but often scarce elsewhere. This is because food distribution is not only uneven across regions, but uneven even within many developing nations as a result of government policies, poor planning, or war.
5. Economic pressures in both developed and developing countries lead to actions that harm the global environment, such as deforestation and industrial pollution. Sustainable, environmentally sound economic growth is possible, but efforts to control and repair environmental damage must take into account economic necessity as well as environmental factors.
6. Even though more of the world is immunized than ever before, many old diseases have proven quite resilient in the face of changing population and environmental conditions, especially in the developing world. AIDS, resurgent diseases such as malaria and tuberculosis, and emerging diseases such as hepatitis B and ebola have taken their toll in both the North and South.
7. The war on drugs is a relatively new phenomenon. Although drugs are produced mostly in the developing world, which initially prompted developed countries to focus their drug-control efforts there, they are consumed in greater quantities in industrialized states. A consensus has begun to emerge as the developed countries realize that they cannot begin to stop the sup-

ply of drugs unless they do more to help the economies of the developing countries and curb demand at home.

8. All countries are vulnerable to terrorism, though many nations support terrorist organizations as part of their foreign policies. International cooperation to stop terrorism is relatively undeveloped, but was boosted by the collapse of the Communist regimes in Eastern Europe and the former USSR.

9. The access of all nations to important natural resources, such as petroleum and water, is threatened by the increased demand resulting from population growth and industrialization. Market mechanisms and political agreements have proven to be fair and efficient systems of allocating scarce resources in many cases, but war often results from conflicts over resources or attempts to cut off supplies of critical resources for political purposes.

10. Interdependence fosters both cooperation and conflict. Experience has shown that international cooperation to resolve global issues is possible, but states must recognize their responsibilities toward one another if they are to live together peacefully in a world where states interact more frequently and closely.

KEY TERMS

Contras
deforestation
desertification

enforcement
terror
eradication
extradition

greenhouse
effect
hydroelectricity

industrial
pollution
interdiction

SOURCE: Courtesy Lockheed Martin

Security

For better or for worse, nations have always been preoccupied with security. Although most of us have never personally experienced war in all its cruelty, violent interstate conflict continues to be a fact of life in the New Era, as best exemplified by the bloody conflict that broke out between the remnants of the former Yugoslavia, including Bosnia, Croatia, and Serbia. Indeed, as long as the international system remains predominantly anarchic, the provision of **national security** will remain a fundamental duty of national leaders, and they will continue to ask or compel their citizens to make sacrifices to provide for the common defense.

In many periods of history national security was such an important value that people were expected to lay down their lives for it without question. This attitude was manifested in the ancient Roman expression, *dulce et decorum est pro patria mori* ("how sweet and beautiful it is to die for the fatherland"). In many parts of the world, this old principle continues to be strongly felt; states threatened by conflicts often have little choice but to devote vast resources to protecting their sovereignty and independence. Even in the New Era, all states face the classic dilemma of "guns or butter"—the need to choose between security on the one hand, and economic and social development on the other, when allocating their scarce resources.

Chapter One introduced the concept of the security dilemma: Measures that states take to make themselves feel more secure will inevitably make other states feel less secure, so other states respond with their own security measures, which in turn make the first state feel less secure, and so on. Chapter Nine discussed how states attempt to escape from the security dilemma by making the international system less anarchic. This chapter will consider how nations try to manage the security dilemma by adopting unilateral strategies of self-protection and by trying to limit arms or prevent arms races from erupting into war. It also examines how the pursuit of security affects international politics: In other words, it looks at how states attempt to protect themselves and how their efforts at self-protection affect their relations with other states. There will be little here about war or battles, which are the province of military history, and not much about defense budgets, which are intimately connected with domestic politics.

Before looking at how states attempt to achieve security, however, it is necessary to understand what it is they are trying to achieve. In other words, what is "national security"?

THE MANY FACES OF SECURITY

The term *security* is used much more frequently than it is precisely defined. In the absence of a generally agreed-upon definition, virtually anybody can invoke the slogan of "national security" for any purpose. As one analyst wrote,

> National security is a modern incantation. As in any incantation the words have both power and mystery. In the name of national security, all things can be threatened. All risks can be taken. All sacrifices can be demanded. . . . The ultimate catch-all term, it can mean anything the user chooses it to mean.[1]

Unfortunately, it is easier to point out why we need a precise definition of security than to actually offer one. One of the main reasons why this is so is that the concept of security has many different aspects and is constantly changing. This can easily be understood if we ask what security means to us as individual human beings. Immediately, it becomes apparent that security means different things to different people in different environments. What security means to a !Kung hunter in the Kalahari Desert might differ from the idea held by a college student in the United States. Even in similar environments, security can be interpreted differently by different individuals. For some students, security will mean assuring one's financing for the next academic year (economic well-being), for others it may have medical connotations (physical health), and for still others it may refer to personal safety in a crime-infested neighborhood (protection from violence).

When we return our analysis to the level of the nation-state, the multidimensional nature of security becomes even more apparent. Like humans, states also differ in the nature of their security predicaments. Poor nations may count provision of adequate food and clean water among their primary security necessities, while more advanced, developing countries may simultaneously face ethnic separatism and foreign military threats, and industrialized countries may fear pollution and the loss of manufacturing jobs to other countries. During the Cold War, the military aspects of security received the most attention, largely because of the ever-present risk of nuclear war. Now that the Cold War is history, decision-makers are under more pressure to address the economic, environmental, and even cultural aspects of security. (Cultural security may seem a strange concept to Americans, but American rock music and fast-food chains have "invaded" far more countries than have American troops.)

External and Internal Threats

Even when considering the military aspects of security, most states face both external and internal security threats. External threats come from beyond a nation's borders and differ according to geopolitical factors. A country such as Israel, which occupies a thin piece of hotly contested real estate along the Mediterranean Sea and is surrounded by adversaries, finds itself in a profoundly different security predicament than a country like Malta, an isolated island in the Mediterranean with few coveted resources. Internal threats are found within national boundaries, and they also vary greatly among states. Countries such as India and Egypt face serious problems with domestic terrorism, while Denmark and Canada experience almost no political violence within their boundaries.

External and internal threats to security are often interrelated. Ironically, an obsession with one can increase the risks from the other. The former Soviet Union serves as a powerful example. Throughout the Cold War, Moscow expended enormous resources on national defense, allegedly to ensure the continued survival of the country and to protect it from foreign aggression. Ultimately, the demise of the USSR had little or nothing to do with foreign intervention but occurred almost spontaneously from within, caused in part by economic tensions exacerbated by defense expenditures. Most analysts now agree that the Soviet Union's huge military budget, rather than strengthening its security, actually contributed to its downfall.

Now that the end of the Cold War has focused the world's attention on common global problems, more attention is being given to dimensions of security that transcend its traditional military-territorial aspects. Transnational threats to the community of nations and the global ecosystem include the issues addressed in Chapter Ten: population pressures, environmental pollution, AIDS, drug trafficking, and terrorism. As one analyst wrote, security means a lot more than just military threat:

> It means an informed electorate, healthy environment, a strong economy, and a just society. We are endangered not just by nuclear weapons, but also by pollution

of our air, rivers, lakes, and oceans, by leaking nuclear waste dumps, by the hole in the ozone layer and by the greenhouse effect. We are endangered not just by foreign economic competition, but also by drugs, illiteracy, and disease, by unregulated corporate greed, and by the wasting of our technical talent in the weapons industry.[2]

Clearly, problems like environmental degradation, exhaustion of natural resources, rapid population growth, and migration can undermine a state's security by overtaxing its political, economic, and social systems, leading to instability or even the wholesale collapse of the state (see Chapters Five and Ten).[3] It is important to recognize, however, that there are dangers in expanding the concept of security to include every problem faced by a nation or the world. Powerful bureaucratic players in many countries have a vested interest in broadening the definition of national security to include any activity that falls under their responsibility. Many ministers and cabinet secretaries responsible for health, education, the environment, or trade policy have been quick to claim that the issues they deal with are matters of national security in order to obtain more resources from the state. A more insidious potential danger in expanding the concept is that national security has traditionally been a favored excuse for governments to suspend or ignore civil rights. Although states may be wise to give more attention to aspects of security outside of military threats, citizens should not allow expanding definitions of national security to erode personal, political, and economic freedom.

Subjective versus Objective Aspects of Security

Another factor complicating the task of defining security is that security and insecurity frequently have a strong subjective dimension. In other words, security is in large part a perception or feeling. At the level of the individual, some residents of New York may feel perfectly safe walking after dark, whereas others might feel constantly threatened. In the international system, some states (such as Stalin's Soviet Union or Kaiser Wilhelm II's Germany) have at times behaved as if they were under an imminent threat for reasons that outsiders could not understand. Conversely, some countries have felt unjustifiably safe in periods when they should have taken the threats that confronted them more seriously, and as a result suffered surprise attacks (such as the United States in 1941).

Subjective perceptions of security show up in nations' defense budgets. Defense spending may be thought of as an insurance policy against the vagaries of the international system. Just as people can take out different types of insurance policies for their cars, states also vary in their approach to risk: They can underestimate danger and not take out sufficient insurance, or they can be paranoid and overinsure. This relationship between objective threat and subjective perceptions of security may be represented as a matrix as shown in Figure 11.1.

In this matrix, the right-hand column represents cases of high objective threat, such as the presence of well-armed expansionist neighbors. Within this column, the top right corner of "underinsurance" (quadrant I) represents a dangerous situation in which a country is objectively in danger but believes itself to be secure.

| Figure 11.1 | Objective and Subjective Aspects of Security |

Figure 11.1 — Objective and Subjective Aspects of Security

		Objective (Real) Threat to Security	
		Secure	Insecure
Subjective Perception of Security	Low Threat	III Overinsurance (USSR, 1980)	I Underinsuranc (France, 1940)
	High Threat	IV Pacifism (Malta, 1998	II Prudence (Israel, 1948–)

A country that fails to correctly evaluate the threats to its security is far less likely to invest sufficient resources into its defense, and it could therefore easily become a victim of aggression. For example, before World War II many European countries believed Hitler could be appeased and thus were not adequately prepared to resist when he attacked. France was especially unprepared; after Hitler invaded Belgium, he was able to bypass France's much heralded defensive fortification, the Maginot Line.

The lower right corner (quadrant II) depicts a state that is objectively in danger and, at the same time, is aware of its insecurity. Israel, for instance, has been surrounded by well-armed adversaries. However, because it remains acutely aware of its situation, for over four decades it has been able to safeguard its security through a mixture of political and military means, which has finally begun to pay off with moves toward peace in the area.

The left-hand column of the matrix represents countries that face few actual threats to their security. States that exist in low-threat conditions and perceive themselves to be secure have small defense budgets (quadrant III). In contrast, however, those states that are not objectively threatened but believe danger is imminent tend to plan on the basis of worst-case assumptions. This often results in "overinsurance" (quadrant IV). Such a country is likely to waste large amounts of resources against an illusory threat. The most salient example of security overinsurance is the Soviet Union after World War II. Despite its possession of nuclear stockpiles, friendly neighboring states, and a huge conventional army, Moscow continued to spend enormous sums of money on security, much to the detriment of its economic system.

The psychological mechanisms behind a country's perception of its security do not readily lend themselves to rational analysis. Intuitively, one might expect that as a country becomes more powerful, it would start to feel more secure. Historically, this proposition has been violated with astonishing regularity. Political scientist Karl Deutsch called this anomaly Parkinson's Law of National Security: "A nation's feeling of *insecurity* expands directly with its power" (italics added).[4] As most nations become more powerful, they acquire more interests that need defending, and more potential adversaries. The United States, for example, had few interests outside the Western Hemisphere when it was an isolationist power before World War I, and accordingly it spent little on defense. After World War II, however, the United States made commitments to defend its allies all over the globe. Its defense budgets rose to unprecedented levels, though few Americans felt any more secure than they had before World War II.

Working Definition of Security

Now that we understand how national security is a partly objective, partly subjective condition, the rest of this chapter will examine the measures states take to survive as independent entities within the international system. A country's security will be defined herein as a condition in which the sovereignty and the territorial integrity of a country are guaranteed.

Given the anarchic nature of the international system, this condition has been difficult for states to achieve. It is an unfortunate but inescapable reality that the history of international relations has been punctuated by innumerable military conflicts, many of which resulted in massive bloodshed. Even in the New Era, many states face threats against their sovereignty or territorial integrity, and as a result they have little choice but to try to protect themselves through various means.

Will the world ever reach a condition in which no country's independence or integrity is threatened? Possibly, but not likely. The international system is composed of states whose internal situations constantly fluctuate. Just as a young family with new children will look for larger living accommodations, states with growing populations and economic needs have looked for more territory, more resources, and so forth. Because most of these resources are scarce commodities, there is always potential for conflict. As a state's internal pressures increase, conflicts are bound to multiply, and if states cannot or will not resolve them by political means, armed aggression might become a temptation for one of the parties and thus a danger to the others. Hence, as pressure mounts, security threats are created, and states must respond to them if they hope to preserve their independence, territory, resources, or values.

SECURITY DILEMMA REVISITED

When threatened, the instinctive reaction of states will be to try to protect their sovereignty and territorial integrity against the pressures created by internal factors, such as uneven development and social upheavals, and external conditions, like armed threats from neighboring countries. For many states, responses to these conditions mean arming themselves against the possibility of aggression or allying with other states that face similar dangers. The Roman author Vegetius summarized this idea in the fourth century B.C. with the famous adage *qui desiderat pacem, preparet bellum* ("let them that desire peace prepare for war"). One of the tragic traits of the international system is the uncertainty of the effects of these defensive efforts—sometimes they work and deter a potential aggressor, other times they backfire and decrease the defender's security (as their neighbors arm themselves in response, and so on). Countries thus face the painful security dilemma discussed in Chapter One: The measures a state takes to increase its own security are likely to decrease the security of other states. If all states take steps to increase their own security, the net effect may be that the security of all is actually diminished.

Here again, the concept is not exclusively restricted to the international system. Our own individual "security policies" may be useful in explaining the basic idea. Consider a person (let's call him Steve) living in an unsafe neighborhood where many muggings and burglaries take place. In the absence of gun-control laws, Steve may decide to purchase a firearm for self-defense, "just to play it safe." Upon hearing that Steve has bought a gun, his neighbor Beth may well do the same, again "just in case." After a period of time, most of the neighborhood's residents are armed. Even if no one in the neighborhood has aggressive intentions, it's not very likely that the residents feel much safer than before, because there are far more guns now floating around. The existence of so many firearms increases the likelihood that someone will use one of them, either deliberately (in a domestic quarrel, perhaps), as a result of poor information (mistaking a roommate entering the house through a window because he lost his keys for a prowler), or accidentally (by a small child or intoxicated person). Thus, even though Steve, Beth, and everybody else bought guns to increase their personal safety, the whole neighborhood has become objectively and subjectively less safe.

A similar situation to this neighborhood arms race occurs in the international system, where all countries face the security dilemma. On the one hand, all nations understandably want to counteract the threat of an expanding neighbor, either by building up their own military strength internally or by allying with third powers who feel equally threatened by the rising state. But, on the other hand, by resorting to these techniques, they may give the ascendant power an incentive (or excuse) to beef up its military strength, which in turn decreases the first country's security. As a result, states get trapped in this vicious action-reaction spiral. Of course, some states will follow a deliberate policy of aggression or coercion, which makes matters even worse. As the old saying goes, even paranoids have real enemies.

One of the best examples of this lethal logic was the start of World War I. No country seemed to really want to start a war, yet an apparently inconsequential act (the assassination of the Austro-Hungarian archduke by a Serbian terrorist) led to a chain reaction of military mobilizations that ultimately led to what was at that point the world's largest war (see Chapter Three). No one country could afford not to mobilize, and when it did, it made mobilization by the other countries even more imperative, leading to a rapid escalation of the crisis into full-blown war.

Why can't all these countries just act rationally? The point is, they are acting rationally. In an anarchic environment where the possibility of conflict is ever present, it makes sense for each state to arm itself, because the risk of preparing for

Clausewitz on War and Politics

A number of strategists and military theorists have expounded their views on the conduct of war through the centuries. For example, the writings of the ancient Chinese General Sun Tzu on the art of war are still studied for their strategic insights. Most of these military thinkers have viewed the conduct of war as a specialized activity, outside the sphere of "normal" activities of a state or society. In the early nineteenth century, the Prussian soldier Carl von Clausewitz (1780–1831) realized that holding this attitude was a good way to lose wars.

Born to a lower-middle-class family, Clausewitz studied literature and philosophy and attended the War College in Berlin, but his experience of war was more than academic. He served in the field during the French Revolutionary and Napoleonic Wars, became a prisoner of war after the crushing Prussian defeat by Napoleon at Jena in 1806, and joined the Russian army to fight against Napoleon's invasion of Russia in 1812. After Napoleon's final defeat inaugurated what became a century of relative peace in Europe, Clausewitz concentrated on the theoretical study of military affairs as a War College professor.

Unlike most other strategists, Clausewitz did not produce a system of guidelines for the conduct of battles or campaigns. Instead, his major work, *On War*, emphasized that mechanistic principles are of little value in carrying out military operations, because war is inherently a risky and uncertain business. Chance, psychological factors, and the "fog of war" (the inability of commanders to have pre-cise information about their own forces, let alone those of the enemy) make war a chaotic enterprise. To be successful, he argued, commanders must adapt to constantly changing conditions (on the battlefield and off) without losing sight of their strategic objectives.

Moreover, Clausewitz wrote, war is fought not just by armies, but by nations. In order to defend itself, a state must mobilize not only its military forces, but its resources and will to fight as well, and it must seek to reduce the enemy's army, industry, and national morale. His famous dictum, "War is nothing but the extension of politics by other means," reminds soldiers and statesmen alike that wars are fought for political objectives and that defeat is far more likely if the nation does not support the underlying goals of a military campaign.

Clausewitz's studies of war had a major impact on strategic thinking throughout the world, and many of his writings are still read at military academies and war colleges. Modern strategists, such as those on the American side in Vietnam, were foolish to ignore his conclusions that the political goals of war must be expressed and maintained. Though he wrote before the era of **"total war,"** Clausewitz warned civilian and military leaders that national security is an activity to which the whole nation must contribute. Clausewitz thus anticipated, and may well have inspired, the well-known remark made by French Prime Minister Georges Clemenceau during the First World War: "War is too important to be left to the generals."

armed conflict seems less than the risks incurred by remaining defenseless. It is therefore extremely difficult to escape from the security dilemma in an anarchic system, and as a result, all states have to adopt a security strategy of one kind or another. (If this section makes you wish for a world government or global police force, see Chapter Nine for a discussion of the problems and prospects of international law and organizations.)

STRATEGIES FOR SECURITY: DETERRENCE AND DEFENSE

There are two basic strategies states may use to protect their sovereignty and territorial integrity from external challengers: **deterrence** and **defense.** These strategies are not mutually exclusive, but they are based on different assumptions and seek to protect the state through different means.

Deterrence

Deterrence attempts to prevent war by discouraging a potential aggressor from attacking. The primary goal for the defender is to convince the challenger that the probable cost of attacking will far exceed any anticipated gain. This is usually accomplished by threatening to militarily retaliate or punish the initiator if it commits the undesired action. More precisely, the defender must signal its **commitment** to punish or retaliate and its **capability** to do so in order to demonstrate the **credibility** of the deterrent threat. If the defender succeeds, the challenger will back down without a shot being fired; if it fails, the challenger will attack.

The concept of deterrence is commonly associated with nuclear weapons, but its application extends to any situation in which one side seeks to prevent another from taking some action that has not already been taken. When a five-year-old boy accosted by bullies attempts to warn them off by threatening, "You better leave me alone or my big brother will beat you up," he is using a strategy of deterrence to deal with a security problem.

Deterrence can also be used by the strong to prevent the weak from trying to overthrow the established order. Its use dates back thousands of years. In A.D. 70, for example, a Jewish rebellion against Roman rule in Palestine was crushed, but a few Jews managed to escape to the mountain fortress of Masada. Although it could easily have chosen to ignore the remaining rebels, Rome painstakingly and expensively assaulted Masada to demonstrate that it "would pursue rebellion even to mountain tops in remote deserts to destroy its last vestiges, regardless of the cost."[5] Rome's purpose was to deter any other groups in the empire from rebelling. In more recent times, the same argument could be made about the Soviet Union's strong-arm tactics in putting down the 1956 Hungarian revolt; Moscow's harsh action was intended to send a strong and clear message to Soviet satellites in Eastern Europe.

Strategists identify four basic types of deterrence. Two kinds, general and immediate, have to do with the time frame of the strategy. **General deterrence** is a long-term strategy intended to "discourage serious consideration of any challenge to one's core interests by an adversary."[6] General deterrence operates all the time, attempting to prevent an adversary from attempting any kind of military challenge because of its expected consequences. **Immediate deterrence,** by contrast, is a response to a specific and explicit challenge to a state's interests. Once an aggressor has begun an attack, general deterrence has failed, but immediate deterrence may still convince it to stop what it is doing and go no further.

As an illustration of the difference between general and immediate deterrence, consider the marshal of a town in the Old West. When he walks around town with his six-guns strapped on, he is exercising general deterrence, tacitly reminding potential lawbreakers that they will have to answer to him if they try to make any trouble. When he sees a desperado about to draw a gun and warns, "Ya better not try it, varmint," he is exercising immediate deterrence, attempting to dissuade the outlaw from taking a specific action.

Two additional types of deterrence deal with the geographic scope of the intended strategy. **Primary deterrence** is intended to dissuade a challenger from attacking a state's own territory, while the objective of **extended deterrence** is to discourage a challenger from attacking an ally or partner. Through its commitments to NATO and Japan, the United States has used extended nuclear deterrence to protect its major allies. As one might guess, extended deterrence runs a greater risk of failure because challengers are more likely to doubt the willingness of one state to risk war (especially nuclear war) over its partner. For this reason, France developed its own nuclear arsenal during the 1960s, as French President Charles de Gaulle argued that France could never be sure that in a confrontation with the Soviet Union, the United States would be willing to "trade New York for Paris" and risk nuclear war to defend France.[7]

An example of extended non-nuclear deterrence was Israel's response to a Syrian threat in 1970. Israel believed that Syria would soon intervene in neighboring Jordan's civil war. (Israel did not want Syrian troops so close to major Israeli cities.) To dissuade Damascus from attacking Jordan and overthrowing King Hussein's government, Israel threatened direct retaliation against Syrian forces. Israel, in effect, made it clear that any attack on Jordan would be treated the same as an attack on Israel. Syrian forces, which had started to intrude, withdrew, and the Syrian air force did not attack—an example of successful extended deterrence.[8]

Defense

A strategy of defense, by contrast to deterrence, attempts to reduce an enemy's capability to damage or take something away from the defender.[9] The purpose of defense is to resist an attack in order to minimize losses after deterrence has failed. It minimizes the damage to the defender and denies its territory, raw materials, or other valued resources to the aggressor. Although a strategy of deterrence aims to provide security by raising the prospective costs of aggression to unacceptable levels, a strategy of defense attempts to thwart the aggressor's aims even if the aggressor decides to attack. In particular, deterrence is primarily psychological and intends to influence the challenger's decision process, while defense is physical and intends to rebuff the challenger.

This distinction can be illustrated by a simple example. Someone who wants to protect an expensive car from theft can seek to discourage potential thieves by installing a car alarm and placing a warning sticker in the window. On the other hand, the owner can put the car in a locked garage where it is physically impossible for someone to steal it. The difference between these strategies of protecting the car is that in the first case, the owner seeks to dissuade the thief by influencing the thief's mental calculations, whereas in the second instance the owner physically tries to deny the thief the valued goods. Both of these strategies are potentially effective, but both have drawbacks. In order for deterrence to be effective, the owner must pay for an alarm, the thief must be convinced that someone will come if the alarm goes off, and if the thief decides to attempt to steal the car anyway, the alarm must actually go off and the thief must either run away or be apprehended before he can make off with the car. In order for defense to work, a garage must be available (the owner may have to add one on to his house), and the owner must remember to lock the garage door—and even then, the thief might still pick the lock.

These strategies for protection against theft can be combined, of course: The owner can set an alarm and lock the car in a garage. But in this case the owner must pay the costs of both strategies, which may be more than he can afford. States, too, have finite resources to devote to security, and so must choose the mix of deterrence and defense that makes the best use of the resources available.

To take nuclear war as an example, although the provision of strategic nuclear weapons such as ICBMs and SLBMs provides a powerful deterrent capability, they cannot shoot down incoming missiles or stop enemy armies from marching across borders. Once war has broken out, deterrence has failed (and nuclear weapons are more or less useless) and defensive resources must be used.

The nuclear exception aside, almost any weapon or type of military unit can be used for defense. Equally important, though, is the fact that most forces usable for defense have some offensive capability as well, which is the very heart of the security dilemma. As long as a nation's soldiers, ships, tanks, artillery, and aircraft are capable of being used to attack as well as defend, its neighbors are likely to find it hard to believe that these forces are intended for purely defensive purposes.

This caveat even applies to seemingly defensive concrete bunkers and trench lines. Rather than make one's neighbors less suspicious, they often increase suspicion by indicating to neighboring states that an attack on them is imminent. Additionally, fortifying territory that another state claims as its own (such as the Golan Heights, annexed by Israel but claimed by Syria) may well be regarded as a warlike act.

Overall, as shown by the car thief example, the two strategies of deterrence and defense are not mutually exclusive—a state's security is a function of both. Defensive measures typically also have some deterrent value; a would-be car thief who sees a well-built garage will probably be deterred from trying to break into it. To guarantee security, countries must pursue a mix of these strategies and not pursue only one at the expense of the other. What constitutes a proper mix is often a major point of debate among policy-makers and military planners.

REQUIREMENTS FOR DETERRENCE

As shown in the previous section, deterrence can be a difficult strategy to implement. It was mentioned that three conditions must be met in order for it to work.

First, the defending state must define behavior that is unacceptable and communicate its commitment to punish the challenger. Second, the defender must possess the capability to punish an attacker. Finally, the defending state must demonstrate that it is willing to carry out its commitment to retaliate against the attacker; that is, the deterrent threat must have credibility.[10]

Commitment

As the first step in successful deterrence, the defending state must make a commitment to punish the challenger if the challenger takes a specified action. In other words, the defender must "draw a line in the sand" and warn the challenger that it will suffer if it crosses it. This commitment must be stated clearly, unambiguously, and before the challenger commits the act of aggression. For example, Israel repeatedly stated that a blockade of the Strait of Tiran, the only waterway passage to its southern port of Eilat, would be regarded as an act of war, and Egyptian attempts to blockade the strait in 1955 and 1967 were contributing factors in both the 1956 and 1967 Arab-Israeli wars.

It is important that deterrence commitments be definite and specific, as ambiguity may elicit probes by challengers interested in testing a defender's resolve. In 1950 the United States omitted South Korea from its announced defense perimeter in the Pacific, and this may have encouraged North Korea to believe that the United States would not respond if it attacked its southern neighbor (see Chapter Four). Likewise, prior to the outbreak of World War I, Britain wavered on its commitment to support the Entente (France and Russia) in the event of war against the Triple Alliance (Germany, Austria-Hungary, and Italy). Had Britain clearly voiced its position, Germany might have been dissuaded from attacking France in 1914.

Deterrence can easily fail when a defender does not properly signal a commitment to punish or fails to specify the precise retaliatory actions to be undertaken in case of aggression. Prior to Argentina's invasion of the Falkland Islands in 1982, for example, Britain failed to issue any verbal warning or to start any military preparations as a deterrent signal.[11] As a result, the ruling Argentine junta probably doubted Britain's interest in defending a small colony left over from its imperial past, and thus was not deterred from seizing the islands. More recently, there has been considerable debate over the mixed signals that the United States sent Saddam Hussein prior to his decision to invade Kuwait, specifically regarding the alleged comments that U.S. Ambassador April Glaspie made to Hussein shortly before Iraq's invasion of Kuwait. She reportedly stated that the United States had "no opinion" on Iraq's border dispute with Kuwait and did not warn Saddam Hussein of the consequences of using force against Kuwait.[12] In this case, deterrence appears to have failed because a defender did not state its commitment to punish or was ambiguous about its position.

Capability

The clearest commitment is useless if a state does not have the means to carry it out. Because deterrence revolves around convincing a challenger that the cost of a certain action is not worth the benefit, the challenger must be convinced (or at least strongly suspect) that the defender has the capability to retaliate. Even if a state's deterrent capability is weak, it may try to convince a challenger that its power to punish is greater than it actually is, just as a homeowner might hope to dissuade trespassers by posting a "Beware of Dog" sign even though she doesn't own a dog. This is one reason why some countries (for example, Israel and pre-1993 South Africa) refuse to reveal their suspected nuclear capabilities; the very possibility that a defender might respond to an attack with nuclear weapons may be sufficient to deter an aggressor.

Deterrence with **conventional weapons** is considerably more difficult, because aggressors can better estimate their capability to inflict punishment. Even though Britain and France had more tanks than Germany in 1940, Hitler believed that German forces could compensate with a lightning campaign. Consequently, he was not deterred from attacking and decisively defeated Allied forces in France. Similarly, America's naval strength in the Pacific in 1941 did not deter the Japanese attack on Pearl Harbor, and the combined armed forces of Egypt and Syria did not deter the Israeli attack in 1967, because Israel and Japan gambled that they could each score a knockout blow with **preemptive strikes.** Israel's gamble paid off; Japan's didn't.

Credibility

Third, a state must convince the aggressor of its resolve and willingness to carry out its commitment to punish. Even if a defender has clearly stated its commitment to punish and has the capability to do so, deterrence can still fail if the challenger doubts the willingness of the defender to risk war. As a result, this commitment to punish must be persuasive to keep from sounding like a bluff. In part, the defender's success will depend upon its reputation, past behavior, and image. With this in mind, Israel has consistently pursued a policy of harsh retaliation in order to foster its credibility, although its failure to respond to Iraqi Scud missile attacks during the Persian Gulf War was disturbing to many Israeli decision-makers, who feared future deterrence would be eroded. Forty years earlier, many believed that the United States had little strategic interest in Korea, but that it had to respond to North Korea's attack to signal American willingness to protect its Pacific and Western European allies from Soviet aggression.

Ironically, the fearsome destructive power of nuclear weapons that makes their retaliatory capability unquestioned also leads to a credibility problem. Would the defender really be willing to sacrifice millions of people in a nuclear war? For example, in June 1948, one year before the Soviet Union exploded its first nuclear bomb, the American nuclear monopoly was still not able to prevent the Soviets from blockading Berlin. Similarly, in both the 1973 Arab-Israeli and the 1982 Falklands wars non-nuclear challengers (Egypt and Syria, and Argentina) doubted the defenders' resolve to retaliate with their nuclear weapons. (As it turned out, neither Britain nor Israel had to resort to nuclear arms to turn back the aggressors.)

In many ways, crises in which nuclear weapons are involved often resemble the game of "chicken." In the classic film *Rebel without a Cause*, James Dean and a rival play this game by racing their cars toward the edge of a cliff; the first to "chicken out" and swerve is the loser, but if neither swerves, both will go over the cliff. In this game, each player wants the other to swerve before he does, but both players prefer swerving away from the edge and letting the other side win to going over the cliff. The object of the game, like the object of deterrence in a confrontation between two nuclear powers, is to prevail by convincing the opposing player of your willingness to risk destruction.

The Cuban missile crisis is often presented as a game of chicken in which the Soviets were the first to blink. If neither side was willing to retreat or "swerve," the outcome would have been war between the nuclear-armed superpowers. This might have occurred if the Soviets had attempted to proceed with their plan of placing more missiles on Cuba and the United States had launched an air strike on Cuba or invaded the island.

To summarize, deterrence can fail because a challenger doubts the defender's commitment, capability, or credibility to punish the aggressor. However, deterrence theory recognizes instances in which the defender clearly signals its commitment to credibly defend its interests, but the challenger then calculates that the benefit or prize exceeds the punishment. In such a case, it is still rational for the challenger to choose to attack. In 1914 Austria-Hungary probably knew that an attack on Serbia would mean war with Russia, but it declared war on Serbia anyway because it believed it would win. If the government in Vienna had known that its empire would be destroyed as a result, it would not have attacked. Deterrence always involves risk and uncertainty. Like Clint Eastwood in the film *Dirty Harry*, defenders point their weapons and ask, "Do you feel lucky?" If the aggressor feels lucky despite the defender's commitment, capability, and credibility, deterrence will fail.

CRITICISMS OF DETERRENCE

The risks and uncertainties inherent in deterrence have prompted a number of scholars and policy-makers to challenge the assumptions of deterrence theory and question its usefulness as a strategy for national security. Similarly, the history of the Cold War indicates to some that deterrence was of limited utility. Even when the United States held a nuclear monopoly, it could not prevent the USSR from taking control of Eastern Europe, nor could it deter non-nuclear powers such as

Vietnam or China from taking undesirable actions. For these reasons, a number of criticisms have been leveled at both the theory and practice of deterrence.

The first criticism of deterrence questions the assumed **rationality** of leaders and their ability to make all the necessary calculations. Deterrence theory assumes that decision-makers are rational, that is, able to make comparisons among the possible options and rank them. Successful deterrence also requires that each party have sufficient, accurate, and up-to-date information about the situation at hand. Critics of deterrence, however, argue that policy-makers are not the perfectly rational beings that deterrence theory makes them out to be. The problem is that humans have limited capacity to obtain, receive, process, and assimilate information about a situation and to evaluate all the policy options in the most thorough and accurate way. In short, critics question the ability of humans to make all the necessary cost-benefit analyses and calculations that deterrence requires.

A second bone of contention between proponents and opponents of deterrence is how to determine whether it has succeeded or failed. Proponents often point to the absence of war as proof of deterrence success, but the absence could be attributable to other factors. Return to the example of the marshal trying to deter crime in his western town. If his jailhouse is empty, it indicates one of two things: Either the marshal is doing a good job and people are obeying the laws, or the marshal is doing a lousy job and no one has been caught. Therefore, the fact that the Soviet Union never attacked Western Europe or the United States during the Cold War does not conclusively demonstrate the effectiveness of deterrence. It may be that despite all of NATO's military hardware, the Soviets never intended to attack Western Europe or the United States in the first place. Instead, all they might have wanted was a secure buffer zone in Eastern Europe. It is difficult to determine whether deterrence worked without knowing the objectives of potential aggressor states. Declassified Soviet records confirm that Stalin had designs on Western Europe in the 1940s, but the means he was willing to use to expand the Soviet sphere of influence may have been limited to internal subversion (which succeeded in Czechoslovakia, but failed in France, Italy, and Greece; see Chapter Four).

A third criticism of deterrence is that even if the defender does everything right, the message the defender is trying to send may be misinterpreted by the challenger. To convince a challenger that you have the commitment, capability, and credibility to carry out a threat, you must at each stage send signals to the challenger, but these signals can be misinterpreted. First, it is particularly easy to misperceive the resolve of the defender if the challenger is strongly intent on taking a particular course of action. For example, prior to Iraq's invasion of Kuwait, the United Arab Emirates (UAE) and the United States held an air-refueling exercise to indicate American support for the security of the Gulf sheikdoms (of which Kuwait is one). However, because Saddam Hussein was bent on invading Kuwait, he may have interpreted the exercise as a signal of limited American interest in that it included only one tanker aircraft. Similarly, a challenger might underestimate the defender's intentions and believe the defender is bluffing when it actually intends to fulfill its threat. During the Korean War, as UN troops pushed the North Korean army back and began to approach China, Chinese officials repeatedly issued warnings that Beijing would enter the conflict if the UN continued north. Discounting the likelihood of Chinese intervention, MacArthur ordered the advance to continue, whereupon China entered the conflict and sent UN troops into full retreat (see Chapter Four).

Additionally, aggressors can underestimate their adversaries' military capabilities and therefore expect an easier fight than actually occurs. When the USSR attacked Finland in 1939, Moscow expected that its 1 million soldiers would easily defeat the 200,000 Finnish troops but was stunned when Finnish forces dealt several heavy blows and held out for almost four months before being forced to meet Soviet demands. Similarly, in 1941, Italy expected a rapid victory in its attack on Greece, but instead underestimated the capabilities of Greek forces, which were able to drive the Italians back into Albania until German forces joined the offensive.

Finally, states may get the impression that their opponents are actually preparing to attack rather than to resist a potential challenge. It can be difficult to convince other states that the tanks, aircraft, and missiles used for deterrence are really intended for that purpose, rather than for offense or intimidation. This problem bedeviled East-West relations throughout the Cold War, as both sides introduced new weapons that they claimed would be used only to deter attack but that the other side perceived as an offensive threat. For example, the USSR built a large number of intermediate-range nuclear missiles (discussed later) in the 1970s and early 1980s and deployed them in Europe, claiming that they were intended to dissuade NATO from launching a preemptive nuclear strike. NATO responded by developing and deploying "Euromissiles" of its own in the 1980s, which it likewise claimed were designed to deter Moscow from attacking with its own intermediate-range weapons. The resulting "missile crisis" brought tensions between the two blocs to levels not seen since the Berlin crises of the 1950s and 1960s (see Chapter Four). In an attempt to avoid this kind of misperception, states may take steps to reassure their rivals that their intentions are really defensive. Examples of such reassurance measures include taking aircraft and missiles and bombers off high alert, and storing artillery or bridging equipment in depots far away from border areas so they could not be used to mount a surprise attack.

To Deter or Not to Deter?

There is no final verdict on the controversies surrounding deterrence. The debate on whether deterrence was responsible for the "long peace" of the Cold War will probably last far into the future. Just as deterrence itself depended on the unknowable (the consequences of attack and retaliation) to prevent the unthinkable (a nuclear war that would have destroyed civilization), the precise reasons why the United States and USSR never went to war between 1945 and 1991 may never be known for certain. Proponents of deterrence will contend that the strategy was successful despite all of its flaws and contradictions (that is, nations that upheld peace, prosperity, and human rights as their highest goals could guarantee their security only by threatening their adversaries with the destruction of millions of people). Deterrence detractors will argue that the strategy was similar to an "elephant repellent" that a con artist might sell to a Midwestern farmer; if the farmer later complains that he never saw any elephants that needed repelling, the con man replies, "Then it must be working." Regardless of the outcome of the deterrence debate, nuclear war did not break out during the Cold War, and we can only hope that whatever prevented nuclear destruction in the past will continue to operate in the future.[13]

Strategy in the Nuclear Age

When most people think of deterrence, they think of nuclear weapons. For many analysts, nuclear missiles represented the ultimate weapon, so powerful that it would make war unthinkable. Gradually this idea spread throughout the international community, and most existing military doctrines changed to place the nuclear weapon at the center of the military universe. Now that the Cold War is over, some historians and political scientists are claiming that nuclear weapons were responsible for the absence of a major war between the two key geopolitical alliances during this period.[14] The domination of nuclear weapons in military strategy changed the focus of the security dilemma. First, the incredible destruction wrought by the use of these weapons raised the stakes of an arms race. Second, the startling offensive potential of these weapons made a long, drawn-out nuclear war (characteristic of eras in which defense dominates) practically impossible. In particular, though, the emphasis on nuclear weapons produced some peculiar concepts of strategy.

A state is said to possess **first-strike capability** if it can launch an attack that destroys the defender's retaliatory capability and prevents the defender from inflicting major damage in return.[15] A situation in which any nation has a first-strike capability would be highly unstable, because that side might feel able to do whatever it wanted, believing that it was **invulnerable** to nuclear retaliation. The other side would then have an incentive to preempt such a situation by attacking with a preemptive strike in the hope of knocking out the adversary's nuclear arsenal while it still could. The most likely outcome of such a situation is a short and catastrophic war.

The solution to this dilemma is to develop and deploy a nuclear force that could be nearly impossible to destroy. Known as **second-strike capability,** the purpose of such a force is to ensure that enough weapons would survive an initial attack to launch a retaliatory second strike that would inflict unacceptable damage on the enemy. For stable mutual deterrence, each side must have the ability to inflict massive damage on the other even if the other side strikes first. This situation would nullify any advantage or incentive for launching a first strike, because destroying a part of an adversary's strategic forces would still invite devastating retaliation.

The acquisition of an assured second-strike capability by both the United States and the USSR by the late 1960s meant that either would be able to retaliate massively if the other attacked. The existence of such a condition was termed mutual assured destruction, referred to by its acronym, MAD. Mutual

The Father of the Atomic Bomb

The Manhattan Project—the huge research and development effort that the United States carried out in 1941–1945 to create the atomic bomb—was not only a major military, industrial, and engineering enterprise but a cutting-edge experiment in nuclear physics as well. Accordingly, many of the leading physicists in the United States participated in the project for scientific reasons as well as patriotic ones. The eminent researchers who were involved included Ernest Lawrence, Edward Teller, Leo Szilard, Hans Bethe, and Enrico Fermi (all except Lawrence had fled to America to escape Nazi persecution). Even the pacifist Albert Einstein had a hand in the bomb's development when he was persuaded by Szilard to sign a letter to President Franklin Roosevelt in 1939 saying that nuclear fission would produce a bomb of tremendous explosive power. (Einstein later confided, "I made one great mistake in my life, when I signed the letter to President Roosevelt.")

The scientist who was in charge of the actual design and construction of the first atomic bomb was J. Robert Oppenheimer (1904–1967). Oppenheimer earned accolades through his research in England, the Netherlands, Germany, and Switzerland before holding academic posts at the California Institute of Technology and the University of California at Berkeley. In 1942 he was asked by the Manhattan Project's director, General Leslie Groves, to set up a laboratory for making the bomb. Oppenheimer chose a site that he had stumbled upon while vacationing in the mountains of New Mexico. Thus, the Los Alamos Ranch School was taken over by the U.S. government and converted to a national laboratory.

Under Oppenheimer's direction, the top-secret laboratory complex became a scientific city of over 5000, where many of the nation's brightest minds labored to create the most formidable and powerful weapon the world had ever known. Throughout the project, Oppenheimer was well aware of the destructive potential (and moral implications) of the forces his team was working to unleash. When he witnessed the first test of the atomic bomb in the desert near Alamogordo, New Mexico, on July 16, 1945, he quoted the words of the Hindu god Shiva: "I am become death, the shatterer of worlds."

After the war, Oppenheimer helped draft the proposals for the international control of atomic energy, which were rejected by the USSR (discussed later in this chapter). Subsequently, as chairman of the Scientific Advisory Committee of the U.S. Atomic Energy Commission, Oppenheimer recommended against the development of the **hydrogen bomb.** When the United States went ahead with the project, Oppenheimer was accused of being a Communist traitor during the "witch hunts" of the McCarthy era (see Chapter Four). He was then investigated, denied access to classified information, and removed from his advisory post. He was later cleared and remained a physics professor for the rest of his life. The fact that the scientist who directed the development of the first atomic weapon became a victim of the atomic spy hysteria, prevalent in the United States in the early 1950s, was one of the many ironies of the Cold War.

J. Robert Oppenheimer and General Leslie Groves, director of the Manhattan Project, inspect the Trinity Site in New Mexico where the first atomic bomb was tested in 1945.

SOURCE: © Associated Press

assured destruction, the highest stage of the nuclear balance (or balance of terror, as Winston Churchill called it) is an uncomfortable but stable situation, because there is no incentive or temptation for either side to strike first or even launch a surprise attack. To do so would mean that both the defender and the initiator would suffer devastating casualties. A second-strike capability was achieved in the United States through the development of the **nuclear triad.** This consists of the ability to "deliver" (a euphemism for "attack with") nuclear weapons by bombers, intercontinental ballistic missiles (ICBMs), and submarine-launched ballistic missiles (SLBMs). In this way, even if the Soviets launched an all-out attack on the United States, and even if this attack destroyed the entire land-based missile force, the other two "legs" of the triad would survive and be able to deliver a devastating blow. The USSR adopted a similar strategy, though it relied most heavily on ICBMs. By the early 1970s, both superpowers possessed thousands of strategic nuclear warheads, and MAD was a strategic fact of life.

Not all nuclear strategists were comfortable with MAD, however, and both the USSR and the United States eventually developed weapons systems designed to attack each other's nuclear forces, which potentially threatened both sides' second-strike capabilities. Because of the security interdependence of nuclear states, however, it was widely believed that it was in the interest of both sides to

DETERRENCE

During the Cold War, both superpowers practiced a policy of Mutual Assured Destruction ("MAD") in order to prevent nuclear war.

SOURCE: © Scott Willis

reduce or or eliminate any systems that weaken a second-strike capability. According to this line of thinking, the second-generation technology of **multiple independently targeted reentry vehicles** (MIRVs), which allowed several warheads to be placed on a missile, and the increased accuracy of ICBMs threatened to undermine an opponent's second-strike capability because of their potential ability to destroy all of an opponent's arsenal on the first strike. In this case, it is offensive, rather than defensive, weapons that weaken an opponent's second-strike capability, thereby destabilizing the balance. For this reason, one of the main goals of the START negotiations was a ban on land-based MIRVed ICBMs, which was finally agreed to in START II.

Defensive Weapons Systems

As stressed earlier, a key aspect of deterrence is credibility, and anything that weakens credibility is destabilizing. For this reason, many strategists regard defensive weapons systems that shoot down incoming missiles as potentially destabilizing because they reduce the effectiveness of mutual deterrence. The controversies over antiballistic missiles (ABM) and the Strategic Defense Initiative (SDI or "Star Wars") illustrate this strategic paradox. Both systems were designed to destroy incoming missiles. This, of course, defied the logic of MAD, which held that possession of a secure second strike by both sides was the bedrock of strategic stability. Nevertheless, in the 1960s the United States contemplated development of an ABM system that could protect U.S. cities from nuclear attack (thereby upsetting mutual deterrence), but eventually it scaled back its plans and settled on a limited system designed to protect missile silos rather than cities. The idea was to safeguard the U.S. second-strike capability without reducing the potential effectiveness of a Soviet second strike, which (as discussed above) would have decreased strategic stability and increased Soviet threat perceptions. Both the United States. and the USSR eventually agreed (in the ABM treaty signed as part of the SALT process; see the section on arms control) to deploy no more than two ABM sites, one around the national capital and one near an ICBM base complex. The USSR went ahead with its system, but the U.S. system never became operational.

SDI, proposed in the 1980s was intended from the start to create a space-based "peace shield" or "nuclear Astrodome" over the United States. Critics in both the United States and USSR immediately contended that such a system would be prohibitively expensive and dubiously reliable, would disrupt mutual deterrence, and would prompt a renewed arms race, as it would leave the USSR with no choice but to build more offensive missiles to overwhelm the system. Some critics of SDI, in fact, argued that deploying the system would encourage the Soviet Union to attack before it became completely operational, because once it was operational, the USSR would be unable to retaliate. SDI remained contentious until the end of the Cold War, when the plan was shelved but not entirely canceled, as Congress continues to appropriate money for research into space-based missile defenses.[16]

More recently, some decision-makers in both the United States and Russia called for the renewed use of a limited SDI-type system, known as Global Protection Against Limited Strikes (GPALS), to defend against missiles launched by terrorists or irrational or suicidal leaders who feel they have nothing to lose (see Chapter Ten). Such a defense system could not completely guard against nuclear terrorism, however, as there are other ways to deliver a nuclear bomb to a target. Terrorists could detonate one in a ship docked in a harbor, for example, or assemble one in the target city if they are able to smuggle in the required nuclear material. GPALS seems unlikely to get off the ground in any sense, but the United States is proceeding with programs to defend military forces in forward areas from ballistic missile attack. These "theater missile defenses" are less controversial than ABM and SDI, as they are not designed for use against strategic weapons, but Russia remains concerned that small-scale theater defense could be adapted for large-scale deployment to weaken its strategic deterrent.

Nuclear Weapons and Conventional Defense

Nuclear weapons are not useful for meeting all the military challenges a state or alliance faces. Responding to a conventional attack with strategic nuclear weapons would be like using a hand grenade to kill houseflies—it might take care of the problem, but it creates a bigger one. For this reason, the superpowers and their allies all maintained substantial conventional forces, and developed strategies for using them, throughout the Cold War. Though theater nuclear weapons had a key role in the strategies of both NATO and the Warsaw Pact, from the mid-1960s onward the military balance in Europe witnessed a continual deemphasizing of nuclear weapons toward a more credible conventional posture.[17]

The trend away from exclusive reliance on nuclear weapons continued after the revolutions in Eastern Europe and the subsequent disintegration of the Warsaw Treaty Organization and the Soviet Union itself. Although these developments have created many new security problems in Europe (as exemplified by the conflicts in the Caucasus and the former Yugoslavia), these new post–Cold War issues seem to be less threatening than the nuclear and conventional confrontation between the Warsaw Pact and NATO during the Cold War. Some theorists, in fact, now contend that nuclear war, once unthinkable because it would mean the end of civilization, is now unthinkable because war itself is obsolete, at least between the major powers.[18] Regional and ethnic conflicts, however, remain deadlier than ever, and many regional powers still possess or seek nuclear arms and other weapons of mass destruction (discussed below). In sum, although the geopolitical configuration of the New Era seems much less likely to provoke a global nuclear war, political fragmentation, continued strains on the ability of developing countries to maintain internal security, and the resurgence of ethnic and nationalist conflict all make conventional war, and possibly regional nuclear war, more likely.[19]

Spotlight

Nukespeak

Can't tell the difference between an ICBM and an SLBM? Don't know your GLCMs from your SLCMs? Need to impress your classmates and relatives? Here's a quick reference guide to nuclear weapons terminology used in this chapter.*

ABM: Antiballistic missile; a missile designed to destroy incoming missiles or their warheads before they hit the designated targets.

ALCM: Air-launched cruise missile; a cruise missile launched from an airplane. *See* Cruise missile.

Atomic weapon: Explosive device that derives its power from nuclear fission, or the "splitting" of atoms (uranium or plutonium).

Ballistic missile: A missile that "coasts" to its target on a free-falling trajectory following a period of powered flight.

Biological weapon: Germ- or bacteria-based weapon, also known as a "living weapon," which spreads disease, infection, or toxins.

Chemical weapon: A weapon that uses a chemical agent to kill or disable military personnel and civilians. These weapons consist of poisoned gas, mists, and powders, and can be effective only when they come into contact with people.

Conventional weapon: Nonnuclear weapon such as a tank, artillery piece, or tactical aircraft (troops that operate these weapons are referred to as conventional forces).

Cruise missile: A missile that resembles a pilotless aircraft and flies on a horizontal trajectory. This missile operates completely within the earth's atmosphere and may be launched from the air, the ground, or from the sea, and can carry conventional, chemical, or nuclear warheads.

First strike: Ability to destroy or decisively weaken an opponent's strategic weapons, or prevent retaliation with an initial attack.

GLCM: Ground-launched cruise missile; a cruise missile launched from land.

Hydrogen bomb: A thermonuclear weapon that uses a hydrogen or fusion reaction in which atoms are fused together to produce an energy release.

MILITARY POWER

The persistence of armed conflict in the New Era reminds us that **military power** remains an essential component of security. Both deterrence and defense require adequate military forces, along with the supporting infrastructure to train, equip, control, and supply them and deploy them when and where they are needed. Moreover, military power has also been one of the traditional measurements of a state's capability directly or indirectly influence world politics. Chinese leader Mao Zedong best expressed this view in his famous aphorism, "Political power grows out of the barrel of a gun." Likewise, when Stalin was once told that the Pope disapproved of one of his policies, he reportedly dismissed the criticism with the question, "How many divisions has the Pope?" Not all leaders share Mao and Stalin's enthusiasm for military power, but its importance to world politics cannot be denied, even in the New Era.

Military power derives from the size of a state's armed forces, their quality and quantity of weaponry, and their training, morale, organization, and leadership. It thus consists both of "hardware" (weapons and equipment) and "soft-

These weapons require a fission reaction that uses uranium or plutonium in order to get the temperature high enough to have the hydrogen atoms react.

ICBM: Intercontinental ballistic missile; a land-based missile able to deliver a nuclear payload to a target more than 3400 miles away (in practical terms, capable of going directly from the United States to Russia, or vice versa).

IRBM: Intermediate-range ballistic missile; a land-based missile with a range of 1700 to 3400 miles.

MAD: Mutual assured destruction; a condition that exists when both sides are able to survive a first strike with sufficient forces to retaliate in a second strike and inflict unacceptable damage on their opponent. Thus both would be destroyed regardless of who struck first, and therefore neither has an incentive to initiate a nuclear war.

MIRV: Multiple independently targeted reentry vehicle; a single ballistic missile with several warheads that can each hit a separate target.

Second strike: Ability to retaliate even after a nuclear attack, and thus punish the initiator of a nuclear war.

SLBM: Submarine-launched ballistic missile; a long-range ballistic missile carried in and launched from a submarine. Examples include the U.S. Poseidon and Trident missiles.

SLCM: Sea-launched cruise missile; a cruise missile launched from a ship or submarine.

Strategic weapon: Weapon that strikes directly at a nation's home territory and the industry, resources, population, or military forces located there.

Tactical weapon: Weapon designed for use on the battlefield, often in support of ground troops.

Thermonuclear weapon: Explosive device that derives its power from nuclear fusion, or the coming together of atoms (usually hydrogen or helium; this is the same process that gives the sun its energy).

Warhead: The bomb that a missile delivers to its target.

*For the technical definitions of this subject, see Norman Polmar, *Strategic Weapons: An Introduction* (New York: National Strategy Information Center, 1982); Lawrence Freedman, *The Evolution of Nuclear Strategy* (London: St. Martin's Press, 1983); Sheila Tobias, et al., *The People's Guide to National Defense* (New York: Morrow, 1982), or Sheikh R. Ali, *The Peace and Nuclear War Dictionary* (Santa Barbara, CA: ABC-CLIO, 1989).

ware" (personnel and their direction), and both must be of high quality in order for a state's armed forces to perform their missions. Because of the importance of the "hardware," it is impossible to divorce military from economic power; throughout history the most developed states often have been the most militarily powerful ones.

For the reasons discussed in the previous section, **strategic nuclear forces** have been the most dramatic measure of a state's military strength. However, just as it is unwise to use machine guns to kill houseflies, nuclear weapons are not useful for all applications of military force, so the size of conventional armies (including soldiers, tanks, military aircraft, and warships) remains a vital part of military capability. As the largest armies are not necessarily the most effective, military expenditure is another means for gauging military power. These aspects of military power are relatively easy to quantify, but other components are not so easy to express but remain important to consider. These factors include training, leadership, morale, and power projection. Another crucial factor, technology, creates its own set of capabilities and challenges (which will be discussed later in a separate section).

It is rarely possible to know beforehand whether numbers, training, or technology will prove decisive in a conflict. One of the world's greatest military geniuses, Napoléon Bonaparte, once claimed that in war, "the moral is as to the physical as three is to one," but he also said that "victory goes to the bigger battalions." Because of this uncertainty, states must pay attention to all elements of military power in order to maintain adequate forces for their security strategies.

Strategic Nuclear Forces

Since 1945 nuclear weapons have dominated military affairs, and a modern state cannot be considered a global military power if it lacks strategic nuclear forces (designed to attack long-range targets, including cities; see the Spotlight box on Nukespeak). The number of strategic nuclear warheads is a useful indicator of the size of a state's nuclear arsenal. Five states—not coincidentally, the permanent members of the UN Security Council—have declared arsenals of strategic nuclear weapons. Table 11.1 shows the numbers of strategic nuclear warheads deployed by these states as of 1996. (India first tested a nuclear device, which it claimed was a peaceful nuclear explosive, in 1974, and in 1998 conducted five further explosions that were openly declared to be tests of nuclear weapons. Pakistan responded with its own series of tests a few weeks later. Although it may be assumed that India and Pakistan have the means to use nuclear weapons against each other and targets in neighboring regions, they do not possess weapons that can strike intercontinental-range strategic targets.)

In addition to strategic forces, most of the nuclear powers possess a number of **tactical nuclear weapons,** which are short- or medium-range weapons designed to be used primarily against military forces. Of these nations, the United States and Russia obviously had by far the largest nuclear inventories. These large (many would say, much too large) nuclear stockpiles are in many ways artifacts of the Cold War, when superpower rivalry between the United States and USSR was the driving force behind the buildup of their strategic arsenals. The end of the Cold War intensified efforts to reduce the arsenals of the two largest nuclear powers, and the numbers of weapons deployed by both states have decreased significantly in recent years (see the section on arms control).

Table 11.1	Strategic Nuclear Weapons, 1996
United States	7350
Russia	7250
France	384
China	250
United Kingdom	160

SOURCE: National Resources Defense Council

Other Weapons of Mass Destruction

The seven declared nuclear powers are not the only states that possess nuclear capabilities. Israel is generally believed to possess nuclear warheads as well, though it has not stated this openly. In addition, a number of other states, motivated by security concerns or political ambitions, have clandestine programs to develop nuclear weapons. Other states, however, have given up their nuclear programs as a result of international pressure or a lessening of regional tensions. Still others maintain **chemical weapons** (nerve gas, poison gases like those used in World War I, or other deadly chemicals) for use against enemy troops or cities, or **biological weapons** (weapons for germ warfare), even though such horrors are now banned by international conventions (discussed later in this chapter). All these weapons of mass destruction are useless without a means to get them where they can do their deadly work—a delivery system, in military parlance. Although some could be taken to their targets by spies or terrorists, ballistic missiles are the system of choice for most countries, because they can strike their targets rapidly and are difficult to intercept.

Because of their destructive potential, nuclear weapons, chemical and biological weapons, and ballistic missiles are all indicators and signals of military strength. Map 11.1 shows the states known to possess, or suspected of possessing, these weapons. Though possession of these devices does not make automatically make a state a major military power, it does show that the state perceives the need, or exhibits the desire, to develop military capabilities beyond those conferred by conventional forces.

Military Personnel

The overall number of military personnel is another important measure of military power. It indicates the total strength of a nation's ground, naval, and air forces, although it does not take into account the often vital factors of quality of equipment, technology, training, morale, command and control, and leadership.

Table 11.2 shows the number of military personnel fielded by selected countries in 1985 and 1995. Over this ten-year period, China, the Soviet Union and its successor Russia, and the United States maintained the largest armed forces—consistent with their roles as leading military powers. Middle-rank military powers, such as India, Britain, France, and Germany, maintain sizable armed forces for both security and political reasons, but as a rising regional power India must "go it alone" on defense, while Britain, France, and Germany can rely on the NATO alliance and so can get by with smaller, higher-quality forces. Nations like Japan that depend on alliances for their security and have no independent military ambitions can maintain relatively small forces. Significantly, all these states have reduced their force levels since the end of the Cold War—dramatically so, in the case of the three largest military powers, which are no longer locked in a global arms

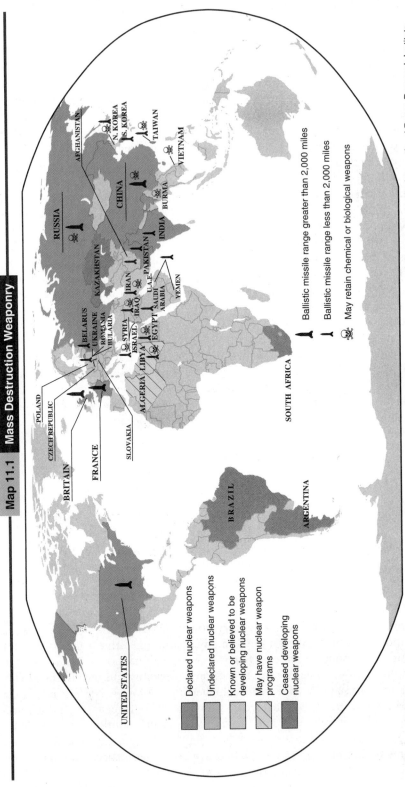

Map 11.1   Mass Destruction Weaponry

SOURCES: U.S. Arms Control and Disarmament Agency; National Resources Defense Council; Federation of American Scientists; Stockholm International Peace Research Institute, *World Armaments and Disarmament: SIPRI Yearbook 1996*; Randall Forsberg et al., *Nonproliferation Primer* (MIT Press, 1995); Aaron Karp, *Ballistic Missile Proliferation* (SIPRI, 1996); and International Institute for Strategic Studies, *The Military Balance, 1996–1997*

Table 11.2	Military Personnel of Selected Countries, 1985 and 1995	

State	Active Military Personnel, 1985	Active Military Personnel, 1995
Major Military Powers		
United States	2,156,600	1,547,300
USSR (1985)/Russia (1995)	5,300,000	1,520,000
China	3,900,000	2,930,000
Middle-Rank Military Powers		
India	1,260,000	1,145,000
France	464,300	409,000
Germany	478,000	339,900
United Kingdom	327,100	239,600
Japan	243,000	239,500
States in Conflict Regions		
Pakistan	482,800	587,000
Israel	142,000	172,000
Syria	402,000	423,000
North Korea	838,000	1,128,000
South Korea	598,000	633,000

SOURCE: International Institute for Strategic Studies, *The Military Balance 1996/1997*

race. On the other hand, states in regions of tension, such as Israel, Syria, Pakistan, and the Koreas, have generally kept their force levels constant or increased their forces, as the Cold War's end has not greatly reduced the potential for conflict in these regions (see Chapter Five).

Note that the numbers in the table indicate military personnel on active duty. Many smaller countries that cannot rely on military alliances, such as Israel, Switzerland, and Sweden, rely heavily on reserve forces that can be mobilized quickly in a crisis. Israel offers a noteworthy example of this strategy, fielding a standing army of 172,000 but maintaining about 430,000 well-trained reservists.[20] Switzerland, following a strict policy of neutrality and well-protected by its mountainous terrain, relies even more heavily on its reserves. In 1996, Switzerland had only 3000 troops in its regular army but could mobilize about 400,000 soldiers within forty-eight hours.[21]

Defense Expenditures

All these troops and weapons come at a price. By comparing defense expenditures, it is possible to see how much economic power a state is attempting to convert into military might. Table 11.3 gives the top ten military spenders in 1994. As we might expect, the three largest military powers are at the top of the table, followed by rich middle-rank powers with large defense budgets. The last two positions in

Table 11.3	Military Expenditures, 1994: Top Fifteen Countries	
State	Military Expenditure 1994	% of GNP
1 United States	$288.1 billion	4.3
2 Russia	$96.8 billion	12.4
3 China	$52.8 billion	2.4
4 Japan	$45.8 billion	1.0
5 France	$44.4 billion	3.4
6 Germany	$36.3 billion	1.8
7 United Kingdom	$34.1 billion	3.3
8 Italy	$20.4 billion	2.0
9 Saudi Arabia	$17.2 billion	14.2
10 South Korea	$13 billion	3.7
11 Taiwan	$11.5 billion	4.9
12 Canada	$9.5 billion	1.8
13 Australia	$8.3 billion	2.6
14 India	$8.2 billion	2.9
15 Spain	$7.4 billion	1.6

SOURCE: U.S. Arms Control and Disarmament Agency, *World Military Expenditures and Arms Transfers 1995*

Table 11.4	Percent of GNP Spent on Military, 1994: Top Fifteen Countries	
State	Military Expenditure 1994	% of GNP
1 North Korea	$5.5 billion	26.3
2 Oman	$1.8 billion	18.1
3 Bosnia and Herzegovina	$916 million	15.3
4 Iraq	$2.7 billion	14.6
5 Yemen	$2.1 billion	14.5
6 Saudi Arabia	$17.2 billion	14.2
7 Croatia	$1.4 billion	12.6
8 Russia	$96.8 billion	12.4
9 Kuwait	$3.1 billion	11.1
10 Mozambique	$104 million	8.7
11 Israel	$6.6 billion	8.6
12 Angola	$515 million	8.4
13 Brunei	$309 million	7.9
14 Rwanda	$114 million	7.6
15 Jordan	$434 million	7.5

SOURCE: U.S. Arms Control and Disarmament Agency, *World Military Expenditures and Arms Transfers 1995*; International Institute for Strategic Studies, *The Military Balance 1996/1997*

the top ten are held by prosperous states in regions of high tension and potential for conflict. The table also indicates military expenditure as a percentage of GNP for each of these states, indicating the fraction of national wealth each spends on security.

Table 11.4, which shows the fifteen countries with the highest defense burdens in terms of military expenditure as a percentage of GNP, tells quite a different story. Although relatively prosperous Israel and oil-rich Oman, Kuwait, Saudi Arabia, and Brunei appear in the rankings, most of the other states in the top fifteen are poor countries that face serious regional conflicts. North Korea, which has maintained high defense expenditures despite economic backwardness and even famine, ranks first, and Bosnia and Herzegovina, ravaged by ethnic conflict and civil war in recent years, ranks second. Russia, despite its persistent economic problems, also holds a place in the top fifteen, along with Mozambique, one of the poorest developing countries. The high defense burdens of strife-torn developing states like Angola and Rwanda underscores how poverty and violent conflict often create a vicious circle.[22] The military threats faced by most of these countries are significant, but considering that a stable economy is an important component of security, one cannot help but wonder if the overall security situation of the poorest of these states might not be improved by spending less on guns and more on butter.

Logistics and Power Projection

Like police forces or fire brigades, military forces must arrive where they are needed, when they are needed, in order to accomplish their missions. The art and science of getting forces and supplies in the right place at the right time is known as logistics, and is an extremely important component of military power. Wars are won, as one Civil War logistician put it, by the side that "gets there firstest with the mostest."

States that can mobilize, supply, and transport sizable forces far from their own borders are in a position to better use military power than states that cannot. This capability for "power projection," like other aspects of military power, requires both hardware (ships, transport aircraft, and land vehicles) and software (skill, experience, and the ability to analyze strategic data). Geography is also a major factor in power projection. States with ports and free access to sea lanes, such as the United States or Britain, can more easily make their power felt all over the globe. Conversely, large nations with restricted access to the sea, such as Russia, often have difficulty getting their forces where they are needed to stop an invasion, and so must compensate by maintaining larger forces at home (which, in turn, make their neighbors nervous). The United States demonstrated the value of mobility and power projection during the Persian Gulf War of 1991, when it was the nation most capable of rapidly deploying and supplying the forces used in Operation Desert Storm.

Qualitative Factors: Equipment, Training and Morale

The levels of nuclear forces, numbers of military personnel, and the amount of money spent on defense are useful numerical indicators of military power. Nevertheless, there are qualitative components of these indicators that are equally important to consider. Aggregate numbers fail to reveal the accuracy, lethality, or reliability of weapons, for example, or the skills and morale of the troops who use them. Does one Israeli tank equal one Syrian tank? Does a twenty-five-year-old plane equal one that is only five years old? How many Iraqi tanks equal an American helicopter? The same problem arises in attempts to compare nuclear weapons. During the Cold War it was hard to determine which side was ahead in nuclear capability because of the numerous ways possible of measuring the utility of nuclear warheads. Should comparisons be based on the numbers of launchers (missiles and aircraft), numbers of warheads, the yield (explosive power) of weapons, or their accuracy? Not surprisingly, by carefully choosing the indicators to examine, it was possible to argue throughout the latter years of the Cold War that either the United States or the USSR had the superior nuclear arsenal.

Even if the preceding problems of measurement could be overcome, numbers could not adequately reflect some of the most important aspects of military power. The training and morale of armed forces have proven crucial to the outcome of many conflicts. In the opening battle of the campaign for North Africa during World War II, for example, 36,000 British Commonwealth troops rapidly defeated 250,000 ill-trained and poorly motivated Italian soldiers; in December 1940 the British were able to capture 39,000 prisoners in three days. Similarly, Allied Coalition forces in the Persian Gulf War of 1991 found that demoralized Iraqi troops surrendered almost faster than they could be captured. Small, professional forces that receive intensive training are usually far more capable than large numbers of draftees who are looking for the first opportunity to desert or surrender once combat has begun. Special forces—commando units such as the U.S. Green Berets and SEALS and the British SAS—show what small groups of highly trained and expertly led soldiers can accomplish by slipping into hostile territory to destroy targets or rescue hostages.

Leadership at every level plays a critical role in both the effectiveness of training and the maintenance of morale under the debilitating stress of combat. Along with competent and experienced leaders, military power requires capabilities for command, control, communications, computers, and intelligence (C4I)—essentially, the ability of leaders to get the information they need, determine how to use their forces, and transmit their orders to front-line units quickly and securely. No matter how plentiful or sophisticated its weaponry, any military force is useless without adequate training for those who use the weapons, and without competent leadership from the people who direct them in battle.

TECHNOLOGY AND SECURITY

The rapid pace of development of both nuclear and conventional weapons since World War II underscores the importance of technology to military power. During the Cold War, frequent innovations in Soviet and American strategic weaponry produced a rough technological parity between the two superpowers but at the same time broadened the gap between them and the smaller nuclear powers. The successful use of high-tech weapons and information technology in the Persian Gulf War suggests that advanced technology is likely to become increasingly

U.S. armored vehicles maneuver en route to an engagement with Iraqi troops in the Gulf War. The poor showing of Saddam Hussein's vaunted military machine against U.S.–led coalition forces suggests the unpredictability of warfare.

SOURCE: © A. Tannenbaum/Sygma

important in conventional military operations as well. Although the pace of technological advance has been quite dramatic since World War II, especially in aerospace and electronics, technical developments have revolutionized warfare many times over since the first time a primitive hominid picked up a rock.

Breakthroughs, Lead Times, and Cost

Historically, three aspects of technological advance have proven particularly important: breakthroughs, lead times, and cost. Technological breakthroughs refer to the introduction of new weapons with potential capabilities so great that they require a new calculation of military strength; in such cases, if other states do not keep up with the innovator, they are quickly left behind in the competition for military power. The introduction of the machine gun in the late nineteenth and early twentieth centuries was such a breakthrough, as was the development of nuclear weapons by the United States at the end of World War II. Technological revolutions can have unpredictable effects, however. In 1906 Britain introduced the dreadnought, a new type of battleship with high-caliber guns and steam turbine engines. Dreadnoughts were so fast and powerful that older battleships quickly became obsolete. This ultimately worked to Britain's disadvantage, however, because it led to intense German efforts to achieve parity with the Royal Navy. A new naval arms race ensued, and Germany proved better able to compete in the construction of the new warships. Ultimately, the expense of conducting a naval arms race damaged the British economy almost as much as the German submarines that were eventually produced.

Although new weapons may initially seem impressive, the effect of a technological breakthrough on warfare is often not realized until a dramatic event or military disaster occurs. European armies did not realize how the machine gun would change the nature of war until the opening months of World War I, when the new weapons caused horrendous casualties and led military planners to abandon hopes for a short war. Although tactical missiles had existed for decades, the 1982 Falklands War demonstrated for the first time their devastating effect in naval combat. Argentina was able to effectively use a French-made air-launched Exocet missile (costing $200,000) to disable a British destroyer (costing $50 million). Britain eventually won the war, but the use of advanced missile technology demonstrated the vulnerability of its naval surface forces to missile attack.

Lead time is the time required between the initial decision to produce a weapon and its operational deployment. The production of weapons systems with long lead times may allow an innovator to widen (or narrow) the gap with its nearest competition, but the whole process carries with it considerable risk. For instance, it may allow a nation's closest competitor to neutralize that weapons system with an innovation of its own, or at least improve its existing weapons. During World War II, Germany devoted substantial technological and material resources to

Pride of the Royal Navy, the guided missile destroyer *Sheffield* sits dead in the water with severe damage during the Falklands War. The ship was hit by a single Exocet missile fired from an Argentine air force jet.   SOURCE: © Sygma

the development of jet fighter aircraft. When the aircraft were developed and deployed, they were clearly superior to anything the Allies could put in the air. While Germany was developing the new weapons, however, the Allies concentrated on the refinement and mass production of tried-and-true designs. By the time the German jet fighters became operational, Allied superiority in numbers made the air war no contest, and Germany's advanced weapons had little impact.

A third important aspect of technological development is cost. High technology usually requires big money, and political and military leaders often face difficult decisions as to whether the new weapons will justify their increased costs. Throughout the 1980s, the increasing costs of the United States' SDI ballistic missile defense system (discussed earlier) threatened that program's budgetary future in Congress, especially because it was not known whether the system would work. Similarly, cost overruns on the B-1 and B-2 bombers led to successive controversies over whether to scale back or cancel production plans, and the United States is unlikely to ever deploy these advanced aircraft in the numbers initially proposed.

The Offense/Defense Balance

Because wars are fought with the weapons of the time, the history of international security has been inextricably linked to the history of military technology. Changing military technology has made territorial acquisition and war more likely at certain points in time and less likely at others. In fact, the history of military technology can be interpreted as a struggle between offense and defense referred to as the offense/defense balance. The argument is that certain periods in history can be characterized by a technological dominance of either the offense or the defense. Whenever the offense is dominant, wars are more likely to occur and can be expected to be shorter in duration and less costly. Conversely, when the defense is dominant, wars are less likely to occur, but if they do break out, they can be expected to last longer and to be more destructive. At the same time, territorial aggrandizement is unlikely to occur, although internal security challenges may arise.[23]

In the heyday of medieval feudalism, for instance, defensive technology reigned. Strongly fortified castles were extremely difficult to capture with existing offensive technology (swords, bows, and catapults) even if the attacker could afford to lay siege to the castle for months or years. This allowed petty overlords to maintain their domains for years without being absorbed by larger states. By the mid-fifteenth century, however, the introduction of gunpowder and cannons shifted the offense/defense balance back toward the offense. Castles and fortified towns could be captured more easily, which led to more frequent and shorter wars that allowed for the forceful absorption of local fiefdoms into new and larger kingdoms and, eventually, nation-states. In this case, the offense/defense balance played an important role not only in the dynamics of military conflict, but in the size and character of geopolitical units as well.

A similar technological shift also occurred in the late nineteenth century with the introduction of the breech-loading rifle and the machine gun. Prior to these developments, it was possible (albeit at an often staggering cost in human lives) to break through defensive lines with a well-organized large-scale offensive, as had been demonstrated many times during the wars of the eighteenth century and the Napoleonic Wars. However, with these new defensive weapons, frontal assaults became tantamount to mass suicide. This became painfully obvious during the American Civil War, but this lesson was ignored by the European powers until the massive carnage of the First World War drove the point home. By World War II, however, defensive dominance was again overturned by the introduction of the tank and aircraft onto the battlefield. These new weapons allowed aggressors once more to quickly break through defensive lines and thus conduct rapid, short wars, most dramatically demonstrated by the German blitzkrieg attacks on Poland and France.

Although certain technological developments seem to make territorial conquest and empire-building easier or harder, it is not always simple to classify a given historical period as offense- or defense-dominant—particularly during the period itself. Although the lessons to be drawn from the defensive wars of the end of the nineteenth century may seem fairly straightforward from hindsight, they were generally unappreciated at the time. In fact, most countries flatly ignored them and continued to believe in the possibility of offensive breakthroughs. It has been argued that this erroneous perception of the offense/defense balance (the "cult of the offensive") was one of the important factors leading to World War I, as Chapter Three points out. Learning the right lessons from technological developments—particularly those which have not yet been extensively used on the battlefield—is a key challenge for strategists and military leaders.

The Cutting Edge

Three recent, related trends illustrate how technology is likely to have an even greater impact on security as the New Era progresses. The first trend is the emergence of space as a theater of military operations. Space has attained great economic and strategic importance through the increased use of satellites to collect and transmit data—the most precious cargo of the information age. Just as seventeenth-century navies struggled for control of the seas and twentieth-century air forces battled for control of the air, twenty-first-century space forces will contest the control of orbital space. This is not science fiction; the U.S. Space Command, which coordinates the operation and protection of U.S. military satellites, can deploy antisatellite missiles to destroy an opponent's space platforms. The growing reliance of military forces on satellites to locate targets, track friendly and hostile forces, transmit information, and coordinate movements will make "space power" as important to military success in the New Era as sea power and airpower were in earlier periods.[24] The first, potentially decisive, actions of future wars may be silent, fierce, and graceful battles fought high above the earth's atmosphere.

The second trend in security technology is the combination of advanced information systems with improved delivery systems, referred to by American analysts as the "revolution in military affairs." (The term itself shows an unfortunate lack of imagination, as the same expression was used over forty years ago by Soviet theorists to describe the changes in military science brought about by nuclear weapons.) Satellite reconnaissance and navigation, "stealth" weapons capable of evading defenses, and "smart" weapons with uncanny accuracy make air, sea, and land battles deadlier than ever.[25] The lethality of these weapons systems was dramatically demonstrated during the Persian Gulf War, where missiles flew through doors and ventilation shafts to their targets while transmitting video images. Weapons guided by computers and directed from space decimated the Iraqi army in the Gulf conflict, leaving the stunned survivors easy prey for coalition forces. The decisive technological advantage of a twenty-first-century military force over troops equipped to World War II standards (supported by a few inaccurate Scud rockets originally designed in the 1950s) was overwhelmingly clear. What will happen when two armies equipped with twenty-first-century technology clash, however, is less clear, as are the potential effects of these new technologies on the balance between offense and defense (discussed earlier). Just as the machine gun stunned the European powers with its lethality at the start of World War I, the "revolution in military affairs" may hold some nasty surprises in store for strategists in future conflicts.

Even more nasty surprises may come from a second high-tech trend, the emergence of **information warfare.** Heavy reliance on computers and instantaneous communications has a downside for both military and civilian users: What happens if hackers break into and disrupt the systems, or a computer virus causes everything to crash? Because so much of the security and productivity of modern states depends on information technology, strategists are busily devising ways to disable enemy information systems and to protect their own. Before the twentieth century, armies were often paralyzed by epidemics, and disease killed more soldiers than the enemy did. In the coming century, computer viruses may lay armies low, and inadequate software safeguards may make aircraft and missiles fatally vulnerable to tampering. Terrorists might attempt information strikes also; consider what could happen if a nation's banking system were suddenly wiped out by a software "bomb." Military forces will often be able to rely on low-tech backup methods if their advanced equipment were suddenly put out of action, but civilian industry could be much more vulnerable. Future information attacks may be faster and stealthier than even the slickest stealth bomber, and computer defenses will have to react with equal speed and sophistication. Conceivably, states or terrorists might fight a future information war in minutes, winning a decisive victory by doing billions of dollars of damage to the enemy's economy without causing a single human casualty.[26]

Though it can confer decisive advantages, technology is only one of several qualitative aspects that must be taken into account when evaluating a state's military power. It is also important to remember that technology requires more than just machines and computer programs, as equipment must be operated and maintained by qualified personnel, who must be led by officers who appreciate the capabilities and limitations of the systems they command. As technology advances, the need for highly trained, educated, and motivated personnel increases. Numbers of missiles, levels of defense expenditure, and sophistication of weapons systems are extremely important components of military power, but morale and leadership at all levels is crucial to military success, and therefore to security. That is why Alexander the Great and Norman Schwartzkopf—two commanders whose victories in the Persian Gulf region were separated by over two thousand years—would both confirm that regardless of the level of technology in battle, human factors are decisive.

ARMS CONTROL AND DISARMAMENT

The creation and deployment of military forces is not the only means states have to achieve their security objectives. As the security dilemma reminds us, too much armament can be as dangerous as too little. The potential dangers of excessive arms became most obvious in the nuclear era, when many began to fear that the nuclear arms race would eventually lead to the destruction of civilization. For these reasons, just as nations have invested their resources in building up adequate defensive capabilities against real or perceived threats, some also have tried to cooperate to control the dangerous and wasteful arms race. The most common way to do so has been through negotiations on arms control and disarmament.

Definitions

Arms control can be defined as "measures, directly related to military forces, adopted by governments to contain the costs and harmful consequences of the continued existence of arms (their own and others), within the overall objective of sustaining or enhancing their security."[27] In other words, the main ambition of arms control is to manage an arms race in such a way as to minimize the most dangerous consequences of the unavoidable security dilemma. Theoretically, this aim could be accomplished without any real decrease in the overall levels of armaments. In this way arms control differs from **disarmament,** in which states actually reduce their overall arms levels. Even though disarmament might seem to be the more desirable strategy, certain types of injudicious disarmament could actually increase the danger of international conflict. Highly asymmetrical disarmament initiatives imposed on a weakened opponent, for instance, could increase the opponent's feeling of subjective insecurity, leading to a renewed cycle of arms races. This is precisely what happened to Germany in the immediate aftermath of World War I. It is also possible to reduce arms below the level needed to deter potential aggressors, as the western powers arguably did in the 1930s (see Chapter Three).

To avoid such paradoxical effects of arms reductions, the primary aim of arms control is strategic stability, meaning a situation in which neither side has an incentive to launch an attack on an opponent or to increase its armaments because of the particular configuration of armed forces. As we will see, this concept was the basis for the CFE (Conventional Forces in Europe) talks and the U.S.–Soviet SALT and START negotiations.

Early Efforts at Disarmament

At the turn of the twentieth century, there was already a widespread feeling in the international community that the existing level of armaments was excessive. Two international peace conferences were convened in The Hague in an attempt to restrict or prohibit the use of certain weapons systems in war, including chemical and germ weapons (see below). The outbreak of war in 1914 ended this first effort at international disarmament, but the movement was revitalized through several disarmament initiatives following four years of World War I's unprecedented carnage and brutality. The most grandiose of these efforts was the Kellogg-Briand Pact (1928), in which almost all the nations of the world agreed to renounce war as an instrument of national policy and instead settle all international disputes by peaceful means. In reality, however, various countries interpreted the obligations of the treaty differently (particularly the one that safeguarded a nation's right to self-defense). Because there were no effective means to ensure compliance, the treaty was a dead letter.

A somewhat more successful set of arms-control agreements were the naval treaties of the 1920s and 1930s, in which the world's leading naval powers (the United States, Britain, Japan, Italy, and France) agreed to quantitative and qualitative restrictions on certain types of warships. These agreements, too, were beset by problems. First, the signatories complied with the letter of the treaty but redirected their efforts into nonregulated areas of warship construction (especially aircraft carriers, which were not covered in the treaties). Second, two major powers were not sufficiently involved: Germany was left out of the negotiations, and Japan withdrew from the treaties in 1934.

The end of World War II saw renewed attempts to achieve far-reaching arms control agreements. One of the most important efforts was the **Baruch Plan,** in which the United States proposed that all atomic-energy activities fall under the control of an international atomic-development authority. The Soviet Union rejected this plan primarily because it believed, with good reason, that the real goal of the plan was to codify and make permanent the existing U.S. monopoly over nuclear weapons.

The enthusiasm for far-reaching arms control agreements waned during the early years of the Cold War, although efforts to regulate the arms race were not abandoned altogether. Negotiations continued over two principal areas: control of weapons of mass destruction (including strategic nuclear weapons, intermediate and tactical nuclear weapons, **nuclear proliferation,** and chemical and biological weapons), and conventional arms control.

Test Bans

The most important efforts to limit weapons of mass destruction have been made in the area of nuclear weapons. The accompanying "At a Glance" box summarizes the relevant treaties. The first significant achievement was the Limited (or Partial) Test Ban Treaty of 1963, which was inspired by the dangerous nuclear face-off during the Cuban missile crisis. In this treaty, the United Kingdom, the United States, and the USSR committed to refrain from nuclear testing except in underground explosion sites. The treaty was subsequently signed by more than 100 states, but two nuclear powers, France and China, refused to adhere to it. The Limited Test Ban Treaty was supplemented in 1974 by the Threshold Test Ban Treaty, which confined the superpowers' underground explosions to an upper limit of 150 kilotons. After two decades of fits and starts, the Comprehensive Test-Ban Treaty, which prohibits all tests of nuclear explosives, was signed in 1996 by more than 100 states, including the five strategic nuclear powers. There is considerable hope that a ban on nuclear tests will become part of customary international law (see Chapter Nine), and thereby be considered binding on nonsignatories as well. Similarly, the United States and other states have declared their support for a global halt to the production of fissile material useable in nuclear weapons (including enriched uranium and plutonium). Nevertheless, significant resistance to test bans remains in the defense communities of the nuclear states, which contend that continued testing is necessary to maintain the safety and reliability of existing weapons.

SALT and START

In the late 1960s the strategic nuclear arsenals of the two Cold War superpowers became symmetrical enough (that is, referring back to the section on nuclear deterrence, both states developed secure second-strike capabilities) to allow for talks on strategic nuclear arms control. The principal negotiations of the process, the Strategic Arms Limitation Talks (SALT), took place in two slow and protracted stages.

The first stage culminated in the signing of the Strategic Arms Limitation Treaty (SALT I) in Moscow in 1972 (see Chapter Four). SALT I consisted of the Interim Agreement and the Anti-Ballistic Missile (ABM) Treaty.[28] The Interim Agreement put a ceiling on the number of land- and sea-based strategic nuclear missiles the two sides were allowed to retain while they were negotiating a more substantive agreement, which was to be signed at a future date. This ceiling froze the number of offensive strategic missiles at their 1972 levels of 2568 for the USSR and 1764 for the United States. The disparity was justified by the exclusion of long-range bombers, of which the United States had many more.

Overall, the Interim Agreement did not require any sacrifices by either side; it simply froze the arsenals at their existing levels and left many loopholes for both superpowers to exploit. The most important of these was the failure to limit the number of warheads per launcher, which allowed for the creation of multiple-warhead missiles (MIRVs) throughout the 1970s. These loopholes aside, the Interim Agreement at least provided ways to verify arms limitations (that is, to make sure the other side didn't cheat) through the use of orbital reconnaissance, or "spy satellites." Because neither side wanted to officially admit that such satellites existed, they were referred to in the treaty as "national technical means" of verification.

The ABM treaty of SALT I proved to be of greater long-term significance. Both parties were limited to not more than two ABM sites (one for the protection of the national capital, another to protect an ICBM complex), with not more than 100 interceptor missiles each. These restrictions did not result in any significant strategic adjustments by either side, because both had become disappointed in the utility of ABMs. However, the ABM treaty did prohibit the deployment of any space-based ABM system, which was an important element in the debate surrounding the Strategic Defense Initiative (See Chapter Four for more on SDI, or "Star Wars").

The follow-up agreement to SALT I, creatively termed SALT II, was signed in 1979 but was never ratified by the U.S. Senate because of the Soviet invasion of Afghanistan (see Chapter Four again). Even so, each side adhered to the guidelines of the treaty, while often accusing the other of noncompliance, sometimes justifiably and sometimes not. The provisions of the treaty were complex, but its central points were an aggregate ceiling of 2250 launchers (including ICBMs, SLBMs, and heavy bombers) for both superpowers, as well as other limits on MIRVs. MIRVs are viewed as extremely destabilizing because they may either tempt an aggressor to strike first or conversely represent extremely valuable targets for a first strike. (If it is possible to knock out a larger percentage of the opponent's arsenal with fewer missiles, this increases the temptation to strike first.) Unfortunately, the ceiling for MIRVed ICBMs still permitted both sides to increase their warheads by more than 40 percent from the initial signing of the treaty.

Indeed, a serious shortcoming of SALT II as a whole was that all of its aggregate limits were significantly higher than the levels existing at the time, thus allowing the superpowers to expand their arsenals to the treaty limits. Although it may have provided more predictability in the nuclear arms race, the SALT process was not particularly successful in curbing it; both qualitative improvements and quantitative increases in the superpower nuclear arsenals were permitted.

When Ronald Reagan assumed the presidency in 1981, the name of the negotiations was changed to the Strategic Arms Reduction Talks (START), to reflect his insistence on mutual and balanced reductions in strategic nuclear forces. The intellectual seeds of the START treaties were planted during the 1986 Reykjavik summit meeting between Reagan and Soviet President Mikhail Gorbachev, but it took negotiators over four years to work out the final provisions of the January 1991 START I treaty. For the first time, an arms-control treaty mandated genuine reductions in strategic arms, also addressing some of the weapons systems that are widely perceived to be destabilizing. The main parameters were set at 1600 launchers and 6000 warheads for each side.

On the negative side, the treaty suffered from several significant problems. It excluded certain weapons systems, had very permissive counting rules for some of the systems that were included, and placed far too few restrictions on modernization of existing systems. In a general sense, although strategic stability was one of the declared goals of the negotiations, the final result was somewhat disappointing because major steps like eliminating MIRVed ICBMs were not taken.

Significant as it was, START I was soon overshadowed by the collapse of the Soviet Union. Indeed, as the Cold War gave way to the New Era, the arms race appeared to turn into an arms-control race. Instead of trying to stay a step ahead of the adversary by developing new weapons systems, both the United States and Russia tried to outdo each other by advancing new proposals for nuclear arms reductions and even by unilaterally implementing cuts. This process led to the signing of START II in January 1993, whereby both sides pledged to reduce their strategic nuclear arsenals to between 3000 and 3500 warheads. In addition, START II "rectified" some of the problems with START I. For example, some of the permissive counting rules were tightened, and potentially destabilizing MIRVed ICBMs were to be eliminated.

By 1998, START II faced serious ratification difficulties in Russia, with some Russian authorities claiming that the treaty is biased (because it bans MIRVed ICBMs, on which Russia relies heavily) and others arguing that it should be rejected to protest the expansion of NATO (see Chapters Five and Nine). Arms control advocates in both Russia and the United States proposed immediately beginning negotiations for START III, which could alleviate these concerns and provide for even deeper cuts. In any event, the debate over START II shows that just as during the Cold War, strategic arms control remains an inherently political process, and progress is difficult to achieve when it is linked to other political issues. Nevertheless, through many disappointments and detours, the SALT and START negotiations finally achieved significant agreements on the reduction of the two largest nuclear powers' strategic arsenals, and further reductions may be possible as the Cold War fades into distant memory.

Intermediate-Range and Tactical Nuclear Weapons

Strategic weapons were not the only nuclear forces considered for reductions in the waning days of the Cold War. In December 1987, after seven years of negotiations, the United States and the USSR signed the Intermediate-Range Nuclear Forces (INF) Treaty, which eliminated all nuclear missiles with a range of 310 through 3400 miles. Although these weapons represented a relatively small portion of both superpowers' nuclear arsenals, the INF treaty marked the first time that an entire class of nuclear weapons had been banned. By June 1991, all such weapons had been destroyed by both sides.

Another class of nuclear weapons lost much of their military significance after the disintegration of the Warsaw Pact and the reunification of Germany in 1990.

Tactical nuclear weapons, with ranges between 95 and 310 miles, and battlefield nuclear weapons, with ranges of less than 125 miles, were no longer of any military importance in Europe. It was no great surprise, then, that both the Soviet Union (and subsequently Russia) and the United States announced unilateral steps to remove many of these weapons as the Cold War wound down to a close. After the August 1991 coup attempt in the Soviet Union, President Bush declared that the United States would unilaterally reduce its short-range nuclear forces. In response, Soviet President Gorbachev also announced similar steps. After the demise of the Soviet Union, the successor states agreed to transfer all of the tactical nuclear weapons on former Soviet territory to storage depots in Russia. By July 1992, the United States and former Soviet states had completed these steps, and by 1997 thousands of these weapons were dismantled without any type of formal arms-control agreement.

Nonproliferation Treaty

In addition to strategic nuclear weapons and intermediate-range and tactical nuclear weapons, a third major area of arms control after World War II concerned the proliferation of nuclear weapons. After the development of the atomic bomb and its use by the United States on Hiroshima and Nagasaki in 1945, nuclear weapons were developed by the USSR, United Kingdom, France, and China. Many more countries embarked upon research programs that gave them the potential to construct their own nuclear weapons.

To stem the danger of proliferation, the UN General Assembly adopted a resolution in 1961 calling on all states to sign a treaty prohibiting the transfer and acquisition of nuclear weapons. The 1968 **Nonproliferation Treaty** (NPT) prohibited states already in possession of nuclear weapons from helping other states to acquire them. Furthermore, non-nuclear weapon states were forbidden to manufacture or otherwise obtain nuclear arms and were to submit their nuclear programs to monitoring by the **International Atomic Energy Agency** (IAEA). Nuclear weapon states were allowed to facilitate the exchange of equipment, materials, and scientific and technical information on the peaceful uses of nuclear energy, and they were encouraged to pursue further negotiations on arms control and disarmament.

Most of the countries signing the NPT had no intention of acquiring nuclear weapons in the first place. Several states with nuclear ambitions at the time (including India, Pakistan, South Africa, and Israel) refused to sign the treaty. Other countries, including Iran, Iraq, and North Korea, signed it but still continued their nuclear weapons programs. To prevent these countries from acquiring the weapons, the major nuclear suppliers began to meet in London in 1975 to develop a common approach to limit their nuclear exports. The "London Club" eventually was able to produce a set of guidelines for the transfer of peaceful nuclear technology. However, as the recent examples of Iraq and North Korea indicate, transfer guidelines remain insufficient to prevent nuclear proliferation.

The fragmentation of the New Era has led many states to rethink their policies toward nuclear proliferation. This has already happened with France and China, both of whom eventually signed the NPT after holding out for more than two decades. Setting other hopeful examples, Brazil and Argentina jointly agreed to halt their nuclear weapons programs in 1991, and South Africa revealed and destroyed its small nuclear capability in 1993. In 1995, the treaty was extended indefinitely, further strengthening the commitment of most states to preventing the spread of nuclear weapons.

On the other hand, the dangers of new states gaining nuclear weapons in a more fragmented international arena has increased. As noted in the section on military power, a number of states are believed to be continuing to develop nuclear weapons. Many of these states (such as North Korea and Algeria) are ruled by unstable regimes, and others (including Libya, Iran, Syria, and Iraq, which might resume its nuclear program if UN monitoring is relaxed) are known or suspected to be major sponsors of terrorists. The possibility that nuclear material or the technical knowledge needed to make nuclear weapons might "leak" out of the former Soviet states, where security measures on nuclear facilities were revealed to be seriously inadequate, has heightened proliferation concerns in recent years, and major international efforts have been launched to prevent this frightening possibility.[29] Though the cause of nonproliferation has come a long way, the possibility that dictators or terrorists will build or buy nuclear weapons, or that nations that have not declared them will use them in regional conflicts, will continue be serious security concerns in the New Era.[30]

Chemical Weapons, Biological Weapons, and Missiles

As terrible as nuclear weapons are, they are neither the first nor the only weapons of mass destruction in evidence today. Chemical weapons, poisons designed to incapacitate or kill people after touching the skin or being inhaled, were first used as a weapon in World War I and have been employed in several wars since, such as in Yemen in the 1960s and in the Iran-Iraq war of the 1980s. In 1925 the Geneva Protocol prohibited the use but not the possession of chemical weapons, allowing many countries to build large stockpiles and continue their research and production programs. In 1980 the UN Conference on Disarmament began work on a treaty that would ban chemical weapons. Since January 1993, more than 150 nations signed the **Chemical Weapons Convention,** which bans their possession, acquisition, production, stockpiling, transfer, and use. The treaty was finally ratified by a sufficient number of states (including the United States and Russia) in 1997, and signatory states must dispose of these weapons within ten years. However, Libya, Syria, North Korea, and other states refused to sign, and they maintain chemical weapons or programs to develop them in spite of international convention.

As if chemical weapons weren't bad enough, biological weapons use viruses, bacteria, or the toxins they produce to strike at an enemy's population through "germ warfare." These weapons are covered by the 1925 Geneva Protocol and the

At a Glance

Major Nuclear Weapons Treaties

Limited Test Ban Treaty, 1963
Nations: United Kingdom, United States, USSR, and more than 100 other states (excluding China and France)

Commitments: Outlawed nuclear explosions in the air, under water, and in outer space. Underground testing is still allowed.

Nonproliferation Treaty (NPT), 1968
Nations: More than 100 states

Commitments: Prohibited "nuclear weapon states" from helping other states to acquire nuclear weapons. "Non-nuclear weapon states" were forbidden to manufacture or otherwise obtain nuclear arms and required to submit their nuclear programs to monitoring by the International Atomic Energy Agency (IAEA). Indefinitely extended in 1995.

Threshold Test Ban Treaty, 1974
Nations: United States, USSR

Commitments: Confined their underground explosions within an upper limit of 150 kilotons.

Strategic Arms Limitation Treaty (SALT I), 1972
Nations: United States, USSR

Commitments: Interim Agreement put a ceiling on the number of land- and sea-based strategic nuclear delivery vehicles the two sides were allowed to have while they were negotiating a more substantive agreement to be signed at some future date. No sacrifices were required by either side because it did not prohibit qualitative improvements such as MIRV. Instead, it froze the number of offensive strategic missiles deployed or under construction for five years as of the date of the signing.

Anti-Ballistic Missile (ABM) Treaty
Restricted both parties to having not more than two ABM sites, with not more than 100 interceptor missiles each. An additional protocol in 1974 further restricted the deployment of a ballistic missile defense system to a single area designated by each country.

SALT II, 1979
Nations: United States, USSR. Never ratified by the U.S. Senate due to the Soviet invasion of Afghanistan.

Commitments: Although not ratified, both sides adhered to the broad guidelines of the treaty, which were an aggregate ceiling of 2400 launch vehicles for each superpower until the end of 1981 and 2250 launch vehicles from the end of 1981 until the treaty expired in 1985. A number of subceilings were designed to put a cap on MIRVs.

Intermediate-Range Nuclear Forces (INF) Treaty, 1987
Nations: United States, USSR

Commitments: Totally eliminated all nuclear missiles with a range of 310 through 3400 miles.

Strategic Arms Reduction Talks (START I), 1991
Nations: United States, USSR

Commitments: First arms-control treaty mandating genuine reductions in strategic weapons. Main parameters were set at 1600 launch vehicles and 6000 warheads for each side.

START II, 1993
Nations: United States, Russia

Commitments: Reduced strategic nuclear arsenals to between 3000 and 3500 warheads by the year 2003. Eliminated MIRVed ICBMs completely and, as a subceiling, limited SLBM warheads to 1750.

Comprehensive Test-Ban Treaty (1996)
Nations: More than 100 states

Commitments: Prohibits testing of any type of nuclear explosive

Spotlight

Hidden Killers

The term "weapons of mass destruction" usually refers to sophisticated means of dealing death, difficult to develop and carried over hundreds or thousands of miles by high-tech aircraft or missiles. For these reasons, nuclear, chemical, and biological weapons have been the most visible topics for deterrence, arms control, and disarmament. But more destruction on a mass scale has been caused by relatively simple devices, easy and cheap to produce, usable even by children, and which do their deadly work literally underfoot.

These small packets of death are antipersonnel mines. Originally developed to stop invading armies, mines have become the weapons of choice in insurgencies and civil wars in developing countries, because they are so inexpensive and easy to use. Buried under roads or vegetation or set as booby traps in buildings, mines kill friend, foe, and innocent civilian indiscriminately, and many remain active years after they have been placed and forgotten. Mines are cheap—many cost less than $1 to make, but can cost $1000 to remove and deactivate—and readily available on the world market. They are produced in more than thirty countries and are often given away as "security assistance" to Third World regimes and their opponents.

Although they can be placed in a matter of minutes by fighters with only rudimentary training, they are difficult and expensive to remove and are often left in place long after a conflict has ended. As a result, over 100 million land mines were lying about in more than seventy countries in 1996 (10 million each in Afghanistan and Cambodia), killing untold thousands annually.* The majority of those killed are children, because most types of mines have small explosive charges and are designed to maim rather than kill. In Angola, where 9 million mines remain hidden, 5000 people lose limbs to them each year. They remain active in more than eighty countries in Africa, Asia, Latin America, and Europe. The United Nations operates mine removal programs in many of these countries involving a total of six thousand personnel, but the task they face is overwhelming.

An international movement to ban antipersonnel mines gained momentum in the 1990s with the start of the Ottawa Process, a program of international negotiations which culminateed in a treaty for a global ban opened for signature in 1997. The U.S.-based International Campaign to Ban Landmines was awarded the Nobel Peace Prize that same year, but much work remains to be done before the movement's ultimate goal can be achieved. The governments of the United States, Britain, Canada, and more than sixty other countries have officially supported the elimination of these miniature murderers, but the United States has stated that it will not sign on to a ban resulting from the Ottawa process,

---

1972 Biological Weapons Convention (BWC), which 134 states had signed by 1993. Each signatory is formally committed to not develop, produce, stockpile, acquire, or transfer biological agents. Although many experts claim that biological weapons have never been successfully used as a military weapon, many countries continue to fund biological-weapons programs, including Iraq, Iran, Libya, Syria, and until its breakup, the Soviet Union. (Some experts claim that a small, highly secret biological weapons program still exists in Russia.) When Baghdad's demand for an end to United Nations inspections of suspected mass destruction weapon sites provoked a confrontation with the United States and Britain in 1998,

■ Children in Sarajevo play next to a minefield (indicated by yellow tape).   SOURCE: AP/Wide World

and China and Russia, major mine producers and exporters, are not taking part in it. In any case, even if production and sales of mines stopped immediately, clearing those already active could cost over $100 billion and would be difficult or impossible in many conflict-prone areas. Meanwhile, a hundred million killers remain hidden, ready and waiting to perpetrate mass destruction one victim at a time.

*Figures quoted in Dan Smith, *The State of War and Peace Atlas*, 3d ed. (1997).

Iraq's potential to deploy biological weapons was cited as a major reason why the inspections must be continued. At the same time, the use of biological weapons by terrorists has become a major security concern in the New Era, and many states began "biodefense" programs in the 1990s to counter this threat.

As noted in the section on military power, chemical and biological weapons, like nuclear weapons, can be delivered by ballistic missiles. Throughout the 1980s concerns rose about the proliferation of ballistic missiles in many regions of the world. In 1983 seven Western nations began negotiations to limit the export of ballistic missile technology. Although they could not agree on a treaty, they did agree on the creation of the Missile Technology Control Regime, which restricted the export of ballistic missiles capable of carrying more than 500 kilograms (considered to be the minimum payload required for a nuclear warhead) over a distance of 300 kilometers or more. This agreement was subsequently strengthened by the inclusion of several key suppliers, including Russia, Israel, Argentina, Brazil, and China, but it is not clear whether Russia's and China are fully committed to fulfilling its provisions.

The missile agreement has not yet succeeded in eliminating missile deployment programs already existing in several countries. It does, however, offer the prospect of significantly restraining exports if its members adhere to their agreements and accept limitations that restrict potential sales. The involvement of a growing number of countries in efforts to control missiles and weapons of mass destruction shows how the spread of military technology has become a global problem curable only through global cooperation.

Conventional Arms Control

The control of conventional arms has remained one of the most difficult areas for arms limitation. Throughout the Cold War, the Warsaw Pact maintained an overwhelming quantitative conventional superiority that led to corresponding NATO buildups. This resulted in a situation in which two enormous armies of over 1 million troops each, equipped with the most sophisticated weapons, confronted each other for more than forty years along the East German–West German border. NATO's worst military nightmare was a Soviet surprise attack across this line with the vast Warsaw Pact army already in Eastern Europe.[31] From 1973 until 1986 both alliances negotiated to little avail over reductions of conventional forces in the Mutual and Balanced Force Reduction (MBFR) talks.

As with the nuclear arms race, the end of the Cold War proved to be a major catalyst for change. In November 1990 NATO and the Warsaw Pact countries signed the Conventional Forces in Europe (CFE) Treaty, one of the most intricate arms-control agreements ever reached. The treaty called for the destruction or removal from Europe of over 125,000 tanks, artillery, armored vehicles, aircraft, and helicopters. In sharp contrast to the protracted MBFR negotiations, it took the twenty-two signatory states only twenty months to complete the treaty. The Soviet Union in particular made large concessions that removed the threat of a blitzkrieg-type Soviet invasion of Western Europe even before the final collapse of the USSR. The demise of the communist superpower, ironically, created new difficulties in implementing the CFE Treaty as the USSR's successor states argued among themselves over the allocation of the remaining weapons permitted under the agreement. Russia also argued that the treaty's "flank limits," which govern the equipment allowed in the northeastern and southeastern portions of the regions covered by the agreement, had to be revised to reflect its new security concerns, but this problem was resolved through the signing of an understanding with NATO in 1997.

CONCLUSION: TO ARM OR NOT TO ARM?

All nations face a security dilemma that they must manage, either through international negotiations, unilateral measures, or both. Regardless of their choice, the pursuit of the various goals that states include in their definition of "national security" consumes a significant portion of their available resources. This is understandable, because one of the primary responsibilities of a state is the provision of security for its citizens. Beyond a certain point, however, the pursuit of security begins to have detrimental effects on a state's relations with its neighbors and the international community, and on the state itself. Determining the point where the proportion of a nation's material and human resources devoted to security becomes self-defeating is a difficult task for its leaders, but an essential one.

Because many aspects of international security are fraught with uncertainty, there is no way to precisely determine how much security is enough. The threats a nation faces and the measures it should adopt in response depend heavily on perceptions. Former President George Bush, an advocate of prudence in security policy, views the resources earmarked for national security as money well spent:

> Throughout our history, our national security has pursued broad, consistent goals. We have always sought to protect the safety of the nation, its citizens, and its way of life. We have also worked to advance the welfare of our people, by contributing to an international environment of peace, freedom, and progress within which our democracy—and other free nations—can flourish.[32]

A proponent of disarmament has a quite different view of security:

> Security has become a god, and a cruel and demanding one. Our tribute to fear now runs at around $1 trillion a year. But the real cost is the diversion of resources needed elsewhere. And our insecurity increases. We live under the shadow of nuclear war, of famine, violence, and human and environmental tragedy.[33]

These views can be difficult to reconcile. Recall the images of world politics introduced in Chapter One. A person who holds the "Star Wars" image of international relations, who is worried about the threat presented by "evil empires" and undemocratic leaders, is more likely to be concerned with national security than someone who believes that all conflicts are simple misunderstandings, because "it's a small world after all." Events may temporarily incline a nation's government or citizenry toward one view or the other, but they are not likely to cause a shift in the underlying difference in perspective. For this reason, debates over how much security a nation should "purchase" for itself are among the most persistent and contentious controversies in democratic societies, and are difficult to resolve even in undemocratic ones.

Ultimately, if national security is defined as the preservation of sovereignty and territorial integrity, the resources a state spends on national security are part of the price of independence. Just as an individual must decide how much health or accident insurance to purchase depending on his or her specific needs, nations must

What Would You Do ?

You are the prime minister of Japan. The time is the present. Your intelligence services inform you that North Korea will complete a secret plutonium reprocessing plant within a matter of months. The reports, confirmed by U.S. and South Korean intelligence, estimate that when the plant becomes operational, North Korea will be able to produce enough plutonium to build ten to twenty nuclear weapons each year.

They suspect, although they cannot be sure, that these weapons could be mounted on ballistic missiles with sufficient range to hit most cities in Japan, including Tokyo.

How should your country respond to this threat? You might ask the United States to destroy the plant with an air strike, but this could easily provoke a second Korean War, and Pyongyang would certainly retaliate, possibly by using terrorists to attack a Japanese city with chemical or biological weapons. You could secretly order the development of your own nuclear weapons, to deter a North Korean nuclear attack, but your efforts would surely be detected and would distress the United States, anger China, and panic South Korea. You could cooperate with the United States and/or South Korea to develop and deploy theater missile defenses, but you could never be sure of their effectiveness, and Russia and China would probably try to block the program. Finally, you could reveal the existence of the plant in hopes of mustering international diplomatic pressure against Pyongyang, but the North Korean regime has never cared about world opinion, and the Japanese public may come to regard your moderate action as a sign of weakness or incompetence.

Each of these options has its own set of attendant risks, and all may seem unpalatable at best, but there are few easy choices where national security is concerned. Perhaps you can come up with a better option, but the clock is ticking.

What would you do ?

consider the threats confronting them and the strategies and resources available when they purchase their "security insurance." If they spend too little, they risk catastrophic losses from aggression not covered by their defense effort; if they spend too much, their other goals or values may suffer.

No matter how much attention a nation gives to these matters, absolute security is impossible to attain. Every security strategy involves risks of one sort or another, even for the most powerful nation. Consequently, states must choose armament or disarmament, deterrence or defense, and multilateral cooperation or unilateral action to meet their security needs, and each option has its own inherent drawbacks. As long as the possibility of conflict exists—and it always will—all nations must assess the threats they face, decide how best to protect their land

and people, and choose the sacrifices they will make and the risks they will accept in the name of national security.

PRINCIPAL POINTS OF CHAPTER ELEVEN

1. The concept of national security can include many elements, such as territorial integrity, economic prosperity, maintenance of basic values, and preservation of the natural environment. For the purposes of this text, security is defined as a condition in which the sovereignty and the territorial integrity of a country are guaranteed.

2. In the anarchic international system, every state faces the security dilemma: The actions a state takes to increase its own security may decrease the security of other states, which may respond by taking actions that decrease the security of the original state.

3. A variety of strategies for protecting national security are available to states:
   a. States may unilaterally build up their armed forces, join with other states in military alliances (such as NATO), or rely on collective-security organizations (such as the UN) to protect them from aggression.
   b. Each nation must also determine the mix of deterrence (persuading opponents not to attack by threatening them with punishment) and defense (resisting or stopping an attack) upon which it will rely.

4. There are two main types of deterrence. General deterrence attempts to dissuade adversaries from attempting any type of challenge to a state's interests, while immediate deterrence is a response to a specific, imminent threat.

5. A distinction may also be drawn between direct deterrence, which threatens punishment for attacks on a nation's own territory, and extended deterrence, which threatens sanctions against attacks on a state's allies.

6. Successful deterrence requires the "three C's": commitment, capability, and credibility. In addition, the opponent must be rational enough to weigh the likely costs and benefits of attacking.

7. Critics of deterrence contend that deterrence often fails because challengers do not accurately perceive the defender's capabilities or commitment, or have limited ability to make cost-benefit calculations when considering an attack.

8. Military technology can have a great impact on the success or failure of security strategies, particularly if it alters the offense/defense balance.

9. The development of nuclear weapons radically changed military strategy in the following ways:
   a. If a state possesses the ability to destroy all of an adversary's nuclear forces with its initial attack, it is said to have a first-strike capability. This is a very dangerous situation, as the state may be tempted to launch a nuclear attack during a crisis.

   b. To preserve the strategic balance and ensure that neither side has an incentive to launch a nuclear attack, states must maintain a second-strike capability by ensuring that enough of their nuclear arsenal will survive a nuclear attack to inflict unacceptable damage on the enemy. The preferred way of doing this is to deploy a nuclear triad of land-based missiles (ICBMs), submarine-based missiles (SLBMs), and bombers.

   c. If both states possess a secure second-strike capability, a condition of mutual assured destruction (MAD) exists, and neither side has an incentive to attack first (as it would be destroyed by the opponent's retaliatory strike).

10. Even though the end of the Cold War has halted the arms race between the United States and Russia, problems with the command and control of nuclear weapons possessed by unstable states and the spread of nuclear weapons, or nuclear proliferation, still remain.

11. States may attempt to enhance their mutual security through arms control or disarmament.

   a. Disarmament seeks to reduce existing levels of weapons as a goal in itself.

   b. Arms control seeks to limit and manage an arms race; this may or may not entail reductions in weapons.

12. Major arms control treaties since 1945 include the following:

   a. The Limited Test Ban Treaty (1963), the Threshold Test Ban Treaty (1974), and the Comprehensive Test-Ban Treaty (1996), which restrict testing of nuclear weapons.

   b. The multilateral Nonproliferation Treaty (1968), designed to control the spread of nuclear weapons, extended indefinitely in 1995.

   c. The first U.S.–Soviet Strategic Arms Limitation Treaty (SALT I) (1972), consisting of the Interim Agreement, which put temporary limits (different for each state) on strategic offensive weapons, and the Anti-Ballistic Missile (ABM) Treaty, which severely restricted the development and deployment of anti-missile systems.

   d. SALT II (1979), signed by the United States and USSR but not ratified by the United States (though both superpowers generally complied with it), which set equal overall ceilings on strategic weapons.

   e. The INF Treaty (1987), in which the United States and USSR eliminated intermediate-range nuclear forces.

   f. The first Strategic Arms Reduction Treaty (START I) (1991), which committed the United States and USSR to reduce their strategic nuclear forces to equal lower levels.

   g. START II (1993), not yet ratified by Russia, which codified further reductions in U.S. and Russian nuclear weapons and banned land-based missiles with MIRVs (multiple warheads).

   h. The agreement on Conventional Forces in Europe (CFE) (1990), limiting conventional (non-nuclear) weapons and forces in Europe and the successor states to the USSR.

i. The multilateral Biological Weapons Convention (1972), which bans germ-warfare weapons.
j. The Chemical Weapons Convention (1993), which bans poison gas and other chemical-warfare agents.
k. Although it is not a formal multilateral treaty, the Missile Technology Control Regime engages key suppliers in the effort to seek limitations on the export of ballistic missile technology.

KEY TERMS

air-launched cruise missle
arms control
Baruch Plan
biological weapons capability
chemical weapons
Chemical Weapons Convention
commitment
compellence
conventional weapons
credibility
cruise missile

defense
deterrence
disarmament
extended deterrence
first-strike capability
general deterrence
hydrogen bomb
immediate deterrence
information warfare
intercontinental ballistic missile
intermediate range ballistic missile

International Atomic Energy Agency
invulnerability
military power
multiple independently targeted reentry vehicles
national security
Nonproliferation Treaty
nuclear proliferation
nuclear triad
preemptive strikes

primary deterrence
rationality
sea-launched cruise missile
second-strike capability
strategic nuclear forces
strategic weapon
tactical nuclear weapons
tactical weapon
thermonuclear weapon
total war
warhead

Theory and Analysis of World Politics

SOURCE: AP/Alexander Zemlianichenko/Wide World

CHAPTER

12

□ □ □ □

Levels of Analysis

A group of psychologists recently met at a Fantasy University conference to explain the behavior of an individual, specifically, a political science undergraduate. Some psychologists put forth the argument that the undergraduate's mental state is primarily controlled by the chemical balance of the brain. Their explanations for the person's behavior were said to derive from the "biochemical" level of analysis. Others emphasized the person's childhood experiences, emotional traumas, and personality traits; these doctors stressed the "personal" level of analysis to explain specific actions. Finally, some of the psychologists concentrated on outside influences such as family, workplace, community, or even the television programs watched. These specialists examined the "environmental" level of analysis to try to understand the person's behavior. The psychologists could not agree on the level at which the most powerful influences were to be found, and as a result their recommendations for modifying the person's behavior differed.

One prescribed drugs, a second advised helping the person work through an emotional problem, and a third suggested doing something to reduce stress on the job or in the family. (No one suggested switching majors.)

This story is not intended to suggest that international politics resembles mental illness. (The reader should draw his or her own conclusion in this regard.) Rather, it is designed to show that when behavior can be influenced by many factors, it must be examined at a number of levels in order to be explained fully. We can apply this principle to international politics this way: The fact that there is a significant number of possible influences on the actions of states means that there will inevitably be disagreement over which factors exert the greatest impact. This chapter will outline various theories derived from the three **levels of analysis** that seek to explain why states do what they do.

The three levels of analysis were first introduced in Chapter One; as you will recall, analysts of global politics find it useful to categorize the many factors that affect international relations according to the level at which they exert their influence. Factors arising from the nature and structure of the world political system (such as the number and relative strength of major powers) fall under the **systemic level of analysis.** These influences are essentially external to the individual states within the international system in that they are attributes of the system itself rather than of the units (the states) within the system. The unique characteristics of nation-states that shape their foreign polices (such as form of government, historical experience, and **ideology**) fall into the **domestic level of analysis.** Finally, the skills, beliefs, personalities, and idiosyncrasies of leaders come into play at the **individual level of analysis.**

A rich and complex body of theory has been developed for each of the three levels of analysis. This chapter can do no more than present a very basic outline of the concepts and leading schools of thought which deal with each level, which students of world politics can fill in and expand upon through further study. To this end, this chapter will undertake a brief "top-down" survey of the various theories that attempt to explain the workings of world politics. As we will see, many of these theories appear to compete with one another, although ultimately they are complementary: They help us comprehend the "big picture" of world politics by identifying its component parts and explaining how they interact.

THE SYSTEMIC LEVEL

As mentioned earlier, systemic arguments contend that factors external to the state will encourage certain actions and discourage others.[1] Accordingly, changes in the nature or structure of the international system will lead to changes in the behavior of states within the system. To examine these ideas in greater detail, the following two sections focus on how systemic factors lead to conflict or facilitate cooperation between states. The first section outlines the realist paradigm, which holds that the distribution of capabilities within the international system (that is, the relative power of states) has a profound effect on how nations act and on the

At a Glance

The Systemic Level: Schools of Thought

Classical Realism

Theory: The world is governed by the "law of the jungle" in which each state must protect its vital interests, political independence, and territorial sovereignty by any means necessary. There is no effective international organization to control individual states.

The System: It is a "dog-eat-dog" world. Some states are inherently expansionist and aggressive, while others have an interest in maintaining the status quo. If a state becomes militarily weaker vis-à-vis other states, its survival might be jeopardized; in this way, the process of the rise and fall of states resembles Charles Darwin's theory of natural selection. In this anarchic world, peace can only be achieved by hegemony or balance of power.

Structural Realism

Theory: The system is anarchic. All states are unitary, rational actors. Their primary concern is survival. Although the international system refers to all states in the world, structural realists are primarily concerned only with the most powerful states or great powers.

The System: The system is described in terms of polarity: unipolarity, bipolarity, or multipolarity. Some contend that movement toward an equal distribution of power is most conducive to international stability, while others argue that movement toward dominance of the system by a single state is the best guarantor of stability.

Classical Liberalism

Theory: The world is not always consumed by warfare, and states pursue goals other than those involving power and security. Because states also value economic well-being and political, social, and cultural values, on which they can often cooperate, the international system is not doomed to be a "dog-eat-dog" environment.

The System: The system is anarchic, but this does not necessarily prohibit cooperation. Not all aspects of world politics may be characterized by a zero-sum game; instead, free trade and democracy make the advantages of cooperation more apparent. Barriers to cooperation will always exist, but these can often (though not always) be overcome through reciprocal agreements.

Neoliberalism

Theory: States do not exist in a "dog-eat-dog" environment, and are in many ways interdependent. There have always been more instances of international cooperation than conflict. The existence, indeed prevalence, of cooperation on many issues demonstrates that more cooperation is possible.

The System: The anarchy and violence of the international system can be overcome through carefully designed institutions for international cooperation. Treaties, international law and regimes, free trade areas, common markets, collective security organizations, and other institutions can encourage states to cooperate on economic, security, environmental, and other issues.

overall stability of the system, and examines the debate within the realist school over what leads to the most stable international system. The second section examines an alternative school of systemic theory, liberalism, which focuses on the barriers to cooperation among states and suggests how these barriers can be overcome to increase the likelihood that states will cooperate with each other in the New Era.

REALISM

The school of thought known as **realism** is the most venerable paradigm in international relations theory. Its roots can be traced back hundreds of years to the Greek historian Thucydides' Peloponnesian War (431–404 B.C.), to Kautilya (around 300 B.C.), a Hindu statesman and philosopher, and to Sun Tzu (500 B.C.), the author of the Chinese classic, *The Art of War*. It also borrows from political theorists such as Niccolò Machiavelli and Thomas Hobbes and academic disciplines such as microeconomics and biology. Modern realist theory is a response to the failure of idealistic attempts during the interwar period (1919–1939) to prevent a new world war (Chapter Three discusses these noble measures and their disappointing results). In rejecting the "naive" and utopian orientation of **idealism**, scholars and policy-makers such as Hans Morgenthau, Reinhold Niebuhr, George Kennan, Henry Kissinger, and John Foster Dulles emphasized the logic of realpolitik (literally the "politics of realism"), power politics, and the evil—or at least amoral and wicked—nature of humans in shaping interstate relations.[2]

At the core of the realist paradigm is a belief in the primacy of national security issues (referred to as **high politics**) over economic and other domestic issues (**low politics**). **Classical realists,** such as Morgenthau and Kissinger, view the world as governed only by the "law of the jungle," wherein each state must protect its own vital interests, political independence, and territorial sovereignty at any cost. In the "dog-eat-dog" world described by the realist paradigm, military power is often a necessary ingredient for national survival. If a state becomes militarily weaker vis-à-vis other states, its survival might be jeopardized; in this way, the process of the rise and fall of states resembles Charles Darwin's theory of natural selection (that is, the survival of the fittest).

In contrast to classical realists, who emphasize the fearful and conflictual nature of humankind, adherents of **structural realism** (also known as **neorealism**) such as Kenneth Waltz and Joseph Grieco focus on the structure of the international system rather than on human nature to account for the behavior of states.[3] Although the international system refers to all states in the world, structural realists are primarily concerned only with the most powerful states, or great powers (see Chapter Twelve). For these theorists, the structure of the international system is defined by the distribution of power among the great powers—or in other words, the number of great powers in the system and their relative capabilities.

The structure of the international system is typically described in terms of polarity, with each major power representing a "pole" of the system. A **unipolar** system is one in which a single dominant power exists, a **bipolar** structure is one with two great powers, and a **multipolar** structure is one with three or more. Structural realists are intensely interested in the shifts in power among the major states and the impact these will have on the stability of the international system. Some contend that movement toward an equal distribution of power (**parity**) is most conducive to international stability, while others argue that movement toward dominance of the system by a single state (**preponderance**) is the best guarantor of stability. We will return to this question later in this section; for now, we will examine in more detail the basic premises and arguments of structural realism, a leading school of thought in the study of international relations.

Principles of Structural Realism

Any school of thought is based on central assumptions or axioms. The three central assumptions of structural realism are:

1. The international system is anarchic.
2. All states within the system are unitary, rational actors.
3. The primary concern of all states is survival.

An anarchic system is one that lacks a legitimate authority to "make and enforce laws, adjudicate disputes, and regulate behavior among states."[4] The international system is thus likened to Thomas Hobbes' "state of nature," where no "world policeman" exists to protect states from one another. (See Chapters Nine and Eleven for more on the effects of anarchy in the international system.)

The second assumption is that the political authority of nation-states is supreme and not subject to any higher political authority. As noted in Chapters Two and Nine, the Peace of Westphalia (1648) ushered in the modern international system by legitimating the state as the ultimate sovereign authority over people and geographic territory. Although we tend to identify a state as something that signs treaties and makes war, states exist only as legal, or juridical, entities. A state's legal status is associated with its monopoly over the legitimate use of force within its territorial confines, as well as its authority to wage war against other states. No supranational organization is authorized to maintain order within state boundaries. The United Nations has been constrained in both peacekeeping and peacemaking efforts by an inability to muster and maintain troops without the permission of its sovereign member states.

In conceptualizing the state as a unitary and **rational actor,** realists recognize that states are sovereign and deemphasize the role of actors within the state (such as political parties or leaders) in shaping the state's actions in the international system. States are often likened to billiard balls on a pool table. Just as players don't care what's inside the balls, so too systems analysts have little concern for domestic factors. In short, structural realists contend that domestic politics do not really matter, because states act as though they are rational individuals by making cost-benefit calculations in determining which policy to pursue. According to this line of reasoning, then, U.S. military intervention in Korea and Vietnam, for example, was neither a result of domestic politics such as congressional or public-opinion preferences, nor a product of Pentagon or State Department maneuvering, nor a product of the individual preferences of American presidents Truman, Kennedy, or Johnson; rather, it was a rational, logical result of the international system of the time. U.S. involvement was necessary to contain Communist expansion, regardless of the wishes of other nations. After all, the very survival of the United States could have been at stake.

The third assumption of structural realism is that the primary objective of all states is survival. Because the international system is an anarchic, self-help system, each state is left alone to guarantee its own survival, because no other state will do so.[5] As a result of this assumption, the "hierarchy" of state interests is dominated by security issues. Realism contends that in an anarchic world, power is the means to security, and therefore states seek to maximize their own power. Realists are not interested in a state's absolute power, but instead they are concerned about changes in its relative power or position with regard to other states. States must always prepare themselves for war or face the risk of annihilation as a sovereign entity. The inherent danger of this situation, of course, is that the heavy emphasis on security issues compels other states in the system to take countermeasures that might ultimately weaken the state's relative position. (For more on the security dilemma and its implications, see Chapter Eleven.)

Shifts in System Structure

The primary contention of structural realism is that shifts in the distribution of power among states will pressure them to respond in a uniform and predictable pattern. According to this argument, a decline in a state's relative position will lead it to try to improve its standing relative to that of the dominant power. In a bipolar system in which two superpowers vie for leadership, this is usually accomplished through **internal balancing** (building up a state's own capabilities), as during the Cold War. In a multipolar system (1648–1945), balancing is accomplished through the formation of alliances and coalitions. In both cases, all states wish to survive, and this desire will lead them to balance by forming a counter-coalition against the dominant power. States will act similarly despite differences between them in political and economic institutions, historical backgrounds, and individual leaders. Hypothetically, realism would predict that had Britain, and not the Soviet Union, emerged as the other superpower after World War II, then the United States would have perceived England as the primary threat to its security. In this view, the Cold War was inevitable, no matter who the contenders were.

A second argument of structural realism is that states rarely cooperate, especially on security-related issues. Concerned about any possible changes in their international ranking, states may hesitate to collaborate out of fear that their partner might get a larger share of the benefits than themselves. Although both may gain in absolute terms, both fear that cooperation may strengthen the other, as today's ally might be tomorrow's enemy. During the Vietnam War, for example, China and North Vietnam cooperated to frustrate U.S. objectives and later even set up a "fraternal" Communist regime in Cambodia. After the United States withdrew its forces in 1973 and Vietnam reunified in 1975, however, conflicts between Beijing and Hanoi quickly resurfaced. Vietnamese forces invaded Cambodia in 1978, and Vietnam and China fought a brief border war in 1979 (see Chapter Six).

Polarity and the Balance of Power

Although they agree that all states seek security through maintenance of a balance of power, realists disagree on the type of international system structure that best promotes stability. One debate centers on whether a balance of power or an **imbalance of power** is preferable. The **parity school** argues that an equal distribution of capability among states, or a balance of power, creates stability and that war is more likely to occur when one state is the dominant power. On the other hand, the **preponderance school** contends that stability is more likely if there is an imbalance of power, where one state dominates the system, than with an equal distribution of power, where war is more likely. (See the boxed feature in Chapter Two for more on the controversy over the balance of power.) The second debate in the realist school exists within the parity version of realism: namely whether a bipolar or multipolar distribution of power is more stable.

However, neither of these debates can be resolved without first defining stability within the international system. A narrow definition of stability is the absence of any war, the continued political independence and territorial integrity of all states in the system, and the maintenance of the status quo, or existing international order. A looser definition would be the absence of war between the great powers, where the system would still be considered stable even if limited wars occurred (that is, war between a great power and a lesser power, or between lesser powers). Using this definition, the Cold War era was relatively stable, despite its numerous regional conflicts, because there was no war between the superpowers (see Chapter Four). Because the realists define the global system by the number of great powers, under the broadest of definitions a particular system is not stable if it ceases to exist when one of the great powers declines, collapses, or is divided or destroyed. Not surprisingly, proponents of different perspectives on the parity/preponderance and bipolarity/multipolarity debates base their arguments on different definitions of stability.

The Case for Parity

Balance-of-power theory argues that an equal distribution of power is more stable than a hegemonic distribution, where one state dominates. Balance-of-power theory is an equilibrium model, intended to prevent the dominance of the system by any single state. According to this argument, when an imbalance does occur, the system is likely to return to an equilibrium; if one state becomes too powerful, other states will form a **counterbalancing coalition** to restore the original balance.

The reason why dominance of the system by a single state is seen as destabilizing is clear. When one state or bloc becomes preponderant, it is tempted to dominate the system and impose its will on the other states by the threat or use of military force. Perhaps the most prominent twentieth-century example was Nazi Germany, from the mid-1930s up until its defeat in 1945. Even if the hegemon (dominant power) is initially benevolent, there is an ever-present danger that it will become dictatorial; as the nineteenth-century English historian Lord Acton wisely noted, "Power tends to corrupt and absolute power corrupts absolutely."[6]

By forming a counterbalancing coalition, states seek to prevent war by deterring the aggressor state. If deterrence fails, however, the members of the counterbalancing coalition must be willing to use military force to restore the balance of power. Remember that states balance not for moral reasons, but for self-preservation. Personal differences among leaders, ideological competition, or historical antagonisms play no role in a state's decision to join a counterbalancing coalition. The mid-twentieth century is full of such cases: the 1939 nonaggression pact between fascist Germany and communist Russia, and the World War II alliance between the Soviet Union and the United States against Germany are two prime examples. When Britain and the USSR became allies, early in the war, Winston Churchill was recognizing the necessity of allying with an ideological adversary to counter even more pressing threats. The British prime minister remarked, "If Hitler invaded Hell, I would at least make a favorable reference to the Devil in the House of Commons."[7]

There are two basic ways that states can balance against a potentially dominant power. The first is through internal balancing. This strategy calls for the domestic mobilization of economic and industrial resources and their conversion into military power in order to match up against the preponderant power's capabilities. Here industrial strength must be converted into military power, which demonstrates the relationship between economic power and military power (see Chapter Eleven). As a result, it is not by chance that the most powerful states have often been the most developed ones.

If one cannot go it alone, the second strategy of balancing entails the formation of a counterbalancing coalition. Under this strategy, if one state becomes too powerful, the remaining states will balance against it by forming an alliance. The purpose of an alliance is to quickly aggregate capability in order to deter the preponderant power, and if this fails, to prepare for war in order to restore the balance of power. Examples of balancing through alliances against the preponderant power include the countercoalitions that formed against Spain during the Spanish-Dutch Wars and during the Thirty Years' War, against France during the War of the Spanish Succession and the Napoleonic Wars, and against Germany in World War I and World War II (see Chapters Two and Three). Table 12.1 summarizes these major alliances and wars.

Historically, Britain has played the role of continental "balancer," throwing its weight on the side opposing the ascending power. For centuries Britain was concerned that one "continental" power would come to dominate Europe, threaten British commercial links with the Continent, and perhaps launch an attack across the English Channel. As balance-of-power theory predicts, Britain's policy was to

Table 12.1	The Balance of Power: Alliances and Major Wars, 1580–1945	

State Seeking Hegemony	Balancing Powers	War against Potential Hegemon
Spain	Britain, France	Spanish-Dutch Wars (1580–1609)
Holy Roman Empire (Spain, Austria)	Britain, France, Sweden, Netherlands	Thirty Years' War (1618–1648)
France	Britain, Netherlands	War of the Spanish Succession (1701–1714)
France	Britain, Austria	War of the Austrian Succession (1740–1748)
France	Britain, Prussia, Austria, Russia	French Revolution and Napoleonic Wars (1792–1815)
Germany	Britain, France, Russia, United States	World War I (1914–1918)
Germany, Japan	Britain, France, USSR, United States	World War II (1939–1945)

SOURCE: Table based on Paul Kennedy, *The Rise and Fall of the Great Powers: Economic Change and Military Conflict from 1500 to 2000* (New York: Vintage Books, 1987)

align with the weaker state or coalition, with little consideration of its political or ideological orientation. Accordingly, Britain balanced against Spain in the seventeenth century, France in the eighteenth and nineteenth century, and Germany in the first half of the twentieth century. As Churchill noted,

> For four hundred years the foreign policy of England has been to oppose the strongest, most aggressive, most dominating power on the Continent. . . . [I]t would have been easy . . . and tempting to join with the stronger and share the fruits of conquest. However, we always took the harder course, joined with the less strong powers . . . and thus defeated the Continental tyrant whoever he was.[8]

Most balance-of-power theorists envision the formation of fluid and shifting alliances that quickly dissipate after they have served their purpose, only to form again at some future point against another preponderant state. During the seventeenth and eighteenth centuries, often referred to as the "golden age of diplomacy," ideology was not a barrier to this process. As a result, as Chapter Two discusses, states freely switched back and forth between alliances with little concern. Even with the rise of the twentieth-century rivalry between the United States and the ideologically rigid USSR, ideological incompatibility was still overcome when a greater danger loomed. During World Wars I and II the United States allied with Russia and the Soviet Union, respectively, to face a common and more threatening enemy, Germany. More recently, in the 1991 Persian Gulf War, the United States allied with Syria against Iraq. Would Israel and the Arab states unite against Iran if it threatened both? Would India and Pakistan mend their significant differences if China posed a common threat to their security? According to balance-of-power theory, the answer should be a resounding "yes."

There are a number of problems associated with balancing against a preponderant power through alliances. The first is the matter of reliability: allies may not fulfill their commitments to aid their partners.[9] In an anarchic system, a state that is "jilted at the altar" will have little recourse against its partner. In the aftermath of World War I, for instance, France made commitments to defend Czechoslovakia if Germany attacked. However, in 1938, when Hitler demanded the return of the Czechoslovak Sudetenland to Germany, France abandoned Czechoslovakia. This is an example of why realists contend that states should be suspicious of alliances and other cooperative-security arrangements.

Second, counterbalancing alliances are often slow to form. Knowing that an effective countercoalition will take time to come together, an expansionist power might be tempted to attack while the window of opportunity still exists (as Japan did in 1941, before the United States and Britain became formal allies in the Pacific).

Third, when faced with a stronger opponent and reluctant or uncooperative potential allies, states may conclude "if you can't beat 'em, join 'em." Through this strategy, known more formally as **bandwagoning**, states ally with an aggressor to avoid being attacked themselves and share in the rewards of conquest. As German power rose in the early years of World War II (see Chapter Three), less powerful states such as Hungary and Romania joined the Axis and participated in the invasion of the Soviet Union and other countries. This strategy can be a dangerous one, however. The leading state in an aggressive alliance may turn on its partners, and they may be defeated and occupied or loose territory if a balancing coalition eventually overcomes the aggressors. (Hungary and Romania both suffered this fate in World War II, surrendering to the Allies before Germany did.)

Additional problems with alliances include the twin dangers of **buck-passing** and **chain-ganging**.[10] Buck-passing refers to the temptation of all parties to "pass the buck" and let other states confront the threatening state. States are tempted to do this because no state wants to bear the high cost, in terms of lives and equipment, of fighting the dominant power. As we saw in Chapter Five, after Bosnia declared independence from Yugoslavia, the European Union (EU) nations avoided trying to curb first Serb and then Croat aggressions in Bosnia, preferring instead that the United States take care of the problem. Not willing to bear the high costs of a military intervention, the United States did not take steps believed to be necessary to halt the fighting, either characterizing the situation as a European problem or leaving it for the United Nations to try to resolve. Chain-ganging describes the danger that a state might get dragged into a war it has no interest in fighting. Picture the prisoners of a chain gang, shackled together at the feet. If the first prisoner falls over a cliff, all of the others will be dragged over, too. In the case of alliances, if an ally goes to war, the other(s) must follow or risk facing the rival alone at some future point. In the case of World War I, it can be argued that once Austria-Hungary went to war, Germany had to follow its partner into war or face the possibility of fighting Britain, France, and Russia alone at some future date.

The Case for Preponderance

Considering all the problems encountered in maintaining a balance of power and the many wars that have occurred when coalitions have attempted to block a powerful state's bid for hegemony, it should come as no surprise that some realists believe that an imbalance of power is more conducive to stability. Thucydides, an early realist, wrote in the fifth century B.C. that what made the Peloponnesian War inevitable was the growth of Athenian power and the fear this caused in Sparta, the other great power. Thucydides was arguing that war is most likely to occur in a system with two great powers of relatively equal strength or when two states are approaching parity. To take this theory one step further, it can be argued that international stability is more likely when one hegemonic state dominates the rest, the rationale being that as long as there is one hegemonic power, no state will challenge it because any challenger is likely to lose.

Power-transition theory recognizes that the responsibilities of acting as a hegemon eventually places a strain on a state that then allows other states to mount an effective challenge. A hegemon is the dominant military and economic power among the states in the international system and often has extensive global commitments. It establishes and enforces a set of rules that govern the international system, and it provides a number of global services to its allies (for example, economic and military aid). Often, and especially in the industrial age, the rising costs of armaments, maintaining the global system, and excessive defense spending weaken the hegemon's position and divert resources from investment. The burden of maintaining an empire eventually drags the hegemon down to a level where rival powers can mount a challenge to it.

From this perspective, international relations resembles a game of "king of the hill." Because a challenger is likely to restructure the international order (that is, the existing territorial, political, and economic arrangements), a declining hegemon will not peacefully relinquish its position to a challenger, and a rising challenger is unlikely to back down. The outcome is often a total (or hegemonic) war over succession between the declining hegemon and the emerging challenger, at the point where their relative power is equal.

Long-cycle theory shares many assumptions with the power-transition model. The theory attempts to explain the curiously regular cycles of world leadership and global war, each of which lasts about 100 years. According to George Modelski and William R. Thompson, the theory's primary proponents, every cycle consists of four phases. Out of a global war, a new dominant world power emerges from the struggle for global leadership and maintains its position through naval power. However, the costs associated with global leadership contribute to the world power's decline, giving way to two new stages: **delegitimation** (decline in relative power) and **deconcentration** (challenge by emerging rivals). Deconcentration proceeds until the new contenders for world leadership attempt to push the declining leader out of its hegemonic position. Overall, periods of hegemony are associated with peace, and periods of hegemonic decline are associated with war. Table 12.2 depicts the five most recent cycles of leadership in world history. According to long-cycle theorists, four states—Portugal, the Netherlands, Britain, and currently the United States—have successively played the role of hegemon, with each cycle of dominance ending in a hegemonic war.

As American economic strength declined relative to that of Japan and the European Union, power-transition theory and long-cycle theory would offer a bleak prediction for the stability of the international system. Based on the length of the phases in a cycle, around the year 2000 the United States could expect to enter the deconcentration phase and be challenged by another power (possibly China), with the global-war phase following about thirty years later.

Table 12.2	Long-Cycle Theory: The Struggle For Global Leadership, 1494–1994			
Phase	Hegemon	Years	War	Challenger
Global war		1494–1516	Italian/Indian Ocean Wars	
World power	Portugal	1516–1539		
Delegitimation		1540–1560		
Deconcentration		1560–1580		Spain
Global war		1580–1609	Spanish–Dutch War	
World power	Netherlands	1609–1639		
Delegitimation		1640–1660		
Deconcentration		1660–1688		France
Global war		1688–1713	Wars of Louis XIV	
World power	Britain	1714–1740		
Delegitimation		1740–1763		
Deconcentration		1764–1792		France
Global war		1792–1815	French Revolution and Napoleonic Wars	
World power	Britain	1815–1849		
Delegitimation		1850–1873		
Deconcentration		1874–1914		Germany
Global war		1914–1945	World Wars I and II	
World power	United States	1945–1973		
Delegitimation		1973–		

SOURCE: Adapted from George Modelski, *Long Cycles in World Politics* (Seattle: University of Washington Press, 1987), p. 40

Before accepting this bleak assessment, it is important to note that several factors might mitigate this outcome. First, the impact of nuclear weapons and nuclear deterrence on this cycle is unclear. (Recall that deterrence and balance-of-power theorists attributed the "long peace" of the Cold War era to the stabilizing role of nuclear weapons.) Second, it is uncertain as to what role **regime type** (that is, whether a state is democratic, authoritarian, communist, and so forth) will play in influencing a nation's behavior toward other states. In particular, many theorists contend that democratic states do not fight one another, and with the proliferation of democratic states, one might expect a peaceful transition to the next long cycle.[11] Finally, not all transitions have resulted in a global war. Power-transition theorist A. F. K. Organski writes that although in decline Britain was willing to peacefully accommodate an emerging United States because it had willingly accepted the established Anglo-French international order.[12] The reader is encouraged to draw his or her own conclusions about the utility of power transition and long-cycle theory.

Polarity

A second debate within realist theory centers on the distribution of power and asks whether a bipolar or a multipolar distribution is more stable. The period from 1648 until 1945 is characterized as multipolar (with three or more great powers), while the period from 1945 to 1991 was bipolar (with two superpowers contending for world leadership). One can also distinguish between a tight bipolar system in which there are only two superpowers, and a loose bipolar system in which there are two superpowers and several great powers as well. The period immediately after World War II would be closer to a tight bipolar period, while period from the 1960s to the end of the Cold War represents a loose bipolar structure because rebuilt Europe, Japan, and China emerged as centers of power.

There are major disagreements within the realist school of thought over which form of polarity is most stable. The absence of war during the Cold War bipolar period and the numerous wars during the multipolar period between 1648 and 1945 are used to support the contention that a bipolar distribution is more stable. Political scientist John Mearsheimer has contended that the world will soon miss the stability of the bipolar Cold War era.[13] Mearsheimer and international relations theorist Kenneth Waltz contend that a bipolar system is more stable for several reasons: It is simple, because there are only two large states, and small states cannot influence either's policies; it is more efficient, because the two powers do not have to rely on allies; and it is more competitive, because through constant jockeying, imbalances of power are less likely to occur.

Proponents of multipolarity, on the other hand, contend that the increased number of interaction opportunities in a multipolar system leads to cross-cutting concerns, which in turn moderate behavior and reduce the likelihood of war. In other words, a member of one alliance might have interests in common with members of the opposing coalition, as well as interests conflicting with those of its own coalition. This condition, it is argued, moderates the behavior of states. In a bipolar configuration, on the other hand, if all the members of one coalition have common interests, none of which are shared by the other coalition, antagonism between blocs is reinforced and exacerbated, further fueling rivalry. For instance, if members of different ethnic groups have little contact with one another, living in segregated neighborhoods and attending segregated schools and social clubs, differences between the factions are reinforced. Accordingly, permanent alliances are seen as destabilizing because they reduce the potential for the formation of cross-cutting concerns. In a multipolar system, though, uncommitted states encourage the formation of cross pressures, which moderate conflict.

Moreover, a multipolar system slows arms races and restrains the security dilemma. A multipolar world is not a zero-sum game. If one state initiates an arms buildup, other states do not have to match it equally, because they can balance against it through an alliance. In a multipolar system, a state can "survive as a second-class power as safely or precariously as it did as a first-class one, provided only that it joins in time the appropriate new alliance or alignment."[14] A multipolar distribution will moderate behavior, too: Because today's enemy might be tomorrow's ally, there is little incentive to impose harsh penalties on a defeated state.

In the bipolar-multipolar debate, there is a clear trade-off in the virtues and vices of both systems.[15] In a bipolar world, wars between the superpowers are less likely to occur, but because of the intense competition and antagonism that exist in that system, wars are likely to be more violent and costly when they do occur. In a multipolar system, great-power wars are more likely to occur, but will usually be less violent. In other words, there will be more "brush-fire" wars, but they will be less likely to burn out of control. States will have an incentive to moderate their behavior and not treat defeated states too harshly, because today's enemy might be tomorrow's ally.

One branch of the realist school of thought argues that the existence of nuclear weapons renders the bipolar versus multipolar debate a moot point. Stability is fostered by the potential destructiveness of a nuclear war, not by the number of great powers. Consequently, a change in the distribution of power would probably have little if any independent impact on the stability of the system. Judging the costs of nuclear war to be intolerable, post–World War II decision-makers, particularly U.S. and Soviet leaders, consistently moderated their behavior, according to this theory. If this is true, then the nuclear age presents an ironic implication: Weapons of mass destruction could be the basis for a lasting international peace. Because the use of nuclear weapons would make any war aim irrelevant, rational decision-makers would always choose to behave moderately. On the other hand, in a multipolar world armed with nuclear weapons, events rapidly become more complicated and changes are harder to predict. It is often not clear which country is the main threat, and uncertainty plays a larger role. In a multipolar system, it is possible for several actors to gang up on a victim and thus nullify the possibility of a second-strike capability. It might therefore be impossible for any single state to ensure that it possesses enough nuclear weapons to survive a first strike and still have the capability to retaliate with a massive second strike against several states (see Chapter Eleven). In this way, nuclear weapons may reverse the traditional strengths and weaknesses of bipolar and multipolar systems.[16]

LIBERALISM

Not all systemic-level theorists believe that states exist in a dog-eat-dog environment. As we know, the world is not always consumed by warfare. There have been many instances of interstate cooperation, and relatively few great powers have been destroyed by war. Indeed, if interactions between states were counted, there would be far more cooperation than conflict. The New Era is a period of state creation and rebirth. If nations were unwilling to coordinate their foreign policies, the multiplicity of interactions between states would be far more chaotic and dangerous than has been the case in the past.

The very existence of international cooperation raises the fundamental question, what makes it possible? The school of thought known as liberalism argues that the inherent anarchy and violence of the international system can be overcome through carefully designed institutions for international cooperation.[17] Liberalism accepts many of the assumptions of realism, such as the supremacy of the nation-state and the anarchic character of the international system, yet it contends that cooperation among states is possible. Liberals reject the idea that the world is a zero-sum game in which one state's gain translates into another's loss, as if they were all dividing up a pie. Instead, liberals contend that world politics is a variable-sum game—that is, it is possible for all states to simultaneously and mutually benefit through cooperation because the size of the "pie" is not fixed; it can grow or shrink, depending on how well states are able to cooperate.

The Prisoners' Dilemma

The game of **Prisoners' Dilemma** serves as a metaphor for the difficulty of achieving international cooperation in an anarchical system.[18] As explained in the boxed feature on this subject, the game shows how two players acting to maximize individual interests can bring about an outcome that neither desires. In arms-control negotiations, for example, both sides would become more secure if they could agree not to deploy a destabilizing weapons system. However, as a result of the higher payoff for defection over cooperation, both have an incentive to cheat on the agreement or not to agree in the first place because they might be able to gain a quick or temporary advantage over the other. In the end, though, if each state acts in this manner, both will suffer. Therefore, the Prisoners' Dilemma is a variable-sum game; both states can benefit, or both can suffer losses, or one can gain and the other lose, depending on how the players act.

The years between 1895 and 1914 saw an intense naval arms race between Britain, the established naval power, and Germany, its emerging challenger.[19] In 1912 both states demonstrated an interest in cooling down the naval race, because the domestic economic costs were becoming more difficult to manage. As the Prisoners' Dilemma model would predict, however, both sides attempted to circumvent the potential restrictions placed on arms control in order to gain the upper hand.[20] The worst outcome for either, of course, was having the other side attain a decisive advantage. Each wanted to avoid their worst outcome and feared the other would cheat, so they both cheated. Instead of ending up with a controlled arms race (the second best outcome for both), the naval race continued, resulting in the second worst outcome for both.

Overcoming the Dilemma

The Prisoners' Dilemma illustrates the problems states face when trying to cooperate without any supranational guarantee that agreements will be enforced. Is it possible to overcome the incentive to cheat and instead obtain an outcome mutually beneficial to both states? Liberals argue that it is, if states can find some way to build confidence that others will not cheat. One way to do this is by encouraging states to focus on the long-term benefits of cooperation rather than the short-term gains of cheating. If a game of Prisoners' Dilemma is played for only one round, it is expected that both players will defect. However, if the game is played over and over again with the same players, and if they value future gains from cooperation, it is possible to achieve a mutually beneficial outcome by employing a tit-for-tat strategy. This strategy, as we noted in Chapter Six, begins with cooperation on the first round, no matter what the other party does, and then mimicking that party's moves on subsequent rounds—cooperating when it cooperates, defecting when it defects. Liberals contend that this strategy of reciprocity shows that cooperation is possible, even in an anarchic system.

Another way to overcome the dilemma of cooperation under anarchy is to

The Prisoners' Dilemma Game

Prosecutors believe that two suspects have collaborated in a major crime. Once captured, they are kept in separate rooms for interrogation. If neither prisoner talks to the police, the authorities have only enough circumstantial evidence to convict the prisoners of a minor offense. The district attorney thus offers both suspects a deal: If one prisoner turns state's evidence and testifies against the other, he or she will be released. The other will receive a life sentence.

The choices the prisoners face are modeled in the matrix. If both prisoners cooperate with each other (tell the police nothing), they each achieve their second-best payoff, spending only six months in jail apiece.* This outcome is represented by the upper left (C, C) cell of the matrix. However, if one turns state's witness against the other (that is, defects), the prisoner who squeals will be set free, and thus gain his/her best possible payoff, while the partner in crime gets his/her worst penalty, life imprisonment. If A cooperates and B defects, the outcome is found in the upper right cell; if A defects and B cooperates, the situation in the lower left quadrant applies. If both defect, then there is no trial because both have confessed, and the prosecutor gives them a medium sentence—ten years.

The game predicts that if both prisoners act in their own self-interest, each will defect—in other words, each prisoner will rat on the other. The consequence is that both end up with their second worst outcome, spending ten years in jail, as indicated in the lower right cell. The irony of the game is that if both had cooperated with each other (exercising their right to remain silent), each would spend only six months in jail, clearly a better outcome than life imprisonment. However, individually, both prisoners can do better by defecting or cheating than by cooperating because neither can be sure of the other's actions. The consequence is that both end up with a worse outcome than they would have secured if they had cooperated.

In the Prisoners' Dilemma game, the structure of the situation shapes and influences the moves of each player. The prisoners defect not because they are immoral or dislike their partner, but because the structure of the game offers an incentive for each to defect or cheat; any rational, self-interested person would defect under these circumstances. The Prisoners' Dilemma model is an attempt to explain why sovereign states, each acting in their own self-interest, will often fail to cooperate even though cooperation offers the potential for substantial gains.

| | | **Prisoner B** | |
		Cooperate	Defect
Prisoner A	**Cooperate**	A jailed for 6 months **C, C** B jailed for 6 months	A imprisoned for life **C, D** B goes free
	Defect	A goes free **D, C** B imprisoned for life	A jailed for 10 years **D, D** B jailed for 10 years

*The payoffs of the Prisoners' Dilemma as presented here are based on punishments. In other Prisoners' Dilemma games, payoffs can—and often do—reflect rewards.

Spotlight

Critical Theory, Constructivism, and Post-modernism

Most systemic theories of international relations can trace their origins to theories and methods in the natural sciences, and therefore use rational calculation, statistics, or empirical data derived from observations of state action to propose and test explanations for the behavior of the international system. Recently, however, a paradigm of scholarship derived from philosophical discourse and literary criticism has arisen to question and challenge core concepts of world politics such as sovereignty and security. This school of thought regards world politics as a process of identity formation and discourse on many levels rather than cooperation and conflict between well-defined actors such as states and international organizations. Branches of this evolving paradigm, which is often termed **critical theory** to reflect its intellectual roots, include **postmodernism**, which rejects many of the rationalist and materialist ideas of the modern era, developed in the nineteenth and twentieth centuries, and **constructivism**, which regards knowledge and truth as socially constructed and therefore subjective, rather than objective.

Critical theorists point out that states, borders, nations, organizations, and institutions, and even events such as peace and war, are not physical phenomena that can be measured with precision. Rather, they are social constructs, built upon the norms and values of the powerful groups or dominant cultures that establish and perpetuate them, and as such privilege some groups (typically the political and economic elites of the industrialized world) and discriminate against others (traditional cultures in the developing world, for example). Central to these constructs are definitions of individual and national identity, which draw artificial boundaries between groups to facilitate the pursuit of political, economic, and social objectives, many of which require distinction between a "self" to be strengthened and protected and an "other" whose very otherness represents a potential threat. Critical theorists claim that in order to understand the systems and structure of world politics, one must first expose the cultural foundations of nationality, independence, sovereignty, security, and prosperity, and decode the value-laden language used to describe international interactions.*

As critical theory, constructivism, and post-modernism are relatively new approaches to understanding international affairs, their potential contributions are not yet clear. In some areas, their advantages over traditional systemic theories will be difficult to prove; however one conceptualizes conflict and war, for example, they have been part of world politics (and indeed of human relations in general) for thousands of years, and redefining them as cultural constructs will not make them go away. Additionally, unless the paradigm can identify cause-and-effect relationships which can be tested with real-world data, it is difficult to see how critical theory can provide useful information for policy-makers. Nevertheless, by exposing and critiquing the cultural foundations of the global political and economic system, and offering alternative explanations for conflict and cooperation from formerly underrepresented perspectives of culture, class, race, and gender, constructivism and other branches of critical theory may add a healthy diversity to the study of world politics.

---

*Representative efforts at postmodern analysis of world politics include Nicholas Onuf, *World of Our Making: Rules and Rule in Social Theory and International Relations* (Columbia, SC: University of South Carolina Press, 1991); R. B. J. Walker, *Inside/ Outside: International Relations as Political Theory* (Cambridge: Cambridge University Press, 1993); and Peter J. Katzenstein, ed., *The Culture of National Security: Norms and Identity in World Politics* (New York: Columbia University Press, 1996).

make the world less anarchic. A branch of liberalism known as **neoliberal institutionalism** focuses on how interdependence leads to the institutionalization of cooperation. Chapters Six and Nine have already discussed how international regimes, international organizations, and international law attempt to create some level of order and predictability in the behavior of nation-states by establishing sets of rules and giving states incentives to follow them. Although the record of the United Nations in achieving cooperation in the field of security has been mixed, economic institutions such as the General Agreement on Trade and Tariffs (GATT) and its successor, the World Trade Organization (WTO), have had considerable success in getting states to cooperate in the economic sphere and to reduce trade barriers. Chapter Ten outlines how states have cooperated on environmental issues and on human rights, and Chapter Eleven details successful efforts at arms control and disarmament.

After World War II, a school of thought referred to as functionalism contended that increased frequency of social, economic, and environmental interactions between states will gradually lead to the creation of supranational regulatory institutions.[21] The many difficulties of European integration (see Chapters Seven and Nine) has led liberals to rethink this idea, and a new school of thought known as intergovernmentalism concentrates on the decisions of states to transfer or "pool" sovereignty over some issues from governments to specialized bodies, such as the European Union's regulatory agencies.[22] Though integration has not proceeded as many liberal theorists predicted, the strength and advantages of common markets and other international economic regimes lead many to conclude that supranational organization is truly the wave of the future. As the next century progresses, liberals argue hopefully, the advantages of cooperation and the ability of international regimes to detect and punish cheaters will increase even further. In their view, growing interdependence will make the variable-sum nature of world politics increasingly obvious, and the decreasing ability of states to exercise sovereign control over their economic and social systems will lead them to prefer institutionalized cooperation over continued anarchy.

STRENGTHS AND LIMITS OF SYSTEMIC ANALYSIS

Whether it is being used to explain cooperation or conflict, one of the main strengths of the international systemic level of analysis is that it is relatively parsimonious (that is, brief and uncomplicated). Systemic theory rarely requires extensive studies of a particular country, its political or economic system, or its leaders and decision-makers in order to predict how a state will behave in the international system. Instead, to draw their conclusions, systems theorists need only study about changes in a state's position or ranking in the international system and the existing distribution of power—that is, the nature of the system itself. The predictions of systemic theory are also often compelling and powerful. Structural realists, for example, are able to make broad and accurate generalizations about state behavior, predictions that are borne out in the real world of global politics.

Systemic theories cannot forecast everything, of course. They are often crude, and their time frames are often vague and broad. Balance-of-power theory, for example, cannot predict which states will balance against a preponderant power, let alone when a given state will do so. Likewise, systemic arguments are better at explaining consistency than change; they can explain why different states respond to a similar situation in a similar fashion, but not why states in a similar situation respond in a different manner. Systemic predictions of state behavior are not unbreakable laws of nature, but only generalizations of how the international system creates pressures that drive the behavior of individual states. As the next two sections will discuss, there are numerous subsystemic factors that can impede the "invisible hand" of the international system from determining the actions of large and small powers alike.

Many observers of world politics contend that systemic arguments, despite their weaknesses, still explain a great deal about state behavior. Systemic arguments can tell us how states will respond to changes in the distribution of power. They can help us explain why cooperation is possible in an anarchic system. In a broader sense, they explain the general patterns of interaction among states, even if they cannot explain the specific policies of a particular state. The dean of structural realists, Kenneth Waltz, makes a comparison to the theory of gravitation, which, though it predicts that objects will fall downward, cannot predict the "wayward path of a falling leaf."[23] Similarly, in order to more accurately account for the specific aspects of a state's behavior in the international system, it is necessary to consider the domestic and individual levels of analysis.

THE DOMESTIC LEVEL

The systemic-level theories discussed above describe how external factors shape and constrain a state's behavior in the international system. These theories are "outside-in" arguments because they contend that the primary source of a state's foreign policy is found in shifts in the distribution of power among states, rather than domestic political forces or the personal characteristics of leaders. As compelling as their arguments may be, there is much that systemic theories cannot explain about state behavior in any given situation. To better understand a state's role in the international system, it is also necessary to look at domestic politics and decision-making. This section surveys theories of decision and action in foreign policy of the "inside-out" variety; that is, they describe how domestic political, economic, and social factors affect the choice of options for a state's foreign policy.

Because state institutions affect society and vice versa, it is impossible to fit many domestic influences on foreign policy into neat categories. Indeed, because a state's political institutions implicitly or explicitly reflect its social structure and cultural norms, all of the explanations for foreign-policy decisions discussed in this chapter combine elements of state and society to some extent. Nevertheless, dividing domestic-level approaches to the study of international relations into statist, societal, and combination approaches can make it easier to grasp how both state institutions and social structures can shape a state's role in international affairs. Many of the systemic approaches discussed in the previous sections consider the process by which states determine their international actions as a "black box,"

At a Glance

Approaches to the Domestic Level of Analysis

Statist

Theory: Domestic political institutions shape the form and substance of a state's foreign policy and can enhance or constrain the state's ability to achieve its objectives in the international system. Government agencies with responsibilities for international affairs attempt to define national interests and evaluate, choose, and carry out strategies for pursuing those interests.

Sample arguments: A state's overall form of government (democratic, authoritarian, socialist, and so on) has a major impact on how that state carries out its dealings with others. Particular political institutions and procedures, including elections, specialized bureaucracies, the legislature, the nature of the executive, and the constitutional division of power and responsibility, shape the interests and behavior of states.

Societal

Theory: State institutions are not autonomous and disinterested, but instead reflect the interests of the most powerful forces in society. Foreign policy reflects the objectives of whichever groups or forces in society exert the most influence over policy-making.

Sample arguments: A state's definition of its national interest is determined by the success of domestic interest groups in promoting their particular needs, concerns, and objectives. In pluralist societies, politics is a wide-open game, and those groups expecting to gain from a specific foreign policy will come into conflict with those most likely to lose.

State/Society as an Integrated Whole

Theory: Many influences that operate at the domestic level encompass both government institutions and social/cultural attributes. Because state institutions affect society and vice versa, it is impossible to fit many domestic influences on foreign policy into neat categories.

Sample Arguments: Ideologies often serve as links between state and society. Norms and ideals embedded in political culture have a major impact on a state's foreign policy. Strong political and social norms have prevented democracies from going to war with one another.

with state interests (input) going into one end and state actions (output) coming out the other. Our task in this section is to open up this "black box" and take a look at its inner workings. The first things we should take out and examine are a number of smaller boxes—all securely wrapped in red tape, of course—which contain the government institutions that do the actual work of formulating a state's foreign policy.

STATIST APPROACHES

Domestic political institutions shape the form and substance of a state's foreign policy in a number of ways and can enhance or constrain the state's ability to achieve its objectives in the international system. The "three branches of government" (executive, legislative, and judicial) all have roles to play in international relations just as they do in domestic politics and policy-making. Even in states where the legislature and courts have little independence from a strong executive, bureaucracies and government officials at many levels can influence the making and implementation of foreign-policy decisions. **Statist approaches** to the study of international relations consider how the form and functioning of state institutions influence a state's interests and actions in the international arena.

At the very least, government agencies with statutory responsibilities for international affairs (such as foreign ministries and congressional or parliamentary committees on foreign relations) attempt to define national interests and evaluate, choose, and carry out strategies for pursuing those interests. At the same time, however, many state agencies pursue their own interests and objectives, and the influence of bureaucracies or legislators can lead to the adoption of foreign policies that do not necessarily reflect the interests of the nation as a whole. For example, many Congressional representatives from U.S. states that depend heavily on the automobile industry consistently push for restrictions on imports of autos, which would result in price increases for American consumers. Thus, policymakers can use government institutions to carry out objectives that do not have widespread public support and may actually be detrimental to the interests of the nation as a whole.

Regime Types

One school of thought within the statist approach focuses on the general structure and underlying philosophy of a state's political system. Regime type refers to a state's basic form of government, whether democratic or authoritarian, liberal or Communist. Proponents of the regime-based approach argue that the type of regime governing a state can exert a powerful influence on the nature of that state's foreign policy.

It is often argued that in states governed by authoritarian regimes, where democratic controls on the state are weak or absent, the state has a freer hand to pursue costly or aggressive foreign policies. Because they are not accountable to the electorate, authoritarian governments with aggressive intentions are less constrained than democratic states from initiating international conflict. Mussolini's fascist government was impervious to any **public opinion** that might have discouraged it from seizing Ethiopia in 1935, and Japanese expansion in Manchuria and China in the 1930s was made easier by the lack of any need to mobilize popular support. Similarly, in 1990 Iraq's autocratic ruler Saddam Hussein did not have to seek legislative approval before ordering the invasion of Kuwait, and the Iraqi regime believed it would be difficult if not impossible for the countries of the U.S.–led coalition to gain public support to reverse the invasion. The Iraqi gamble did not pay off, however, as leaders of the coalition states were able to convince their citizens that driving Iraqi forces out of Kuwait would be worth the economic and human cost. The absence of the deterrent effect of public opinion can give dictators additional bargaining power in crisis situations, as it enables them to risk war with greater credibility. Hitler exploited this advantage at the Munich

Conference in 1938, when widespread aversion to war among the British and French populations was a major factor in their governments' decisions to make concessions rather than threaten to fight.

In contrast, individuals and **interest groups** in democratic governments have much more influence on foreign policy, and particularly on trade policy, because government officials are politically accountable to the electorate. Constitutional guarantees of political and civil rights enable groups outside government to voice their perspectives on and interests in foreign policy. In democratic regimes, domestic conflicts of interest are more likely to "spill over" into a state's foreign relations. For example, the access of agricultural interest groups to the foreign policy-making process in the United States, Japan, and the European Union countries has been a continuing source of trade friction, as farmers lobby for protection against imports of farm products. In contrast, farmers in closed authoritarian states such as Syria and Myanmar have little say in the food import or export policies of their respective governments.

Executive-Legislative Relations

The executive (for example, the president, prime minister, or cabinet) is usually at the center of a state's foreign-policy apparatus. Most countries have some sort of legislature or parliament, but these bodies vary enormously in the degree to which they genuinely represent the wishes of the public and act as a check against executive power. Under most one-party dictatorial regimes, parliamentary bodies do little more than "rubber stamp," or legitimatize for foreign-relations purposes, the decisions made by party leaders. Legislative constraints on executive authority, by contrast, are prominent features of domestic political institutions in democratic societies. In most democratic states, legislatures can actively participate in foreign-policy decisions or oversee the government's conduct of foreign affairs. In Germany, Israel, and Italy, for example, leaders of ruling parties or coalitions are severely constrained in their foreign-policy actions by the need to maintain the confidence (support) of their parliament, which if lost could lead to the fall of the government. Israeli governments, in particular, must take into account the various positions of that nation's multiplicity of parties when negotiating peace with neighboring Arab states and when formulating policy on the occupied territories (see Chapter Five).

In the United States, the Constitutional separation of powers allows the Congress to compel or constrain executive action, depending on its collective view of national interests. Perhaps the best-known historical example of this was the Senate's refusal to approve the original version of the League of Nations charter (see Chapter Three). The League was significantly weakened without U.S. membership, and it subsequently failed to resolve the international conflicts that preceded the outbreak of World War II. Similarly, the legislatures of several European and North American states have often been unwilling to endorse the lowering of trade barriers provided for in the WTO and other trade agreements painstakingly negotiated by their countries' leaders and diplomats.

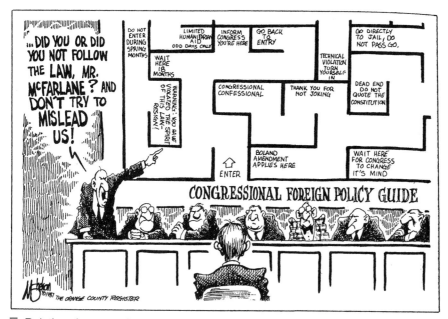

Relations between the executive and legislative branches of the U.S. government can become quite complicated. Former National Security Advisor Robert McFarlane was the object of congressional scrutiny for his role in the Iran-*Contra* affair.

SOURCE: © King Features

Electoral Politics and Foreign Policy

A state's electoral system has a major impact on executive-legislative relations, and this in turn affects the foreign-policy process. In the United States, where both the executive and legislators are elected for fixed terms, the president often schedules foreign-policy initiatives around the electoral calendar. Debates over contentious issues, including free-trade agreements (such as NAFTA) or economic relations with countries where human rights abuses are endemic (such as the former Soviet Union, China, and South Africa under the apartheid regime) are usually scheduled for years when there are no presidential or congressional elections, in the hope that unpopular decisions will be less fresh in the minds of the voters when they go to the polls. In election years, presidents tend to avoid risky foreign-policy initiatives that could be criticized by political challengers or opponents in Congress, and instead travel around the globe to summit meetings, which they hope will generate cheering crowds and lots of photo opportunities making them look like respected world leaders. Of course, events can force a president to make difficult decisions in election years. Richard Nixon's triumphant meetings in Beijing and Moscow in 1972 were one factor in his landslide victory in that year's election, but Jimmy Carter's need (and failure) to handle the Iranian hostage crisis successfully in 1979–1980 dealt a crippling blow to his campaign in 1980.

In most parliamentary systems, by contrast, legislators do not serve for fixed terms, though the government must hold elections within a specified time limit. On the one hand, this enables the party in power to call elections at politically opportune moments in order to make the most of a major foreign-policy triumph or military success. When Margaret Thatcher called elections shortly after Britain's victory in the Falkland Islands War in 1982, her party won handily, but George Bush was unable to capitalize on the U.S.–led coalition's victory in the Gulf War in 1991, because by the time of the 1992 presidential election, domestic economic problems had become the electorate's primary concern. On the other hand, parliamentary governments can be brought down at any time because of a vote of no confidence. This can make it very difficult for prime ministers who govern with small majorities or in a coalition government to stay in power while pursuing controversial foreign policies. During the delicate negotiations between Israel and the PLO in 1993–1994, Israeli Prime Minister Yitzhak Rabin often had to tread carefully to avoid alienating any of his government's coalition partners, who might have defected to the opposition if they had believed the outcome of the talks would harm their values or constituencies.

Political Parties

Political parties often make a major difference in a state's foreign policy through the electoral process. In Israel, the Labor party is more prepared to relinquish at least a part of the occupied territories; the Likud party much less so. In Britain, the Conservative party has been more cautious than the Labour party in integrating Britain's economy into the EU. In Russia, reformist parties argue for the development of trade and political links with Europe and the United States, while nationalist parties contend that Moscow must be prepared to use military and political muscle to protect the rights of Russians living in the former republics of the USSR even if the United States and Europe object.

Often, interest groups seek influence across the political spectrum so they can win no matter who gets elected, which accounts in part for the oft-noted similarities between supposedly competing parties in democracies. In the United States, for example, both Democrats and Republicans support continued defense spending—as long as the money continues to be spent in their districts. (Efforts to reduce U.S. defense spending after the Cold War by closing domestic military bases became very contentious, as even legislators who had consistently voted to cut overall defense budgets attempted to save bases in their own districts and close bases in others, and a special process that presented rounds of closures in a "take it or leave it" package had to be adopted.) Both parties also get massive campaign contributions from agricultural and manufacturing interests. Other interest groups form long-term alliances with specific parties. Most labor unions supply strong support to the Democrats, while fundamentalist Christians, who oppose foreign-aid programs that fund abortions, tend to back the Republicans. The major parties in Germany and France have consistently supported full integration into the EU even though public opinion on the subject has often been divided.

Moreover, parties may themselves represent a national consensus on particular is-sues or they may reflect a national style, such as the Japanese reliance on leading bureaucrats no matter who is in power or the vaunted influence of the British civil service.

Parties also reflect the institutional characteristics of a state's political system. In multiparty states such as Israel and Russia, the need to maintain a governing coalition of parties complicates the process of making foreign policy. In Israel's case, this has led to dramatic shifts in the government's approach to the peace pro-cess, particularly when a Likud-led government must keep the allegiance of reli-gious parties in order to hold its coalition together. By contrast, in states where one party has dominated for an extended period (as the Liberal Democratic party did in Japan from the 1950s to the early 1990s), a consistent foreign-policy line is easier to achieve—but the lack of partisan debate over foreign-policy issues strengthens the power of government bureaucrats.

Bureaucracies

This last consideration reminds us that in addition to elected executives and legis-lators, unelected bureaucrats can have great influence on a state's foreign policy— too great, many would argue. Bureaucratic organizations such as the U.S. State Department and National Security Agency can facilitate the evaluation of foreign-policy options by acting as information processors for decision-makers. Ideally, these agencies can channel timely, unbiased information enabling calculations of costs and benefits of various policy options. Unfortunately, many studies of bu-reaucratic organizations suggest that the way various departments are organized and interrelated is not always conducive to the making of policy decisions that maximize a nation's goals. When confronted with a foreign-policy problem, large organizations tend to follow a set of decision-making guidelines and make routine recommendations without calculating the advantages and drawbacks of all avail-able options. This often makes organizational behavior appear rigid, inflexible, and unimaginative, qualities that rarely contribute to the creative resolution of international conflicts.

A related view of bureaucratic influence argues that decision-making outcomes represent neither a rational value-maximizing calculation of the state's interest nor the simple output of an organizational routine. This model contends that foreign policy results from political competition among government agencies.[24] According to this argument, a bureaucrat's policy stance will reflect his or her or-ganizational affiliation. Organizational interests shape and constrain an official's preferences and range of policy recommendations. An old Washington proverb is, "Where you stand [on an issue] depends on where you sit [within the federal bureaucracy]."

It is easy to observe how this plays out in real life. Military organizations de-velop defense plans, diplomatic staffs try to manage political relations between countries, intelligence agencies create information-gathering networks, and eco-nomic departments make trade and investment recommendations. In the United

Spotlight

Organizational Process in 1914

The rigid mobilization plans that helped draw the European powers into war in 1914 (see Chapter Three) are tragic examples of bureaucratic rigidity and inertia. The German Schlieffen Plan, in particular, called for an attack on France through Belgium in order to capture the strategic railroad juncture at Liege. After rapidly defeating France, the German army would attack Russia. The basis of this plan was that it would take Russia six weeks to fully mobilize. As a consequence, in order to ensure that Germany did not fight a two-front war (Russia and France were allies), Germany would have to defeat France during this six-week window.

The commitment of the German military bureaucracy to the Schlieffen Plan was so steadfast that the General Staff offered the kaiser the stark choice between its immediate implementation and no action at all. At the same time, Tsar Nicholas of Russia did not realize that partial mobilization of his troops could not be carried out in response to Austria-Hungary's ultimatum to Serbia, as the Russian army had plans only for full mobilization. When the tsar ordered partial mobilization, he was informed mobilization would have to be total,

thereby triggering a set of **organizational processes** that had disastrous consequences. The German General Staff believed that once Russia mobilized, Germany would have to mobilize immediately in order to carry out its plan to avoid the dreaded two-front war.

Because European armies of the period believed that the first side to initiate an effective large-scale offensive operation would win the war, the armies of the great powers would not respond to mobilization without attacking. The necessity of a response to Russia's mobilization prompted Germany to implement its offensive plan against France and Belgium, which drew Britain into the conflict in order to back up its guarantee of Belgian neutrality and independence. Thus, when the crisis came to a head in July 1914, organizational constraints did not allow for intermediate options; mobilization meant war.*

---

* For more on the influence of offensive doctrine on the outbreak of World War I, see Stephen Van Evera, "The Cult of the Offensive and the Origins of the First World War," *International Security* 9, no. 1 (Summer 1984), pp. 58–107.

States, managing U.S.–Japanese economic relations, for example, requires involvement of, at a minimum, the Department of State, the Department of Commerce, and the Office of the U.S. Trade Representative, and sometimes the Departments of the Treasury, Labor, and Agriculture as well. Bureaucrats in these different agencies often view trans-Pacific relations from different perspectives; the Defense Department worries that trade friction could damage the U.S.–Japanese strategic alliance, while the Labor Department fears that imports of Japanese products will destroy American jobs.[25] On the other side of the Pacific, bureaucrats from the Japanese Ministry of International Trade and Industry and the Ministry of Finance are the key players in trade negotiations, and reaching trade agreements without their support is effectively impossible.

One danger of **bureaucratic politics** is that such policies sometimes send mixed and contradictory messages to other states. In 1989 the U.S. Department of Agriculture extended credits to Iraq for the purchase of U.S. agricultural exports. The Bush administration approved these credits, which allowed Iraq to use other funds to purchase weapons prior to its 1990 invasion of Kuwait. A major controversy broke out in 1992 when it was revealed that the credits were approved even after the CIA had reported that Iraq had organized a secret network to buy components for ballistic missiles and nuclear, chemical, and biological weapons. Congressional critics of the Bush administration charged that one U.S. government agency was thereby indirectly financing Iraqi aggression at the same time that other agencies were trying to deter it. The White House contended that it was trying to use U.S. aid to persuade Iraq to pursue less aggressive policies. This explanation could not hide the contradictory results of the "pulling and hauling" among government agencies.[26]

The Cuban Missile Crisis (discussed in Chapter Four) is often used as an example of how government department act to further their own interests rather than national objectives. Beginning in 1961, Kennedy had ordered U.S. missiles to be removed from Turkey several times, but because the Turkish government wanted them to stay, various U.S. government agencies delayed removal of the missiles, so they were still in Turkey at the time of the crisis. Because Khrushchev had demanded the removal of the missiles from Turkey in return for withdrawing Soviet missiles from Cuba, many felt that a Soviet strike against the Turkey-based missiles would be seen as legitimate retaliation for any U.S. strike against the Cuban-based rockets. The continued presence of U.S. missiles in Turkey in spite of his repeated orders to remove them caused Kennedy to lose his temper at one point in the crisis: "Get those frigging missiles off the board!" he reportedly shouted (though his original expletive was probably different).[27]

SOCIETAL APPROACHES

Although the statist approach treats the state as the dominant institution in the decision-making process, the **societal approach** suggests that foreign policy reflects the objectives of whichever groups or forces in society exert the most influence over policy-making. In pluralist societies, politics is a wide-open game, and those groups expecting to gain from a specific foreign policy will come into conflict with those most likely to lose. In this view, state institutions are not autonomous and disinterested, but instead reflect the interests of the most powerful forces in society. Public opinion also reflects and is influenced by policy debates and controversies involving the media, policy elites, government officials, and major interest groups. Throughout the policy-making process, a state's **political culture** can shape policy by defining the values and goals that governments are expected to pursue and policy-makers are expected to uphold.

Interest Groups

Interest groups in the largest sense of the word include business groups, military organizations, veterans groups, environmental lobbies, labor unions, agricultural interests, issue-specific groups, groups organized around ethnic interests, and the media. Groups in society may be concerned with foreign affairs directly, or their involvement in foreign policy may originate in their domestic economic or political interests.

Examples of interest groups in the United States that are directly interested in world politics include the Arms Control Association and the American Israel Public Affairs Committee (AIPAC). AIPAC, for example, supports efforts to increase U.S. aid to meet Israel's economic and security needs and presents arguments for the compatibility of American and Israeli interests. To achieve these ends, it organizes letter-writing campaigns, encourages its members to support candidates for Congress and the presidency who are believed to be sympathetic to Israel, and lobbies Congress to support its preferred policies. Sometimes AIPAC gets its way, while other times Arab-American lobbies are more successful. Similarly, many African-American groups take great interest in U.S. policy toward South Africa, and called for economic sanctions against that state's regime of racial separatism (Apartheid) until the system was dismantled after political reforms and multiracial elections in 1994. Greek-American groups frequently push for limitations on U.S. aid and strategic ties to Turkey, and Americans with ethnic origins in Eastern Europe lobbied for the expansion of NATO to include Poland, the Czech Republic, and Hungary in 1996–1998.

Other interest groups become involved in international politics for economic reasons. Defense firms in many countries seek to promote the sales of their equipment to foreign governments. These products are often exported to nations that then use the weapons in a way that threatens the security of the defense contractor's home nation; Western exports to Iraq before the Gulf War are a recent example. The motives of textile manufactures are also economic. They often try to restrict imports of foreign-made garments even when their policies lead to higher prices for consumers. Labor unions typically oppose free trade, fearing that it could result in the "export of jobs." Many labor groups in the United States and Canada opposed NAFTA and GATT in the 1990s for this reason (see Chapter Seven). Similarly, farmers' lobbies in the United States, the EU, and Japan consistently pressured governments to slap tariffs on agricultural products coming into their countries. Computer and software firms, aerospace manufacturers, and other high-tech companies have become powerful players in the politics of international trade in the New Era. Many of these companies, striving to gain market access in China, oppose efforts to impose trade and other sanctions intended to persuade Beijing to improve its policies on labor and human rights.

In most industrialized states, environmental interest groups are becoming increasingly active in foreign policy-making. With the Green party in the vanguard, Germany initiated EU legislation to reduce vehicle and industrial plant emissions during the 1980s and also sought international restrictions on carbon dioxide emissions at the 1992 UN Conference on Environment and Development. Environmental groups like the Sierra Club in the United States opposed NAFTA on environmental grounds, and supported U.S. ratification of treaties on the law of the sea and on limiting greenhouse gases (see Chapter Ten).

Although the impact of interest groups on foreign policy in open societies is undeniable, this does not necessarily mean that the national interest can be defined as the outcome of political competition between specific interests. For one thing, it is difficult to separate the national interest, however defined, from the interests of individual citizens and social groups, or even to identify factors constituting individual, group, and national interests. For example, while all Americans benefit from lower automobile prices, competition from foreign automakers may force U.S. companies to close plants and lay off workers, who would not be able to benefit from lower new car prices if unemployed. Higher unemployment would be detrimental to the U.S. economy, but higher automobile prices would harm U.S. consumers. And consider the complexities of energy policy. Imports of oil from the Middle East help keep U.S. gasoline prices down, but dependence on foreign oil may oblige the United States to intervene militarily to protect oil-exporting nations, despite their undemocratic governments. Furthermore, the availability of cheap imported oil reduces the incentive to develop alternative energy sources, which would pollute the environment less. The varied and conflicting interests involved in foreign policy can be as difficult to untangle as the complex international conflicts that characterize the New Era.

The Military-Industrial Complex

The relationship between private interests and public institutions is particularly strong in the defense sector, and as a result many observers have questioned what they consider to be an excessive level of influence exercised by defense industries and their bureaucratic allies. Military organizations have close working relationships with the industries that produce military hardware in most nations, but charges that these relationships result in undue influence over foreign and defense policy arise most frequently in the liberal democracies, especially Britain and the United States. According to critics, the danger is that the military-industrial complex will support an active and aggressive military posture, because both the military and industry will benefit. In some instances, it has even been blamed for inciting warfare.[28]

An early critic of the military-industrial relationship was the mid-nineteenth-century British statesman Richard Cobden. In his 1861 book, *Three Panics, An Historical Episode,* Cobden noted that each of the British "invasion scares" of the preceding twenty years had been provoked by sensational stories in newspapers and that they mysteriously subsided after the government allocated generous shares of the national budget to the Royal Navy. This pattern continued throughout the nineteenth century, and by 1900, many Britons were concerned with the power exerted by the nation's well-established defense industries and the nature of their relationship with the national government. Meanwhile, across the Atlantic, the military-industrial complex was coming under increasing criticism, particularly after U.S. entry into World War I led to huge profits for manufacturers of war matériel. The American public remained focused on the arms industry in the interwar period, and advocates of disarmament inveighed against an international conspiracy of "merchants of death." War profiteers were satirized in American culture as well, and military industrialists who enjoyed rich rewards while soldiers died on the battlefields were the inspiration for Daddy Warbucks, the archetypal "fat cat" character in the popular comic strip *Little Orphan Annie*.

The role of the defense sector in federal budgets and the U.S. economy burgeoned enormously after the Korean War. By 1960 even President Dwight Eisenhower, who had been the supreme commander of Allied Forces in the European theater during World War II, was concerned at the growth of military spending. Responding to Democratic charges that the United States was not spending enough on conventional armed forces and had allowed a strategic missile gap to occur, Eisenhower criticized large military expenditures as "just negative stuff adding nothing to the earning capability of the country" and denounced the "almost hysterical fear among some elements of the country" that prevented reductions in the defense budget.[29] In his farewell address, Eisenhower warned against "the acquisition of unwarranted influence, whether sought or unsought, by the military-industrial complex."

The Cold War continued to drive U.S. defense budgets upward, and America's defense industries continued to grow. By 1980, according to one author's estimates, the jobs of 18 million people in the armed forces, government, and industry depended on the level of defense spending for that year. During the Vietnam War, defense spending accounted for as much as 40 percent of annual federal spending, and the figure remained at 20 percent or more from 1970 to 1990.[30] By 1998, the share of defense spending in the federal budget had declined to 15 percent.

The end of the Cold War has called the continued influence of the military-industrial complex into question. First, whatever political power arms manufacturers had was not enough to block U.S.–Soviet agreements on arms limitation. Second, now that the Soviet-American competition for global political influence has given way to the economic, political, and social challenges of the New Era, the share of human and material resources solely devoted to defense purposes in the West is declining. Nevertheless, defense-related industries and their corresponding government organizations are likely to continue to be important factors in the formulation of foreign policy. The issues of whether and how to keep defense production lines running, preserve skills and technology that will be needed to meet security challenges, or undertake expensive "defense conversion" programs to shift workers and factories from military to civilian production remain important in both the United States and Russia. In the New Era, while they will certainly continue to lobby policy-makers, the influence that defense industry groups will be able to exercise remains uncertain.

Public Opinion

Despite the influence that industrial, labor, or environmental lobbies can exert on foreign policy, participation in politics and policy-making is not limited to powerful special interests, especially in democratic states. Since the nineteenth century, public opinion has been an important part of the foreign-policy process in advanced industrial states, and even more so since the extension of the franchise to larger proportions of the population.

Perhaps the most obvious way in which the public affects a democratic state's foreign policy is through the election of policy-makers, including the chief executive. The anxieties of many Israelis regarding terrorism and the creation of a Palestinian state contributed to the victory of the Likud party, led by Binyamin Netanyahu, in the Israeli elections of 1996. Politicians in democracies take great pains to stay apprised of public opinion and frequently commission and consult polls on foreign-policy issues. (President Lyndon Johnson was known to carry the results of public opinion polls in his pajama pockets.) Although politicians do not necessarily allow public opinion to dictate their policies, they certainly consider it before selecting a particular policy from among a menu of options. Generally, democratic leaders tend to eliminate the options least palatable to the voting public. Thus, public opinion often constrains the set of options open to selection.[31]

Another way in which the electorate can participate in formulating foreign policy is through referenda, which governments may call to obtain a popular mandate for major changes in policy or constitutional structure. The initial rejection of the Maastricht treaty on closer unification within the European Union by Danish voters in 1992, and that treaty's narrow approval in France later that year, led EU member states to reconsider the pace and depth of European union. Many European governments had regarded closer unification as a foregone conclusion until the general public voiced its concerns over the issue. Similarly, in 1994, the electorates of Sweden and Finland voted to join the EU, but a referendum in Norway rejected EU membership. Continued concerns over a proposed economic and monetary union (EMU), which would establish a common currency for all EU members, led Britain's new Labor government to announce in 1997 that British membership in EMU would require a referendum. (See Chapter Seven for more on EMU.)

In most countries, the media (especially television) also play a progressively critical role in mobilizing public opinion on a host of key issues. People are influenced by the pictures they see. The British and Israeli publics, for example, have been deeply influenced by news reports of IRA, Palestinian, or Islamic fundamentalist terrorism. It was difficult for Western governments—especially the Bush administration—to resume business as usual with China after the televised massacre at Tiananmen Square in 1989. The United Nations might never have intervened in Somalia in 1992 except for the pictures of starving men, women, and children on international television. Yet people can also become accustomed to violence, as suggested in the 1990s by the delayed Western response to the crises in Bosnia and Haiti, and by inaction in the face of violent chaos in Liberia and Sierra Leone and genocide in Rwanda. Despite these cases, certainly the media today frames public debates and discussions of foreign policy in distant lands that might otherwise be barely recognized, even by elite opinion.

LINKS BETWEEN STATE AND SOCIETY

Other domestic influences on foreign policy operate both within government institutions and in the broader context of society as a whole. Ideology and political culture affect how both the state and society are organized to interact with the outside world. By the same token, the prevalence of peace among democratic states seems related to both the political systems and cultural traditions of democratic societies.

Ideology

Ideology refers to the **belief systems** on which states and groups within states base their actions—in other words, the grand ideals that provide a system of values for a state's institutions and foreign policy-making process. Ideological influence on foreign policy can have deep roots. In England and the United States, the origins of democracy and individual liberty in political institutions can be traced from the Magna Carta (a written agreement between King John and his feudal barons signed in 1215) to the American Declaration of Independence and the U.S. Constitution, and right down to the present. Consequently, these nations often frame their foreign policy (forthrightly or otherwise) in an ideological context, such as the need to protect democracy throughout the world. As we saw in Chapter Two, similar ideals grounded in the eighteenth-century Enlightenment inspired the French Revolution in 1789, which smashed the monarchical *ancien regime;* and during the subsequent Napoleonic Wars, French arms and diplomacy spread the new concepts of liberalism, egalitarianism, and nationalism throughout Europe. Chapter Three relates how, after the Bolshevik Revolution of 1917, the Soviet Union sought to foment Communist revolutions in the belief that overthrowing the capitalist system would lead to world peace and social justice.

As we discussed in Chapter Four, Soviet and American foreign policy took an especially strong ideological cast during the Cold War. Some argue that post–World War II American foreign policy represented an attempt to extend to the rest of the world the ideas of John Locke (who argued that people have a natural right to own and use property for individual enrichment) and Adam Smith (who contended that the free market is the most efficient, and therefore the most just, system for distributing rewards). In order to do so, the United States had to prevent the encroachment of the ideas of Marx and Lenin. To this end the United States used its political, economic, and military strength to stop Communist movements from taking over Western Europe and to assist other countries in strengthening their domestic economies. The United States acted even when this effort meant erecting trade barriers against American products, which ran counter to the more open trade system sought by the GATT accords.

Soviet postwar foreign policy, on the other hand, was ostensibly driven by the belief that a powerful Soviet Union was required to protect the achievements of socialism and hasten the collapse of the exploitative capitalist system. Accordingly, this led the USSR to install compliant Communist regimes in Eastern Europe, form the Warsaw Pact, build up its industrial and military infrastructure, and support "wars of national liberation" in Cuba, Vietnam, Angola, Nicaragua, and elsewhere. Regardless of the degree to which Soviet and American policies were influenced by their respective ideologies, their ideological conflict certainly reinforced mutual perceptions of threat, served their security interests, and intensified the global political competition during the Cold War.[32]

In another context, the theocracy established after the Iranian revolution of 1979 represented a conscious repudiation of Western Enlightenment ideology. The 1979 revolution ushered in a fundamentalist Islamic theocracy in which political and religious law were to be merged into one. In terms of foreign policy, Iran's new government led by religious mullahs justified violence when it declared that the United States was the "Great Satan," intent on destroying Islam and denying basic human rights to the people of developing nations. (The officially atheistic USSR was awarded the title of "Little Satan" as a second prize.) Therefore, terrorism against Americans was not only justified but also would ensure a martyr's place in heaven. This ideology is practiced through Iranian support of terrorist organizations throughout the Middle East and the backing of radical Islamic parties in Central Asia and North Africa. Thus, ideologies developed within states or adapted from ideas originating elsewhere often become the source of—or at least justification for—actions a particular regime pursues in its foreign policy.

Political Culture

Political culture fuses a nation's historical traditions to its cultural institutions and values to form a national style of politics and policy-making. One aspect of a nation's culture that can shape its foreign policy is its cultural vision of its proper role in the world. In the fifteenth and sixteenth centuries, for example, Spain viewed itself as champion and defender of the Roman Catholic Church. In response, Spain sent out explorers and conquistadors, including Columbus, Cortés, and Pizarro, in an effort not only to open new trade routes and settle new territory, but also to win souls for the Church and thereby gain glory for the Spanish Crown. Three centuries later, England tried to bring liberal democratic ideals to the indigenous populations of present-day Africa and Asia in fulfillment of what English author Rudyard Kipling (born in British India) called "the white man's burden." France, too, established colonies and imposed its language and form of government on Africans and Asians as part of carrying out *la mission civilistrice*— the "civilizing mission."

Other states' foreign policies have been similarly affected by historical and cultural traditions. Islamic fundamentalism has inspired efforts (heroic or fanatical, depending on one's point of view) to rid the Middle East of American influence, drive Soviet forces out of Afghanistan, and combat or destroy the state of Israel. To consider another example, some observers have argued that Japanese traditions of deference to authority, avoidance of direct confrontation, and preoccupation with achieving group consensus have had an impact on Tokyo's recent foreign policy, which has been relatively unassertive despite Japan's great economic strength.

Many scholars perceive the American style of foreign policy as characterized by a conflict between a crusading idealism to change the world in America's image and an isolationist impulse to disengage from international politics altogether.[33] The interventionist spirit may be traced to the Puritan ideals of many

English settlers in colonial America and to the nineteenth-century concept of America's "manifest destiny" to dominate North America and transform the world for the better:

> [The American claim] is by the right of manifest destiny to overspread and to possess the whole of the Continent which Providence has given us for the development of the great experiment of liberty and federative self government entrusted to us.[34]

Interestingly, one author finds that America's "colossal liberal absolutism . . . is inspired either to withdraw from 'alien' things or to transform them: it cannot live in comfort constantly by their side."[35] Another author suggests that the American style of foreign relations exhibits the irresolvable dualistic tendency to speak two languages simultaneously: one of power and the other of community and harmony. "Only a symbolic eagle can hold both the arrows and the olive branch easily at the same time . . . the impulse of violence and the thrust toward harmony are both escapes from the unbearable reality of inevitable conflict."[36] Over the years, the tension between trying to transform international relations into a harmonious whole through intervention and then retreating into isolationism when other countries do not want to conform to the U.S. vision has made American foreign policy appear inconsistent, if not schizophrenic.

Peace among Democracies

The idea that it is more difficult for a state to engage in war when its leaders are accountable to the public forms the basis of a theory with far-reaching implications. In his essay *Perpetual Peace,* the eighteenth-century philosopher Immanuel Kant wrote that democracies are much less likely than other types of states to go to war with each other. According to Kant, "If the consent of the citizens is required to decide whether or not war is to be declared, it is very natural that they will have great hesitation in embarking on so dangerous an enterprise."[37]

Since the time of Kant's writing, democracies have participated in war about as often as authoritarian states, but they have gone to war against one another only very rarely (or never, some argue). Freely elected high-level policy-makers are accountable to society and constrained by a public that demands justification for war; when both states in a conflict are democratic, political constraints are doubled, making war even less likely.

Contemporary theorists have concluded that the power of independent domestic interest groups and political institutions contributes only one part of what restrains democracies from rushing headlong into battle. **Normative influences** constitute the other source of restraint. Democratic polities operate under norms of peaceful conflict resolution, through debate, elections, and judicial judgments. Thus, all democratic states share a common democratic political culture, and all expect to apply its method of resolving conflict at home to resolving international disputes amicably, without recourse to war. Democracies therefore try to externalize their norms of political competition, compromise, and peaceful transfer of

Gender and International Relations

A cliché once held that "It's a man's world"; in the words of pioneering feminist Simone de Beauvior, "Representation of the world, like the world itself, is the work of men; they describe it from their own point of view, which they confuse with absolute truth." * In recent decades, feminist scholars have challenged traditional concepts of international relations, contending that gender-biased theories and analysis offer an incomplete and distorted picture of world politics. They argue that because, until very recently, the overwhelming majority of actors in international conflict, politics, and economics have been men, the study of world affairs has been biased toward the "high politics" of war, adversarial bargaining, and realpolitik, which grow out of men's experience. Conversely, roles and concerns traditionally ascribed to women, such as health, education, child care, and home and community economics, have been considered irrelevant to the workings of the international system. As a result, both the theory and practice of international relations have overemphasized security, power, hierarchy, and domination, in keeping with the privileged status of values that society ascribes to men and defines as primarily male pursuits.

Feminist theorists of international relations seek to change all this. In the 1990s, scholars such as Judith Ann Tickner, Anne Sisson Runyan, Rebecca Grant, and Kathleen Newland began to develop an approach to world politics that takes the perspectives, values, and concerns of women explicitly into consideration.† In an effort to balance or overcome traditional gender biases in the study of international relations, their studies show how focusing on the experiences of women can offer insights into the needs of citizens and behavior of states, particularly in the areas of health, population, and the environ-

ment. Feminist perspectives can particularly deepen our knowledge of the world economy, as women are typically affected first and most strongly in times of economic hardship. Feminist scholars also seek to challenge or redefine core concepts of international relations such as security, power, and sovereignty, claiming that these ideas are based in values traditionally associated with masculinity and constructed to exclude women from full participation in world politics. For example, many feminist critics contend that realist theories, which conclude that states must be self-reliant and seek military power to preserve their security, are generalizations from male values and experience that do not reflect the perceptions and concerns of women.

As more women take leading roles in governments, economic enterprises, and international institutions, the systems and structures of world politics may take on more gender-inclusive forms. However, the extent to which women will change world politics, or will be changed by it, is not yet clear, as female policy-makers are socialized into the same institutions and confront the same problems as their male colleagues. In any event, by analyzing world events through a gender-sensitive lens, feminist scholars offer an alternative view of the world that can bring the needs and experiences that lead to cooperation and conflict into sharper focus.

---

* Simone de Beauvior, *The Second Sex* (New York: Knopf, 1953) p. 161.
† To begin exploring these perspectives, see Rebecca Grant and Kathleen Newland, *Gender and International Relations* (Bloomington, IN: Indiana University Press, 1991); Judith Ann Tickner, *Gender in International Relations: Feminist Perspectives on Achieving Global Security* (New York: Columbia University Press, 1993); and V. Spike Peterson and Anne Sisson Runyan, *Global Gender Issues* (Boulder, CO: Westview, 1993).

power. When two democracies confront each other, the argument goes, they are able to draw upon democratic norms to prevent international conflicts from escalating into war.[38]

A number of major studies contend that democracies do not go to war against one another.[39] Overall, though, there is no clear consensus that democratic countries are inherently more peace-loving than authoritarian or other types of states.[40] Regardless, history has repeatedly demonstrated that democracies are willing to engage in wars with nondemocratic states. One consequence of the need to garner public support for military action is that leaders of democratic states frequently attempt to justify wars by "overselling" them, making it difficult to stop short of complete victory. Thus, although it appears that democracies are at peace with one another, it is difficult to conclude confidently that democratic regimes are inherently more peaceful.

Norms of political behavior and democracy take time to develop institutional and cultural roots, and the world may experience a period of violent conflict before a lasting peace among democratic states emerges. It is still too early to tell, but the argument that democracies do not go to war with one another may not hold for fledgling democracies without a democratic tradition within their societies. If the argument does hold true for even these newly democratic states, then the recent democratization of many states in Eastern Europe, the former Soviet Union, Latin America, and Africa bodes well for international stability.

Conclusions from the Domestic Level

This section has examined the ways in which the unique attributes of states and societies can influence how states behave in the international system. The previous section on the systemic level of analysis, on the other hand, focused on how states were alike in their power, security, and prosperity, and outlined how these similarities lead states to act in similar ways. The question that arises is, which are more important, the similarities or the differences? Are the actions of states in the international system affected more by the distribution of capabilities among them or by the character of their individual political, economic, and social systems? And if countries' unique attributes are the driving forces behind their foreign policies, which of the many attributes exert the greatest influence?

Perhaps the best way to answer this question is by drawing an analogy between states and persons. The physiological structure of every human being is essentially similar, and humans share many common needs, wants, desires, and fears. At the same time, each individual is unique in many important respects, as each has a unique combination of special concerns, hopes, and dreams. The similarities among people lead to common patterns of behavior (any person who is hungry will attempt to get food), but differences in capabilities, resources, values, and attitudes prompt individuals to pursue commonly held goals in distinctive ways (a variety of factors will determine whether a hungry person goes to a restaurant or goes out hunting). Thus, although knowledge of human behavior makes it possible to offer statistical predictions of what people are likely to do in a given situation, the factors that cause a person to act in a specific manner in a specific situation may be difficult, if not impossible, to ascertain.

The study of world politics involves many controversies, and the relative impact of the international system and domestic concerns is one unlikely to be resolved soon. Nevertheless, just as the inability to predict the actions of individuals with absolute certainty does not make the study of human behavior a useless enterprise, the existence of contending theories on why states act as they do does not mean that the study of international relations is pointless. Improving our knowledge of how domestic-level influences shape foreign policy can help governments avoid many past mistakes—or at least leave them free to make new mistakes.

The parallels drawn here between international relations and human behavior remind us that although the language of global politics often refers to abstract entities—states, regimes, forces, and so forth—political decisions are always made and carried out by individuals. With this in mind, the next sections will consider how individual leaders can affect foreign policy and world politics in the New Era.

THE INDIVIDUAL LEVEL

Theories that approach international politics from the systemic and domestic levels of analysis hold that a decision-maker's foreign-policy choices are shaped either by the nature of the international system or by forces in state and society. Proponents of these approaches do not claim that their theories can predict the decisions that will be made, but they do contend that factors operating over leaders' heads, behind their backs, or under their feet—the balance of power and anarchic nature of the international system for systemic-level theorists, and the nation's political institutions and social forces for domestic-level theorists—create the context for decisions on foreign policy and determine the range of options available to policy-makers. Even the most ardent systemic or domestic theorist will concede, of course, that individuals have at least some influence on the foreign policy ultimately chosen. But just how important is the individual? This is an issue fervently debated by analysts of international politics. The final sections of this chapter will consider how the characteristics and roles of individual leaders can be of critical importance in shaping their nations' course in world affairs and interactions with other states.

Personal Experience and Leadership Style

Very often, in spite of all the impact of political systems and the international balance of power, critical foreign-policy decisions must be made by a single individual. Though bureaucracies and legislatures might try to "pass the buck" on difficult issues, a sign on the desk of President Harry Truman reminded everyone that "the buck stops here." This section will examine the leadership style of several important individuals, their strengths and weaknesses, their skills and flaws.

Leadership style consists of the individual's considerations of ends (for example, one's desired role in the foreign policy-making process; one's country's role in global affairs) and means (for example, the methods one uses to define and play out those roles; one's approach and organization—whether one delegates authority or not). To illustrate how experiences affect beliefs and decisions, the following pages will compare and contrast leaders from Western, Communist, and Third World societies. What should become apparent is that even within the same political system, leadership style will vary widely across individuals, often with important policy implications. This approach to ends and means is combined with the particular idiosyncratic background and personal traits an individual brings to specific decisions to produce a powerful influence over the fate of a particular nation and often over other states with which it interacts.[41]

Two American Presidents

Harry Truman, Pragmatist   Harry S. Truman became president upon the death of Franklin Delano Roosevelt in 1945, with no experience in foreign affairs. As vice president, he had been kept "out of the loop" on many strategic decisions during World War II; indeed, he was told about the existence of the atomic bomb only after being sworn in as president. However, he had great experience in hardball politics and logrolling in Congress and his home state of Missouri, where he built a reputation for integrity and incorruptibility. Consequently, Truman formed his ideas about international relations through his experience in domestic politics. For instance, because Soviet Premier Joseph Stalin reminded him of Boss Thomas Pendergast, his mentor in Missouri Democratic Party politics, Truman initially believed that, like the Missouri machine politician, the Russian dictator could be trusted to keep a deal despite his anti-Western ideological rhetoric.[42] This belief led to bitter disappointment in Stalin's behavior after World War II, such as when the Kremlin leader reneged on his promise to withdraw Soviet troops from Iran within six months of the end of the war. This duplicity led Truman to conclude that Communists could not be trusted, a belief that influenced the types of solutions he sought to Cold War crises. As in his response to the Berlin blockade and in the establishment of NATO, he tried to create *faits accomplis* without relying on the word of the Soviets, which he had concluded they would break anyway.

Truman was a hands-on decision-maker, but he also took pride in his ability to delegate responsibility, and he backed up those he trusted. Accordingly, he was willing to take the political fallout from ending aid to the Chinese Nationalists in 1949 and from the refusal to escalate the Korean War after the Chinese Communist intervention. He also established the National Security Council in 1947, creating a more formal and bureaucratic framework for the making of U.S. foreign and defense policy. His inexperience with the niceties of international diplomacy did not prevent him from articulating a consistent position on America's role in

Harry S. Truman had no experience with foreign policy when he became president, but his leadership helped define America's new role in the post–World War II world.
SOURCE: UPI/Corbis/Bettmann

the world and setting precedents that exerted profound influence on U.S. strategy throughout the Cold War.

George Bush, Diplomat   Despite George Bush's experience with the give and take of congressional politics, or perhaps because of it, he displayed a great distaste for cutting deals, an innate sense of caution, a distrust of grand ideas, and a great loyalty to friends. Thus, he preferred to surround himself with a close group of trusted aides, like Secretary of State James Baker and National Security Advisor Brent Scowcroft. Bush had gained diplomatic experience as U.S. representative to the UN and to China, but unlike Ronald Reagan, he did not promote a sweeping vision of America's role in the world, concentrating instead on managing the practical problems of adjusting America's foreign policy to the end of the Cold War. Bush acted decisively during the Persian Gulf crisis and war of 1990–1991

As president, George Bush made effective use of his experience in diplomacy and international business.

SOURCE: Sygma

and deftly secured the approval of the UN Security Council for the use of military force against Iraq, but he was unable to translate the allied victory into foreign-policy successes as America entered the New Era.

Like Roosevelt, Bush was born a patrician. He felt comfortable dealing with other world leaders on an informal, personal basis, frequently calling friendly heads of governments for spontaneous discussions over the phone. Bush's policies were much more successful abroad than they were at home, and he much preferred the genteel world of diplomacy to the rough-and-tumble bargaining of domestic politics. He summarized succinctly one reason why many presidents have found foreign policy more absorbing and satisfying than domestic politics:

> Some people say, why can't you bring the same kind of purpose and success to the domestic scene as you did in Desert Shield and Desert Storm? And the answer is, I didn't have to get permission from some old goat in the United States Congress to kick Saddam Hussein out of Kuwait. That's the reason.[43]

Two Egyptian Leaders

Gamal Abdel Nasser, Pan-Arabist   On July 23, 1952, a group of young military officers, part of the clandestine Free Officers Society, overthrew King Farouk

Egyptian President Gamal Abdel Nasser waves to the crowd at a sporting event in December 1961. Nasser's ability to inspire his countrymen was one of his greatest leadership qualities.   SOURCE: © UPI/Bettmann

of Egypt. Among this group was Egypt's first long-term president, Gamal Abdel Nasser, in office from 1954 to 1970, and his successor, Anwar el-Sadat, who served between 1971 and 1981. Nasser, the son of an Alexandria postal clerk, got his break in 1937 when the Royal Military Academy allowed young men without palace or aristocratic connections to enter the officer corps. For many from lower-class families, the academy was an opportunity to rise to a modest rank based on merit. Yet, dissatisfaction among the junior officers with their superiors and the unsuccessful attempt to prevent the establishment of Israel in 1948 created a hotbed of political activism.

Although Nasser rose from the ranks of the lower middle class and instituted many programs that benefited them, there is evidence of dualism in his personal beliefs. Although appealing to the masses, he also distrusted them, destroying all political parties except the state party and severely curtailing freedom of the press. Although supporting the notion of a democratic Egypt, Nasser believed that Egypt was still in a pre-democratic stage and required authoritarian rule. He therefore employed a large corps of domestic spies to monitor the behavior of both friend and foe. As one author notes, Nasser could be "dictatorial or deferential, charismatic or suspicious, ingenuous or crafty."[44]

For many in the Arab world, Nasser stood for defiance of the West. In 1954 he forced the British to withdraw their army of 80,000 from the Suez Canal Zone; in 1955 he acquired Soviet arms; in 1956 he recognized Communist China and in the same year nationalized the British-controlled Suez Canal Company. Nasser was able to convert the military defeat that Egypt suffered as a result of the Suez Crisis (see Chapter Six) into a political victory, because the United States joined the USSR in condemning the British-French-Israeli attack on Egypt. This victory further elevated Nasser's status in the Arab world and in the Nonaligned Movement. Even when he attempted to resign after the disastrous Arab defeat in the Six-Day War of 1967, massive street demonstrations by his supporters and a vote of confidence by the National Assembly allowed Nassser to remain in power.

Nasser's successes—or more accurately, his survival—contributed to the emergence of **Nasserism,** a personality cult that made the Egyptian leader seem bigger than life. He became identified with a new revolutionary nationalism and effectively promoted **Pan-Arabism,** a movement to unify the Arab world into a single state. Toward this end, from 1958 to 1961, Egypt and Syria unified to form the United Arab Republic, with Nasser at the helm. Yet, although many viewed Nasser as a champion of the Arab cause, Western states and conservative Arab monarchies in Jordan and the Gulf region perceived Nasser's bullying as an ambitious attempt to extend Egyptian influence throughout the region.[45] When Nasser died of a heart attack in 1970 shortly after mediating an end to a civil war in Jordan, his country faced a host of economic, social, and diplomatic problems. He was widely praised as a hero, though his dream of Pan-Arabism had fallen far short of its goal. Regardless of the final verdict on Nasser, it is clear that he played the critical role in shaping Egyptian foreign policy during nearly twenty tumultuous years.

Anwar el-Sadat, Peacemaker   Nasser's particular policies were not inevitable, as was soon demonstrated when he was succeeded as president of Egypt by Anwar el-Sadat. Although following on the heels of a revered hero, Sadat reversed many of Nasser's policies and at the same time revived Egypt's sagging fortunes. Although Nasser spoke of "Egypt for the Arabs," Sadat's actions reflected his belief in "Egypt for the Egyptians," often with little concern for outside Arab opinion. An example is the way Sadat dealt with the strong political pressure to reverse the defeat Egypt had suffered in the 1967 war with Israel. Although he named 1971 the "Year of Decision," meaning the year the lost territory would be recovered by political means if possible and by military instruments if necessary, he was unwilling to be cajoled into action before Egypt was prepared for war. Moreover, when Egypt and its ally Syria finally attacked Israel in 1973, Sadat did not attempt to achieve a complete defeat of the Jewish state, but instead he wanted to demonstrate that Jerusalem could never be secure without making peace with Cairo. He accomplished this goal by ordering Egyptian troops to cross the Suez Canal and maintain a beachhead in the Sinai.

The surprise attack in October 1973 was typical of Sadat's decision-making pattern: procrastination followed by a sudden and dramatic turnabout in policy. After the war, he switched superpower allies from the Soviet Union to the United States, and began to move his country away from Nasser's authoritarian version of "Arab socialism." In 1977, seeking to break the impasse with Israel, Sadat made a historic visit to Jerusalem and appeared before the Israeli Knesset. A number of Arab leaders criticized his unilateral action, but he was not swayed by their

Anwar el-Sadat launched the October War in 1973, but later he took the bold step of making peace with Israel and paid the ultimate price for this courageous move.   SOURCE: AP/Wide World

stance. Shortly thereafter, Sadat made an even more historic decision to "go it alone" and sign with Israel the Camp David Accords, which led to the return of the Sinai peninsula to Egypt in exchange for a peace treaty with Jerusalem. Although Sadat established a basis for a stable relationship between Egypt and Israel and for closer ties between his country and the United States, many in the Arab world never forgave him for signing a separate peace with the "Zionist enemy." Egypt was expelled from active participation in the Arab League, and Sadat himself paid the ultimate price for peace: he was assassinated in 1981. Despite Sadat's controversial legacy, few Third World leaders have made as much of an impact on foreign affairs.

Two Soviet Leaders

Nikita Khrushchev, Demagogue   The leadership styles of the two Soviet premiers who successively held power in the Kremlin through almost three decades of the Cold War are a study in contrasts. Nikita Sergeyevich Khrushchev, Ukrainian by

Soviet Premier Nikita Khrushchev pounds the table at the UN General Assembly in October 1960.
SOURCE: Archive Photos

birth, was outgoing, demonstrative, and confrontational. During his tenure from 1958 to 1964, he rarely shied away from taking risks, either in domestic politics or foreign policy. Khrushchev loved a good argument and was fond of making dramatic gestures. Under his leadership, the USSR temporarily took the lead in the "space race" by orbiting Sputnik and launching the first human voyagers into space.

Khrushchev's bombastic pronouncements, grandiose claims, and bluffs often caused alarm in the Western world. He once boasted, for example, that communism would "bury" the West with superior production, and during the Suez Crisis in 1956 his government threatened Britain and France with nuclear devastation. Khrushchev delighted in what politicians in later years would call "photo opportunities." He took full advantage of public appearances to unleash barrages of Cold War rhetoric (accenting a speech at the UN by banging his shoe on the rostrum) or to promote an image of himself as a warm personality who empathized with the man and woman on the street (as when he extolled the progressive Soviet attitude toward women to visiting U.S. Vice President Richard Nixon in the so-called Kitchen Debate).

Khrushchev's combative stance with respect to the West was reflected in the frequent East-West crises that erupted during his tenure in office. His pronouncements during the Suez, Taiwan Straits, Berlin, and Cuban crises (see Chapter Four) symbolized the sharpness of the Cold War's ideological conflict. Yet, his passionate speeches did not prevent him from developing a respectful relationship with Eisenhower during his 1959 visit to the United States. Reflecting Khrushchev's mercurial style, the new relationship with Eisenhower was in turn ruined by the U-2 crisis the following year. At the same time, Khrushchev's conflict with a fellow Communist, China's Mao Zedong, was often played out on a personal level, and the poor relationship between Khrushchev and Mao certainly did nothing to lessen the growing rift between Moscow and Beijing in the late 1950s and early 1960s. Ultimately, Khrushchev's risky moves at home and abroad (such as cutting the Soviet conventional defense budget in favor of nuclear weapons, pumping resources into the "virgin lands" agricultural development fiasco, and precipitating a frightening nuclear crisis by attempting to place missiles in Cuba) alienated too many of his colleagues in the Soviet Communist Party, and he was removed from power in 1964.[46]

Leonid Brezhnev, Party Hack   Although Khrushchev could be pushy, rude, boorish, and cruel, he was never dull. Boring, however, is the adjective that best describes the leadership style of the next Soviet ruler, Leonid Ilyich Brezhnev, who served from 1964 to 1982. In appointing Brezhnev, the Soviet party leaders hoped for stability and predictability, and they got plenty of both. Brezhnev was a deliberate, cautious leader, who was careful to consult other Politburo members before making important decisions in an effort to build consensus for his policies. He avoided risks whenever possible, and he cautiously made preparations for every contingency before taking actions that could alarm the West, such as the invasion of Czechoslovakia in 1968 or the deployment of Soviet air defense personnel, pilots, planes, and surface-to-air missiles to Egypt in 1970.

Although Brezhnev's monotonous constancy and aversion to risk and change prevented him from reversing the economic and social stagnation of the USSR in the 1970s and early 1980s, they were arguably assets to Soviet foreign policy in the decade of détente, the 1970s. Many in the West who were suspicious of the USSR conceded that under Brezhnev, the Communist superpower was at least predictable and would be unlikely to make risky moves that could provoke crises such as those that dominated the Cold War of the 1950s and early 1960s. Brezhnev and Nixon, who had once been fervent ideological opponents, were able to establish a working relationship. Although not without its problems, their personal connection helped facilitate the signing of SALT I in 1972 and the movement toward the East-West economic and cultural exchange that followed.

In retrospect, it is ironic that one of Moscow's most startling foreign-policy actions occurred under Brezhnev's leadership. Because the USSR's foreign policy had been as staid and predictable as its leader in the mid-1970s, the Soviet invasion of Afghanistan in 1979 came as a rude shock. Some Soviet analysts later pointed to the decision to send troops into Afghanistan as the one hasty and incautious decision that Brezhnev ever made. By the time of his death in 1982, Brezhnev had become the embodiment of a moribund Communist system that would disintegrate within ten years.[47]

Leonid Brezhnev, shown between fellow Politburo members Nikolai Podgorniy (left) and Alexi Kosygin (right) reviewing a May Day Parade from the Rostrum of Lenin's Mausoleum in Moscow, was a cautious, unimaginative leader of the Soviet Union who rarely took risks.

SOURCE: AP/Wide World

GENERATIONAL EXPERIENCE

Sometimes the experiences that shape leaders' attitudes on the nature of world politics are those that have affected the entire generation to which the leader belonged.[48] In other words, events that have a powerful impact on a generation's consciousness may be uppermost in the minds of its members who rise to political power and gain the responsibility for making foreign policy. This kind of **generational experience** sometimes leads to misguided policies. Let's travel back in time to Europe to look at several examples. As explained in Chapters Two and Three, the stunning results of Bismarck's wars of German unification against Austria (1866) and France (1870–1871) led European leaders (and much of the European public) to enter the 1914 crisis with a shared image of war as glorious, short, and beneficial.[49] When war broke out that August, many leaders believed that their soldiers would be "home before the leaves fell," and military plans were predicated on the idea that if mobilization could be accomplished quickly enough, an offensive would quickly overwhelm defensive forces.[50] The European leaders, however, could not foresee the implications of new technologies, and the resulting war turned into a bloody four-year conflagration. Demonstrating how generations as a whole can get caught up in an error, leaders focused on Bismarck's rapid and relatively cost-free victories and ignored other available lessons from conflicts that were dismissed as peripheral, such as the American Civil War, the Russo-Japanese War of 1904–1905, and the Boer War (1899–1902) between Britain and the Afrikaner republics of South Africa. All of these experiences showed that war could be quite prolonged and costly.

The tragedy of World War I left no European untouched and imbued a generation of leaders with the moral imperative to prevent such a disaster from ever happening again. This imperative helped sway British and French leaders to adopt the policy of appeasement in dealing with the German and Italian aggression of the 1930s. When British Prime Minister Neville Chamberlain returned to London after the Munich Conference in 1938, his declaration that the Munich Agreement had secured "peace in our time" at the cost of concessions to Hitler reflected the hope that appeasement could stave off another catastrophic war. This wish was shared by the majority of British and French citizens at the time; their leaders may have suspected that the hope was a forlorn one, but their generation's experience of conflict made it difficult to maintain peace by preparing for war.

Appeasement, of course, failed miserably (see Chapter Three). After World War II, the Munich analogy became the lesson of choice for a succession of leaders who had fought in or otherwise experienced the war. British Prime Minister Anthony Eden used the analogy in advocating the use of force against Egypt when Nasser ordered the nationalization of the Suez Canal in 1956. Recalling Chamberlain's experience with Axis leaders at Munich, Eden argued that anything short of an armed response would constitute appeasement and called Nasser the "Mussolini of the Nile." Thirty-four years later, President Bush likened Iraqi leader Saddam Hussein to Hitler and incorporated his own experiences as a young pilot during World War II into his admonitions to avoid another Munich. By contrast, the experience of the Vietnam War taught a more recent generation of Americans that the use of force can easily cause more problems than it solves. American fears of "another Vietnam" were reflected in the country's reluctance to become involved in the conflicts following the breakup of Yugoslavia in the early 1990s, as well as the turmoil in Rwanda, Somalia, and Haiti.

The generation of Soviet leaders from Joseph Stalin to Konstantin Chernenko (Mikhail Gorbachev's immediate predecessor) vividly recalled another "lesson" from the appeasement of Hitler: The Soviet Union must maintain a buffer zone of states it controlled around its periphery, especially its European border, to prevent invasion. With this lesson in mind, the USSR occupied Eastern Europe and the Kuril Islands off Japan, secured the neutrality of Austria and Finland, suppressed worker demonstrations in East Germany in 1953, engineered the Warsaw Pact's invasions of Hungary in 1956 and Czechoslovakia in 1968, maintained a huge force on the border with China after the Sino-Soviet split, and invaded Afghanistan in 1979. On the other hand, Gorbachev was unconvinced of the correctness of these policies; he was old enough to remember World War II, but too young to have fought in it. The positive effects of the "thaw" in U.S.–Soviet relations during the Khrushchev era (when many of Stalin's draconian measures were muted or reversed), and of détente under Brezhnev, may have taught Gorbachev that Soviet security could be safeguarded by political as well as by military means and that the USSR's huge military arsenal made other nations fear and distrust it. These impressions may have made it more palatable for the new generation of Soviet leaders to negotiate the arms reductions provided for in the INF, CFE, and START treaties, to withdraw Soviet troops from Afghanistan, to abandon the Soviet empire in Eastern Europe, and to improve the USSR's image in world public opinion shortly before its final collapse.

PSYCHOLOGICAL ASPECTS OF DECISION-MAKING

Just as individuals differ in their beliefs, goals, and experiences, they also vary in their ability to process information and make decisions, particularly under stress or time constraints. These capacities have been the focus of a number of psychological theories of decision-making, which attempt to capture how individuals' capabilities, attitudes, biases, reactions to stress, and miscellaneous idiosyncrasies influence how they process information and, equally important, the ramifications these characteristics can have on policy choices.

Operational Codes

Some psychologists contend that people develop their own mental flowcharts, which contain sets of rules enabling them to more easily process information, invent and appraise options, and choose the action that seems best in the face of uncertainty. They argue that policy-makers subconsciously use these flowcharts, termed **operational codes**, as a way to translate their fundamental moral and political beliefs into policy decisions.[51] An individual leader's operational code contains his or her fundamental beliefs about the nature of international politics and conflict, perceptions of the extent to which future developments can be shaped by intelligent or misguided action, and maxims regarding correct strategy and tactics for dealing with political adversaries and allies. The operational code thus has both a philosophical and an instrumental content; it is both a belief system and a guide to action.

To illustrate these concepts, it is useful to briefly compare the operational codes of Soviet and American leaders during the Cold War. Western studies found that the operational codes of the original Communist leaders of the Soviet Union closely resembled one another and appeared to be heavily influenced by Marx's ideas on dialectical materialism and class struggle.[52] These leaders believed, for instance, that the political universe was one of acute conflict, with a capitalist opponent inherently hostile toward and determined to destroy the Soviet Union. Thus, capitalism itself must be decimated if the Soviet Union was to escape destruction. Distrust of opponents aside, the Bolshevik code was basically optimistic, because it was predicated on a belief in the inevitability of the eventual global triumph of communism. This optimism was balanced by an awareness of the possibility of catastrophe—the idea that miscalculation by Bolshevik leaders could lead to disaster. Intelligent action would be important, in the short term to reduce the likelihood of miscalculations and in the long term as a means of expediting the historical process from capitalism to communism. In accordance with these beliefs, the Communist Party was obliged to seize any opportunity to advance history in the right direction.

American leaders, in contrast, tended to believe that the conflict between the superpowers could be moderated, and perhaps eventually overcome, if the two sides limited their objectives.[53] This belief was the basis for the American concept of limited war, fought by limited means for limited objectives, which was developed after the failed attempt to forcibly unify Korea during the Korean War. During subsequent conflicts, U.S. policy-makers sought to communicate to their opponents that American objectives were limited, and that they were not intent on their adversaries' total destruction. In the Vietnam War, for example, U.S. aircraft were ordered to avoid striking targets in "bombing sanctuaries" around Hanoi in order to demonstrate that the United States did not want to destroy North Vietnam completely. In the Persian Gulf War, President Bush limited American objectives to driving Iraqi forces out of Kuwait; he stopped allied military operations without advancing on Baghdad or destroying the Iraqi army. Bush also avoided announcing that coalition forces would attempt to remove Saddam Hussein from power, instead calling on Hussein's opponents to do this themselves. Bush's operational code, it would seem, contained maxims that the use of force is justified only if the opponent is evil, but even then, unity among allies should not be jeopardized by opportunistic attempts to exceed agreed-upon objectives.

Effects of Stress

The risks and uncertainties inherent in important decisions often create stress for the people who make them. Of all the challenges faced by foreign-policy decision-makers, international crises are the most formidable because they create the highest degree of tension and stress. Crises have a number of stress-inducing characteristics: usually they come as a surprise, they threaten important values and interests, they require quick decisions, and therefore they impose emotional and physical fatigue on top decision-makers.[54] In their memoirs of the Cuban Missile Crisis, participants Robert Kennedy and Theodore Sorensen both claimed that pressure to decide what to do about the Soviet missiles in Cuba was intense. For Kennedy, "that kind of [crisis-induced] pressure does strange things to a human being, even to brilliant, self-confident, mature, experienced men. For some it brings out characteristics and strengths that perhaps they never knew they had, and for others the pressure is too overwhelming."[55] Sorensen reports that during the week-long crisis, he witnessed "how brutally physical and mental fatigue can numb the good sense as well as the senses of normally articulate men."[56]

Throughout history, various leaders have suffered near- or total breakdowns under the intense pressure of international crises. There is evidence that British

Prime Minister Anthony Eden during the 1956 Suez crisis, Indian leader Jawaharlal Nehru in the 1962 Sino-Indian war, and both Israeli Chief of Staff Yitzhak Rabin and Egyptian President Gamel Abdel Nasser during the 1967 Arab-Israeli conflict all became temporarily incapacitated, mentally and physically, as a result of tremendous crisis-induced stress.[57] But perhaps a more illuminating example is the behavior of Soviet Premier Joseph Stalin at a key turning point in World War II. In June 1941 Stalin broke down and became temporarily paralyzed after hearing about Germany's invasion of the Soviet Union, an action he had thoroughly believed Hitler would never risk. One of Stalin's aides reported that "from the moment of the attack by Germany, Stalin locked himself in his study, would not see anybody, and did not take any part in state decisions."[58] At a meeting of the Politburo convened to discuss Soviet options, Stalin sat silent, cradling his unlit pipe, his mind apparently somewhere else. This indecision allowed the German advance to continue and exact a heavy toll in Soviet lives and territory.

Cognitive Consistency and Dissonance

Crisis-induced stress is not the only factor that can lead policy-makers to make bad decisions, of course; sometimes, they make mistakes in the ordinary day-to-day formulation of foreign policy. Some of these errors can be attributed to conscious or unconscious psychological biases. For example, some theorists contend that people often try to simplify difficult decisions by seeking **cognitive consistency**. That is, they tend to see what they expect to see and thus assimilate incoming information according to the beliefs and images that they have already formed—they make the facts fit their theories. **Cognitive dissonance** theory tells us that "inconsistencies [dissonance] within the cognitive system cause an uncomfortable state of tension that people are then motivated to reduce or eliminate."[59] Individuals often try to resolve the tension between their deeply held beliefs and contradictory information by discrediting or ignoring the source of the information, reinterpreting the information, or replacing it with other information more consistent with their beliefs.

Excessive consistency seeking can lead to serious policy miscalculations. Prior to the Nazi invasion of the Soviet Union in 1941, Stalin had sufficient information about Hitler's military disposition and plans, but he still refused to believe that Hitler would launch an attack. Stalin's image of Hitler, possibly derived from their negotiations over the 1939 Nazi–Soviet Pact, supported the Soviet leader's belief that Hitler would almost certainly engage in a bargaining game before deciding on the need to use force.[60] Stalin seriously miscalculated the fuhrer's intentions, and the result was a near-disaster for the USSR. Similarly, when Egypt nationalized the Suez Canal in 1956, British leaders believed that the Egyptians would not be able to operate the canal. The pilots who navigated ships through the waterway were European, and they were expected to quit if nationalization took place. As a result of these assumptions, the British cabinet mistakenly concluded that the canal would have to be shut down; they overlooked the fact that it took minimal training to produce competent pilots.[61]

Some argue that cognitive consistency seeking on the part of U.S. leaders also exacerbated the Cold War, especially in the face of acute domestic political pressure. Political scientist Deborah Larson asserts that cognitive-dissonance theory could account for abrupt changes in the attitudes of American policy-makers toward the USSR after World War II:

> Washington officials changed their estimate of Soviet foreign policy intentions in February 1946, a few months after the Truman administration had decided to adopt a "tougher" stance toward the Soviets in response to Republican criticism of the so-called "appeasement" policy. American policy-makers would have been reluctant to admit to themselves that, for illegitimate political motives, they had diminished the chances for Soviet-American cooperation and increased the risks of war. Accordingly, they would have been motivated to change their attitudes toward the Soviet Union, to make them more consistent with the public "hard-line" policy.[62]

Generally, decision-makers who engage in consistency seeking are responding to some sort of difficult value trade-off inherent in domestic or international politics. In other words, when decision-makers realize that two or more values will come into direct conflict with one another, they tend to react by downplaying or ignoring some of the values in order to avoid the psychological discomfort that occurs when important interests or morals seem to be sacrificed. Decision-makers may engage in a process of **cognitive restructuring** by turning aside information that calls attention to or aggravates a value conflict. Thus, they may "discount, deny, forget, or unintentionally misinterpret information about some of the competing values."[63] In their own minds, they may also "devalue" one of the interests that they or others close to them hold dear. As a result of restructuring their values, decision-makers may refuse to consult advisors who they suspect hold the devalued interests, or may fail to credit their information, or even belittle them in front of others.

The way in which decision-makers frame an issue can also create **cognitive biases**. A body of psychological theory known as prospect theory emphasizes that the point around which decision-makers frame losses and gains is crucially important to their decision process. Leaders challenging the status quo are especially likely to experience an "instant endowment effect" whereby they quickly consider the gains resulting from a recent challenge to be part of the status quo, and thus take greater risks to protect their newly realized gains.[64] Iraq's attempt to absorb Kuwait in 1990–1991 is a perfect illustration of this pattern: the "offensive" goal of taking Kuwait, from which Baghdad might have been deterred, was immediately transformed in the mind of Saddam Hussein into the "defensive" goal of holding on to Iraq's "Nineteenth Province," for which the Iraqi leader was willing to risk a devastating war.

Attribution Theory

Another way to examine the role of psychological factors in decision-making is provided by **attribution theory**, which considers decision-makers to be "problem-solvers" or "naive scientists." In contrast to the "consistency seeker," the "naive scientist" is "relatively open-minded in the search for truth, untrammeled by the need to maintain a favorable self-image or preserve a favored belief." [65] Even though this model at first glance seems to view decision-makers in a more positive (and perhaps unrealistic) light, it does acknowledge that particular aspects of the decision-making process are subject to certain biases. For example, attributional biases occur when decision-makers must infer, or guess, the motivations of other actors. One of the most common attributional biases is known as **fundamental attribution error,** which consists of applying a double standard in which one's own inappropriate behavior is attributed to situational variables (related to circumstances beyond one's control), while an adversary's are attributed to dispositional variables (related to character and fundamental goals). Similarly, one's own positive behavior is attributed to strong moral character but an opponent's to outside pressures. [66]

George Kennan, the author of America's Cold War containment strategy, warned against allowing fundamental attribution error to guide U.S. policy toward the Soviet Union: "Now is it our view that we should take account only of their [Soviets'] capabilities, disregarding their intentions, but we should expect them to take account only of our supposed intentions, disregarding our capabilities?" [67] U.S. policy-makers frequently ignored Kennan's warning. In the early postwar period, many State Department officials viewed Soviet attempts to establish an exclusive sphere of influence in Eastern Europe as evidence of Soviet expansionist aims, refusing to consider that the USSR might have had valid concerns for its own security. At the same time, these officials maintained that Central and South America—an area far larger than Eastern Europe—remained off-limits for the new UN Security Council. [68]

To consider another example, both sides in the Arab-Israeli conflict have tended to make fundamental attribution errors. A summary of one author's analysis of the double-standard behavior of the Arabs and Israelis follows:

View of Self

1. The explanation for one's own "good" behavior, by both Arabs and Israelis, is usually dispositional. Good actions are seen as proof of inherent good character.
2. However, when explaining actions of which the opponent disapproves, situational terms predominate. Circumstances are used to excuse one's own poor behavior.

View of Opponent

1. When the opponent behaves well in a particular instance, the tendency of both Arabs and Israelis is to explain it in situational terms. Neither would concede that the opponent may have positive dispositional elements.
2. When the opponent is found behaving badly, it is offered as evidence of

inferior disposition. Situational factors are discounted as a possible explanation.[69]

Heuristics and Schemas

Another bias stems from the overuse of **heuristics** (rules of thumb or mental shortcuts) in processing large flows of information and assessing the likelihood that certain policy options will be successful.[70] One such rule of thumb is the availability heuristic, which suggests that policy-makers are prone to expect a situational outcome that is most easily remembered or imagined on the basis of past experience. A second is the representativeness heuristic, which refers to the proclivity to expect an outcome that is most consistent with or most resembles the salient features of the situation in question. After the Iraqi invasion of Kuwait in 1990, for example, many American policy-makers believed that the situation in the Persian Gulf closely resembled the one that existed in Europe before the 1938 Munich Conference (the availability heuristic). Believing that Hussein resembled Hitler in methods and motivation, they expected that unless the occupation of Kuwait was reversed, Hussein would make ever increasing demands on neighboring countries (the representativeness heuristic).

Both of these cognitive shortcuts reflect a tendency to recall concrete historical analogies—the "lessons" of history—in diagnosing a new situation and surveying the options for dealing with it. These analogies are termed **schemas**, generic concepts stored in an individual's memory that refer to objects, situations, events, or people.[71] Schemas allow a decision-maker to select what is important out of a large flow of data, thus providing an economical means of storing memories of objects and events. They enable an individual to go beyond the information given and, using the lessons drawn from a similar previous experience, make useful inferences about an object or situation. Finally, they even permit a decision-maker to envision and carry out a sequence of actions to achieve a particular goal.

It is worth noting that important bits of data can be lost in this process, leading to misperceptions and sometimes inappropriate behavior. The experience of war, for instance, is often burned deeply into the memory of those who live through it. Consequently, there is a tendency for strategists and policy-makers to assume that the next war will closely resemble the last one and to make plans accordingly. The events of the late nineteenth and early twentieth centuries are illustrative. Because of the rapid defeat of France in the Franco-Prussian War of 1870–1871, European military planners assumed that the next war would be won by the side that mobilized first. The race to mobilization went on to become a decisive factor in the outbreak of World War I. This assumption proved wrong, however, as the Great War dragged on for years of grinding trench warfare. The situation repeated itself before the outbreak of the next war. Most strategists of the 1920s and 1930s expected the next war would be fought in the trenches, like the last one. When World War II erupted, their analogies again proved inappropriate, and in 1940 France was defeated more rapidly and thoroughly than it had been in 1871.[72]

Leadership Within Systematic Constraints

The "great man" theory of history contends that individuals are the driving force behind momentous events. This idea contrasts with the concept of history expressed in the writings of Russian novelist Leo Tolstoy, who believed that the relentless ebb and flow of events swept up both the weak and powerful, and heroes and leaders were merely individuals fortunate enough to be in the right place at the right time. Clearly, the truth about the role of individuals in world politics lies somewhere in between these extremes. But where? How much impact do the decisions and characteristics of individuals have, relative to the larger **structures of the international system** or domestic institutions? For example, Nixon opened new relations with China, causing a major change in the patterns of international politics at the time. Was he only recognizing the reality of the system—that anyone else as president of the United States would have similarly identified—or was he acting as a figure uniquely capable of altering the policy because of his past opposition to China? Similar questions can be asked about French President Charles de Gaulle's decision to leave Algeria; Gorbachev's policies of *glasnost* and *perestroika*; President F. W. de Klerk's abolishment of apartheid in South Africa. Were these unique figures whose vision and personality changed history, or were they simply accepting the inevitable imposed by the international system or domestic conditions as most other leaders of their country would have done at about the same time?

These questions, like all major questions in the study of international relations, are far from easy to answer. The careers of leaders such as Napoléon or Bismarck clearly changed not only the course of world politics, but its essential nature as well. On the other hand, leaders like Neville Chamberlain and Lyndon Johnson had their otherwise distinguished careers ended by failure to overcome the constraints that international and domestic politics placed on their policies. Systemic and state-level factors have an undeniably powerful influence on the foreign policies adopted by decision-makers. Their impact is rarely absolute, however, as leaders usually have some freedom of action to make policy choices, even when they publicly claim that the situation gives them "no choice." There are many instances when uncertainty or ambiguity requires leaders to make judgment calls on the risks, benefits, or morality of specific policies. In order to understand how individual decision-makers are likely to use what freedom of action they have, it is necessary to consider what they are like as human beings—their mental and physical limitations, and their unique beliefs, goals, and character.

CONCLUSION: WHAT DO THE LEVELS OF ANALYSIS EXPLAIN?

Our discussion thus returns to its original question: How much can be explained by the individual, state, and systemic levels of analysis? Let's look back at the causes of World War I as an example. Systemic-level theories argue that World

What Would You Do ?

You are a U.S. senator. The president favors continuing most-favored-nation trade status for China (see Chapter Six for a review of MFN), but your own party is divided on this question. Some analysts, arguing from the systemic level, contend that a new cold war with China is coming, so the United States should not do anything that would strengthen China's economic position or boost Chinese technological capabilities even if this means forgoing the benefits of trade. Other experts, however, say that free trade with Beijing will be an important step towards China's integration into international institutions such as the World Trade Organization, which will moderate China's international ambitions and help prevent a new cold war from breaking out.

On the domestic level, many U.S. companies would profit from trade with China if MFN is continued and would show their gratitude by increasing their contributions to your campaign fund. Other supporters of free trade argue that trade and increased prosperity will prompt China to reform its political system and eventually lead to democratization. Labor unions, however, oppose MFN, arguing that it would destroy American jobs and would result in the import of goods made by slave labor in prison camps. Religious groups and human rights organizations also oppose MFN, to protest China's persecution of Christians and dissidents, as do environmental organizations, which fear that MFN will encourage U.S. companies to transfer production to China to circumvent environmental regulations. The State and Commerce Departments and the Office of the U.S. Trade Representative favor MFN, but the Labor and Defense Departments are opposed. Your party's majority leader would like to hand the president a defeat, but he has not put major pressure on you to vote against MFN, and your party has no official position on the issue. Public opinion in the United States and your own constituency is divided on the MFN question, so taking any position involves some political risk and some potential political benefits.

On the individual level, you have met many of China's leaders yourself, and you believe that they can be trusted to keep a trade agreement. However, some of your Senate colleagues point out that in past trade negotiations, Beijing's rulers have made promises to improve tolerance for dissidents and reform of their intellectual property laws, but have not lived up to them. Although the president has little foreign-policy background and is primarily concerned with the domestic consequences of trade, he would like to be seen as an effective leader, so he may be willing to make a deal to gain your support.

How will you vote? Which level of analysis offers the best guide to action?

What would you do ?

War I represents the outcome of a classic security dilemma that led to an arms race. Domestic-level theories contend that factors such as the cult of the offensive (discussed in Chapter 3) fueled the security dilemma by biasing each state's military planning in favor of all-out mobilization. The individual level of analysis argues that it was the idiosyncrasies and incompetence of many European leaders that caused them to horribly mismanage the crisis that broke out in July 1914, initiating a chain of events leading to the bloodiest war the world had yet experienced.

Now let's look at the Cold War. At the most general, international level, one could argue that bipolarity created the U.S.–Soviet rivalry and that the collapse of Soviet power ended it. Or, at the state level, that the Russian Revolution ushered in a Marxist system fundamentally opposed to capitalism and democracy and that only the liberalization of Russia brought about the Cold War's demise. Or, at the individual level, that Stalin's and Truman's misperception and distrust of each other's intentions set into motion a competitive spiral that deescalated only after Mikhail Gorbachev and Ronald Reagan developed a cooperative relationship that turned their countries' relations in a more positive direction. The interpretation you believe to be most correct may depend, like many other political questions, on your own beliefs and assumptions. Thus, the answers to questions on international relations depend to a great extent upon the views and goals of the observer, as well as of the participants. In this manner, political science is not too different from the other social and natural sciences—that is, it has its element of subjectivity—as much as practitioners of those disciplines may be loath to admit it.

The approach one takes to explaining world politics also depends on the specific question one is trying to answer. Systemic theories are most useful for explaining long-term trends or broad relationships, such as the connection between system structure and stability. Domestic theories can help explain specific policy outcomes that result from a decision-making process, such as a state's position on WTO or entry into the European Union. Finally, individual-level explanations tell us a great deal about what happens when leaders must make quick decisions, when there is no time for substantial public or legislative debate, as when John F. Kennedy and his advisors were suddenly confronted with a Soviet attempt to secretly station ballistic missiles in Cuba. Understanding variations on or deviations from a consistent theme in a state's foreign policy—such as the relaxation and resumption of Cold War tensions during Khrushchev's tenure in the Kremlin—may require an approach that combines several levels of analysis.

In any field of inquiry, it is usually easier to identify patterns of causal relationships than it is to explain an event fully. "What is the effect of X on Y?" is a relatively straightforward question that lends itself to classification according to a level of analysis. (In international politics, this question may take forms such as, "How does polarity affect stability?" "What role has the War Powers Act played in decisions to commit American troops to combat?" or "Did Eden's illness during the Suez Crisis affect his judgment?") Questions of the form "Why did X happen rather than Y?" are inherently more complex and controversial. They involve more variables, not all of which may be identifiable, and they require the analyst to consider counterfactuals (a fancy term for things that might have been: what might have happened if Chamberlain had called Hitler's bluff at Munich, for example). Both types of questions are nevertheless useful, and in fact both must be asked in order to attempt a better understanding of world politics. After all, a good question for scientific inquiry is one that, when answered, not only adds to our knowledge of events, concepts, and processes, but also produces more good questions.

PRINCIPAL POINTS OF CHAPTER TWELVE

1. The systemic level of analysis looks at how features of the international system external to individual nations influence the behavior of states. Although systemic-level arguments are parsimonious and powerful in their ability to predict the broad outlines of state behavior, they are often not very specific and have other limitations.

2. One of the leading schools of thought in systemic theory is realism. Classical realists emphasize the logic of realpolitik, power politics, and the evil nature of humans in shaping interstate behavior. Structural realists, or neorealists, focus on changes or shifts in the distribution of power among states in the international system.

3. Balance-of-power theory argues that an equal distribution of power is stable and that balancing is accomplished either through internal buildup or through alliance formation. Conversely, preponderance theories contend that a hegemonic distribution of power (dominated by a single state) is more stable.

4. Many realists contend that a bipolar distribution of power (where two superpowers dominate the international system) is more stable than a multipolar distribution (where there are three or more great powers). Other realists, however, conclude that a multipolar system is more stable, because the complexity of the system breeds caution, creates cross-cutting concerns, encourages moderation, and dampens arms races.

5. Liberalism contends that cooperation is possible among states, even in the absence of a centralized global organization. For liberals, the main barrier to cooperation is the temptation of each state to maximize its individual gains, which results in an outcome that no state desires. (This situation is modeled in the Prisoners' Dilemma.) However, liberals (and particularly neoliberal institutionalists) contend that it is possible to achieve robust international cooperation in a number of ways, including a tit-for-tat strategy, international regimes, and international law.

6. Analyses on the domestic level focus on how attributes of individual states affect their actions in the international system.

7. The statist approach focuses on domestic political institutions that shape the preferences and behavior of states, including regime type, executive-legislative relations, political parties, and bureaucracies.

8. Societal approaches examine how groups, social structures, and cultural features outside government, including interest groups and public opinion, can affect a state's international relations.

9. Some domestic influences on foreign policy directly combine aspects of both state institutions and social norms and structures. Chief among these are ideology, political culture, and the prevalence of peace among democracies.

10. The individual level of analysis examines how people can make a difference in world politics. It considers how traits shared by all human beings, and traits unique to individuals, shape the decisions and actions taken by leaders and citizens.

11. The personal style, background, and experience of leaders often color their perceptions and affect the decisions they make. Different persons, confronted with the same facts and acting within the same political system, can interpret a given situation in diverse ways producing markedly different results.

12. Certain formative experiences, such as wars, economic depressions, or political upheaval, can be shared by a generation of leaders and may give rise to distinct generational perceptions and attitudes.

13. A number of psychological factors can have profound effects on the decisions made by national leaders. These include operational codes, the effects of stress, cognitive biases, attributional errors, and heuristics and schemas.

14. The level of analysis most useful for explaining an aspect of international relations depends upon the specific question to be answered, the time scale involved, and the nature of the issue or event being examined (for example, decisions in a crisis, the outcome of debates over trade policy, or strategic alignment over the course of a century). Contentions between the levels of analysis can be difficult to resolve, but can help analysts gain a richer picture and deeper understanding of world politics.

KEY TERMS

attribution theory
belief systems
buck-passing
bureaucratic politics
chain-ganging
classical realists
cognitive biases
cognitive consistency
cognitive dissonance

cognitive restructuring
constructivism
counterbalancing coalition
critical theory
deconcentration
delegitimation
domestic level of analysis
fundamental attribution error

generational experience
heuristics
high politics
idealism
ideology
imbalance of power
individual level of analysis
interest groups
internal balancing

levels of analysis
long-cycle theory
low politics
multipolar
Nasserism
neoliberal institutionalism
neorealism
normative influences
operational codes

organizational
  processes
Pan-Arabism
parity
parity school
polarity
political culture

postmodernism
power-transition
  theory
preponderance
preponderance
  school
Prisoners'
  Dilemma

public opinion
rational actor
realism
regime type
schemas
societal
  approach
structural
  realism

structure of the
  international
  system
systemic level of
  analysis
unipolar

SOURCE: UN/DPI/John Isaac

The Future of International Politics

Our examination of world politics past and present has revealed a constant tension between increased interdependence and cooperation among states on the one hand and continuing fragmentation and conflict on the other. As has been shown, these processes are not mutually exclusive; several contradictory trends exist in the world simultaneously. It is clear, however, that these trends do not move at the same rate in all parts of the globe. Some parts seem mired in intractable and violent conflict, while others appear to be absolutely rushing toward economic and political integration. A television viewer surfing between CNN, showing a live report on a civil war in Africa, and MSNBC, featuring a discussion on how to use Internet to promote transpacific trade, may feel like she has switched worlds rather than just channels. Is there any way of knowing which channel gives a clearer picture of where the international system is headed?

This book cannot provide a remote control for world politics, but we can offer a viewer's guide. The historical chapters in Part II of this text described how the international sytem has changed over the centuries. Part III gave an overview of the economic aspects of world politics, while Part IV considered how issues such as security, human rights, and the environment are played out on the global stage through international regimes and institutions. So far in Part V, Chapter Twelve has outlined various theories, approaching world politics from different levels of analysis, that seek to link cause and effect in the international system and that can help explain trends and anomalies. This chapter will go a step further by using the three levels of analysis to construct scenarios for the future of world politics, each of which derives from a different conception, or vision, of the forces that shape world events. Two scenarios will be derived from the systemic level, one from the liberal perspective and one from the realist perspective on international affairs. Next, another pair of scenarios, the first considerably rosier than the second, will begin with the premise that developments at the domestic level will prove to be most consequential for the future of world politics. Finally, we will consider what the individual level can tell us about the future of the global political and economic system; this vision will necessarily be the fuzziest, as we have no way of knowing what kind of leaders will be at the helm at future turning points in world history.

No such catalog of possible futures can hope to be complete, and none should try to be too specific, as not even the most highly developed theories can predict the future with fine detail. Indeed, the reader should not regard this chapter as an attempt at prediction, but as an exercise in speculation, designed to help clarify ideas about how the international system does, can, or should work. Which of the following scenarios is most likely? Which is most positive? Which is most frightening? By considering these questions about the future, the student of world politics can gain a richer understanding of the present and develop ideas on how to deepen that understanding still further.

THE BIG PICTURE: SCENARIOS FROM THE SYSTEMIC LEVEL

As we learned in Chapter Twelve, systemic-level theories of international relations contend that the structure and nature of the international system, rather than individual countries or leaders that act within it, most profoundly affect world politics. Nation-states and national leaders retain some freedom of action, but their policy choices are constrained by systemic-level factors. The most important of these factors, for systemic theorists of all stripes, is the degree of anarchy in the system—or, to put it another way, the level of transnational authority exerted, implicitly or explicitly, by international institutions and regimes. From the systemic level, the ability of these regimes to regulate conflict and promote cooperation, and the ability of states to maintain their traditional sovereignty in the economic and security spheres, are the key questions for the future.

One World, Ready or Not

The title of a recent book by William Greider suggests that these questions have already been decided.[1] This scenario for the future of world politics contends that economic interdependence has already increased past the point where nation-states can control their own trade and industrial policies. From this viewpoint, the world has become an integrated economic whole, with trade and production organized by multinational corporations and regulated by international regimes. As liberal institutionalists have predicted (see Chapter 12), interdependence, the advantages of specialization, and global economies of scale will make cooperation rather than conflict the norm in the international system, but the result will not be exactly what most liberals had in mind.

In the Information Age, the most important factor of production—information itself—is the most mobile, though capital flows almost as quickly and even labor is more mobile than ever before. When states attempt to buck the trend of global integration by insisting on their own standards for, say, workplace safety or environmental protection, capital moves elsewhere with the speed of the Internet. Multinational firms, which control vital technology and skills, shop around for tax breaks and regulatory easements, and can threaten to move to more business-friendly countries just like National Football League teams threaten to leave cities that refuse to build new stadiums. Countries have little choice but to design their fiscal, industrial, and labor policies to maximize competitiveness in the global marketplace, but the competition takes place at the level of the firm, not that of the state. Essentially, in this scenario, states transfer some of their sovereignty not to a world government, but to a decentralized international economic regime. It is too early to say exactly what form this regime and the institutions that embody it will take, but it will probably look more like the Internet than the League of Nations.

Transfer of sovereignty is unlikely to apply only to economics and trade, however. Harmonization of environmental and social policies soon follows the standardization of trade regulations, as states dare not burden production facilities with the costs of greater environmental protection, more comprehensive health care, or increased retirement pensions. As a result, states cannot afford to have cleaner air or more generous social security systems than their neighbors. Eventually, states will be driven to create a workable system of collective security, if only because they cannot afford to stay competitive while maintaining an independent defense establishment. Not even the most powerful states will be willing to give their allies a security "free ride" if it means the loss of jobs and the concentration of research and development efforts on an unproductive defense sector. Collective security "clubs" are therefore inevitable, but their members are likely to blackball any states that refuse to play by the rules of international democratic capitalism. Such states, like present-day Cuba, Libya, and North Korea, may come to be regarded as international rogues or pariahs and may try to form a global "counterculture" to oppose the dominant system, but the advantages of reforming and conforming to international regimes will be great. Thus, economically, politically, and socially, states will become ever more similar as they grow increasingly inter-dependent.

As boundaries lose their functionality, sovereignty over territory will lose its meaning, and eventually may become a liability. With the growing importance of skills, knowledge, capital, and advanced technology, the relative value of natural resources, and the advantages of control over them, will steadily decrease. Large populations and extensive territory, which once were the foundations of eco-nomic, political, and military power (see Chapters Six and Eleven), may mean only increased concerns for and costs of health care, welfare, and environmental man-agement. Although the most powerful states of the twentieth century were two superpowers with vast territories, in the twenty-first century they may be "virtual states," trade and financial capitals with hardly any territory (see Chapter Five). Many of these Information Age versions of Renaissance-era Venice could wield influence far greater than their size.[2] (Some of the "smart" money has already bet on Singapore.)

This auto worker, assembling vehicles for export at a General Motors plant in Mexico, personifies the globalization of manufacturing and increased economic interdependence in the New Era.

SOURCE: AP/Wide World

It is easy to find evidence pointing to the realization of this "one world" scenario. More and more states, even authoritarian giants like China, clamor to join the World Trade Organization and move to reduce barriers to trade and investment. The European Union moves, albeit fitfully and incrementally, toward common environmental and safety regulations, a common currency, and even a common "social charter." Other regional trade groups like ASEAN, MERCOSUR, and NAFTA seem determined to expand despite the difficulties of integration and opposition by labor and environmental groups (see Chapters Seven and Eight). The institutionalization of cooperation and international norms has been slowest in the security sphere, but that is to be expected, given the manifest risks of a failure of collective security. Nevertheless, trends in military policy, training, and budgets point to increased emphasis on international cooperation for peacekeeping and peace enforcement, exemplified by NATO's deployment of IFOR and subsequently SFOR in the former Yugoslavia (see Chapter Five). In the eyes of the international community—especially the international business community, which may matter most—the use of force will become legitimate only when authorized by a "concert of powers" which will probably look very much like the UN Security Council.[3] In this scenario, the potential for conflict will still exist, but economic interdependence will greatly reduce the incentives for conflict (at least between Information Age societies), and the response to conflict is more likely to be collective rather than unilateral.

Many would regard this version of the future as a rosy scenario, but the rose has thorns. Labor advocates (including Greider) have described the integrated global economy as capital run wild in search of labor, resulting in decreased health and safety protection for workers and the downward standardization of wages to Third World Levels. Though the statistics are debated, it is likely that the wages of unskilled and semiskilled workers have stagnated or declined because of the huge pool of labor available in developing countries. Even skilled workers are not immune to international competition; experienced software engineers in Mumbai, India, will work for much less than their counterparts in Seattle. Thus, globalization may increase in total output and overall efficiency, but it can also result in heightened economic inequality between workers and investors. This trend may be balanced by two considerations, however. First, although monetary wages may decline, free trade can be expected to increase purchasing power as it allows consumers access to less expensive goods and services. Labor activists may lament the transfer of production outside the United States, but union members can buy inexpensive imports at Wal-Mart to make their paychecks go further. Second, because increased access to the global market creates more jobs in developing countries, the globalized economy could also be described as labor run wild in search of capital. Investment follows productivity in the global market, allowing workers in successful developing countries such as Taiwan, South Korea, and Hungary to enjoy lifestyles about which their grandparents could only dream. In other developing states, such as Mexico and India, jobs in export industries allow many families to live in greater security and comfort, if not in luxury. Although the use of child or forced labor certainly violates international norms and may deserve trade sanctions, the availability of less expensive labor in the South has an upside for both developed and developing states.

Environmental concerns may be a sharper thorn in this rosy scenario. Manufacturers may cut back on environmental safety to increase export profits, while governments look the other way for fear of undermining competitiveness. Decreasing prices for fossil fuels may encourage burning more coal and oil, which may contribute significantly to global climate change (see Chapter Ten). Demand for wood products can lead to accelerated deforestation, particularly in tropical rain forests, with a consequent loss of biodiversity, increase in desertification, and other negative environmental and economic consequences. Moreover, global competitive pressures may lead to slackening of environmental standards in both developed and developing regions.

In any case, regardless of whether they are primarily concerned with labor, agriculture, the environment, or other issues, domestic interest groups will probably have less influence on internationalized processes of policy-making and will have to organize at the international level to maintain their effectiveness. These concerns raise one of the most serious questions in the One World scenario: will globalization mean that environmental regulations, labor laws, and social protection will be standardized upward or downward? Can international institutions enforce stricter standards at the global level, or will environmental, labor, and consumer safety regulations sink to the lowest common denominator? Liberal institutionalism may develop theories capable of addressing these questions, but the answers are not yet clear.

One example, perhaps somewhat trivial on the global scale but to which many students can relate, may serve as a metaphor for the One World scenario. In Germany, brewers were held to strict standards of quality for over three centuries by a purity law, the *Reinheitsgebot*. No beer that failed to meet its standards, which many non-German beers did not, could be sold in Germany. However, European Union rules mandated the standardization of food and drug laws, so the venerable *Reinheitsgebot* was eventually struck down by the European bureaucracy. Germans now enjoy freer trade in beer, at the cost of a once-cherished piece of cultural identity. The One World scenario certainly raises more serious questions on the effects of globalization, especially about collective security, income disparities, and the environment. The demise of the *Reinheitsgebot* points out how increased international interdependence and institutionalization may result in unprecedented prosperity, but can have unintended consequences.

Forward into the Past

Although many liberals thus see a bright future from a systemic viewpoint, realists, true to form, see a darker picture. Recall from Chapter Twelve that realists contend that the search for security in an anarchic system is the overriding dynamic of international relations, and that structural realists conclude that the character of the system and the behavior of the major units within it is shaped by the distribution of power. For realists, economic globalization and information technology have changed the components of power, but they have not changed the nature of power itself nor robbed it of its utility. The economic role of the state may have declined, but states cannot abdicate their responsibility to provide security in the absence of an effective world government. Therefore, realist visions of the future of world politics will continue to be dominated by the necessity of power and the mechanics of power balancing.[4]

As always, from the realist perspective, the distribution of power between the major actors in the system will be crucial. The number of major actors and their relative strength will determine the character of the system. At present, the world may be described as a unipolar or hegemonic system, with the United States clearly the strongest power (see Chapters Five and Twelve). The European Union, Japan, and China are also major economic powers, and as such are potential challengers to American hegemony. China's rapid economic growth, Japan's continued economic strength, and Europe's gradual progress toward ever-closer union are likely to result in a more even distribution of economic power in the coming century. The key questions of the New Era, for realists, are whether these great powers will attempt to convert their economic strength into military capability, and how many of them will emerge as serious rivals for global power.[5]

Some analysts have already concluded that a bipolar competition between the United States and China is inevitable.[6] In their view, the world is on an unalterable course toward a new Cold War between Washington and Beijing. China may never see the need to build an arsenal of strategic nuclear weapons equal to that of the United States, and trying to do so could prove to be a strategic blunder equivalent to Germany's ambitious naval construction program of 1905–1914, which ensured the enmity of Britain and contributed to the outbreak of World War I (see Chapter Three). Likewise, China may not try to match U.S. military technology or challenge American capabilities in space (see Chapter Eleven). Nevertheless, China may come to dominate East Asia militarily and present a serious strategic threat to the United States as well as its Asian and Pacific neighbors (see Chapter Five).

Moreover, China may sooner or later overtake the United States in total economic output, if not per capita income, and may present itself as a rising force in world politics as the Soviet Union did in the 1950s and 1960s (see Chapter Four). Increases in Chinese military and economic power will inevitably make Japan, South Korea, Vietnam, and other regional states feel increasingly threatened, and these states may face an uncomfortable choice between bowing to Beijing (bandwagoning, in realist parlance) or balancing Chinese strength with their own military forces or closer military ties with the United States. A regional arms race with global implications would be the likely result, and indeed is already underway. With fewer cultural similarities to ameliorate hostility, and little apparent likelihood of a Chinese economic collapse to parallel that of the USSR, a Sino-American cold war could become very cold indeed. Although Japan and Europe would almost certainly stay in the American camp in such a bipolar confrontation, the alignments of regional powers like Russia, India, Pakistan, Iran, Vietnam, Brazil, and South Africa could be subject to destabilizing shifts. Taiwan, of course, would be the most likely flash point of a Sino-American confrontation. China's

In a show of strength directed at Taiwan, Chinese soldiers take part in maneuvers in March 1996. Realists predict that China's growing military power will lead to increased regional tensions and challenges to the United States. SOURCE: AP/Wide World

unequivocal goal of reunification, balanced against the pressure on America to uphold deterrence, could easily make Taiwan crises in the twenty-first century even more dangerous than the Berlin and Cuban crises, which brought the twentieth century to the brink of nuclear disaster.

If Japan, Europe, Russia, India, or other states attempt to pursue an independent course and challenge both U.S. hegemony and Chinese ascendancy, the international system may come to resemble the classic multipolar system of the nineteenth century. Perhaps the United States would take on Britain's classic role as balancer, preventing one state from becoming hegemonic without attempting to dominate the others militarily. Shifting alignments and balancing maneuvers would become the order of the day, and future Bismarcks and Metternichs will come into their own as masters of the "great game" of world politics. The game would be played for even higher stakes, however, as all of the players would be armed with nuclear weapons. It may be hoped that weapons of mass destruction would make them more cautious than their Victorian predecessors, but this remains to be seen. Continued multipolar machinations could encourage more players to get into the game, leading to accelerated proliferation of missiles and other advanced weapons and increasing the risks of regional confrontations.

The creation of a "concert of powers," such as a restructured UN Security Council, might help moderate conflict and stabilize the system, but this concert would operate very differently than the liberal version described above. Rather than an institution for collective security, it would function primarily as a bargaining table for the great powers, an arena for conflict and compromise rather than a mechanism for providing for the common good. Systemic theory cannot predict whether such an arrangement would promote a new "golden age of diplomacy" or a new dark age of power politics, but nuclear warheads and ballistic missiles would leave even less tolerance for error than the thin margin that existed in 1914. As John Mearsheimer and others have argued, diplomats in this version of the future might even become nostalgic for the comparative safety and stability of the Soviet-American Cold War.[7]

PRIDE AND PREJUDICE: SCENARIOS FROM THE DOMESTIC LEVEL

Readers may find some of the possibilities considered in the systemic-level visions of the future to be inconsistent with the history and culture of some of the states involved. Would Europe, so closely tied to the United States economically and culturally, really play America off against China? Could China abandon centuries-old traditions and open its economy and society to the world? Furthermore, won't Russia's foreign-policy course depend most strongly on whether it continues to build democracy? By asking these questions, one enters into the domestic level of analysis, which as we saw in the last chapter looks at how the political systems, economic attributes, culture, and other unique characteristics of states affect their policies and relationships in the international arena. From the domestic level, the nature of states within the international system determines the nature of the system. Therefore, scenarios guided by domestic-level theories depend heavily on the ideology, values, and goals of the leading contenders for power and influence in world politics.

A Perpetual Peace

This scenario takes its title and its central premise from the eighteenth-century philosopher Immanuel Kant, who argued that the shared values, goals, procedures, and habits of democracy would cause democratic states to refrain from war against each other. As we saw in Chapter Twelve, contemporary analysts have bolstered Kant's contention with empirical and theoretical studies, though their conclusions have not gone unchallenged.[8] For the sake of argument, let us accept the conclusion that democracies will never, or almost never, fight wars with each other. What would the future of world politics look like if Kant were correct?

On the surface, it might look much the same as it does now. Democratic states would not need transnational institutions to avoid war and negotiate compromises; they would do so naturally. Intergovernmental organizations would exist to facilitate negotiation and to help coordinate policies of mutual interest, more or less like the present-day UN and WTO. Cultural similarities between the democratic states would help prevent misperceptions from aggravating disagreements (see Chapter Twelve), and democratic norms would prevent egregious abuses of human rights. Robust democratic structures would likewise prevent the rise of new Hitlers who might seek to wage aggressive war. Indeed, many argue that if democratic structures had been stronger in Germany's Weimar Republic, the original Hitler would never have been able to threaten Germany's neighbors (see Chapter Three). Disputes and conflicts over trade and territory would still exist, but democratic states would resolve them peacefully.

In this scenario, there might not be a need for collective security, because the likelihood of aggression between democratic states would be vanishingly small. Democracies would certainly look to one another for help in deterring or defending against undemocratic aggressors, and they would probably form alliances for collective defense. These alliances, or perhaps a single global democratic alliance, would probably resemble NATO—indeed, NATO could have a clear and continuing mission in this scenario. Smaller states would continue to try to "free ride" on the collective good of security provided by the major democratic powers, but a demonstrably robust democratic peace would make the costs of defending small democracies more bearable, and the value of intervention to protect or restore democracy more apparent. Would the United States, EU, and NATO been more likely to intervene to prevent ethnic violence in Yugoslavia if that state had been an established democracy rather than a socialist conglomerate? The answer is probably yes, although if Yugoslavia had been democratic, military intervention might not have been necessary.

This future looks very bright for the democratic states, but what about states that are not democracies? The outlook in this scenario is not nearly so good for states that cannot, or will not, adhere to democratic norms. The possibility of violent conflict with democratic states will remain, particularly if the democracies see no need for a global system of collective security. Indeed, an intergovernmental security organization that included both democratic and authoritarian states, like the Concert of Europe (see Chapter Two), might be doomed to failure, because the democracies would be loath to risk their citizens' lives to save a threatened dictatorship. If an instance of aggression against a nondemocratic state threatened the vital interests of the influential democracies, a collective response could be organized under the auspices of the UN, just as it was during the Persian Gulf War (see Chapter Five). But civil wars that did not threaten to spread to members of the democratic club would probably be allowed to play out, much as the conflicts in Liberia, Rwanda, Zaire, and Sierra Leone were in the 1990s. Even when faced with the loss of trade or access to key resources, democracies could prove reluctant to intervene in the kind of conflict that British Prime Minister Neville Chamberlain described in 1938 as "a quarrel in a far-off country among people of whom we know nothing." Chamberlain's words, as Chapter Three describes, signaled the failure of the leading democracies to come to the defense of one of their own, Czechoslovakia, with catastrophic consequences.

The realities of this scenario would likely push borderline democracies to join the democratic club, but the experience of many developing states has shown that the requirements for membership can be difficult to meet. Chapters Eight and Ten discuss how persistent underdevelopment, exploding populations, and shortages of capital and skilled labor can undermine the foundations of a democratic system. Even states that complete the transition to democracy may find the established democracies reluctant to extend economic and security guarantees. The experience of the former communist states of Eastern Europe may be particularly instructive, as Western Europe has proven perhaps too eager to admit these states to NATO while seeking to slow their admission to the European Union (see Chapter Five).

In this scenario, the path China will take is especially critical. Japan, North America, and Europe would probably fall over each other in their rush to strengthen trade and political ties with a China which embraced democracy and adopted international norms of human rights. However, an unrepentantly authoritarian China, even one with liberal trade policies, would seem increasingly threatening to democratic states as its economic and military strength grew. Continued tensions between an unreformed China and the democratic states could easily produce an outcome similar to the new bilateral cold war described in the section on systemic theory, with one crucial difference: alignments would be determined not by strategic interests, but by ideology and domestic political structures. A democratic India, under this scenario, would not be tempted to align with an authoritarian China, but would stay resolutely within the economic and security umbrella of the democratic camp. Conversely, an Iran that maintained its hostility to Western democracy would move even closer to the "leader of the unfree world." The democratic status of developing countries such as Turkey and Serbia, which share borders with more established democracies, would have particular strategic importance. In any case, according to domestic-level arguments, the alignment of developing states would be determined by the character of their domestic political systems, rather than by the whims and maneuverings of leaders like Tito or Nasser.

Thus, the Perpetual Peace is a hopeful scenario as far as it goes. The strength of the democratic peace would ultimately be determined by the strength of democracy in influential and pivotal states, and the ability of democratic states to support threatened democracies. Clearly, the democratic peace would need not only visionary philosophers like Kant, but also pragmatists like Harry Truman and George Marshall, who steadfastly advocated aid to teetering democracies in Europe after World War II (see Chapter Four).

A Clash of Civilizations

The Perpetual Peace scenario postulates that the shared cultural values of civic democracy will promote cooperation. Another domestic-level view of the future, however, contends that cultural differences and the impetus to preserve cultural autonomy will be powerful forces for fragmentation and conflict. This scenario owes its outlook to Samuel Huntington, who, echoing the works of theorists of history such as Arnold Toynbee and Oswald Spengler, has written that the major political conflicts of the coming century will take place along cultural fault lines. Huntington argues that the world is already dividing itself into groups of cultural nations (as opposed to nation-states) distinguished by their historical memory and cultural heritage.[9] Each of these "civilizations" (Western, Slavic, Islamic, Confucian, Hindu, African, and Latin American) has a distinct set of ideological, political, economic, and moral values that shape the world-view of its leaders and citizens and that are embedded in and preserved by its cultural institutions, including governments, corporations or their equivalents, and religious organizations. In many cases, racial divisions reflect and reinforce cultural conflict. From this perspective, ideological controversies are only the most visible intellectual manifestations of deeper cultural conflicts. The net result, according to this scenario, is that the different values, outlooks, and goals of these civilizations will inevitably lead to misunderstandings and conflict as states seek to defend their fundamental cultural principles.

The most striking cultural divide in this view, one that several analysts have predicted will lead to continued conflict, is the gulf between Western culture and Islamic civilization.[10] Based on a strictly defined and strongly held set of religious and cultural principles, Islamic civilization often perceives the secularism and materialism of Western culture as a serious threat. In many Islamic states, Muslim clerics, who often play key political as well as religious roles, fear that Islamic social, cultural, and spiritual values are under constant attack from the West, and conclude that democracy and capitalism must be resisted lest they undermine the Islamic foundations of society. Most Islamists view state, culture, economy, and society as an integrated whole, so an ideological threat to one is a threat to all. In a sense, this view is the mirror image of modernization theory (discussed in Chapter Eight), which holds that cultural and political change go hand in hand with economic development. Islamists agree, and they are determined to prevent cultural change even at the cost of economic and political conflict with the secular West. This viewpoint, and consequently the potential for conflict with neighboring cultures, is strongest in Islamic republics such as Iran and Sudan and is widely held among Islamic insurgent or opposition groups in Algeria, Egypt, Afghanistan, and elsewhere in the Middle East, Africa, and Central Asia.

This scenario holds that culture-driven conflicts will not be limited to the struggle between Islam and the West, however. Conflict is most likely in regions where one civilization borders on another. In Eastern Europe, Slavic cultural values clash with Western ideas, leading to opposition between "Slavophiles" and "Westernizers" in Russia and tension between Western Germans and Slavic Poles. To the south, Turkey straddles the divide between Islam and the West and faces a perpetual internal struggle between the two. The situation is worse in the former Yugoslavia, viewed as a misbegotten attempt to unite Western Croats and Slovenes with Slavic Serbs and Islamic Bosnians, which predictably collapsed into open warfare. Israel is seen as an attempt to force Western culture on the heart of Islamic civilization, and as such must be destroyed (or must, from the opposite viewpoint, kill or be killed). In South Asia, Islamic Pakistan clashes with predominantly Hindu India, which is in turn threatened by China, the fountainhead of Confucian culture. Leaders in Singapore restrict political freedoms in the name of safeguarding Confucian values. The African civilization clashes with the Islamic in the Sudan and resists Western encroachment, in the form of neocolonialism,

The aftermath of Hindu-Muslim rioting in Bombay, India, July 1997. Tensions between Hindus and Muslims present a vivid example of the "clash of civilizations."

SOURCE: AP/Wide World

throughout the continent. Meanwhile, Latin American civilization is engaged in continuous economic and cultural conflict with the United States, which exemplifies the best and worst of Western culture. Tensions between civilizations in the Western hemisphere underlie Latin American resistance to U.S. economic domination, American discomfort with Hispanic immigration, and the reluctance of the North American public to admit Mexico and Chile into NAFTA.

Surely, however, these clashing civilizations share some common interests. Can't we all just get along? In this scenario, the answer is no, not really, because cultures must either expand or die. Unless civilizations increase their scope and strength, they are bound to contract and crumble under pressure from more dynamic cultures. Once-great civilizations such as the Egyptian, Classical Greek, and Arab collapsed because they could not stand up to the economic, political, and ideological force of aggressive civilizations, such as the Roman Ottoman, which in turn were destroyed or assimilated by other rising cultures. Cultural compromise always entails the abandonment of fundamental values, and if its fundamental values are not upheld a civilization is lost. Thus, although civilizations can coexist for a time and may conclude a truce, they can never really make peace. Because the basic problems preventing reconciliation lie within societies, they are not resolvable by tinkering with the relations between states. In the long run, the only way to deal with the threat from rival civilizations is to convert them or destroy them. The dog-eat-dog, Darwinian view of world politics under this scenario makes the power-driven realist paradigm, in which peace can be achieved through a balance of power, look benign by comparison.

Some commentators regard the resurgence of ethnic conflict following the Cold War as a regression to nationalism or even tribalism. In a struggle between ethnic nations, however, there is at least a possibility for coexistence. Two groups may dispute territory, resources, or rights within a political system, but the continued existence of one does not inherently threaten any others, so at some point they may decide to resolve their differences through compromise or partition, and live in peace. The Clash of Civilizations scenario admits no such possibility, as all civilizations are built on values that are held to be universal, and a universal truth must prevail against others to prove its own validity. Mere cultures can coexist, but civilizations must conquer or die. Conflict, whether military, economic, or cultural, is therefore inevitable in an international system driven by a struggle between civilizations, until and unless one comes to dominate the entire world. Many Marxists, you will recall from Chapters Two and Six, argued that the rival ideologies of communism and capitalism were also locked in mortal struggle, but the Marxists were confident that communism would prevail and throw capitalism onto the ash heap of history. In the Clash of Civilizations scenario, however, there is no guarantee that any one civilization will eventually triumph, though it is certain that some civilizations that now seem strong and vigorous will join their glorious predecessors in the ashes.

THE DEFINING MOMENT: THE FUTURE FROM THE INDIVIDUAL LEVEL

What can the individual level of analysis say about the future of world politics? The previous sections have mentioned the kind of leaders who would be required in various scenarios, but do leaders make the times, or do the times make the leaders? On the one hand, if systemic or domestic-level theorists are correct, individuals will not have a significant impact on the nature of the international system regardless of their political power and cultural influence. Impersonal forces will determine the fundamental character of international politics, and leaders will be able to make only temporary, minor adjustments. Successful leaders, regardless of whether they are technocrats or demagogues, will be people who fit the times, selected for characteristics that make them most effective in the prevailing international environment. On the other hand, if factors at the individual level really matter—if individual leaders will set the tone and shape the structure of global politics—how can we guess where the international system is headed without knowing whose hands are on the wheel?

Yet the individual level may have more to say about the future than we might observe at first glance. From this perspective, even if systemic or state-level forces determine the basic structure of world politics, change in the international system does not come about through a smooth, seamless, self-regulating process. Rather, the evolution of world politics is a punctuated equilibrium, wherein one system exists until it suffers a profound shock, then collapses into chaos and conflict until it is replaced by a new, stable system. In order for the new system to function, however, its structure must be clarified and its rules must be codified. In other words, a regime that embodies the new system must be constructed. History shows us that the leaders who guide that process of construction can have an influence on the nature of the new system that is far from trivial. In other words, the individuals who are "present at the creation" (as Truman's foreign policy advisor Dean Acheson put it) of a new world order can shape and define that order, for better or worse.

At the Congress of Vienna in 1815, for example (see Chapter Two), representatives of the European great powers hoped to create institutions that would help avoid a recurrence of the turmoil and devastation of the Napoleonic Wars. Metternich, Talleyrand, and Castlereagh shared a belief that major wars were caused by domestic instability, so they tried to design a system that would prevent or contain upheavals like the French Revolution. France, the power that many had seen as the main source of disruption and aggression, was represented at the Congress even though it had been defeated by the other powers, and it was thereby recognized as an essential part of the solution to instability as well as a contributor to the problem. As a result, the institution created by the Congress, the Concert of Europe, functioned for a time to prevent internal problems and rivalries among the great powers from escalating into another devastating general war. Of course, the Concert had flaws and limitations; most obviously, it gave short shrift to the smaller nations within Europe and almost no thought to the peoples outside it. The arrangements made at Vienna were eventually undermined by Industrial Revolution, demographic changes, the unification of Italy and Germany, and the weakening and collapse of the multinational Austrian, Russian, and Ottoman Empires. It is difficult to imagine, however, how any institution could survive unaffected by the wrenching changes that transformed nineteenth-century Europe. In any case, the fact that the Concert worked as well as it did was due in large part to the foresight and moderation of the leaders who established it.[11]

The same could not be said of the Versailles settlement more than a century later (see Chapter Three). Although most of the great powers contributed to the start of World War I in one way or another, Germany and Austria, who lost the war, were branded as aggressors and were left out of the Versailles negotiations, as were Bolshevik Russia and the soon-to-be-extinct Ottoman Empire. Leaders of the victorious Western Allies like Britain's David Lloyd George and France's Georges Clemenceau sought to punish Germany and ensure its continued weakness, and in doing so burdened the infant Weimar Republic with crushing reparations payments, ignoring German perceptions of a threat from revolutionary Russia. At the same time, the Allies squabbled among themselves for a division of colonial spoils from the former Ottoman and German empires in the Middle East and Africa. They intended the League of Nations to function as a new and improved Concert of Europe, but Germany and Russia were excluded, and President Woodrow Wilson's moralistic arguments did not convince the traditionally isolationist United States to join the new institution. The "war to end wars" thus ended with a "peace to end peace," which paved the way for the rise of Hitler and blocked the path to effective collective security.[12] Within a generation, conflicts in Europe exploded into the most destructive war in history.

At the end of World War II, Churchill, Roosevelt, and Stalin, although they each had their separate motives, hoped the United Nations would be able to maintain the peace that the League of Nations could not keep.[13] As Chapter Four explains, however, their plans fell by the wayside when it became clear that an exhausted Britain could neither maintain its traditional role as the balancer in Europe nor block Soviet plans to expand Communist influence in Eastern Europe, the Mediterranean, the Middle East, and East Asia. The German question also threatened to ignite future conflicts if a stable resolution could not be found in the new bipolar world. The UN might have become an impotent facade, or the war-weary but essentially undamaged United States might have retreated back into isolationism. However, the leaders of the Western Allies recognized that the stability of the nascent system would require unprecedented levels of U.S. economic aid and a continued American security presence in Europe. Through diplomacy, legislation, and public relations, the Allies developed a system of institutions that would maintain the balance of power in Europe without alienating Germany. Although the UN could act to enforce collective security only with the consent of all the major powers (which it rarely received in the ensuing decades), policies such as the Truman Doctrine and Marshall Plan and new institutions like NATO and the European Community prevented the Cold War from escalating into a hot war in Europe. In the Middle East, Africa, East Asia, and elsewhere, where the institutional basis for the new international system was not as well defined, regional tensions posed serious threats to global peace, but the United Nations at least provided a framework within which the superpowers could contain regional conflicts (see Chapter Five).

The fall of the USSR and the rise of China threatened to create new tensions, though the threat of nuclear conflagration receded with the end of the Cold War. Chapter Five relates how Iraq's attempt to take over Kuwait and the disintegration of Yugoslavia presented new security challenges, or perhaps represented a resurgence of traditional problems engendered by regional and ethnic conflict. Although the transitional generation of post–Cold War leaders like George Bush, Helmut Kohl, Margaret Thatcher, and Boris Yeltsin did not share a common world-view, they were finally able to use the United Nations as an institution for containing and managing conflict in a manner similar to that intended by the organization's founders. Civil wars in Bosnia, Somalia, Chechnya, Liberia, Rwanda, and all too many other places quickly showed that existing institutions could not cope well with intrastate conflicts, and it soon became clear that collective security would have to be limited in application in order to be effective. Peace enforcement would be attempted only in cases of overt international aggression in areas of widespread, vital economic or security interest; otherwise, peacekeepers would continue to be deployed only after conflicting parties agreed on at least a temporary peace. Meanwhile, the strengthening of the European Union and the World Trade Organization established a trend toward international governance

Leaders of the G-7 states and Russia meet in Denver in 1997. Such summit meetings remind us that the character and beliefs of leaders can have a profound impact on world politics. Pictured left to right are Canadian Prime Minister Jean Chretien, U.S. President Bill Clinton, British Prime Minister Tony Blair, Russian President Boris Yeltsin, and German Chancellor Helmut Kohl.   SOURCE: AP/World Wide

on transnational issues, especially in the economic sphere, and summits held by members of the Organization for Economic Cooperation and Development and the Asia-Pacific Economic Cooperation group pointed the way toward broad, if not always deep, support for freer trade.

Perhaps because the most recent shock to the international system was, fortunately, not as severe as previous upheavals, the outlines of a new system have been slower to form. The process of institutional design, of setting precedents for international action, and of ensuring that new regimes and organizations function as they are intended is still going on. Observers of the individual level in world politics would probably agree that future summits may not be as dramatic as those in Vienna or Versailles, but the work they undertake will be equally important. As Chapter Nine points out, future roles for global and regional organizations, and indeed for the nation-state, in world politics have yet to be determined.[14] It remains to be seen whether leaders at the start of the twenty-first century will craft innovative political institutions and agree on new rules for the global economy, or fall back into age-old patterns of conflict and compromise. Moreover, periods of systemic transition are not the only times when leaders and leadership can have a profound impact. As we saw in the historical chapters of this book, leaders such as Napoléon, Bismarck, Hitler, Chamberlain, Gorbachev, and Reagan all played decisive roles in the world politics of their respective eras.

Theorists from the individual level cannot tell us what kind of leaders the world will have, but they can tell us how they can make a difference. There is no way to know ahead of time if the leaders who will shape the emerging international system will be open-minded and visionary, shortsighted and selfish, or some combination of all the above. One thing is certain, however: more of them will be women. As the pressure to reform the UN and other institutions continues, more of them will also represent the developing regions of the South. What difference, if any, these differences will make is open to debate (see Chapter Twelve). Nevertheless, increased diversity among the leaders who will build a new system raises hopes that the institutions they construct, unlike some previous regimes that have reflected the interests and beliefs of narrow elites in traditional centers of power, will be more equitable for humankind as a whole. From the individual level, however, the crucial attributes of future leaders will not be group characteristics such as race, gender, or class, but unique individual qualities such as values and beliefs, personal experience, and style of leadership. After all, systems, institutions, ideologies, and culture are all abstractions; individuals make the policies and decisions that shape world politics.

CONCLUSION: CHOOSE YOUR FUTURE

Discussion of the individual level naturally brings us back to the point from which we began our introduction to world politics in Chapter One: the growing impact of international affairs on our individual lives. How will world events affect our own goals and values? Can we expect a future dominated by increased cooperation or intensified conflict? What impact will globalization and fragmentation have on our security, our prosperity, and our cultural identity? How will international regimes and interdependence transform our communities and our countries? How can theories of world politics from any level of analysis help us answer any of these questions?

By now, the student of world politics should be able to tackle this last question using the information and concepts presented in this book. One way to begin is to choose one of the scenarios for the future considered in this chapter—perhaps the most interesting, the most hopeful, or the most disturbing. Then consider how closely the scenario resembles your apprehension of the world. How well does it describe the international events you observe? Does it help explain trends and patterns? Do current developments seem to validate the scenario, or to argue against it? Can we point to any evidence that indicates that the international system is taking the form that the scenario describes? Which of your perceptions and ideas on world politics does the scenario confirm, and which does it challenge? Overall, does today's international environment make more sense, or less, when viewed from the scenario's conceptual lens? Answers to these questions will help determine how well the theories upon which the scenario is based capture the structure and operation of contemporary world politics.

Next, think about the scenario's resemblance to periods of history considered in this book. Have we seen this world before? What events transpired to bring about a system similar to that described in the scenario? How was that system maintained? What were the defining events and conflicts of the period? Was it stable or unstable? How and why did it break down, and what followed it? Was it historically unique, or did it resemble other periods in important ways? Questions like these can be used to examine how well various approaches to the study of international politics can enhance our understanding of historical events, and to trace connections between previous episodes and current trends.

Finally, consider the assumptions and antecedents of the scenario in the light of what you know about the present and what you have learned about the past. How valid is the scenario's fundamental premise? What are the necessary conditions for its realization, or in other words, what would have to happen in order for it to come about? What are the variables and turning points that would shape the development of the system the scenario describes? Which problems and conflicts are likely to be resolved under the scenario, and which are likely to get worse? Does the scenario imply accelerated globalization, increased fragmentation, or both? Do currently observable trends make the scenario appear more likely or less possible? Is the scenario an impossible dream, an all-too-probable nightmare, or somewhere in between? These questions can be explored to see what the scenario can tell us about the future of world politics. With further study, the theories underlying each scenario can be applied directly to investigate historical or current events, and to construct new scenarios and other possible futures.

All these questions can help us think about the future of world politics, but there is one more we must ask ourselves: What can we *do* about it? Regardless of how one conceptualizes world politics, or which approach one adopts to analyze and understand it, we all have a responsibility to appreciate how world affairs affect our lives, and vice versa. We all have choices to make as citizens, as producers and consumers, as beneficiaries of cultural traditions, and as guardians of an environmental heritage.

Looking at the momentous events and great leaders in the history of world politics, or at the supranational institutions that regulate the global economy, might make us feel rather small and inconsequential, but it shouldn't. We are all inheritors of a common historical and intellectual legacy, and the most powerful institutions will ultimately fail if they do not meet our human needs. Moreover, in an increasingly interdependent world, our actions can have a global impact on the lives of others and on future generations. In this sense, we all are world leaders, and we all have a responsibility to choose a vision of the future and to do what we can to help achieve it.

So go ahead—use the building blocks for the study of world politics this book has offered as tools to build an understanding of the events, forces, trends, and connections that make up the international system. In your further study of international relations, construct an appreciation of the complex process of change that continuously reshapes world politics, the global environment, and the world economy. Learn how to take an active role in that process. Choose your future.

Notes

Chapter 1

1. Lyrics from "It's a Small World" (Sherman).
2. Lyrics from "Russians" (Sting).
3. Lyrics from "Imagine" (Lennon).
4. For a more detailed discussion of the role of natural resources in world politics, see Chapter 7 of Richard Rosecrance, *The Rise of the Trading State* (New York: Basic Books, 1986), or Daniel Yergin, *The Prize: The Epic Quest for Oil* (New York: Simon & Schuster, 1991).
5. Figures reflect direct investment at market value, quoted in Russell B. Scholl, "The International Investment Position of the United States in 1995," *Survey of Current Business* 76/77 (July 1996), pp. 36–44.
6. This breakdown follows that presented by Kenneth Waltz in *Man, the State, and War: A Theoretical Analysis* (New York: Columbia University Press, 1959).

Chapter 2

1. For analyses of political and economic trends during this period, see W. H. McNeill, *The Rise of the West* (Chicago: University of Chicago Press, 1967) and *The Pursuit of Power: Technology, Armed Forces and Society Since 1000 AD* (Chicago: University of Chicago Press, 1983); Albert Hirschmann, *The Passions and the Interests* (Princeton, NJ: Princeton University Press, 1977); and E. L. Jones, *The European Miracle* (Cambridge: Cambridge University Press, 1981).
2. For an overview of early European imperial motives and strategies, see Carlo Cipolla, *Guns and Sails in the Early Phase of European Expansion* (London: Pantheon, 1965).
3. The Spanish Empire is described in C. Gibson, *Spain in America* (New York: Harper & Row, 1966); and J. H. Parry, *The Spanish Seaborne Empire* (London: Hutchinson, 1966). For a dramatic account of Spain's conquest of Mexico, see Hugh Thomas, *Conquest* (New York: Simon & Schuster, 1993).
4. The story of Anglo-French imperial rivalry is told in J. H. Parry, *Trade and Dominion: The European Overseas Empires in the Eighteenth Century* (London: Weidenfeld and Nicolson, 1971) and C. G. Reynolds, *Command of the Sea: The History and Strategy of Maritime Powers* (New York: Morrow, 1974).
5. For more on social and political conditions in eighteenth-century Europe, see J. C. D. Clark, *English Society 1688–* (Cambridge: Cambridge University Press, 1985); and C. B. A. Behrens, *Society, Government, and the Enlightenment* (New York: Harper & Row, 1985).
6. On the causes and nature of wars in the eighteenth century, see Kalevi J. Holsti, *Peace and War: Armed Conflicts and International Order 1648–1989* (Cambridge: Cambridge University Press, 1991); Geoffrey Parker, *The Military Revolution* (Cambridge: Cambridge University Press, 1988); and Jeremy Black, *European Warfare, 1660–1815* (New Haven, CT: Yale University Press, 1994).
7. The relative strengths and weaknesses of the eighteenth-century European powers are discussed in Paul Kennedy, *The Rise and Fall of the Great Powers* (New York: Random House, 1987), pp. 73–142.
8. For an overview of the major wars in eighteenth-century Europe, see Michael Howard, *War in European History* (New York: Oxford University Press, 1976).
9. Gordon A. Craig and Alexander L. George, *Force and Statecraft* (New York: Oxford University Press, 1983), pp. 19–20.
10. Quoted in Derek McKay and H. M. Scott, *The Rise of the Great Powers, 1648–1815* (London: Longman, 1983), p. 164.
11. For more on the development of the idea of nationalism and its role in the French Revolution, see Eric Hobsbawm, *Nations and Nationalism since 1780* (Cambridge: Cambridge University Press, 1990) and Lia Greenfeld, *Nationalism* (Cambridge, MA: Harvard University Press, 1992). For more on the spread of revolutionary ideas, see George Rude, *Revolutionary Europe 1783–1815* (London: Collins, 1964).
12. Quoted in Gunther Rothenberg, "The Origins, Causes, and Extension of the Wars of the French Revolution and Napoleon," *Journal of Interdisciplinary History* 28, no. 4 (Spring 1988), p. 780.

13. There are more books on Napoléon than any other real person, with the possible exception of Jesus of Nazareth. Some of the most useful works on the man and his time are Louis Bergeron, *France Under Napoleon*, trans. by R. R. Palmer (Princeton, NJ: Princeton University Press, 1981); J. C. Herold, *The Age of Napoleon* (London: Weidenfeld and Nicholson, 1963); J. M. Thompson, *Napoleon Bonaparte: His Rise and Fall* (Cambridge, MA: Blackwell, 1990); David Chandler, *The Campaigns of Napoleon* (New York: Macmillan, 1966); and Alistair Horne, *How Far From Austerlitz? Napoleon 1805–1815* (New York: St. Martin's, 1996).

14. Gordon Craig, *Europe since 1815* (New York: Holt, Rinehart and Winston, 1974), pp. 12–13.

15. Ibid., p. 13.

16. For more on the changes wrought by the Industrial Revolution, see W. O. Henderson, *The Industrial Revolution in Europe, 1815–1914* (Chicago: Quadrangle, 1961); David Landes, *The Unbound Prometheus* (Cambridge: Cambridge University Press, 1969); and Sidney Pollard, *Peaceful Conquest: The Industrialization of Europe, 1760–1970* (Oxford University Press, 1981).

17. Geoffrey Best, *War and Society in Revolutionary Europe, 1770–1870* (New York: St. Martin's Press, 1982) discusses the wide-ranging impact of the industrialization of warfare.

18. This pivotal period in the history of France is explored in Maurice Agulhon, *The Republican Experiment, 1848–1852*, trans. Janet Lloyd (New York: Cambridge University Press, 1983).

19. For comprehensive appraisals of the events of 1848 and their aftermath, see Priscilla Robertson, *Revolutions of 1848: A Social History* (New York: Harper Torchbooks, 1960); and L. B. Namier, *1848: The Revolution of the Intellectuals* (London: Oxford University Press, 1962).

20. Napoléon I's son, also called Napoléon, lived out most of his short life as a pampered prisoner in Vienna. No Napoléon II ever ruled France.

21. Carl von Clausewitz, *On War*, rev. ed., ed. and trans. by Michael Howard and Peter Paret (Princeton, NJ: Princeton University Press, 1984), p. 69.

22. Quoted in Henry W. Littlefield, *History of Europe Since 1815* (New York: Barnes and Noble, 1963), p. 48. The life and career of the Iron Chancellor are presented in Edward Crankshaw, *Bismarck* (New York: Viking, 1981); and Otto Pflanze, *Bismarck and the Development of Germany: The Period of Unification, 1815–1871* (Princeton, NJ: Princeton University Press, 1973).

23. Michael Howard describes how and why Prussia won the war in *The Franco-Prussian War* (New York: Macmillian, 1961).

24. Jack Snyder studies the temptations of empire and the consequences of succumbing to them in *Myths of Empire* (Ithaca, NY: Cornell University Press, 1991). For another view, see Michael Doyle, *Empires* (Ithaca, NY: Cornell University Press, 1986).

25. J. Gallagher and Ronald Robinson examine this phase of British imperialism in *Africa and the Victorians* (New York: St. Martin's, 1961), as does Bernard Porter in *The Lion's Share: A Short History of British Imperialism 1850–1970* (London: Longman, 1976).

26. For a classic account of imperial machinations beyond Europe in the late nineteenth century, see William L. Langer, *The Diplomacy of Imperialism* (New York: Knopf, 1935).

27. France's colonial policies are discussed in Winfired Baumgart, *Imperialism: The Idea and Reality of French Colonial Expansion* (New York: St. Martin's Press, 1961).

28. The story of the many-sided struggle over Central Asia is told in Peter Hopkirk, *The Great Game* (New York: Kodansha, 1994).

29. L. L. Farrar assesses the effectiveness of Bismarck's policies and the system of European alliances in general in *Arrogance and Anxiety: The Ambivalence of German Power, 1848–1914* (Iowa City: University of Iowa Press, 1981).

Chapter 3

1. René Albrecht-Carrié, *A Diplomatic History of Europe Since the Congress of Vienna* (New York: Harper & Row, 1973), p. 295.

2. For contending perspectives on the expansion of German power before the First World War, see Fritz Fischer, *War of Illusions: German Policies from 1911 to 1914*, trans. by Marian Jackson (New York: Norton, 1975); and John A. Moses, *The Politics of Illusion: The Fischer Controversy in German Historiography* (New York: Barnes & Noble, 1975). For more on the Anglo-German naval arms race, see Robert K. Massie, *Dread-*

nought: Britain, Germany, and the Coming of the Great War (New York: Random House, 1991).

3. Albrecht-Carrié, *A Diplomatic History of Europe,* pp. 212–214.

4. A. J. P. Taylor, *The Struggle for Mastery in Europe,* (Oxford: Clarion Press, 1957), p. 427; and Paul Kennedy, *The Rise and Fall of the Great Powers* (New York: Vintage, 1987), pp. 215–219.

5. James L. Stokesbury, *A Short History of World War I* (New York: Morrow, 1981), p. 11.

6. Taylor, *The Struggle for Mastery in Europe,* pp. xxix–xxxi.

7. These trends are discussed in Kennedy, *The Rise and Fall of the Great Powers,* pp. 194–249.

8. European colonialism is discussed in more detail in Chapters Five and Six; for more on this subject, the reader is referred to J. Gallagher and Ronald Robinson, *Africa and the Victorians: The Climax of Imperialism in the Dark Continent* (New York: St. Martin's, 1961); and Wilfred Baumgart, *Imperialism: The Idea and Reality of British and French Colonial Expansion* (New York: Oxford, 1982).

9. Quoted in Gordon A. Craig, *Germany, 1866–1945* (Oxford: Clarendon Press, 1978), p. 246.

10. For more on this belief and its origins see Stephen Van Evera, "The Cult of the Offensive and the Origins of the First World War," *International Security* 9 (Summer 1984), pp. 58–107.

11. Cited by J. M. K. Vyvyn in "The Approach of the War of 1914," in *The New Cambridge Modern History,* vol. 12 (Cambridge: Cambridge University Press, 1968), p. 160.

12. Richard Lebow, *Between Peace and War: The Nature of International Crisis* (Baltimore: Johns Hopkins University Press, 1981), pp. 232–233.

13. Charles F. Horne, ed., *Source Records of the Great War* (U.S.A.: National Alumni, 1923), p. 348.

14. Stokesbury, *A Short History of World War I,* p. 29.

15. For more on the outbreak and initial stages of World War I, see Lafore, *The Long Fuse; Joll, The Origins of the First World War;* and Barbara Tuchman, *The Guns of August* (New York: Macmillan, 1962).

16. An outstanding comprehensive account of World War I is B. H. Liddel Hart's *History of the First World War, 1914–1918* (London: Faber & Faber, 1938). John Keegan presents a gripping ground-level description of trench warfare in *The Face of Battle* (New York: Penguin, 1976).

17. John Keegan, *The Face of Battle* (New York: Viking, 1986), pp. 255, 280.

18. Brian Bond, "The First World War," in *The New Cambridge Modern History,* vol. 12 (Cambridge: Cambridge University Press, 1968), p. 194. Kennedy, *The Rise and Fall of the Great Powers,* pp. 271–274.

19. Kennedy, pp. 255, 280.

20. Estimates taken from D. H. Aldcroft, *From Versailles to Wall Street: The International Economy in the 1920s* (Berkeley, CA: University of California Press, 1977), pp. 13–14.

21. For a firsthand account of the squabbling, see Harold Nicolson, *Peacemaking 1919* (London: Constable, 1933).

22. For more on the Versailles settlement's impact on the Middle East and Eastern Mediterranean, see David Fromkin, *A Peace to End All Peace: The Fall of the Ottoman Empire and the Creation of the Modern Middle East* (New York: Avon, 1989).

23. Archibald Wavell, quoted in David Fromkin, *A Peace to End all Peace: The Fall of the Ottoman Empire and the Creation of the Modern Middle East* (New York: Avon, 1989). The Versailles treaty is analyzed in detail from a number of perspectives in Ivo J. Lederer, *The Versailles Settlement: Was It Doomed to Failure?* (Boston: Heath, 1960).

24. Mussolini, his party, and his fascist philosophy are described by James Gregor in *Italian Fascism and Developmental Dictatorship* (Princeton, NJ: Princeton University Press, 1979); and *Young Mussolini and the Intellectual Origins of Fascism* (Berkeley, CA: University of California Press, 1979).

25. Germany's difficulties during this period are outlined in S. W. Halperin, *Germany Tried Democracy: A Political History of the Reich from 1918 to 1933* (New York: Norton, 1965).

26. For more on the causes and effects of the Great Depression, see C. P. Kindelberger, *The World in Depression, 1929–1939,* rev. ed. (Berkeley, CA: University of California Press, 1986).

27. This division follows that of William Manchester in *The Caged Lion,* (London: Michael Joseph, 1988), pp. 52–53.

28. There are a great many works on Hitler and on Germany during the Nazi period. Among the most interesting are William Shirer, *The Rise and Fall of the Third Reich* (New York: Simon & Schuster,

1960); Alan Bullock, *Hitler: A Study in Tyranny*, rev. ed. (New York: Harper & Row, 1964); John Toland, *Adolf Hitler* (Garden City, NJ: Doubleday, 1976); Walter Laqueur, ed., *Fascism: A Reader's Guide* (Berkeley, CA: University of California Press, 1976); and Hanna Arendt, *The Origins of Totalitarianism*, 2d ed. (Cleveland: World, 1958).

29. Kennedy, *The Rise and Fall of the Great Powers*, p. 332.

30. Kennedy, *The Rise and Fall of the Great Powers*, p. 296.

31. The Munich agreement and its implications are discussed in A. J. P. Taylor, *The Origins of the Second World War* (New York: Atheneum, 1965); Henri Nogueres, *Munich*, trans. by Patrick O'Brien (New York: McGraw-Hill, 1965); and P. M. H. Bell, *The Origins of the Second World War in Europe* (London: Longman, 1986). Churchill is quoted from his speech to the House of Commons, October 5, 1938.

32. World War II is arguably the most important event in world history. It is certainly the most recounted, documented, and analyzed. Outstanding among the many books devoted to it are Gordon Wright, *The Ordeal of Total War, 1939–1945* (New York: Langer, 1968); J. F. C. Fuller, *The Second World War* (New York: Meredith, 1968); and B. H. Liddel Hart, *History of the Second World War* (New York: Putnam, 1971).

33. The grand strategies of the major powers during World War II are extensively covered in Gerhard L. Weinberg, *A World At Arms: A Global History of World War II* (New York: Cambridge University Press, 1994).

34. The fall of France is analyzed in detail in Alistair Horne, *To Lose a Battle: France 1940* (Boston: Little, Brown, 1969).

35. Basil Collier, *The Battle of Britain* (New York: Macmillan, 1962) is a classic study of the air war over England.

36. For the planning and execution of the attack on Pearl Harbor, see Walter Lord, *Day of Infamy* (New York: Holt, Rinehart and Winston, 1967).

37. Estimated in Kennedy, *The Rise and Fall of the Great Powers*, p. 332.

38. For analysis of Japan's entry into the war, see Ike Nobutake, ed., *Japan's Decision for War* (Stanford: Stanford University Press, 1967). Axis and Allied campaigns in the Pacific are described in John Toland, *The Rising Sun* (New York: Random House, 1970); and Samuel Eliot Morrison, *Rising Sun in the Pacific* (Boston: Little, Brown, 1975).

39. For a compilation of figures, see Kennedy, *The Rise and Fall of the Great Powers*, pp. 352–357.

40. The strained relations between the Soviet Union and the Western Allies are discussed from different perspectives in John Lewis Gaddis, *Strategies of Containment* (New York: Oxford, 1982), pp. 3–24; and Walter LaFeber, *America, Russia and the Cold War 1975–1990* (New York: McGraw-Hill, 1991), pp. 8–28.

41. For a superb account of the development of the first atomic weapons, see Richard Rhodes, *The Making of the Atomic Bomb* (New York: Simon & Schuster, 1988).

42. For alternative views on the decision to use the atomic bombs, see Barton M. Bernstein, "Roosevelt, Truman, and the Atomic Bomb, 1941–1945: A Reinterpretation," *Political Science Quarterly*, no. 3 (Spring 1975), pp. 23–69; Martin J. Sherwin, *A World Destroyed: The Atomic Bomb and the Grand Alliance* (New York: Random House, 1987); Paul Fussell, *Thank God for the Atom Bomb, and Other Essays* (New York: Ballantine, 1988); and Gar Alperovitz, "Hiroshima: Historians Reassess," *Foreign Policy* 99 (Summer 1995), pp. 15–34.

43. These approximate figures, estimated by Soviet and Western sources, are cited in Kennedy, *The Rise and Fall of the Great Powers*, p. 362.

Chapter 4

1. Quoted in David Holloway, *The Soviet Union and the Arms Race* (New Haven: Yale, 1983), p. 20.

2. Quoted in Joseph Nogee and Robert Donaldson, *Soviet Foreign Policy since World War II* (New York: Macmillan, 1992), p. 96.

3. Deborah Welch Larson, *Origins of Containment: A Psychological Explanation* (Princeton, NJ: Princeton University Press, 1985), p. 76.

4. To sample the range of views on the origins of the Cold War may be found in John Lewis Gaddis, *The United States and the Origins of the Cold War, 1941–1947* (New York: Columbia University Press, 1972); Daniel Yergin, Shattered Peace: The Origins of the Cold War, 2d ed. (New York: Penguin, 1990); Thomas G. Paterson and Robert J.

McMahon, eds., *The Origins of the Cold War,* 3d ed. (Lexington, MA: D. C. Heath, 1991); Melvyn P. Leffler and David S. Painter, eds., *Origins of the Cold War: An International History* (London: Routledge, 1994); and R. C. Raack, *Stalin's Drive to the West, 1938–1945: The Origins of the Cold War* (Stanford, CA: Stanford University Press, 1995).

5. Adam B. Ulam, Expansion and Coexistence: *Soviet Foreign Policy 1917–1973* (New York: Holt, Rinehart and Winston, 1974), p. 428.

6. Winston Churchill, "The Sinews of Peace," March 5, 1946, in *Vital Speeches of the Day,* vol. 12, March 15, 1946, p. 332.

7. William Fox exemplifies this perspective in *The Super-Powers: The United States, Britain, and the Soviet Union—And Their Responsibility for Peace* (New York: Harcourt Brace, 1944).

8. Adapted from Dean Acheson, *Present at the Creation* (New York: Norton, 1969), p. 196.

9. William A. Williams, *The Tragedy of American Diplomacy,* rev. ed. (New York: Delta, 1962), pp. 269–270.

10. "Text of President Truman's Speech on New Foreign Policy," *New York Times,* March 13, 1947, p. 2.

11. Harold F. Gosnell, *Truman's Crises: A Political Biography of Harry S. Truman* (London: Greenwood, 1980), p. 351.

12. *Department of State Bulletin,* June 15, 1947, pp. 1159–1160.

13. Quoted in telegram from U.S. Embassy Moscow to Secretary of State Marshall, May 26, 1947, papers of Joseph Jones, Truman Library.

14. Joan Spero, *The Politics of International Economic Relations* (New York: St. Martin's Press, 1985).

15. U.S. Senate, Committee on Foreign Relations and Committee on Armed Services, *Hearings: Military Situation in the Far East* (Washington: Government Printing Office, 1951), p. 10; and John W. Spanier, *The Truman-MacArthur Controversy and the Korean War* (Cambridge, MA: Belknap, 1959), p. 67.

16. Dwight David Eisenhower, *Mandate for Change* (New York: Doubleday, 1963), p. 181.

17. Ulam, *Expansion and Coexistence,* p. 540.

18. Quoted in William Zimmerman, "Russia and the International Order," *Survey* 58 (January 1966), pp. 209–213.

19. Tom Gervasi, *The Myth of Soviet Military Supremacy* (New York: Harper & Row, 1986), pp. 411–412.

20. Walter LaFeber, *America, Russia, and the Cold War: 1945–1990* (New York, McGraw-Hill, 1991), p. 205.

21. See Malcom Kerr, *The Arab Cold War: Gamal Abdel Nasser and His Rivals* (London: Oxford University Press, 1971).

22. Quoted in Arthur Schlesinger, Jr., *A Thousand Days* (Boston: Houghton Mifflin, 1965), p. 769.

23. For more on the Cuban Missile Crisis, see Graham T. Allison, *Essence of Decision: Explaining the Cuban Missile Crisis* (Boston: Little, Brown, 1971); and James G. Blight and David A. Welch, *On the Brink* (New York: Hill & Wang, 1989).

24. Robert Dallek, *The American Style of Foreign Policy: Cultural Politics and Foreign Affairs* (New York: Oxford University Press, 1983), p. 231.

25. Dallek, *The American Style of Foreign Policy,* p. 241.

26. R. Ernest Dupuy and Trevor N. Dupuy, *The Encyclopedia of Military History, from 3500 B.C. to the Present,* rev. ed. (New York: Harper & Row, 1977), p. 1221.

27. John Lewis Gaddis, *The United States and the End of the Cold War* (New York: Oxford University Press, 1993), p. 231.

28. Address at the commencement exercises of Notre Dame University, May 22, 1977, in *Department of State Bulletin,* June 13, 1977, pp. 621–625.

29. Ronald Reagan, remarks to the National Association of Evangelicals, March 8, 1983, in Strobe Talbott, *The Russians and Reagan* (New York: Vintage, 1984), p. 116.

30. Mikhail Gorbachev, *Perestroika: New Thinking for Our Country and the World* (New York: Harper & Row, 1987), pp. 216–218.

31. Francis Fukuyama, *The End of History and the Last Man* (New York: Free Press, 1992).

32. For a range of analytical perspectives on the end of the Cold War, see Michael R. Beschloss and Strobe Talbott, *At the Highest Levels* (Boston: Little, Brown, 1993), Raymond L. Garthoff, *The Great Transition* (Washington: Brookings, 1994); Richard Ned Lebow and Janice Gross Stein, *We All Lost the Cold War* (Princeton, NJ: Princeton University Press, 1994); Ralph Summy and Michael E. Salla, eds., *Why the Cold War Ended: A Range of*

Interpretations (Westport, CT: Greenwood, 1995); and Jay Winik, *On the Brink: the Dramatic, Behind-the-Scenes Saga of the Reagan Era and the Men and Women Who Won the Cold War* (New York: Simon & Schuster, 1996).

Chapter 5

1. U.S. strategic options and challenges in the New Era are discussed in Barry R. Posen and Andrew L. Ross, "Competing Visions for U.S. Grand Strategy," *International Security* 21, no. 3 (Winter 1997), pp. 5–53.

2. China's potential power is discussed in Denny Roy, "Hegemon on the Horizon?" *International Security* 19/1 (Summer 1994) pp. 149–168; Richard Bernstein and Ross H. Munro, "China I: The Coming Conflict with America," *Foreign Affairs* 76, no. 2 (March/April 1997), pp. 18–32; and Robert S. Ross, "China II: Beijing as a Conservative Power," in the same issue, pp. 33–44.

3. Noteworthy assessments of the emerging structure of the international system may be found in the contributions from William C. Wohlforth, Kenneth N. Waltz, John J. Mearsheimer, and Christopher Layne collected in Michael Brown et al., eds., *The Perils of Anarchy* (Cambridge, MA: MIT Press, 1995).

4. For wide-ranging speculation on the economic, political, and social impact of the information revolution, see Alvin Toffler, *Powershift: Knowledge, Wealth, and Violence on the Edge of the 21st Century* (New York: Bantam, 1991).

5. These themes are discussed in Joseph S. Nye, Jr., *Bound to Lead: The Changing Nature of American Power* (New York: Basic Books, 1991); Paul Kennedy, *Preparing for the Twenty-First Century* (New York: Random House, 1993); Joseph S. Nye, Jr., and William A. Owens, "America's Information Edge," *Foreign Affairs* 75, no. 2 (March/April 1996), pp. 20–36; and Eliot A. Cohen, "A Revolution in Warfare" in the same issue, pp. 37–54.

6. Richard Rosecrance and Arthur Stein, "Interdependence: Myth or Reality?" World Politics 25, no. 3 (October 1973), pp. 1–27.

7. This definition is taken from Kenneth N. Waltz, *Theory of International Politics* (New York: Random House, 1979).

8. Both dimensions of interdependence are taken from Robert Keohane and Joseph Nye, *Power and Interdependence* (Boston: Scott, Foresman, 1989), p. 12–13.

9. Richard Rosecrance, "The Rise of the Virtual State," *Foreign Affairs* 75, no. 4 (July-August 1996), pp. 45–61. For more on the decline of the nation-state as an economic unit, see Jessica T. Mathews, "Power Shift," *Foreign Affairs* 76, no. 1 (January-February 1997), pp. 50–66; Susan Strange, *The Retreat of the State* (Cambridge, UK: *Cambridge Studies in International Relations* 49, December 1996); and Kenichi Ohmae, *The End of the Nation-State* (New York: Free Press, 1995).

10. Boutros Boutros-Ghali, *An Agenda for Peace* (New York: United Nations, 1992).

11. Outstanding among the many works on ethnic conflict and its resolution in an international context are Donald L. Horowitz, *Ethnic Groups in Conflict* (Berkeley, CA: University of California Press, 1985); Michael E. Brown, ed., *Ethnic Conflict and International Security* (Princeton, NJ: Princeton University Press, 1993); and David A. Lake and Donald Rothchild, *Ethnic Fears and Global Engagement: The International Spread and Management of Ethnic Conflict* (Princeton, NJ: Princeton University Press, 1998).

12. Figures from World Bank, *World Development Report 1992*, pp. 218–219.

13. For more on the interrelated balances of power in the Middle East, see L. Carl Brown, *International Politics and the Middle East* (Princeton, NJ: Princeton University Press, 1984); Malcom Kerr, *The Arab Cold War*, 3d ed. (London: Oxford, 1971); and Alan Taylor, *The Arab Balance of Power* (Ithaca, NY: Syracuse University Press, 1982).

14. David Fromkin provides an excellent study of the machinations over the Middle East during and after the First World War in *A Peace to End All Peace: The Fall of the Ottoman Empire and the Creation of the Modern Middle East* (New York: Avon, 1989). Mark Tessler, *A History of the Israeli-Palestinian Conflict* (Bloomington: Indiana University Press, 1994) offers a thorough and balanced analysis of that dispute.

15. The story of the Six-Day War and its aftermath is told in David Kimche and Dan Bawly, *The Sandstorm: The Arab-Israeli War of June 1967* (New York: Stein and Day, 1968); Nadav Safran, *From War to War: The Arab-Israeli Confrontation,*

1948–1967 (New York: Pegasus, 1969); and Edgar O'Ballance, *The Third Arab-Israeli War* (London: Faber & Faber, 1972).

16. For more on the economic, political, and strategic importance of oil and the efforts of many countries to gain and wield the power it provides, see Daniel Yergin, *The Prize* (New York: Simon & Schuster, 1991).

17. The events surrounding the 1973 war are detailed in Chaim Herzog, *The War of Atonement: October, 1973* (Boston: Little, Brown, 1975); and Edgar O'Ballance, *No Victor, No Vanquished: The Yom Kippur War* (San Rafael, CA: Presidio Press, 1978).

18. The complex relationships between the United States, the USSR, and Middle Eastern states in the 1970s and 1980s are explored in Moshe Efrat and Jacob Bercovitch, eds., *Superpowers and Client States in the Middle East* (London: Routledge, 1991); and Steven L. Spiegel, *The Other Arab-Israeli Conflict* (Chicago: University of Chicago Press, 1985).

19. For the inside story of the negotiations at Camp David, see William B. Quandt, *Camp David: Peacemaking and Politics* (Washington, DC: Brookings, 1986).

20. For discussions of the implications of the end of the Cold War on the Middle East from different perspectives, see John Lewis Gaddis, "Toward the Post-Cold War World," *Foreign Affairs* 70, no. 2 (Summer 1991), pp. 102–122; Michael Hudson, "The Middle East Under Pax Americana: How New, How Orderly?" *Third World Quarterly* 13 (1992), pp. 301–316; and Nikkie Keddie, "The End of the Cold War in the Middle East," *Diplomatic History* 16 (1992), pp. 95–103.

21. For more on the Middle East peace process since the Madrid summit see William B. Quandt, *Peace Process: American Diplomacy and the Arab-Israeli Conflict since 1967* (Washington: Brookings, 1993) and David Makovsky, *Making Peace with the PLO* (Boulder, CO: Westview, 1996).

22. For more on the conflict over Kashmir, see Lorne J. Kavic, *India's Quest for Security* (Berkeley and Los Angeles: University of California Press, 1967); J. Bandyopadhaya, *The Making of India's Foreign Policy* (New Delhi: Allied, 1970); and Mushtaqur Rahman, *Divided Kashmir* (London: Lynne Rienner, 1996).

23. The origins and aftermath of the Sino-Indian conflict are discussed in John S. Dalvi, *Himalayan Blunder* (Bombay: Thacker, 1969); and Neville Maxwell, *India's China War* (Garden City, NY: Doubleday, 1972).

24. For more on international relations in South Asia during this period, see Gunnar Myrdal, *Asian Dilemma* (New York: Pantheon, 1968); and Karunaka Gupta, *India in World Politics: A Period of Transition* (Calcutta: Scientific Books, 1969).

25. Details on the Indian-Pakistani war may be found in Robert Jackson, *South Asian Crisis: India, Pakistan, and Bangladesh* (Boulder, CO: Praeger, 1975).

26. Regional relations in South Asia since the end of the Cold War are discussed in Hafeez Malik, ed., *Dilemmas of National Security and Cooperation in India and Pakistan* (New York: St. Martin's, 1993); and Marvin G. Weinbaum and Chetan Kumar, eds., *South Asia Approaches the Millennium: Reexamining National Security* (Boulder, CO: Westview, 1995).

27. See Chapter Four for more on the Korean War. For an analysis of the events leading up to the war and of Sino-American antagonism after 1949, see Tsou Tang, *America's Failure in China, 1941–1950*, 2 vols. (Chicago: Phoenix, 1963); Bruce Cummings, *The Origins of the Korean War* (Princeton, NJ: Princeton University Press, 1981); and Sergei N. Goncharov, John W. Lewis, and Xue Litai, *Uncertain Partner: Stalin, Mao, and the Korean War* (Stanford, CA: Stanford University Press, 1993).

28. Classic studies of the falling out between Moscow and Beijing include O. Edmund Clubb, *China and Russia* (New York: Columbia University Press, 1971); and Donald Zagoria, *The Sino-Soviet Conflict, 1956–1961* (Princeton, NJ: Princeton University Press, 1962).

29. Robert Sutter, *Chinese Foreign Policy after the Cultural Revolution* (Boulder, CO: Westview, 1978), outlines the developments in the region's politics during this period.

30. For more on how this alignment came about, see Raymond L. Garthoff, *Détente and Confrontation* (Washington, DC: Brookings, 1985); and Warren I. Cohen, *America's Response to China*, 3d ed. (New York: Columbia University Press, 1989).

31. Two useful essays on the relationship between China and the other major powers in East Asia after 1989 are Robert Gilpin, "International Politics in the Pacific Rim Area," in Steven L. Spiegel,

ed., *At Issue: Politics in the World Arena,* 6th ed. (New York: St. Martin's, 1991), pp. 130–143; and Marie Gottschalk, "China After Tiananmen: The Failure of American Policy," in the same volume, pp. 173–188.

32. The story of North Korea's nuclear program and the tensions created by it is told in Michael J. Mazarr, *North Korea and the Bomb* (New York: St. Martin's, 1995).

33. To explore security issues in the Asia-Pacific region in the New Era, see Michael Brown, et al., eds., *East Asian Security* (Cambridge, MA: MIT Press, 1996); Gary Klintworth, ed., *Asia-Pacific Security* (New York: St. Martin's, 1996); and Susan L. Shirk and Christopher P. Twomey, eds., *Power and Prosperity: Economics and Security Linkages in Asia-Pacific* (London: Transaction, 1996).

34. This image is graphically presented by Robert D. Kaplan in *The Ends of the Earth: A Journey at the Dawn of the 21st Century* (New York: Random House, 1996).

35. The transformation of the role of the state is examined in James N. Rosenau and Ernst-Otto Czempel, *Governance Without Government: Order and Change in World Politics* (New York: Yale University Press, 1992); David A. Lake, "Anarchy, Hierarchy, and the Variety of International Relations," *International Organization* 50, no. 1 (Winter 1996) pp. 1–34; Stephen D. Krasner, "Compromising Westphalia," *International Security* 20, no. 3 (Winter 1995–96), pp. 115–152; and Brad Roberts, ed., *Order and Disorder after the Cold War* (Cambridge, MA: MIT Press, 1995).

Chapter 6

1. For a more detailed introduction, see Thomas D. Lairson and David Skidmore, *International Political Economy: The Struggle for Power and Wealth* (Fort Worth, TX: Harcourt Brace, 1993), pp. 11–34. For more advanced discussions, see Robert Gilpin, *The Political Economy of International Relations* (Princeton, NJ: Princeton University Press, 1987); and Joan Edelman Spero, *The Politics of International Economic Relations,* 4th ed. (New York: St. Martin's Press, 1990).

2. This is the standard definition of comparative advantage using the Heckscher-Ohlin model. For an in-depth analysis of comparative advantage and other variants of the concept, see Paul Krugman and Maurice Obstfeld, *International Economics: Theory and Policy* (New York: HarperCollins, 1991), pp. 9–118; and James R. Markusen et al., *International Trade: Theory and Evidence* (New York: McGraw-Hill, 1995).

3. David Ricardo, *The Works and Correspondence of David Ricardo,* Piero Sraffa, ed. (Cambridge: University Press for the Royal Economic Society, 1951).

4. Hundreds of books and thousands of articles have been written from both sides of the free trade versus protectionism debate. Good surveys of the arguments from both sides are collected in Jeffry A. Frieden and David A. Lake, eds., *International Political Economy: Perspectives on Global Power and Wealth,* 3d ed. (New York: St. Martin's, 1995). For a strong presentation of the case for free trade, see Jagdish Bhagwati, *The World Trading System at Risk* (Princeton, NJ: Princeton University Press, 1991); for arguments critical of free trade, see Paul Krugman, *Rethinking International Trade* (Cambridge, MA: MIT Press, 1990); William Greider, *One World, Ready or Not: The Manic Logic of Global Capitalism* (New York: Simon & Schuster, 1997); and Dani Rodrik, *Has Globalization Gone Too Far?* (New York: Institute for International Economics, 1997).

5. For more on the Great Depression's effect on the world economy, see Charles Kindelberger, *The World in Depression, 1929–1939* (Berkeley, CA: University of California Press, 1973).

6. There is also a statistical discrepancy due to some inaccuracy in measuring this data. For more on the balance of payments, see Lairson and Skidmore, *International Political Economy,* pp. 15–20.

7. For more detailed analyses of these three schools of thought, see Gilpin, *The Political Economy of International Relations,* pp. 25–41.

8. Do not confuse this "classical" liberalism with "liberal" thought as it is used in contemporary American politics. Many advocates of government intervention to mitigate the ill effects of market failure or to redistribute wealth are called "liberals" today, but these ideas are not liberalism as the term is used in discussion of international political economy.

9. Spero, *The Politics of International Economic Relations,* pp. 5–6.

10. Duncan Snidal, "Limits of Hegemonic Stability

Theory," *International Organization* 39 (Autumn 1985), pp. 579–614.

11. Karl Marx, *Capital,* ed. Friedrich Engels. *Manifesto of the Communist Party,* by Karl Marx and Friedrich Engels, 2d ed. (Chicago: Encyclopedia Britannica, 1990).

12. For a political argument, see Ronald Rogowski, *Commerce and Coalitions: How Trade Affects Domestic Political Alignments* (Princeton, New Jersey: Princeton University Press, 1989). For the economic underpinnings, see Wolfgang F. Stolper and Paul Samuelson, "Protection and Real Wages," *The Review of Economic Studies* 9, no. 1 (1941), pp. 58–73.

13. Jeffrey A. Frieden, "Invested Interests: The Politics of National Economic Politics in a World of Global Finance," International Organization 45, no. 4 (Autumn 1991), pp. 425–451.

14. Data on estimated proved oil reserves drawn from *International Petroleum Encyclopedia* (Tulsa, Oklahoma: Pennwell Publishing Company, 1992), pp. 270–271.

15. For data on amount of arable land available to individual countries, see *UN Food and Agriculture Organization Yearbook,* 1990, pp. 6–34.

16. Ibid., pp. 22–34.

17. World Bank, *World Development Report 1992,* pp. 218–219.

18. Ibid., p. 221.

19. Ibid., p. 253.

20. In the late 1980s, the United States had 1.4 million scientists, the Japanese 400,000, and the West Germans 100,000. The United States had 2.2 million engineers, the Japanese 1.1 million, and the West Germans 500,000. Comparisons of U.S., Japanese, and West German R&D efforts, 1986–1989, from Joseph S. Nye, Jr., *Bound to Lead: The Changing Nature of American Power* (New York: Basic Books, 1991), p. 166.

21. Joseph Grieco, *Cooperation among Nations: Europe, America, and Non-Tariff Barriers to Trade* (Ithaca, NY: Cornell University Press, 1990), p. 22.

22. See Robert Keohane, *After Hegemony: Cooperation and Discord in the World Political Economy* (Princeton, NJ: Princeton University Press, 1984); and Stephen Krasner, ed., *International Regimes* (Ithaca, NY: Cornell University Press, 1983).

23. This position is taken in Susan Strange, "Cave! Hic Dragones: A Critique of Regime Theory" in Krasner, *International Regimes,* pp. 337–354.

24. Stephen Krasner, "State Power and the Structure of Foreign Trade," *World Politics* (April 1976), pp. 317–347.

25. Duncan Snidal, "The Limits of Hegemonic Stability Theory," *International Organization* 39, no. 4 (Autumn 1985), pp. 579–614.

26. See Kindelberger, *The World in Depression.*

Chapter 7

1. See Rondo Cameron, *A Concise Economic History of the World from Paleolithic Times to the Present,* 2d ed., (Oxford: Oxford University Press, 1993) for a comprehensive survey.

2. A.G. Kenwood and A.I. Lougheed, *The Growth of the International Economy 1820–1990,* 3d ed. (London: Routledge, 1992).

3. For more details, see Cameron, *A Concise Economic History,* pp. 163–190; and David S. Landes, *The Unbound Prometheus: Technological Change and Industrial Development in Western Europe from 1750 to the Present* (Cambridge: Cambridge University Press, 1969), pp. 41–123.

4. P. J. Cain and A.G. Hopkins, "The Political Economy of British Expansion Overseas, 1750–1914," *Economic History Review* 33, no. 4 (November 1980), p. 472.

5. McCloskey, "The Industrial Revolution," p. 112.

6. See Cain and Hopkins, "The Political Economy of British Expansion Overseas," pp. 474–475. In fact, the Americas (the United States plus Latin America) accounted for roughly 60 percent of the cumulative increase in British exports between 1783 and 1812.

7. Gilpin, *The Political Economy of International Relations,* p. 31.

8. Cain and Hopkins, "The Political Economy of British Expansion Overseas," p. 475.

9. Cameron, *A Concise Economic History,* p. 279.

10. See Kenwood and Lougheed, *The Growth of the International Economy,* pp. 12–13.

11. Cameron, *A Concise Economic History,* pp. 242–248.

12. For more background, see Sidney Pollard, *The Industrialization of Europe, 1760–1970* (Oxford: Oxford University Press, 1982), pp. 172–183.

13. Kenwood and Lougheed, *Growth of the International Economy,* pp. 70–73.

14. Aaron Friedberg, *The Weary Titan: Britain and the*

Experience of Relative Decline (Princeton, NJ: Princeton University Press, 1988).

15. For more on this period, see Peter Gourevitch, *Politics in Hard Times: Comparative Responses to International Economic Crises* (Ithaca, NY: Cornell University Press, 1986).

16. Lairson and Skidmore, *International Political Economy*, p. 52.

17. Barry J. Eichengreen, *Golden Fetters: the Gold Standard and the Great Depression, 1919–1939* (New York: Oxford University Press, 1992).

18. See Alan Milward, *War, Economy and Society, 1939–1945* (Berkeley, CA: University of California Press, 1977), p. 67.

19. Kenwood and Lougheed, *Growth of the International Economy*, p. 245.

20. For more on the establishment of the Bretton Woods institutions, see Lairson and Skidmore, *International Political Economy*, pp. 65–66; and Spero, *The Politics of International Economic Relations*, pp. 21–27.

21. See Spero, *The Politics of International Economic Relations*, pp. 68–73, for details.

22. John Odell, *U.S. International Monetary Policy* (Princeton, NJ: Princeton University Press, 1982), pp. 203–205.

23. For an in-depth discussion of the oil crisis in the early 1970s, see Daniel Yergin, *The Prize: The Quest for Oil, Money, and Power* (New York: Simon & Schuster, 1991), pp. 563–652, Joel Darmstadter and Hans H. Landsberg, "The Crisis," in *The Oil Crisis,* edited by Raymond Vernon (New York: Norton, 1976), pp. 20–33; and Simon Bromley, *American Hegemony and World Oil* (University Park, PA: Pennsylvania State University Press, 1991).

24. Yergin, *The Prize*, p. 588.

25. For more on the increasing importance of trade politics (along with a good introduction to the modern global trading system), see John H. Jackson, *The World Trading System*, 2d ed. (Cambridge, MA: MIT Press, 1997).

26. Noteworthy analyses of the competitiveness of nations and firms in the modern world economy include Michael Porter, *The Competitive Advantage of Nations* (New York: Free Press, 1990); Jean Claude Derain, *America's Struggle for Leadership in Technology* (Cambridge: MIT Press, 1990); and William J. Baumol, *Productivity and American*

Leadership: The Long View (Cambridge: MIT Press, 1991).

27. Lairson and Skidmore, *International Political Economy,* p. 101.

28. For detailed explanations of the economic failure of socialism in Eastern Europe and the former USSR, see Charles Gati, *The Bloc That Failed* (Bloomington: Indiana University Press, 1990); and Bartlomiej Kaminski, *The Collapse of State Socialism* (Princeton, NJ: Princeton University Press, 1991).

29. John Pinder discusses the economic links between Eastern and Western Europe in *The European Community and Eastern Europe* (London: Pinter, 1991).

30. For more on the successes and failures of G-7 summits, see Robert Putnam and Nicholas Bayne, *Hanging Together: Cooperation and Conflict in the Seven-Power Summits* (Cambridge: Harvard University Press, 1987); Martin Feldstein, *International Economic Cooperation* (Chicago: University of Chicago Press, 1988); and Richard N. Cooper et al., *Can Nations Agree? Issues in International Economic Cooperation* (Washington, DC: Brookings, 1989).

31. Lairson and Skidmore, p. 113.

32. For more on the development and organization of the European Community, see Nicholas Colchester and David Buchan, *Europower* (New York: Times Books, 1990); and John Pinder, *European Community* (Oxford: Oxford University Press, 1991).

33. The potential benefits and drawbacks of EMU are evaluated in David Currie, "The Pros and Cons of EMU" (London: Economist Intelligence Unit, 1997).

34. For background on NAFTA, see Jeffrey Schott, ed., *Free Trade Areas and U.S. Trade Policy* (Washington:, DC: Institute for International Economics, 1989); and William A. Orme, *Understanding NAFTA* (Austin, TX: University of Texas Press, 1996).

35. Figures cited in Sidney Weintraub, "NAFTA at Three: A Progress Report" (Washington, DC: Center for Strategic and International Studies, 1997). For a broad economic, social, and environmental critique of NAFTA, see Ralph Nader, ed., *The Case Against Free Trade: GATT, NAFTA, and the Globalization of Corporate Power* (New York: North Atlantic Books, 1993).

36. Felix Pena discusses MERCOSUR's successes and setbacks in "New Approaches to Economic Integration in the Southern Cone," *Washington Quarterly* 18/3 (Summer 1995), pp. 113–122.

37. Various preliminary answers to this question are offered in T. David Mason and Abdul M. Turay, eds., *Japan, NAFTA, and Europe* (New York: St. Martin's, 1995).

Chapter 8

1. For a discussion of this issue, see Robert Gilpin, *The Political Economy of International Relations* (Princeton, NJ: Princeton University Press, 1987), pp. 263–305.

2. Classic works of modernization theory include Gabriel Almond and James Coleman, eds., *The Politics of the Developing Areas* (Princeton, NJ: Princeton University Press, 1960); W. W. Rostow, *Stages of Economic Growth: A Non-Communist Manifesto* (Cambridge: Cambridge University Press, 1960); David Apter, *The Politics of Modernization* (Chicago: University of Chicago Press, 1965); Samuel Huntington, *Political Order in Changing Societies* (New Haven: Yale University Press, 1968); Lucian Pye, *Communications and Political Development* (Princeton, NJ: Princeton University Press, 1963); and Dankwart Rostow, *A World of Nations: Problems of Political Modernization* (Washington, DC: Brookings, 1967).

3. World Bank, *World Development Report 1997,* pp. 188–189.

4. Ibid., pp. 188–189.

5. Ibid., p. 198.

6. Leading critiques of modernization theory are offered in Gunnar Myrdal, *Economic Theory and Underdeveloped Regions* (New York: Harper & Row, 1971); Ragnar Nurske, *Problems of Capital Formation in Underdeveloped Countries* (New York: Blackwell, 1953); and Raul Prebisch, "Commercial Policy in the Underdeveloped Countries," *American Economic Review* 49 (May 1959), pp. 251–273.

7. This criticism is advanced in Arrighi Emmanuel, *Unequal Exchange: A Study of the Imperialism of Trade* (New York: Monthly Review Press, 1972), rebutted in Paul Samuelson, "Illogic of Neo-Marxist Doctrine of Unequal Exchange,"
Inflation, Trade, and Taxes, edited by David Belsey et al. (Columbus, OH: Ohio State University Press, 1976), pp. 96–107; and discussed in Sven Grassman and Erik Lundberg, eds., *The World Economic Order—Past and Prospects* (London: Macmillan, 1981).

8. Howard Wiarda, "Toward a Nonethnocentric Theory of Development: Alternative Conceptions from the Third World," *Journal of Developing Areas* 17, no. 4 (July 1983), p. 437.

9. Outstanding works on dependency theory include Henrique Cardoso and Enzo Faletto, *Dependency and Development in Latin America* (Berkeley: University of California Press, 1979); David Collier, *The New Authoritarianism in Latin America* (Princeton, NJ: Princeton University Press, 1979); Theotonio Dos Santos, "The Structure of Dependence," *American Economic Review* 60 (1970), pp. 235–246; Peter Evans, *Dependent Development: The Alliance of Multinational, State, and Local Capital in Brazil* (Princeton, NJ: Princeton University Press, 1979); Andre Gunder Frank, *Latin America: Underdevelopment or Revolution* (New York: Monthly Review Press, 1969); and Osvaldo Sunkel and Pedro Paz, *El subdesarrollo latinoamericano y la teoria del desarrollo* (Mexico City: Siglo Veintiuno, 1970).

10. See Immanuel Wallerstein, *The Modern World-System: Capitalist Agriculture and the Origins of the European World-Economy in the Sixteenth Century* (New York: Academic Press, 1976).

11. This argument is set forth in Joseph L. Love, "Raul Prebisch and the Origins of the Doctrine of Unequal Exchange," *Latin American Research Review* 15, no. 3 (1980); and Joan Robinson, "Trade in Primary Commodities" in *International Political Economy: Perspectives on Global Power and Wealth,* 2d. ed., Jeffrey A. Freiden and David Lake, eds. (New York: St. Martin's, 1991), pp. 376–385.

12. Robinson, "Trade in Primary Commodities," pp. 378–379.

13. Joan Spero, *The Politics of International Economic Relations,* 4th ed. (New York: St. Martin's, 1990), p. 131.

14. Thomas D. Lairson and David Skidmore, *International Political Economy: The Struggle for Power and Wealth* (Fort Worth, TX: Harcourt Brace, 1993), p. 252.

15. Rhys Jenkins, *Transnational Corporations and*

Uneven Development (New York: Meuthen, 1987), p. 10.

16. Lairson and Skidmore, *International Political Economy*, p. 260.

17. Spero, *The Politics of International Economic Relations*, p. 287.

18. See Volker Bornschier and Christopher Chase-Dunn, *Transnational Corporations and Underdevelopment* (New York: Praeger, 1985).

19. For critical reviews of dependency theory, see David Ray, "The Dependency Model of Latin American Underdevelopment: Three Basic Fallacies," Journal of Interamerican Studies and World Affairs 15, no. 1 (February 1973); Sanjaya Lall, "Is Dependence a Useful Concept in Analyzing Underdevelopment?" *World Development* 3, no. 11 (November 1975); and Tony Smith, "The Underdevelopment of the Development Literature: The Case of Dependency Theory," *World Politics* 32, no. 2 (January 1979).

20. See World Bank, *Global Economic Prospects and the Developing Countries 1994* (Washington: World Bank, 1994); and "Poor Relations: Are Third-World Commodity Producers Condemned to Eternal Poverty?" *The Economist,* April 16, 1994, p. 76.

21. See Guillermo O'Donnell, *Modernization and Bureaucratic-Authoritarianism* (Berkeley, CA: University of California Press, 1979).

22. Robert Alexander offers an evaluation of import-substitution industrialization in "Import Substitution in Latin America in Retrospect" in *Progress Toward Development in Latin America: From Prebisch to Technological Autonomy,* edited by James L. Dietz and Dilmus D. James (Boulder, CO: Lynne Rienner, 1991).

23. John Macomber discusses this strategy in "East Asia's Lessons for Latin American Resurgence," *World Economy* 10, no. 4 (December 1987).

24. For more details, see Lairson and Skidmore, *International Political Economy,* pp. 204–205.

25. Robin Broad and John Cavanagh "No More NICs," *Foreign Policy* 72, no. 1 (Fall 1988).

26. See *World Resources 1992–93,* pp. 41–56; and World Bank, *World Development Report 1992* (which focuses on the environmental costs and benefits of development), for discussions of this issue. More details will also be found in Chapter Ten.

27. For more on the NIEO, see Robert Mortimer, *The Third World Coalition in International Politics,* 2d. ed. (Boulder, CO: Westview, 1984); Jeffrey Hart, *The New International Economic Order* (New York: St. Martin's Press, 1983); Stephen Krasner, *Structural Conflict: The Third World Against Global Liberalism* (Berkeley: University of California Press, 1985); and Robert Tucker, *The Inequality of Nations* (New York: Basic Books, 1977).

28. Mortimer, *The Third World Coalition in International Politics,* p. 44. For more on OPEC, see Ian Skeets, *OPEC: Twenty-Five Years of Prices and Politics* (Cambridge: Cambridge University Press, 1988); and Daniel Yergin, *The Prize* (New York: Simon & Schuster, 1991).

29. See Krasner, *Structural Conflict,* for a discussion of the Group of 77's efforts.

30. World Bank, *World Development Report 1997,* p. 192.

31. OECD figures quoted in "U.S. Loses Rank in Global Giving," *Washington Post,* June 18 1996, p. A10.

32. World Bank figures quoted in *The Economist,* September 25, 1993, special section on Third World finance, p. 12.

33. For analysis of the debt crisis from a variety of perspectives, see Miles Kahler, ed., *The Politics of International Debt* (Ithaca, NY: Cornell University Press, 1985); Vinod Aggarwal, "International Debt Threat: Bargaining Among Creditors and Debtors in the 1980s," *Policy Papers in International Affairs,* no. 79 (Berkeley, CA: University of California Press, 1987); Barbara Stallings and Robert Kaufman, eds., *Debt and Democracy in Latin America* (Boulder, CO: Westview, 1989); and Gianni Vaggi, ed., *From the Debt Crisis to Sustainable Development: Changing Perspectives on North-South Relations* (New York: St. Martin's, 1993).

34. Clyde Farnsworth, "U.S. Will Tie Aid to Exports in Bid to Curb the Practice," *New York Times,* May 14, 1990.

35. "Playing the Aid Game," *World Press Review,* February 1989, p. 51.

36. Judith Tendler discusses this problem in *Inside Foreign Aid* (Baltimore: Johns Hopkins University Press, 1975).

37. Natasha Bechorner, "Water and Instability in the

Middle East," *Adelphi Paper* 273, presented at International Institute for Strategic Studies, London, (Winter 1992–1993), p. 49.

38. For summaries of the pros and cons of NAFTA, see D. K. Brown, A. V. Deardorff, and R. M. Stern, "A North American Free Trade Agreement—Analytical Issues and Computational Assessment," *World Economy* 15, no. 1 (January 1992), pp. 11–29; and the debates in *Foreign Affairs* 72, no. 5 (November–December 1993), and *Foreign Policy* 93 (Winter 1993–1994).

39. For a balanced assessment of the economic effects of NAFTA, see Sidney Weintraub and Julius L. Katz, "NAFTA at Three: A Progress Report" (Washington, DC: Center for Strategic and International Studies, 1997). For the labor critique of NAFTA, see Max Green, *Epitaph for American Labor* (Washington, DC: American Enterprise Institute, 1997).

40. For an overview of the uneven progress of political and economic reform in Latin America, see "Gestures Against Reform," *The Economist* (London), Nov. 30 1996.

41. Max Singer and Aaron Wildavsky, *The Real World Order: Zones of Peace, Zones of Turmoil* (Chatham, NJ: Chatham House, 1993).

42. See Stephan Haggard, *Pathways from the Periphery: The Politics of Growth in the Industrializing Countries* (Ithaca, NY: Cornell University Press, 1990); and Lawrence H. Summers and Vinod Thomas, "Recent Lessons of Development," *World Bank Research Observer* 8, no. 2 (July 1993), pp. 241–254.

Chapter 9

1. This definition comes from Hedley Bull, *The Anarchical Society* (New York: Columbia University Press, 1977), p. 127.

2. For a more detailed introduction to these principles of international law, see Paul Sieghart, *The International Law of Human Rights* (Oxford: Clarendon, 1983), pp. 10ff.

3. Robert F. Drinan, *Cry of the Oppressed: The History and Hope of the Human Rights Revolution* (San Francisco: Harper & Row, 1987).

4. *A Report on the Development Concerning the Deployment of United States Forces to Panama on December 20, 1989* (Washington, DC: U.S. Government Printing Office, 1990), p. 1.

5. For more on the use of the tit-for-tat (or TFT) strategy in international relations, see Robert Axelrod, *The Evolution of Cooperation* (New York: Basic Books, 1984).

6. These aspects of customary law are discussed in Paul Sieghart, *The Lawful Rights of Mankind* (Oxford: Oxford University Press, 1985), pp. 48–62.

7. Sieghart, *The International Law of Human Rights,* p. 11.

8. Quoted in *Los Angeles Times,* February 23, 1993, p. A9.

9. Sieghart, *The Lawful Rights of Mankind,* p. 32.

10. For good discussions of the special human rights concerns of women, see World Health Organization, *Women's Health: Across Age and Frontier* (New York: United Nations Press, 1992); "Violence Against Women," *UN Chronicle,* June 1995, p. 48; and Oloka Onyango, "Women, War, and Rape," *Human Rights Quarterly* 17 (1995), pp. 650–690.

11. For more on the Peltier case, see *New York Times,* April 3, 1988, p. 6A.

12. For estimates of the casualties caused by the fighting in the former Yugoslavia, see Milan Andreevich, "Bosnia & Herzegovina: In Search of Peace," *Radio Free Europe/Radio Liberty Research Report,* June 5, 1992, pp. 5–9; and Patrick Moore, "Ethnic Cleansing in Bosnia: Outrage but Little Action," *Radio Free Europe/Radio Liberty Research Report,* August 28, 1992, pp. 11–15.

13. Nicholas Rengger, *Treaties and Alliances of the World,* 5th ed. (Detroit: Gale Research, 1990). Also see *UN Chronicle* 30, no. 1 (March 1993), p. 93.

14. Union of International Associations, ed., *Yearbook of International Organization 1992/1993* (Munich: Saur, 1992).

15. For more on the objectives and formation of the League, see Edward Hellet Carr, *The Twenty Years' Crisis* (New York: Harper & Row, 1964).

16. Hans Morgenthau, *Politics among Nations,* 5th ed. (New York: Knopf, 1978), p. 200.

17. "On the Lines: The UN Role in Preventing and Containing Conflict," *United Nations Association of United States of America News,* 1985; and "Report of the 18 UN Issues Conference," 1987, Stanley Foundation.

18. See "Settling Some Old Scores in Cambodia," *New York Times,* July 13, 1997; and "The Game the Khmer Rouge Played and Lost," *New York Times,* June 25, 1997. For views on the UN's mission in Cambodia, see *Los Angeles Times,* February 23, 1993, pp. H1–2; William Branigin, "UN Performance at Issue as Cambodian Vote Nears," *Washington Post,* May 20, 1993, A25; and William Branigin, "Tarnishing UN's Image in Cambodia," *Washington Post,* October 29, 1993, A33.

19. See *The Blue Helmets: A Review of United Nations Peacekeeping,* 2d ed. (New York: United Nations, 1997).

20. *UN Chronicle,* June 1993, p. 73.

21. The possibilities and problems with UN peacekeeping are debated in William Durch and Barry Blechman, "Keeping the Peace: The United Nations in the Emerging World Order" (Washington: Henry L. Stimson Center, March 1992); John Blodgett, "The Future of UN Peacekeeping," *Washington Quarterly* 14, no. 3 (Winter 1991); and a special issue of *Survival* 32, no. 3 (May–June 1990), which includes contributions from Brian Urqhardt, Aleksandr Belonogov, and Augustus Norton and Thomas Weiss among others.

22. See David Baldwin, *Economic Statecraft* (Princeton, NJ: Princeton University Press, 1985).

23. For more on the Arab League, see *Yearbook of International Organizations 1992/1993,* p. 1166ff.

24. CSCE's role in the Yugoslav crisis is discussed in James E. Goodby, "Peacekeeping in the New Europe," *The Limited Parnership: Building a Russian–U.S. Security Community* (Oxford: University Press, 1993).

25. Figures from U.S. Department of State, "Patterns of Global Terrorism: 1990," *Terrorism* 14 (1991), pp. 253–254.

26. Thomas Hobbes, *Leviathan,* Michael Oakeshott, ed. (New York: Collier, 1962), p. 100.

Chapter 10

1. Figures from Population Reference Bureau, *World Population Data Sheet 1997;* projections from U.S. Bureau of the Census, *World Population Profile 1994,* p. 5.

2. Council of Europe, Directorate of Economic and Social Affairs, "The Changing Age Structure of the Population and Future," *Population Studies* 18 (1985).

3. U.S. Bureau of the Census, *World Population Profile 1996,* pp. 1–2.

4. "Mexico City, Sao Paulo Likely to Rank as World's Largest Cities Soon," *UN Observer & International Report* 13, no. 2 (February 1991), p. 3.

5. Mark S. Hoffman, ed. *The World Almanac & Book of Facts* (New York: World Almanac, 1994).

6. Sadik, "The 1990s: The Decade of Decision," *Populi* 17, no. 2 (1990), pp. 10–19.

7. Sadik, "The 1990s: The Decade of Decision," pp. 17, 22.

8. See McGeorge Bundy, "Population: An Inescapable Problem," *Populi* 17, no. 1 (1990), pp. 20–24.

9. Figure on undocumented aliens from U.S. Immigration and Naturalization Service; on the sources and destinations of migrants, see Organization on Economic Cooperation and Development, *Trends in International Migration 1996.*

10. For more on female migrant workers, see Shirley Hune, "Migrant women in the context of the International Convention on the Protection of the Rights of All Migrant Workers and Members of Their Families," *International Migration Review* 25/4 (1991), pp. 800–815; and Cynthia Enloe, *Bananas, Beaches, and Bases* (Berkeley: University of California Press, 1989), pp. 181–194.

11. Anne-Christine D'Alesky, "UNHCR: Facing the Refugee Challenge," *UN Chronicle* 28, no. 3 (September 1991), p. 43.

12. United Nations High Commission on Refugees (UNHCR) estimate, 1997.

13. U.S. Committee for Refugees, *Refugee Reports,* December 31, 1992, pp. 9–13.

14. *Refugee Reports,* pp. 9–13.

15. "Convention on Migrant Worker Rights Adopted," *UN Chronicle* 28, no. 1 (March 1991), pp. 80–81.

16. D'Alesky, "UNHCR: Facing the Refugee Challenge," p. 46.

17. "Iraqi Refugee Tragedy Steers UN on New Path to Humanitarian Aid," *UN Observer & International Report* 13, no. 6 (August 1991), p. 4.

18. D'Alesky, "UNHCR: Facing the Refugee Challenge," pp. 53–54.

19. U.S. Committee for Refugees, *World Refugee Survey 1992,* p. 35.

20. Figures taken from FAO "Food, Agriculture, and

Food Security: The Global Dimension" (Technical paper 96/TECH/1), 1996. See also N. Alexandratos, ed., *World Agriculture: Towards 2010* (Rome: FAO, 1995).

21. Robert C. Johansen, "A Human World Community," in Robert J. Art and Robert Jervis, eds., *International Politics* (Glenview, IL: Scott, Foresman, 1985), p. 76.

22. Good discussions of future world food supplies may be found in Lester R. Brown and Hal Kane, *Full House: Reassessing the Earth's Population Carrying Capacity* (New York: Norton, 1994); Tim Dyson, *Population and Food: Global Trends and Future Prospects* (London: Routledge, 1996); and Donald O. Mitchell et al., *The World Food Outlook* (New York: Cambridge University Press, 1997).

23. FAO, *Global Watch,* July 22 1997.

24. For a detailed explanation of why this occurs, see "Somalia, Operation Restore Hope: A Preliminary Assessment" (London: African Rights, May 1993); and Peter Madden, "Brussels Beef Carve-up: EC Beef Dumping in West Africa" (London: Christian Aid, April 1993).

25. Kidron and Segal, *The New State of the World Atlas,* 4th ed., (New York: Simon & Schuster, 1991), pp. 106–107.

26. FAO estimates quoted in M. Bied-Charreton, P.G. Reichert, and K. Janz, "The Role of Remote Sensing in FAO's Global Forest Assessment and Monitoring Programme" (Rome: FAO, 1996).

27. Harrison, "Beyond the Blame-Game: Population-Environment Links," pp. 19–20.

28. R. Paul Shaw, "Population Growth: Is It Ruining the Environment?" *Populi* 16, no. 2 (1989), p. 22.

29. Estimates cited in U.S. Council on Environmental Quality and Department of State, *The Global 2000 Report to the President,* vol. 2, p. 331.

30. Sadik, "The 1990s: The Decade of Decision," pp. 8–9.

31. World Resources Institute, *World Resources 1996–1997* (New York: Oxford University Press, 1996), Ch. 14.

32. Estimate quoted in Kidron and Segal, *The New State of the World Atlas,* 4th ed., p. 107.

33. World Resources Institute, *World Resources 1996–1997* (New York: Oxford University Press, 1996), Ch. 14; and Sadik, "The 1990s: The Decade of Decision," pp. 8–9.

34. The prediction is made by George W. Rathjens in "Energy and Climate Change," in Jessica T. Matthews, ed., *Preserving the Global Environment* (New York: Norton, 1990), p. 169.

35. See Harrison, "Beyond the Blame-Game," p. 17; and Bruce Babbit, "Earth Summit," *World Monitor* (January 1990) p. 30.

36. Hiroshima Nakajima, "Epidemiology and the Future of World Health," *Epidemiological Bulletin* 12, no. 4 (1990), p. 4.

37. Barry R. Bloom, "Vaccines for the Third World," *World Health* (June–July–August 1990), p. 13.

38. William H. Foege, "International Health Developments after the Elimination of Smallpox," *World Medical Journal* 38, no. 1 (January–February 1991).

39. Foege, "International Health Developments after the Elimination of Smallpox."

40. The reemergence of malaria is described in Ellen Ruppert Shell, "Resurgence of a Deadly Disease," *Atlantic Monthly,* August 1997, pp. 45–60.

41. World Health Organization, World Health Organization, *Weekly Epidemiological Record,* August 21, 1992, pp. 258–259.

42. Sharyl Stolberg, "Afflictions Expected to Kill 4 Million Annually by 2010," *Los Angeles Times,* March 30, 1990, p. A30.

43. Estimates from WHO primer on AIDS quoted in *Public Health Reports* 111/1 (January–February 1996), p. 7.

44. James Slack, "Responding to the Global Epidemic of AIDS," *Policy Studies Journal* 20, no. 1 (1992), pp. 125–126.

45. Ivan Gillibrand, "AIDS in Africa," *World Medical Journal* 35, no. 2, (March–April 1988), p. 18.

46. WHO primer on AIDS, 1996, and WHO data cited in *Index to International Statistics 1996.*

47. Estimates given in WHO primer on AIDS, 1996.

48. Alan Whiteside and David Fitsimmons, *The AIDS Epidemic: Economic, Political, and Security Implications* (Conflict Series, no. 251) (London: Research Institute for the Study of Conflict and Terrorism, 1992), p. 6.

49. Kimball, "AIDS: The Global Epidemic," p. 299.

50. Ivan Gillibrand, "AIDS in Africa," *World Medical Journal* 35, no. 2 (March–April 1988), p. 18.

51. WHO press release, Aug. 24, 1995. Emerging diseases are surveyed in disturbing detail in Laurie Garret, *The Coming Plague: Newly Emerging*

Diseases in a World Out of Balance (New York: Farrar, Strauss, and Giroux, 1994).

52. Nakajima, p. 2.

53. Foege, "International Health Developments after the Elimination of Smallpox," p. 7.

54. Jose Antonia Najera-Morrondo, "Malaria Control: History Shows It's Possible," *World Health* (September–October 1991), p. 32.

55. WHO press release, May 20, 1996.

56. Estimates from National Narcotics Intelligence Unit, Strategic Intelligence Section, "The Availability of Southwest Asian Heroin in the United States," May 1996.

57. See William H. Overbolt, "Dateline Drug Wars: Burma—the Wrong Enemy," *Foreign Policy* 77 (Winter 1989–1990), pp. 72–191.

58. Rachel Ehrenfeld, *Narco-Terrorism* (New York: Basic Books, 1990), pp. 63–64.

59. Marjorie Miller, "New Bosses Taking Over Cocaine Traffic," *Los Angeles Times*, February 20, 1993, pp. A10–A11.

60. Ehrenfeld, *Narco-Terrorism*, pp. 52–73.

61. Rensselaer W. Lee III, "The Political Economy of the Andean Cocaine Industry" in *At Issue: Politics in the World Arena*, edited by Steven L. Spiegel (New York: St. Martin's, 1991), p. 272.

62. William Drozdiak, "World Crime Groups Expand Cooperation, Spheres of Influence," *New York Times*, October 5, 1992, pp. A12, A16.

63. Eve Kouidri Kuhn, "Grim Assessment Greets Arrival of the UN's New Narcotics 'Czar,'" *UN Observer & International Report* 13, no. 3 (March 1991), p. 10.

64. Joseph Treaster, "Smuggling and Use of Illicit Drugs Are Growing, UN Survey Finds," *New York Times*, January 13, 1992, p. A6.

65. Kuhn, "Grim Assessment," p. 10.

66. Ehrenfeld, *Narco-Terrorism*, pp. 1–19.

67. Carey Goldberg, "Russian Police Warn of Cocaine Blizzard," *Los Angeles Times*, February 27, 1993, p. A7.

68. International Narcotics Trafficking and Money Laundering Task Force, *Causes and Cures, A National Campaign on the Narcotics Epidemic* (Washington, DC: GPO, 1991).

69. Figures from U.S. Department of Health and Human Services, "National Household Survey on Drug Abuse Main Findings 1995."

70. Michael Isikoff, "30 Nations Join in Attacks on Drug Cartels," *Washington Post*, August 31, 1988, p. A4.

71. "What America's Users Spend on Illegal Drugs, 1988–1991." U.S. Office of National Drug Control Policy, August 1993.

72. Bruce Michael Bagley, "Dateline Drug Wars: Colombia—The Wrong Strategy," *Foreign Policy* 77 (Winter 1989–1990), pp. 159–160.

73. For examples of some of these efforts, see Tracy Wilkinson, "Central Americans Vow War on Drugs at Belize Summit," *Los Angeles Times*, February 20, 1993; and Gabriel Marcell and Donald E. Schulz, "U.S. Drug Czar's Praise Hints at Likely Certification for Mexico," *Los Angeles Times*, January 30, 1997.

74. For details on this case, see David Lauter, "Mexico Leader Scolds Quayle Over Abduction," *Los Angeles Times*, April 27, 1990, pp. A1, A13.

75. Lee, "The Political Economy of the Andean Cocaine Industry," pp. 277–278.

76. Ehrenfeld, *Narco-Terrorism*, pp. 86–87.

77. See Lucia Mouat, "War on Drugs Becomes More Cooperative, Global," *Christian Science Monitor*, January 29, 1992; "The Enemy Within: Drugs Policy," *The Economist*, May 15, 1993, p. 31; and Global Policy Project, United Nations Association of the United States of America, "The Global Connection: New International Approaches for Controlling Narcotic Drugs" (1992).

78. Wilkinson, p. A11.

79. "War on Illicit Narcotics," *UN Chronicle* 27, no. 2 (June 1990), p. 54.

80. "Stronger International Response to Drug Problem Needed, UN Board States," *UN Chronicle* 28, no. 3 (September 1991), p. 62.

81. "Drugs Know No Boundaries," *UN Chronicle* 27, no. 2 (June 1990), p. 54.

82. Michael Isikoff, "World Drug Problem Worsening, UN Reports," *Washington Post*, January 11, 1990, p. A24.

83. "General Assembly Message to World: Reduce Drug Demand," *UN Chronicle* 27, no. 2 (June 1990), pp. 53–60.

84. "Developed Nations Promised Aid to Curtail Drug Demand," *UN Chronicle* 27, no. 3 (September 1990), pp. 60–64.

85. Dan Fisher, "Drug Conference Calls for Global Effort Against Traffickers," *Los Angeles Times*, April 12, 1990, p. A6.

86. U.S. Department of State Bureau of International Narcotics Matters (BINM), *International Narcotics Strategy Report* (Washington, DC: U.S. Government Printing Office, 1992), pp. 22–25.

87. *International Narcotics Strategy Report,* p. 26.

88. Stephen Flynn, "Worldwide Drug Scourge: The Response," Part II, *Brookings Review* (Spring 1993).

89. Sean Anderson and Stephen Sloan, *Historical Dictionary of Terrorism* (London: Scarecrow Press, 1995), p. 8.

90. Paraphrased from George Rosie, *Directory of International Terrorism* (Edinburgh: Mainstream Publishing, 1996), p. 18.

91. Kent Layne Oots, *A Political Organization Approach to International Terrorism* (Westport: Greenwood Press, 1986), p. 22.

92. U.S. Department of State, "Patterns of Global Terrorism 1996" (April 1997).

93. Paul Wilkinson, "Terrorist Targets and Tactics: New Risks to World Order" (Research Center for the Study of Conflict and Terrorism, December 1990).

94. Anderson and Sloan, p. 9.

95. U.S. Department of State, "Patterns of Global Terrorism 1996."

96. John Dinse and Sterling Johnson, "Ideologies of Revolutionary Terrorism," in Henry Han, ed., *Terrorism and Political Violence* (New York: Oceana Publications, 1993).

97. Richard Clutterbuck, *Terrorism in an Unstable World* (London: Routledge, 1994), p. 3.

98. D. P. Sharma, *Countering Terrorism* (New Delhi: Lancers, 1992), p. 154.

99. Ibid., pp. 157–158.

100. Figures from *British Petroleum* 1997 *Statistical Review of World Energy,* quoted in *Mining Journal,* July 18, 1997, p. 50.

101. International Energy Association, *Energy Policies of IEA Countries 1996,* p. 14

102. Figures taken from *UN World Economic and Social Survey,* 1996.

103. For more on the IEA, see Robert O. Keohane, *After Hegemony: Cooperation and Discord in the World Political Economy* (Princeton, NJ: Princeton University Press, 1984) pp. 217–237.

104. See Robert J. Lieber, "Oil and Power after the Gulf War," *International Security* 17/1 (Summer 1992).

105. *Energy Policies of IEA Countries 1991,* pp. 9, 70.

106. Ibid., p. 304.

107. Ibid., pp. 43, 295.

108. Ibid., p. 14.

109. Daniel Yergin explores the role of oil and energy in international politics in *The Prize: The Epic Quest for Oil* (New York: Simon & Schuster, 1991).

110. Figures from "The Earth Summit," *UN Chronicle* (June 1992), p. 60.

111. See Ewan W. Anderson, "Water: The Next Strategic Resource" in *The Politics of Scarcity: Water in the Middle East,* Joyce R. Starr and Daniel C. Stoll, ed. (Boulder, CO: Westview Press, 1988); and Joyce R. Starr, "Water Wars," *Foreign Policy* 82, no. 2 (Spring 1991). For a contrary view, see Peter Beaumont, "The Myth of Water Wars and the Future of Irrigated Agriculture in the Middle East," *Water International* 10/1 (1994) pp. 9–21.

112. For more on the plan and its reception by the Arab League, see David Wishart, "The Breakdown of the Johnston Negotiations over the Jordan Waters," *Middle Eastern Studies* 26, no. 4 (October 1991), pp. 536, 546; and Selig A. Taubenblatt, "Jordan River Basin Water: A Challenge in the 1990s," in Starr and Stoll, *The Politics of Scarcity,* p. 46.

113. These issues are outlined in Frederic C. Hof, "The Water Dimension of Golan Heights Negotiation," *Middle East Policy* 5/2 (May 1997), pp. 129–141.

114. For more on Israeli-Palestinian water issues, see Jad Isaac, "Core Issues of the Palestinian-Israeli Water Dispute" (Applied Research Institute of Jerusalem, 1996); and Ralph H. Salmi, "Water, The Thin Red Line: The Interdependence of Palestinian and Israeli Water Resources," *Studies in Conflict & Terrorism* 20 (Summer 1997), pp. 15–65.

115. See Thomas Naff, "Information, Water, and Conflict: Exploring the Linkages in the Middle East," *Water International* 22/1 (March 1997), pp. 16–27; and Mary Morris, "Water and Conflict in the Middle East: Threats and Opportunities," *Studies in Conflict & Terrorism* 20 (Summer 1997), pp. 15–65.

116. Taubenblatt, "Jordan River Basin Water: A Challenge in the 1990s," p. 13.

117. Serdar Guner, "The Turkish-Syrian War of Attri-

tion: The Water Dispute," *Studies in Conflict & Terrorism* 20 (Summer 1997), pp. 105–116; and Starr, "Water Wars," pp. 28–31.

118. Servet Multu, "The Southeastern Anatolia Project (GAP) of Turkey: Its Context, Objectives, and Prospects," *Orient* 37/1 (1996), pp. 59–86; and Robert Olson, "Turkey-Syria Relations Since the Gulf War: Kurds and Water," *Middle East Policy* 5/2 (May 1997), pp. 168–193.

119. Raj Krishna, "The Legal Regime of the Nile River Basin" in *The Politics of Scarcity,* Joyce R. Starr and Daniel C. Stoll, ed. (Boulder, CO: Westview Press, 1988), pp. 28–30.

120. Starr, "Water Wars," pp. 22–23; and Alan Cooperman, "Egypt Clones a Nile," *U.S. News & World Report,* May 19, 1997, pp. 33–36.

Chapter 11

1. Richard J. Barnet, "Challenging the Myths of National Security," *New York Times Magazine,* April 1, 1979, p. 25.

2. Robert M. Bowman, "Bush Era Begins," *Space and Security News,* January 1989, p. 1.

3. A broad definition of security is articulated in Norman Myers, *Ultimate Security: The Environmental Basis of Political Stability* (New York: Norton, 1993). For the good discussions of the relationship of environmental problems to security, see Marc A. Levy, "Is the Environment a National Security Issue? *International Security* 20/2 (Fall 1995) pp. 35–62; and the chapters by Thomas F. Homer-Dixon, Peter H. Gleick, and Miriam R. Lowi in Sean M. Lynn-Jones and Steven E. Miller, eds., *Global Dangers: Changing Dimensions of International Security* (Cambridge, MA: MIT Press, 1995).

4. Karl W. Deutsch, *The Analysis of International Relations* (Englewood Cliffs, NJ: Prentice-Hall, 1968), p. 88. "Parkinson's Law" was formulated by British historian Cyril Parkinson, who observed that work expands to fill the time available for its completion.

5. Edward Luttwak, *The Grand Strategy of the Roman Empire* (Baltimore: Johns Hopkins University Press, 1976), p. 4.

6. Patrick Morgan, *Deterrence: A Conceptual Analysis* (Beverly Hills: Sage Publications, 1977), pp. 27–47.

7. An outstanding work on primary and extended deterrence and the policies designed to achieve both is Alexander L. George and Richard Smoke, *Deterrence in American Foreign Policy: Theory and Practice* (New York: Columbia University Press, 1974).

8. Paul Huth, *Extended Deterrence and the Prevention of War* (New Haven, CT: Yale University Press, 1988), pp. 86–97. Although technically a limited number of Syrian tanks and troops had already intervened, the Israelis clearly deterred a full-scale invasion.

9. Glenn H. Snyder, *Deterrence and Defense: Toward a Theory of National Security* (Princeton, NJ: Princeton University Press, 1961), p. 3.

10. For more on these requirements, see Richard Ned Lebow and Janice Gross Stein, "When Does Deterrence Succeed and How Do We Know?" (Toronto: Canadian Institute for International Peace and Security, 1990).

11. Richard Ned Lebow, and Janice Gross Stein, *Psychology and Deterrence* (Baltimore: Johns Hopkins University Press, 1985).

12. See "Missed Signals in the Middle East," *Washington Post Magazine,* March 17, 1991, pp. 19–41. Glaspie challenges the accuracy of the Iraqi transcript and contends that it excluded her warnings that the "United States would protect its vital interests in the area."

13. This challenge to deterrence is articulated in Richard Ned Lebow and Janice Gross Stein, *We All Lost the Cold War* (Princeton, NJ: Princeton University Press, 1994).

14. See, for example, John Mearsheimer, "Back to the Future: Instability in Europe after the Cold War" in *The Cold War and After: Prospects for Peace,* Sean M. Lynn-Jones, ed. (Cambridge, MA: MIT Press, 1991), pp. 141–192.

15. For more on this and other concepts of nuclear strategy, see Freedman, *The Evolution of Nuclear Strategy.*

16. The heated debate over SDI produced a large number of works for and against the system; for reasonably balanced summaries of these arguments, see The Ethics and Public Policy Center, *Promise or Peril: The Strategic Defense Initiative* (1986); or Steven W. Guerrier and Wayne C. Thomson, eds. *Perspectives on Strategic Defense* (Boulder, CO: Westview, 1987).

17. Changes in NATO strategy are surveyed in Richard Smoke, *National Security and the Nuclear Dilemma*, 2d. ed. (New York: Random House, 1987).

18. The utility of war in the New Era is discussed in Karl Kaysen, "Is War Obsolete?" in Lynn-Jones, *The Cold War and After*, pp. 81–103.

19. See Mearsheimer, "Back to the Future: Instability in Europe after the Cold War."

20. International Institute for Strategic Studies, *The Military Balance 1996/97*, pp. 134–135.

21. Ibid., p. 100.

22. The concentration of armed conflict in poor regions is noted in Dan Smith, *The State of War and Peace Atlas*, 2d ed. (New York: Penguin, 1997).

23. For an overview of this concept, see Jack S. Levy, "The Offensive/Defensive Balance of Military Technology: A Theoretical and Historical Analysis," *International Studies Quarterly* 28, no. 2 (June 1984), pp. 219–238.

24. Concepts of war in space are presented in Thomas Karas, *The New High Ground* (New York: Simon and Shuster, 1984); United States Air Force, "New World Vistas" (1995); and Dana J. Johnson et al., *Space, Emerging Options for National Power* (Santa Monica, CA: RAND, 1997)

25. The U.S. vision of how these technologies will affect warfare is outlined in United States Army, *Fighting Future Wars* (New York: Brassey's, 1994).

26. For more on information warfare, see Winn Schwartau, *Information Warfare: Chaos on the Electronic Superhighway*, 3d ed. (New York: Thunders' Mouth Press, 1996); and Stuart J. D. Schwartzstein, ed., *The Information Revolution and National Security* (Washington, DC: Center for Strategic and International Studies Signficant Issues Series vol. 18, 1997).

27. Patrick Morgan, "Elements of a General Theory of Arms Control" in *Conflict and Arms Control: An Uncertain Agenda*, Paul Viotti, ed. (Boulder, CO: Westview Press, 1986), p. 285.

28. For details on the SALT I agreement and the negotiations that led up to it, see John Newhouse, *Cold Dawn: The Story of SALT* (New York: Holt, Rinehart and Winston, 1973).

29. The threat of "leakage" of nuclear material from the former USSR and means to address it are discussed in James R. Schlesinger et al., *Nuclear Energy Safety Challenges in the Former Soviet Union* (Washington, DC: Center for Strategic and International Studies, 1995); and Oleg Bukharin, "Security of Fissile Materials in Russia," *Annual Review of Energy & Environment* 21 (1996), pp. 467–496.

30. For good discussions of the challenges of proliferation and some possible responses to them, see United States Office of Technology Assessment, *Proliferation of Weapons of Mass Destruction: Assessing the Risks* (Washington, DC: GPO, 1993); Randall Forsberg et al., *Nonproliferation Primer* (Cambridge, MA: MIT Press, 1995); and Mitchell Reiss, *Bridled Ambition: Why Countries Constrain Their Nuclear Capabilities* (Washington, DC: Woodrow Wilson Center Press, 1995).

31. Not all analysts agree that Warsaw Pact forces held the upper hand throughout this period. For a contrary argument, see Tom Gervasi, The Myth of Soviet Military Supremacy (New York: Harper & Row, 1986).

32. George Bush, *National Security of the United States: 1990–1991* (Washington, DC: Brassey's, 1990), p. 3.

33. Frank Barnaby, ed., *The Gaia Peace Atlas: Survival into the Third Millennium* (New York: Doubleday, 1988), p. 14.

Chapter 12

1. Robert Keohane, "Theory of World Politics: Structural Realism and Beyond," in Robert Keohane, ed., *Neorealism and Its Critics* (New York: Columbia University Press, 1986), p. 166.

2. Modern classics of the realist paradigm include Edward Hallett Carr, *The Twenty Years' Crisis: 1919–1939* (New York: Harper & Row, 1964); and Hans J. Morgenthau, *Politics among Nations* (New York: Knopf, 1973).

3. See Kenneth Waltz, *Theory of International Politics* (New York: Random House, 1979), Joseph Grieco, *Cooperation among Nations: Europe, America, and Non-Tariff Barriers to Trade* (Ithaca, NY: Cornell University Press, 1990); and David A. Baldwin, ed., *Neorealism and Neoliberalism: The Contemporary Debate* (New York: Columbia University Press, 1993).

4. Jack Levy, "The Causes of War: A Review of Theories and Evidence" in *Behavior, Society and Nu-*

clear War, vol. 1 (New York: Oxford University Press, 1989), p. 224.

5. John Mearsheimer, "Back to the Future: Instability in Europe after the Cold War," *International Security* 15, no. 1 (Summer 1990), p. 12.

6. Letter to Bishop Mandell Creighton, April 5, 1887.

7. Quoted in Winston S. Churchill, *The Second World War: The Grand Alliance,* vol. 3 (Boston: Little, Brown, 1950), p. 370. Compare this statement with a remark by then-Senator Harry Truman before the United States entered World War II: "If we see that Germany is winning the war, we ought to help Russia, and if Russia is winning the war, we ought to help Germany, and that way let them kill as many as possible."

8. Quoted in Stephan Walt, *The Origins of Alliances* (Ithaca, NY: Cornell University Press, 1987), p. 18.

9. This difficulty is discussed in Alan Ned Sabrosky, "Interstate Alliances: Their Reliability and the Expansion of War" in *The Correlates of War,* J. David Singer, ed. (New York: Free Press, 1980), pp. 161–198.

10. Thomas J. Christensen and Jack Snyder, "Chain Gangs and Passed Bucks: Predicting Alliance Patterns in Multipolarity," *International Organization* 44, no. 2 (Spring 1990), pp. 137–168.

11. See, for example, Randall Schweller, "Domestic Structure and Preventive War: Are Democracies More Pacific?" *World Politics* (1992), pp. 235–269.

12. A.F.K. Organski, *World Politics,* 2d. ed. (New York, Knopf, 1968), p. 362.

13. John Mearsheimer, "Back to the Future: Instability in Europe after the Cold War," *International Security* 15, no. 1 (Summer 1990), pp. 5–56.

14. Karl Deutsch and J. David Singer "Multipolar Power Systems and International Stability," *World Politics* 16, no. 3 (April 1964), pp. 390–406.

15. Richard Rosecrance, "Bipolarity, Multipolarity and the Future," *Journal of Conflict Resolution* 10, no. 3 (September 1966), pp. 314–327.

16. This position is discussed in Mearsheimer, "Back to the Future: Instability in Europe after the Cold War," and John Lewis Gaddis, "The Long Peace: Elements of Stability in the Postwar International System, *International Security* 11, no. 4 (Spring 1988), pp. 99–142.

17. See, for example, Robert Keohane, *After Hegemony: Cooperation and Discord in the World Political Economy* (Princeton, NJ: Princeton University Press, 1984); Robert Axelrod, *The Evolution of Cooperation* (New York: Basic Books, 1984); Axelrod and Keohane, "Achieving Cooperation Under Anarchy: Strategies and Institutions," *World Politics* 38, no. 1 (October 1985), pp. 226–54; and Charles Lipson, "International Cooperation in Economic and Security Affairs," *World Politics* 37, no. 1 (October 1984), pp. 1–23.

18. See Charles Kindleberger, *The World in Depression, 1929–1939* (Berkeley, CA: University of California Press, 1973).

19. J. H. Maurer, "The Anglo-German Naval Rivalry and Informal Arms Control, 1912–1914," *Journal of Conflict Resolution* 36, no. 2 (June 1992), p. 285.

20. Deborah Welch Larson, "Crisis Prevention and the Austrian State Treaty," *International Organization* 41, no. 1 (Winter 1987), p. 32.

21. Classic works of functionalism include David Mitrany, *A Working Peace System* (Chicago: Quadrangle Books, 1966 [1943]; Karl Deutsch, *Political Community and the North Atlantic Area* (Princeton, NJ: Princeton University Press, 1957); Ernest Haas, *The Uniting of Europe: Political, Social, and Economic Forces, 1950–1957* (Stanford: Stanford University Press, 1958); and J. P. Sewell, *Functionalism in World Politics* (Princeton, NJ: Princeton University Press, 1966).

22. The intergovernmentalist position is articulated by Andrew Moravcsik in "Preferences and Power in the European Community: A Liberal Intergovernmentalist Approach," *Journal of Common Market Studies* 31 (1993), pp. 473–524.

23. Waltz, *Theory of International Politics,* p. 121.

24. Graham Allison presents the bureaucratic politics model in *Essence of Decision* (Chicago: Scott Foresman, 1971), pp. 144–184. Not all analysts agree with the premises of the bureaucratic politics paradigm; for a contrary view, see Steven D. Krasner, "Are Bureaucracies Important? (Or Allison Wonderland)," *Foreign Policy* 7 (Summer 1972), pp. 159–179.

25. See for example, "China Computer Sale Causes Split," *Los Angeles Times,* December 5, 1992, A16. The State and Commerce Departments favored the proposed sale of a U.S. high-speed supercomputer to China, while the Defense Department sought to block it, warning of the computer's potential military uses.

26. The Iraqi loan controversy is detailed in Kenneth I.

Juster, "The Myth of Iraqgate," *Foreign Policy* 94 (Spring 1994), pp. 105–119; and Bruce Jentleson, *With Friends Like These: Reagan, Bush, and Saddam 1982–1990* (New York: Norton, 1994).

27. Quoted in Allison, *Essence of Decision,* pp. 141–142.

28. These arguments are collected in Benjamin F. Cooling, ed., *War, Business, and American Society* (New York: Kennikat Press, 1977).

29. Cited in Anne Trotter, "Development of the 'Merchants of Death' Theory," in Cooling, *War, Business, and American Society,* pp. 93–94.

30. Figures cited in Tom Kemp, *The Climax of Capitalism: The U.S. Economy in the Twentieth Century* (London: Longman, 1990), pp. 163–164.

31. See John H. Aldrich, John Sullivan, Eugene Borgida, "Foreign Affairs and Issue Voting: Do Presidential Candidates 'Waltz before a Blind Audience'?" *American Political Science Review* 83, no. 1 (March 1989), pp. 123–141; K. T. Gaubatz, "Election Cycles and War," *Journal of Conflict Resolution* 35 (1991), pp. 212–244; and Barry Hughes, *The Domestic Contents of American Foreign Policy* (San Francisco: Freeman, 1978).

32. For more on the role of ideology in the origins of the Cold War, see Chapter Four.

33. This theme is developed in Louis Hartz, *The Liberal Tradition in America* (New York: Harcourt Brace Jovanovich, 1991); and Stanley Hoffmann, *Gulliver's Troubles, or the Setting of American Foreign Policy* (New York: McGraw-Hill, 1968); and Walter McDougall, *Promised Land, Crusader State: The American Encounter with the World Since 1776* (New York: Houghton Mifflin, 1997).

34. John O'Sullivan, cited in Frederick Merk, *Manifest Destiny and Mission in American History* (New York: Vintage, 1963), p. 259.

35. Hartz, *The Liberal Tradition in America,* pp. 285–286.

36. Hoffmann, *Gulliver's Troubles,* pp. 178–181.

37. Quoted in Kant's *Political Writings,* Hans Reiss, ed. (Cambridge, MA: Cambridge University Press, 1970), p. 100.

38. For examples of this argument, see Zeev Maoz and Nasrin Abdolali, "Regime Types and International Conflict," *Journal of Conflict Resolution* 33, no. 1 (March 1989), pp. 3–36; Harvey Starr, "Why Don't Democracies Fight One Another?" *Jerusalem Journal of International Relations* 14, no. 4 (December 1992), pp. 41–59; and Bruce M. Russett, *Grasping the Democratic Peace* (Princeton, NJ: Princeton University Press, 1993).

39. Michael Doyle, "Liberalism and World Politics," *American Political Science Review* 80, no. 4 (December 1986), pp. 1151–1169, offers a pioneering presentation of this thesis. For an outstanding analysis of the philosophic roots of this position, see Michael Howard, *War and the Liberal Conscience* (New Brunswick: Rutgers University Press, 1978).

40. For an oustanding discussion of the relationship between democracy and peace, see Michael E. Brown, Sean M. Lynn-Jones, and Steven E. Miller, eds., *Debating the Democratic Peace* (Cambridge, MA: MIT Press, 1996).

41. See James M. Goldgeier, *Leadership Style and Soviet Foreign Policy: Stalin, Khrushchev, Brezhnev, Gorbachev* (Baltimore: Johns Hopkins University Press, 1994).

42. See Deborah Welch Larson, *Origins of Containment: A Psychological Explanation* (Princeton, NJ: Princeton University Press, 1985).

43. Quoted in Douglas Jehl and James Gerstenzang, "The Mind of the President," *Los Angeles Times Magazine,* October 11, 1992, p. 62.

44. Arthur Goldschmidt, Jr., *A Concise History of the Middle East* (Boulder, CO: Westview, 1979), p. 281.

45. Carl Brown, *International Politics and the Middle East: Old Rules, Dangerous Game* (Princeton, NJ: Princeton University Press, 1984), p. 164.

46. Khrushchev tells his own story in three volumes of memoirs, *Khrushchev Remembers* (Boston: Little, Brown, 1970), *Khrushchev Remembers: The Last Testament* (Boston: Little, Brown, 1974), and *Khrushchev Remembers: The Glasnost Tapes* (Boston: Little, Brown, 1990). A more balanced appraisal of his years in power may be found in Roy A. Medvedev, *Khrushchev* (Garden City, NY: Anchor, 1983).

47. For an assessment of Brezhnev's leadership at the height of his power, see John Dornberg, *Brezhnev: The Masks of Power* (New York: Basic Books, 1974). George Breslauer compares the styles of the two Soviet premiers in *Khrushchev and Brezhnev as Leaders* (London: Allen & Unwin, 1982).

48. See Michael Roskin, "From Pearl Harbor to Vietnam: Shifting Generational Paradigms and Foreign Policy," *Political Science Quarterly* 89, no. 3, (Fall 1974), pp. 563–587; and Robert Dallek, *The*

American Style of Foreign Policy: Cultural Politics and Foreign Affairs (New York: Oxford University Press, 1983).

49. Richard Ned Lebow, *Nuclear Crisis Management: A Dangerous Illusion* (Ithaca, NY: Cornell University Press, 1987), pp. 247–254.

50. Stephen Van Evera, "The Cult of the Offensive and the Origins of the First World War," *International Security* 9 (Summer 1984), pp. 58–107.

51. Nathan Leites, *The Operational Code of the Politburo* (New York: McGraw-Hill, 1951).

52. See Leites, *The Operational Code;* and Alexander George, "The 'Operational Code': A Neglected Approach to the Study of Political Leaders and Decision-Making," *International Studies Quarterly* 13, no. 2 (June 1969), p. 197.

53. For example, see Stephen Walker, "The Interface between Beliefs and Behavior: Henry Kissinger's Operational Code and the Vietnam War," *Journal of Conflict Resolution* 21, no. 1 (March 1977), pp. 129–161; Ole Holsti, "The Operational Code Approach to the Study of Political Leaders: John Foster Dulles' Philosophical and Instrumental Beliefs," *Canadian Journal of Political Science* 3 (1970), pp. 123–157.

54. See Alexander L. George, *Presidential Decisionmaking in Foreign Policy: The Effective Use of Information and Advice* (Boulder, CO: Westview, 1980); and Michael Brecher with Benjamin Geist, *Decisions in Crisis* (Berkeley, CA: University of California Press, 1980).

55. Robert F. Kennedy, *Thirteen Days* (New York: Norton, 1969), p. 22.

56. Theodore Sorensen, *Decision Making in the White House* (New York: Columbia University Press, 1964), p. 76.

57. For an overview of the effects of crisis-induced stress, see George Herek, Irving Janis, and Paul Huth, "Decision Making during International Crises: Is Quality of Process Related to Outcome?" *Journal of Conflict Resolution* 31, no. 2 (June 1987), pp. 203–226; and Lebow, *Nuclear Crisis Management,* pp. 144–145.

58. Ivan Maisky, cited in Adam Ulam, *Expansion and Coexistence* (New York: Praeger, 1968), p. 315. Similar incidents are recounted in Georgii Zhukov, *The Memoirs of Marshal Zhukov* (New York: Delacorte, 1971), pp. 234–238; and Voitech Mastny, "Stalin and the Prospects of a Separate Peace in World War II," *American Historical Review* 77 (December 1972), pp. 1365–1388.

59. See Leon Festinger, *A Theory of Cognitive Dissonance* (Stanford, CA: Stanford University Press, 1957); Deborah Welch Larson, *Origins of Containment;* and Fred Wehling, *Irresolute Princes: Soviet Decision Making in Middle East Crises, 1967–1973* (New York: St. Martin's, 1997).

60. George, *Presidential Decisionmaking,* p. 68.

61. Ibid., p. 64.

62. Larson, *Origins of Containment,* p. 32.

63. George, *Presidential Decisionmaking,* pp. 32–33.

64. On the development and application of prospect theory, see Amos Tversky and Daniel Kahneman, "The Framing of Decisions and the Psychology of Choice," *Science,* 2/11 (1981), pp. 453–458; Jack S. Levy, "An Introduction to Prospect Theory" and "Prospect Theory and International Relations: Theoretical Applications and Analytical Problems" *Political Psychology* 13/2 (June 1992), pp. 171–186, 283–310; and Levy, "Loss Aversion, Framing, and Bargaining: The Implications of Prospect Theory for International Conflict." *International Political Science Review* 17 (1996), pp. 177–193.

65. Larson, *Origins of Containment,* p. 35.

66. George, *Presidential Decisionmaking,* p. 58; and Larson, *Origins of Containment,* pp. 37–38.

67. Quoted in Holsti, "Models of International Relations," p. 37.

68. Larson, *Origins of Containment,* p. 38.

69. Adapted from Daniel Heradstveit, *The Arab-Israeli Conflict: Psychological Obstacles to Peace* (Oslo: Universitetsforlaget, 1979), pp. 48–75.

70. See George, *Presidential Decisionmaking,* pp. 60–66; and Ernest R. May, *"Lessons" of the Past: The Use and Misuse of History in American Foreign Policy* (New York: Oxford University Press, 1973), pp. 44–45.

71. Larson, *Origins of Containment,* pp. 50–57. For more on the use of historical analogies to inform and misinform decision making, see Richard E. Neustadt and Ernest R. May, *Thinking in Time: The Uses of History for Decision-Makers* (New York: Free Press, 1986).

72. Robert Jervis, *Perception and Misperception in International Politics* (Princeton, NJ: Princeton University Press, 1976), pp. 266–270.

Chapter 13

1. William Greider, *One World, Ready or Not: The Manic Logic of Global Capitalism* (New York: Simon & Schuster, 1997).

2. See Rosecrance, "The Rise of the Virtual State," *Foreign Affairs* 75/4 (July-Aug. 1996), pp. 45–61.

3. Richard Rosecrance discusses how such a body might function in "A New Concert of Powers," *Foreign Affairs* 71, no. 2 (Spring 1992), pp. 64–82.

4. Kenneth N. Waltz, "The Emerging Structure of International Politics." *International Security* 18 (Fall 1993), pp. 44–79.

5. For instructive speculations on these questions, see Paul Kennedy, *Preparing for the Twenty-First Century* (New York: Random House, 1993); and Christopher Layne, "The Unipolar Illusion: Why New Great Powers Will Rise," *International Security* 17, no. 4 (Spring 1993), pp. 5–51.

6. See Richard Bernstein and Ross H. Munro, *The Coming Conflict with China* (New York: Knopf, 1997).

7. John Mearsheimer makes this point in "Back to the Future."

8. Both sides of this question are explored in Michael E. Brown, Sean M. Lynn-Jones, and Steven E. Miller, eds., *Debating the Democratic Peace* (Cambridge, MA: MIT Press, 1996).

9. Samuel P. Huntington, *The Clash of Civilizations and the Remaking of World Order* (New York: Simon and Schuster, 1996).

10. This viewpoint is articulated in Mark Juergensmeyer, *The New Cold War? Religious Nationalism Confronts the Secular State* (Berkeley, CA: University of California Press, 1993); and Graham E. Fuller and Ian O. Lesser, *A Sense of Siege: The Geopolitics of Islam and the West* (Boulder, CO: Westview, 1995).

11. For more on the Concert of Europe and the diplomats who negotiated its establishment, see Richard B. Elrod, "The Concert of Europe: A Fresh Look at an International System," *World Politics* 28/2 (January 1976), pp. 159–174; and Henry M. Kissinger, *Diplomacy* (New York: Simon & Schuster, 1994).

12. For an assessment of the Versailles treaty from several perspectives, see Ivo J. Lederer, *The Versailles Settlement: Was It Foredoomed to Failure?* (Boston: Heath, 1960).

13. Herbert Feis, *Churchill, Roosevelt, Stalin* (Princeton, NJ: Princeton University Press, 1957) offers a classic study of relations between the "Big Three" during World War II and their ideas for a postwar settlement. For another thorough study, see Gerhard L. Weinberg, *A World at Arms* (New York: Cambridge University Press, 1994).

14. For varying perspectives on the role of leaders in the New Era, see Brad Roberts, ed., *Order and Disorder after the Cold War* (Cambridge, MA: MIT Press, 1995); and Michael Brown et al., eds., *The Perils of Anarchy* (Cambridge, MA: MIT Press, 1995).

Glossary

Absolute advantage A situation in which one country is more efficient than others in producing a certain good. One party can have an absolute advantage in all goods.

Air-launched cruise missile (ALCM) A cruise missile launched from an airplane. See *cruise missile.*

Amnesty International (AI) A humanitarian NGO that works on behalf of prisoners of conscience around the world. It seeks the release of political prisoners and the abolition of torture, investigates abuses of human rights, and organizes campaigns for the release of persons jailed for political activity.

Anarchy A concept of systems theory contending that the international system is chaotic and unpredictable, with no legitimate international law-enforcement mechanism.

Antiballistic missile (ABM) A missile designed to destroy incoming missiles or their warheads before they hit the designated targets.

Appeasement One-sided concessions to a potential opponent.

Arable land Land usable for agriculture.

Arms control Agreements between two or more states or unilateral actions to regulate the research, manufacture, or deployment of weapons or troops on the basis of number, type, and/or location.

ASEAN Free Trade Area (AFTA) A fifteen-year plan launched by the members of the Association of Southeast Asian Nations (ASEAN) in 1992 in response to fears that NAFTA and the EU would divert global investment to Europe and North America. This plan calls for reducing tariffs among members on products in fifteen categories.

Asia-Pacific Economic Cooperation (APEC) A loose conglomeration of more than twelve Pacific Rim countries, including the United States, China, Japan, and Australia, that concentrates on improving economic ties and cooperation.

Association of South-East Asian Nations (ASEAN) A general-purpose IGO founded in 1967 that encourages peaceful cooperation and economic development among its members (Brunei, Indonesia, Malaysia, the Philippines, Singapore, and Thailand).

Atomic weapon An explosive device that derives its power from nuclear fission, or the "splitting" of atoms (uranium or plutonium).

Attribution theory A theory whereby decision-makers attempt to discern the attributes of other actors, to infer the causes of salient events, and to predict historical trends and the behavior of other people, all to understand and exercise more control over the outcomes of particular situations; decision-makers are seen to be "problem-solvers" or "naive scientists."

Balance of payments The "balance sheet" of a nation's transactions with the rest of the world. These national accounts tell us a country's trade balance (exports of goods and services minus imports of goods and services), how much money locals earned overseas, the amount of foreign currency invested in the domestic economy, the level of official foreign aid given to other countries, and the amount of foreign currency held by the central bank.

Balance of power A system of international relations in which states seek security through internal buildup of power or alliances with other states. Used to prevent one state (or group of states) from accumulating too much power. An equilibrium, or at least a rough equivalent used specifically in reference to the relative economic and military strength of nations, by which stability can be achieved. According to some analysts, a condition of equilibrium reduces the likelihood of war or domination.

Balfour Declaration A statement issued by Great Britain in 1917 promising support of a Jewish homeland in Palestine as long as the "civil and religious rights" of existing non-Jewish communities there were not prejudiced.

Ballistic missile A missile that "coasts" to its target on a free-falling trajectory following a period of powered flight.

Bandwagoning An alliance in which a state, instead of joining a counterbalancing coalition, joins the stronger state or coalition.

Baruch Plan A post–World War II proposal that would have placed all atomic energy activities under the control of an international atomic development authority. This proposal was rejected by the USSR primarily because it would have made permanent the existing U.S. monopoly over nuclear weapons.

Beggar-thy-neighbor policy A situation in which Country B raises tariffs on Country A's goods in retaliation for Country A's raising its tariffs on Country B's exports. These countervailing tariffs can eventually lead to declining international trade.

Belief systems A conviction that certain ideas are true, including basic values like morals, religious beliefs, and the fundamental philosophies by which policy-makers operate.

Bilateral aid Direct aid in the form of grants or loans from a single developed country to a specific developing state, typically handled by governments of the donor and the recipient.

Biological weapon A germ- or bacteria-based weapon, also known as a "living weapon," that spreads disease, infection, or toxins.

Bipolar system (Bipolarity) An international system dominated by two actors of relatively equal power that overshadow all of the rest.

Bismarckian system A succession of alliances sought by Otto von Bismarck in the twenty years after his defeat of France in 1871; these were pursued to moderate the demands of Germany's allies, prevent the formation of opposing coalitions, and prevent local conflicts from escalating into general war.

Blitzkrieg Literally translated as "lightning war." The Nazi employment of this strategy included armor and air attacks that were directed at overwhelming the intended target in a quick victory.

Blue Helmets UN peacekeeping and truce supervision forces dispatched at the invitation of parties to a local conflict. Their primary mission is to serve as armed sentries, separating combatants in order to make violation of a peace agreement more difficult. Also known as "Blue Berets," they wear UN headgear but retain their respective national uniforms.

Bretton Woods system See International Bank for Reconstruction and Development, and International Monetary Fund.

Buck-passing The temptation by members of an alliance to avoid the high cost in lives and equipment of fighting an opposing power by letting other members confront the threatening state.

Buffer stocks Funds provided to countries that participate in international commodity agreements and experience balance of payment difficulties because of fluctuations in the price of primary goods.

Bureaucratic politics model A model of decision-making that sees foreign policy outcomes as a result of political competition (turf battles) among government agencies, not the rational value-maximizing calculation of the state's interest or the simple output of an organizational standard operating procedure. Therefore, a bureaucrat's policy stance depends on his organizational affiliation and a desire to protect agency interests as he strives to maintain and improve its position in the government. This results in policy made through "pulling and hauling" among bureaucratic chiefs.

Capability The aspect of deterrence that refers to the ability to do great harm to an aggressor. A state's ability to retaliate against a challenger should the defending nation deem the challenger's actions to be unacceptable. Also used more broadly as the capacity to act in world politics.

Capital-intensive technology Highly advanced equipment that lessens the need for manual labor. Frequently brought by MNCs to developing countries.

Capitalism A belief that the means of production of goods and services should be owned privately, so that the desire for profit will lead to greater efficiency and thus benefit both consumers and producers.

Casualties Members of the armed forces who have been killed, wounded, captured, are interned, sick or missing, and, therefore, no longer a part of active duty.

Chain-ganging The danger that a state, by virtue of its membership in an alliance, might be dragged into a war that it has no interest in fighting.

Chemical weapon A weapon that uses a chemical agent to kill or disable military personnel and civilians. These weapons consist of poison gases, mists, and powders and can be effective only when they come into contact with people.

Chemical Weapons Convention (CWC) Treaty signed in 1993 that prohibits the production, use, or stockpiling of chemical weapons.

Chlorofluorocarbons (CFCs) A primary agent of ozone depletion found mostly in aerosols and refrigerants.

Classical realism A philosophy that the international system is anarchic and that each state must protect its own vital interests, political independence, and territorial sovereignty at any cost.

Cognitive bias A psychological bias related to the cognition, or reasoning, processes that attempt to make new information fit into an individual's preexisting knowledge and beliefs.

Cognitive consistency An attempt by people to simplify difficult decisions by changing the facts to fit their theories.

Cognitive dissonance A situation in which consistency seekers attempt to maintain their beliefs in the face of discordant information.

Cognitive restructuring A situation in which decision-makers set aside information that calls attention to or aggravates a value conflict.

Collective action problem A complication with collective arrangements that refers to the problem that all member states might pass responsibility to other members of the coalition rather than abide by their commitments.

Collective security A system of mutual action to ensure global security in which an agreement is reached between a group of states that provides for unified opposition to any member state that illegally violates the peace.

Colonialism A policy by which a nation maintains or extends its control over foreign dependencies. The two main types of colonialism are (1) movement of people from the mother country to form a new political institution in the designated distant land, and (2) ruling of the less developed indigenous peoples by outside powers.

Commitment The first step in deterrence that must be stated clearly and unambiguously before a challenger carries out an act of aggression. The defending state must make clear its determination to punish a challenger if the challenger takes a specified action that the defender considers unacceptable (such as drawing a line in the sand).

Commodity cartels Southern nations producing a particular product that have banded together in the hope of increasing their collective bargaining power, the most famous being OPEC (Organization of Petroleum-Exporting Countries).

Common markets Political or economic organizations characterized by common external trade barriers and uniform internal trade barriers.

Commonwealth of Independent States (CIS) The organization of successor states to the former Soviet Union.

Communism In theory, the organization of society—based on collective ownership of the means of production—that assumes an equitable distribution of goods, services, and wealth. In practice, the organization of both the society and polity based on a centralized and totalitarian state which owns all property. A privileged elite controls the state in the name of the workers.

Comparative advantage A situation in which even when one country has an absolute advantage over all goods produced abroad, that country benefits from trade by specializing in its most efficiently produced domestic goods and purchasing other goods abroad.

Compellence A strategy that attempts to force an adversary to reverse some action that has already been undertaken. Compellence is almost always more difficult than deterrence because the defender must convince or force an adversary to retreat.

Concert of Europe A special system of consultation used by the great powers of Europe after the Napoleonic Wars. A great power could initiate international conferences when it believed that the security and peace of Europe were compromised.

Conditionality Requirements, in the form of economic reforms, attached to loans from international lending institutions to developing countries.

Conference on Security and Cooperation in Europe (CSCE) Created in 1975 as part of the Helsinki negotiations, CSCE is composed of most NATO and former Warsaw Pact nations, including the United States, Canada, and Russia. Its purpose is to guarantee European security and human rights. Known since 1994 as the Organization on Security and Cooperation in Europe (OSCE).

Constructivism Analytical approach that regards knowledge and truth as socially constructed and therefore subjective, rather than objective.

Containment U.S. foreign policy during the Cold War aimed at halting Soviet expansion through American military and economic power.

Contras Anticommunist rebels and counter-revolutionary opponents of the 1980s Nicaraguan Sandinistas, organized and armed by the CIA, that were supported by the Reagan administration even after Congress prohibited direct military aid.

Conventional weapon A non-nuclear weapon such as a tank, artillery piece, or tactical aircraft (troops that operate these weapons are referred to as conventional forces).

Corn Laws A set of tariffs and other restrictions on agricultural imports that protected British landowners in the late 1700s and early 1800s. Repeal of these laws in 1846 helped facilitate a boom in international trade.

Council of Mutual Economic Assistance (CMEA or COMECON) A Soviet-led institution that solidified trade relations in the East during the Cold War.

Counterbalancing coalition A way to balance a potentially dominant power by which all or most of the remaining states form an alliance to quickly aggregate capability to deter the preponderant power or, upon failure, to prepare for war in order to restore the balance of power.

Credibility The resolve and willingness of the defending state to carry out its commitment to punish the unacceptable actions of the aggressor state. One aspect of deterrence, credibility is necessary to convince an adversary that its capabilities will be used if the adversary attacks.

Critical Theory School of thought, originating in various branches of philosophy and literary criticism, that regards world politics as a process of identity formation and discourse rather than cooperation and conflict between actors such as states and international organizations. Includes postmodernism, constructivism, and feminist theory.

Cruise missile A missile that resembles a pilotless aircraft and that flies on a horizontal trajectory. This missile operates completely within the earth's atmosphere and may be launched from the air, the ground, or the sea and can carry either a conventional, chemical, or nuclear warhead.

Cult of the Offensive A belief of strategic analysts before World War I that the party that attacked first would win, encouraging immediate mobilization and attack in case of a crisis.

Current account balance The sum total of a nation's imports, exports, foreign aid, and other government transactions, and investment income and payments.

Customary practices International customs represent the established and consistent practices of states in international relations; one of the main sources of international law.

Dawes Plan A plan to alleviate the economic pressure on Germany caused by reparations imposed after World War I. Under this agreement, American banks would lend money to Germany for its reparations payments to the Allies. These payments could then be transferred to the U.S. government from the Allies in order to service war loans.

Deforestation Conversion of forested land to other uses, such as cropland, shifting cultivation, or urban and industrial use.

Deconcentration A stage in long-cycle theory in which a dominant power is challenged by emerging rivals.

Defense A strategy that attempts to reduce an enemy's capability to damage or take something away from the defender. The purpose is to resist an attack and minimize losses after deterrence has failed. Defense is physical and intended to rebuff the challenger.

Delegitimation A stage in long-cycle theory in which the costs associated with global leadership contribute to a dominant power's relative decline.

Demographic transition A change from the high birth and death rates characteristic of traditional societies to the low rates associated with industrialized nations; typically occurs until birth and death rates stabilize at lower levels.

Dependency theory A theory of international economics, following upon the works of Karl Marx, that views the world as divided between industrialized "core" countries and underdeveloped "periphery" countries. It focuses on a country's assigned role in the global economic system, where the core exploits the periphery and stunts industrialization.

Dependicistas Supporters of dependency theory.

Desertification The process by which an area becomes a desert. The rapid depletion of plant life and topsoil at desert boundaries and in semiarid regions, usually caused by a combination of drought and overexploitation by humans of grasses and other vegetation. Also called desertization.

Détente French for "relaxation of tensions," the reduction of tensions between two or more countries. During the Cold War, détente between the United States and Soviet Union referred to cooperation on areas such as arms control, trade, and technology.

Deterrence The attempt to prevent war by discouraging a potential aggressor. The primary goal of the defender is to convince the challenger that the probable cost of attacking will far exceed any anticipated gain. For deterrence to function effectively, the defender must signal its commitment to punish or retaliate and possess the capability to do so in order to demonstrate the credibility of the deterrent threat. Deterrence is psychological and intended to influence the challenger's decision-making process.

Diplomatic immunity Freedom from arrest and prosecution for accredited diplomats.

Disarmament The reduction or elimination of a state's overall arms levels.

Domestic level of analysis A method of analyzing international relations according to the unique characteristics of specific nation-states, including government institutions, society, and the links between them.

Dumping A situation in which one country sells (dumps) its products on a foreign market at a price below the cost of production, thereby harming another country's domestic producers.

East Asian Economic Caucus (EAEC) A group of newly industrialized East Asian nations, the activities of which are devoted to rapid economic growth in their region.

Economic and Social Council (ECOSOC) A UN organ

responsible for coordinating the work of the UN "family" of more specialized agencies and organizations.

Economic bloc An economic arrangement between states designed to promote high levels of internal cooperation and to enhance competitiveness with the rest of the world.

Economic interdependence The mutual dependence of national economies.

Empire Domination of a single state over other states in the international system to the extent that they are legally subordinate to the dominant state.

Enforcement terror Terrorism carried out by a government or a government-backed agency against its own citizens.

Eradication A method for restricting the supply of illegal drugs. It consists of destroying crops that are eventually processed into illegal drugs.

European Community See *European Union*.

European Free Trade Area (EFTA) Originally founded in 1959 by the British as a counterweight to the French-dominated EEC. Most members are now members of the EU or have applied for membership.

European Union The world's most highly integrated economic bloc. Originally known as the European Economic Community (EEC) and later as the European Community (EC), it was organized in the 1957 Treaty of Rome.

Export-led industrialization The promotion of development by working within, rather than against, the global economic system through emphasizing export production as an engine for economic growth.

Extended deterrence A policy that seeks to discourage a challenger from attacking an ally or a partner.

External subsidies Government payments that allow producers to compete in the international market.

Extradition A process wherein a country surrenders an individual accused of a crime to another country for trial.

Factor approach An analytical framework for understanding how conditions in the international economy affect domestic politics. Factor approach hypothesizes that every society has three basic interest groups: landholders, capital owners, and workers. Conflicts arise between those groups that benefit from international conditions and those that are harmed.

Fascism A doctrine promoted by the far right seeking an authoritarian society built around the rule of an elite led by a dictator or supreme leader. Fascists usually gain power through a coup d'état during a period of revolution, or as a consequence of economic crises.

First-strike capability Ability to destroy or decisively weaken an opponent's strategic weapons, or prevent retaliation, with an initial attack.

First World Industrialized countries of North America, Western Europe, and Japan that account for four-fifths of global GNP (with one-fifth of the world's population), characterized by export of services and manufactured goods and by high standards of living.

Fixed exchange-rate system A regime in which nations agree to establish a set of currency rules. All currencies in this system are valued at fixed rates against each other. Two examples of this system are the Gold Standard (1870–1914) and the Bretton Woods system (1945–1973). This regime makes the international economy more stable and predictable, but it can also force governments to pursue harmful policies when the currency's value goes in one direction and the economy's health in the other.

Flexible Response A Kennedy administration strategy that replaced the Massive Retaliation doctrine of the Eisenhower administration. This revised strategy called for sufficient NATO military capability to counter Soviet offensives at each step of the escalation ladder: the conventional level, the battlefield nuclear level, and the strategic nuclear level.

Floating exchange-rate system The value (price) of a currency is allowed to fluctuate in relation to other currencies. This regime accurately reflects an economy's well-being but it also creates additional uncertainty in the world economy.

Food and Agriculture Organization (FAO) A UN humanitarian organization under the ECOSOC umbrella.

Foreign policy The actions and positions on key issues taken by an individual state regarding other states or groups outside its boundaries.

Fossil fuels Forms of energy—oil, coal, and natural gas—that are derived from the remains of living organisms.

Fragmentation Breakup of a country or other governing body.

Free-trade areas Economic arrangements that are generally characterized by uniform internal trade barriers among members states.

Free trade International movement of goods based on supply and demand without government intervention.

Free ride The use of a public good without making any contribution to its upkeep.

Fundamental attribution error Explaining one's own inappropriate behavior with situational variables (related to circumstance beyond one's control) while attributing an adversary's undesirable actions to dispositional variables (related to one's character or fundamental goals). On the other hand, one's own appropriate behavior is explained using dispositional variables while the opponent's good behavior is seen in situational terms.

General Agreement on Tariffs and Trade (GATT) An agreement established in 1947 to encourage freer trade. Several rounds of GATT rules negotiations since its founding have progressively lowered tariffs and nontariff barriers to trade among member states.

General deterrence This long-term strategy operates at all times and attempts to prevent an adversary from attempting any kind of military challenge because of its expected consequences.

Generational experience A phenomenon in which a group of political leaders are influenced by the events and experiences of the generation to which they belong.

Glasnost Russian for "openness," referring to the political policies that followed Mikhail Gorbachev's 1985 rise to power in the USSR. Gorbachev increased political freedom dramatically, freed a number of political prisoners, and loosened state control of the news media.

Globalization A process by which increasing interdependence and communication between states and varying parts of the world lead to shared experiences and common identification of global issues.

Gold standard A fixed exchange-rate system in which each nation's currency value is set to gold. The periods between 1870–1914 and 1945–1971 were at least partial examples of gold standard systems.

Great power A state that possesses, exercises, and defends interests throughout the world. Great-power status may be quantitative, such as a certain level of GNP or the size of its armed forces. It may instead be qualitative, demonstrated by a high level of industrialization or the capability to make and use nuclear weapons. Great powers may also be distinguished by institutional recognition, such as that accorded by the League of Nations or by the UN.

Great power unanimity A concept that holds that on all resolutions and proposals before the UN Security Council, a veto by any one of the five permanent members (China, France, the United Kingdom, Russia, and the United States) will kill any proposal.

Greenhouse effect An increase in the earth's average temperature caused by the emission of "greenhouse gases" (especially carbon dioxide and methane) that trap and retain the sun's heat in the atmosphere.

Gross domestic product (GDP) The total sum of goods and services produced by a nation, not including goods and services produced abroad by domestic individuals or firms.

Gross national product (GNP) The total sum of all goods and services produced by a nation.

Ground-launched cruise missile (GLCM) A cruise missile launched from land. See *cruise missile*.

Group of Seven (G-7) The seven leading industrialized member nations of the Organization for Economic Cooperation and Development (OECD). Members include the United States, the United Kingdom, France, Germany, Italy, Canada, and Japan. The leaders and economic ministers of member nations meet regularly to discuss economic policy and resolve their differences.

Guerrilla warfare An irregular style of warfare fought by small groups against a larger invading army or an established government.

Hegemonic stability theory A theory stating that a global hegemon, in an international system, allows for more stability than a system based on several great powers. Acting in its own interests, this dominant "hegemon" sets and enforces rules for the global economy. In a hegemonic period the international economic system works because a dominant state pays the costs of providing economic stabilizers (free flow of international goods, providing international security arrangements, and stabilizing world currencies).

Hegemony/Hegemon/Hegemonic theory The dominant military and economic power among states within a regional or global system.

Heuristics Rules of thumb, or mental shortcuts, used in processing large flows of information to assess the likelihood that certain policy options will be successful.

High politics Part of the realist paradigm of the systemic level of analysis that places emphasis on national security issues over economic and other domestic issues.

Hydroelectricity Electricity generated by water power, a frequently touted alternate energy source.

Hydrogen bomb A thermonuclear weapon that uses hydrogen atoms in a fusion reaction to produce an energy release. These weapons require a fission reaction to achieve a temperature high enough to cause the hydrogen atoms to react.

Hyperinflation A situation with an extreme, rapid, and uncontrolled rise in prices. Also, an uncontrollable decline in the value of a currency.

Idealism A set of beliefs rooted in the assumption that cooperation is possible in the international system. The game of international relations may not always be zero-sum; interdependence may make it necessary and possible for countries to collaborate in order to solve common problems. If the structure of the international system or human nature leads to recurrent conflict, perhaps either or both can be improved in order to create an environment more favorable to cooperation.

Ideology The set of beliefs on which states and groups within states base their actions. It shapes a state's political institutions and its political, social, and economic relations.

Imbalance of power An unequal distribution of capability between states in which one state or coalition dominates the international system.

Immediate deterrence A strategy of response to specific and explicit challenges to a state's interests.

Imperialism A superior-inferior relationship in which one state controls the people and territory of another area.

Import quotas Trade barriers erected by a state to limit the number of imports from the rest of the world.

Import-substitution industrialization An attempt to industrialize by protecting domestic industries from foreign imports via price protection, thereby mitigating competition.

Imported conflicts Conflicts that are extensions of Northern ideas and problems that affect conditions in the South.

Indigenous conflicts Conflicts that have long histories in a society, predating the era of European imperialism.

Individual level of analysis A method of analyzing international relations that focuses on the skills, beliefs, personalities, and unique characteristics of the leaders who make decisions within each state. It considers what role, if any, "human nature" plays in world affairs and whether or not it can be changed to make the world a less conflictual and violent place.

Industrial pollution Environmental ills such as smog, acid rain, and high levels of carbon dioxide and chlorofluorocarbons (CFCs) caused by urbanization and industrialization.

Infant mortality rate The ratio of infants who die before reaching their first birthday versus those who survive; usually higher in developing countries.

Influence A political actor's ability to impact the behavior of others in a direction it favors.

Information UN warfare Military use of computer networks to attack an opponent's capabilities for receiving, processing, and communicating information.

Intercontinental ballistic missile (ICBM) A land-based missile able to deliver a nuclear payload to a target more than 3400 miles away (in practical terms, capable of going directly from the United States to Russia or vice versa).

Interdependence As nations modernize and society becomes more complex, states begin to interact more frequently with other states for a variety of reasons and in a variety of ways, such as trade and diplomacy. Economies become linked to those of other states, creating an interrelatedness of the societies of the world in relation to socioeconomic and technological issues. The nations of the world are mutually sensitive and vulnerable, thus they will behave to attain cooperation rather than conflict over security issues.

Interdiction A method for restricting the supply of drugs, it entails stopping shipments, usually via customs inspections, before they enter the country.

Interest groups A group of people who share a common belief and seek government support. These groups operate through lobbying activities with the help of paid professionals.

Intergovernmental organizations (IGOs) Groups of states or governments created through treaties and organized for a common purpose. Examples include OPEC, OECD, and NATO.

Intermediate-range ballistic missile (IRBM) A land-based missile with a range of 1700 to 3400 miles.

Internal balancing A method for states to balance a potential competitor power through the mobilization of domestic, economic, and industrial resources—and their conversion to military power.

Internal subsides (price supports) Government payments that allow producers to compete against imports in the home market.

International Atomic Energy Agency (IAEA) A specialized UN agency that monitors nuclear weapons proliferation, safety of nuclear power plants, use of nuclear fuels, and disposal of nuclear waste.

International Bank for Reconstruction and Development (IBRD, or World Bank) Established as part of the Bretton Woods system, the World Bank was initially created to help finance reconstruction after World War II. Since the 1950s and 1960s, it has lent money to lesser developed countries to finance development projects and humanitarian needs.

International Children's Emergency Fund (UNICEF) A UN humanitarian organization under the umbrella of ECOSOC.

International division of labor An economic theory proposed by *dependencistas*, in which the South does the "dirty work" of producing raw materials while the North gets the "good jobs" in manufacturing and services; it is believed to encourage developing countries to continue exporting primary goods and discourage development of a modern manufacturing sector in Third World countries.

International law The law of nations; a body of rules that binds states and other agents in world politics in their relations with one another.

International Monetary Fund (IMF) Established as part of the Bretton Woods system, IMF is a global lending agency that originally was to aid industrialized nations in stabilizing their economies after the shocks of the Great Depression and World War II. Its goals today are promotion of market economies, free trade, and high growth rates.

International Committee of the Red Cross A humanitarian NGO that acts as an international relief agency and maintains strict neutrality in order to alleviate suffering without being involved in politics. Its main activities include disaster and famine relief and efforts to ensure humane treatment of prisoners of war.

International Relations The totality of interactions, both political and nonpolitical, among states and nonstate actors.

International system All the states of the world—including the international organizations to which they belong; the general setting of politically relevant relations between nation-states.

Internationalism A belief that states have no choice but to participate actively in world politics to pursue their basic interests. Problems in one part of the globe, if left unchecked, can eventually spread to every corner, so states ignore the outside world at

their own peril. Nations must open their doors and minds to the world whether they like it or not.

Interpol The International Criminal Police Organization (Interpol) created in 1923 and based in Lyons, France. Its purpose is to promote mutual assistance between all police authorities, within the limits of existing law in each country, and in the spirit of the Universal Declaration of Human Rights.

Intifada The Palestinian uprising in the Israeli-occupied West Bank and Gaza Strip, beginning in 1987.

Invulnerability The ability of a significant portion of a state's arsenal to survive an attack, thus guaranteeing a second strike. In the nuclear arena, both sides must have a secure second strike capability for Mutual Assured Destruction to be effective.

Irredentism Conflicts between states caused by one state claiming territory that is controlled by another state, whether for historical reasons or because the population of that territory shares the nationality of the aggrieved state.

Isolationism A belief that engagement with other nations is an inherently risky enterprise that affords more dangers than opportunities. Because the world is such a complex and unpredictable place, and each state's resources are limited, it is better to concentrate on solving problems at home and improving the welfare of one's own citizens. Isolationism promotes noninvolvement in the international system and the "live and let live" idea in foreign policy.

Junker Wealthy landowners, especially in East Prussia, descended from medieval German knights who held a monopoly of civilian and military offices during the reign of Frederick the Great. A conservative group, *Junkers* led the unification of Germany in 1871, contributed to the rise of Adolf Hitler, and helped the Nazis undermine and overthrow the Weimar Republic in 1933.

Laissez-faire French for "leave well enough alone," Adam Smith's economic theory that a market free from government interference produces the most benefits for all.

Lend-Lease A plan designed by the United States early in World War II to assist those countries fighting against the Axis powers. According to this act, which became law on March 11, 1941, the president of the United States could transfer weapons, food, or equipment to any nation whose fighting against the Axis powers aided U.S. defense.

Least-developed country (LDC) A country with a per

capita income of less than $3700 and one with low standards of living. Also referred to as the Third World, "developing countries," underdeveloped countries, and the South.

Levels of analysis Categories of variables that can help decide where to begin the search for answers to questions relating to world affairs.

Limited war A conflict fought for limited goals by limited means (that is, a war fought for less than total destruction of the enemy and less than unconditional surrender). Limited war was practiced during the Cold War as even though the superpowers possessed nuclear weapons, they did not use them in conflicts, and conflicts were kept isolated to specific locations.

Long-cycle theory A power transition theory that attempts to explain the regular cycles of world leadership and global war, each of which lasts for approximately 100 years.

Low politics Politics dealing with economic and domestic issues rather than national security.

Maginot Line An extensive system of defensive fortifications established by France in 1930 along its border with Germany.

Maquiladoras Factories located in Mexico that assemble components produced in the United States into goods that are reexported to the U.S. market.

Massive retaliation The Eisenhower administration's strategic doctrine that Soviet-sponsored aggression would be countered with large-scale nuclear retaliation.

Mercantilism An economic theory that trade is a zero-sum game with the objective to gain profits at the expense of one's trading partners. Protective tariffs and other economic measures are undertaken to enhance a nation's power.

MERCOSUR (Southern Cone Common Market) Common market formed by Argentina, Brazil, and Uruguay in 1991.

Military power The factor of power relating to the size of a state's armed forces, its quality and quantity of weaponry, training, morale, organization, and leadership.

Modernization theory A theory that domestic, social, and political structures are key factors in national development. Supporters of this theory examine the transition from a traditional agrarian economy to a modern capitalist economy, and contend that it can be achieved via open markets and investment in physical, financial, and human capital.

Monopsony A condition in which only one buyer exists for a product; the buyer therefore effectively sets the price.

Most-favored-nation status (MFN) A principle of granting equal treatment to all signatories participating in a trade agreement. The countries involved in such an agreement promise each other that both countries' goods will receive the best terms available in their respective markets.

Multilateral aid Aid channeled to countries through international organizations, specifically the World Bank and the International Monetary Fund (IMF), usually in the form of loans from the international organization to the recipient government.

Multilateral Involving more than two parties.

Multinational corporations (MNCs) Large corporations with branches in many countries, headquarters in the North, and huge investments throughout the world. Examples include General Motors, Pepsi Co., IBM, Sony, and Shell Oil.

Multiple independently targeted reentry vehicle (MIRV) A single ballistic missile with several warheads that can each hit a separate target.

Multipolar system (Multipolarity) A structure of the international system in which more than two states, roughly equal in power, dominate.

Mutual and Balanced Force Reductions (MBFR) Talks that strove fruitlessly from 1973 to 1986 to reduce NATO and Warsaw Pact conventional forces.

Mutual assured destruction (MAD) A condition that exists when both sides are able to survive a first strike with sufficient nuclear forces to retaliate in a second strike and inflict unacceptable damage on their opponent. Thus, both would be destroyed regardless of which struck first, and therefore neither has an incentive to initiate a nuclear war.

Nasserism A cult of personality that made Egyptian President Gamal Abdel Nasser appear to be the leader of all Arabs in the 1950s and 1960s; it became identified with a new revolutionary nationalism and promoted Pan-Arabism.

Nation A group of people that views itself as having a common heritage, destiny, and sense of mutual identification based on language, history, and culture.

Nation-state A state structure in which a nation resides and exists (ideally) to protect and promote the interests of that nation. Examples include France, Turkey, Japan, and Brazil.

Nationalism The belief that all nations should have their own state.

National security A state's perception of the balance between the threats it faces (to its population, sovereignty, and territorial integrity) and its capabilities to meet those threats.

Natural law The approach to international law which claims that universal principles can be derived from human nature or "the mind of God" through the use of human reason. This notion of unchangeable laws as eternal verities leads to an emphasis on human rights.

Neoliberal institutionalism A school of thought contending that the anarchy of the international system can be overcome through carefully designed institutions for international cooperation.

Neorealism See *Structural realism.*

New International Economic Order (NIEO) A 1974 declaration on the establishment of a New International Economic Order adopted by the UN General Assembly. The proposals were originally advanced by countries of the South for eliminating the economic inequities between them and the advanced industrial nations of the North.

Newly industrialized countries (NICs) Developing countries that are characterized by rapid growth of manufactured goods; includes states such as Brazil, Mexico, and the Four Tigers (Hong Kong, Singapore, Taiwan, and South Korea); Asian NICs come closest to bridging the gap between the First and Third Worlds.

Nongovernmental organizations (NGOs) Groups not directly related to governments but that are organized to take an active part in international affairs. Examples include terrorist, religious, and humanitarian organizations.

Nonproliferation Treaty Signed in 1968, the treaty provides that signatory nations without nuclear weapons will not seek to build them and will accept safeguards to prevent diversion of nuclear material and technology from peaceful uses to weapons programs. Nations in possession of nuclear weapons at the signing of the treaty agreed not to help non-nuclear states gain access to nuclear weapons, but to offer access to peaceful nuclear technology.

Nonaligned Movement During the Cold War, a movement through which leaders of some states did not pursue a formal alliance with one superpower, but rather found it beneficial to play off one against the other in the hope of gaining aid from both. Leaders of the Nonaligned Movement included Jawaharlal Nehru of India, Gamal Abdel Nasser of Egypt, and Marshall Josip Broz Tito of Yugoslavia.

Normative influences A source of restraint that prevents democracies from rushing into conflict. Proponents argue that democratic states share a common democratic political culture, and all expect to apply its method of resolving conflict at home to resolving international disputes amicably, without resorting to war. Therefore, the argument holds that democratic nations draw upon their democratic norms (elections, compromise, debates, and judicial judgment) to prevent international conflicts from escalating into war, at least between them.

Norms General rules and principles established by international regimes to facilitate cooperation between states. Norms are frequently formalized in treaties, which in turn often create institutions and/or organizations to provide states with opportunities to meet and discuss their common problems.

North American Free Trade Agreement (NAFTA) An agreement between Canada, the United States, and Mexico that created a free-trade area within North America and that went into effect January 1, 1994.

North Atlantic Treaty Organization (NATO) A formal security agreement between the United States, Canada, and the nations of Western Europe, established in April 1949 to deter Soviet aggression.

NSC-68 A document prepared by the U.S. National Security Council in early 1950 to address the issue of what should be done to counter the spread of international communism. NSC-68 called for expansion of America's armed forces, adding an important military dimension to the economic and political means of containment.

Nuclear proliferation States acquiring nuclear weapons that did not formerly possess them.

Nuclear triad Three-pronged capability to deliver nuclear weapons using manned bombers, ICBMs, and SLBMs. This defense posture seeks to preserve a capability to answer a first strike; should one leg of the triad be attacked and destroyed, the other two legs would survive.

Observer mission One of the three types of UN missions; international forces that are present to observe a cease-fire organized by or for the opposing forces in a dispute.

Operational codes Both a system of beliefs and a guide

to action used by policy makers as a way to translate their fundamental moral and political beliefs into policy decisions.

Organization for Economic Cooperation and Development (OECD) Composed of advanced industrial states, OECD was formed in 1961 to promote economic and social welfare in member countries and to stimulate and harmonize efforts on behalf of developing nations.

Organization of African Unity (OAU) A general purpose IGO that promoted decolonization in Africa and that now focuses on regional development and the settlement of regional disputes.

Organization of American States (OAS) An organization that includes most nations of the Western Hemisphere, it addresses a number of regional concerns.

Organization of Petroleum Exporting Countries (OPEC) An intergovernmental cartel of oil exporting countries whose goal is to collectively raise the price of crude oil on the world market.

Organizational process model (OPM) When confronted with a foreign-policy problem, organizations follow a prescribed set of decision-making guidelines, or standard operating procedures (SOPs). This almost mechanical process for formulating routine recommendations does not necessarily calculate the advantages or disadvantages of available options. Indeed, it can contribute to policy inertia and behavior that appears rigid, inflexible, and unimaginitive.

Ostpolitik West German Chancellor Willy Brandt's eastern policy, begun in 1969, that signaled Western aspirations for more contact with, and more independence for, Eastern Europe through conciliation rather than confrontation. Part of *Ostpolitik* involved reversing previous policy by accepting the existence of East Germany and West Germany's post-1945 borders.

Pan-Arabism The idea that all Arabs should belong to a single state.

Panchsheel Jawaharlal Nehru's set of foreign-policy principles, which included respect for other countries' sovereignty and territorial integrity, nonaggression, noninterference in the internal affairs of others, equality and mutual benefit, and peaceful coexistence.

Pariah states States that consistently prove they cannot be trusted at their word and thereby become ostracized by the world community.

Parity An equal distribution of power among a group of states in the international system.

Parity school A division of realism contending that an equal distribution of capability among states creates stability and that war is much more likely to occur when one state is the dominant power.

Peace-enforcement mission One of the three types of UN missions; these troops observe, act as a buffer, and as a last resort, are allowed to use military force to keep the peace in a particular locale.

Peace of Westphalia The 1648 treaty that ended the Thirty Years' War and marked the beginning of the modern international system by legitimizing the state as the ultimate sovereign authority over people and geographic territory.

Peacekeeping mission One of the three types of UN missions; these troops not only observe a cease-fire, but also act as a buffer between the two sides of a conflict.

Perestroika Mikhail Gorbachev's policy for restructuring the economy of the Soviet Union, it promoted democratization, increased privatization of the economy, and created free markets.

Plebiscite A vote used to determine the desire of a population concerning an area of great public interest.

Polarity A term referring to the number of major powers, or "poles," in the international system.

Political culture The fusing of a nation's historical traditions to its cultural institutions and values to form a national style of politics and policy making.

Positive law A belief that international law exists only through those rules to which states have consented in writing, usually in treaties, or otherwise clearly recognized.

Postmodernism School of thought that rejects many of the rationalist and materialist ideas of the modern era, developed in the nineteenth and twentieth centuries in favor of analysis of identity formation and discourse.

Power The ability to convince another state to do what it would not normally do.

Power projection The ability of a state to deploy its military forces to distant locations.

Power transition theory A theory arguing that as the gap in power between rival states narrows and they become more equal in strength, war is likely to occur, since both the challenger and the dominant state believe they are likely to prevail in a conflict.

Preemptive strike A defensive attack carried out when a fundamental threat to vital interests is identified or when an attack by an opponent is believed to be imminent. The underlying motivation holds that "the best defense is a good offense."

Preponderance Dominance of the international system by a single state.

Preponderance school A division of realism contending that stability is more likely when one state dominates the system, rather than when there is an equal distribution of power.

Price inelasticity An economic principle that people purchase goods regardless of price.

Primary deterrence A strategy intended to dissuade a challenger from attacking a state's own territory. It is synonymous with deterrence.

Primary products Raw materials and agricultural goods upon which most developing nations' economies depend for foreign hard currency through exports.

Prisoners' Dilemma A model derived from game theory designed to explain the difficulties states experience cooperating in the international system. If both actors in the Prisoners' Dilemma act in their self-interest, each will defect, leading to an unfavorable outcome.

Private aid International aid donated by individuals and groups through nongovernmental organizations so as to bypass the government, usually for humanitarian purposes or economic development projects.

Privatization The sale of firms owned by the government to the private sector.

Protectionism An economic theory pertaining to a system of trade barriers erected to protect domestic industries from foreign competition. Also known as "managed trade," proponents believe barriers should be erected to protect important industries and high-paying jobs, even if consumers must pay higher prices for goods or pay subsidies through increased taxes.

Public opinion Views and attitudes on national issues held by the people of a nation, with particular emphasis placed on elite views and media influence. The role of the public in shaping foreign relations can take the form of elections, referenda, or work slowdowns.

Rational actor model A model of decision-making that sees a perfectly rational decision-maker who gathers all relevant facts, weighs all available evidence, and selects a course of action offering the greatest benefits in relation to costs.

Rationality The ability of a decision-maker to make and rank cost-benefit comparisons among possible options.

Reagan Doctrine The Reagan administration's abandonment of détente and return to an assertive form of containment. This was characterized by both direct U.S. intervention and especially by indirect support of anticommunist insurgencies.

Realism A theory contending that distribution of relative power within the international system has a profound effect on how nations act and on overall stability of the system. A view of world politics that states that in the anarchic international system, states have no choice but to preserve their vital interests through whatever means are available.

Realpolitik Literally, the "policy of realism" or power politics, a promotion of policies that seek to maximize a nation's security and power in a cold, cruel world in which all other states have no choice but to do the same.

Reciprocity A response in kind. A mutual exchange, particularly involving privileges between two countries.

Regime type The general structure and underlying philosophy of a state's political system (democratic, authoritarian, liberal, Communist, and so on). Many domestic level theorists argue that the type of regime that governs a state can exert a powerful influence on the nature of that state's foreign policy.

Regime A neoliberal institution in which rules or practices are generally accepted by a group of states to help them work together in an otherwise anarchic world.

Relative power A state's power in comparison to other states in the international system.

Revanchism The desire for revenge, especially after a loss in war.

Schemas Generic concepts stored in an individual's memory that help process information more quickly and efficiently. They refer to objects, situations, events, or people.

Schlieffen Plan Strategic plan, developed by German Chief of Staff Alfred von Schlieffen and put into operation at the beginning of World War I, which directed German forces to knock out France with a fast-moving offensive, then shift by rail to the eastern front to fight Russia.

Sea-launched cruise missile (SLCM) A cruise missile launched from a ship or submarine. See *cruise missile*.

Second-strike capability Ability to retaliate, even after a nuclear attack, and thus punish the initiator of a nuclear war.

Second World A term used especially during the Cold War to apply to the bloc of countries consisting of Communist nations of the former Soviet Union and Eastern Europe. The Second World has varying standard-of-living levels and is currently dealing with problems in the transition from communism to a market-oriented economic system.

Sector approach An analytical framework for understanding how conditions in the international economy affect domestic politics. This approach focuses on sectors of the economy (that is, groups of related industries). It assumes that capital is fixed in a particular industrial sector, meaning that increased foreign competition might hurt some capital owners more than others.

Security Council The principal organ of the United Nations responsible for the preservation of peace and security. It is charged with organizing collective security operations and dispatching observer missions and peacekeeping troops around the world. This body has the right to investigate any dispute or situation that might lead to international friction, and to recommend methods of settlement.

Security dilemma The situation that arises when a state feels insecure and decides that its best policy in the anarchic context of world politics is to increase its military strength. As its potential adversary does the same, an unintended spiral occurs as every nation grows more and more insecure and seeks to stay equal to its neighbors in military strength.

Sensitivity A dimension of interdependence referring to the speed and extent with which changes in one country can bring about changes in another.

Smoot-Hawley Tariff Act A tariff passed by Congress in 1930 in an attempt to protect U.S. jobs. This act raised prices on all imports by 19 percent; some reached as high as 55 percent. Foreign countries responded by raising tariffs of their own, thereby spreading and deepening the Great Depression. Such a course of action is called a "beggar-thy-neighbor policy."

Socialism A belief that productive assets should be owned collectively (which in practice means by the state) in order to maximize the benefits to society.

Societal approach Arguments contending that the state's national interest is reflected by the strength of organized domestic interests (agricultural, industrial, environmental, and so on). Therefore, the state's national interest is determined by the success of domestic interest groups in promoting their needs, concerns, and objectives.

Solidarity A popular labor union begun in the 1970s in Poland led by Lech Walesa. Solidarity made political and economic demands on the Communist government for many years before winning elections and assuming power under a new constitution in 1989.

Sovereign Independent of all others; possessing supreme political authority.

Spheres of influence A region influenced by one great power. In a sphere of influence, the dominant power does not have sovereignty but imposes its will over several neighboring states, restricting the maneuverability of local territorial leaders.

Stagflation A combination of low or stagnant economic growth, coupled with high rates of inflation.

Standard operating procedures (SOPs) Entrenched routines used by organizations (bureaucracies) to evaluate specific policies and their options. When making these evaluations, organizations follows set guidelines that can lead to inertia, or inflexible and rigid solutions. Once triggered, SOPs can be difficult to reverse.

State An independent political entity with institutions and authority in a specific territory.

Statist approach Theories that focus on the foreign policy implications of a state's institutional and governmental structures. The statist theory contends that the state's form of government (democratic, socialist, authoritarian, and so on) and/or political institutions (electoral process, specialized bureaucracies, legislature, character of its executive, and constitutional division of power and responsibility) shape the interests and behavior of states in the international arena.

Strategic Defense Initiative (SDI) A 1980s U.S. program that proposed the creation of a highly ambitious ballistic missile defense system that would produce a total defense against strategic nuclear weapons and missile systems. Also known as "Star Wars," SDI threatened to upset the nuclear balance of power by giving the United States an ability to launch a first strike without fear of a Soviet counterattack. Its potential effectiveness was controversial.

Strategic nuclear forces Nuclear forces designed to attack long-range targets, including cities.

Strategic weapon A weapon that strikes directly at a nation's home territory and the industry, resources, population, or military forces located there.

Structural adjustment programs Policies undertaken to meet the conditions placed on loans from international lending institutions. These include opening markets to imports, devaluating overvalued currencies, and reducing government spending, price controls and subsidies, and direct state ownership of industries.

Structural realism A philosophy that contends the structure of the international system, rather than innate human aggressiveness, accounts for the behavior of states. Also known as Neorealism, structural realism places emphasis on the actions of the most powerful states, the "great powers."

Structure of the international system The distribution of power among the major actors in the international system, characterized by the number of great powers in the system and their relative capabilities.

Submarine-launched ballistic missile (SLBM) A long-range ballistic missile carried in and launched from a submarine.

Subsidies Government payments to domestic industries that allow producers to price their goods below the cost of production without going out of business.

Subsistence agriculture Hand-to-mouth farming for direct consumption by one's family.

Systemic level of analysis A method for analyzing international relations according to factors that arise from the nature and structure of the world political system. The factors that influence individual states are external to the states, coming from the attributes of the system itself.

Tactical nuclear weapons Weapons designed to attack short- or medium-range (between 95 and 310 miles) targets, primarily conventional military assets.

Tactical weapon A weapon designed for use on the battlefield, often in support of ground troops.

Tariff A tax imposed on an imported good.

Terms of trade The ratio of export prices to import prices. If a country's export prices are rising faster than prices of the goods it imports, its terms of trade are increasing; if import prices are increasing faster than export prices, its terms of trade are declining.

Thermonuclear weapon An explosive device that derives its power from nuclear fusion, or the coming together of atoms (usually hydrogen or helium; this is the same process that gives the sun its energy). Also called a hydrogen bomb.

Third World More than 160 underdeveloped/developing nonwestern nations in Africa, Asia, Latin America, and the Middle East, accounting for three-fourths of the global population. Third World nations frequently depend on the export of a single commodity or raw material.

Tit-for-tat A neoliberal institutional practice of cooperating with another actor on the first round, and then mimicking its moves on all subsequent rounds to convince it that you will cooperate when it does—as well as cheat when it does. These practices are designed to encourage cooperation.

Total war War fought to obtain the political objective of complete victory over the enemy. In order to achieve this goal, full mobilization of a country's military, economic, and social resources is undertaken (as in World War II).

Trade deficit A balance of trade in which imports exceed exports.

Trade surplus A balance of trade in which exports exceed imports.

Transfer pricing mechanisms Schemes pursued by MNCs to transfer profits to countries where taxes are lower.

Treaties Documents similar to written contracts in that they impose obligations only on the parties that sign them. Also known as charters, pacts, conventions, or covenants, they are some of the main sources of international law.

Treaty of Versailles The agreement signed in 1919 at Versailles, France, that formally ended World War I.

Truman Doctrine A strategy outlined in a speech given before Congress by President Harry Truman on March 12, 1947. The Truman Doctrine pledged U.S. military and economic aid to countries (initially Greece and Turkey) to resist communism. This doctrine is regarded by many as a U.S. "declaration of the Cold War."

Unipolarity A structure of the international state system in which a single state dominates the system.

United Nations (UN) A worldwide IGO established in 1945 as the successor to the defunct League of Nations for the purpose of promoting international peace, security, and cooperation in a variety of diplomatic, economic, and social fields.

United Nations Convention on the Law of the Sea (UNCLOS) A 1982 agreement that divides the world's oceans into public (free access) and private (regulated access) property zones for the purpose of regulating competition over the finite resources of the world's oceans.

United Nations Educational, Scientific, and Cultural Organization (UNESCO) A specialized agency of the United Nations that attempts to improve literacy rates in the Third World, promote scientific and cultural exchange, and facilitate the distribution of information.

Urbanization Rapid growth of cities that is frequently accompanied by overcrowding, unemployment, and crime; a major consequence of demographic transition and industrialization.

Voluntary export restrictions (VERs) A situation in which a state sometimes compels another nation to "voluntarily" limit its exports in order to protect the domestic economy.

Vulnerability The degree to which a state can suffer costs imposed by external events even after policies have been altered in response to them.

War of attrition A strategy that aims to defeat the opposition by wearing it out. Attrition can be costly in terms of men and matériel. World War I is a classic example.

War of secession A situation in which disagreements are so profound and intractable that one or more competing national groups deny the very legitimacy of the state and attempt to break away from it and form a new state, or join another state.

War of unification A war waged to create a single nation-state for an ethnic group previously divided among several states.

Warhead The explosive device that a missile delivers to a target.

World Bank See International Bank for Reconstruction and Development.

World Health Organization (WHO) A humanitarian organization established in 1948 under the ECOSOC umbrella of the UN. WHO aids in the development of national health administrations and provides advisory services.

World politics The competition for, and exercise of, power and authority in the international system.

Zero-sum game A situation in which one state's gain is seen as another's loss, encouraging intense competition between the two powers.

Zionism A political, religious, and social movement that called for the establishment of a national homeland for the Jewish people in the region of the Middle East known as Palestine. Today, Zionists promote political, economic, financial, and military support for Israel and the resettlement of Jews in Israel.

Zollverein A German customs union that abolished tariffs between German states. Established January 1, 1834, the *Zollverein* resulted in increased industrial prosperity, German economic unity, and beginning in 1867, a common German parliament for economic matters. It marked a significant step in the process of political unification, which was completed with the proclamation of the German empire in 1871.

Chronology

1453: Ottoman forces under Mehmet the Conqueror capture Constantinople, destroying the Byzantine Empire and cutting off Western European access to trade with India and China.

1469: The two major Spanish kingdoms are unified through the marriage of Isabella I of Castile and Ferdinand II of Aragon.

1487–1488: Portuguese explorer Bartholomeu Dias leads the first European expedition to round the Cape of Good Hope.

1492: Sailing for the Spanish crown, Columbus makes the first known European landing in the Western Hemisphere; Isabella I and Ferdinand II attempt to "ethnically cleanse" their kingdom by decreeing that all Jews must convert to Christianity or leave the country.

1494: Spain and Portugal agree to the Treaty of Tordesillas, dividing up the world.

1497–1498: Vasco da Gama rounds the Cape of Good Hope and establishes sea route between Portugal and India.

16th Century: Spanish conquistadors topple Aztec and Inca empires in Mexico and Peru.

1500–1920: European colonization of the Southern Hemisphere creates relationship of Southern subservience to the North.

1513: Niccolò Machiavelli's *The Prince* argues that security is possible only when government is strong and that man's innately selfish and aggressive nature motivates state behavior.

1529: Ottoman Empire reaches height of imperial expansion, but fails to capture Vienna.

1533–1584: Russian Empire expands during the rule of Ivan the Terrible.

1545: A major silver vein is discovered in what is now Bolivia.

1588: Spanish Armada is defeated by the British; leads to Spanish decline and opens world to English trade and colonization.

1602: Dutch East India Company is founded to expand spice trade in Asia.

1607: First area of English overseas colonization occurs at Jamestown, Virginia, followed by other colonies in North America.

1648: Peace of Westphalia ends Thirty Years' War and inaugurates modern nation-state system.

1648–1945: International relations are characterized by a multipolar system.

Mid-1600s: Dutch replace Portuguese as naval hegemon in Asian waters.

1652–1674: Sporadic Anglo-Dutch wars occur; one result, Dutch lose New York and Delaware.

1654–1715: French "Sun King" Louis XIV's strong personal rule brings about an extension of France's boundaries, a decline in the power of the nobility, and the promotion of industry and art.

1689–1725: Rule of Peter the Great in Russia.

1699: Austrian armies acquire Hungary from Ottoman Empire.

1701–1714: War of the Spanish Succession checks French expansion in Europe and prevents France from acquiring Spanish possessions in North America.

1721: Treaty of Nystadt between Russia and Sweden definitively establishes Russia as a European power.

1740–1748: War of the Austrian Succession establishes Prussia as a major power in central and eastern Europe.

1756–1763: Seven Years' War occurs; Austria fails to defeat Prussia; most of French territory in North America ceded to Britain; British secure domination in India.

1760–1830: British Industrial Revolution occurs, making Britain the dominant economic power in the world.

1776–1783: American Revolution occurs; United States gains independence from Britain.

1789: American Bill of Rights and French Declaration of the Rights of Man provide a legal framework for fundamental rights and freedoms.

1789–1799: French Revolution occurs; France is declared a republic; Louis XVI is executed.

1790–1920: Great Britain is the world's leading naval power.

1795: Philosopher Immanuel Kant, in *Perpetual Peace,* hypothesizes that democratic regimes are unlikely to go to war with one another; Poland is partitioned out of existence as an independent state by Russia, Prussia, and Austria.

1795–1796: British seize Ceylon from the Dutch.

1798: Thomas Malthus publishes *Essay on the Principle of Population.*

1799: Napoléon Bonaparte seizes power in France.

19th Century: British add Burma and Malaya in Asia and parts of Africa to their empire, and colonize Australia and New Zealand; French add colonies in Africa, Indochina, and a number of Pacific Islands.

1803: United States purchases the Louisiana Territory from Napoléon.

1803–1815: Napoleonic Wars occur; Napoléon becomes emperor of the French, establishes temporary French domination of continental Europe, but after failure of Russian and Spanish campaigns is defeated and exiled.

1804: Rebellion occurs in Serbia against Ottoman rulers.

1806: British seize the Cape Colony in southern Africa from the Dutch.

1810–1825: Latin Americans gain independence from Spain.

1815: Napoléon makes a short comeback; Austrian Prince Metternich is instrumental in establishing the Concert of Europe, which replaces the balance of power with a collective security arrangement.

1819: United States acquires Florida from Spain.

1822: Brazil gains independence from Portugal; Dom Pedro announces formation of the independent Brazilian Empire.

1828–1829: Russia defeats the Ottomans and receives part of what is today Romania.

1830: Serbia gains autonomy; Greece and Belgium become independent; France conquers Algeria.

1834: Prussia's *Zollverein* creates a German common market, establishing an economic basis for subsequent German unification.

1839–1842: Opium War opens Chinese market to western states.

1845: Republic of Texas is admitted to the United States.

1846–1848: Mexican-American War occurs; U.S. gains California and American southwest.

1848: United States establishes military dominance in the Western Hemisphere, providing a measure of stability to Latin America; Karl Marx and Friedrich Engels publish *The Communist Manifesto,* calling for laborers to revolt against an exploitative capitalist system; Revolutions occur throughout Europe; Second Republic is proclaimed in France, led by Louis Napoléon.

1850–1864: China's Taiping Rebellion occurs.

1850–1875: European and American industrialization, technical innovations, and the rapid expansion of foreign trade expedite the growth of the world economy.

1853–1854: American Commodore Perry travels to Japan; ends Japanese isolation and establishes friendly relations.

1853–1856: Crimean War demonstrates weaknessess of Concert of Europe.

1856: Declaration of Paris clarifies the rights of neutral vessels, an early agreement on the conduct of warfare.

1860: Britain and France sign the Cobden-Chevalier Treaty to remove tariffs on each nations' products; it includes a most-favored-nation clause.

1861: Italian states are unified in kingdom of Italy.

1864: Prussia and Austria defeat Denmark in war created by the Schleswig-Holstein crisis.

1868: Japan begins rapid modernization during the Meiji Restoration.

1870s: Growth of railroads in the United States allows American wheat to be sold in Europe, reducing prices and leading to protectionism.

1870–1914: World economy remains relatively stable under the gold standard.

1871–1890: Bismarck's system of Austrian alliances maintains fragile peace in Europe.

1878: Congress of Berlin ends Russo-Turkish War and outlines temporary Balkan settlement; Bulgaria becomes autonomous; Montenegro, Serbia and Romania recognized as independent; Austria-Hungary occupies Bosnia and Herzegovina.

1880s: "Scramble for Africa" takes place among European powers.

1884: Delegates from fourteen nations at the Berlin Conference on African affairs agree to work for the suppression of slavery and the slave trade.

1885: Decline of the Ottoman Empire leaves a power vacuum that contributes to the first of several Balkan wars.

1889: Hague Convention outlaws the use of poisonous gases, expanding bullets, and explosives discharged from balloons.

1890s: American manufacturers begin investing in plants overseas.

1892: The Sierra Club is founded in the United States to protect America's natural environment.

1895–1914: A naval arms race between Britain and Germany mimics the Prisoner's Dilemma.

1898: Spanish-American War occurs; Spain gives up Cuba and cedes Guam, Puerto Rico, and the Philippines to the United States.

1899–1902: Boer War occurs in South Africa.

1901–1909: Presidency of Theodore Roosevelt; the United States takes its first steps toward involvement in European affairs and reinforces American military hegemony in the Western Hemisphere.

1903: U.S. supports Panamanian independence from Colombia, and then signs treaty with Panama to build Panama Canal.

1904: Fearing potential German hegemony, Great Britain and France put aside their historical rivalry in the Anglo-French Entente.

1904–1905: Russo-Japanese War occurs; Japan defeats Russia and becomes dominant power in northeastern Asia.

1905: First Moroccan Crisis increases Franco-German tensions.

1906: Britain's technological breakthrough, the dreadnought, leads to a renewed naval arms race with Germany.

1908: Austria annexes Bosnia and Herzegovina; crisis ensues.

1909: Turkey and Serbia recognize Austria's annexation of Bosnia and Herzegovina.

1910: Japan annexes Korea.

1911: Second Moroccan Crisis occurs.

1912–1913: Balkan Wars break Ottoman power in Europe.

1914: World War I begins, precipitated by assassination of heir to Austro-Hungarian throne, Archduke Franz Ferdinand, in Bosnia by Serbian nationalist; Central Powers (Germany and Austria-Hungary, joined later by Ottoman Empire) fight Allies (Britain, Russia, France, Japan, Belgium, and Serbia).

1915: Italy joins Allies; Bulgaria joins Central Powers.

1917: United States enters war on Allied side; Britain issues the Balfour Declaration supporting a Jewish homeland in Palestine.

1917–1922: Bolshevik Revolution occurs in Russia; leads to civil war, expansion of territory, and formation of USSR.

1918: Bolsheviks end war with Central Powers; Armistice ends World War I; Germany is defeated.

1919: Treaty of Versailles breaks up Austro-Hungarian empire, creates new states and extensive territorial changes in Europe, imposes harsh penalities on Germany, and creates League of Nations.

1920: President Wilson's self-righteousness and inflexibility contributes to a rejection of the Treaty of Versailles by the U.S. Senate; Britain and France assume control of Middle East after defeat of Ottoman Empire.

1920–1923: Turkish nationalists under Ataturk drive Allied forces out of Turkey; Treaty of Lausanne acknowledges abolition of Ottoman Empire and creation of republic of Turkey.

1921–1922: Britain grants home rule to most of Ireland.

1922: USSR is created; Benito Mussolini becomes prime minister of Italy and begins to institute fascist dictatorship.

1923: International Criminal Police Organization (Interpol) is created to promote international cooperation between police authorities.

1924: Dawes Plan establishes a monetary cycle of loans, reparations, and loan payments to Germany, the Allies, and the United States, respectively; the United States passes the Immigration Act, which establishes a national origins quota system.

1925: Geneva Protocol outlaws the use of chemical weapons.

1926: League of Nations Slavery Convention seeks an end to slavery around the world.

1927: The Second Report of the Malarial Commission of the League of Nations reveals difficulties in its anti-malarial campaign.

1928: Federal Reserve Bank in the United States raises interest rates, breaking the Dawes Plan cycle and leading to a collapse of Germany's economy; Stalin gains control of the Soviet Union—his paranoia leads to severe repressions at home and widespread suspicion of other states.

1929: Stock-market crash in United States precipitates Great Depression.

1930: Smoot-Hawley Tariff in the United States leads to countervailing tariffs and a worldwide collapse of export industries, accelerating and deepening the Great Depression.

1931–1932: Japan seizes Manchuria and establishes it as an independent protectorate called Manchukuo.

1933: Adolf Hitler becomes chancellor in Germany; National Socialist (Nazi) dictatorship replaces Weimar Republic—ultimately leading to expansive policy and world war.

1934: Publication of Engelbrecht and Hanighen's *The Merchants of Death* leads to congressional committee hearings to investigate charges that banks and arms manufacturers led the United States into World War I.

1935: Hitler remilitarizes the Rhineland; Italy invades Ethiopia.

1936–1939: Spanish Civil War fought; fascist Francisco Franco becomes dictator of Spain.

1937: Japan invades China.

1938: Germany annexes Austria; Munich Conference

and policy of appeasement allow German annexation of Sudetenland.

1939: Stalin and Hitler's ideological differences are set aside in the signing of the Nazi-Soviet Nonaggression Pact; Germany invades Czechoslovakia; World War II begins with German invasion of Poland.

1940: In its invasion of France, Germany easily bypasses the Maginot Line despite French confidence in it as a defense perimeter; German forces overrun Denmark, Norway, the Netherlands, Belgium, and France, leaving Britain without allies; Italy, Hungary, and Romania join Axis powers; Battle of Britain won by the British; North African campaign begins.

1941: U.S. naval strength in the Pacific fails to deter Japan from bombing Pearl Harbor; Bulgaria joins Axis powers; Germany conquers Yugoslavia and Greece and invades Soviet Union.

1941–1945: Manhattan Project results in the creation of the atomic bomb.

1942: Axis advances halted at battles of Stalingrad (Russia), Midway (central Pacific), and El Alamein (Egypt).

1943: Allied forces drive Axis out of North Africa; Italy surrenders.

1944: Invasion of Normandy opens second front in Europe; Allied forces gain momentum in Pacific.

1945: Germany surrenders; United States drops atomic bombs on Hiroshima and Nagasaki; Japan surrenders, ending World War II; United Nations is created to safeguard the independence and integrity of member states and to promote international law.

1945–1948: USSR under Stalin sets up communist regimes in Eastern Europe.

1945–1973: Bretton Woods system creates an international monetary system based on a gold/dollar standard; United States is considered a hegemon in economics and in providing international security arrangements for its allies.

1945–1991: A bipolar system with nuclear weapons prevents direct military confrontation between the United States and the Soviet Union.

1946: Nazi leaders are prosecuted for "crimes against humanity" at the Nuremberg Trials; World Bank begins operation; initially created to help finance reconstruction after the war, its primary task eventually becomes lending money to underdeveloped countries; U.S. grants independence to Philippines.

1947: Mohandas "Mahatma" Gandhi's dream of Indian independence is realized, due in large part to his campaign of civil disobedience against British colonial rule; United States announces the Truman Doctrine, which pledges to assist countries opposing Communist insurgencies, and proposes Marshall Plan to rebuild Europe; General Agreement on Tariffs and Trade (GATT) is established, providing basic rules and procedures for reducing tariffs; includes a most-favored-nation clause; International Monetary Fund (IMF) begins operation to fix exchange rates and provide international loans to war-torn countries; Independence of India and Pakistan, accompanied by ethnic and nationalist conflict and dispute over Kashmir, leads to war.

1947–1991: During the Cold War, the United States and Soviet Union use economic aid to further their geopolitical and strategic interests.

1948: British departure from Palestine and the subsequent founding of Israel results in the first Arab-Israeli War; Tito, the leader of Yugoslavia, separates from Soviet communism; Afrikaner Nationalist Party in South Africa wins election and creates a legal system of rigid hierarchy, eventually known as apartheid; Burma and Ceylon gain independence from Britain; Convention on the Prevention and Punishment of the Crime of Genocide is agreed to by UN General Assembly; Universal Declaration on Human Rights is signed; the International Union for the Protection of Nature, now the World Conservation Union, is created to work toward global environmental goals; the World Health Organization is organized to control the spread of disease.

1948–1949: Soviet blockade of Berlin is thwarted by Allied airlift.

1949: Soviets test atomic bomb, ending American nuclear monopoly; Communists led by Mao Zedong win civil war and establish People's Republic of China; NATO is established; Indonesia gains independence from the Netherlands.

1950–1953: Korean War occurs, providing the first opportunity for UN Security Council-sponsored military action.

1951–1954: United States signs security treaties with the Philippines, Japan, Australia, New Zealand, South Korea, and Nationalist China (Taiwan).

1952: Puerto Rico is granted commonwealth status.

1952–1953: Senator Joseph McCarthy undertakes a campaign based on accusation and innuendo intended to root out alleged Communists within the U.S. government, which leads to widespread anticommunist hysteria throughout the country.

1953: Stalin dies, leading to internal Soviet succession crisis.

1954: Battle of Dien Bien Phu occurs in Vietnam, leading to France's departure from Indochina and the partition of Vietnam along the 17th parallel between a Communist North and a pro-Western South.

1955: Austrian State Treaty makes Austria neutral.

1956: Soviet forces brutally suppress anticommunist revolt in Hungary; Suez Crisis occurs after Nasser nationalizes the Suez Canal.

1957: Soviets launch Sputnik; Treaty of Rome inaugurates the European Economic Community.

1958: Gamal Abdel Nasser gets the Soviet Union to finance and build the Aswan Dam for Egypt.

1959: Khrushchev's strong Communist ideology does not prevent him from developing a respectful friendship with Eisenhower during his visit to the United States; Antarctic Treaty is signed, banning military activity and setting guidelines for scientific research in Antarctica; forces led by Fidel Castro overthrow Fulgencio Batista in Cuba; a water-sharing agreement between Egypt and Sudan regulates the use of the Nile.

1960: American U-2 spy plane is shot down over Soviet territory; leads to breakup of Paris summit meeting and cancellation of Eisenhower's visit to Moscow; Organization of Petroleum Exporting Countries (OPEC) is formed to gain higher prices and greater control over the petroleum production of member states; first run on the dollar occurs, leading the United States to abandon unilateral management of the monetary system in favor of multilateral management to promote stability; France detonates its first atomic bomb in southwestern Algeria, thus joining the "atomic club" of the United States, the USSR, and Britain.

1960s: Second-strike capability by the United States and the Soviet Union opens the threat of mutual assured destruction (MAD), providing a stable nuclear deterrence.

1960s–1970s: Many Southern countries nationalize their mineral and agricultural export sectors, wresting control of these industries from multinational corporations.

1961: Sino-Soviet split is finalized; Castro thwarts Bay of Pigs invasion; following the Second Berlin Crisis, the Soviets erect the Berlin Wall to stem the flow of refugees from Communist East Berlin to democratic West Berlin.

1962: Independence for most African colonies becomes complete; France leaves Algeria after years of war between Muslims and French; United States and Soviet Union are brought to the brink of nuclear war following the discovery of Soviet missiles in Cuba; the Cuban Missile Crisis leads to a temporary thaw in relations.

1963: Limited Test Ban Treaty signed by the United States, the Soviet Union, and the United Kingdom limits nuclear testing to underground explosions.

1964: Nuclear proliferation occurs as China gains nuclear capability, prompting India and Pakistan to follow suit in subsequent years.

1965: U.S. forces begin large-scale intervention in Vietnam; President Lyndon Johnson orders a military intervention in the Dominican Republic; India and Pakistan clash in continuing dispute surrounding the control of Kashmir.

1965–1973: U.S. involvement in Vietnam War fails despite its greater economic and military power.

1966: The International Covenant on Civil and Political Rights; The International Covenant of Economic, Social, and Cultural Rights; and the Optional Protocol strengthen provisions of the Universal Declaration of Human Rights.

1967: During the Six-Day War, Israel captures West Bank from Jordan, the Golan Heights from Syria, and the Sinai peninsula and Gaza Strip from Egypt; Association of Southeast Asian Nations (ASEAN) is formed for economic and cultural cooperation; Outer Space Treaty bans territorial claims in space and space-based weapons of mass destruction; The United Nations High Commissioner of Refugees defines refugee status.

1968: Nonproliferation Treaty prohibits states possessing nuclear weapons from helping others to acquire them and forbids non-nuclear states that adhere to the treaty from manufacturing or otherwise obtaining nuclear arms; the Club of Rome, a multinational group of economists and other specialists, is formed to warn of the dangers of continued population growth and pollution; Soviet Union invades Czechoslovakia to thwart liberalization of Czech government.

1969: European *ostpolitik* and U.S. overtures to China herald the beginning of détente; Soviet and Chinese forces clash along the Ussuri River.

1969–1970: Military confrontations known as the War of Attrition occur between Israel and Egypt along the Suez Canal.

1970: Israel practices non-nuclear deterrence by

threatening Syria with retaliation should it attack Jordan.

1970s: United Nations-sponsored African census program illustrates the full dimensions of the population problem.

1971: East Pakistan declares its independence as Bangladesh; West Pakistani troops invade Bangladesh but are defeated when India intervenes; UN votes to expel Nationalist China (Taiwan) and admit Communist China; United States suspends its commitment to convert dollars into gold and resorts to protectionism, indicating the decline of its hegemony.

1972: Nixon visits China and USSR; United States and USSR sign SALT I arms limitation treaty; UN Conference on the Human Environment in Stockholm approves Declaration on the Human Environment.

1972–1979: Détente creates economic and cultural ties between the United States and the Soviet Union, lessening the incentives for conflict.

1973: Egypt enjoys initial successes against Israel during the Yom Kippur War, which permits Egyptian President Anwar el-Sadat to reverse his policy and become the first Arab leader to begin public negotiations with Israel; War Powers Act is adopted by Congress, restricting flexibility of the president in committing U.S. forces to long-term, large-scale operations.

1973: Bretton Woods regime fails, and currency rates float in financial markets; Arab nations of OPEC impose an oil embargo on the United States, raising oil prices dramatically; G-7 leaders attempt to restore international economic stability; United States involvement in Vietnam ends after the United States and South Vietnam sign cease-fire with North Vietnam; Arab-Israeli War leads to energy crisis.

1974: UN Declaration on a New Economic Order (NIEO) aims at reducing economic inequalities between the North and the South; the Abu Nidal Organization, a terrorist group, is founded; the United Nations Environmental Program and the United Nations Conference on Trade and Development meet in Mexico to discuss environmental problems and the distribution of the world's resources; the International Energy Agency is created among major industrial states to develop an emergency system for sharing oil.

1974–1975: Independence occurs for Portugal's colonies in Africa: Guinea-Bissau, Angola, and Mozambique.

1975: Conference on Security and Cooperation in Europe is finalized; South Vietnam surrenders to Communist Viet Cong and North Vietnam; Cambodian and Laotian governments fall to Communist insurgents.

1977–1978: Somalia's invasion of the Ogaden region of Ethiopia fails.

1978–1979: Vietnam invades Cambodia and creates a Vietnamese-backed Communist government.

1979: Reacting to Vietnam's invasion of Cambodia, China initiates a short border war with Vietnam; Iranian Revolution overthrows the shah and establishes a fundamentalist Islamic government led by the Ayatollah Khomeini; Egypt and Israel sign peace treaty; United States and USSR sign SALT II, but it is not ratified by U.S. Senate.

1979–1984: Global recession exacerbates the debt crisis in developing countries.

1979–1989: Soviet Union invades and occupies Afghanistan, which leads to war with Muslim rebels.

1980: The United States imposes a grain embargo on the Soviet Union in retaliation for its invasion of Afghanistan; World Health Organization announces that it has reached its goal of eradicating smallpox; United States demands that Japan enact voluntary export restrictions on automobiles to protect domestic auto producers; Federal Reserve Bank raises interest rates to fight inflation; more than 100,000 people are allowed to flee Cuba to other countries by Fidel Castro during the Mariel boat lift; United States agrees to accept political prisoners released by Cuba, some of whom are later discovered to be criminals and mental patients.

1980s: China opens coastal areas to foreign investment for the first time; several Asian states experience rapid economic growth.

1980–1988: Iran-Iraq War is triggered by Iraqi invasion of Iran.

1981: The U.S. grain embargo against the Soviet Union is lifted.

1981–1982: United States experiences a severe recession that spreads worldwide, causing President Reagan to push for economic deregulation and tax cuts—while increasing spending—leading to large budget deficits.

1981–1989: United States supports anticommunist forces in Nicaragua and Afghanistan under Reagan Doctrine.

1982: UN Convention on the Law of the Sea regulates the finite resources of the ocean; Britain's weak reputation prompts Argentinian invasion of the Falkland Islands; war ensues.

1984: Nicaragua wins 15–0 decision from the International Court of Justice against the United States for mining of the Managua harbor, blockading of its ports, and supporting counterrevolutionary activities (*Contras*); UN General Assembly adopts the Convention against Torture and Other Cruel, Inhuman, or Degrading Treatment or Punishment.

1985: Live Aid benefit concert raises funds for short-term relief of famine in Africa; Vienna Convention establishes framework of worldwide cooperation for pollution control; Mikhail Gorbachev assumes power in the Soviet Union and inaugurates reforms; Single European Act accelerates economic integration of EU members.

Mid-1980s: Famine throughout the Horn of Africa caused by drought and exacerbated by political and economic crises in local countries leads to extensive suffering.

Mid-1980s–present: Japanese-American disputes over their respective economic policies lead to continued feuding between Tokyo and Washington over such matters as trade practices and financial issues.

1986: Mexico joins GATT, lowering its tariffs and dramatically increasing trade with the United States; the world's worst nuclear reactor accident occurs at Chernobyl in the former USSR; large amounts of radioactive material are released into the atmosphere.

1986–1993: Farmer's lobbies in the EU, particularly France, and Japan pressure governments to continue nontariff barriers in the form of subsidies on agricultural products entering their countries, thereby delaying the Uruguay round of GATT negotiations.

1987: The Montreal Protocol requires signatory states to phase out the use and importation of chlorofluorocarbons; Turkey imposes a water embargo on Syria in retaliation for its support of Kurdish terrorists in Turkey; Intermediate-range Nuclear Forces Treaty signed, for the first time banning an entire class of nuclear weapons; Intifada in the West Bank and Gaza Strip reflects Palestinian frustration and discontent with Israeli rule.

1988: The U.S.–sponsored International Drug Enforcement Conference is put into operation.

1989: Series of revolutions in Eastern Europe replace Communist governments; Berlin Wall is dismantled; United States sends approximately 24,000 troops into Panama to oust and arrest Manuel Noriega;

China cracks down on student demonstrators in Tiananmen Square; Helsinki declaration proposes halting production and use of chlorofluorocarbons by 2000.

1989–1994: During the tenure of F. W. de Klerk, South Africa's system of apartheid is dismantled, culminating in the election of Nelson Mandela as president in 1994.

1990: Iraq occupies Kuwait; UN Security Council approves military action to restore Kuwait's sovereignty; UN World Summit for Children is held in New York; Germany is reunified; UN General Assembly convention seeks to protect the human rights of migrant workers; NATO and Warsaw Pact countries sign the Conventional Forces in Europe Treaty, limiting conventional forces in Europe and removing the threat of a blitzkrieg-type Soviet invasion of Western Europe.

1990–1991: Persian Gulf War occurs, in which a U.S.–led coalition removes Iraqi invaders from Kuwait and severely impairs Iraq's potential to gain a dominant position in the Persian Gulf.

1991: After coup intended to oust Gorbachev fails, collapse of USSR brings the Cold War to an end and creates transition in the international system; Russia and the other former republics become independent states; United States and Soviet Union sign START I, reducing for the first time the number of nuclear arms; Maastricht Treaty among EC states sets basis for monetary union and increased political cooperation; UN begins peacekeeping in Cambodia.

1991–1992: Somalia suffers a famine that threatens more than 4 million people with starvation.

1991–1994: Slovenia, Croatia, and Bosnia secede from Yugoslavia, resulting in civil war.

1992: UN imposes sanctions and initiates peace-keeping operation in attempt to stop bloodshed in Yugoslavia; UN Conference on Environment and Development (the "Earth Summit") convenes in Rio de Janeiro; Maastricht treaty comes into force, EC becomes European Union (EU), but initial rejection of the treaty by Denmark and its narrow passage in France lead member states to reconsider the pace and depth of integration.

1993: North American Free Trade agreement is ratified; rare peaceful separation occurs when Czechoslovakia becomes the Czech Republic and Slovakia; Maastricht Treaty is ratified; Israel and PLO sign mutual recognition accord in Oslo; Uruguay Round of

GATT is successfully concluded, establishing the World Trade Organization; more than 120 nations sign the Chemical Weapons Convention to ban production, stockpiling, and use of chemical weapons; United States and Russia sign START II, further reducing strategic nuclear arsenals and eliminating MIRVed ICBMs; Asia-Pacific Economic Cooperation group formed.

1994: United States and Russia stop aiming their nuclear missiles at each other and agree to speed up dismantling of nuclear weapons ahead of START II schedule; Nelson Mandela elected President of South Africa in first election in which all people, regardless of race or color, are allowed to vote; Israel and Jordan sign peace treaty; North American Free Trade Agreement goes into effect in Canada, Mexico, and the United States, beginning the process of eliminating internal trade barriers; IRA agrees to a cease-fire in Northern Ireland; Russian troops invade Chechnya, a republic in southern Russia; civil war ends in Angola.

1995: Israel, PLO sign new accords; UN approves peace-keeping in Haiti; UN peacekeepers leave Somalia; truce ends fighting in Chechnya; Israeli Prime Minister Yitzhak Rabin assassinated; Presidents of Bosnia-Herzegovina, Sebia, and Croatia sign Dayton Accords to end nearly four-year-old civil war; UN holds Fourth World Conference on Women in Beijing.

1996: UN, Iraq sign oil-export agreement; Comprehensive Nuclear Test-Ban Treaty opened for signature; Israeli-Palestinian peace process falters over security and territorial issues.

1997: Chinese President Deng Xiaoping dies; Hong Kong reverts to Chinese control; Poland, Hungary, and Czech Republic invited to join NATO; IRA renews cease-fire; Chemical Weapons Convention signed by the United States and enters into force; Israeli-Palestinian peace process restarts.

1998: India conducts underground tests of nuclear devices, announces its status as nuclear weapons state. Pakistan follows suit.

Index

Credits